AF723943

Criminal Justice and Law Enforcement Books of

WEST PUBLISHING COMPANY

St. Paul, Minnesota 55102

December, 1977

CONSTITUTIONAL LAW

Maddex's Cases and Comments on Constitutional Law by James L. Maddex, Professor of Criminal Justice, Georgia State University, 816 pages, 1974.

Maddex's 1976 Supplement.

CORRECTIONS

Burns' Corrections—Organization and Administration by Henry Burns, Jr., Professor of Criminal Justice, University of Missouri–St. Louis, 578 pages, 1975.

Kerper and Kerper's Legal Rights of the Convicted by Hazel B. Kerper, Late Professor of Sociology and Criminal Law, Sam Houston State University and Janeen Kerper, Attorney, San Diego, Calif., 677 pages, 1974.

Killinger and Cromwell's Selected Readings on Corrections in the Community, 2nd Edition by George G. Killinger, Chairman, Board of Pardons and Paroles, Texas and Paul F. Cromwell, Jr., Director of Juvenile Services, Tarrant County, Texas, 357 pages, 1978.

Killinger and Cromwell's Readings on Penology—The Evolution of Corrections in America by George G. Killinger and Paul F. Cromwell, Jr., 426 pages, 1973.

Killinger and Cromwell's Selected Readings on Introduction to Corrections by George G. Killinger and Paul F. Cromwell, Jr., about 450 pages, 1978.

Killinger, Cromwell and Cromwell's Selected Readings on Issues in Corrections and Administration by George G. Killinger, Paul F. Cromwell, Jr. and Bonnie J. Cromwell, San Antonio College, 644 pages, 1976.

Killinger, Kerper and Cromwell's Probation and Parole in the Criminal Justice System by George G. Killinger, Hazel B. Kerper and Paul F. Cromwell, Jr., 374 pages, 1976.

Krantz' The Law of Corrections and Prisoners' Rights in a Nutshell by Sheldon Krantz, Professor of Law and Director, Center for Criminal Justice, Boston University, 353 pages, 1976.

Rubin's Law of Criminal Correction, 2nd Edition (Student Edition) by Sol Rubin, Counsel Emeritus, Council on Crime and Delinquency, 873 pages, 1973.

Rubin's 1977 Supplement.

CORRECTIONS—Continued

Smith & Berlin's Introduction to Probation and Parole by Alexander B. Smith, Professor of Sociology, John Jay College of Criminal Justice and Louis Berlin, Chief, Training Branch, New York City Dept. of Probation, 250 pages, 1975.

CRIMINAL JUSTICE SYSTEM

Kerper's Introduction to the Criminal Justice System by Hazel B. Kerper, 558 pages, 1972.

Senna and Siegel's Introduction to Criminal Justice by Joseph J. Senna and Larry J. Siegel, both Professors of Criminal Justice, Northeastern University, 540 pages, 1978.

Study Guide to accompany Senna and Siegel's Introduction to Criminal Justice by Roy R. Roberg, Professor of Criminal Justice, University of Nebraska-Lincoln, 187 pages, 1978.

CRIMINAL LAW

Dix and Sharlot's Cases and Materials on Basic Criminal Law by George E. Dix, Professor of Law, University of Texas and M. Michael Sharlot, Professor of Law, University of Texas, 649 pages, 1974.

Ferguson's Readings on Concepts of Criminal Law by Robert W. Ferguson, Administration of Justice Dept. Director, Saddleback College, 560 pages, 1975.

Gardner and Manian's Principles, Cases and Readings on Criminal Law by Thomas J. Gardner, Professor of Criminal Justice, Milwaukee Area Technical College and Victor Manian, Milwaukee County Judge, 782 pages, 1975.

Heymann and Kenety—The Murder Trial of Wilbur Jackson: A Homicide in the Family by Philip Heymann, Professor of Law, Harvard University and William Kenety, Instructor, Catholic University Law School, 340 pages, 1975.

LaFave's Principles of Criminal Law by Wayne R. LaFave, Professor of Law, University of Illinois, about 600 pages, 1978.

Loewy's Criminal Law in a Nutshell by Arnold H. Loewy, Professor of Law. University of North Carolina, 302 pages, 1975.

CRIMINAL PROCEDURE

Davis' Police Discretion by Kenneth Culp Davis, Professor of Law, University of Chicago, 176 pages, 1975.

Dowling's Teaching Materials on Criminal Procedure by Jerry L. Dowling, Professor of Criminal Justice, Sam Houston State University, 544 pages, 1976.

Ferdico's Criminal Procedure for the Law Enforcement Officer by John N. Ferdico, Assistant Attorney General, State of Maine, 372 pages, 1975.

Israel and LaFave's Criminal Procedure in a Nutshell, 2nd Edition by Jerold H. Israel and Wayne R. LaFave, 372 pages, 1975.

Johnson's Cases, Materials and Text on The Elements of Criminal Due Process by Phillip E. Johnson, Professor of Law, University of California, Berkeley, 324 pages, 1975.

CRIMINAL PROCEDURE—Continued

Kamisar, LaFave and Israel's Cases, Comments and Questions on Basic Criminal Procedure, 4th Edition by Yale Kamisar, Professor of Law, University of Michigan, Wayne R. LaFave, Professor of Law, University of Illinois and Jerold H. Israel, Professor of Law, University of Michigan, 790 pages, 1974. Supplement Annually.

EVIDENCE

Gardner's Criminal Evidence by Thomas J. Gardner, Professor of Criminal Justice, Milwaukee Area Technical College, about 640 pages, 1978.

Klein's Law of Evidence for Police, 2nd Edition by Irving J. Klein, Professor of Law and Police Science, John Jay College of Criminal Justice, about 600 pages, 1978.

Markle's Criminal Investigation and Presentation of Evidence by Arnold Markle, The State's Attorney, New Haven County, Connecticut, 344 pages, 1976.

INTRODUCTION TO LAW ENFORCEMENT

More's The American Police—Text and Readings by Harry W. More, Jr., Professor of Administration of Justice, California State University at San Jose, 278 pages, 1976.

Police Tactics in Hazardous Situations by the San Diego, California Police Department, 228 pages, 1976.

Schwartz and Goldstein's Law Enforcement Handbook for Police by Louis B. Schwartz, Professor of Law, University of Pennsylvania and Stephen R. Goldstein, Professor of Law, University of Pennsylvania, 333 pages, 1970.

Sutor's Police Operations—Tactical Approaches to Crimes in Progress by Inspector Andrew Sutor, Philadelphia, Pennsylvania Police Department, 329 pages, 1976.

JUVENILE JUSTICE

Cromwell, Killinger, Sarri and Solomon's Text and Selected Readings on Introduction to Juvenile Delinquency by Paul F. Cromwell, Jr., George G. Killinger, Rosemary C. Sarri, Professor, School of Social Work, The University of Michigan and H. N. Solomon, Professor of Criminal Justice, Nova University, 502 pages, 1978.

Faust and Brantingham's Juvenile Justice Philosophy: Readings, Cases and Comments by Frederic L. Faust, Professor of Criminology, Florida State University and Paul J. Brantingham, Professor of Criminology, Florida State University, 600 pages, 1974.

Fox's Law of Juvenile Courts in a Nutshell by Sanford J. Fox, Professor of Law, Boston College, 286 pages, 1971.

Johnson's Introduction to the Juvenile Justice System by Thomas A. Johnson, Professor of Criminal Justice, Washington State University, 492 pages, 1975.

Senna and Siegel's Cases and Comments on Juvenile Law by Joseph J. Senna, Professor of Criminal Justice, Northeastern University and Larry J. Siegel, Professor of Criminal Justice, Northeastern University, 543 pages, 1976.

CRIMINAL JUSTICE BOOKS

MANAGEMENT AND SUPERVISION

Gaines and Ricks' Selected Readings on Managing the Police Organization by Larry K. Gaines and Truett A. Ricks, both Professors of Criminal Justice, Eastern Kentucky University, about 500 pages, 1978.

More's Criminal Justice Management: Text and Readings, by Harry W. More, Jr., 377 pages, 1977.

Souryal's Police Administration and Management by Sam S. Souryal, Professor of Criminal Justice, Sam Houston State University, 462 pages, 1977.

Wadman, Paxman and Bentley's Law Enforcement Supervision—A Case Study Approach by Robert C. Wadman, Rio Hondo Community College, Monroe J. Paxman, Brigham Young University and Marion T. Bentley, Utah State University, 224 pages, 1975.

POLICE-COMMUNITY RELATIONS

Cromwell and Keefer's Readings on Police-Community Relations, 2nd Edition by Paul F. Cromwell, Jr., and George Keefer, Professor of Criminal Justice, Southwest Texas State University, 506 pages, 1978.

PSYCHOLOGY

Parker and Meier's Interpersonal Psychology for Law Enforcement and Corrections by L. Craig Parker, Jr., Criminal Justice Dept. Director, University of New Haven and Robert D. Meier, Professor of Criminal Justice, University of New Haven, 290 pages, 1975.

VICE CONTROL

Ferguson's the Nature of Vice Control in the Administration of Justice by Robert W. Ferguson, 509 pages, 1974.

Uelman and Haddox' Cases, Text and Materials on Drug Abuse Law by Gerald F. Uelman, Professor of Law, Loyola University, Los Angeles and Victor G. Haddox, Professor of Criminology, California State University at Long Beach and Clinical Professor of Psychiatry, Law and Behavioral Sciences, University of Southern California School of Medicine, 564 pages, 1974.

LAW OF EVIDENCE
FOR
POLICE

SECOND EDITION

By

IRVING J. KLEIN, B.S. in S.S., J.D.
Associate Professor of Law and Police Science
John Jay College of Criminal Justice
the City University of New York

CRIMINAL JUSTICE SERIES

WEST PUBLISHING CO.
St. Paul • New York • Los Angeles • San Francisco
1978

COPYRIGHT © 1978 By WEST PUBLISHING CO.
50 West Kellogg Boulevard
P.O. Box 3526
St. Paul, Minnesota 55165

All rights reserved

Printed in the United States of America

Library of Congress Cataloging in Publication Data
Klein, Irving J
Law of evidence for police.
(Criminal justice series)
Includes index.
1. Evidence, Criminal—United States. 2. Evidence (Law)—United States.
I. Title. II. Series.
KF9660.K55 1978 345'.73'06 78-279
ISBN 0-8299-0149-3

DEDICATION

This book is dedicated to three women who have been most responsible for its production by their assistance and forebearance. They are my deceased wife, Sylvia H. Klein, my present wife, Dr. Marta Arias Klein, and my Girl Friday and secretary, Marion Berenson.

*

PREFACE

The second edition has been made possible because so many professors in colleges throughout the land have been good enough to accept my offering of the first edition as the required text for their course. Just as the Ford Motor Car Company product produced today is far superior to the initial production of the Model T, so I have endeavored to improve the second edition of this book in the same way. I have updated the various principles of the Law of Evidence, expanded the topics covered to include a full chapter on Circumstantial Evidence, a chapter on Personal and Family History and another on Real Evidence. I have also enlarged the chapter dealing with Illegally Obtained Evidence and renamed it to read: Unconstitutionally Obtained Evidence.

The idea of including cases in civil law has not been wholly abandoned in the second edition but in response to some constructive criticism, more cases in criminal law have been included in Part II.

Much thanks is given to the following persons whose help and encouragement have been invaluable:—to my deceased wife, Sylvia H. Klein, for her moral support while I attended law school when I was a Sergeant in the New York City Police Department; to my dear wife, Dr. Marta Arias Klein, who had to do without my attention for many hours because of the time spent in writing this book and for her help in making pertinent suggestions to improve its contents; to my son, Dr. Michael R. Klein, Assistant Professor of Criminal Justice at Nassau Community College, Nassau County, New York, for his counsel as to the content of the second edition; to my secretary, Marion Berenson (Mrs. Irwin Berenson) for her devotion and excellent editorial and typing skills; to the staff of West Publishing Company for their excellent cooperation; to President Gerald A. Lynch and Professor Leo Loughrey of John Jay College of Criminal Justice, Vice-Chancellor Richard (Dick) Ward of the University of Illinois at Chicago Circle, and Professor John Sullivan, Chairman of the Department of Criminal Justice and Public Safety of Mercy College, Dobbs Ferry, New York, whose advice has been most welcome; and finally, to all of the teachers of the Law of Evidence throughout the country who have been so cooperative in sending me letters indicating the strengths and weaknesses of the first edition.

IRVING J. KLEIN

New York City, N. Y.
February, 1978

*

SUMMARY OF CONTENTS

*

TABLE OF CONTENTS

Chapter II. Examination of Witnesses and Trial Procedures—Continued

TABLE OF CONTENTS

TABLE OF CONTENTS

Chapter XVI. Real Evidence—Continued

Chapter XIX. Unconstitutionally Obtained Evidence—Cont'd

PART II. JUDICIAL DECISIONS RELATING TO PART I

TABLE OF CONTENTS

TABLE OF CONTENTS

†

LAW OF EVIDENCE FOR POLICE

PART I

CHAPTER I

INTRODUCTION

§ 1.1 Many cultures have made efforts to determine the guilt or innocence of persons charged with infractions of the rules of that society. These cultures developed legal systems for the ascertainment of the truth. Some of these legal systems were founded on a rational basis and they continued for many centuries. England used parts of earlier methods of determining the guilt or innocence of offenders in its building of a body of law of evidence.

With the development of a jury system, England developed a complete set of rules for determining the admissibility of evidence. The development of this law of evidence was not an overnight development. It was based upon trial and experience.

The United States adopted the rules of evidence of the English courts but over the years, the rules in the United States courts and English courts have been changed by the courts and legislative bodies. We find that today the rules of evidence in the United States are more strict than in England.

The law of evidence is an everchanging law. As society and our government seek better methods for determining guilt or innocence so too will our rules of evidence change to protect the weak from the strong and the strong from the weak.

The rules of evidence are not perfect and probably never will be perfect as Hon. Justice Sutherland stated in Funk v. U. S., 290 U.S. 371, 381, 54 S.Ct. 212, 78 L.Ed. 369, 93 A.L.R. 1136 (1934). The fundamental basis upon which all rules of evidence must rest—if they are to rest upon reason, is their adaption to the successful development of the truth. And, since experience is of all teachers the most dependable, and since experience is a continuous process, it follows that a rule of evidence at one time thought necessary to the ascertainment of the truth should yield to the experience of a succeeding generation whenever that experience has clearly demonstrated the fallacy or wisdom of the old rule.

Frequently, police officers firmly believe that grave injustices have been done when they are not permitted to testify to certain parts of the facts of a given situation because the defense attorney has objected to the introduction of such evidence and the objection is sustained by the judge.

When a judge sustains an objection by opposing counselor, the evidence is not permitted into the record of the case and the trier of the facts, be it the judge himself or the jury, depending upon the nature of the case, does not consider this testimony in the deliberation of the issue.

However, a ruling by a judge excluding evidence from the trial record may be the gravamen of a reversal when the case is heard on appeal. In order for the trial counsel to make his point appealable, he is required, in most instances, to voice his exception to the judge's ruling on the record. Some jurisdictions have taken the position that when a judge overrules an objection, there is no further necessity for the objecting counsel to record his exception on the record.

Another method to preserve the record for appeal is by a device known as an "offer of proof". If this means of preserving the record occurs in a jury trial, the trial counsel will ask for a side bar conference to make an offer of proof. The judge should then request counsel for all sides and the court stenographer to approach the bench and in a tone of voice not audible to the jury, the attorney will place on the record the offer of proof by indicating that his purpose in asking the question of the witness was to enable him to show to the court and jury some facet of the case which he believes to be material to the litigated issues and which he believes are admissible in evidence pursuant to some rule of law which he usually quotes. The judge at that time may reverse his previous ruling or, in the alternative, either indicate his reasons for his ruling or stand by his previous ruling without comment. In any case, the jury is never privy as to what conversations are taking place at the side bar conference. They are, however, advised before the commencement of the trial that such conferences may take place and that the rules of evidence developed over the centuries as a means of ascertaining truth, dictate that such conferences be conducted out of the hearing of the jury.

An incorrect ruling from the bench, however, may also be revised by an appellate court if there is a plain error affecting a substantial right. Even though it was not brought to the attention of the court, the appellate court may reverse on its own discovery of the error. See Rule 102 Federal Rules of Evidence.

The rules of evidence may vary from one state to another, but they are substantially the same in all states. Since the passage of the Federal Rules of Evidence, effective July 1, 1975, it appears that there has been a trend toward even greater uniformity in the rules of evidence throughout the nation.

From time to time, words may be used in this book which will not be initially familiar to many readers. This is to be expected, but if you furnish yourself with a legal dictionary and use it as soon as an unfamiliar word or phrase is used, you will have no difficulty in understanding the thought expressed. In a short time, you will find that you will have little need for the legal dictionary.

The study of law of evidence is a fascinating study if one keeps in mind that it is similar to a puzzle or a game. Just as one tries one method or another to reach a desired goal in a puzzle, so too in the law of evidence, the goal reached is to have the evidence admitted into the record of the case. There may be many roadblocks but very often if the road to admissibility is blocked by one obstruction, the possibility exists that by clever maneuvering, the obstruction may be circumvented and the evidence is admitted.

§ 1.2 COMMON LAW AND STATUTORY LAW

The law of evidence is based on both common law and statutory law. The common law concept is Anglo Saxon in origin. It is distinguished from the Roman law, the modern civil law, the canon law and other systems. The common law is that body of law and juristic theory which was originated, developed, and formulated and is administered in England, and has obtained among most of the states and peoples of Anglo Saxon stock. Lux v. Haggin, 69 Cal. 255, 10 Pac. 674 (1886).

You will note that in the preceding paragraph we have expressed a definition of common law and immediately after the definition, you read the name of a case with numbers and abbreviations following it. This is known in law to be a citation. Therefore Lux v. Haggin, 69 Cal. 255, 10 Pac. 674 (1886), means that the statement immediately preceding the citation was written down word for word in the decision of the court in the case of Lux against Haggin and the full decision may be read by looking at volume 69 of the California Reports beginning on page 255 and it may also be found in volume 10 of the Pacific Reporter. In New York State, the student often has difficulty in his first encounter with the abbreviation for New York Supplement which is cited as N.Y.S. Frequently a reciting student will read this as New York State. This is incorrect. For example, the case often cited for a good definition of the manner in which incompetent evidence should be objected to is Bell v. Bumstead, 60 Hun 580, 14 N.Y.S. 697 (1891). This citation means that the decision of the case of Bell v. Bumstead may be found in volume 14 New York Supplement page 697 and it may also be found in volume 60 Hun's New York Supreme Court Reports page 580.

Sometimes the citation will indicate that a second series has been published beginning with volume number 1 and continuing e. g. 10 N.Y.S.2d 457. In addition to the above, one may find the following as a citation, Michelson v. United States, 335 U.S. 469, 69 S.Ct. 213, 93 L.Ed. 168 (1949). This means that the case may be read in volume 335 of the United States Reports on page 469, also to be found in volume 69 Supreme Court Reporter, page 213, also to be found in volume 93 Lawyers' Edition of the United States Supreme Court Reports on page 168.

A further refinement may sometimes be found in the following citation wherein proper evidence is described as something capable of being weighted in scales of reason and compared and estimated with other matter of the probative sort. Pa.—Neely v. Provident Life & Accident Ins. Co. of Chattanooga, Tenn., 322 Pa. 417, 185 A. 784, 788 (1936).

The student now can see that the case may be read in volume 322 of the Pennsylvania Reports on page 417. S/He may also find it in volume 185 of Atlantic Reporter wherein the case begins on page 784 but the exact phrase quoted may be seen on page 788.

It was said in a preceding paragraph that the law of evidence is built on both common law and statutory law and a definition of common law was presented to you with a citation following it.

§ 1.3 COMMON LAW

A further examination of the theory of common law becomes necessary in order for the student to have a knowledge of the fundamental concepts of the law of evidence. Common law then is a body of law built up over centuries by the decisions of learned judges in Anglo Saxon and American courts. It is very much like building a house and each succeeding judicial decision may be compared to the foundation of the building. It is seldom that a dispute arising between parties in one case is exactly similar to a dispute arising between other parties at a different time and place. However, very often points of similarity may be seen and the judge will rely on these points of similarity in coming to a judicial decision.

Inasmuch as there are seldom two cases which have the exact same factual pattern, the decisions are constantly changing. In aid of the changing decisions is the change in the personnel of the judiciary and the change in their thinking, their mores and their customs. Hence, if the reader will look at the chart on the opposite page, Exhibit 1, he may more readily understand the concept of gradual change in our law where the factual pattern of each case coming before the court is slightly different and the case is said in law "not to stand on all fours with the previous case".

After viewing the chart on the opposite page, the reader can see that our law is capable of slowly changing through ordinary legal means in a slow evolutionary manner.

The basic foundation of the law of evidence in the United States is the common law based on court decisions. This is described by the Latin phrase "Stare Decisis" which has been defined as: to abide by, or adhere to, decided cases. It is further defined as policy of courts to stand by precedent and not to disturb a settled point. Ill.—Neff v. George, 364 Ill. 306, 4 N.E.2d 388, 390, 391 (1936).

EXHIBIT "1"

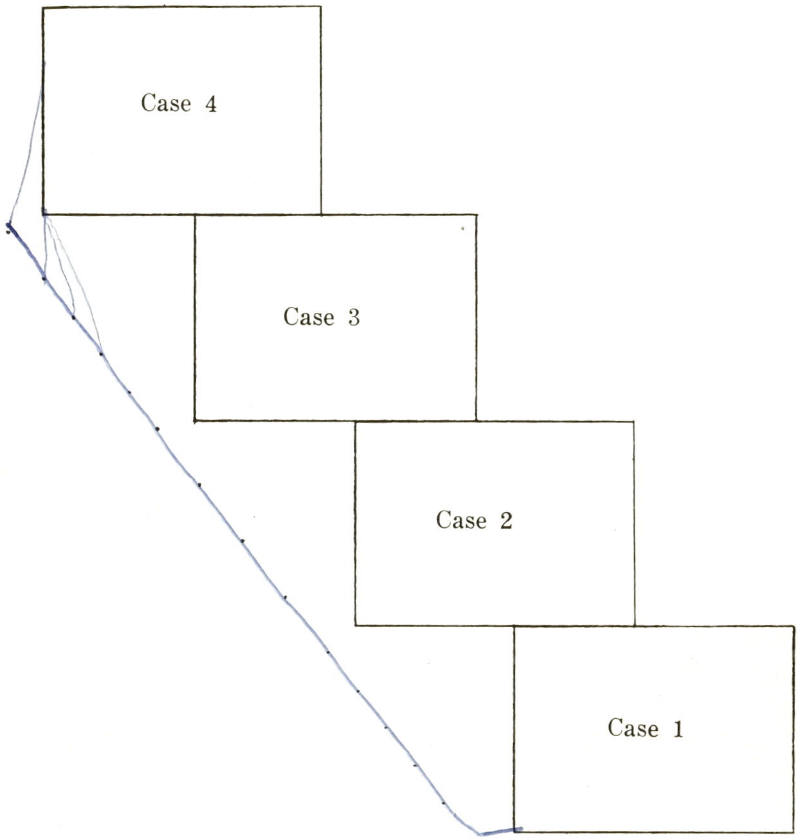

THE CHANGING LAW

[A7365]

Mention has been made of the connection of statutory law to the law of evidence but statutory law has not been explained.

§ 1.4 STATUTORY LAW

Statutory law is that law which has been reduced to writing and has been passed by the legislative branch of our government and acceded to in one form or another by the executive branch of the government. Another way of describing it is, an act of the legislaure declaring, commanding, or prohibiting something; a particular law enacted and established by the will of the legislative department of government; the written will of the legislature, solemnly expressed according to the forms necessary to constitute it the law of the state. Federal Trust Co. v. East Hartford Fire Dist., 283 F. 95, 98 (2d Cir. 1922). It can therefore be understood by the reader, that a faster way to change the law is by statutory enactment rather than by the slower process of stare decisis.

Accordingly, legislatures have often taken this fiat and changed the rules of evidence when in their opinion such change was necessary.

The rules of evidence have as their basic concept that they are established in aid of the search for the truth. They are the aggregate of rules and principles regulating the admissibility, relevancy, and weight and sufficiency of evidence in legal proceedings.

§ 1.5 STATE RULES OF EVIDENCE

The Tenth Amendment to the United States Constitution, commonly referred to as the reserved powers amendment, provided that the powers not delegated to the United States by the Constitution nor prohibited by it to the States, are reserved to the States respectively, or to the people. The United States government being a government of delegated powers, and no delegation having been made in the Constitution as to the police powers governing the health, welfare and morals of the people, the states were free to set up their own courts and their own judicial and evidentiary procedures.

The Federal government has not interfered with the administration of the State court system except when a substantial right of a citizen of the United States has been interfered with. Mapp v. Ohio, 367 U.S. 643, 81 S.Ct. 1684, 6 L.Ed.2d 1081 (1961). Accordingly, each state may have its own rules of evidence but they tend to be substantially the same in each state which bases its rules on the common law.

§ 1.6 THE FEDERAL RULES OF EVIDENCE

The law of evidence in many state jurisdictions however, is based on both common law and statutory law. The trend in recent years has been towards the statutory codification of the rules of evidence leading to a hopeful uniformity in the courts of the United States. Before July 1, 1975, a Federal court sitting in California might have been operating under a different rule of evidence from the same type of court sitting in North Carolina. Up to that time each Federal court would operate under the rules of evidence being practiced in the state in which the court convened. This led to unequal justice in many cases and some confusion, notwithstanding the fact that the basic concepts of the law of evidence practiced throughout the United States were substantially the same.

To avoid this possible confusion, a thirteen year study was made, beginning in 1961, by distinguished jurists, Congress, lawyers and others interested in the administration of justice in Federal courts.[1]

Unlike most legislation, this was a joint effort by Congress and the United States Supreme Court. During March 1969, the Judicial

1. U. S. Congress. House. Federal Rules of Evidence. Report No. 93–1277 to accompany H.R. 5463, 93rd Cong., 2nd Sess., 1974.

Conference printed and circulated widely a preliminary draft of a proposed "Federal Rules of Evidence" accompanied by notes. Revisions were made and a final draft was forwarded to the Supreme Court in October 1971. In 1972, the Supreme Court promulgated the "Federal Rules of Evidence" pursuant to various enabling acts in the United States Code. These rules became P.L. 93–12 enacted by Congress in 1974 to become effective July 1, 1975. The rules govern proceedings in the courts of the United States and before United States magistrates, to the extent and with the exceptions stated in rule 1101 of the "Federal Rules of Evidence". For a more detailed explanation, it is suggested that the reader refer to Rule 1101 in the Appendix.

One by one, the states are adopting codified rules of evidence, primarily based on the "Federal Rules of Evidence". It is anticipated that changes will be made from time to time in accordance with the principle of law expounded by Mr. Justice Sutherland in Funk v. United States, 290 U.S. 371, 54 S.Ct. 212, 78 L.Ed. 369 (1934), when writing of the rules of evidence he indicated "Those rules being founded in reason, one of the oldest maxims is, that where the reason of the rule ceases the rule also ceases".

§ 1.7 DEFINITIONS

In order for a student of the law of evidence to communicate with another in the rules of evidence, he must learn a new language. The language, of course, is based on the English language but the vocabulary is enlarged and sometimes we will find that words may have several meanings depending upon the way the word is used. For example, the word "issue" which you will frequently see in this book, may have several meanings depending upon the context in which it is used. It may mean the children of a man and woman. They may be referred to in the law as the issue of Mary and John. On the other hand, if we say that the issue on trial is whether or not a defendant entered a premises to commit a crime therein, or if he entered the premises to get shelter from inclement weather, the word "issue" here is used to indicate a disagreement between two versions of what occurred.

In the law of evidence, the word "issue" is a single certain and material point, deduced by the pleadings of the parties, which is affirmed on the one side and denied on the other. Pa.—Whitney v. Borough of Jersey Shore, 266 Pa. 537, 109 A. 767, 769 (1920).

If there was a dispute between a contractor of building siding with respect to the square footage of aluminum siding which he installed on your home, resulting in a court action, a witness who might be called to testify as to the square footage of your plot of land would not be testifying relating to facts in issue between you and the contractor. Therefore all testimony relating to the square footage of your plot of land is incompetent because it is immaterial and irrelevant to the issue between you and the contractor, i. e. the square footage of the outside of your home covered with aluminum siding.

The word "evidence" has been defined to include all the means by which any alleged matter of fact, the truth of which is submitted to investigation, is established or disproved. N.Y.—Dibble v. Dimick, 143 N.Y. 549, 38 N.E. 724, 725 (1894).

§ 1.8 ADMISSIBLE EVIDENCE

All evidence to be admissible must stand certain tests. If these tests are passed, then the evidence is admissible.

There are two basic concepts in the common law of evidence which were enunciated by Thayer in his Preliminary Treatise on Evidence (1898). He wrote:

1. That nothing is to be received which is not logically probative of some matter requiring to be proved; and
2. That everything which is thus probative should come in, unless a clear ground of policy or law excludes it.

To explain this another way, one might say that:

1. No evidence is admissible unless it is logically relevant;
2. All logically relevant evidence is admissible unless it is barred by an exclusionary rule.

Another way to describe admissible evidence is to consider all evidence as liquid. This liquid is to pass through a funnel (see Exhibit 2) (infra). At the top of the funnel we have an opening through which we pour the liquid evidence. In the funnel we have obstacles which prevent the evidence from going to the bottom of the funnel. If the evidence is not filtered out by the obstacles then the evidence goes to the bottom and is admissible.

The first and foremost obstacle is relevancy. If the evidence is not relevant or irrelevant as it is sometimes called, then the evidence will not be admitted.

To understand the concept of relevancy I would like to return your thoughts to the issue of the size of the aluminum siding necessary to cover the walls of your home. If the witness were to testify as to the square footage of your plot of land, it would not be relevant to what we are looking for. We are looking for the size of the area that was covered by aluminum siding, not the size of the plot.

There are many other obstacles in our funnel which we will discuss in later chapters. To mention just a few that are indicated in Exhibit 2, they are:

1. Immaterial and irrelevant;
2. Opinion evidence by lay witness;
3. Dying declaration improperly given;
4. Hearsay statement—not subject to exception;
5. Self-serving declaration;

6. Character evidence improperly solicited;
7. Privileged communications;
8. Self-incriminatory statements;
9. Best evidence rule;
10. Parol evidence rule;
11. Unconstitutionally obtained evidence.

EXHIBIT "2"

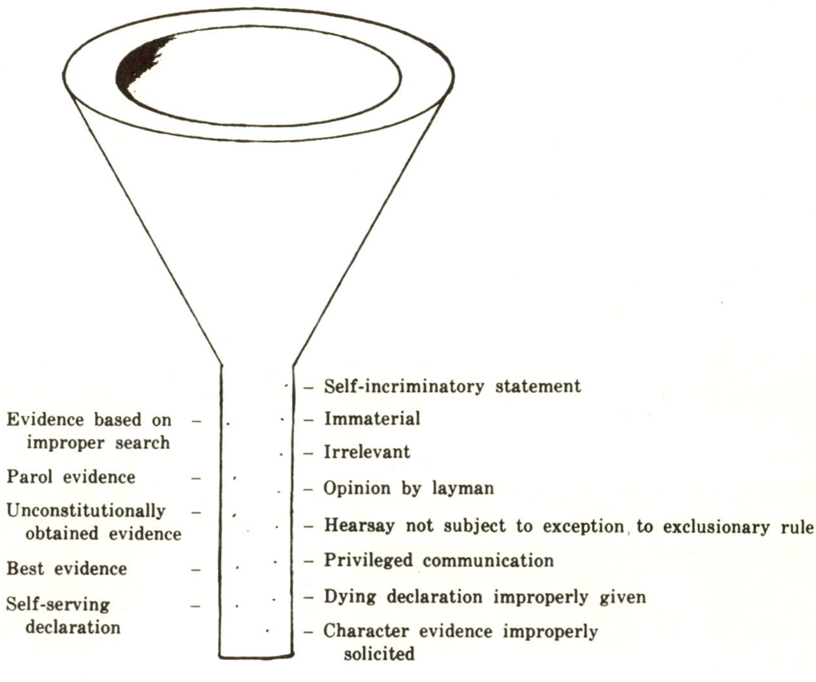

§ 1.9 EXCLUSIONARY RULES

As discussed earlier in this chapter, certain rules of evidence have been developed over the centuries to ferret out the truth. Since certain types of testimony have been found to be less reliable than others, rules were developed by court decision and by statute to exclude that type of testimony which experience has taught men of good intellect and reason to believe that untruths may be testified to even if there was no motive or intent on the part of the witness to testify falsely. This type of evidence was then kept out of the record and is not to be considered by the triers of the facts in their deliberations.

There are other reasons why evidence may be excluded from the record. Some of these are that it may confuse the jury, cause undue surprise, be unduly prejudicial, unduly prolong the trial, be remote, uncertain, conjectural, or speculative or be in violation of constitutional safeguards of the 4th, 5th, or 6th Amendment to the United States Constitution, as interpreted by the Supreme Court of the United States or other reasons which will be developed later in this book. Therefore we say that a body of evidence rules have evolved which excludes certain types of testimony because it is subject to an exclusionary rule and is not admissible. We sometimes refer to this type of testimony as inadmissible. We will discuss each of the exclusionary rules referred to in much greater detail, in subsequent chapters.

§ 1.10 EVIDENCE ADMISSIBLE FOR A PARTICULAR PURPOSE ONLY

Sometimes evidence may be admissible for a particular purpose only and not for any other purpose. Evidence may be admitted merely to show that a particular statement was made without regard for the truth of the statement e. g., in a will probate contest where the issue was the testamentary capacity of a testator, a witness may be permited to testify that the testator had said to the witness "Did you know that I abdicated the throne of England so that I could marry?"

This, from a person who never set foot in England and who never was offered the job is however admissible to show the state of mind of the testator.

§ 1.11 FUNCTION OF JUDGE AND JURY

As you no doubt know, the parties to a court action are known as the litigants. Their respective attorneys are characterized as adversaries. The Judge is referred to as the Court. If there be more than one judge sitting at a trial, one judge is designated as the presiding judge and the other judge or judges are known as associate judges. Each jurisdiction designates its judge either as a judge or a justice. Therefore the judge of a U. S. Circuit Court is designated as a judge whereas a Justice of the United States Supreme Court is designated as a Justice. Whether the person conducting the trial be given the title judge or justice, his/her function remains the same, namely to conduct an impartial trial adhering to the law of evidence, the rules of the court, ruling on the admissibility of evidence and deciding issues of law.

Sometimes the judge or justice presiding is given the authority by the litigants to decide both questions of law and of fact. This occurs where the parties waive a jury trial. In effect they are saying to the judge that we will rely on your decision with respect to the facts as well as the law of this case. If either litigant demands a jury trial, he is entitled to it in most jurisdictions in both criminal and civil trials. The jury determines questions of fact only and applies the law as explained to it by the judge. An illustration of this concept is as follows:

"A" is arrested and tried for the offense of burglary. The facts are that "A" was an alcoholic and he was in an intoxicated condition on the date of the alleged offense. In order to get out of the inclement weather, he entered the premises of a cleaning store whose proprietor had closed at the end of the day and had mistakenly left the front door ajar. "A" seeing this, entered the premises and promptly fell asleep. "O", the officer on foot patrol in the area made his rounds and tried doors on his post. When he arrived at the cleaning store, he found the door opened and "O" entered the store in the company of a fellow officer. Both officers came upon "A" who was found asleep on the pressing table of the store. He was arrested and charged with burglary. The prosecution contended that "A" had entered the premises with intent to steal clothing but when he saw that he was about to be apprehended, he acted as if he were sleeping. If this statement of the facts are true he would be chargeable with a higher degree of crime than the one which "A" contends he is guilty of (trespass). The jury hears the evidence presented by both sides and then comes to a conclusion as to what the facts of this incident are. If the jury finds that "A" did not enter the premises with intent to steal, the judge will then apply the law of the crime of trespass in rendering the sentence.

§ 1.12 EVIDENCE—DEFINITION

Before discussing the different types of evidence, it is best that we know what evidence is. It has been defined as any species of proof, or probative matter, legally presented at the trial of an issue, by the act of the parties through the medium of witnesses, records, documents, concrete objects, etc., for the purpose of inducing belief in the minds of the court or jury as to their contention. Hotchkiss v. Newton, 10 Ga. 560; Black's Law Dictionary (Revised Fourth Edition 1968).

Evidence includes all means by which any alleged matter of fact is submitted to investigation and is established or disproved. N.Y.—Dibble v. Dimick, 143 N.Y. 549, 554, 38 N.E. 724, 725 (1894). Proof is the belief or conclusion arrived at by a consideration of the evidence. Evidence is further subdivided into legal evidence, direct evidence, circumstantial evidence, real evidence, testimonial evidence, documentary evidence, relevant evidence, irrelevant evidence, competent evidence, incompetent evidence, corroborative evidence, prima facie evidence, and hearsay evidence. Each of these will be more thoroughly discussed in later chapters but the student should familiarize himself or herself with the general meaning of these terms, at this time, to enable him/her to understand the concepts and examples explained in the later chapters.

§ 1.13 REAL EVIDENCE

Real evidence is that evidence furnished by things themselves on view or inspection, as distinguished from a description of them by the mouth of a witness. Black's Law Dictionary (Revised Fourth Edition 1968).

§ 1.14 LEGAL EVIDENCE

Legal evidence is defined in Black's Law Dictionary (Revised Fourth Edition) (1968) as a broad general term meaning all admissible evidence including both oral and documentary, but with a further implication that it must be of such a character as tends reasonably and substantially to prove the point, not to raise a mere suspicion or conjecture. Conn.—Curtis v. Bradley, 65 Conn. 99, 31 A. 591, 594, 28 L.R.A. 143 (1895). Legal evidence is also defined as that which is used or is intended to be used at a trial or at hearings before courts, judges, commissioners, referees, arbitrators, hearing officers etc.

§ 1.15 RELEVANT EVIDENCE

Relevant evidence is evidence which logically tends to prove or to disprove one or more of the principle facts in issue. N.Y.—People v. Nitzberg, 287 N.Y. 183, 187, 38 N.E.2d 490 (1942). Material evidence is that measure of proof which affects a fact or issue of the case in a significant way. To be competent, evidence must be legally adequate and sufficient. It is really an omnibus term used for all of the exclusionary rules.

An example of a relevant competent or material evidence problem is as follows:

Let us assume that there is a contractual dispute with respect to the floor measurements of your living room. The carpet dealer from whom you just purchased wall to wall carpeting tells you that your room was 18 feet wide by 18 feet long and that he used 36 square yards to carpet your living room and the roll of carpet was from an 18 foot roll. Your contention is that he only used 25 square yards in that your living room is 15 x 15 and you refuse to pay him for the 36 square yards. He sues you and a trial of the issue between you (the size of the room) results. You get someone to measure the width of your home and this witness takes the stand. You ask this witness "What, if any, is your means of earning a living? " He answers that he is a carpet salesman and measures the size of rooms for the purpose of furnishing carpeting to prospective customers. After showing the court that he has been so employed for five years the court accepts him as an expert in measuring for the purpose of furnishing carpet. You now ask him whether or not he measured the size of your home. There is an instant objection from your adversary because he tells the judge that the size of your home is not relevant, competent or material to the issue i. e. the size of your living room. You argue that it is relevant, competent and material and you ask the judge to accept this testimony "subject to connection". The judge answers that he will accept it "subject to connection" but if it is not connected later he will direct the jury to disregard the testimony in their deliberations. The expert then testifies that the width of your house is 16 feet and the house is rectangular in shape. Inasmuch as the carpet vendor had already testified in his direct case that he sold you carpeting for an 18 foot wide room, you have now introduced testimony which is relevant, material and competent and is proof of the fact that the room could not be 18 feet by 18 feet. It is therefore connected to the issue of the case.

Another way of describing relevant evidence is such evidence as relates to, or bears directly upon, the point in issue and proves or has a tendency to prove the proposition alleged.

Still another way of describing material evidence is evidence which has an effective influence or bearing on the question in issue.

The terms material and relevant are generally used interchangeably although it is possible that evidence may be logically relevant but immaterial. Evidence which is so remote as to be of no practical value in determining the issues is immaterial even though it may have some logical relevancy to the issues involved.

In actual practice, the distinction between relevancy and materiality is obscure and in most cases whether it is characterized as irrelevant or immaterial makes little practical difference.

§ 1.16 DIRECT EVIDENCE

Direct evidence is that method of proof which tends to show the existence or non-existence of a disputed fact without the intervention of proof of another fact. Ky.—Stark's Adm'x v. Herndon's Adm'r, 292 Ky. 469, 166 S.W. 828 (1914). Another court held "direct evidence" when strictly defined, means that which immediately points to the question at issue, or is evidence of the precise fact at issue and on trial, by witnesses who can testify that they saw the act done or heard the words spoken which constituted the facts to be proved. Mo.—Stern v. Employers' Liability Assur. Corporation, Limited, of London, England, 249 S.W. 739 (App.1923).

I like to think of direct evidence as something that the witness can testify to what he saw, smelled, tasted, heard or felt which is directly related to the issue between the litigants.

Let us hypothecate that a police officer was on routine motor patrol when he received a report of a stolen vehicle bearing a particular make, model, color and license plate marker. Shortly after he received this alarm he observed "D" and "B" seated in the wanted vehicle. "D" was in the driver's seat and "B" was in the front passenger seat. The vehicle was standing in a "no standing" zone in front of the entrance to a National Bank which was located on a street having considerable pedestrian traffic. The bank was open for business. The officer observed "B" walk into the bank while "D" remained in the driver's seat with the motor running.

After signalling for assistance, the officer parked his police vehicle to the rear of the stolen vehicle and remained in his car waiting for reinforcements.

"D" and "B" had planned to perpetrate a robbery of the National Bank. As part of this plan, if something went wrong on the outside, "D" was to "honk" the vehicle's horn twice and try to get away from the scene on foot. While "B" was waiting in line to reach a teller, he heard two "honks" on the horn of the stolen vehicle.

The perpetrators further arranged beforehand that if the horn was sounded before "B" had made his demands known, he was to ask the teller for change of ten dollars and disappear into the crowd.

"B", having heard the horn, followed the scheduled procedure.

Shortly after the horn was sounded, another officer arrived at the scene just in time to see "D" seated in the vehicle and emerging from it.

The second officer on the scene apprehended "D" and frisked him, only to find no contraband. This officer charged "D" with larceny of the motor vehicle and possession of stolen property. The officer did not see "D" steal the vehicle. He could not testify that he saw him commit larceny. He did, however, observe him in the driver's seat with the motor running. This is direct evidence that he saw, heard and possibly smelled (exhaust fumes). These observations could be testified to by the officer to satisfy some of the elements of the offense "possession of stolen property". Most jurisdictions require such a defendant to go forward with the evidence when he is found with the recent and exclusive possession of stolen property. N.Y.—Knickerbocker v. People, 57 Barb. 365, affirmed 43 N.Y. 177 (1870). In this hypothesis, one may find several inferences that other crimes were about to be committed. We will discuss them in the next section.

§ 1.17 CIRCUMSTANTIAL EVIDENCE

Circumstantial evidence is evidence which does not directly prove the existence of a fact but merely gives rise to a logical inference that it exists; such evidence is admissible if it affords a basis for a reasonable inference of the existence of the fact. N.C.—Wilkerson v. Clark, 264 N.C. 439, 141 S.E.2d 884, 887 (1965). "Circumstantial evidence" is the proof of facts which have a legitimate tendency from the laws of nature, the usual connection of things, and ordinary transactions of business, etc. to show the reasonable mind that the disputed fact was or was not in existence. Del.—Fahey v. Niles, 7 Boyce 454, 108 A. 135 (1919).

Let us return now to our hypothetical attempted bank robbery. Let us suppose that the first officer on the scene knew that "D" and

"B" were acquainted and observed "B" coming out of the bank. By prearrangement, each officer was to apprehend one of the participants. When "B" was apprehended and frisked, he was found to possess a fully loaded revolver. When "D" was frisked, he was "clean" (had no contraband on his person).

When the prosecutor heard the full information, he decided to charge both "D" and "B" with (1) attempted robbery, (2) possession of stolen property, (3) unauthorized use of a motor vehicle, (4) possession of a revolver in violation of law, (5) conspiracy and, lastly, with (6) standing a motor vehicle in a "no standing" zone. In short, he decided to "throw the book" at the defendants.

The officers could testify what they directly observed and leave the inferences to be drawn by the fact finder to ascertain whether or not the defendants committed the crimes for which they are charged. The inferences that will be drawn by the presence of the stolen vehicle in a "no standing" area, with motor running, with "D" in the driver's seat, with "B" in the bank with a fully loaded revolver, with "B" having arrived at the bank in the vehicle with "D", with the signal on the vehicle's horn, with the dispersal plan executed, all lead to the inference that a bank robbery was being attempted.

Each of the enumerated acts taken together, circumstantially tend to prove the commission of the attempted robbery and the conspiracy.

§ 1.18 RELATIVE WEIGHT OF CREDIBILITY

We have all seen the symbol of law as a blindfolded woman holding a weight scale in her hand. It is to be presumed that she does not see who or what is being placed on either side of the scale but eventually one side of the scale should be heavier than the other. It is also to be presumed that the side which has the heavier weight is the side which prevails in a law suit. A more detailed discussion of the quantum of proof required to prevail is undertaken in the next chapter.

For our purposes, at this juncture, we should know that when witnesses testify, some of their testimony will be believed more by the trier of the facts than other testimony. We refer to this concept as the weight of testimony. When a witness testifies to a material fact at issue and the trier of the fact believes the testimony of the witness, we say in law, "The testimony of that witness was heavy".

The greater number of witnesses testifying for a particular side in a law suit does not necessarily tip the scale in favor of the litigant for whom they are testifying. There is always the issue of credibility of the testimony.

Frequently a witness who is aged may be, but need not necessarily be, regarded as untrustworthy. In weighing testimony, the old age of a witness may support a presumption that his memory is to a considerable extent untrustworthy with respect to recent events. U.S.—Bentley v. Phelps, 3 F.Cas.No. 1, 331 (C.C.Mass.). A witness of mature age may well remember facts that occurred in his childhood but his testimony should be received with caution. Ill.—Moffett v. South Park, 138 Ill. 620, 28 N.E. 975 (1891).

Confidence in the testimony being greatly reduced if the witness was of extremely tender years. La.—Flettrich v. State Farm Mutual Ins. Co., 238 So.2d 220 (App.1970).

The witness may not be believed because he might be biased towards one of the litigants. United States—Pritchett v. U. S., 185 F.2d 438 (D.C.Cir., 1950), certiorari denied 341 U.S. 905, 71 S.Ct. 608, 95 L.Ed. 1344, or the weight to be given to evidence of character depends largely on the facts involved in a particular case and is a question for the jury to determine. Fla.—Mitchell v. State, 43 Fla. 188, 30 So. 803 (1902).

There are many reasons which cause a jury to disbelieve a witness. Some additional reasons may be that the reputation of the witness for veracity is bad; or he has testified to inconsistent statements; or he is intoxicated; or under the influence of narcotics while testifying; or while at the scene of the occurrence; or that his perceptive ability is poor; or that he is a paid expert who earns the bulk of his income by testifying for a particular type of litigant; or his demeanor on the witness stand does not favorably impress the trier of the facts; or for a variety of other reasons which produce a "gut" reaction in the mind of the trier of the facts.

§ 1.19 TESTIMONIAL EVIDENCE

We frequently refer to testimony as all forms of evidence which is admitted in a trial. However this is an inaccurate use of the term "testimony". Testimony is more accurately defined to designate only a particular kind or species of evidence, namely which comes to the tribunal through living witnesses speaking under oath or affirmation in the presence of the tribunal. Ark.—Poe v. State, 95 Ark. 172, 129 S.W. 292 (1910); Tex.—Ex parte Jackson, 470 S.W.2d 679 (Cr.App. 1971); Neb.—Meyers v. State, 112 Neb. 149, 198 N.W. 871 (1924). However, testimony need not necessarily be made to a judicial tribunal. Police departments frequently have disciplinary trials wherein a superior officer brings charges against a subordinate for a violation of department rules and regulations. This is not a judicial tribunal but it is an administrative hearing. When the superior officer or any other complainant is sworn and begins to testify, his presentation to the administrative hearing officer constitutes testimony and hence he is giving testimonial evidence.

There are other situations of a non-judicial character which result in the same type of testimonial evidence being presented.

It has been said that what witnesses say under oath is testimony but only so much of it as impresses the mind of the court trying the facts is "evidence". N.J.—Mick v. Mart, 65 A. 851 (Ch. 1907).

§ 1.20 COMPETENT EVIDENCE

Competent evidence means evidence which tends to establish the fact in issue and does not rest on mere surmise or guess. La.—Clifton v. Arnold, 87 So.2d 386 (App.1956). One must develop a logical feel for the competency or incompetency of evidence. The evidence must be logically probative of the fact in issue but sometimes we find that competent evidence is not admissible because it is not the character of proof which the law permits in a particular case. See N. Y.—Porter v. Valentine, 18 Misc. 213, 41 N.Y.S. 507 (1896), for a discussion of this point. Evidence is incompetent if not fit for the purpose for which it is offered. Me.—Torrey v. Congress Square Hotel Co., 145 Me. 234, 75 A.2d 451 (1950). We often hear the standard hoop skirt (covers all but touches nothing) objection of "I object on the grounds that the testimony is incompetent, immaterial and irrelevant."

This is a standard objection and sometimes works to the advantage of the objector to exclude certain evidence which he feels might be damaging to his case or which might raise collateral issues not before the court.

§ 1.21 DOCUMENTARY EVIDENCE

Documentary evidence is that furnished by written instruments, inscriptions and documents of all kinds. N.Y.—Ticknor v. Ticknor, 23 Misc.2d 257, 200 N.Y.S.2d 661 (1960). The term includes every form of writing and applies to both public and private documents. R.I.—Arnold v. Pawtuxet Valley Water Co., 18 R.I. 189, 26 A. 55, 19 L.R.A. 602 (1893). In the private document sector, we might find deeds, wills, agreements, etc. In the public document area, we might find public records, birth, marriage and death certificates, election registers, motor vehicle accident reports and licenses. Woltin v. Metropolitan Life Ins. Co., 167 Misc. 382, 4 N.Y.S.2d 296 (1938).

The usual manner to present this into evidence is to have the lawyer who is interested in getting the document admitted ask the Court to direct the stenographer to mark the document for identification. After it has been so marked, reference is then made to the identification number in phrasing a question to the witness, thusly:

> "Mr. (Witness' name), When, if ever, have you seen People's exhibit A for identification before?"

After the witness indicates that he has seen the exhibit previously, he is asked the circumstances under which he saw this exhibit. If the exhibit is established to be competent, material and relevant to the issue at trial, the attorney then offers "People's exhibit 'A' for identification in evidence as People's exhibit 'A' in evidence."

The exhibit is then shown to his adversary who has an opportunity to object to the introduction in evidence of this particular exhibit.

If the objection is sustained, the exhibit is not introduced into evidence and the triers of the facts shall not consider the exhibit as part of the evidence in their deliberations, notwithstanding the fact that certain testimony was elicited while it was introduced as People's exhibit "A" for identification.

The procedure outlined above might be used for all types of inanimate objects which are necessary for the trier of the facts to consider in the deliberations of the issues between the litigants.

§ 1.22 VIDEO TAPE—DEPOSITION (DEPOVISION)

One of the more recent innovations in the law of evidence has been the use of video tape in the court room. It is no secret that the court calendars are overcrowded and that much delay is experienced in the trial of cases both criminal and civil. In an effort to remedy this problem and to make the best use of available resources, experiments have been conducted to introduce the use of video tape in the court room.

Historically, our rules of law and more particularly, our rules of evidence, change very slowly. Many roadblocks are placed in the way of change. Practitioners are set in their ways whether they be judges or trial counsel, but more and more the organized bar is accepting the challenge to make changes. In all fairness, it must be said that change comes slowly in the law also to insure that justice is done and that changes are not made merely for the sake of change itself.

Many jurisdictions, now allow the use of depovision of expert witnesses. Frequently a litigant is unable to obtain a fair trial because the cost of having an expert appear in the court room has been too expensive. Accordingly, provision has been made for an expert to be examined in a place other than the court room, with the opportunity being given to all litigants for direct, cross, redirect and recross examination. Objections to testimony are recorded and the witness is permitted to answer. The judge views the testimony in chambers before the jury sees the video tape and the judge makes rulings on the objections at that time. The tape is then edited to omit the testimony that the judge has ruled inadmissible and at the proper time in the trial, the video tape is shown to the jury.

This procedure is presently being used in an experimental setting for ordinary lay witnesses.

§ 1.23 HYPNOTIC INDUCED TESTIMONY—TRUTH SERUM

As indicated previously, the rules of evidence are founded upon the search for truth. Surely a person who is testifying and who is under the hypnotic influence of another, cannot be thought to be testifying to the truth. Some effort has been made to gain a certain modicum of respectability for the use of truth serums or narcoanalysis, as well as the use of hypnosis. No court, known to the author, has permitted the use of these methods. For an extended review see Teitlebaum, Admissibility of Hypnotically Adduced Evidence and The Arthur Nebb Case, 8 St. Louis L.J. 205 (1963), also Polen, The Admissibility of Truth Serum Tests in Court, 35 Temp.L.Q. 401 (1962).

§ 1.24 PRIMA FACIE EVIDENCE

The officer often hears that s/he has the responsibility of providing the evidence to prove a prima facie case in order for him/her to be free of a possible judgment against him/her for false imprisonment. The prosecutor might be heard to say that all s/he needs to hold the defendant is a prima facie case. The question now is, what is a prima facie case?

Naturally we know that "prima facie" has a Latin derivation. A literal definition might be "at first view or on its face". When we combine "prima facie" with "case", we mean, one which, in the absence of explanation or contradiction, constitutes an apparent case sufficient in the eyes of the law to establish the fact, and if not rebutted, remains sufficient for that purpose. Idaho—Miller v. Belknap, 75 Idaho 46, 266 P.2d 662 (1954).

When the prosecutor/rix "puts in" his/her prima facie case in the initial hearing, s/he does not try to buttress this up with additional testimony. The reason for this method is that s/he does not require the additional testimony at the initial hearing and s/he does not have to give his/her adversary all the evidence s/he has against the defendant at this time.

However, the trend is for the prosecution to be required to disclose whatever information the government has whether exculpatory or inculpatory, as the case progresses towards trial.

§ 1.25 CORROBORATIVE EVIDENCE

Evidence which strengthens, confirms or makes certain other evidence is corroborative evidence. It is additional evidence of a different character about some point which will support, strengthen, or confirm evidence already received. Many jurisdictions require corroboration of a female's testimony for a rape conviction. It was much too easy for a female to disarray her clothing or injure herself before reporting the rape. However, the pendulum swung too much in favor of our male population in that it became almost impossible to convict a defendant of rape because most rapes are not conducted under the watchful eye of disinterested witnesses. Accordingly, many jurisdictions have removed the necessity of corroboration for conviction in the crime of rape. If the trier of fact believes the victim in these states, the defendant can be convicted on the victim's testimony alone. For a more detailed analysis of the use of corroboration the reader is referred to 45 A.L.R.2d 1316, 7 Wigmore Evidence 2056–2060 (3rd Ed. 1940), 60 A.L.R. 1124, 100 A.L.R.2d 612, 21 A.L.R.2d 1013.

§ 1.26 HEARSAY EVIDENCE

A good portion of this text will include exceptions to the hearsay exclusionary rule. The rule basically states that if the testimony is hearsay, it should not be admissible on a trial. However, as with most legal rules, there are exceptions which are founded on reason and logic. The most frequently met exceptions will be spelled out in great detail in the pages which follow.

CHAPTER II

EXAMINATION OF WITNESSES AND TRIAL PROCEDURES

§ 2.1 INTRODUCTION

In the trial of a law suit, whether it be of a criminal nature or of a civil nature, one party is arguing against the other. This is known as an adversary proceeding. In such a proceeding, the party who is making the charge has the burden of proving his case before the trier of the facts. In law, it is said that the moving party has the burden of proof. There are various degrees of proof which can best be shown by looking at the following scale. As you will note the scale is supposed to be the scale of justice and at the beginning of a trial the scale is exactly balanced. As the trial progresses one side or the other begins to drop with the corresponding rise on the other side of the scale. Sometimes the evidence will be very heavy on one side causing that side to be momentarily very heavy. Then, a barrage of excellent cross-examination of the witness may cause the scale to balance towards the other side. The trier of the facts theoretically has a scale of justice in his/her or their mind (depending on whether or not it is a jury trial) and when the trial is finally over, s/he or they make a determination in favor of one side or the other. If a jury makes this determination we refer to it as a jury's verdict. If a judge makes the determination we refer to it as a judgment.

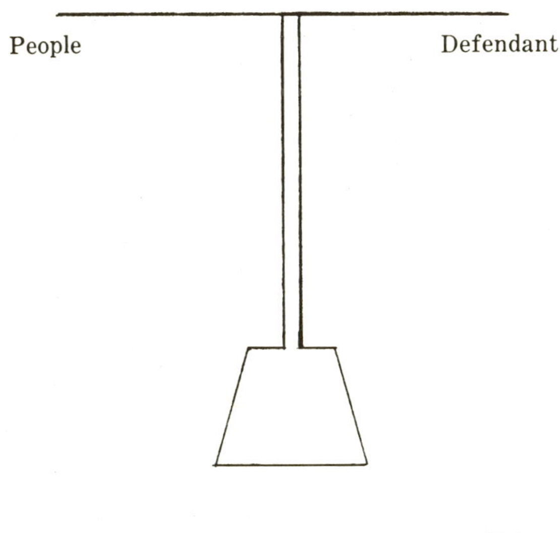

[A7367]

Whether it be a criminal trial, an administrative hearing or a civil trial, we have what is known as the quantum of proof. This basically means the weight of the evidence sufficient to get a determination of the case for one side or the other. There are different quanta of proof required for the three types of trials heretofore named. A defendant in a criminal trial must be proven guilty beyond any reasonable doubt. All that is necessary is that a reasonable or average person would have no reasonable doubt that the defendant is guilty. If the prosecution cannot prove this, then the defendant is entitled to have the charge or indictment dismissed and he will be permitted to go free. We like to show this on the scale of justice in the following manner.

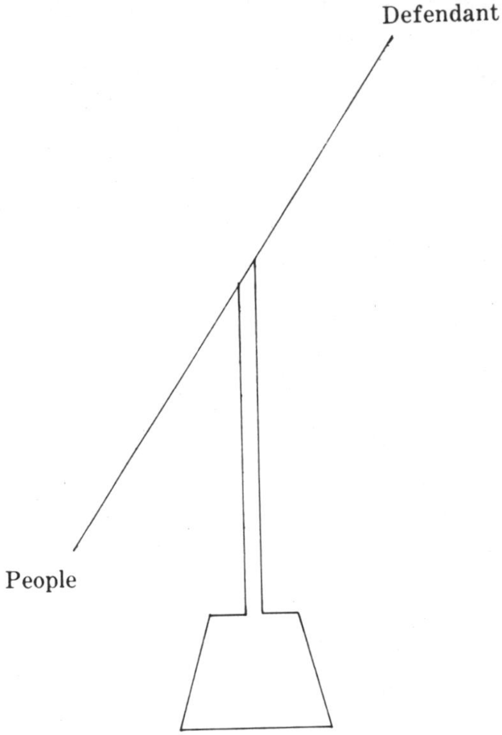

BEYOND ANY REASONABLE DOUBT

[B6886]

If it would be necessary to prove the defendant guilty beyond all doubt the scale would look thus.

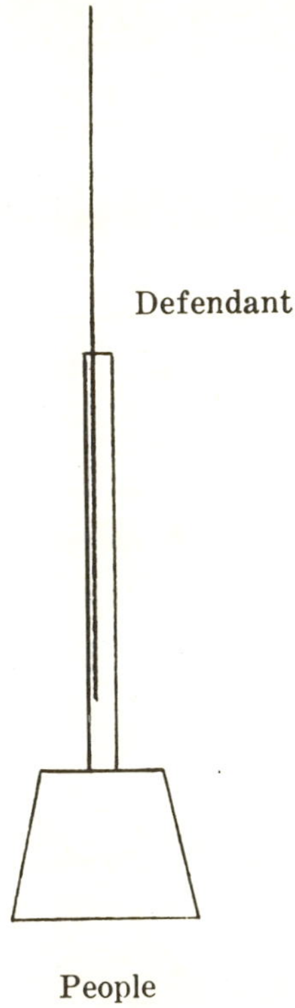

BEYOND ALL DOUBT

[A7369]

In a criminal case, the burden of proof does not shift but when the government establishes a prima facie case, it is then for defendant to overcome inferences reasonably to be drawn from the proven facts. United States—Wallace v. U. S., 281 F.2d 656 (4th Cir. 1960).

Even where State establishes a prima facie case, the burden of proof in a criminal case does not shift, but accused is only required to overcome the inference the State has established. S.C.—State v. Attardo, 211 S.E.2d 868 (1975).

Reasonable doubt is not mere guess or surmise that a man may not be guilty; it is such a doubt as a reasonable man may entertain after a fair review and consideration of the evidence. A doubt for which some good reason arising from the evidence can be given. N.Y.—People v. Friedland, 2 App.Div. 332, 37 N.Y.S. 974 (1896). Another case held that a reasonable doubt exists if the doubt is of such a substance as to cause the prudent man to hesitate and pause in matters of importance in his own affairs.

Probable cause is a term used in criminal law where an officer, acting and thinking as a reasonable person, might have cause to make an arrest. It is more than mere suspicion but less than beyond a reasonable doubt. Thus a police officer might have probable cause to make an arrest which would make a prima facie case, yet he may not be able to prove the defendant guilty beyond a reasonable doubt. U.S.—United States v. Leaphart, 513 F.2d 747 (10th Cir. 1975).

§ 2.2 SUBSTANTIAL EVIDENCE

What is substantial evidence? The answer of Chief Justice Hughes is, "Substantial evidence is more than a mere scintilla. It means such relevant evidence as a reasonable man might accept as adequate to support a conclusion."[1] Mere uncorroborated hearsay or rumor does not constitute substantial evidence. The evidence must be such as a reasonable mind would accept[2] though other like minds would not do so. Substantial evidence is the quantum of proof required for a prosecution to prevail in an administrative hearing.

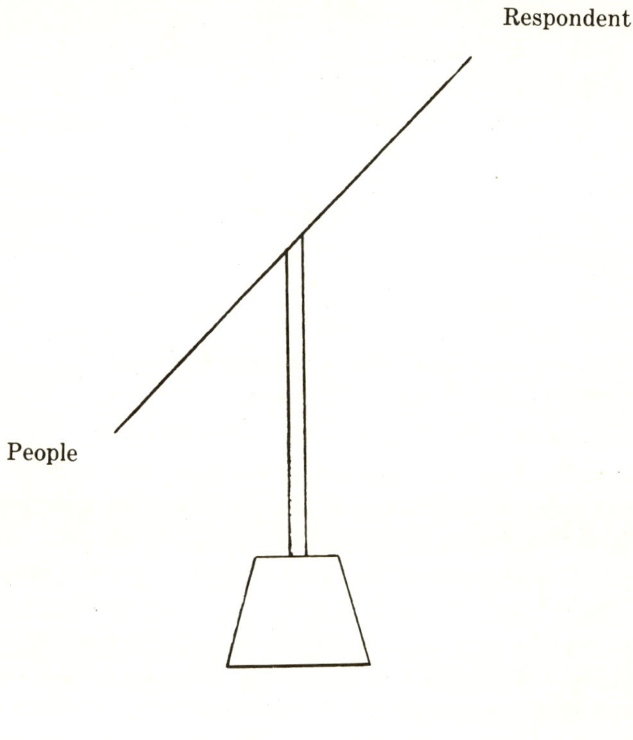

ADMINISTRATIVE HEARING

[A7370]

1. U.S.—Consolidated Edison Co. v. N. L. R. B., 305 U.S. 197, 229–230, 59 S.Ct. 206, 83 L.Ed. 126 (1938).

2. U.S.—International Assoc. of Machinists v. N. L. R. B., 110 F.2d 29, 35 (D.C.Cir. 1939), affirmed 311 U.S. 72, 61 S.Ct. 83, 85 L.Ed. 50.

Civil trials, however, require still another quantum of proof. This is known as the preponderance of evidence theory. All the successful party must do at the close of the case is to tip the scale in his favor, thus:

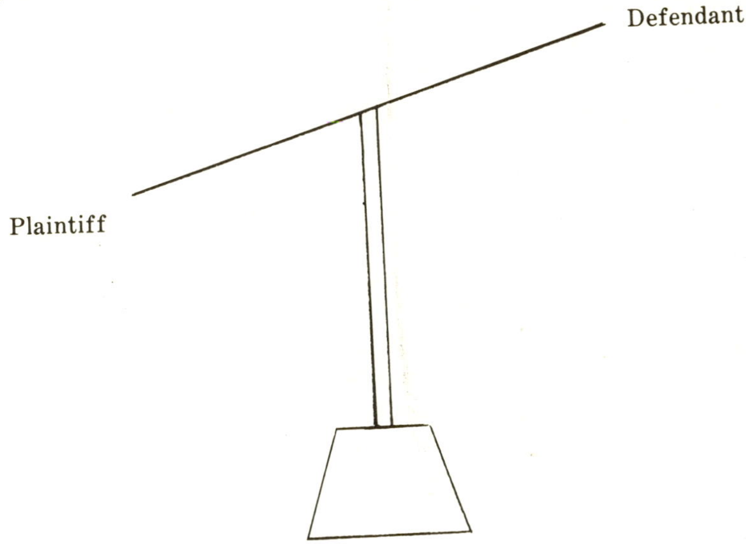

CIVIL CASE

[A7371]

You may have noticed that in the scale diagrams the right side of the scale in the four previous diagrams were indicated by different nomenclature. In the criminal and the civil cases we called the person against whom the action was directed as the defendant. In the 3rd (Administrative Hearing or trial) we called this person, "the Respondent." On the left side of the four previous scales we also had indicated different appellations. In the criminal trial we indicated the word "People" as the moving party. We meant that the District or County Attorney of the county or the Attorney General of the State or Federal Government is the moving party. The non law enforcement person who is making the charge against the defendant is known as the complainant.

Similarly in an administrative proceeding, the word people is used to represent an agent of government who is prosecuting the respondent. The nongovernmental person who is making this charge is known as the complainant. In some administrative hearings, an officer of government becomes the complainant. This is the situation in police department disciplinary trials where very often a superior officer is making a charge of a violation of a department rule against a subordinate. The superior officer is the complainant and the subordinate is the respondent.

Finally, the civil case deserves our attention. This is an action between two or more persons, natural or corporate, to determine their respective rights to property. These actions may be known as torts (private wrongs) or breach of contract actions or equitable actions (e. g. injunctions) or probate proceedings, and other actions to determine the rights and privileges of parties. In the tort and breach of contract actions, the moving party is called the plaintiff and the other party is called the defendant. In equitable actions, the moving party is designated as petitioner and his adverse party is designated as respondent. In probate proceedings, one party is designated as the proponent and the other is designated as the contestant.

In subsequent chapters of this book, cases will be assigned to the student. In order to fully comprehend the meaning of these cases, it is imperative that the student familiarizes himself with common terms often used in law. To assist the student to do this we have spent considerable time to explain what many of these terms mean. It is inconceivable that we would be able to explain every term or word that the student will encounter in his reading. It is therefore recommended that each student avail himself of a legal dictionary and as he reads case material, he constantly refers to the legal dictionary when he is in doubt as to the meaning of a word. In this way the student will better understand what he is reading and it will add to his enjoyment of the course.

§ 2.3 THE ORDER OF THE TRIAL

The order of the trial usually proceeds by the party having the burden of proof putting his side of the controversy first, before the trier of the facts.

S/He does this in several ways depending upon whether the trier of the facts is a judge or whether it is a jury. If the trier of the facts be a jury, the attorney representing the plaintiff in a civil action or the attorney representing the people or government in a criminal action will "open to the jury."

This simply means that he will introduce himself and the parties and their counsel to the jury and briefly explain the factual situation surrounding the cause of action and explain what his side intends to prove.

Local court procedures vary but usually the side which has the burden of proof may not waive the opening to the jury.

The defendant's attorney also has an opportunity to open to the jury after his/her adversary has finished. S/He will espouse his/her clients' cause in this opening statement. In some jurisdictions, the defendant alone may waive his right to open to the jury.

The side which has the burden of proof (the people in a criminal action, the plaintiff in a civil action) then must place his/her first witness on the stand and in question and answer form must elicit proof to substantiate his/her claim if s/he is to prevail in the outcome of the case. S/He is required to ask questions in a particular form which will be explained later in this book. If s/he deviates from the prescribed form, and if his/her adversary objects, the court may sustain the objection and the witness would be directed by the court, not to answer the question.

After the attorney who has the burden of proof completes his/her questioning of the witness, s/he may say to his/her adversary "You may inquire". This means that s/he has completed his/her direct questioning of the witness and now gives his/her adversary an opportunity at cross-examination.

Cross-examination questions may be phrased differently from direct examination questions. The manner in which these questions may be asked will be more fully explained in later sections.

After the cross-examination of the witness is concluded the attorney who initially called the witness to the stand may attempt to rehabilitate the witness by asking him/her further questions. This is known as redirect. Then the other attorney may ask questions of the witness which is known as re-cross. This may continue according to the needs of the attorneys and the discretion of the presiding judge.

This procedure continues with the side having the burden of proof calling other witnesses for direct examination, then cross, then redirect, then re-cross etc.

When the attorney for the side that has the burden of proof feels that s/he has proven his/her case s/he will call no further witness. If the case is a criminal case, the prosecutor/rix will announce to the court "Your honor, that is the peoples case" or s/he may use similar language to the same import.

If it is a criminal case, the defendant's attorney will move to dismiss the charges on the ground that the people have failed to prove a prima facie case.

This means that on the testimony adduced at the trial, as a matter of law (as opposed to as a matter of fact) the people have failed to prove that the defendant was guilty of the crime charged. It is rare that this motion is granted because the prosecutor/rix usually has carefully caused testimony to be elicited which covers the elements of the crime charged.

Assuming that the defendant's motion for dismissal is denied, the defendant may remain mute, may take the stand in his/her own defense, may bring witnesses to testify in his/her favor or need not bring witnesses to testify in his/her behalf.

If s/he decides not to have witnesses testify in his/her behalf and to remain mute, his/her attorney may move the court to dismiss on the ground that the people have failed to prove him/her guilty beyond any reasonable doubt. This motion is sometimes granted at the end of the people's case.

If s/he decides to take the stand and testify in his/her own defense or if s/he has witnesses in his/her behalf take the stand and testify, s/he and his/her witnesses will be subjected to direct examination by defense counsel, then cross-examination by the prosecutor/rix, then re-direct, then re-cross etc. in the same manner as the prosecutor's witnesses were questioned. The only difference is that each of the defendant's witnesses will first be questioned by the defense attorney and later by the prosecutor/rix.

At the conclusion of the parade of witnesses for the defense, the defense attorney will say to the court "The defendant rests." Thereupon the prosecutor may ask the court for permission to reopen his/her direct case with newly found evidence and the court in its discretion may permit this to occur.

There is also a procedural device known as prosecution's rebuttal. The prosecution is limited to testimony which might refute the evidence presented by the defendant. New witnesses may be called but only witnesses whose testimony might negate the defendant's witnesses' testimony. If, for example, the defense raises the issue of insanity or infancy, the prosecution may offer evidence to show that the defendant was not insane or was not an infant respectively. Even these witnesses may be cross-examined by the defendant or his/her counsel.

If the prosecution uses a rebuttal, the defendant may have the opportunity to introduce evidence contrary to that introduced by the prosecution as rebuttal. This is known as a rejoinder. Naturally this give and take is subject to the discretion of the trial judge.

If both sides rest, the court will finally determine this and it is so indicated on the record of the case. Motions will then be entertained by the court. This is usually done outside of the presence of the jury but in open court. The jury is excused, normally while these arguments of counsel are placed before the court.

It is sometimes good practice for the defendant's attorney to renew his motion to dismiss because of failure of the prosecutor to prove a prima facie case even though it was previously denied. The judge may reverse his prior decision based on new testimony which he heard at the trial. In any event the judge may ask the attorney for the grounds of his motion and the attorney will explain the reasons for his asking for the dismissal and he may cite court decisions to support his contentions. The judge may then ask the other attorney as to what he has to say to counter these arguments.

This same procedure is followed with respect to the next motion i. e. the motion to dismiss on the grounds that the people have failed to prove the defendant guilty beyond any reasonable doubt.

Assuming that the judge denies these motions, the attorneys will then give their summation to the jury. In most jurisdictions the defendant's attorney will "sum up" first, followed by the prosecutor/rix. The summation consists of a speech to the jury recalling parts of the testimony of the trial and placing special emphasis on the testimony that favors the position of his/her client.

The next step in the order of trial is the judge's charge to the jury. This usually occurs when the courtroom doors are locked to prevent spectators moving in and out of the courtroom. The judge usually reads from a prepared text in which s/he explains the law of the case but leaves the determination of the facts to the jury. If the charge were one of intentional murder the judge may charge that if you find that the defendant intentionally killed the victim, then you are to come back with a verdict of guilty of murder, but if you find that the defendant killed the victim in the heat of passion, you are to return to this court with a verdict of manslaughter.

After the charge is over, the jury goes out of the courtroom to the deliberation room. When they have made their decision (in a criminal case some jurisdictions require a unanimous decision, others are now requiring 5 jurors agreement in a 6 person jury or 10 persons agreement in a 12 person jury) they return and the foreman of the jury is asked by the Court Clerk as to whether they have reached a verdict. The jury foreman who is standing will say "We have." The Court Clerk will ask "What is your verdict?" The jury foreman will reply either Guilty of Murder first degree or Guilty of Manslaughter or Not Guilty or whatever the jury may have decided.

After the initial shock has worn off the losing attorney may make what are known as Post Trial Motions. The only one which should interest the reader of this book is the motion to poll the jury. The judge will ask the court clerk to poll the jury and the court clerk will ask each juror by name as to how he voted and each juror will reply.

The jurors are then discharged by the judge who will usually thank them for their services.

The procedure described above will vary slightly in different jurisdictions but generally this is the order of a trial. The order of trial has been included in this book so that you might be more aware of the safeguards that are included in an orderly trial where the ultimate goal is equal justice under law.

§ 2.4 OATH OR AFFIRMATION REQUIRED FROM EACH WITNESS

Every witness is asked, upon his entry into the witness box to swear or affirm that he will testify truthfully. This is done in a manner to impress upon his mind his duty to do so. This procedure is designed to provide flexibility in dealing with religious cults, atheists, mental defectives, children and conscientious objectors.

§ 2.5 INFANT AS A WITNESS

When an infant is a necessary witness, a special problem arises as to the question of whether the infant is capable of understanding the nature of an oath or affirmation. This problem is often resolved by the judge in camera. The child is taken into the judge's chambers or robing room, and testimony is taken in the presence of the litigants, their attorneys and a court reporter. The situation is informal and the judge usually sits at his/her desk and may or may not be clothed in his/her robe. The judge conducts what is known as a voir dire of the prospective infant witness.

The usual procedure is for the judge to introduce himself/herself to the infant in a kindly manner and proceed to ask questions relative to the child's school; his/her accomplishments in school; whether the child attends a church or synagogue; if so, how often does s/he attend; whether s/he has ever told a lie; if so, how often has s/he told a lie. If s/he admits to having told a lie, the judge may ask him/her what lies s/he has told. The judge may ask the child who would punish him/her if s/he tells a lie. Sometimes the child will say that God will punish him/her or his/her mother or father will punish him/her. The judge may then ask how would God or the parent punish him/her. The judge usually gives an opportunity to all trial counsel to examine the infant prior to the judge making a determination as to whether s/he will take the child's testimony under oath or affirmation or merely permit the child to testify not under oath or affirmation. In United States v. Spoonhunter, 476 F.2d 1050 (10th Cir. 1972) the voir dire of the trial judge was as follows:

THE COURT: I'll ask her a few questions. Donna, how old are you?

DONNA: Seven.

THE COURT: You are seven?

DONNA: Uh-huh.

THE COURT: What grade are you in school?

DONNA: Second.

THE COURT: Do you think you remember what occurred on the night of July 13, 1971?

DONNA: Yes.

THE COURT: Do you know what it is to tell the truth when you raise your hand and are sworn?

DONNA: Yes.

THE COURT: And if I administer the oath to you, you will swear to tell the truth and you know that you can be punished if you don't tell the truth? You understand that?

DONNA: Yes.

THE COURT: I think she is qualified. You raise your right hand then (Sworn).

THE COURT: Do you so swear, do you?

DONNA: Yes.

THE COURT: Very well.

It has been held that a child's unsworn testimony is inadmissible in a civil action. N.Y.—Stoppick v. Goldstein, 174 App.Div. 306, 160 N.Y.S. 947 (1916); People ex rel. Niebuhr v. McAdoo, 184 N.Y. 304, 144 N.Y.S. 306 (1913); People v. Oyola, 6 N.Y.2d 259, 189 N.Y.S.2d 203 (1959).

In criminal prosecutions, most jurisdictions permit a child who does not understand the nature of an oath to testify without being sworn if he appears to be of sufficient intelligence to justify the reception of evidence. However, in New York, a conviction cannot be had upon such testimony which is not supported by other evidence, given by a child of less than 12 years of age.

New York Criminal Procedure Law cited hereafter, as N.Y.—CPL § 60.20 reads as follows:

60.20 Rules of evidence; testimonial capacity; evidence given by children

1. Any person may be a witness in a criminal proceeding unless the court finds that, by reason of infancy or mental disease or defect, he does not possess sufficient intelligence or capacity to justify the reception of his evidence.
2. Every witness more than twelve years old may testify only under oath unless the court is satisfied that such witness cannot, as a result of mental disease or defect, understand the nature of an oath. A child less then twelve years old may not testify under oath unless the court is satisfied that he understands the nature of an oath. If the court is not so satisfied, such child or such witness over twelve years old who cannot as a result of mental disease or defect, understand the nature of an oath may nevertheless be permitted to give unsworn evidence if the court is satisfied that the witness possesses sufficient intelligence and capacity to justify the reception thereof.
3. A defendant may not be convicted of an offense solely upon unsworn evidence given pursuant to subdivision two.

There is a rebuttable presumption that a child over 14 is competent to be sworn in a civil case, but in fact there is no rule of law which qualifies an infant to be sworn at any particular age. United States—Wheeler v. U. S., 159 U.S. 523, 16 S.Ct. 93, 40 L.Ed. 244 (1895).

Anyone who has had experience with the testimony of children can understand that one must be overly careful if they accept their testimony as the truth. This is not to say that their testimony is not to be accepted but children frequently have great imaginations, which tend to color their testimony, particularly in the area of sex offenses where their testimony should be carefully weighed. The courts have held that in sexual offense cases the evidence must be "more than usually clear and convincing". N.Y.—People v. Oyola, 6 N.Y.2d 259, 189 N.Y.S.2d 203 (1959).

§ 2.6 IDENTITY OF WITNESS

When a witness takes the stand the trier of the facts is looking for an introduction. He may ask himself who this person is who is testifying, where does he live, and/or how long has he lived there, and/or what is his employment history, and/or what is his marital status and/or what school he attends, and/or what grade in school has he achieved, and/or how long he has been a member of the police department, and/or what assignments did he have etc? These questions are frequently asked by the attorney who summoned him to the stand to testify. The extent to which the attorney may go is limited by his/her adversary's sustained objections or by the discretion of the presiding judge. The ostensible intent of the attorney who summons a witness to testify is to give the impression that the witness is a responsible member of society who is worthy of belief.

Many times a complaining witness does not wish to divulge where s/he lives because of fear of reprisal from the defendant or his/her cohorts. For this reason, the prosecution may attempt to have a witness testify without stating where s/he lives. This practice is permissible but when the witness is asked on cross-examination "Where do you live?" s/he is under a duty to tell where s/he lives or in the alternative all of his direct examination may be struck from the record. "The question 'Where do you live?' was not only an appropriate question preliminary to the cross-examination of the witness but on its face, without any such declaration of purpose as was made by counsel here, was an essential step in identifying the witness with his environment, to which cross-examination may always be directed."[3] A witness's prior address must also be disclosed.

However, it sometimes occurs that to divulge the location of the residence of the witness might endanger the life of the witness or members of his family. When this issue is raised, the court may conduct a preliminary examination out of the hearing of the jury and defendant.

The threat however, must be actual and not the result of conjecture. U.S.—Shaw v. Illinois, 394 U.S. 214, 89 S.Ct. 1016, 22 L.Ed. 2d 211 (1969). If the court determines that the true name, address and place of employment of the witness are not critical enough to deny effective cross-examination, the witness will not be required to reveal this information. However, if the judge concludes that the defendant is not entitled to this information, the defendant is entitled to ask any other relevant question which may aid the jury in weigh-

3. U.S.—Alford v. U. S., 282 U.S. 687, 51 S.Ct. 218, 75 L.Ed. 624 (1931).

ing the witness's credibility. U.S.—United States v. Palermo, 410 F.2d 468 (7th Cir. 1969).

§ 2.7 UNDERCOVER INFORMER AS A WITNESS

The situation respecting the use of undercover informers is very tricky. The prosecution may not need the testimony of the informer in order to spell out a prima facie case against a defendant. However, this is not always the situation. In such a case, the prosecutor/rix is faced with a dilemma. If s/he exposes the informer or undercover police officer to the defendant, there are some cases in which the witness will not live to testify at the trial, his/her death being caused by natural or unnatural causes. In other cases, the witness himself/herself may be fearful about testifying. In still others, the usefulness of the informer or undercover police officer in future arrests is nullified by the prosecutor divulging his/her identity to the defense. A prosecutor/rix is not compelled to reveal the identity of the informer or undercover police officer.

In McCray v. Illinois, 386 U.S. 300, 87 S.Ct. 1056, 18 L.Ed.2d 62 (1967), and also in Spinelli v. U.S., 393 U.S. 410, 89 S.Ct. 584, 21 L.Ed. 2d 637 (1969), it was held that the revelation of the identity of the informer was not required on the facts of those cases if the trial judge is convinced by evidence submitted in open court that the officers did rely in good faith upon creditable information supplied by a reliable informant. However, the court indicated that there might be some circumstances in which such a revelation might be required.

If the informer is a material witness on the trial of the action if the prosecution wishes to prevail, the informer must be produced to give the defendant an opportunity of cross-examination as is guaranteed to every defendant by the Sixth Amendment of the United States Constitution which was made applicable to State and Federal trials by virtue of the Fourteenth Amendment. U.S.—Pointer v. Texas, 380 U.S. 400, 85 S.Ct. 1065, 13 L.Ed.2d 923 (1965).

The Supreme Court has only granted this right to trials and not to preliminary hearings, grand jury proceedings or sentencing hearings. Since these proceedings are not to determine guilt or innocence the Supreme Court has held that the Sixth Amendment is not applicable. The Court said in Pointer v. Texas (Supra), "We must remember also that we are not dealing with the trial of the criminal charge itself. There the need for a truthful verdict outweighs society's need for an informer privilege."

However, where there is a threat to the life of a witness, the right of the defendant to have the witness's true name and address and place of employment is not absolute. The threat must be actual and not the result of conjecture. U.S.—Shaw v. Illinois, 394 U.S. 214, 89 S.Ct. 1016, 22 L.Ed.2d 211 (1969). The government bears the burden of proving to the district judge the existence of such a threat. The trial judge can then ascertain the interest of the defendant in the answer and exercise an informed discretion in making his ruling. U.S.—United States v. Palermo, 410 F.2d 468 (7th Cir. 1969).

In McCray v. Illinois, 386 U.S. 300, 87 S.Ct. 1056 (1967), it was held that an Illinois statute which gave discretion to the presiding judge on a preliminary (motion to suppress) hearing as to whether or not an informer's identity need be disclosed was constitutional. In Nutler v. State of Maryland, 8 Md.App. 635, 262 A.2d 80 (1970), the court said:

> "The State has the privilege to withhold from disclosure the identity of persons who furnish information to police officers concerning the commission of crimes. However, the privilege is not absolute. On the issue of guilt or innocence (not on Fourth Amendment issues) and only upon demand by the defendant, the trial court may, in the exercise of its judicial discretion compel such disclosure upon determination that it is necessary and relevant to a fair defense. Factors to be considered in ascertaining whether such disclosure is necessary and relevant to a fair defense include the nature of the crime charged; the importance of the informer's identity to determination of innocence, as for example, whether the informer was an integral part of the illegal transaction and the possible significance of his testimony; and the possible defenses. Whether the privilege must yield depends upon the facts and circumstances of the particular case. But if the informer testifies for the State the privilege may not be invoked by it."

As a practical manner then, the prosecutor/rix has the alternative of concealing the identity of the informer or undercover police officer when the prosecutor/rix feels that his/her usefulness would be wasted on a small offender. Hopefully, the undercover officer or informer will give information which will lead to the "big fish" in the operation. If the prosecutor/rix fails to continue the prosecution at this point, there is always the spectre of civil liability hanging over the government as well as the prosecutor/rix individually. However, where no malice is proved, the probability of the defendant recovering under such a situation is nil.

It is interesting to note that the one who has most to lose under this problem, i. e. the informer or undercover officer, has little input as to whether s/he will have to testify. The privilege of not divulging the identity is that of governmental authority, not that of the informant. The government alone may waive the privilege. United States v. Reynolds, 345 U.S. 1, 73 S.Ct. 528, 97 L.Ed. 727 (1953).

Probably it is most difficult for anyone not directly involved in this problem to fully appreciate the feelings that an undercover police officer has when s/he is confronted with the requirement that s/he testify in open court. The author has had experience in such a problem but no amount of writing about it will fully place the reader in the shoes of such a person. As a change in the popular phrase goes, "Try it, you won't like it."

§ 2.8 EXCLUSION OF WITNESSES FROM COURTROOM

Very often an astute attorney will move the court to exclude from the courtroom all persons who will be called as a witness in the instant case. It should be quite evident to the reader that this is a very effective means to prevent collusion among the various witnesses as to how the facts of the case occurred. In most jurisdictions, this is a motion which is addressed to the court's discretion. If the request is made in good faith however, there is ordinarily no reason why it should be denied.[4] In many jurisdictions statutes now provide for the exclusion of witnesses on examination of the accused before committing magistrates. However in New York a party to the action is entitled to be present during trial and his counsel may not be excluded [N.Y.Const. Art. I, Section 6]. If a witness fails to leave the courtroom upon direction by a judge he may be punished for contempt of court (interference with the business of the court).

§ 2.9 USE OF MEMORANDUM

Many times a witness, particularly a police officer witness, has no independent recollection of the facts which are involved in the instant case. The common law and the statutory law of some states provide that his/her memory may be refreshed by the use of memorandum. This writing may be used to revive his/her recollection. In the case of the police officer witness, it is proper upon application to the presiding judge, that the officer look at departmental forms such as reports which s/he prepared at the time of the instant case and after reading this matêrial, s/he may answer the questions put to him/her by counsel. When, however, a witness has so far forgotten the facts that he cannot recall them, even after looking at the memorandum of them, and he testifies that he once knew them and made a memorandum of them at the time or soon after they transpired, which he intended to make correctly, and which he believes to be correct, such memorandum in his own handwriting may be received as evidence of the facts therein contained although the witness has no present recollection of them.[5] It is not necessary to the use of the memorandum that it should have been made by the witness himself since it is not the memorandum that is the evidence, but the recollection of the witness.[6] A witness may refresh his recollection from a memorandum made by others. Conn.—Neff v. Neff, 114 A. at 128.

4. N.Y.—Philpot v. Fifth Avenue Coach Co., 142 App.Div. 811, 128 N.Y.S. 35 (1911).

5. N.Y.—McCarthy v. Meaney, 183 N.Y. 190, 76 N.Y.S. 36 (1902); Conn.—State v. Masse, 1 Conn.Cir. 381, 186 A.2d 553 (1962).

6. N.Y.—Taft v. Little, 178 N.Y. 127, 70 N.E. 211 (1904).

§ 2.10 PAST RECOLLECTION RECORDED ADOPTED BY WITNESS AS HIS TESTIMONY

A memorandum of a past recollection is not, of itself independent evidence of the facts contained therein. However it may be received in evidence provided it is connected to the testimony of the witness. The witness swears to the facts contained in the memorandum, because of his confidence in the accuracy of his written memorandum. The writing therefor becomes a present evidentiary statement of the witness verified by his oath. Now the contents may be read to the trier of the facts and taken together as equal to a present positive statement of the witness as he affirms the truth of the facts stated in the memorandum.[7]

§ 2.11 USE OF MEMORANDUM FOR CROSS-EXAMINATION

If the witness uses a memorandum to refresh his recollection, even though it may not be shown to the jury evidentially, it may be used by opposing counsel in that he has a right to inspect it and use it to test the credibility of the witness.[8]

The reader will recall that in Section 2.9, supra, a police officer frequently is required by department rules and regulations to make a memorandum of the nature of police business that s/he has attended to. The trial of the issues of this police business may not take place until a considerable time after the event, thereby dulling the police officer's recollection of the happening. With the permission of the presiding jurist, the officer may refresh his/her recollection by reading to himself/herself the entries contained in the memorandum. However, once s/he uses the memorandum in this way, s/he opens the door for the opposing counsel to inspect the memorandum for the purpose of cross-examination.

The prosecutor/rix should carefully look at the memorandum first to see that no information not relevant to the issues of the case and not testified to by the police officer on his/her direct examination is made available to defense counsel. This irrelevant material may be blocked out with adhesive tape providing application is made to the Court and the application is granted. Care should be taken that no injury is done to the blocked out portions so that it is available for an appellate court to inspect, should conditions warrant.

§ 2.12 USE OF PRETRIAL STATEMENT MADE BY PROSECUTION WITNESS

Sometimes the prosecution in a criminal action will ask its witness to sign statements during the investigatory stage of the proceeding. In both Federal courts and State courts, the defendant has a

7. Wis.—Manning v. School District No. 6, 124 Wis. 84, 102 N.W. 356 (1905).

8. N.Y.—People v. Gezzo, 307 N.Y. 385, 121 N.E.2d 380 (1954).

right to inspect and to use for purposes of impeachment on cross-examination any pretrial statement given by the witness to the authorities provided the statement relates to the witness's testimony, and provided also "that the necessities of effective law enforcement do not require the statement be kept secret or confidential".[9]

Congress, as a result of the Jencks v. United States decision, enacted Section 3500 of Title 18 of the U.S. Code which reads as follows:

§ 3500. Demands for production of statements and reports of witnesses

(a) In any criminal prosecution brought by the United States, no statement or report in the possession of the United States which was made by a Government witness or prospective Government witness (other than the defendant) to an agent of the Government shall be the subject of subpoena, discovery, or inspection until said witness has testified on direct examination in the trial of the case.

(b) After a witness called by the United States has testified on direct examination, the court shall, on motion of the defendant, order the United States to produce any statement (as hereinafter defined) of the witness in the possession of the United States which relates to the subject matter as to which the witness has testified. If the entire contents of any such statement relate to the subject matter of the testimony of the witness, the court shall order it to be delivered directly to the defendant for his examination and use.

(c) If the United States claims that any statement ordered to be produced under this section contains matter which does not relate to the subject matter of the testimony of the witness, the court shall order the United States to deliver such statement for the inspection of the court in camera. Upon such delivery the court shall excise the portions of such statement which do not relate to the subject matter of the testimony of the witness. With such material excised, the court shall then direct delivery of such statement to the defendant for his use. If, pursuant to such procedure, any portion of such statement is withheld from the defendant and the defendant objects to such withholding, and the trial is continued to an adjudication of the guilt of the defendant, the entire text of such statement shall be preserved by the United States and, in the event the defendant appeals, shall be made available to the appellate court for the purpose of determining the correctness of the ruling of the trial judge. Whenever any statement is delivered to a defendant pursuant to this section, the court in its discretion, upon applica-

9. U.S.—Jencks v. United States, 353 U.S. 657, 77 S.Ct. 1007, 1 L.Ed.2d 1103 (1957).

tion of said defendant, may recess proceedings in the trial for such time as it may determine to be reasonably required for the examination of such statement by said defendant and his preparation for its use in the trial.

(d) If the United States elects not to comply with an order of the court under paragraph (b) or (c) hereof to deliver to the defendant any such statement, or such portion thereof as the court may direct, the court shall strike from the record the testimony of the witness, and the trial shall proceed unless the court in its discretion shall determine that the interests of justice require that a mistrial be declared.

(e) The term "statement", as used in subsections (b), (c) and (d) of this section in relation to any witness called by the United States, means—

(1) a written statement made by said witness and signed or otherwise adopted or approved by him; or

(2) a stenographic, mechanical, electrical, or other recording, or a transcription thereof, which is a substantially verbatim recital of an oral statement made by said witness to an agent of the Government and recorded contemporaneously with the making of such oral statement. Added Pub.L. 85–269, Sept. 2, 1957, 71 Stat. 595.

As a practical matter however, the United States Attorney often makes this information available to defense counsel at least one day prior to the anticipated date on which the witness is scheduled to testify. In this way, the defense counsel has no valid grounds to ask the court for a continuance in order to have sufficient time to study the statements or report. The lawyers refer to this as 3500 material.

§ 2.13 INTERPRETERS

The usual procedure is to require the witness to answer questions directed at him/her in English and to respond in the English language. However, those who are unable to speak the English language, or who do not have a good command of the English language or who are deaf and dumb persons, may testify through court appointed interpreters. If the witness is a deaf mute, the interpreter must be familiar with the code signs employed by the witness. An interpreter must be sworn to interpret properly and truly. Testimony repeated on the witness stand of what an interpreter, not on the witness stand, said when the police examined the accused is hearsay and hence inadmissible.[10]

The student should have some understanding of what procedures exist in foreign countries with respect to this problem in order to

10. N.Y.—People v. Sing, 242 N.Y. 419, 152 N.E. 248 (1926).

fully appreciate the fundamental fairness which American courts provide in this area of the law. It is urged upon the student if he has occasion to visit a foreign non-English speaking jurisdiction that he goes to a court and observes what transpires when an English speaking defendant is brought before the court. The author was shocked at what he observed in a Canadian court in Quebec Province. Fortunately, he was not the defendant in the case which was observed but it certainly made him appreciate more fully the American system of providing interpreters when necessary.

§ 2.14 MODELS, DIAGRAMS, MAPS, ETC.

The parties have a right to introduce properly authenticated models, diagrams, and maps to illustrate and explain the testimony of witnesses.[11]

However, if it is not essential to an understanding of the testimony and it is merely cumulative in effect, the judge has discretion as to whether or not to permit it.

There is a distinction between the use of a map or drawing for purposes of illustration as opposed to its admission in evidence. If it is used for the purpose of illustration alone, it is said that the testimony of the witness is the evidence. On the other hand, if it is used with intent to have it admitted as evidence, then it possesses within itself evidentiary characteristics tending to establish a particular fact. Ala.—Crocker v. Lee, 261 Ala. 439, 74 So.2d 429 (1917).

The use of a blackboard for illustration purposes or to aid trial counsel in his arguments is within the discretion of the trial judge. However, it is improper to photograph it in the presence of the jury for purpose of the record on appeal. Fla.—Ratner v. Arrington, 111 So.2d 82 (1959).

Generally a map, diagram or sketch must be accurate in order to warrant its admission. The paper must correctly represent the situation as it existed at the time under consideration. Ark.—Arkansas Louisiana Gas Co. v. Lawrence, 235 Ark. 365, 389 S.W.2d 431 (1965); Va.—Cowles v. Zahn, 20 Va. 743, 146 S.E.2d 200 (1929).

It has been held that it is not essential that the person making the map, diagram or the like, testify to its correctness but any person acquainted with the facts may do so. Miss.—Crawford v. City of Meridian, 186 So.2d 250 (1939).

Therefore, as a practical matter, a cartography section of a law enforcement agency could make the diagram, etc. and any officer or representative familiar with the facts could refer to it and/or testify to its accuracy for its admission.

11. Wyo.—Grayson v. Williams, 256 F. 2d 61 (10th Cir. 1919); Cal.—Smith v. Addiego, 54 C.A.2d 230, 129 P.2d 953 (1913).

§ 2.15 LEADING QUESTIONS

A witness may testify in a narrative response to a general question explaining what s/he saw or heard at a particular time and place. S/He may also give his/her response to a series of specific questions. The former type of questioning is inherently more dangerous because the witness may testify to facts which are wholly incompetent, immaterial and irrelevant. The latter method is far more suitable for trial purposes because only necessary testimony will be included in the trial. The questions and the method used to ask the question is within the discretion of the trial judge. Like all other discretionary acts of a governmental official, it is subject to review by a higher tribunal and may be overturned if the discretion used was arbitrary, discriminatory or prejudicial.

When a question is asked in such a manner as to suggest an answer, the question is known as a leading question. Whether a leading question may be put to the witness rests in the trial judge's discretion. However, generally, subject to well defined exceptions, leading questions may not be used in the direct examination of a witness although they may be used in cross-examination.

Even though the question may call for a yes or no answer, it may not necessarily be leading unless it is so worded that, by permitting the witness to answer yes or no, he would be testifying in the language of the interrogator rather than his/her own.

A question is a leading one when it indicates to the witness the real or supposed fact which the examiner expects and desires to have confirmed by the answer. e. g., "Do you live at 360 Park Avenue South, in the City of New York?" "Have you not lived there for 10 years?"

It is not apparent on every occasion whether or not a question is a leading question. Many times it may become a leading question by the intonation of the questioner's voice.

In Steer v. Little, 44 N.H. 613, the court divided leading questions

1. Questions calling for no answers other than "yes" or "no".
2. Questions so framed as to suggest to the witness the answer desired.
3. Questions which assume facts in controversy.

As indicated above, the test of whether a question is leading is not one of form, but rather whether the question does in fact suggest the answer.

A question framed to suggest an answer to the witness is illustrated in the following: "Did you not hear the defendant say, 'I'll kill John when I see him?' " However, the alternative form, "Did you or did you not hear the defendant say 'I'll kill John when I see him?' "

is an acceptable question because it does not suggest a yes answer to the witness.

A question which assumes a controverted fact is also a leading question. e. g., What did the defendant do when he was driving the car at the scene of the homicide? This is leading and objectionable when the issue, among others, is that there is a question as to whether or not defendant was driving the car at the scene of the homicide.

§ 2.16 LEADING QUESTIONS ADMITTED AS INTRODUCTORY MATTERS

Leading questions, however, are admissible under certain controlled conditions. Leading questions are permissible when they relate to introductory matter and tend to carry the witness quickly to matters material to the issue. Accordingly, a witness may be asked "Were you in the vicinity of 10th Avenue and 59th Street in the County of New York on a specified time and date?" (yes) "Did you make any observations at that time and place with respect to the defendant?" (yes).

Both of these questions are clearly leading questions but are admissible because they lead the witness up to the facts of the time at issue and this facilitates the movement of the trial without any corresponding reduction in the veracity of the witness's testimony.

§ 2.17 LEADING QUESTIONS—HOSTILE WITNESSES

A leading question is permitted, even in direct examination, where the witness appears to be hostile, biased or an unwilling witness. A hostile witness conceals much and reveals as little of the truth as his/her skill and intellect will permit and it is therefore concluded that there is no danger of coloring the witness's testimony by suggesting desired answers.

If a witness is unwilling to testify he may also be led by the question. This often occurs in the prosecution of sex crimes where the witness is embarrassed. U.S.—Antelope v. United States, 185 F.2d 174 (10th Cir. 1950). In a prosecution for statutory rape, permitting district attorney to ask prosecutrix leading questions was not reversible error where prosecutrix was a young, timid Indian girl and was in strange surroundings and the questions were embarrassing to her, and she testified in a timid halting manner. U.S.—United States v. Spoonhunter, 476 F.2d 1050 (10th Cir. 1973). In the final analysis, the judge makes the decision as to who is biased, hostile or unwilling to testify and s/he alone decides whether or not to permit leading questions.

§ 2.18 LEADING QUESTIONS—ELDERLY, CHILDREN OR MENTALLY DEFICIENT WITNESSES

In its quest for the truth, the court, in its discretion, will permit a trial counsel to assist an elderly person, a child or a mentally deficient person who may be nervous when testifying or who may have a fleeting recollection of the facts in issue, to testify by means of responses to leading questions on direct examination. N.Y.—Nicoletti v. Dieckmann, 89 Misc. 131, 151 N.Y.S. 520 (1956). It should be noted however, that if a person is so mentally retarded as to make him an incompetent witness, his testimony should not be admitted unless his testimony was merely cumulative. N.Y.—People v. Rensing, 14 N.Y.2d 210, 199 N.E.2d 489 (1936).

§ 2.19 LEADING QUESTIONS—PATENTLY ERRONEOUS STATEMENTS

When it is apparent that a witness has inadvertently answered a question incorrectly or that he did not understand the question, a leading question may be used on direct examination to give the witness an opportunity to correct the mistake. Va.—Hargrow v. Watson, 200 Va. 30, 104 S.E.2d 37 (1958).

§ 2.20 LEADING QUESTIONS—FACTS NOT REMEMBERED

Where the witness has exhausted his recollection, suggestions of the interrogator are allowed to assist his memory. Suggestions with respect to name, date or itemized lists are permitted. For example, it is unrealistic to expect a police officer to remember dates and what took place in a complicated police occurrence. For the purpose of assisting the officer to testify the questioner may say something like this, "You made a written report of this occurrence at the scene shortly after the time of the occurrence, didn't you?". After an affirmative answer, the next question might be, "You have this report on your person now?". Both of these questions call for a yes or no answer and if asked on direct examination both suggest an affirmative answer. They are usually permitted by the court in its discretion. The questions are not critical questions going to the gravamen of the main issue and no harm can be done to the adversary by their inclusion in the trial record.

§ 2.21 LEADING QUESTIONS—MEMORANDUM

If a memorandum is used to refresh the recollection of the witness, a leading question with respect to this memorandum is admissible, e. g. "Did you make a memorandum of this event in the normal course of your business?"; "Was it a normal course of your business to make such a memorandum?"; "Was this memorandum that you made of this event in the normal course of your business?", etc.

§ 2.22 LEADING QUESTIONS—CROSS-EXAMINATION

The witness to be cross-examined is a hostile witness and therefore the interrogator may use leading questions. N.Y.—People v. Sexton, 187 N.Y. 495, 80 N.E. 396 (1907). If, however, the witness who is to be cross-examined is, in fact, biased in favor of the cross-examiner, leading questions may not be permitted. A situation such as this might occur where a plaintiff calls the defendant to the stand as his witness and the witness is then cross-examined by his own counsel.

A cross-examiner who elicits new matter from the witness, however, is placed in the same position as one who is directly examining and therefore cannot use leading questions.

§ 2.23 LEADING QUESTIONS—THE COURT

The court may, in its discretion, ask leading questions of a witness provided the trial judge does not impress the jury with his opinion as to which of the parties is entitled to judgment. Tenn.—Parker v. State, 132 Tenn. 327, 178 S.W. 438 (1915).

§ 2.24 LEADING QUESTIONS—DISCRETION OF TRIAL COURT

The trial court has great discretion whether or not to permit leading questions and the appellate courts are reluctant to interfere with this discretion.

Some cases state the rule to be that the discretion of the court in this matter is subject to being reviewed but that the determination of the trial court will not be regarded as error unless the discretion is abused. N.Y.—Budlong v. Van Nostrand, 24 Barb. 25. Other cases have stated that if an established rule of law has been violated, the party injured has an undoubted right to relief, and the court should feel no reluctance in such a case to grant it.

The New York Court of Appeals has gone so far as to indicate that the trial court's discretion to determine whether a question is leading and also whether it should be permitted, even though leading, is not subject to review or appeal. N.Y.—Walker v. Dunspaugh, 20 N.Y. 170, 7 N.Y.S. 781 (1890). However, if the judge shows his own opinion on the factual issue when he asks the leading question, the case may be reversed. N.Y.—People v. Mendes, 3 N.Y.2d 120, 164 N.Y.S.2d 401 (1917).

§ 2.25 LEADING QUESTIONS—THE FEDERAL RULE

The Federal Rules of Evidence have prescribed for the use of leading questions as follows:

> **Rule 611(c): —Leading questions.**—Leading questions should not be used on the direct examination of a witness except as may be necessary to develop his testimony. Ordinarily leading questions should be permitted on cross-examination. When a party calls a hostile witness, an adverse party, or a witness identified with an adverse party, interrogation may be by leading questions.

§ 2.26 CROSS–EXAMINATION

The purpose of direct examination is to get the witness to tell the court whatever relevant and competent knowledge he may know respecting the issues of the trial. Leading questions are not generally permitted on direct examination except under certain exceptional conditions as heretofore explained. However, on cross-examination, we find that there are reasons for permitting leading questions.

We must always remember that the reason that we have rules of evidence is that over the centuries, these rules have proven most reliable in eliciting the truth. If we have a rule and then an exception to the rule, the exception is permitted because there is necessity and a high probability of reliability.

Therefore in the admissibility of the exceptions to the leading question exclusionary rule there is always present a necessity and a high degree of reliability.

In cross-examination we are attempting to do three things

1. to challenge the credibility of the direct examination;
2. to bring out additional facts relating to those elicited as direct examination in addition to the facts which were favorable to the opposing party;
3. to give the triers of the fact an opportunity to observe the witness under stress.

In such a climate, the witness becomes a hostile witness and as said previously, a hostile witness may be asked leading questions.

The right of cross-examination is so fundamental to our law that it is included in the Sixth Amendment to the United States Constitution. If the opposing party is denied the right of cross-examination, all of the direct examination is to be expunged from the record. Ala.—Wray v. State, 154 Ala. 36, 45 So. 697 (1908).

This right also is given to the prosecution in a criminal trial to cross-examine defense witnesses.

§ 2.27 CROSS–EXAMINATION—EXTENT

The extent to which the cross-examiner may go rests within the discretion of the trial judge. Only if his rulings are arbitrary, capricious, unreasonable or prejudicial will an appeal court overrule him. This is seldom done. It is therefore apparent that the trial court has great authority in conducting a trial.

If a cross-examiner asks questions which were not brought out on direct examination he makes the witness his own witness and he is bound by his answers.

Shutting off cross-examination by a trial judge, has been held not to abuse his discretion when he shuts off a continuation of cross-examination into collateral and immaterial matters. United States v. Hall, 342 F.2d 849 (4th Cir. 1965).

Answers to certain collateral cross-examination questions need not be adopted by interrogator even though it may introduce new matter. For example, a witness may be asked whether or not he has ever been convicted of a crime. If he answers negatively, the statutes of many jurisdictions provide that the judgment of conviction is admissible to effect his credibility. New York CPLR 4513, New York CPL § 60.60(1). See Harris v. U. S., 371 F.2d 365 (9th Cir. 1967), for further qualifications.

§ 2.28 IMPEACHMENT OF WITNESSES

Impeachment is a term employed to attempt to attack the credibility of a witness by convincing the jury or trier of th efacts that the testimony may not be truthful.

There are various methods of impeachment, some of which are as follows:

1. Showing that the witness has been convicted of a crime after his/her denial of such conviction. (Recent law is limiting this method—see Section 2.30 infra.)
2. Surprise witness—showing that the witness had made other statements to interrogator on previous occasion.
3. Interrogation regarding an immoral, vicious or criminal act of his/her life which may affect his/her character and tend to show that s/he is not worthy of belief.
4. Introduction of extrinsic evidence.
5. Showing his/her bias against the cross-examiner or the party s/he represents.
6. Showing that either at the time of the occurrence to which s/he has testified or at the time of giving the testimony, s/he was under the influence of drugs, or alcohol, or was sick, or was mentally incompetent or was incompetent to testify because of lack of the appreciation of the solemnity of an oath or because of other physical or mental incapacity.
7. Showing his/her general bad reputation with respect to truth and veracity.
8. Showing that s/he was in an improper position or location to make the observation that s/he testified to.
9. Impeachment of experts from the literature in the field of knowledge.
10. Qualifications of expert witnesses.
11. Specific instances of misconduct.
12. Show defect in perception.

13. Showing other similar acts which s/he has done to negate defense of mistake or accident, to infer motive, to show intent, to prove identity, or to show a common scheme or plan.

§ 2.29 IMPEACHMENT BY SHOWING THAT THE WITNESS HAS BEEN CONVICTED OF A CRIME

A witness may be asked in direct or cross-examination whether or not he has been ever convicted of a crime. When this is used in direct examination it may be for the following reasons.

1. To show the jury that they have before them a person who has never been convicted of a crime and therefore is worthy of belief.
2. To show the jury that he has previously been convicted of a crime but that this does not mean that he committed the instant crime.
3. To lessen the blow that might be expected on cross-examination when the adversary asks the question.

For impeachment purposes, as indicated previously, a witness may also be asked this question to attack his credibility. If s/he answers falsely in the negative, statutory authority in most jurisdictions permits the questioner to present into evidence a properly certified copy of a conviction of the witness. This then affects his/her credibility.

When this occurs, his/her own lawyer may, with court permission, engage in redirect examination to attempt to rehabilitate his/her witness. The witness may testify that s/he plead guilty but s/he did not believe that this was a conviction. S/He thought that a conviction only occurred after a trial.

There has been a movement away from this theory of questions. People v. Mallard, 78 Misc.2d 858, 358 N.Y.S.2d 913 (1974), adopted the concept of People v. Sandoval, 34 N.Y.2d 371, 357 N.Y.S.2d 849, 314 N.E.2d 413 (1974), in not permitting cross-examination of a defendant's prior criminal record unless its purpose is to directly relate it to the crime charged.

§ 2.30 FEDERAL RULE—PREVIOUS CRIMINAL CONVICTIONS

Rule 609 Federal Rules of Evidence, reads as follows:

Rule 609: Impeachment by evidence of conviction of crime

(a) General rule.—For the purpose of attacking the credibility of a witness, evidence that he has been convicted of a crime shall be admitted if elicited from him or established by public record during cross-examination but only if the crime (1) was punishable by death or imprisonment in excess of one year under the law under which he was convicted, and the court determines that the probative value of admitting this evidence outweighs its prejudicial effect to the defendant, or (2) involved dishonesty or false statement, regardless of the punishment.

(b) Time limit.—Evidence of a conviction under this rule is not admissible if a period of more than ten years has elapsed since the date of the conviction or of the release of the witness from the confinement imposed for that conviction, whichever is the later date, unless the court determines in the interests of justice, that the probative value of the conviction supported by specific facts and circumstances substantially outweighs its prejudicial effect. However, evidence of a conviction more than 10 years old as calculated herein, is not admissible unless the proponent gives to the adverse party sufficient advance written notice of intent to use such evidence to provide the adverse party with a fair opportunity to contest the use of such evidence.

(c) Effect of pardon, annulment, or certificate of rehabilitation.—Evidence of a conviction is not admissible under this rule if (1) the conviction has been the subject of a pardon, annulment, certificate of rehabilitation, or other equivalent procedure based on a finding of the rehabilitation of the person convicted, and that person has not been convicted of a subsequent crime which was punishable by death or imprisonment in excess of one year, or (2) the conviction has been the subject of a pardon, annulment, or other equivalent procedure based on a finding of innocence.

(d) Juvenile adjudications.—Evidence of juvenile adjudications is generally not admissible under this rule. The court may, however, in a criminal case allow evidence of a juvenile adjudication of a witness other than the accused if conviction of the offense would be admissible to attack the credibility of an adult and the court is satisfied that admission in evidence is necessary for a fair determination of the issue of guilt or innocence.

(e) Pendency of appeal.—The pendency of an appeal therefrom does not render evidence of a conviction inadmissible. Evidence of the pendency of an appeal is admissible.

§ 2.31 SURPRISE WITNESS—SHOWING THAT THE WITNESS HAD MADE OTHER STATEMENTS TO INTERROGATOR ON PREVIOUS OCCASIONS

After a proper foundation is laid, a witness who has made a prior inconsistent statement may be asked questions relating to what he had stated or written on a previous occasion.

By laying a proper foundation is meant that the witness must just be asked whether

1. s/he made such a statement;
2. did s/he make it to a specified person;
3. did s/he make it at a particular time and place.

The purpose of the foundation is to furnish the witness with specific enough information about the former statement that s/he can recall it.

If the witness admits having made the statement, the impeaching attorney cannot adduce any extrinsic evidence of the prior inconsistent statement. If the witness admits having made the statement but offers an explanation for the apparent inconsistency, e. g., "the former statement was signed by him unread," the explanation will be permitted for what the jury thinks it is worth.

The Federal Rules of Evidence treat this problem in Rule 613(a) in a different manner:

> **Rule 613: Prior statements of witness**
>
> (a) Examining witnesses concerning prior statement. In examining a witness concerning a prior statement made by him, whether written or not, the statement need not be shown nor its contents disclosed to him at that time, but on request shall be shown or disclosed to opposing counsel.

§ 2.32 INTRODUCTION OF EXTRINISIC EVIDENCE

Extrinsic evidence is elicited not on cross-examination (from the witness' own mouth or suggested by the cross-examiner) but rather through the introduction of the testimony of independent witnesses or perhaps tangible evidence directed at attacking the credibility of the witness who is being impeached. This type of impeachment is usually introduced when it is the impeacher's turn to put on his/her case. Sometimes the intent is to discredit a particular statement made by the witness rather than to discredit the person generally e. g., to show that a clergyman of great reputation in the community made an error in his testimony yet the impeacher does not want to discredit this clergyman's total person.

However, according to Rule 613(b) of the Federal Rules of Evidence, extrinsic evidence of a prior inconsistent statement by a witness is not admissible unless the witness is afforded an opportunity to explain or deny the same and the opposite party is afforded an opportunity to interrogate him thereon, or the interests of justice otherwise require. This provision does not apply to admissions of a party opponent as defined in Rule 801(d)(2).

§ 2.33 SHOW BIAS AGAINST CROSS-EXAMINER OR AGAINST PARTY THAT HE REPRESENTS

In New York, the Court of Appeals stated in Schultz v. Third Avenue R. R. Co., 89 N.Y. 242, 250 (1882), that the evidence to show hostile feelings of a witness "should be direct and positive, and not very remote and uncertain, for the reason that the trial of the main issues in the case cannot be properly suspended to make out the case of hostile feeling by mere circumstantial evidence from which such hostility or malice may or may not be inferred." In other cases it has been held that the extent to which a cross-examiner may go to show bias or hostility rests with the trial judge but a trial judge abuses his discretion if he rules out all questions to show hostility or bias.

The party cross-examining a witness has the same right to show bias or hostility that the party who called the witness to the stand has in calling him.

Many techniques and reasons may be demonstrated to show bias or hostility. A previous quarrel, jealousy, overzealous police officer, prejudice for particular race or religion, close friend of one of the parties, political publicity, sexual desire for the mate of the defendant, breach of a commercial agreement by one of the adversaries, higher insurance premium to witness if other party is successful, loss of money if other party is successful, are only a few of the types of motivation which might conceive bias or hostility.

§ 2.34 SHOWING THAT EITHER AT THE TIME OF THE OCCURRENCE OR AT THE TIME OF TESTIFYING, WITNESS WAS UNDER INFLUENCE OF DRUGS, ALCOHOL, NARCOTICS, ILL MENTALLY AND/OR PHYSICALLY, DID NOT UNDERSTAND THE NATURE OF ANY OATH, OR OTHER PHYSICAL OR MENTAL INCAPACITY

Assuming that the witness is an honest witness, we may impeach him/her on his/her ability to perceive what he has observed. Many of us will look at a person and fail to remember what color tie he wore or what color dress she wore. When we look at a situation and perceive all of the details of that situation to the extent we can turn our head away and look in another direction and verbalize what we have previously observed we can thus say we have perceived what we have seen.

This area of testimony is particularly well suited to impeachment procedure in normal healthy individuals. It is particularly well suited to persons whose perceptive ability is impaired through the use of narcotics or alcohol or illness. If it can be shown that the witness' perception was incapacitated by the use of drugs, or narcotics, or alcohol or physically incapacitated (e. g., color blindness, poor eyesight, poor hearing, lack of proper illumination) or mentally defective, the weight of the witnesses testimony is lessened in the eyes of the jury.

Often, a child or mentally retarded adult is permitted to testify. If this witness is shown not to understand the seriousness of an oath or affirmation, this too may affect the weight of the witness' testimony.

§ 2.35 SHOWING WITNESS' BAD REPUTATION FOR TRUTH AND VERACITY

A witness may have a reputation in the community for being a congenital liar. If this is so, his testimony may be refuted by other witnesses who may testify that they have heard rumors or reports in the community that the witness cannot be believed.

All authorities agree however, that testimony as to the reputation of a witness with respect to any specific trait of character, other than veracity is not admissible for the purpose of impeaching the creditability of a witness e. g., a complaining witness in an assault may not be impeached by testimony of his general bad reputation for not paying his just debts.

The time that the reputation is flooding the community need not be very recent nor should it be too remote. See N.Y.—Sturmwald v. Schreiber, 69 App.Div. 476, 74 N.Y.S. 995 (1948).

Specific examples of misconduct may not be introduced in the direct examination of the character witness but it may be asked of the witness on cross-examination.

§ 2.36 SHOWING THAT WITNESS WAS IN AN IMPROPER POSITION TO MAKE OBSERVATIONS THAT HE TESTIFIED TO

Frequently a witness will testify that he observed a gun in the right hand of the defendant or that he observed the traffic light to be green for a particular party. A cross-examiner might be able to show that the witness was in such a location at the time of the incident that s/he only heard the noise of the gun shooting, or the collision of the vehicles and then ran to the location of the incident and concluded that the facts were as s/he had testified without actually seeing them occur because s/he was in a location which was out of the line of sight of the situs of the instant case.

§ 2.37 SHOW ENTRAPMENT OF DEFENDANT

Frequently a defendant's attorney will raise the defense of entrapment to save his/her client from being convicted. There is a popular misconception as to what the word "entrapment" means. Black's Law Dictionary, Revised 4th Edition, defines entrapment as: The act of officers or agents of government in inducing a person to commit a crime not contemplated by him for the purpose of instituting a criminal prosecution against him. Falden v. Commonwealth, 167 Va. 549, 189 S.E. 329 (1937). The mere act of an officer in furnishing the accused an opportunity to commit a crime, where the criminal intent was already present in the accused's mind, is not ordinarily entrapment. Wash.—State v. Cowling, 167 Wash. 519, 297 Pac. 172 (1931).

Many statutory prohibitions exist prohibiting law enforcement officers from entraping defendants. They are an outgrowth of the federal standards as set forth in Sorrells v. United States, 287 U.S. 435, 53 S.Ct. 210, 77 L.Ed. 413 (1933), and Sherman v. United States, 356 U.S. 369, 78 S.Ct. 819, 2 L.Ed.2d 848 (1958). In essence a law enforcement officer cannot successfully encourage a person to commit a crime unless that person was previously disposed to commit that crime. An illustration may make this concept clearer.

Let us assume that because of a rash of auto burglaries in the vicinity of a hospital where out-of-town visitors were accustomed to park their cars leaving valuables within the vehicle, the local police set up a "stake-out". They parked a vehicle in the street near the hospital with a camera and a woman's pocketbook plainly visible on the front seat. Officers were stationed in jeans and sport shirts near the car and played a game of cards on a stoop of a building located near the subject vehicle. "C" and "D" were seen to be walking along the street looking into parked vehicles as they walked. As they came to the designated car, they stopped, had a short conversation and then "D" took instruments from his right coat pocket and proceeded to pick the lock. "C" assisted by taking one of the instruments from "D" and inserted it into the lock to keep the dust cover of the lock open while "D" did his picking. After a time, the door was opened and entry was made. "D" picked up the camera and "C" picked up the woman's handbag. At this point the officers sprang to action and the arrests were made.

One may think that this was a clear case of entrapment. This, however, was not entrapment because they had an apparent previous disposition to commit the crime. Accordingly, if the defense of entrapment is raised, the prosecutor would have to elicit testimony as to what the defendants were doing prior to the burglary as they walked down the street looking at cars. This could be brought out on redirect examination or he could have the officers testify to it on direct examination. In United States v. Russell, 411 U.S. 423, 93 S.Ct. 1637, 36 L.Ed.2d 366 (1973), the United States Supreme Court held that there is no defense of entrapment available to a defendant previously disposed to commit the crime where the government agent supplies a necessary ingredient to manufacture a controlled substance. In the 1976 Term of the Court, it decided Hampton v. United States, 425 U.S. 484, 96 S.Ct. 1646, 48 L.Ed.2d 113 (1974), where a 5–4 decision held that where a defendant had a predisposition to commit a crime, the defense of entrapment may still be available if there was "outrageous police conduct". There was no definition of what outrageous police conduct might be. In the *Hampton* case, the defendant was accused of distribution of heroin and both the suppliers and the purchasers were government agents or informers.

§ 2.38 IMPEACHMENT OF EXPERTS FROM THE LITERATURE IN THE FIELD

Certain disciplines have books which are recognized authorities in the area of the alleged expertise of the expert witness. Frequently the witness will make statements which are at variance to the theories of practices expressed in the works of the recognized authorities in the discipline. The expert witness may be confronted with these statements if s/he recognized them as authoritative in the field where s/he claims his/her expertise. Frequently embarrassing encounters result when the witness' statements are at variance with some statement s/he has made in a publication. This, of course, lessens the weight of his/her testimony in the minds of the jury.

However, a medical book or treatise must be shown to be a recognized authority before it can be used in cross-examination of an expert medical witness. N. J.—Ruth v. Fenchel, 37 N.J.Super. 295, 117 A.2d 284 (1955), affirmed 21 N.J. 171, 121 A.2d 373, but the cross-examination must be confined to legitimate impeachment of what the witness has testified to, to showing such deficiency in the knowledge of the expert as to the science about which he is testifying as is calculated to impair the weight of his testimony. Tex.—Gulf, C & S.F.R. Co. v. Farmer, 102 Tex. 235, 115 S.W. 260 (1909).

§ 2.39 QUALIFICATIONS OF EXPERT WITNESS

Witnesses who are experts are first required to establish their credentials to the satisfaction of the trial judge before they may be called upon to answer a question which requires a conclusion. When the judge is satisfied that the witness is an expert, he may then testify on direct examination with respect to conclusions in the area of his expertise.

On cross-examination in a voir dire examination the interrogator may delve more thoroughly into the witness's qualifications to testify as an expert and may elicit information that the witness' experience in the discipine is not sufficiently extensive to warrant that s/he testify as an expert.

It may be timely to note that a voir dire examination is conducted upon application to the judge by the adversary before the expert witness is permitted to testify as an expert and is almost like a cross-examination but is different in that the adversary inquires only to the fitness of the witness to testify as an expert and at that juncture does not inquire into the facts of the instant case. Cal.—Eble v. Peluso, 80 C.A.2d 154, 181 P.2d 680 (1947); N.J.—Carbone v. Warburton, 11 N.J. 418, 94 A.2d 680 (1953); Pa.—Hoffman v. Berwind-White Coal Mining, 265 Pa. 476, 109 A. 234 (1920).

§ 2.40 SPECIFIC INSTANCES OF MISCONDUCT

In New York a specific act of misconduct relevant only as tending to impair the witness' credibility can only be elicited on his cross-examination; it may not be proved by extrinsic evidence. If the witness denies committing the act, the cross-examiner cannot refute his answer by calling other witnesses or producing other evidence. N.Y.—People v. McCormick, 303 N.Y. 403, 103 N.E.2d 529 (1952). However, the cross-examiner may, if in good faith, continue the cross examination of the witness on the chance that he may change his answer. N.Y.—People v. Sorge, 301 N.Y. 198, 93 N.E.2d 637 (1950). The specific act of misconduct must have some relevancy to show that the witness is a person of moral turpitude. N.H.—Curtice v. Dixon, 74 N.H. 586, 68 A. 587 (1908); N.Y.—People v. Montlake, 184 A.D. 578, 172 N.Y.S. 102 (1958).

§ 2.41 SHOW DEFECT IN PERCEPTION

As indicated previously, a person may see something occur but s/he may be unable to verbalize the occurrence because s/he did not perceive it. Perception has been defined as a mental impression or the act or ability to become aware of something. It is therefore possible for a witness to see something with his/her eyes and yet not become mentally aware of what s/he sees. The author has used a method with some success in cross-examination when he would turn his back on the witness and ask the witness to describe what color shirt and tie he was wearing and what distinctive characteristics could be found in the author's face. If the witness was unable to identify these objects or characteristics after having been questioned by the author for a lengthy period of time prior to the perception test, this fact would be brought out to the jury in summation to discredit the witness's perceptive ability.

§ 2.42 IMPEACHMENT OF ONE'S OWN WITNESS

In common law a party calling a witness to the stand in effect vouched for the truth and veracity of his testimony and could not impeach his testimony. N.Y.—Bulkley v. Kaolin Products Co., 187 A.D. 103, 175 N.Y.S. 219 (1919); Colo.—Scott v. Shook, 249 P. 259, 80 Colo. 40, 47 A.L.R. 1108 (1926).

This has been modified by statute in some jurisdictions e. g., N.Y. CPLR 3117; CPLR 4514, CPL § 60:35(i) where a witness who makes a contradictory statement on the witness stand may be impeached by the party who called him to testify providing the witness previously made either a written statement signed by him or an oral statement under oath, said statement being contrary to his testimony from the stand at the present time.

However, a party whose witness has testified to contradictory information and who has not made a prior statement under oath or a written prior statement signed by the witness available to him, may prove his claim by other evidence and is not bound to his witness' testimony. Conn.—Nicholson Realty, Inc. v. Libby, 144 Conn. 555, 135 A.2d 738 (1927); Pa.—Frew v. Barto, 345 Pa. 217, 26 A.2d 905 (1942); Ill.—Wisniewski v. Shimashus, 176 N.E.2d 781, 22 Ill.2d 451 (1961); N.Y.—Quick v. American Can Co., 205 N.Y. 330, 98 N.E. 480 (1912).

The Federal Rules of Evidence Rule 607 spells out this deviation from the common law practice very clearly. It provides in Rule 607 that the creditability of a witness may be attacked by any party, including the party calling him. The same result is found in California Evidence Code § 785, Kansas Code of Civil Practice § 60–420 and New Jersey Evidence Rule 20.

§ 2.43 SHOWING OF OTHER SIMILAR ACTS

A defendant may be prone to do certain acts which standing alone may not demonstrate criminal behavior but, if considered collectively, they may logically infer that the intent of the subject was to violate the law. In this category of behavioral patterns we may find an inference:

1. To show motive.
2. To show intent.
3. To show absence of mistake.
4. To show common scheme or plan.
5. To show identity of person charged.

§ 2.44 OTHER SIMILAR ACTS—MOTIVE—INTENT

A motive has been defined as an inner reason for doing a given act. Intent is defined as having the mind closely fixed on a subject. A person may have a reason to steal to support his family without resorting to public assistance. Therefore his motive is to support his family. His intention therefore is to steal. If it can be demonstrated that he desperately needed money this fact would be admissible in a larceny trial.

Another example of this principle might occur if shortly after the homicide of a husband, the defendant married the wife of the deceased. The fact of the marriage could be introduced to show motive on the part of the defendant to commit the homicide. In order for this type of testimony to be admissible, it must have a logical relation to the commission of the crime charged. N.Y.—People v. Namer, 309 N.Y. 458, 131 N.E.2d 734 (1956); Conn.—Lomartira v. Lomartira, 159 Conn. 558, 271 A.2d 91 (1971); Fla.—River Hills Inc. v. Edwards, 190 So.2d 415 (App.1966); Ky.—Flynn v. Songer, 399 S.W.2d 491 (1960).

However, subsequent acts may not be considered as showing previous fraudulent intent. Mich.—Sachs v. Karos, 310 Mich. 577, 17 N.W. 2d 759 (1945), certiorari denied 326 U.S. 794, 66 S.Ct. 483, 90 L.Ed. 482.

§ 2.45 OTHER SIMILAR ACTS—TO SHOW ABSENCE OF MISTAKE

A defendant may have made a mistake and the wrongdoing that he committed is excusable. However, if this alleged "mistake" occurred with some frequency, it might be admissible to introduce other similar acts which would negate the defense of mistake.

For example, if a defendant was charged with the homicide of his mother and his defense was that he was awakened in the middle of the night by his mother requesting medicine for a heart palpitation attack. He went to the medicine cabinet in the bathroom and returned with a brown medicine which his mother had told him was in the medicine cabinet. He administered the medicine to his mother and immediately both he and she realized that it was the wrong medicine. He had given her a preparation to be used to remove warts. When he realized his mistake he called the police to get a stomach pump to his mother immediately. His mother died within a short time after he gave her the medicine. The medicine which he should have given her was in a similar bottle and similar in appearance to the wart remover. If there was a similar type of occurrence previously with this same defendant, it could have been introduced into evidence to show that it was not a mistake. It may interest the reader to know that such a situation as this occurred and that the author was the police officer who responded to the call.

The overriding concept of the reason for admission of other similar acts—absence of mistake—is based on two theories:

1. Probability theory—The greater the repetition, the less probable that it was a mistake.
2. Knowledge theory—As the number of the acts increase, there is a greater opportunity to gain knowledge.

§ 2.46 OTHER SIMILAR ACTS—TO SHOW COMMON SCHEME OR PLAN

Other similar acts may be introduced into evidence to show a common scheme or plan. There are two types of situations which should be considered. In the first type there will be at least two crimes committed but there will be at least one objective. The second type envisages the commission of several crimes with relation of time and space being very close.

An example of more than one crime with one objective may occur if three persons are co-conspirators and rob a bank. The agreement between them was that they would divide the proceeds of the robbery equally. After the successful completion of the robbery, two of the participants agree to murder the third in order to divide his portion among them. They murder the third person and then the defendant felt that this was an easy way to get rich so he murdered the second participant. At the trial of the defendant for either of the murders, evidence may be introduced that his objective was to get all the proceeds for his own use and therefore testimony of the first murder could be introduced. This is very close to motive and almost indistinguishable.

An example of the commission of several crimes with relation of time and space being very close might be the apprehension of a burglar in an apartment of an apartment house containing forty apartments, two of which reported burglaries having taken place on the same evening that the defendant was apprehended and the defendant having been caught with the proceeds of the other burglaries on his person. In order to grasp this concept clearly, the student should ask himself:

1. Is it relevant?
2. Does it have substantial relevancy?
3. If it does, will the substantial relevancy outweigh the undue prejudice?

§ 2.47 OTHER SIMILAR ACTS—TO SHOW IDENTITY OF PERSON CHARGED

The Federal Rules of Evidence have codified the principles in Rule 404(b) where it reads as follows:

> b. Other crimes, wrongs or acts.—Evidence of other crimes, wrongs or acts is not admissible to prove the character of a person in order to show that he acted in conformity therewith. It may, however, be admissible for other purposes, such as proof of motive, opportunity, intent, preparation, plan, knowledge, identity or absence of mistake or accident.

Other similar acts may be introduced to show the identity of the person charged. An example of this concept might be if a burglar has been leaving his trademark by defecating on top of the bedspread which is on the bed in the master bedroom of the burglarized premises. The burglar is later apprehended coming out of the rear window of a burglarized home. Inspection by the police officers revealed that there was fresh feces on the bedspread in the master bedroom. Evidence might be introduced in the trial of this defendant for the other burglaries that he defecated in each of the burglaries in a peculiar manner. This would tend to logically infer that the same person committed all of the burglaries and that the defendant was that person.

For a thorough discussion of these principles, the reader is referred to N.Y.—People v. Molineux, 168 N.Y. 264, 61 N.E. 286, 62 L.R.A. 193 (1901); U.S.—Drew v. United States, 331 F.2d 85 (D.C.Cir. 1964).

CHAPTER III

CIRCUMSTANTIAL EVIDENCE

§ 3.1 DEFINITION

Perhaps the best way to understand the concept of circumstantial evidence is to contrast it with direct evidence. Direct evidence means that which immediately points to the question at issue, or is evidence of the precise facts at issue and on trial, by witnesses who can testify that they saw the act done, or heard the words spoken, which constitute the facts to be proved. Mo.—Stern v. Employers' Liability Assur. Corporation, Limited of London, England, 249 S.W. 739 (App. 1929). Another definition of direct evidence is a recital of facts testified to by eyewitnesses constitutes positive or "direct evidence". Ohio —Rio Bar Inc. v. State, 117 N.E.2d 522 (Comm.Pl.1918). Whereas circumstantial evidence is evidence which, without going directly to prove the existence of a fact, gives rise to a logical inference that such fact does exist. N.C.—Wilkerson v. Clark, 264 N.C. 439, 141 S.E.2d 884 (1965); Or.—LaBarge v. United Ins. Co., 221 Or. 480, 349 P.2d 822 (1960).

Let us hypothecate that a witness heard screams coming from a room in a house other than the one in which the witness was presently in. The witness ran to the room where the noise emanated and saw the defendant standing over the body of the deceased holding a bloody nine inch knife in his right hand. The deceased, although still alive, was unable to talk because of a pre-existing organic problem. The deceased was bleeding profusely from his stomach and head and his body was surrounded by a pool of thick blood. When the witness entered the room, he almost fell to the ground by stepping into the blood, causing the soles of his shoes to lose traction. The defendant denied that he had committed the homicide. The witness testified as to gory facts as I have related them. The jury could logically infer that the defendant committed this crime even though he was not seen to directly plunge the knife into the deceased.

§ 3.2 CIRCUMSTANTIAL EVIDENCE—ADMISSIBILITY

The admissibility of circumstantial evidence is within the wide discretion of the trial court. Great latitude generally is allowed in admitting it. Or.—Byrd v. Lord Bros. Contractors Inc., 256 Or. 421, 473 P.2d 1018 (1970); Fla.—Baugher v. Boley, 63 Fla. 75, 58 So. 980 (1912). However, the facts offered as circumstantial evidence must afford a reasonable inference of the existence or non-existence of the fact sought to be proved. N.Y.—In re Dale's Will, 159 Misc. 578, 288 N.Y.S. 564 (1936).

§ 3.3 CIRCUMSTANTIAL EVIDENCE—EXCLUSIONARY RULES

Throughout the study of the law of evidence, the student will encounter what are known as exclusionary rules. These rules will exclude certain type of evidence in the interest of justice. The courts, in their search for truth, have found it desirable to exclude evidence which, although relevant and competent, may tend to be too slight, remote or conjectural to have any legitimate influence in determining the issues between the parties. N.Y.—People v. Feldman, 299 N.Y. 153, 85 N.E.2d 913 (1949). A decision may not be rested on remote inference. Tenn.—Quaker Oats Co. v. Davis, 33 Tenn.App. 373, 232 S.W.2d 282 (1950). There are situations where the trial judge will refuse to permit the introduction of evidence where the danger of its admission would prolong the trial to an unreasonable extent without any corresponding advantage; or would confuse the issues and mislead the jury; or unfairly surprise a party or create substantial danger of undue prejudice to one of the parties. N.Y.—People v. Harris, 209 N.Y. 70, 102 N.E. 546 (1913); Thayer, Preliminary Treatise on Evidence at the Common Law (1898) p. 516.

§ 3.4 CIRCUMSTANTIAL EVIDENCE—INFERENCE

An inference has been defined as a deduction from the facts given, which is usually less than certainty but which may be sufficient to support a finding of fact; a process of reasoning by which a fact or proposition sought to be established is deducted as a logical consequence from other facts, by virtue of the common experience of man which will support but will not compel such deductions.

A. *Remoteness*: As explained in § 3.3 supra, evidence which is too remote will not be admitted. So, too, with inferences which are too remote. An inference must be reasonably drawn from, and supported by, the facts on which it purports to rest. Tex.—Dotson v. Royal Indemnity Co., 427 S.W.2d 150 (1968); Va.—Virginia Transit Co. v. Schain, 205 Va. 373, 137 S.E.2d 22 (1964).

B. *Prejudice*: The fact that evidence may prejudice the adverse party in the minds of the jury will in itself, be insufficient grounds to exclude the admissibility of evidence. A party cannot be deprived of the benefit of evidence which is relevant and material because it may also have a tendency to prejudice the adverse party in the eyes of the jury. Kan.—Harmon v. Electric Theatre Co., 111 Kan. 352, 206 Pac. 875 (1922); Ga.—Fuller v. Fuller, 107 Ga.App. 429, 130 S.E.2d 520 (1963). However, where there is a possibility of unfair prejudice the court may exclude such evidence. N.Y.—People v. Harris, 209 N.Y. 70, 102 N.E. 546 (1913); N.H.—Bunten v. Davis, 83 N.H. 304, 133 A. 16 (1926).

C. *Conjectural*: If evidence is too conjectural so that many different deductions may be drawn, it should be excluded. It cannot be based on surmise, speculation, conjecture or guess. Ark.—Glide v.

Arkhola Sand & Gravel Co., 212 Ark. 838, 208 S.W.2d 4 (1948); N.J.—Rivera v. Columbus Cadet Corps. of America, 59 N.J.Super. 445, 158 A.2d 62 (1960). However, whenever the evidence is such that fair-minded men may draw inferences, a measure of speculation and conjecture is required on the part of those whose duty it is to choose the most reasonable of inferences. N.Y.—Rocco v. N.Y. Central System, 6 A.D.2d 828, 176 N.Y.S.2d 234 (1919). Therefore, the trial court must exercise discretion in weighing whether the conjecture to be drawn would cover too many logical deductions to be reliable.

D. *Confuse Jury*: The jury usually is composed of laymen with average intelligence. When we speak of average intelligence, we might analogize it to the height of the average man. Let us assume that the average height of the American male is 5′10″. There are many American males who are 6′2″ and many who are 5′5″. So too with the intelligence of the person who is called upon to perform jury duty. It is hoped that the collective intelligence of the jury is that of the average intelligence of man. Since the attorneys who select the jury are limited by the array that is before them, they are not always fortunate enough to get an intelligent body of jurors. Accordingly, the evidence that is introduced should not be of such a nature as to confuse the jury so that it may erroneously apply it. N.J.—Ginden v. Baron, 16 N.J.Super. 1, 83 A.2d 790 (1951).

E. *Unduly prolong the trial*: The history of calendar delay in the trial of lawsuits in the United States and State courts is well known. While it is important to our system of government to afford every litigant his day in court, for all practical purposes it is impossible to give a fair trial to all if the trials which are to be tried go on and on and include evidence which, while relevant, will on balance be outweighed by the danger that its admission would prolong the trial to an unreasonable extent without any corresponding advantage. Md.—Huber v. State, 2 Md.App. 245, 234 A.2d 264 (1967); Pa.—Sunshine Packing Corp. v. Com., 45 Erie 231 (1961), motion denied 45 Erie 237.

F. *Unfair surprise*: The concept of unfair surprise is a nebulous one. We cannot expect an adversary to tell the other side in advance of trial exactly what his offense or defense will be. However, court rules in various jurisdictions are requiring extensive disclosures on the part of all litigants. It is presumed that if each side of a controversy exposes its case prior to trial, there will be a greater disposition to settle the case and thus avoid the time and expense of a trial and subsequent appellate processes. Where a litigant is required by law or court rule to disclose a certain evidentiary item and fails to do so, his subsequent attempt to introduce that item at trial is subject to a successful objection. However, where counsel for proponents of a Will had ample opportunity to inspect hospital records at the trial in County Court which admitted the Will to probate, admission of hospital records in evidence in subsequent trial in District Court was not objectionable on ground that proponents had been unfairly surprised by failure of contestants to deliver copy of the records a reasonable time before trial in District Court. Tex.—Greene v. Watts, 332 S.W.2d 419 (Civ.App.1960).

§ 3.5 CIRCUMSTANTIAL EVIDENCE—CHARACTER

In a criminal prosecution a defendant may introduce reputation evidence as to his own good character for the purpose of raising an inference that he would not be likely to commit the offense charged. N.Y.—People v. Van Gaasbeck, 189 N.Y. 408, 82 N.E. 718, 22 L.R.A. (N.S.) 650 (1907). Defendant, whom law does not invest with the presumption of good character, is accorded the privilege or option of initially introducing evidence of his good character on the theory that such circumstantial evidence as may bear on probability that he did not commit the crime charged. U.S.—Brown v. Haynes, 385 F. Supp. 285 (D.C.Mo.1974). An accused has the right to offer evidence of his good character, inferred from reputation testimony, to show that he was unlikely to have acted in the manner and with the intent charged in the indictment. U.S.—United States v. Lewin, 467 F.2d 1132 (7th Cir. 1972).

From a reading of the cases cited above, the student can understand how circumstantial evidence of good character may be introduced into a trial to raise an inference that the defendant did not commit the crime for which he is charged. This is not to say, however, that character traits wholly unrelated to the crime charged, may be introduced. It may only be introduced if it relates to the trait of character which makes it probable or improbable that the accused would have done the kind of fact which is alleged to have constituted a crime. U.S.—Springer v. United States, 148 F.2d 411 (9th Cir. 1945). A further treatment of character evidence will be found in Chapter VI of this text.

§ 3.6 CIRCUMSTANTIAL EVIDENCE—SKILL

If a defendant was found to be in possession of stolen articles which had been unlawfully taken from a locked trunk of an automobile, the fact that the defendant had completed a course of study as a locksmith is relevant to show that he possessed the necessary skill to open the trunk and therefore is inferentially not only guilty as a receiver of stolen property but also of the actual burglary and larceny. In this way the fact that the defendant possessed the necessary skill, considered together with other factors is relevant. Existence of a skill may be shown by prior acts indicative of its possession. Ky.—Paducah First National Bank v. Wisdom, 111 Ky. 135, 63 S.W. 461 (1901).

§ 3.7 CIRCUMSTANTIAL EVIDENCE—PHYSICAL CAPACITY

If a male has a history of sexual impotence, it is logical to infer that the possibility of that person committing a rape on a female is unlikely. Likewise, if a person who is crippled to the extent that he is unable to walk and must move only with the aid of a wheelchair, the likelihood of his running from one section of a street block of about 1/20th of a mile length in 18 seconds, is improbable. This type of evidence is therefore admissible to prove that the defendant may have been incapable of committing the crime with which he is charged.

§ 3.8 CIRCUMSTANTIAL EVIDENCE—MENTAL CAPACITY

One is presumed to know those things which are matters of common knowledge. Ill.—Schaefer v. Stamm, 68 Ill.App.2d 42, 215 N.E.2d 9 (1966). A party is presumed to know, or is chargeable with knowledge of, matters which he had an opportunity to know. Fla.—Kennedy v. Vandine, 185 So.2d 693 (1966). It therefore may be inferred that a defendant knew matters of common knowledge and he is therefore obliged in his defense to go forward with the evidence to show that he did not have the knowledge requisite to make him liable for the commission of the offense.

§ 3.9 CIRCUMSTANTIAL EVIDENCE—THREATS

On the issue of whether a defendant acted in self-defense in inflicting a mortal wound on the deceased, it is permissible to introduce evidence which indicated that the deceased had made threats upon the life of the defendant. Declarations are admissible to prove the inference of a particular motive on the mind of the declarant. Mass.—Leach v. Wilbur, 91 Mass. (9 Allen) 212 (1864); Ga.—Conoly v. Imperial Tobacco Co., 63 Ga.App. 880, 12 S.E.2d 398 (1941).

§ 3.10 CIRCUMSTANTIAL EVIDENCE—MEANS TO ACCOMPLISH ACT

When a defendant has the means to perform an act, this fact may be introduced as circumstantial evidence tending to prove that he did commit the act. In the case of People v. Molineux, 168 N.Y. 264, 61 N.E. 286, 62 L.R.A. 193 (1901), the defendant was a pharmacist who had chemicals at his disposal. Evidence was introduced to show this fact in a homicide case where the decedent had been poisoned. Also see N.Y.—People v. Soper, 243 N.Y. 320, 153 N.E. 433 (1926).

§ 3.11 CIRCUMSTANTIAL EVIDENCE—TECHNICAL KNOWLEDGE

The fact that a defendant had the technical knowledge to commit a crime may also be shown, to prove that the defendant did, in fact, perpetrate the offense. People v. Molineux (supra). Knowledge may be established by circumstantial evidence, even if the defendant claims ignorance. Ala.—Liberty Nat. Life Ins. Co. v. Weldon, 267 Ala. 171, 100 So.2d 696, 61 A.L.R.2d 1346 (1958); Mo.—Fireman's Fund Ins. Co. v. Trippe, 402 S.W.2d 577 (App.1966).

§ 3.12 CIRCUMSTANTIAL EVIDENCE—CONDUCT AS EVIDENCE OF GUILT

Police officers very often develop what is known as a sixth sense. The officer might say when speaking of the defendant, "He just didn't look right to me". What the officer is really saying is that the defendant participated in some course of conduct which aroused suspicion on the part of the officer. However, as will be more fully treated in Chapter 19, suspicion alone is insufficient to cause an arrest.

There are situations however, where conduct could be circumstantial cause for an arrest. Let us suppose that an officer on patrol hears the crash of an auto accident but does not see the actual crash. As the officer proceeds to the location of the collision, he observes a youth running away from the scene. Instead of directly going to the scene, he stops the youth and questions him. The officer handcuffs the youth after the suspect cannot give a satisfactory explanation of why he is running from the scene. The operator of one of the vehicles cannot be found. The passenger in the other vehicle was ejected from the vehicle after hitting his head on the windshield, subsequently resulting in his death. Witnesses saw one unidentified youth run from the vehicle which had no driver but cannot positively identify the apprehended youth as the one who fled the scene. The fact that the apprehended youth was running away from the scene of the collision may be introduced in evidence to prove circumstantially that he was the driver of the now driverless vehicle. Accordingly, the identity of a person is a fact to be proved like any other fact and may be proved by circumstantial evidence. Conn.—State v. Couture, 2 Conn. Cir. 683, 205 A.2d 387 (1965); Pa.—In re Lupenski's Estate, 57 Berks 204, 15 Fiduciary 548 (1965); Fla.—Stettler v. Huggins, 134 So.2d 534 (App.1962).

§ 3.13 CIRCUMSTANTIAL EVIDENCE—EVIDENCE OF OTHER CRIMES

A prosecutor/rix must be particularly careful when introducing evidence of other crimes alleged to have been committed by a defendant. It is axiomatic that every defendant is entitled to a fresh start at the bar of justice. The fact of his/her previous criminal behavior may be so prejudicial so as to result in a reversal when the case goes on appeal. There are situations however, where the courts have permitted the introduction into evidence of the commission by the defendant of other similar crimes to circumstantially prove that the defendant committed the crime for which he is being tried in the instant case. The cases where this is allowed are usually cases where the other similar crimes have an inherently unique quality to them. Such a situation occurred in People v. Seaman, 107 Mich. 348, 65 N.W. 203 (1895), where on a prosecution for manslaughter in committing an abortion, it was proper to receive evidence that the defendant had performed other abortions in the same house to negate the defense of abortion due to accidental causes.

The trial judge must balance all of the relevant factors in order to decide whether the prejudicial character of the introduction of other crimes outweighs the probative value of the evidence.

§ 3.14 CIRCUMSTANTIAL EVIDENCE—OTHER FALSE REPRESENTATION

Frequently a defendant falsely represents a certain fact in order to cause an unsuspecting victim to part with his money. Let us suppose that a defendant is charged with larceny of the sum of $50.00. His modus operandi was to frequent a location in a large city where there was a high concentration of bars and bawdy houses. He would size up a likely prospect, usually a visiting stranger looking for some extra curricular fun. He would accost the victim and furtively give him a glimpse of what appeared to be a diamond ring and ask the victim if he would like to buy it for $100.00. Sometimes he would indicate in some manner that it was "hot" (recently stolen) and that he wanted some quick cash for it. The victim, having a little larceny in his soul, offers him $50.00 for it and the defendant would give the ring to the victim in exchange for the $50.00. After having the ring appraised and finding that he was swindled this stranger makes it his life work to bring the defendant to the bar of justice. Instead of watching the neighborhood for the defendant to put him in the arms of the law, the victim changes his appearance and "cases" (follows) the defendant for several days. He sees the defendant make several sales of similar merchandise to others. The initial victim introduces himself to the other victims, explains to them that they too had been swindled. They exchange identification and agree that they will not report the theft to the police immediately but will wait until ten people who were victimized agreed to prosecute. Then the defendant will be arrested and all will cooperate in the prosecution. When the tenth victim agrees to this scheme, the first victim points out the defendant to the police who assist in arresting the defendant initially on the complaint of the first victim.

At the trial, the other victims could testify as to what had happened to them to prove circumstantially that the false representation happened to the victim in the case on trial.

The preceding case was hypothetical but could conceivably take place. In an actual case, a defendant charged with interstate transportation of a stolen vehicle, who rented automobiles approximately one month prior to committing the offense in the case at bar by identifying himself with a stolen credit card, was prosecuted by the admission into evidence of the prior transaction involving substantially the same method as alleged in the instant case. U.S.—United States v. Coleman, 410 F.2d 1133 (10th Cir. 1969).

§ 3.15 CIRCUMSTANTIAL EVIDENCE—POSSESSION OF THE FRUITS OF THE CRIME

There is an expression among many law enforcement people that goes like this: "The prisoner was caught with his hand in the till." This means that he was caught either with his hands in the cash register or he was caught with the "goods" (stolen property) on his person or in a location under his control. When this occurs, the defendant is required to go forward with the evidence to overcome the presumption of guilt. N.Y.—People v. Langan, 303 N.Y. 474, 104 N.E.2d 861 (1952). Note that the prosecution continues to have the burden to prove the defendant guilty beyond a reasonable doubt. Further treatment of this topic will be found in Chapter 17 infra.

§ 3.16 CIRCUMSTANTIAL EVIDENCE—CRIME OF CONSPIRACY

The least serious type of crime of conspiracy is defined in the New York Penal Law which reads as follows:

> 105.00 Conspiracy in the fourth degree—A person is guilty of conspiracy in the fourth degree when, with intent that conduct constituting a crime be performed, he agrees with one or more persons to engage in or cause the performance of such conduct.
>
> Conspiracy in the fourth degree is a class B misdemeanor.

Like so many criminal statutes, if one looks to its practical application, it might be difficult to successfully prosecute this statute unless the prosecutor/rix invokes the aid of circumstantial evidence. There is little likelihood that direct evidence can be obtained overhearing two or more defendants actually agreeing to commit a crime. With the exception perhaps, of a legal wiretap or electronic device, or an officer with the ability of reading lips or one with a vivid "imagination" to overhear conversations, direct evidence of the agreement to commit a crime is almost non-existent.

The use of circumstantial evidence, however, wherein a course of criminal conduct is observed which is entered into by two or more persons acting together, or independently as part of an over-all scheme, can be spelled out as a conspiracy. The individual members of the conspiracy need not know the others who are involved in order to spell out the commission of this offense. It is a jury question to determine the intent of the parties. N.Y.—People v. Flack, 125 N.Y. 324, 26 N.E. 267, 11 L.R.A. 807 (1891). The conspiracy itself could be established by evidence of particular acts, which taken together furnished a basis for a finding that a conspiracy existed. N.Y.—People v. Connolly, 253 N.Y. 330, 171 N.E. 393 (1930).

§ 3.17 CIRCUMSTANTIAL EVIDENCE—OTHER SEX CRIMES

The question often arises in the prosecution of crimes of rape or sodomy, whether the victim is making the complaint because of a nefarious reason. Often there is a long standing relationship between the parties wherein they frequently have indulged in sexual contact with each other but because of a disagreement, a complaint is made by the alleged wronged party. In such a case, circumstantial evidence may be introduced to show the prior sexual contact between them where such evidence has a legitimate tendency to show the disposition between the parties at or about the time of the offense charged in the indictment. Evidence of such acts, whether prior to or subsequent to the act in question, is admissible where they are so related by brevity of time or continuity of disposition or otherwise to the principal act as to indicate the mutual disposition of the parties. N.Y.—People v. Thompson, 212 N.Y. 249, 106 N.E. 78 (1914).

It should be noted however, that a forceful sodomy could take place notwithstanding the existence of prior or subsequent sexual contact between the parties. This fact should be brought to the attention of the jury in their deliberations of the factual conditions of the case at bar.

§ 3.18 CIRCUMSTANTIAL EVIDENCE—REPETITION IN DEFAMATION ACTION

There are actions in civil law known as actions for libel or actions for slander. The person who brings the action complains that because of the acts of the defendant in spreading certain knowledge about the plaintiff, the plaintiff was injured in a monetary way. If the defendant is alleged to have placed this information in writing for others to read, it is called an action in libel. If the defendant is alleged to have disseminated this information by word of mouth, it is called slander. Both libel and slander have been characterized as actions for defamation. There are defenses against these actions such as truth of the declaration or fair comment with respect to public officials. As law enforcement persons are particularly prone to such an action, one should be careful in his contacts with members of the public to avoid spreading false information which might injure the persons in a financial way. In a recent case, a potentially aggrieved person brought an action for damages and declaratory relief against city and county police officials under 42 U.S.C.A. § 1983 which creates a right of action against a person who, under color of state law, subjects another to the deprivation of any right secured by the Federal Constitution. The plaintiff had been arrested for shoplifting and his picture was included in a police flyer of "active shoplifters", distributed to merchants. The petitioner could have brought his action for defamation in Kentucky courts but chose instead to invoke the aid of the federal courts pursuant to the aforementioned statute. The United States

District Court permitted the "flyer" evidence into the trial but dismissed the action on other grounds.

This case found its way to the United States Supreme Court which held that the words "liberty" and "property" as used in the Fourteenth Amendment do not single out reputation as a candidate for special protection over and above other instruments that may be protected by state law. U.S.—Paul v. Davis, 424 U.S. 693, 96 S.Ct. 1155, 47 L.Ed.2d 405 (1976). This is not to say that Davis did not have a remedy in state court which he did not avail himself of. In any event, the evidence was relevant and was admissible in the District Court and there was no question as to the repetition of the photos being shown to many shopkeepers.

§ 3.19 CIRCUMSTANTIAL EVIDENCE—VALUE OF PERSONAL PROPERTY STOLEN

The value of personal property at a given time is a nebulous concept. When we speak about the monetary value of personal property, we really mean the amount of money that an average bona fide purchaser would pay for this property if it were put up for sale. Anyone who has ever tried to sell an automobile has a good insight into this problem. Therefore, when we speak about the value of personal property, we are speaking about an approximate amount of money.

Let us imagine that you own a motor vehicle for which you just paid $7300.00. You take it out of the dealer's showroom and drive it for one day consisting of about 60 miles. The second day you decide to take the new vehicle for a ride and as you proceed through a cross-street near your home, a vehicle travelling at an excessive rate of speed approaches the intersection from the right, goes through a stop sign and totally demolishes your vehicle. You were wearing a seat belt which prevented your ejection from your vehicle and major personal injury. However, your car was totally damaged. While you were being treated in the emergency room of the local hospital, a tow truck unlawfully hoists the remains of your vehicle on its crane and removes it from the scene.

Three miles from the scene a police officer stops the tow truck to determine if the driver of the truck had proper authority to tow your vehicle. Upon learning that the operator of the tow truck had no authority to remove your vehicle, he is arrested and charged with grand larceny. In this jurisdiction, the threshold between grand larceny or petty larceny is $500.00.

At the trial, the prosecutor is obliged to demonstrate that the value of this wreck was over $500.00. The defense will contend that this was junk and had a salvage value of less than $100.00.

In this hypothetical case, the value of the automobile for the purpose of proving your damages in a civil action against the owner and driver of the other vehicle who caused the damage, and the value of the vehicle remains which the tow truck took from the scene are different. Each side in both court actions will attempt to prove their position by testimony of experts who will testify what they believe the auto could have been sold for at the particular point of time involved in each case. They will base their opinions on what price other vehicles with similar virtues or disabilities were sold for in that locality in the recent past, prior to the time of the occurrence. This type of evidence is admissible as circumstantial evidence, Anderson v. Friendship Body & Radiator Works Inc., 112 R.I. 445, 311 A.2d 288 (1973); Mo.—Bader v. Hylarides, 374 S.W.2d 616 (App.1964). In an action on a burglary policy, a witness may be permitted to testify as to the value of perfect diamonds of a similar size to those which were burglarized. Fla.—New Amsterdam Gas Co. v. James, 122 Fla. 710, 166 So. 813 (1936).

§ 3.20 CIRCUMSTANTIAL EVIDENCE—REPUTATION OF THE VICTIM OF THE CRIME

The reputation of the victim in certain crimes might tend to prove or disprove that the crime was committed. If a deceased in a violent homicide case had a reputation for being involved in street muggings and the accused contends that he killed the deceased in the course of being mugged by the decedent, it is relevant to prove the issue of self-defense or justifiable homicide that the deceased had perpetrated an attempted mugging on the defendant. The defendant may have been acting lawfully in killing the deceased. This is circumstantial evidence, introduced to tend to prove that the occurrence took place as the defendant argues. Where the issue was self-defense in a murder trial, the court said that "the accused, after giving evidence to show that he acted in self-defense, may prove that the general reputation of the deceased was that of a quarrelsome, vindictive or violent man and that such reputation had come to his knowledge prior to the homicide". N.Y.—People v. Rodawald, 177 N.Y. 408, 70 N.E. 1 (1904). The reputation of the deceased is admissible only to show the state of mind of the defendant. It therefore is necessary that the reputation of the deceased is known to the defendant at the time of the homicide. A different rule prevails however, if threats were made to others that the deceased was going to kill the defendant. This is not reputation evidence but tends to prove circumstantially that the deceased was the aggressor. N.Y.—People v. Taylor, 177 N.Y. 237, 69 N.E. 534 (1904).

§ 3.21 CIRCUMSTANTIAL EVIDENCE—EFFECT ON OTHER OCCASIONS

It frequently becomes necessary to determine the cause of a situation without anyone having actually observed it. For example, it is generally known that if persons are sleeping in a room which is air tight, the heating of this room by a gas range will eventually use up all of the oxygen in the room and the occupants are likely to die. We therefore can infer as an initial presumption, subject to later forensic examinations, that persons found dead in such a setting died because of asphyxiation caused by the flame using all of the oxygen in the room.

Where a poison is administered which produces distinctive symptoms in the victim, it may circumstantially be inferred that the second victim ingested the same poison as the first. N.Y.—People v. Molineaux, 168 N.Y. 264, 61 N.E. 286, 62 L.R.A. 193 (1901); N.Y.—People v. Feldman, 296 N.Y. 127, 71 N.E.2d 433 (1947). Motive and intent may be proved by circumstances from which intent may be reasonably inferred. N.Y.—Kramer v. Skiatron of America, 32 Misc. 2d 1022, 323 N.Y.S.2d 283 (1971); U.S.—United States v. Brettholz, 485 F.2d 483 (2d Cir. 1973).

§ 3.22 CIRCUMSTANTIAL EVIDENCE—DOGS, TRACKING WITH

The dog, known as man's best friend, has been taking on a more important role in apprehension of criminals as the years pass by. The keen olfactory sense possessed by certain dogs combined with great intelligence has made them a very useful tool in law enforcement. For many years dogs have been used to follow the path of a malefactor as he fled from the scene of a crime. These dogs were characterized as bloodhounds. In recent years dogs have been trained to detect drugs and explosives. The problem arises however, when the prosecutor/rix attempts to get the dog's findings into evidence. For this purpose the courts have required that a proper foundation be laid. The dog's handler must first testify as to his own qualifications and experience. He must testify with respect to the dog's ability to do the task which is relevant to the case at bar. He must testify as to the training that the dog received and if it is a tracking case, he must testify that the trail was fresh and had not been interfered with by others prior to the tracking. If it is a tracking case, the dog must be placed at an initial position where it is definitely known that the perpetrator of the crime was previously present. When this foundation is laid, evidence may then be introduced with respect to the actions of the dog which inferentially lead to the conclusion that the defendant is the perpetrator. This evidence must be corroborated by other evidence tending toward identification. Such tracking evidence has been held to be admissible in both civil and criminal cases providing the proper foundation has been laid. Minn.—Crosby v. Moriarity, 148 Minn. 201, 181 N.W. 199 (1921).

§ 3.23 SUFFICIENCY OF CIRCUMSTANTIAL EVIDENCE

For many years, a criminal conviction could not be based wholly on circumstantial evidence unless the trier of the facts was convinced that the circumstances must be so clearly proven that they point not merely to the possibility of guilt, but to a moral certainty of guilt and inference which may reasonably be drawn from the facts proven as a whole, must not only be consistent with guilt, but inconsistent with every reasonable hypothesis of innocence. U.S.—Ah Ming v. United States, 300 F.2d 202 (5th Cir. 1962). In recent years however, there has been a noticeable but slow change in this rule of law as was found in United States v. Moore, 505 F.2d 620 (5th Cir. 1975), certiorari denied 421 U.S. 918, 95 S.Ct. 1581, 43 L.Ed.2d 785, where the court said that the proper test of sufficiency of evidence in all cases, including those involving circumstantial evidence, is not whether trial court or appellate court is able to find evidence inconsistent with every hypothesis of innocence, but is whether a reasonably minded jury could so conclude. Another case held that the "rule" that the facts must exclude every other hypothesis than that of guilt is simply another form of the rule that the jury must be convinced beyond a reasonable doubt of the guilt of the defendant. U.S.—United States v. Lewin, 467 F.2d 1132 (7th Cir. 1972). Some states adhere steadfastly to the old rule but their number is diminishing.

§ 3.24 CIRCUMSTANTIAL AND DIRECT EVIDENCE CREDIBILITY COMPARISON

The student has now been exposed to the difference between direct and circumstantial evidence. The question sometimes arises as to which is more credible. It is the author's belief that it depends on the circumstances of each case and as to who was testifying. Many persons viewing a factual situation will verbalize different recollections of that fact pattern, and this would be an example of direct evidence. In a circumstantial evidence problem, we sometimes encounter similar variances as to the inference to be drawn by designated conduct.

§ 3.25 CIRCUMSTANTIAL EVIDENCE—FEDERAL RULE

The Federal Rules of Evidence do not specifically indicate that circumstantial evidence is admissible but Rule 402 reads:

> **Rule 402. Relevant Evidence Generally Admissible: Irrelevant Evidence Inadmissible:** All relevant evidence is admissible, except as otherwise provided by the Constitution of the United States, by act of Congress, by these rules, or by other rules prescribed by the Supreme Court pursuant to statutory authority. Evidence which is not relevant is not admissible.

Furthermore Rule 404(3)(b) reads as follows:

> Other crimes, wrongs or acts.—Evidence of other crimes, wrongs, or acts is not admissible to prove the character of a person in order to show that he acted in conformity therewith. It may, however, be admissible for other purposes, such as proof of motive, opportunity, intent, preparation, plan, knowledge, identity or absence of mistake or accident.

The circumstantial relevance of habit is referred to in Rule 406 where it reads:

> **Rule 406. Habit; Routine Practice:** Evidence of the habit of a person or of the routine practice of an organization, whether corroborated or not and regardless of the presence of eye witnesses, is relevant to prove that the conduct of the person or organization on a particular occasion was in conformity with the habit or routine practice.

Therefore, we see that the Federal Rules of Evidence do permit the introduction of all evidence whether direct or circumstantial, which is relevant to a determination of the issues of the case at bar.

CHAPTER IV

OPINION EVIDENCE

§ 4.1 OPINION TESTIMONY

Generally, witnesses may testify as to what they heard, saw, smelled, tasted or touched. In other words they may testify as to facts, but they may not testify generally as to a conclusion which they made as a result of the experience of using any one of the five senses. Necessity, however, has dictated that there be exceptions to this general rule.

There are two characterizations which are given to witnesses with respect to this problem. One type of witness is designated as an "expert witness" and the other is a "lay witness."

An expert witness is permitted to testify as to conclusions which s/he arrived at as a result of using one or more of his/her five senses. In some situations, a "lay witness" may also testify as to a conclusion. Another way to state this principle is to say that the general rule excluding opinion evidence has many important exceptions which may be classified into two divisions.

1. Opinions of "expert witnesses."
2. Opinions of "lay witnesses."

§ 4.2 REASON FOR OPINION RULE

The reason that we have an opinion evidence rule is that it is intended to protect against the danger of invasion of the province of the jury. "Opinion testimony in its broadest sense encroaches upon the province of the jury to determine for themselves the ultimate facts of the case." Neb.—McNaught v. N. Y. Life Insurance Co., 143 Neb. 213, 12 N.W.2d 108 (1944).

However if found by the trial court to be of aid to the jury, an opinion may be admitted notwithstanding it bears directly on the main issue. Ala.—Glover v. City of Birmingham, 255 Ala. 596, 52 So.2d 521, 522 (1951); Neb.—Drahota v. Wieser, 183 Neb. 66, 157 N.W.2d 857 (1968).

§ 4.3 SKILLED OR EXPERT WITNESSES

Many old decisions have held that an inference opinion or conclusion of a skilled or expert witness ordinarily is excluded. However, modern tendency clearly seems to be away from that rule. Ill.—Wawryszyn v. Illinois Cent. R. Co., 10 Ill.App.2d 394, 135 N.E.2d 154, 61 A.L.R.2d 801 (1956). It therefore has been held that where the matter under inquiry is properly the subject of expert testimony it is no objection that the opinion sought to be elicited is on the issue to be decided. U.S.—Miller's Nat. Ins. Co., Chicago, Ill. v. Wichita Flour Mills Co., 257 F.2d 93 (10th Cir. 1958); Pa.—Whigham v. Metropolitan Life Ins. Co., Com.Pl., 35 Berks 457, modified on other grounds 343 Pa. 149, 22 A.2d 704 (1941). Therefore expert witnesses may be permitted to testify, in the discretion of the trial judge, where issues to be determined by the jury could not be intelligently determined by them without the aid of expert advice. Tenn.—Phillips v. Newport, 28 Tenn.App. 187, 187 S.W.2d 965 (1945).

§ 4.4 EXPERT WITNESS—DETERMINATION OF COMPETENCY

Whether a particular witness has the necessary qualifications to testify as an expert and hence testify as to his opinions, is a question to be determined by the Court (Judge) and not by the jury or a witness. Cal.—Applegate v. Wilson, 156 Cal.App.2d 330, 319 P.2d 401 (1958). This is determined by a preliminary examination of the witness by the proponent's lawyer and also by the presiding judge. The adversary, through his attorney, has an opportunity at an examination known as a voir dire. (Section 2.39, supra.)

Many times the adversary will try to cut the proponent short in his preliminary examination by saying that "To save the time of the court, the defendant will accept Mr. X as an expert." Make no mistake about it, he is not trying to save the time of the court but he is trying to hide the knowledge of the expert's unusually high qualifications from the trier of the facts. Cases have held that where the party calling the expert as a witness insists, he has a right to have the expert testify regarding his qualifications so that the jury might better evaluate the weight of his testimony.

The court has reasonably wide discretion to accept or reject a witness as an expert. It has been held that a witness may qualify as an expert on the basis of study alone. This situation occurs where a qualified person, such as a physician, may study a particular area of medicine and not be examined on it by any licensing authority. N.Y.—People v. Benham, 160 N.Y. 402, 441, 55 N.E. 11, 24 (1899). However, a person cannot become an expert in a specialized area by mere reading of the literature if he has no previous background and training in the general subject. Cal.—Hutter v. Hommel, 213 Cal. 677, 3 P.2d 554 (1931); Conn.—Stressman v. Vitiello, 114 Conn. 370, 158 A. 879 (1932). This does not mean that the court may be arbitrary, unreasonable and/or capricious in its determination.

§ 4.5 EXPERT OPINIONS IN CRIMINAL CASES

In criminal law we often find a necessity for expert opinion. The advances made in the study of criminalistics, police science, forensic science, and related disciplines have improved the certainty of solving many crimes. Accordingly, there is need to draw on the expertise of those trained in these disciplines to enlighten the trier of the facts to conclusions which they might not otherwise be able to arrive at. The necessary requirements before an expert may testify however remain similar to those found in a civil action. These are:

1. Is the subject concerning which s/he is to testify, one upon which the opinion of an expert can be received? i. e., beyond the knowledge of the average layman.
2. What qualifications should an expert possess to qualify to give his/her opinion?
3. Does the witness have these qualifications?
4. Will his/her testimony aid the jury in its search for the truth?

It must be stated at this juncture that the jury may accept or reject the conclusion of the expert witness.

§ 4.6 SUBJECTS OF TESTIMONY OF EXPERT WITNESSES

The subjects of testimony of expert witnesses are not limited to the professions but special knowledge or experience in any line of human activity not presumably shared by the average jury, may authorize a conclusion to be drawn by the expert and testified to by him. D.C.—McReynolds v. National Woodworking Co., 26 F.2d 975 (D.C. Cir. 1928). It is not necessary for the skill or experience to be along desirable or even moral lines. Hence a prostitute could be called to the stand to testify as to certain vocabulary used in her profession. It is impossible to precisely state a general rule as to subjects on which evidence may be received. However, it is generally agreed that matters of art, science or technical training are proper subjects of testimony by experts. N.Y.—Goldstein v. Equitable Life Assur. Soc. of U. S., 160 Misc. 364, 289 N.Y.S. 1064 (1968); Pa.—Pastelak v. Glenn Alden Coal Co., 108 Pa.Super. 89, 164 A. 846 (1960).

§ 4.7 EXPERT WITNESS—AUTOMOBILE ACCIDENT

Police officers frequently are called upon to testify as to how an auto accident happened, after the damage has been observed by them, even though they made no observation with respect to the actual coming together of the vehicles. Many large police departments frown on or discourage the use of their officers in civil actions between the parties because of the time lost to the department by the appearance of the officers in court. However, police administrators and officers should remember that in addition to their sworn duty to enforce the law they have the additional duty to see that justice is done. The officer's presence in court in civil actions is equally important as his appearance in the criminal court. He should constantly bear the thought, "that there, but for the grace of God, go I" and he could be a defendant or a plaintiff in a civil action and he would be looking for equal justice under law.

Usually a police officer will not be accepted as an expert in this area unless he has special qualifications, e. g., a patrolman who had fifteen years experience as a highway patrolman, during which time he had investigated a considerable number of automobile accidents and who had kept abreast of the field of automobile accident investigations by attending various refresher courses, was qualified as an expert to testify as to the speed of automobiles involved in an accident. U.S.—Bonner v. Polacari, 350 F.2d 493 (10th Cir. 1965). It is proper for an expert witness to reconstruct an accident by basing his opinion upon exhibits showing the physical facts as well as numerous photographs. Mo.—Edwards v. Rudowicz, 368 S.W.2d 503 (App.1963).

§ 4.8 PROBABILITY—NOT SUFFICIENT WHEN STANDING ALONE

The issues that require expert opinions are often those involving variable conclusions. We would not require an expert in mathematics to explain that in his opinion, if one adds 10 bushels of wheat to a truck which already had only 10 bushels of wheat in it, the resultant number of bushels would be 20 bushels. There is no probability that the final count of bushels of wheat in the truck would be 19 or 21. However, where uncertainties are involved in a conclusion, the court, in its search for the truth, may draw upon the expertise, experience and reasoning powers of the expert. The expert, however, does not have to be certain in his conclusion. He may testify, for example, that in his considered opinion that to a reasonable medical certainty or based on medical probabilities, the patient will sustain pain in the future. Wis.—Peterson v. Western Cas. & Sur. Co., 5 Wis.2d 535, 93 N.W.2d 433 (1959).

In most jurisdictions, however, testimony that a certain cause or effect is possible, conceivable or reasonable does not constitute substantial evidence, or is of little or no probative value. Ill.—Manion v. Brant Oil Co., 85 Ill.App.2d 129, 229 N.E.2d 171 (1967); Pa.—Marushock v. Associated Transport, Inc., 65 Lack.Jur. 145. The weight that a jury should give to the testimony of an expert witness who testifies that a certain result is probable presents a serious question. However, in the case of a blood test to establish paternity, where medical science has definitely determined negative results—i. e., that it is not possible for a particular person to have fathered the child, an expert may not testify that it is possible that the respondent fathered the child but he may testify that it is impossible for the respondent to have fathered the child. N.Y.—J. v. J., 35 Misc.2d 243, 228 N.Y.S.2d 950 (1962). It must be held in mind that mere possibility is not a basis for a finding of fact, it must be more than mere possibility. In the case of the blood test for paternity it must be established that

1. the blood and the person from whom it was taken are clearly identified;
2. that the test is performed by competent and qualified medical technicians.

§ 4.9 EXPERT WITNESS—AIRPLANE CRASHES

Most police departments do not have qualified personnel to testify as experts in the causes of airplane accidents. Even if they had, it is usually the responsibility of federal law enforcement officers to investigate this type of occurrence. However, the same rules apply in this area as apply to automobile accidents in that the mere fact that a person is a pilot and has been one for many years and has flown many miles does not necessarily qualify him to be an expert to reconstruct the facts surrounding an airplane crash. He must have more knowledge and training than that to reconstruct the occurrence.

However, a witness who had flown over eleven thousand hours during twenty-two years, had visited numerous airfields and had supervised preparation and operation of several airfields, was qualified to state opinion whether a particular field was a safe place for planes to land, and to draw inference from wheel tracks, although he lacked technical training and could not claim familiarity with laws relating to maintenance of airports. U.S.—Beck v. Wings Field, 35 F.Supp. 953 (D.C.Pa.1940), modified on other grounds 122 F.2d 114 (1941).

One who had many years as an assistant flight engineer with previous experience of investigation in more than thirty cases of airplane engine overspeed, who made a study of numerous airplane crashes and who was an inventor of devices concerned with propeller vibration and featherability was held to be a qualified expert witness in an action arising from an airplane accident where an overspeeding propeller was not able to be feathered. U.S.—Noel v. United Aircraft Corp., 342 F.2d 232 (3d Cir. 1964).

§ 4.10 EXPERT WITNESS—BALLISTICS—FINGERPRINTS

Many homicides have been solved by identifying the particular gun from which the bullet was fired and from the fingerprints present on the suspect gun. The problem is to get these items into evidence and thus make them part of the trial record. The average layman is not qualified to identify grooves and lands of a bullet to compare them with a comparison bullet nor is he qualified to ascertain the similarity of a suspected fingerprint pattern with a comparison fingerprint. In this area the role of the scientific crime fighter is most important. Therefore a ballistic expert may express an opinion as to whether a particular bullet was fired from the gun which has been placed in evidence. N.Y.—People v. Soper, 243 N.Y. 320, 153 N.E. 433 (1926). Likewise a fingerprint expert may express his opinion as to whether or not the fingerprints in question are those of defendant. N.Y.—People v. Roach, 215 N.Y. 592, 109 N.E. 618 (1915).

§ 4.11 EXPERT WITNESS—BLOOD GROUPING TEST

The problem of blood grouping to determine paternity is one which does not ordinarily concern the law enforcement officer in his official duty. Some states have codified this by statutes. Results of blood grouping tests are admissible only to establish the impossibility or exclusion of a claimed relationship. N.Y.—J. v. J., 35 Misc.2d 243, 228 N.Y.S.2d 950 (1928); Ohio—State ex rel. Freeman v. Morris, 156 Ohio St. 333, 102 N.E.2d 450 (1952). However in one case of a prosecution for rape, a defendant made a motion for a blood grouping test and the court granted it saying "While it is true that in this prosecution for rape the matter of paternity of the child born to the complainant is not in issue, it nevertheless bears directly upon the question of the credibility of the complainant, for the complainant in her preliminary examination testified that she never had sexual intercourse with anyone except the defendant." N.Y.—People v. Tashman, Sup., 233 N.Y.S.2d 744, 745 (1962).

§ 4.12 EXPERT WITNESS—FORENSIC SCIENCE

There are many other types of experts who have been permitted to express their conclusions in the profession of forensic science. These include experts in determining the origin of blood, the part of the body that blood came from, identification of human and animal blood, identification of a particular person's blood, identification of semen, problems of broken windows, problems of attacks with firearms, identification of hair, identification of teeth, traces of vehicles, traces of teeth, footprints, questioned documents, speed detection by use of radar and vascar, alcohol blood test and handwriting identification.

§ 4.13 EXPERT WITNESS—POLYGRAPH

The modern tendency to rely on the infallibility of machines and computers has led many people to believe that the time has come to supplant all testimony at trials and administer a lie detector test to the suspect. The results so they think, should resolve the issue without error and we would have no need for courthouses, judges, lawyers, court personnel and jurors.

They had no need for the aforementioned personnel or buildings when other modes of trial were used in ancient times, such as trial by ordeal, or the extraction of confessions by torture etc. Few, if any, polygraph experts would wish to be the subject of a polygraph trial if they were accused of the commission of a heinous crime and they were innocent. The natural retort to such a situation is that "It can't happen to me." However, as one lives he realizes more and more that things can happen to him. This is particularly appropriate in the profession of law enforcement where the enforcer may be the accused. Very often the enforcer is accused wrongfully because s/he has been too efficient as a police officer and the malefactors in our society, with no good reputation to lose and who are judgment proof, point the finger at the police officer as having engaged in some nefarious activity.

Fortunately, courts have not generally admitted the results of lie detector tests on the ground that such tests are not yet sufficiently reliable and still too much in the experimental field. Ga.—Wallace v. Moss, 121 Ga.App. 366, 174 S.E.2d 196 (1970); Pa.—Stape v. Civil Service Comm. of City of Philadelphia, 404 Pa. 354, 172 A.2d 161 (1961). They are ordinarily inadmissible regardless of whether submission to the tests is by voluntary agreement, by direction of the court, or by coercion. Mich.—Stone v. Earp, 331 Mich. 606, 50 N.W.2d 172 (1952). However, in a civil case it has been held admissible where it was agreed to by both parties. U.S.—Herman v. Eagle Star Ins. Co., 283 F.Supp. 33 (D.C.Cal.1968). Where evidence was introduced to the effect that a party had submitted to a lie detector test, the court may, in its discretion, admit evidence of the result of the test, at least to the extent necessary to remove any unfair prejudice which might otherwise have ensued from the original evidence. U.S.—California Ins. Co. v. Allen, 235 F.2d 178 (5th Cir. 1956).

In an interesting lower court civil case, N.Y.—Walther v. O'Connell, 72 Misc.2d 316, 339 N.Y.S.2d 386 (1973), it was held that the results of a court ordered lie detector test may be held admissible. Accordingly, where the testimony of the parties was diametrically opposed, the result of a lie detector test, administered at the direction of the court by a competent expert, was held admissible.

§ 4.14 EXPERT WITNESS—BLOOD, URINE, BREATH

It is safe to assume that every jurisdiction has a statute which provides that a defendant's blood may be tested to ascertain whether or not a designated amount of percent of alcohol is present in the blood to determine whether or not the driver was intoxicated at the time that he was apprehended. Police departments have provided for this contingency by training certain members of their personnel to use various instruments which are available for this purpose. After they are given the necessary training and are also trained in the field, they qualify to testify as experts in this area. Various jurisdictions will require a different percentage of alcohol to be present to provide prima facie evidence of the fact that the defendant was intoxicated. Federal and State courts have held that the privilege against self-incrimination of the United States Constitution offers no protection against compulsion to submit to photographing, fingerprints, or to speak, or to stand, or to make a particular gesture. U.S.—U. S. v. Wade, 388 U.S. 218, 87 S.Ct. 1926, 18 L.Ed.2d 1149 (1967), or to submit to a blood examination providing all possible medical safeguards have been taken to insure that the proposed defendant is not injured in any way by the taking of the blood sample. U.S.—Schmerber v. California, 384 U.S. 757, 86 S.Ct. 1826, 16 L.Ed.2d 908 (1966). The blood examination for intoxicated drivers requires certain corroborating factors. The demeanor of the defendant and his/her general appearance must be that of an apparently intoxicated person. Most states have enacted laws for a driver of a vehicle which deem that the driver has given his/her consent to be tested with respect to the alcoholic content of his/her blood if there are reasonable grounds to believe that s/he is driving while intoxicated. Should s/he refuse to take this test, his/her license may be suspended or revoked.

The National Safety Counsel and the American Medical Association has made recommendations to State Legislatures for enactment of legislation to determine the percent of alcohol in a person's blood which should determine prima facie, various degrees of intoxication. The recommendations never suggested a strict line of demarcation to be used as a sole criterion by which to judge whether an individual was intoxicated and thus unfit to drive an automobile. The suggestion is thus made to combine the blood test with other evidence. For many years, this was done by the arresting officer testifying as to what actions he had observed in the defendant. Some jurisdictions are now bolstering this chemical and oral testimony with motion pictures taken of the defendant while s/he was being examined in the place of detention.

The taking of blood from an intoxicated driver when taken under clean scientific conditions by qualified personnel, has been held not to be contrary to the Fourth Amendment and did not offend a sense of justice. U.S.—Breithaupt v. Abram, 352 U.S. 432, 1 L.Ed.2d 448, 77 S.Ct. 408 (1957); Schmerber v. California, 384 U.S. 757, 16 L.Ed.2d 908, 86 S.Ct. 1826 (1966). Such evidence is admissible where there is corroborating evidence of intoxication. Kan.—Williams v. Hendrickson, 189 Kan. 673, 371 P.2d 188 (1962).

Breath tests, which are easier to administer, also have been held admissible. It has been held that before breath tests are admissible, the burden is on the prosecution to show:

1. That the chemicals were compounded to a proper percentage for use in the machine.
2. That the operator of the machine and the machine were under periodic supervision of one who has an understanding of the scientific theory of the machine.
3. The witness is qualified to calculate and translate the reading of the machine into percentage of alcohol in the blood.

Tex.—Hill v. State, 158 Tex.Crim. 313, 256 S.W.2d 93 (1953). See also N.D.—McDonald v. Ferguson, 129 N.W.2d 348 (1964).

Urine tests to prove intoxication have also been admissible under similar circumstances to the blood and breath tests. D.C.—Bungardeanu v. England, 219 A.2d 104, 16 A.L.R.3d 739 (App.1966).

§ 4.15 EXPERT WITNESS—HANDWRITING COMPARISON

The examination and comparison of handwriting does not precisely lend itself to conclusions solely by experts in the field. It has been held that in the absence of statute that the issue of authorship of a disputed signature or writing, other writings established as genuine may be admitted or compared. Ky.—Belcher v. Somerville, 413 S.W.2d 620 (App.1967); N.D.—United States Industries, Inc. v. Borr, 157 N.W.2d 708 (Sup.1968), and that the comparison may be made by the jury; Ind.—State ex rel. Winslow v. Fisher, 109 Ind.App. 644, 37 N.E.2d 280 (1941), or by the court or referee trying the case without a jury. Conn.—Shakro v. Haddad, 149 Conn. 160, 177 A.2d 221 (1962), or by expert witnesses. Ala.—Phillips v. Catts, 220 Ala. 332, 124 So. 884 (1930).

The United States Supreme Court has held that submitting handwriting specimens for comparison purposes does not violate the constitution. A suspect may even be compelled to give handwriting specimens and it did not violate fifth amendment protection against self-incrimination. U.S.—Gilbert v. California, 388 U.S. 263, 87 S.Ct. 1951, 18 L.Ed.2d 1178 (1967).

§ 4.16 EXPERT WITNESS—RADAR IN THE DETECTION OF SPEEDING VEHICLES

The public is aware of the widespread use of radar in detecting the speed of vehicles, yet few people are conversant with the scientific facts of radar which determines the speed of vehicles. It is not the intent of the author to explain the Doppler effect which utilizes continuous beams of microwaves sent out at fixed frequency. However, suffice it to say that the readings of a radar speed meter are now accepted in evidence, just as the courts have accepted other scientific devices. The courts take judicial notice of these items and therefore they require no further proof. Mo.—State v. Graham, 322 S.W. 2d 188 (1959). However, there is a trend among defense attorneys to challenge the reliability of radar readings and they are meeting with some success.

§ 4.17 EXPERT WITNESS—VASCAR IN THE DETECTION OF SPEEDING VEHICLES

Vascar is of more recent vintage than radar. It is a mnemonic for Visual Average Speed Computer and Recorder. Many states have adopted Vascar and courts have given judicial notice to its reliability in detecting the speed of moving vehicles. Vascar computes the average distance involved between two locations, usually previously designated. Again, it is not the intention of the author to burden the student with the scientific basis for an expert's conclusion but suffice it to say that experts may come to conclusions based upon their scientific knowledge.

§ 4.18 EXPERT WITNESS—SPECTOGRAPH FOR VOICEPRINTS

Michigan State University Department of Audiology and Speech Sciences has been in the forefront of a study to explore the possibility of voice printing. They have met with great success in developing voiceprints as a method of identification. Courts, however, were very reluctant to recognize this technique as being valid and therefore spectograms were not admitted in evidence for many years.

Courts are notorious in their inability to effect a fast change in concepts and procedures. Perhaps it is better this way so that change only occurs after testing and retesting to insure accuracy and justice.

Voiceprints are now admissible in many State and Federal courts as a means of identification. Mass.—Commonwealth v. Lykus, 327 N.E.2d 671, 17 Cr.L. 2013 (1974); Cal.—Hodo v. Superior Court, 30 Cal.App.3d 778–781, 106 Cal.Rptr. 547 (1973); U.S.—United States v. Baller, 519 F.2d 463, 17 Cr.L. 2306 (5th Cir. 1975); U.S.—State v. Reed, Mont.Cty., 18 Cr.L. 2011 (4th Cir.); N.Y.—People v. Rogers, N.Y.L.J. (5/21/76).

The author suggests that a student who is seriously interested in the admissibility of voiceprint identification obtain and read a report of the Annual Meeting of the Criminal Justice Section of the American Bar Association held in Honolulu, Hawaii, August 4, 1974 on voiceprint identification. The report is now available from the A.B.A. Criminal Justice Section, 1800 M Street N.W., Washington, D.C. 20036. A very comprehensive analysis also appears in the decisions of Commonwealth v. Lykus (supra) and People v. Rogers (supra).

In March of 1977, the Supreme Court of the State of Pennsylvania in Commonwealth v. Topa held that spectogram techniques with respect to identification of voices have not been generally accepted by the scientific community. This decision represented a serious setback to the technique. The court also held that the reading of spectograms was subjective and went on to say "Thus, as with the lie detector, there is danger that the trial judge or jury will ascribe a degree of certainty to the testimony of the expert spectography witness which may not be deserved.

With this decision, it cannot be said that all jurisdictions are accepting voiceprints in evidence. The reader is cautioned to ascertain the latest appellate decisions in his/her jurisdiction as a guide inasmuch as the rule of admissibility of voiceprint identification is in such a state of indecision.

The mere fact that voiceprint identification is admissible should not, however, be considered as conclusive by the trier of the facts. Such testimony should be and is subject to the usual cross-examination procedure and the final determination is up to the trier of the facts to make the ultimate determination of truth or falsity of the identification. Fla.—Coppolino v. State, 223 So.2d 68 (App.1969). In Fla.

—Alea v. State, 265 So.2d 96 (App.1972), the court held that testimony of experts concerning their spectographic voiceprint identification of defendant and voiceprints upon which experts' opinions were based, were admissible but the evidentiary value of spectographic voiceprints upon which experts based their identification of defendant as person who made allegedly extraordinary telephone calls was for trier of facts. Also see United States v. Raymond, 337 F.Supp. 641 (D.D.C.1972); United States v. Wright, 17 U.S.C.M.A. 183, 37 C.M.R. 447 (1967). This was refined further in a case which required corroboration of defendant's identification by other means. Worley v. State, 263 So.2d 613 (Fla.App.1972), 4th D.C.A. filed May 19, 1972.

§ 4.19 EXPERT WITNESS—TYPEWRITING COMPARISON

It is most likely apparent to everyone who drives an automobile that although your vehicle may be the same model as your friends and you may have all the same extra equipment, and it may have been purchased at the same time and place, yet after a short time, an experienced driver will get a different feel of driving one vehicle as compared to the other. This same result occurs in typewriters. Therefore where initially each typewriter had the same typewriting pattern, after use, each typewriter assumes its own peculiarities. Accordingly, after examining a document which has been typewritten on a particular typewriter, and comparing it with the document in question, a qualified expert may express his opinion as to whether the instrument in question was written on the same typewriter. N.Y.—People v. Storrs, 207 N.Y. 147, 100 N.E. 730, 45 L.R.A.(N.S.) 860 (1913). Okl.—In re Cravens Estate, 206 Okl. 174, 242 P.2d 135, 34 A.L.R.2d 615 (1952).

§ 4.20 EXPERT WITNESS—PHYSICAL AND MENTAL CONDITION

It sometimes becomes necessary to seek the assistance of an expert to determine if, to a reasonable medical certainty, the defendant was capable of doing the act that he is being charged with. This is usually accomplished by having a physician examine the defendant and report his findings to the court. A person skilled in medicine and physiology may state his inference or judgment relating to the physical condition of another person. Ga.—Gahring v. Barron, 108 Ga.App. 530, 133 S.E.2d 389 (1964); Wis.—Fehrman v. Smirl, 20 Wis.2d 1, 121 N.W.2d 255 (1963), rehearing denied 20 Wis.2d 1, 122 N.W.2d 439.

The aid of a psychiatrist is looked for if there is suspicion that a defendant does not understand the nature of the offense with which he is charged and is unable to assist in his defense. The New York Criminal Procedure Law provides for this determination in Section 730.20 et seq. wherein the court, district attorney or defense attorney may move for the appointment of two psychiatrists or one psychiatrist and one psychologist, at state expense, to examine the defendant with respect to his fitness to stand trial. If the defense attorney wishes to dispute the findings of the state appointed psychiatrist, he may do so and a hearing is scheduled to determine the issue of fitness alone. At this hearing, the state appointed psychiatrist is permitted to testify as to his findings and he will be subject to cross-examination by defendant's attorney. The defendant may have his own psychiatrist testify in his own behalf. The defendant's psychiatrist is also subject to cross-examination. If there is a dispute as to the opinions of the psychiatrists, it is for the trier of the facts to make the proper determination. Each jurisdiction may vary slightly in this procedure but suffice it to say that the opinions of psychiatrists and psychologists are admissible in these cases.

§ 4.21 EXPERT WITNESS—PHYSICIAN

Like the psychiatrist, who is a medical doctor with special training in psychology, the physician may be qualified as an expert to give an opinion with respect to medical diagnosis and prognosis and is entitled to great weight. La.—Bass v. Travelers Indem. Ins. Co., 173 So.2d 399 (App.1965); Mo.—Wiener v. Mutual Life Ins. Co. of New York, 170 S.W.2d 174 (App.1943), reversed on other grounds 179 S.W.2d 39. However, when scientific or medical theories or explanations have not become an accepted medical fact, opinions based thereon are no stronger or more convincing than the theories. Wis.—Puhl v. Milwaukee Auto Ins. Co., 8 Wis.2d 343, 99 N.W.2d 163 (1959).

§ 4.22 EXPERT WITNESS—ACCOUNTANT

In white collar crimes, the law enforcement officer is often confronted with a lack of expertise in analyzing the entries of accounts and the general bookkeeping procedures employed by business. In these cases it becomes necessary to seek the aid of an accountant. Some states have what are known as Registered Public Accountants who have been licensed under "grandfather" clauses in legislation. These people were accountants for many years and by virtue of their extensive experience they are granted licenses as "Registered Public Accountants".

Another category of accountant is the Certified Public Accountant. These too are licensed by the State but they must go through rigorous academic training and pass an acknowledged difficult examination.

In any event, the opinions of Registered Public Accountants and Certified Public Accountants in matters pertaining to the keeping of business records is given great weight. He may state the results of his examination of books and schedules of account. Ariz.—Collison v. International Ins. Co., 58 Ariz. 156, 118 P.2d 445 (1941); Ga.—Payne v. Franklin Co., 155 Ga. 219, 116 S.E. 627 (1923).

§ 4.23 EXPERT WITNESS—NEUTRON ACTIVATION ANALYSIS

Neutron Activation Analysis is a recent type of scientific breakthrough which detects the presence of traces of elements in a suspected sample of real evidence. Its adaptation to forensic science is relatively new. For example, if arsenic poison is suspected the expert in neutron activation analysis may conduct tests which will reveal even minute quantities of arsenic. The process was approved and the results thereof were admitted in evidence. U.S.—United States v. Stifel, 433 F.2d 431 (6th Cir. 1970); N.Y.—People v. Pieropan, 72 Misc. 770, 340 N.Y.S.2d 31 (1973). For a detailed discussion of the process the reader is referred to American Jurisprudence "Proof of Facts".

§ 4.24 CROSS–EXAMINATION OF EXPERTS

As has been indicated previously, a fundamental right is guaranteed to every litigant to have the opportunity to cross-examine a witness. If the right is denied, the direct examination is struck from the trial record. So too with the testimony of the expert witness. The fact that he may have attained certain intellectual heights does not preclude the idea that he might be mistaken, or even that he might be lying. The law of evidence therefore gives the opportunity to the adverse party to cross-examine the expert concerning his knowledge of articles, text books, treatises, current publications and other information in his discipline of expertise. He may be confronted with extracts from them and asked whether he is familiar with them and whether he agrees with them.

The reason for this rule is that such cross-examination tests the expert's creditability and reliability by inquiring as to the extent of his familiarity with authorities in his specialty and by asking whether or not he agrees with them. The abstracts with which the witness is confronted on cross-examination do not become affirmative evidence in the case. U.S.—Stottlemire v. Cawood, 215 F.Supp. 266 (D.C.D.C.1963).

The cross-examination should ordinarily be confined within the general scope of the direct examination. Conn.—Floyd v. Fruit Industries, Inc., 144 Conn. 659, 136 A.2d 918, 63 A.L.R.2d 1378 (1958); Ill.—Young v. Miller, 79 Ill.App.2d 463, 223 N.E.2d 854 (1967). The use of a newspaper clipping has been held to be improper. U.S.—Halsey, Stuart & Co. v. Farmers' Bank of McSherrystown, 37 F.2d 476 (3d Cir. 1930).

The cross-examiner may direct the attention of the expert to others in his/her field who have written a contrary opinion. This is permitted not to prove the contrary opinion but merely to call into question the weight to be attached by the jury to the opinion of the witness. The cross-examiner may do this even if the writing is not relied on by the witness. He may be asked whether he has relied on or considered any authorities in formulating his opinion. Cal.—Hope v.

Arrowhead and Puritas Waters, Inc., 174 Cal.App.2d 222, 344 P.2d 428 (1959). He may be asked to name the authorities on which he has based his testimony. Ill.—Wilcox v. International Harvester Co. of America, 278 Ill. 465, 116 N.E. 151 (1917).

§ 4.25 EXAMINATION OF AN EXPERT WITNESS

Expert witnesses may be examined in two basic ways:

1. Through testimony of the witness based on his/her personal knowledge or observation,
2. Through testimony of the witness based upon a hypothetical question addressed to him/her, in which the pertinent facts are assumed to be true, or assumed to be so found by the jury.

The facts included in a hypothetical question must be based on evidence tending to establish them, but the facts need not be uncontroverted or clearly proved and the court may permit the inclusion of facts as to which the party intends subsequently to offer proof. A question may be allowed even though there is a strong preponderance of evidence against the facts assumed. Ind.—Mounsey v. Bower, 78 Ind.App. 647, 136 N.E. 41 (1922); Cal.—Foremost Dairies, Inc. v. Industrial Accident Commission, 237 Cal.2d 560, 47 Cal.Rptr. 173 (1965).

In order that a witness be allowed to compare two writings and state an inference as to whether or not they were written by the same person, it usually must be shown to the reasonable satisfaction of the court, that the witness is sufficiently qualified as a skilled observer or expert to make his inference admissible as an aid to the jury. Pa.—In re Martin's Estate, 51 Dauph. 322 (Orph.Ct.1941). However, a lay witness may compare the disputed writings with other writings proved or admitted to be genuine to refresh his memory and if he is then able to testify from his memory, as refreshed, his statement may be received. Pa.—McNair v. Commonwealth, 26 Pa. 388 (1856). When it becomes necessary to prove handwriting, a witness acquainted with the handwriting of the supposed writer, may be permitted to testify with respect to an opinion as to whether the writing in question was written or signed by him unless it appears that the writing, if made by him, was not in his usual and accustomed handwriting. Pa.—McClure v. Redman, 263 Pa. 405, 107 A. 25 (1919). Opinions as to the genuineness of handwriting should be received only from one whose qualifications have been properly established by proof that he is acquainted with the writing of the writer of the document in question. In order for an ordinary witness to testify with respect to his opinion as to the genuineness of a particular writing, proof of the fact that he was acquainted with the handwriting of the supposed writer, is sufficient to warrant reception of his testimony even though he is not skilled in matters of handwriting. A claim of knowledge of handwriting is prima facie sufficient to show qualification but the fact of knowledge may appear otherwise than claimed. A witness whose knowledge of a person's handwriting was derived from having seen such person write may state an opinion as to whether a particular document was written by such person. Cal.—Armstrong v. Kline, 64 Cal.App.2d 704, 149 P.2d 445 (1944). To render a witness competent, Conn.—Phoenix State Bank & Trust Co. v. Whitcomb, 121 Conn. 32, 183 A. 5 (1936), the ordinary witness is permitted to testify on the subject of a person's handwriting from a mental standard created by the receipt of letters or other documents from such person even though he never had seen such person. The genuineness of the documents received by the witness must be established. N.Y.—Dunklin v. Riegelmann, 155 N.Y.S. 561 (1915), 22 C.J. p. 627 Notes 44, 45, C.J.S. Evidence § 546(20)b.(3). A witness who in the course of official business or any other way has acquired by experience a knowledge of a person's handwriting may state as to whether a particular writing was made by such person. A witness may be deemed sufficiently qualified of the knowledge of the handwriting of the person in question by having seen writings of such person admitted by him (Pa.—Hershberger v. Hershberger, 345 Pa. 439, 29 A.2d 95 (1943). Knowledge may be acquired by paying out money on the signature of the person in question. Cal.—Gibson v. Mailhebuau, 96 Cal.App. 455, 274 P. 566 (1929). Ordinarily the time when a witness acquired knowledge of a person's handwriting does not affect his competence or by the fact that his knowledge of the handwriting of the person in question was not acquired until after the instrument in consideration was written. Although these matters are proffered for consideration as bearing on the weight to be accorded to his testimony. Pa.—Wilson v. VanLeer, 17 A. 1097, 127 Pa. 371 (1889). To recapitulate the qualifications required for an ordinary witness to testify with respect to handwriting comparison are as follows:

1. He must have general knowledge of the handwriting of the supposed writer of the document in question.

§ 4.26 OPINIONS OF LAY WITNESSES

It sometimes becomes necessary for a lay witness to form a conclusion for without it it would be impossible for the witness to testify to pertinent facts to enable the trier of the facts to form a conclusion. Accordingly, an ordinary lay witness may be called upon to give his/her opinion on a question at issue whenever the facts involved cannot be so described to enable persons who are not eyewitnesses to form a proper conclusion with respect to them without the conclusion of the lay witness. In such a case there is no other way than by permitting the lay witness to express his conclusions with respect to observations made by him. N.M.—State v. Pruett, 22 N.M. 223, 160 Pac. 362, L.R.A.1918A, 656 (1916). Usually the qualification of an ordinary witness in this type of situation consists of just common ordinary knowledge, without other qualification. The opinions of lay witnesses where he may give his opinion have been accepted by the courts in the following cases.

1. S/He may see the person write but it is not essential.
2. S/He may have received documents which created a mental image of receipt of such documents from such person.
3. S/He may have acquired experience with respect to a knowledge of the subject person's handwriting.
4. The time lapse between acquiring knowledge and the testimony does not affect its admissibility.

In testifying to handwriting, certainty is not essential. His statement may be allowed to go to the jury if the witness testifies to a belief, an impression, an opinion, or even a thought or states that he perceives a resemblance although he declines to swear positively with respect to the matter. Mass.—Commonwealth v. Andrews, 143 Mass. 23, 8 N.E. 643 (1886), 22 C.J. p. 630, C.J.S. Evidence § 546(20)c.

§ 4.27 TESTIMONY OF LAY WITNESS—HANDWRITING COMPARISON

A bank teller who cashes checks and/or gives out money to depositors when they present signed withdrawal slips is not necessarily schooled in handwriting comparison. They are thus considered as skilled laymen with regard to the recognition of the handwriting of the persons who present these articles to them for payment. Notwithstanding that fact, they, as laymen, have to come to a conclusion in their recognition of the validity of signatures presented to them. You will note that some banks require more than one teller to look at the signature and compare it with the signature that the bank has on file before payment is made.

You will remember that an expert witness may draw conclusions to aid the jury in its determination. The jury may accept or reject the opinion of the expert. In the area of comparison, the jury may also make its own determination as to the identity of the person from the handwriting specimens which are admitted in evidence. However, a witness who is not necessarily a professional handwriting student or expert, may testify as to the genuineness of written instruments and signatures if he can reasonably satisfy the court that the witness is a skilled observer who can aid the jury in its determination. N.C.—Clayton v. Prudential Ins. Co. of America, 4 N.C.App. 43, 165 S.E.2d 763 (1969); N.Y.—Daniels v. Cummins, 66 Misc.2d 575, 321 N.Y.S.2d 1009 (1971); R.I.—Wooddell v. Hollywood Homes Inc., 105 R.I. 280, 252 A.2d 28 (1969).

In some cases, non-expert witnesses were not permitted to express an opinion as to handwriting based on a comparison of the document in question. Pa.—In re Martin's Estate, 51 Dauph. 322 (Orph. Ct.1941); Ill.—Yelm v. Masters, 81 Ill.App.2d 186, 225 N.E.2d 152 (1967).

As you can understand from the above, there is great disparity in the acceptance by the courts of non-expert witness testimony in handwriting comparison. Accordingly, whether a witness may testify as to handwriting comparison is largely within the discretion of the trial court. Idaho—Lowe v. Skaggs Safeway Stores, 49 Idaho 48, 286 Pac. 616 (1930); N.C.—State v. Cofer, 205 N.C. 653, 172 S.E. 176 (1934).

§ 4.28 TESTIMONY OF LAY WITNESS—EMOTION

A lay witness may testify as to the state of a person's emotions manifested by a person, e. g., whether he appeared to be angry or jesting, N.Y.—Blake v. The People, 73 N.Y. 586 (1878), however, the motive, intention or belief may not be the subject of testimony based on opinion since this involves recital of someone else's state of mind. Testimony may not be allowed to the effect that the deceased person had gone to a certain street for a particular purpose. N.Y.—Bogart v. The City of New York, 200 N.Y. 379, 93 N.E. 937 (1911).

§ 4.29 TESTIMONY OF LAY WITNESS—SENSATIONS

An ordinary witness may testify as to his/her own sensory experiences such as taste, e. g., a certain beverage which he drank appeared to be whiskey, N.Y.—People v. Marx, 128 App.Div. 828, 112 N.Y.S. 1011 (1908), or that he felt intoxicated, N.Y.—In re Ronny, 40 Misc.2d 194, 242 N.Y.S.2d 844 (1963), or that he felt heat or cold.

§ 4.30 TESTIMONY OF LAY WITNESS—PHYSICAL CONDITION OF A PERSON

A lay witness may testify as to the apparent strength, vigor, feebleness, illness of a person. He may testify concerning physical injury or conditions susceptible to observation by an ordinary person. Cal.—Pacific Employers Ins. Co. v. Industrial Accident Commission, 47 C.A.2d 494, 118 P.2d 334 (1941).

§ 4.31 TESTIMONY OF LAY WITNESS—IDENTIFICATION BY VOICE

A witness who is conversing with the voice of another may testify that he knew the voice of the other person, that he had spoken with this person previously on the telephone and could positively identify the person he spoke of as being the voice of his adversary. There is sufficient identification if the witness knew the speaker and recognized his voice at the time of the telephone conversation. N.Y.—Murphy v. Jack, 142 N.Y. 215, 217, 36 N.E. 882, 883 (1894). Even if the witness was not acquainted with the speaker and did not recognize his voice at the time of the telephone conversation, the telephone conversation is admissible if the witness testifies that he met the speaker for the first time thereafter and then recognized his voice as the voice he heard over the telephone. The difference affects the weight rather than the competency of the evidence. N.Y.—People v. Strollo, 191 N.Y. 42, 83 N.E. 573 (1908); Ga.—Jones v. Britt, 75 Ga. App. 142, 42 S.E.2d 648 (1942).

§ 4.32 TESTIMONY OF LAY WITNESS—INTOXICATION

Under most authorities a lay witness may testify as to whether or not another person was intoxicated at a particular time or place provided he had a suitable opportunity for observation. N.Y.—Donahue v. Meagley, 220 App.Div. 469, 221 N.Y.S. 707 (1927); N.J.—Searles v. Public Service R. R. Co., 100 N.J.Law 222, 126 A. 465 (1924). If a witness testifies that the person was intoxicated, he may state the extent of his intoxication, Iowa—State v. Cather, 121 Iowa 106, 96 N.W. 722 (1903), or a witness may state whether a person had been drinking. Md.—Cumberland & Westernport Transit Co. v. Metz, 158 Md. 424, 149 A. 4 (1930), reargument denied 158 Md. 424, 149 A. 565 (1930). On the other hand, testimony that a person was sober at a particular time has been held a mere conclusion. Ill.—Klopp v. Benevolent Protective Order of Elks, Lodge 281, 309 Ill.App. 145, 33 N.E.2d 161 (1941). A police officer's testimony with respect to observation of intoxication has been held admissible. Facts on which the opinion is based must be stated. Ga.—Hill v. Rosser, 102 Ga.App. 776, 117 S.E.2d 889 (1961).

§ 4.33 TESTIMONY OF LAY WITNESS—MENTAL CONDITION OR CAPACITY OF A PERSON

Although there is some contrary authority, as a general rule an ordinary or nonexpert witness who through acquaintance or association has had reasonably adequate opportunity to observe another person and to form a conclusion or opinion as to the mental condition of such person, may on the basis of such facts in his knowledge and observation thereof, state his opinion as to the mental condition of such person. Pa.—In re Owens' Estate, 167 Pa.Super. 10, 74 A.2d 705 (1950).

However, it has been held that opinions as to the mental condition or capacity of a person, expressed by a qualified lay witness, may possess substantial evidentiary value. La.—Succession of Chopin, 214 So.2d 248 (App.1968), or in another court case it was held to possess great weight where the witness was an attorney who drafted a will. Pa.—In re Masciantonio's Estate, 392 Pa. 362, 141 A.2d 362 (1958); Va.—Forehand v. Sawyer, 147 Va. 105, 136 S.E. 683 (1927) or where the witness was a subscribing witness to a will. W.Va.—Floyd v. Floyd, 148 W.Va. 183, 133 S.E.2d 726 (1964).

§ 4.34 TESTIMONY OF LAY WITNESS—RATIONAL OR IRRATIONAL NATURE OF A PERSON'S CONDUCT

An ordinary witness may testify as to whether a person's conduct was rational or irrational but he may not testify that the person was of sound or unsound mind except in the case of a witness who is a subscribing witness to a will. N.Y.—Holcomb v. Holcomb, 95 N.Y. 316 (1884); Mich.—Henderson v. Henderson, 206 Mich. 36, 172 N.W. 623 (1919); N.Y.—Falkides v. Falkides, 40 A.D.2d 1074, 339 N.Y.S.2d 235 (1973).

§ 4.35 TESTIMONY OF LAY WITNESS—IDENTITY

An ordinary witness may under proper circumstances where he is shown to be possessed of adequate knowledge and the capacity to apply it, be allowed to state his inference or opinion on the question of identity, whether the inquiry relates to the identity of human beings, or of animals, or inanimate things. The witness may also state an inference as to the correspondence of footprints. N.C.—State v. Reitz, 83 N.C. 634 (1880); Ill.—Starkey v. Lindsey, 8 Ill.App.3d 871, 290 N.E.2d 649 (1973).

§ 4.36 TESTIMONY OF LAY WITNESS—SPEED OF MOVING VEHICLES

An ordinary witness may testify to the rate of speed that a vehicle was moving but he must first show some experience in observing the rate of speed of moving objects or give some other perspectory reason. N.Y.—Penny v. Rochester R. R. Co., 7 App.Div. 595, 40 N.Y.S. 172 (1896), affirmed 154 N.Y. 770, 49 N.E. 1101; S.C.—Livingston v. Oakman, 251 S.C. 611, 164 S.E.2d 758 (1969).

§ 4.37 REVIEW OF OPINION EVIDENCE OF ORDINARY WITNESS

In Hardy v. Merrill, 56 N.H. 227, 22 Am.Rep. 441, 448–449 (1875), the court said the opinions of ordinary witnesses may be received as follows: "Courts and text writers all agree that, upon questions of science and skill, opinions may be received from persons specially instructed by study and experience in the particular art or mystery to which the investigation relates . . . all concede the admissibility of the opinions of non-professional men upon a great variety of unscientific questions arising every day, and in every judicial inquiry. These are questions of identity, handwriting, quantity, value, weight, measure, time, distance, velocity, form, size, age, strength, heat, cold, sickness and health; questions also, concerning various mental and moral aspects of humanity, such as disposition, . . . intoxication, veracity, general character, and particular phases of character, and other conditions and things, both moral and physical. . . ."

From the above, the reader can see that there are many areas in which a lay witness may express a conclusion. The conclusions are those which ordinary people make in their daily lives and are the common experience of most persons.

Like the opinions of experts, the jury or judge, trying the facts may either accept or reject the conclusions of the lay witness and substitute other conclusions in the findings of fact.

§ 4.38 FEDERAL RULE

Rule 701 Federal Rules of Evidence, provides:

Rule 701: Opinion testimony by lay witness

> If the witness is not testifying as an expert, his testimony in the form of opinions or inferences is limited to those opinions or inferences which are (a) rationally based on a perception of the witness and (b) helpful to a clear understanding of his testimony or the determination of a fact in issue.

This rule gives the judge wide discretion in permitting opinions by lay witnesses. Witnesses often find difficulty in expressing themselves in language which is not a conclusion or an opinion. It is thought that the adversary system of cross-examination will point up weakness if the judge overreaches his discretion in allowing conclusions of lay witnesses to be admitted in evidence. Similar provisions are to be found in California Evidence Code 800, Kansas Code of Civil Procedure 60–456(a), New Jersey Evidence Rule 56(1).

CHAPTER V

THE BEST EVIDENCE RULE

§ 5.1 THE BEST EVIDENCE RULE

The rule of evidence commonly known as "The Best Evidence Rule" is that the highest degree of proof of which a case from its nature is susceptible must, if accessible, be produced, or, in other words, that no evidence shall be received where there is an apparent possibility that the party who offers it can obtain better evidence. This elementary principle of law of evidence embraces every issue which may be in controversy but it applies exclusively to documentary evidence. Pa.—Perry v. Ryback, 302 Pa. 559, 153 A. 770 (1931). It is for the court to determine. The best evidence rule goes only to the competency of the evidence, not its materiality, relevancy or weight. Minn.—Stevens v. Minneapolis Fire Dept. Relief Assoc., 219 Minn. 276, 17 N.W.2d 642 (1945); Me.—Morgan v. Paine, 312 A.2d 178 (1974); Minn.—Buffalo Ins. Co. v. United Parking Stations Inc., 277 Minn. 134, 152 N.W.2d 81 (1967).

§ 5.2 THE REASON FOR THE BEST EVIDENCE RULE

The reason for the Best Evidence Rule is that it prevents fraud which might be attempted if the parties were able to prove the contents of a writing by all evidence which is referred to in the law of evidence as parol evidence. It also prevents inaccuracies in the copying of the original writing and mistakes in reading it and when the writing itself is presented in the trial, these dangers are averted. The Best Evidence Rule is aimed at only excluding evidence concerning the contents of the testimony but questions as to its existence or identity may be admissible. Best evidence must always be equated to what one is trying to prove; it has a strong relation to reliability. U.S.—N. L. R. B. v. International Union of Operating Engineers, Local 12, 243 F.2d 134 (9th Cir. 1957).

§ 5.3 ADMISSIBILITY OF BEST EVIDENCE OBTAINABLE

Where the evidence offered, while not of the highest degree or of the most satisfactory kind is otherwise competent and is the best which under the circumstances that can be produced and there is no evidence of a higher degree or more conclusive character available to the party seeking to prove the fact in issue, it is admissible. However, it still must be competent to the fact in issue. If for any reason it is incompetent, it may not be admissible. Thus, an affidavit of a justice of peace who tried case as to bases of action would not be competent as secondary evidence of contents of last records of justice courts. N.C.—Higgs-Taft Furn. Co. v. Clark, 191 N.C. 369, 131 S.E.

731 (1926). Letters or documents written in duplicate are written by the same mechanical act if a carbon copy is produced. Accordingly the carbon copy is known as a duplicate original. Ky.—Davis v. Williams Bros. Construction Co., 207 Ky. 404, 269 S.W. 289 (1925); Minn.—International Harvester Co. v. Elfstrom, 101 Minn. 263, 112 N.W. 252, 12 L.R.A.(N.S.) 243 (1907). Printing press copies and all reproductions from the same setting of type are considered as originals. N.Y.—Huff v. Bennett, 6 N.Y. (2 Seld.) 337 (1852); La.—Joseph Durst Corp. v. Coastal Development Co., 248 La. 420, 179 So.2d 17 (App.1965); Ga.—Ennis v. Atlas Finance Co., 120 Ga.App. 849, 172 S.E.2d 482 (1965); Utah—James Mfg. Co. v. Wilson, 15 Utah 2d 210, 390 P.2d 127 (1964).

§ 5.4 PHOTOCOPY

Modern office practice has discontinued the use of carbon copies as wasteful. It is far less expensive to have a secretary prepare an original and then photocopy the original for file records. This presents a problem in the law of evidence because photocopies are not considered the best evidence because they are not made by the same mechanical act. The student must constantly bear in mind that the rules of evidence are designed to bring forth the truth according to the best knowledge and experience of man. It is a simple matter to change the contents of the original in printing a photocopy and accordingly common law courts will not accept these in evidence. 142 A.L.R. 1270, 76 A.L.R.2d 1356.

However since this practice is so widespread today, it is considered to be done in the regular course of business and many states have enacted statutes which are in derogation of the common law and recognize this practice and consider the photocopies to be sufficiently trustworthy to be treated as an original for the purpose of the best evidence rule. N.Y.—CPLR 4539, Hospital and medical records, CPLR 2306–A, Books or papers of a library department or bureau of a municipal corporation or of the state, 2307–B, Public Officers Law 64–a, General Municipal Law 51–a.

§ 5.5 PRIMARY AND SECONDARY EVIDENCE

If an original document is placed in evidence it is considered to be primary evidence of its contents. However, a copy of the document or the oral statements of a witness regarding its contents are designated as secondary evidence. This usually occurs when the original has been lost or destroyed. The foundation must show that reasonable search has been made for the original in the place where it is most likely to be (the last place that it was seen) and inquiry should be made of persons most likely to have some knowledge of its whereabouts. Naturally, it must be shown that the original was not destroyed with fraudulent intent or intentionally destroyed. The court may permit a party to follow any order of proof to establish

1. that the writing had been in existence;

2. its genuineness, if its authenticity is in question;
3. a proper excuse for its not being produced;
   (a) without fault of the party desiring to prove the fact;
   (b) lost or destroyed by party against whom the evidence is offered;
   (c) inaccessible to party seeking to show the facts
   (d) held by court in same jurisdiction and primary evidence cannot be secured for trial.
   (e) held by a third party not within the jurisdiction of the court.
   (f) failure of adverse party to produce primary evidence on notice. 32A C.J.S. Evidence § 813 et seq.

§ 5.6 INADMISSIBILITY OF PRIMARY EVIDENCE

Secondary evidence of the contents of a writing cannot be introduced where it appears that for any reason the writing would not be admissible. For example, if the original writing constituted a privileged communication it could not be admitted against the party to whom the privilege ran. Ill.—Krumin v. Bruknes, 255 Ill.App. 503. A fortiori, after a writing itself has been offered in evidence and rejected, parol evidence of its contents cannot be received. Ga.—Crider v. Woodward, 162 Ga. 743, 135 S.E. 95 (1926).

§ 5.7 FAILURE OF ADVERSE PARTY TO PRODUCE PRIMARY EVIDENCE ON NOTICE

Secondary evidence is admissible where the primary evidence of a fact which a party desires to prove is in the possession or control of his adversary who fails or refuses to produce it after being notified or requested to do so. Mass.—Bresky v. Rosenberg, 256 Mass. 66, 152 N.E. 347 (1926); N.J.—North Jersey Discount Co. v. Aetna Insurance Co., 125 N.J.Law 7, 13 A.2d 226 (1940); N.Y.—Harmon v. Matthews, 27 N.Y.S.2d 656 (Sup.1941), or who after such notification or request fails to explain why he did not produce the primary evidence. Me.—Norton v. Heywood, 20 Me. 359.

§ 5.8 EFFECT OF PRODUCTION OF ORIGINAL MATERIAL

Secondary evidence is not admissible where primary evidence is produced but the introduction of secondary evidence on failure to produce the primary evidence is not rendered erroneous by the subsequent production of the primary evidence. Ind.—Phenix Ins. Co. v. Jacobs, 23 Ind.App. 509, 55 N.E. 778 (1900).

§ 5.9 DEGREES AND KINDS OF SECONDARY EVIDENCE

Secondary evidence of the contents of a writing may be furnished by the testimony of witnesses. U.S.—Conkling v. N. Y. Life Ins. & Trust Co., 262 F. 620 (D.C.Cir.1919), or by the production of a copy. There is much conflict with respect to whether there are degrees of secondary evidence. It is universally accepted however that where a proper case has been made for the introduction of secondary evidence any kind of secondary evidence is competent which is admissible by other rules of law unless it is shown by the nature of this evidence itself or is made to appear by the objecting party that other or more satisfactory evidence is known to the producing party and can be produced by him. However, courts have rejected the argument of counsel against the introduction of oral testimony of the contents of the original writing where a proper foundation was laid for the non-production of the original and a copy was available. In rejecting this argument the court said "Although the argument is plausible, it is apparent on a moment's reflection that proof of an instrument by proving a copy is merely one form of parol testimony as to its contents, and I am not aware of any rule of law that makes a distinction of grade in secondary evidence." N.Y.—Rosenbaum v. Podolsky, 97 Misc. 614, 162 N.Y.S. 227 (1917).

§ 5.10 RECORDS AND JUDICIAL DOCUMENTS

Where the fact to be proved is one which the law requires to appear of record, the general rule is that the record itself or a properly authenticated copy is the best evidence and parol evidence cannot be received to prove the fact except where the record is lost or destroyed, or is for other reasons inaccessible, and a properly authenticated copy cannot be obtained. Conn.—State ex rel. Capurso v. Flis, 144 Conn. 473, 133 A.2d 901 (1957); Fla.—Milk Commission v. Dade County Dairies, 145 Fla. 579, 200 So. 83 (1941). The judgments and decrees of courts of record cannot be proved by parol unless the record is lost or destroyed or is otherwise inaccessible and a properly authenticated copy or transcript thereof cannot be obtained. N.Y.—In re Diaz-Albertini's Will, 2 A.D.2d 671, 154 N.Y.S.2d 422 (1956); Cal.—Sills v. Forbes, 33 Cal.App.2d 219, 91 P.2d 246 (1939); Conn.—Beers v. Bridgeport Hydraulic Co., 100 Conn. 459, 124 A. 23 (1924). Therefore when a witness while testifying denies that he has ever been convicted of a crime and the prosecution knows that the witness has been previously convicted of a crime, the prosecutor may ask for a continuance to allow sufficient time for him to bring into court a certified copy of the transcript of judgment.

This question may only be asked in a limited type of situation by United States Attorneys and by many state prosecutors pursuant to statute. See Rule 609 Federal Rules of Evidence.

§ 5.11 VOLUMINOUS WRITINGS

Sometimes it is necessary to establish the result of voluminous writings or entries. In this case a qualified person, such as an accountant may testify to a summary of the documents on the condition that these documents have been made available to the other side in sufficient time for him to adequately inspect them. N.Y.—Public Operating Corp. v. Weingart, 257 App.Div. 379, 13 N.Y.S.2d 182 (1939); Ariz.—Collison v. International Ins. Co., 58 Ariz. 156, 118 P.2d 445 (1941).

§ 5.12 LEARNED TREATISES

When an expert testifies he is subject to cross-examination. When the expert's testimony is at variance with what is written in a learned treatise, it becomes necessary to impeach his conclusions by the use of a learned treatise on the subject.

Let us suppose that a police scientist is testifying as to the direction that a bullet shot from a revolver took as it pierced a window glass of an automobile. Let us further assume that he testifies that when a bullet pierces such a window, the side from which the bullet enters the window appears like a crater of a volcano with numerous small flakes of glass missing while the side where it exits the window is a round hole with the approximate circumference of the bullet.

On cross-examination, the expert may be asked whether he himself has done experiments to substantiate these conclusions. Upon an affirmative answer, he may be asked if he is familiar with a recognized book or treatise in forensic science, such as Introduction to Criminal Investigation by Richard H. Ward. If he denies familiarity with the named book or treatise, he may be asked about others. If he denies familiarity with all of those named, he may be asked what book or treatise on the subject that he is familiar with. Hopefully the trial counsel has the book or treatise available to him. If he does not immediately have it, he may ask for a continuance or ask the court to recall the witness at a subsequent date.

When the trial counsel has the book or treatise in his possession, which the witness claims familiarity with, he may ask that it be marked for identification and then ask the witness to read the contradictory material silently, or he may ask the court for permission to read it into evidence himself.

If, as in the hypothetical case indicated above, the book reads that the cone shaped opening of the window is on the side from which the bullet exits, he will ask the witness if he would like to change his testimony. If the witness persists in his testimony, the attorney may ask the court for permission to read the contradictory material into evidence.

Notwithstanding the fact that such information is hearsay, courts have permitted the introduction of such evidence on the issue of the existence of the statement itself and not the truth of the statement. Miss.—Catholic Diocese of Natchez-Jackson v. Jaqueth, 224 So.2d 216 (1969). However, if a witness can be produced to vouch for the general authenticity of a publication, it may be introduced as admissible hearsay. Wash.—Most Worshipful Prince Hall Grand Lodge of Wash. v. Most Worshipful Grand Lodge, A.F. & A.M., 62 Wash.2d 28, 381 P.2d 130 (1963), certiorari denied 375 U.S. 945, 84 S.Ct. 352, 11 L.Ed. 2d 275.

This theory of admitting learned treatises as an exception to the hearsay exclusionary rule has been codified in Rule 803(18) of the Federal Rules of Evidence.

§ 5.13 RULE IN CRIMINAL CASES

In a criminal case the rule with respect to a demand to produce is different because of the constitutional protections.

The defendant's silence or refusal would cause serious injurious inferences against him. Therefore where an incriminating document appears prima facie to be in the possession of the defendant, the people may submit secondary evidence of its contents sans the necessity of just asking the defendant to produce the original. For example, a person who is in possession of lottery numbers in some states is in violation of the gambling statute. If a person is found to be in possession of a blank paper and this paper contains impressions of lottery numbers which resulted from writing on another paper in pencil or ball point pen, the original of which has been placed on top of the impressioned paper when the writing had been done, the second copy of impressioned paper could be admitted in evidence. Photographs of the paper done with oblique lighting could then be introduced to explain the primary (impressioned paper) evidence. In this case the photographs would be considered as secondary evidence. The defendant could not be required to produce the original paper containing the lottery numbers.

§ 5.14 FEDERAL RULE

The Federal Rules of Evidence treat the issue of the Best Evidence Rule in Sections 1002 and 1003 and 1004 as follows:

Rule 1002. Requirement of original

To prove the content of a writing, recording or photograph, the original writing, recording or photograph is required, except as otherwise provided in these rules or by act of Congress.

Rule 1003. Admissibility of duplicates

A duplicate is admissible to the same extent as an original unless (1) a genuine question is raised as to the authenticity of the original or (2) in the circumstances it would be unfair to admit the duplicate in lieu of the original.

Rule 1004. Admissibility of other evidence of contents

The original is not required, and other evidence of the contents of a writing, recording or photograph is admissible if—

(1) Originals lost or destroyed.—All originals are lost or have been destroyed, unless the proponent lost or destroyed them in bad faith; or

(2) Original not obtainable.—No original can be obtained by any available judicial process or procedure; or

(3) Original in possession of opponent.—At a time when an original was under the control of the party against whom offered, he was put on notice, by the pleadings or otherwise, that the contents would be a subject of proof at the hearing, and he does not produce the original at the hearing; or

(4) Collateral matters.—The writing, recording or photograph is not closely related to a controlling issue.

CHAPTER VI

HEARSAY AND CHARACTER EVIDENCE

§ 6.1 INTRODUCTION

I doubt that there is a reader of this book who has not heard that there is is a rule of evidence which excludes hearsay evidence from the trial record. The problem is first to recognize hearsay when you hear it and secondly to be certain that the hearsay which you hear does not come within the scope of the various exceptions to the hearsay exclusionary rule.

Always keep in mind that the rules of evidence have as their object the revelation of the truth. We can therefore easily understand that when a person testifies to something which another person is alleged to have said there is a great possibility for the unintentional distortion of the original statement. How many of us have been the recipient of half truths from the gossiping tongues of acquaintances only to find that by the time the facts are passed from one mouth to the other through successive persons, the final statement has no resemblance to the original statement?

To guard against this type of situation, the rules of evidence have precluded the introduction of hearsay evidence except for certain exceptions to the hearsay exclusionary rule.

These exceptions are predicated in each instance by the following:

1. The necessity for its introduction.
2. The great probability of reliability.

§ 6.2 HEARSAY DEFINED

It is extremely difficult to define precisely what hearsay is. However, we may say that hearsay is a statement, other than one made by the declarant while testifying at a trial or hearing, offered in evidence to prove the truth of the matter asserted. (Rule 801(c) Federal Rules of Evidence.) Another definition of hearsay might be a statement made out of court which is not made in the course of the trial or hearing in which it is offered, if offered for the truth of the fact asserted in the statement where there is no opportunity for cross-examination.

It is important to note that sometimes a statement may appear to be hearsay but if the counsel's intention is not to offer it as proof of the fact that the statement is true but that it is only offered for the fact that the statement was made, it is not hearsay. For example, upon trial for the purpose of showing that "A" had acted in the heat of passion with no intent to kill, "A" was permitted to testify that, just before the killing of his wife, she had told him that she was pregnant by reason of her relations with another man. N.Y.—People v. Harris,

209 N.Y. 70, 102 N.E. 546 (1913), but the case was reversed because the Court of Appeals held that probative value was outweighed by danger that its admission would unreasonably prolong the trial, it would confuse the jury, unfairly surprise a party and create substantial danger of prejudice.

§ 6.3 REASON FOR THE RULE

When a person testifies in open court, the adversary has an opportunity for cross-examination. The purpose of the cross-examination is to inquire into

1. ability to recall past events correctly;
2. accuracy of his perception;
3. veracity of the witness.

When a statement is made out of court, out of the particular trial and is offered for the truth of the assertion contained therein, there is no opportunity for cross-examination and hence no opportunity to probe the full truth from the witness. Hence, it is the deprivation of the right of cross-examination which is the primary reason for the existence of the hearsay exclusionary rule. Some cases give as an additional reason that the declarant was not under oath. However, even if the hearsay statement is made under oath, it is still not admissible. N.Y.—Bookman v. Stegman, 105 N.Y. 621, 11 N.E. 376 (1887); Conn.—Henry v. Kopf, 104 Conn. 73, 131 A. 412 (1926); Fla.—Smith v. Frisch's Big Boy, Inc., 208 So.2d 310 (App.1968).

§ 6.4 EXCEPTIONS TO HEARSAY RULE

The hearsay exclusionary rule is not absolute in that exceptions to the rule have always existed and are recognized. Many times these exceptions to the rule are by authority of a state statute and other times, the common law has provided these exceptions because of necessity and the great probability of reliability, public policy and the trustworthiness which experience has taught, or the circumstances indicate, and the probability of veracity. However, necessity alone has never been considered as a sufficient reason of itself to open the door to hearsay evidence. N.M.—Brown v. General Ins. Co. of America, 70 N.M. 46, 369 P.2d 968 (1962). The burden rests on a person seeking to base hearsay evidence admitted under an exception to the hearsay rule to show clearly that the evidence falls within such exception. Pa.—Carney v. Pennsylvania R. Co., 428 Pa. 489, 240 A.2d 71 (1968). Many exceptions to the hearsay exclusionary rule will be dealt with more particularly later in this book. The Federal Rules of Evidence in Rules 803 and 804(b) list twenty eight exceptions to the hearsay exclusionary rule.

§ 6.5 NEGATIVE HEARSAY

A negative form of hearsay has been recognized as where testimony of a court clerk to the effect that no cases of a particular type, other than the instant one, had been filed. Colo.—Hadden v. Gateway West Pub. Co., 130 Colo. 73, 273 P.2d 733 (1954), or testimony of a party that the records do not show a divorce of particular persons. Ala.—Jordan v. Copeland, 272 Ala. 336, 131 So.2d 696 (1961).

§ 6.6 WRITTEN OR PRINTED HEARSAY

Hearsay is not limited to oral testimony or statements, the rule applies to written as well as oral statements. Cal.—Weaver v. Bay, 216 Cal.App.2d 559, 31 Cal.Rptr. 211 (1963); Conn.—General Motors Acceptance Corp. v. Capitol Garage, Inc., 154 Conn. 593, 227 A.2d 548 (1967); N.Y.—Kaplan v. City of N. Y., 10 A.D.2d 319, 200 N.Y.S.2d 261 (1960).

§ 6.7 WRITTEN STATEMENTS IN JUDICIAL MATTERS—HEARSAY

Written statements have been held inadmissible under the rule excluding hearsay evidence where the form is judicial or relates to judicial matters such as affidavits. N.J.—Union Co. Savings Bank v. Kolpenitsky, 125 N.J.Eq. 125, 4 A.2d 413 (1939).

§ 6.8 OTHER WRITINGS—HEARSAY

Letters have been held inadmissible as hearsay. Ill.—Kane v. City of Chicago, 392 Ill. 172, 64 N.E.2d 506 (1946); Conn.—Purcell v. Purcell, 101 Conn. 422, 126 A. 353 (1924); Cal.—Stoneking v. Briggs, 254 Cal.App.2d 563, 62 Cal.Rptr. 249 (1962); N.Y.—Lindt v. Henshel, 25 N.Y.2d 357, 306 N.Y.S.2d 436, 254 N.E.2d 746 (1970). Postal cards, telegrams, match covers, memorandum, bulletins, diaries, notices, and surveyor's field notes have been held to be hearsay and inadmissible.

§ 6.9 REPUTATION EVIDENCE—EXCEPTION TO HEARSAY RULE—PUBLIC OR GENERAL RIGHT

Reputation evidence consists of the general statements of members of the community with relation to a particular fact, and hence may be regarded as a species of composite hearsay. N.C.—In re Nelson's Will, 210 N.C. 398, 186 S.E. 480, 105 A.L.R. 1441 (1936). A sort of distinction is allowed between hearsay and reputation. Yet reputation is nothing more than hearsay derived from those who had the means of knowing the fact, and may exist when those best acquainted with the fact are dead. Me.—Scott v. Blood, 16 Me. 192, 196 (1848).

The reputation which is admissible, however, must refer to a public or general right and not a particular exercise of it. Mass.—Enfield, Inhabitants of v. Woods, 212 Mass. 547, 99 N.E. 331 (1912). Evidence as to common reputation of ownership is admissible where claims to public lands and to water on such lands are involved but the reputation must be that of a past generation. Where evidence as to ancient common reputation as to ownership of water rights was admissible, the most that could be shown by a witness was that there was ancient common reputation in the community relative to the division and use of water for some beneficial purpose, stating what that reputation was, and to ask the witness to state who was reputed to be the owner of "springs" could only mislead, since there can only be ownership of a right to take and use water and not the corpus of the water.

Facts of genealogy stand in a peculiar position as a matter of quasi-public concern, and, where the race to which a person belongs is in issue, proof of general reputation is competent. Tex.—Stewart v. Profit, 146 S.W. 563 (Civ.App.1912). Reputation evidence cannot ordinarily be received where the fact involved is of only special or limited interest. Such facts within this rule include, individual's position in the community, their financial, mental or physical condition. Cal.—Simons v. Inyo Cerro Gordo Minery & Power Co., 48 Cal.App. 524, 192 P. 144 (1920). General reputation cannot establish the existence of moral qualities such as loyalty. Tenn.—Hart v. Reynolds, 48 Tenn. (1 Heisk) 208 (1870), except where proof of character is permitted in case of a party.

§ 6.10 THE DIFFERENCE BETWEEN CHARACTER AND REPUTATION

Character and reputation are not synonymous. Character is what a person is morally, while reputation is what a person is reputed to be. A person may be a scoundrel but if few people know of this fact, his reputation may be that of a good man. A person's general character has always been proved by general reputation. N.Y.—People v. Van Gaasbeck, 189 N.Y. 408, 82 N.E. 718, 22 L.R.A., N.S. 650 (1907). Another way of distinguishing the difference is by stating that character is what a person is, while reputation is what people believe s/he is.

§ 6.11 CHARACTER OF A WITNESS

A defendant's character may not be attacked until s/he opens the issue of his character on the defendant's case. This is usually done by the testimony of a witness, not a party to the action, who will testify with respect to the good character of the defendant for the trait at issue in the case.

If a defendant has taken the stand in his own defense in a criminal case, he necessarily places his own veracity at issue. He may, under this situation, have another witness testify that the defendant has an excellent reputation in the community for truth and veracity in all of his dealings.

The prosecutor, when faced with this situation, may attempt to impeach the character of the witness who is designated as a character witness, or he may impeach the standards upon which the witness relies in assessing the character of the defendant. In Federal trials, the prosecutor may attack the character of a witness by showing a prior conviction of a crime wherein the crime was punishable by death or imprisonment in excess of one year, or the crime involved dishonesty or a false statement regardless of the punishment. This is limited however by a time factor. It is not admissible if more than ten years have elapsed since the date of the conviction or the release of the witness from confinement imposed for the conviction, whichever is the later date, unless the court determines that in the interests of justice that the probative value of the conviction supported by specific facts and circumstances, substantially outweighs its prejudicial effect. See Rule 609 Federal Rules of Evidence for further amplification of this thought.

Many state courts do not limit the impeachment device of eliciting prior crimes from the mouth of the witness. Hence in some states once a person was convicted as a felon, he would be incapable of belief and he would be adjudged an infamous person. In other states, he is permitted to testify but his testimony is subject to impeachment by the introduction into evidence that he was convicted of a crime. The theory being that if he did not admit to the previous conviction, and the conviction was proved, he is therefore more likely to be testifying to falsehoods in other testimony. The courts were careful to point out that this was not an attack on the character of the witness but on his credibility. With the adoption of the Federal Rule 609, this practice is limited in Federal courts and many states are falling into line in adopting the same procedure.

A prosecutor may impeach the standards upon which the character witness relies by bringing to the attention of the witness the fact that the defendant had been implicated in some prior wrongdoing and ask the witness whether he knew of this fact. He must be very careful in doing this. It may not be introduced merely for the purpose of showing the accused to be a man of bad character likely to commit the crime charged. U.S.—United States v. Brettholz, 485 F.2d 483 (2d Cir. 1973).

In Michelson v. United States, 335 U.S. 469, 69 S.Ct. 213, 93 L.Ed. 168 (1949), the United States Supreme Court said:

> "Wide discretion is accompanied by heavy responsibility on trial courts to protect the practice from any misuse. The trial judge was scrupulous to so guard in the case before us. He took pains to ascertain, out of the presence of the jury that the target of the question was an actual event, which would probably result in some comment among acquaintances if not injury to defendant's reputation. He satisfied himself that counsel was not merely taking a random shot at a reputation imprudently exposed or asking a groundless question to waft an unwarranted innuendo into the jury box."

Under the Federal Rules as enacted, many scholars feel that the Michelson rule should be re-interpreted in the light of Rules 405 and 608. That is, that the Federal Rules now only permit inquiry into the subjects indicated infra and do not encompass all prior bad acts. Most states still permit the inquiry into all prior bad acts. An old case in New York held that a witness may be interrogated upon cross-examination with respect to any immoral, vicious or criminal act of his life which may affect his character and show him to be unworthy of belief. N.Y.—People v. Webster, 139 N.Y. 73, 34 N.E. 730 (1893).

In most state courts however, when a witness is called to the stand to testify on behalf of a side of the controversy, the litigant who calls that witness to the stand is in effect vouching for the credibility of that witness. Accordingly, if that witness testifies to some unexpected response, the litigant who has called the witness to the stand may not impeach his own witness. This situation has been changed by statute in the Federal Rules of Evidence (Rule 607) and at this writing a few states are now permitting impeachment of one's own witness.

Since the prevailing rule in state courts is that one cannot impeach his own witness, it is of paramount importance to ascertain the background and character of the witness before he takes the stand because if his personal history is bad, it might influence the trier of the facts against the side who called the witness to testify. The ultimate objective of a trial conducted in conformity with the rules of evidence is to seek out the truth. Therefore if a witness once plead guilty to stealing an automobile, this fact should not affect his credibility as a witness. Nevertheless, states have allowed inquiry along these lines by statute, (N.Y.CPLR 4513) where the fact of the commission of the crime may affect the weight of the testimony of the witness. There is a movement away from this theory. The Federal Rules of Evidence support this view in Rule 608.

Rule 603. Evidence of character and conduct of witness

(a) Opinion and reputation evidence of character.—The credibility of a witness may be attacked or supported by evidence in the form of opinion or reputation, but subject to these limitations: (1) the evidence may refer only to character for truthfulness or untruthfulness, and (2) evidence of truthful character is admissible only after the character of the witness for truthfulness has been attacked by opinion or reputation evidence or otherwise.

(b) Specific instances of conduct.—Specific instances of conduct of a witness, for the purpose of attacking or supporting his credibility, other than conviction of crime as provided in Rule 609, may not be proved by extrinsic evidence. They may, however, in the discretion of the court, if probative of truthfulness or untruthfulness, be inquired into on cross-examination of the witness (1) concerning his character for truthfulness or untruthfulness, or (2) concerning the character for truthfulness or untruthfulness of another witness as to which character the witness being cross-examined has testified.

The giving of testimony, whether by an accused or by any other witness, does not operate as a waiver of his privilege against self-incrimination when examined with respect to matters which relate only to credibility.

For the time being, it is safe to say that most state courts will permit cross-examination of a witness as to his previous commissions of crime and his character with respect to truthfulness or untruthfulness for the purpose of impeaching his credibility.

§ 6.12 REPUTATION OF A PARTY IN A CIVIL ACTION—EXCEPTION TO HEARSAY RULE

Ordinarily in a civil action the character of a party is deemed by the law to be irrelevant in determining the merits of the controversy. Character may be a relevant fact apart, and where this is the case, evidence of the character of the person in question is admissible. For example, in a contest for custody of a minor child, the character of contesting parents becomes a matter in issue and is a proper subject of proof. Iowa—Herr v. Lazor, 238 Iowa 518, 28 N.W.2d 11 (1947). Character evidence is admissible, however, in a civil case if it is relevant for some purpose other than to raise an inference that the party did or did not do the act in issue. An apparent exception to that rule has occurred in a civil action for assault and battery where evidence may be admitted to show that the defendant acted in self-defense, and then evidence as to the violent and dangerous character of the deceased, is admitted, Ark.—York v. Hampton, 229 Ark. 301, 314 S.W.2d 480 (1958), or the person charged to have been assaulted; Cal.—Northrup v. Baker, 202 Cal.App.2d 347, 20 Cal.Rptr. 797 (1962), is admissible. Other civil cases where character evidence has been held admissible are (a) libel, (b) slander, (c) malicious prosecution. However, in recent years, courts have expanded the use of character evidence in civil cases where the character of the party or the witness has been attacked. In that case, the one attacked may introduce evidence to negate the attack. Ill.—Werdell v. Turzynski, 128 Ill.App.2d 139, 262 N.E.2d 833 (1970), Federal Rule 608.

§ 6.13 CHARACTER OF DEFENDANT IN A CRIMINAL TRIAL—EXCEPTION TO HEARSAY RULE

It is well settled in a criminal prosecution that the defendant may introduce reputation evidence as to his own good character for the purpose of raising an inference that he would not be likely to commit the offense charged. N.Y.—People v. Van Gaasbeck, supra. Each defendant is assumed to have started his/her life afresh at the bar of justice and if s/he chooses, by refraining from introducing character witnesses in his/her own behalf or if s/he fails to exercise his/her right to take the stand in his/her own defense, the prosecution is precluded from introducing evidence relating to the bad character of the defendant. On the other hand, once the defendant opens the door by calling a character witness in his/her behalf or by taking the stand, the prosecution may introduce testimony relating to the defendant's infamous past. The rule is based upon the possibility of introducing evidence which will unduly prejudice the defendant. If the defendant committed a rape heretofore, he may still be innocent of the rape charge in the instant case. However, if he is a previous rapist, and he introduces evidence in a rape case that he has a reputation in the community as being a moral home loving father and husband, the prosecution is justified to introduce his previous conviction, for if the defendant's character is relevant to prove his innocence, it is also relevant to prove his guilt. Character evidence, if believed, may when considered with all the other evidence in a case, create a reasonable doubt when without it none would exist. U.S.—Edgington v. United States, 164 U.S. 361, 17 S.Ct. 72, 41 L.Ed. 467 (1896); N.Y.—People v. McDowell, 9 N.Y.2d 12, 210 N.Y.S.2d 514, 172 N.E.2d 279 (1961).

§ 6.14 CHARACTER EVIDENCE—MODE OF PROOF

Evidence of general reputation as proof of character may be probatively weak but it makes a comparatively simple issue and one which the person affected may be supposed to be able to meet without surprise. N.C.—Nixon v. McKinney, 105 N.C. 23, 11 S.E. 154 (1890).

The accepted method of proving character is by establishing the general reputation as to the particular trait involved. Nev.—Davis v. Davis, 54 Nev. 267, 13 P.2d 1109 (1932), 22 C.J. p. 480, note 76, C.J.S. Evidence § 434.

The reputation which is admissible is the common report which others make concerning the person in question, i. e., the talk about him which shows the opinion which is held in his community. Ky.—Asher v. Beckner, 19 Ky.Law Rep. 521, 41 S.W. 35 (1898). The general reputation of a person cannot be proved by a statement of one or two persons but it must be such as is generally current in the community. Iowa—State ex rel. Seeburger v. Pickett, 202 Iowa 1321, 210 N.W. 782 (1926).

As a general rule, the character of a person cannot be proven from the personal knowledge of the witness, Ohio—Lakes v. Buckeye State Mut. Ins. Ass'n, 110 Ohio App. 115, 168 N.E.2d 895 (1960), 22 C.J. p. 485, note 65, C.J.S. Evidence § 433, and the personal or individual opinion of the witness is not admissible. Tex.—Tarwater v. Donley County State Bank, 277 S.W. 176 (Civ.App.1926), 22 C.J. p. 484, note 65, C.J.S. Evidence § 433(b), usually, the reputation must be confined to the defendant's reputation in the community in which he resides, N.Y.—People v. Van Gaasbeck, supra, or where he has resided. Ky.—Louisville Times Co. v. Emrich, 252 Ky. 210, 66 S.W.2d 73 (1934), 22 C.J. p. 480, note 93, C.J.S. Evidence § 434.

The rules of evidence have had to accommodate to present day situations. In this exception to the hearsay rule, the courts have taken into consideration that the increase of population and the decrease in communal living in small towns has resulted in a slight change with respect to the area from which a party may draw to bring in his character witness. In large cities it is not uncommon for persons to live in an apartment for years and not know the neighbor in the adjoining apartment. In such a case a person may not be known in the community in which he lives and his opportunity to create a reputation "good or bad, is among his associates in his particular activities, or in the personal contacts of his life where he actually lives it." N.Y.—People v. Gitlow, 234 N.Y. 132, 138, 136 N.E. 317 at 319 (1922).

Character evidence may also be shown by negative evidence. A witness may testify that he has lived for a considerable length of time in the same neighborhood as the defendant and has never heard anything against him in respect to peaceableness, or honesty or whatever other trait might be relevant. N.Y.—People v. Van Gaasbeck, supra; Pa.—In re Horton's Estate, 357 Pa. 30, 52 A.2d 895 (1947).

When a person of previous good reputation is indicted and the news is disseminated through the community, his reputation suffers. Therefore, because of this type of situation, the rules of evidence preclude the use of character testimony for the period after the event for which the defendant is presently on trial. Ind.—In re Darrow, 175 Ind. 44, 92 N.E. 369 (1910), 22 C.J. p. 480, note 90, C.J.S. Evidence § 434.

There has been a movement towards deleting the use of an opinion by the character witness and in its stead substituting actual knowledge, wherein a witness would be expected to say that he knows that the party has an excellent character based upon his own dealings with the subject. This concept was debated thoroughly by the House Committee on the Judiciary and in the Congress of the United States. Notwithstanding the fact that the Committee on the Judiciary deleted the provision for making proof by testimony in the form of an opinion, it was defeated on the floor of the House of Representatives and the old rule prevails, namely, that character is to be proved by the opinion of the witness.

However, where character is an essential element of the charge, claim or defense, the defense may prove specific instances of conduct. For example, if a defendant is charged with forceful rape, the defense may introduce specific instances where the complainant has engaged in illicit sexual intercourse with the defendant. The defense being that a woman of previous chaste character is more likely to resist a rape than one who is known to be of loose sexual morality. See 140 A.L.R. 364 for an extensive discussion of this problem.

§ 6.15 CHARACTER OF VICTIM IN A CRIMINAL TRIAL

As a general rule, the victim's character is only relevant as to his/her reputation for veracity. The veracity of the testimony of a witness is always subject to impeachment and the reputation of the witness in the community for telling falsehoods is certainly relevant. The issue is sometimes presented where the victim is dead at the time of the trial, as a result of the wrongful act of the defendant. In these cases the character of the victim is admissible under limited conditions, more fully explained in Section 6.19, infra. In rape cases, the character of the victim is sometimes relevant and admissible. This too is explained more fully in Section 6.20, infra.

§ 6.16 CHARACTER AS AN AID TO PROVE INNOCENCE

A defendant is sometimes faced with an accusation that he/she committed a crime and anyone who knew the defendant would say that in their view it is absolutely impossible that the defendant was the perpetrator because his/her personality and character all point to his/her innocence. The law has provided for this contingency wherein it was stated that character evidence, if believed, may, when considered with all the other evidence in the case create a reasonable doubt when without it none would exist. N.Y.—People v. Helmbrecht, 297 N.Y. 789, 77 N.E.2d 798 (1948); U.S.—Edgington v. United States, 164 U.S. 361, 17 S.Ct. 72, 41 L.Ed. 467 (1897). An accused has the right to offer evidence of his good character, inferred from reputation testimony, to show that he was unlikely to have acted in the manner and with the intent charged in the indictment. U.S.—United States v. Lewin, 467 F.2d 1132 (7th Cir. 1972).

In prosecution for conspiracy to violate narcotic laws, instruction by court that jury could consider evidence of good character and reputation and determine its weight together with all other evidence in case in arriving at their verdict as to defendant's innocence or guilt was proper. Poliafico v. United States, 237 F.2d 97 (6th Cir. 1956), certiorari denied 352 U.S. 1025, 77 S.Ct. 590, 1 L.Ed.2d 597.

§ 6.17 FEDERAL RULES RELATING TO CHARACTER EVIDENCE

Rule 404 is as follows:

Rule 404. Character evidence not admissible to prove conduct; exceptions; other crimes

(a) Character evidence generally.—Evidence of a person's character or a trait of his character is not admissible for the purpose of proving that he acted in conformity therewith on a particular occasion, except:

1. Character of accused.—Evidence of a pertinent trait of his character offered by an accused, or by the prosecution to rebut the same;
2. Character of victim.—Evidence of a pertinent trait of character of the victim of the crime offered by an accused, or by the prosecution to rebut the same, or evidence of a character trait of peacefulness of the victim offered by the prosecution in a homicide case to rebut evidence that the victim was the first aggressor;

3. Character of witness.—Evidence of the character of a witness, as provided in Rules 607, 608 and 609.

(b) Other crimes, wrongs, or acts.—Evidence of other crimes, wrongs, or acts is not admissible to prove the character of a person in order to show that he acted in conformity therewith. It may, however, be admissible for other purposes, such as proof of motive, opportunity, intent, preparation, plan, knowledge, identity or absence of mistake or accident.

§ 6.18 IMPEACHMENT OF CHARACTER WITNESS

A character witness for defendant may be asked whether he had heard that the defendant ever had a reputation in the past for being so brazen that he would steal a red hot stove (assuming the present charge was shoplifting or a similar offense). If his answer is "yes but that was a long time ago", it is a means of impeaching the credibility of the witness. It would materially affect the weight of the direct testimony wherein the witness testified that the defendant is well known in the community as an honest law abiding citizen. The witness may be asked whether he has heard rumors or reports in the community which may be derogatory to the defendant's reputation. The witness may also be impeached by showing his bad reputation for veracity by another witness who is qualified by reason of residence, or other qualifying circumstance. N.Y.—People v. Colantone, 243 N.Y. 134, 152 N.E. 700 (1926). The personal opinion of the witness is not admissible for this purpose. N.Y.—Brill v. Muller Bros., Inc., 13 N.Y.2d 776, 242 N.Y.S.2d 69, 192 N.E.2d 34 (1963).

The witness, on cross-examination, may also be asked whether he has heard of particular instances of conduct pertinent to the trait in question. Michelson v. United States, 335 U.S. 469, 69 S.Ct. 213, 93 L.Ed. 168 (1949). It is quite obvious that such questions must be asked by the prosecutor in good faith. If, for example, the prosecutor in an attempt to impeach a character witness who on direct examination had testified that the defendant had an excellent reputation in the community for honesty, questioned the witness as to a non-existent larceny that the defendant had committed, it would be prejudicial to the defendant in a very substantial way and might justify a reversal.

§ 6.19 CHARACTER OF DECEASED IN HOMICIDE

The defense of a homicide case is often that the defendant did the act but he was justified in doing this act by reason of the fact that he acted in self-defense of his own life or the life of someone in his company at the time. In such a case it has been held to be perfectly proper to introduce the character of the decedent if that character was that of a quarrelsome, vindictive or violent man and that reputation had come to the knowledge of the defendant prior to the homicide. N.Y.—People v. Druse, 103 N.Y. 655, 8 N.E. 733 (1886).

Evidence of this type is not admissible to show that decedent was the aggressor but only to show that the defendant acted on the reasonable and honest belief that his life or the life of someone in his company at the time was in peril. N.Y.—People v. Rodawald, 177 N.Y. 408, 70 N.E. 1 (1904). Always bear in mind that the reputation of the decedent must have been known by the defendant before the event because it is introduced to show the state of mind of the defendant and the inference that the decedent was the aggressor. N.Y.—Stokes v. People, 53 N.Y. 164 (1873).

§ 6.20 CHARACTER OF VICTIM OF RAPE

The character of a victim in a forceable rape prosecution is very material and relevant for the presumption is that a victim of a forceable rape who is a person of unchaste character is less likely to fight her assailant than one of previous chaste character. Non-consent, being an element of the crime, the defendant is permitted to show that the plaintiff was a common prostitute or that her reputation for chastity was bad. Previous acts between the complainant and the defendant which were acts of immorality can also be shown to give rise to the inference that she did not resist. N.Y.—Woods v. People, 55 N.Y. 515, 14 Am.Rep. 309 (1874).

This is not to stand for the premise that a prostitute, or one whose reputation for chastity was bad cannot be the subject of a rape. This is still a matter to be evaluated by the trier of the facts, be it a jury, or a judge in the absence of a jury based on a waiver of a jury trial.

§ 6.21 HABIT—ROUTINE PRACTICE

There are certain actions which people do that are routine. They do these without thinking very much about it. A person may be combing his/her hair or shaving every morning using his/her right hand and s/he does not think very much about it until s/he has a misfortune to that hand and realizes what s/he had been doing with it for years. There is a good argument made that when a person develops a habit of doing something in a particular manner, testimony as to this behavior should be admissible in a trial because it is most likely that the behavior at the time in question was done in the routine manner.

There is much confusion in the court decisions with respect to the admissibility of habit. Particularly when direct evidence can be produced regarding the incident, the court will reject the admission of habit. N.D.—Glatt v. Feist, 156 N.W.2d 819, 28 A.L.R.3d 1278 (1968).

On the other hand, it has been felt that the existence of a habit, causing a more or less settled or automatic reaction to physical or mental stimulus, presents a stronger relevancy as to what happened on a particular occasion than would the mere doing of an isolated act of a similar nature at another time. Mo.—Meller v. State, 438 S.W.2d 187 (1969); Wash.—Breimon v. General Motors Corp., 8 Wash.App. 747, 509 P.2d 398 (1973). Therefore in some circumstances proof of habit may be received. Cal.—Webb v. Van Noort, 239 C.A.2d 472, 48 Cal.Rptr. 823, 29 A.L.R.3d 781 (1966); Tex.—Allstate Insurance Co. v. Smith, 471 S.W.2d 620 (Civ.App.1971).

§ 6.22 OFFERS TO PLEAD AND WITHDRAWAL

State courts have attempted to deal wtih overcrowded court calendars by offering a defendant an opportunity to plead to a lesser included offense in satisfaction of the larger offense. The Federal Courts modify this by permitting the defendant to plead to one of the counts of an indictment and the prosecutor withdraws the prosecution of the other pending counts of the indictment. Prosecutors have wide latitude in what crimes they will prosecute. This mechanism is known as plea bargaining and will be discussed more fully in Chapter XIX, infra.

Many times a defendant pleads guilty to the offense and after the court orders an investigation and report thereof through the probation services, the court will not agree to sentence the defendant in accordance with the previously arranged disposition of the case. When this occurs, most jurists will permit the defendant to withdraw his/her plea of guilty and stand trial, but it is a discretionary act of the judge. The Federal Rules of Criminal Procedure, Rule 11, 18 U.S.C.A., U.S.—United States v. Gonzalez-Hernandez, 481 F.2d 648 (5th Cir. 1973). This is not an absolute right of defendant. It is within the sound discretion of the trial court. Federal Rules of Criminal Procedure Rule 32(d) 18 U.S.C.A., U.S.—United States v. Presley, 478 F.2d 163 (5th Cir. 1973).

When a defendant withdraws his plea of guilty and is later tried, the fact that he had originally plead guilty is not admissible before the trier of the facts in the trial. U.S.—Harris v. Anderson, 364 F.Supp. 465 (D.C.N.C.1973). Evidence of a plea bargain is not admissible in a civil or criminal proceeding against a person who made a plea or offer if the bargain was subsequently rejected by the judge. United States v. Gallington, 488 F.2d 637 (8th Cir. 1974), certiorari denied 416 U.S. 907, 94 S.Ct. 1613, 40 L.Ed.2d 112.

§ 6.23 FEDERAL RULE RELATING TO HABIT EVIDENCE

Rule 406 of the Federal Rules of Evidence provides as follows:

> **Rule 406. Habit; Routine practice**—Evidence of the habit of a person or of the routine practice of an organization, whether corroborated or not and regardless of the presence of eyewitnesses, is relevant to prove that the conduct of the person, or organization on a particular occasion was in conformity with the habit or routine practice.

CHAPTER VII

HEARSAY—ADMISSION EXCEPTION

§ 7.1 ADMISSIONS—EXCEPTION TO HEARSAY EXCLUSIONARY RULE

An admission is a statement made or an act done by a party or his agent within the scope of his authority, said statement or act being inconsistent with his present position at trial. For example, if a defendant, after being given proper warnings by a law enforcement officer, said that he was with a deceased on the night of the homicide, and at the trial he testified that he was not with the deceased on the night of the homicide, the prior statement to the law enforcement officer is an admission. As you can observe, the prior statement to the law enforcement officer was inconsistent with his position at trial.

This is distinguished from a confession in that a confession is a direct acknowledgment of guilt, i. e., the defendant says, "Yes I killed John Doe and I am guilty of murder." Mo.—State v. Thompson, 396 S.W.2d 697 (1966).

An admission is an exception to the hearsay exclusionary rule because it is a statement made or an act done by a party who is not presently on the witness stand and may in fact never take the witness stand and it is offered for the truth of the assertion. Naturally, if the party does not take the stand, the party making the admission may not be subject to cross-examination except that the person testifying to the admission is subject to cross-examination. It is admissible but the weight to be given to the admission is not as great as testimony coming from the mouth of a witness. All admissions must be scanned with care, and verbal admissions should be received with great caution. Ga.—Howard v. Hall, 112 Ga.App. 247, 145 S.E.2d 70 (1965).

Nevertheless, admissions are admissible, as an exception to the hearsay exclusionary rule because of the great probability of reliability. An admission is evidence which tends to prove truth of matter admitted which jury or court may believe as against other evidence, and in no sense are admissions to be considered conclusive. Cal.—Frankenheimer v. Frankenheimer, 231 Cal.App.2d 101, 41 Cal.Rptr. 636 (1965). Admissions are words or acts of a party opponent offered as evidence against him. Ill.—McNealey v. Illinois Cent. R. Co., 43 Ill. App.2d 460, 193 N.E.2d 879 (1963). Thus the court has held that acts too, may be held to be admissions.

Let us assume that a police officer is on routine patrol when he suddenly hears a bell from a fire alarm box ring. He looks towards the source of the ringing and sees a youth, the only person in the vicinity, running away from the fire box. When the youth is apprehended, he states that he was running to catch a train. Is the act of running away from the fire box at the time the bell began to ring an admission? Yes, it is, because courts have held that acts as well as words may constitute admissions, McNealey v. Illinois, supra, but evidence of flight or concealment is relevant and admissible only if there are facts pointing to the crime charged as the motive which prompted it. N.Y.—People v. Reddy, 261 N.Y. 479, 185 N.E. 705 (1933). Showing consciousness of guilt may be used to strengthen "other and more tangible evidence" of guilt, it is not alone sufficient to sustain a conviction. N.Y.—People v. Troche, 14 A.D.2d 361, 221 N.Y.S.2d 288 (1961).

§ 7.2 TYPES OF ADMISSIONS

There are two general types of admissions; one is designated as a judicial admission and the other as an extrajudicial admission. A judicial admission is one which is made directly in connection with a judicial proceeding. It need not necessarily be on the transcript of a trial but it may be made on the pleadings. There is some authority for the position that pre-trial statements whether in the form of statements given to police or answers to interrogatories do not assume the status of judicial admissions but constitute evidentiary admissions and a party is not precluded from presenting evidence which is at variance with pretrial statements but he does run the risk of being impeached by so doing. Cal.—Weiss v. Baba, 218 Cal.App.2d 45, 32 Cal.Rptr. 137 (1963). All admissions not on the court record nor connected with the court procedure are designated as extrajudicial admissions.

§ 7.3 FORMAL JUDICIAL ADMISSIONS

A formal judicial admission is a formal act done in the course of the prosecution of judicial proceeding which obviates the necessity to produce certain evidence by conceding for the purpose of the litigation that a fact alleged by the adverse party is true. Police officers frequently experience this when they are a participant in an unauthorized use of a motor vehicle case. The officer may hear the prosecutor ask defense counsel to stipulate, for the purpose of the hearing or even for the trial, that the defendant did not have authority from the true owner of the vehicle to use the vehicle. The defense attorney will usually stipulate to this and hence makes a formal judicial admission on behalf of his client. The fact that the true owner did not give him permission to use car therefore need not be proved. The defendant may have affirmative defenses such as the fact that s/he purchased the vehicle from someone s/he thought to be the true owner, or s/he was riding as a passenger with one s/he thought to be the true owner. Formal judicial admissions are conclusive of the facts admitted in the action in which they are made. N.Y.—Coffin v. President, etc., Grand Rapids Hydraulic Co., 136 N.Y. 655, 32 N.E. 1076 (1893).

§ 7.4 INFORMAL JUDICIAL ADMISSIONS

An informal admission includes facts incidentally admitted in the course of a trial or judicial proceeding, e. g., statements made by a party who is testifying as a witness or statements made in an affidavit [1] by a party or a deposition [2] by a party which may be received in evidence as admissions in the same or any subsequent litigation.

A formal judicial admission in one action may become an admission in another action and should be classified as an informal judicial admission.[3]

A police officer frequently gives out a traffic summons to a participant of an auto accident. The fine is usually very minimal and the person summoned may plead guilty to the traffic infraction just to get rid of the problem. Later this person may be sued civilly for money damages by another participant in the accident. In the other action, the fact that the person had plead guilty to the traffic infraction is admissible in the civil trial. In the first trial, it is an admission or more correctly stated, a confession. In the second trial it is called an informal judicial admission and may be used against him. Evidence of a plea of guilty is not admissible where the issues in the criminal and civil actions are not the same. Cal.—Skelton v. Fekete, 120 Cal.App.2d 401, 261 P.2d 339 (1953).

An informal judicial admission is not conclusive, it is merely evidence of the facts admitted. Thus, in the situation of the driver who plead guilty to the traffic infraction, the fact that s/he plead guilty is admissible in the subsequent civil action merely for the fact that s/he went into traffic court and plead guilty. It is not conclusive of the fact that s/he was guilty.

§ 7.5 EXTRAJUDICIAL ADMISSIONS

All admissions not made in the course of a judicial proceeding are extrajudicial admissions. Therefor, any oral or written statement or conduct of a party, or his agent which is contrary to his position on trial and is not made in the course of a judicial proceeding is an extrajudicial admission. Iowa—Anderson v. Halverson, 126 Iowa 125, 101 N.W. 781 (1905). Oral admissions of a party are competent evidence against him. Cal.—California Home Extension Ass'n v. Hilborn, 37 Cal.2d 459, 235 P.2d 369 (1951); Del.—Conner v. Brown, 9 W.W.Harr. 529, 3 A.2d 64 (1939). In order to be admissible, however, an admission must be voluntary. Pa.—Logue v. Gallagher, 133 Pa.Super. 570, 3 A.2d 191 (1939). An admission may be contained in a writing made

1. N.Y.—Morrell v. Cawley, 17 Abb.Pr. 76 (1863); Iowa—Davenport v. Cummings, 15 Iowa 219 (1863).

2. Cal.—Mayhood v. La Rosa, 58 Cal. 2d 498, 24 Cal.Rptr. 837, 374 P.2d 805 (1962); N.H.—Cote v. Sears Roebuck & Co., 86 N.H. 238, 166 A. 279 (1933).

3. N.Y.—Ando v. Woodberry, 8 N.Y.2d 165, 203 N.Y.S.2d 74, 168 N.E.2d 520 (1960).

by a party as his authorized agent or adopted by him. N.Y.—Prout v. Chisolm, 21 App.Div. 54, 47 N.Y.S. 376 (1897).

§ 7.6 ADMISSIONS BY CONDUCT

A defendant's flight from the scene of an accident is tantamount to an admission of responsibility. Conn.—Kotler v. Lalley, 112 Conn. 86, 151 A. 433 (1930). This, of course, could also be applied to flight from the scene of a crime. The principle of admission by conduct simply means that any act or conduct on the part of a party which may fairly be interpreted as an admission against interest on a material issue may be shown in evidence against him. N.Y.—People v. Mendel, 10 A.D.2d 767, 197 N.Y.S.2d 484 (1959), appeal denied 11 A.D.2d 605, 204 N.Y.S.2d 110, reargument and appeal denied 11 A.D. 2d 962, 207 N.Y.S.2d 250.

§ 7.7 ADMISSION—ATTEMPTS TO SUBORN PERJURY OR SUPPRESS EVIDENCE

A person who wilfully procures or induces another to commit perjury is guilty of subornation of perjury. Evidence of attempts to suborn perjury is evidence that the cause of the party by whom such attempt was made or to whom it is attributable is unjust. Pa.—McHugh v. McHugh, 186 Pa. 197, 40 A. 410, 65 Am.St.Rep. 849, 41 L.R.A. 805 (1898). Mo.—Pennington v. Kansas City Rys. Co., 201 Mo.App. 483, 213 S.W. 137 (1919). The suppression [4] or destruction [5] of documents is in the nature of an admission that they are unfavorable to the party having control of them.

§ 7.8 ADMISSION BY SILENCE

A party who is under arrest need not deny an accusation made against him and the fact that he failed to deny the accusation is not admissible as an admission. N.Y.—People v. Rutigliano, 261 N.Y. 103, 184 N.E. 689 (1933). However silence when one would naturally be expected to speak in nonarrest situations is significant as an express admission but the party must have had knowledge and an opportunity to reply. Ga.—Swain v. Barton, 210 Ga. 24, 77 S.E.2d 507 (1953). Where no opportunity is available to reply to a statement, silence is not evidence of an admission of the truth of the statement. N.J.—Ollert v. Ziebell, 96 N.J.Law 210, 114 A. 356 (1921); N.Y.—People v. Pollock, 226 A.D. 406, 235 N.Y.S. 553 (1929). Whether the situation was one from which the jury may reasonably find a party's conduct relevant to a fact in issue is a preliminary question for the court's discretion. C.J.S. Evidence § 296.

4. Cal.—Ross v. San Francisco, Oakland Term. Rys. Co., 47 Cal.App. 753, 191 P. 703 (1920).

5. Ala.—Powell v. Smith, 209 Ala. 254, 96 So. 135 (1923).

§ 7.9 ADMISSION BY AGENTS OR SERVANTS

An agent is a person who represents a principal and who is possessed of discretionary powers within the scope of the agency, whereas a servant represents a master, having no discretionary authority, but merely performs ministerial services. With this definition in mind, one can easily see that an admission within the scope of his authority of an agent might tend to bind the principal and likewise the admission of a servant within the scope of his services would bind his master. You will remember that an admission may be created by an act as well as the spoken word.

To establish the responsibility to the principal, the fact of the agency must first be introduced into evidence. To accomplish this, it must be sufficiently proved, directly or inferentially, by evidence other than the statements of the declarant, that he was the agent of the party to be charged with the admission and that he was acting within the scope of his authority, Idaho—Callahan v. Wolfe, 88 Idaho 444, 400 P.2d 938 (1965); La.—Bobo v. Sears, Roebuck & Co., 308 So.2d 907 (App.1974); Pa.—Geesey v. Albee Pennsylvania Homes, Inc., 211 Pa. Super. 215, 235 A.2d 176 (1967), but the court in its discretion may permit the admission to be introduced before the proof of the agency. Mo.—Fielder v. Production Credit Ass'n, 429 S.W.2d 307 (App.1968). The agency need not be conclusive but it must justify a finding that the relation existed. Fla.—Lan-Chile Airlines, Inc. v. Rodriguez, 296 So.2d 498 (App.1974); La.—Bobo v. Sears, Roebuck & Co. (supra).

The rules with respect to servants are similar to those of agents except that one must keep in mind that a servant never has any discretionary authority to bind his/her master but may make admissions through acts or statements, oral or written, nevertheless. For example, a servant may make admissions binding his master by the preparation of an accident report. Ky.—City of Louisville v. Padgett, 457 S.W.2d 485 (1970).

§ 7.10 UNANSWERED WRITTEN COMMUNICATIONS—NOT AN ADMISSION

There is no rule of law which forces the recipient of a written communication to reply to this communication. A failure to answer adverse assertions in the absence of further circumstances making an answer requisite or natural has no effect as an admission. U.S.—Leach & Co. v. Peirson, 48 S.Ct. 57, 275 U.S. 120, 72 L.Ed. 194 (1927).

§ 7.11 OFFERS OF COMPROMISE—NOT AN ADMISSION

A compromise has often been described by lawyers as a situation where no one is completely happy with the result, yet no one loses the case and no one wins the case and everyone goes away from the bargaining table thinking that maybe he could have done better by trying the case to a conclusion. The law however, encourages compromise of litigation because it speeds the wheels of justice and most often there is a little bit of right and a little bit of wrong attached to both sides of the controversy. In order to facilitate compromises, any efforts to compromise the litigation are never admissible against any of the parties. If the contrary situation was permitted, no litigant would make an offer of compromise for fear of having this fact used against him/her as an admission. There are situations, however, where parts of an offer to compromise may be considered as an admission. Such a situation might occur when an admission of fact is made in the course of a negotiating session. This applies more to civil law compromises and is not relevant to the purpose of this book but is mentioned only in passing, e. g., where a defendant's liability is so clear that he makes an offer to liquidate damages without even discussing liability thus tacitly admitting it. N.Y.—Brice v. Bauer, 108 N.Y. 428, 15 N.E. 695 (1888). The fact that a party admits that he made an offer of compromise does not render such offer admissible in evidence. N.C.—Stein v. Levins, 205 N.C. 302, 171 S.E. 96 (1933).

§ 7.12 WEIGHT OF ADMISSIONS

Evidence may be considered as admissible and may be entered on the trial record but different types of evidence may have different weight with respect to the outcome of the litigation. It has been stated that oral admissions are evidence of the weakest and least satisfactory character. N.Y.—Wheeler v. Lewis, 203 A.D. 222, 196 N.Y.S. 817 (1923); Mich.—Tincknell v. Ward, 285 Mich. 47, 280 N.W. 104 (1938); Mo.—Scherffius v. Orr, 442 S.W.2d 120 (App.1969). Verbal admissions should be received with caution and subjected to careful scrutiny, as no class of evidence is more subject to error or abuse. Witnesses having the best motives are generally unable to state the exact language of an admission and are liable, by omission or change of words, to convey a false impression of the language used. Furthermore no other class of testimony affords such temptations or opportunities for unscrupulous witnesses to distort the facts, or to commit open perjury, as it is often impossible to contradict their testimony at all, or at least by any other witness than the party himself. Mont. —Sylvain v. Page, 84 Mont. 424, 276 Pac. 16, 63 A.L.R. 528 (1929).

However, admissions are to be considered like all other evidence with the ultimate determination as to value, effect or weight thereof being for the trier of the facts. Cal.—Kohlhauer v. Bronstein, 21 Cal. App.2d 4, 67 P.2d 1078 (1937); Conn.—Russo v. Metropolitan Life Ins. Co., 125 Conn. 132, 3 A.2d 844 (1939).

§ 7.13 FEDERAL RULE—ADMISSIONS

The Federal Rules of Evidence Rule 803, prescribes twenty-four exceptions to the hearsay exclusionary rule. While the word "admission" is not specifically referred to, it is included in exceptions number 1 and number 24 which read as follows:

Rule 803. Hearsay exceptions; Availability of declarant immaterial—the following are not excluded by the hearsay rule, even though the declarant is available as a witness:

1. Present sense impression.—A statement describing or explaining an event or condition made while the declarant was perceiving the event or condition, or immediately thereafter.

2. Excited utterance.—A statement relating to a startling event or condition made while the declarant was under the stress of excitement caused by the event or condition.

3. Then existing mental, emotional, or physical condition.—A statement of the declarant's then existing state of mind, emotion, sensation, or physical condition (such as intent, plan, motive, design, mental feeling, pain, and bodily health), but not including a statement of memory or belief to prove the fact remembered or believed unless it relates to the execution, revocation, identification, or terms of declarant's will.

4. Statements for purposes of medical diagnosis or treatment.—Statements made for purposes of medical diagnosis or treatment and describing medical history, or past or present symptoms, pain or sensations, or the inception or general character of the cause or external source thereof insofar as reasonably pertinent to diagnosis or treatment.

5. Recorded recollection.—A memorandum or record concerning a matter about which a witness once had knowledge but now has insufficient recollection to enable him to testify fully and accurately, shown to have been made or adopted by the witness when the matter was fresh in his memory and to reflect that knowledge correctly. If admitted, the memorandum or record may be read into evidence but may not itself be received as an exhibit unless offered by an adverse party.

6. Records of regularly conducted activity.—A memorandum, report, or data compilation, in any form, of acts, events, conditions, opinions, or diagnoses, made at or near the time by, or from information transmitted by, a person with knowledge, if kept in the course of a regularly conducted business activity, and if it was the regular practice of that business activity to make the memorandum, re-

port, record, or data compilation, all as shown by the testimony of the custodian or other qualified witness, unless the source of information or the method or circumstances of preparation indicate lack of trustworthiness. The term "business" as used in this paragraph includes business, institution, association, profession, occupation, and calling of every kind, whether or not conducted for profit.

7. Absence of entry in records kept in accordance with the provisions of paragraph 6.—Evidence that a matter is not included in the memoranda reports, records, or data compilations, in any form, kept in accordance with the provisions of paragraph 6, to prove the nonoccurrence or nonexistence of the matter, if the matter was of a kind of which a memorandum, report, record, or data compilation was regularly made and preserved, unless the sources of information or other circumstances indicate lack of trustworthiness.

8. Public records and reports.—Records, reports, statements, or data compilations, in any form, of public offices or agencies, setting forth (A) the activities of the office or agency, or (B) matters observed pursuant to duty imposed by law as to which matters there was a duty to report, excluding, however, in criminal cases matters observed by police officers and other law enforcement personnel, or (C) in civil actions and proceedings and against the Government in criminal cases, factual findings resulting from an investigation made pursuant to authority granted by law, unless the sources of information or other circumstances indicate lack of trustworthiness.

9. Records of vital statistics.—Records or date compilations, in any form, of births, fetal deaths, deaths, or marriages, if the report thereof was made to a public office pursuant to requirements of law.

10. Absence of public record or entry.—To prove the absence of a record, report, statement, or data compilation, in any form, or the nonoccurrence or nonexistence of a matter of which a record, report, statement, or data compilation, in any form, was regularly made and preserved by a public office or agency, evidence in the form of a certification in accordance with Rule 902, or testimony, that dili-

gent search failed to disclose the record, report, statement, or data compilation, or entry.

11. Records of religious organizations.—Statements of births, marriages, divorces, deaths, legitimacy, ancestry, relationship by blood or marriage, or other similar facts of personal or family history, contained in a regularly kept record of a religious organization.

12. Marriage, baptismal, and similar certificates.—Statements of fact contained in a certificate that the maker performed a marriage or other ceremony or administered a sacrament, made by a clergyman, public official, or other person authorized by the rules or practices of a religious organization or by law to perform the act certified, and purporting to have been issued at the time of the act or within a reasonable time thereafter.

13. Family records.—Statements of fact concerning personal or family history contained in family Bibles, genealogies, charts, engravings on rings, inscriptions on family portraits, engravings on urns, crypts, or tombstones, or the like.

14. Records of documents affecting an interest in property.—The record of a document purporting to establish or affect an interest in property, as proof of the content of the original recorded document and its execution and delivery by each person by whom it purports to have been executed, if the record is a record of a public office and an applicable statute authorizes the recording of documents of that kind in that office.

15. Statements in documents affecting an interest in property.—A statement contained in a document purporting to establish or affect an interest in property if the matter stated was relevant to the purpose of the document, unless dealings with the property since the document was made have been inconsistent with the truth of the statement or the purport of the document.

16. Statements in ancient documents.—Statements in a document in existence twenty years or more the authenticity of which is established.

17. Market reports, commercial publications.—Market quotations, tabulations, lists, directories, or other published compilations, generally used and relied upon by the public or by persons in particular occupations.

18. Learned treatises.—To the extent called to the attention of an expert witness upon cross-examination or relied upon by him in direct examination, statements contained in published treatises, periodicals, or pamphlets on a subject of history, medicine, or other science or art, established as a reliable authority by the testimony or admission of the witness or by other expert testimony or by judicial notice. If admitted, the statements may be read into evidence but may not be received as exhibits.

19. Reputation concerning personal or family history. —Reputation among members of his family by blood, adoption, or marriage, or among his associates, or in the community, concerning a person's birth, adoption, marriage, divorce, death, legitimacy, relationship by blood, adoption, or marriage, ancestry, or other similar fact of his personal or family history.

20. Reputation concerning boundaries of general history.—Reputation in a community, arising before the controversy as to boundaries of or customs affecting lands in the community, and reputation as to events of general history important to the community or State or nation in which located.

21. Reputation as to character.—Reputation of a person's character among his associates or in the community.

22. Judgment of previous conviction.—Evidence of a final judgment, entered after a trial or upon a plea of guilty (but not upon a plea of nolo contendere), adjudging a person guilty of a crime punishable by death or imprisonment in excess of one year, to prove any fact essential to sustain the judgment, but not including, when offered by the Government in a criminal prosecution for purposes other than impeachment, judgments against persons other than the accused. The pendency of an appeal may be shown but does not affect admissibility.

23. Judgment as to personal, family or general history, or boundaries.—Judgments as proof of matters of personal, family or general history, or boundaries, essential to the judgment, if the same would be provable by evidence of reputation.

24. Other exceptions.—A statement not specifically covered by any of the foregoing exceptions but having equivalent circumstantial guarantees of trustworthiness, if the court determines that (A) the statement is offered as evidence of a material fact;

(B) the statement is more probative on the point for which it is offered than any other evidence which the proponent can procure through reasonable efforts; and (C) the general purposes of these rules and the interests of justice will best be served by admission of the statement into evidence. However, a statement may not be admitted under this exception unless the proponent of it makes known to the adverse party sufficiently in advance of the trial or hearing to provide the adverse party with a fair opportunity to prepare to meet it, his intention to offer the statement and the particulars of it, including the name and address of the declarant.

CHAPTER VIII

HEARSAY—RES GESTAE EXCEPTION

§ 8.1 INTRODUCTION

A lay person who is testifying from the witness stand is permitted to testify as to what he heard, saw, smelled, tasted or touched but usually is not permitted to testify to what he heard someone else, other than a party to the action, said or did. This type of evidence we previously called hearsay and it is generally not admissible in evidence except for well defined and long used exceptions which over the years have been proved to be of necessity and have a great probability of reliability. We have previously discussed admissions of a party as an exception to the hearsay exclusionary rule. The concept of res gestae is another such exception. Literally translated from the Latin it means "the thing done."

The courts have employed the theory of res gestae in many types of situations and hence it is not possible to formulate a comprehensive definition of the term. The most practical method for the student to understand the idea of res gestae is for the student to become acquainted with situations where the courts have admitted evidence which was clearly hearsay but which is customarily admissible under the res gestae exception to the hearsay exclusionary rule.

§ 8.2 HEARSAY—DEFINED

The general rule excluding hearsay evidence cannot be fully understood unless the student has a clear understanding of what hearsay is. For that reason, we repeat that hearsay is

1. a statement made outside of court (this particular trial);
2. which is offered in the trial to prove the facts which are contained in it.

If it is offered for the mere fact that the statement was made without regard for the truth of the assertion, it is not hearsay.

Let us assume that Mr. "W" is testifying on the witness stand in the courtroom. Let us further assume that the trial is a murder trial wherein Mr. "V" was killed and Mr. "D" is the defendant. Mr. "W" would not be permitted to testify that he heard Mr. "A" say that he (Mr. "A") had seen Mr. "D" pick up a gun from a table and shoot Mr. "V" through the chest by the use of this gun. This is clearly a hearsay situation because Mr. "W" did not see, hear, smell, touch anything directly connected with the commission of the crime. He only heard about it from someone else and the probability of reliability in such a situation is poor. It is common knowledge that as a description is told orally from one person to another, each person carrying the description on to another is likely to change it slightly so that when the final person hears the account, it may, and more than likely, does not have the slightest resemblance to the original account of this occurrence. Anyone who has seen the theatrical production of "Fiddler on the Roof" will remember how the gossiping women in the small town of Russia would change the account of what was happening as it went from one to the other and the final version had no resemblance to the original.

Another method of getting the "feel" to recognize hearsay is "if you can't cross-examine the original person making the statement and it is offered for the truth of the assertion, it is hearsay."

The statement was made in the preceding paragraph that if the statement were offered not for the truth of the assertion but merely to show that it was made, it should be admitted even though it is an out of court statement, not subject to cross-examination. Let us assume that Mr. "D", a half hour before shooting Mr. "V" was heard to have said "I am the King of England and the great British Empire and I demand that all who come before me bow down and pay homage to me." This statement is relative on the trial to the issue of insanity. The statement was not true for Mr. "D" did not possess such a stature in life but it would be admissible for the fact that it was said by him and relevant on the issue of insanity to assist the jury to come to a determination of that issue. This is not hearsay.

Let us take the same statement, and change the timing of it. Let us assume that it was said immediately before the shooting and Mr. "V" declined to bow down and pay homage to Mr. "D". Here too, it would be admissible, not for the truth of the statement but because it would be a part of the transaction evidencing a state of mind. This is one of the situations where res gestae is employed to permit the statements of others who are not necessarily subject to cross-examination. Always remember at this juncture that a defendant in a criminal action need not take the stand in his own defense and this fact shall not be interpreted against his presumption of innocence.

§ 8.3 REASON FOR HEARSAY RULE, REITERATED

The reason for the rule excluding hearsay is to afford an opportunity for cross-examination to examine the witness with respect to

1. veracity;
2. accuracy of perception;
3. ability to recall past events correctly.

§ 8.4 RES GESTAE—DEFINITION

There is probably no term used in the law of evidence which defies a strict definition more than the term "res gestae". The literal definition in translation from the Latin language is "the thing done". In practice, its use has little relevance to its literal translation.

Some courts have defined "res gestae" as those circumstances which are the undersigned incidents of a particular litigated act and which are admissible when illustrative of that fact. Ill.—Perzovsky v. Chicago Transit Auth., 23 Ill.App.3d 896, 320 N.E.2d 433 (1974). The same court in the same case defined it as meaning the circumstances, facts and declarations which grow out of the main fact and serve to illustrate its character and which are so spontaneous and contemporaneous with the main fact as to exclude the idea of deliberation or fabrication *a fortiori,* Okl.—Gulf Oil Corp. v. Harris, 425 P.2d 957 (1967); Pa.—Eller v. Work, 233 Pa.Super. 186, 336 A.2d 645 (1975).

In examining most cases, the statement or declaration concerning which testimony is offered must, in order to be admissible as part of the res gestae, possess at least the following essential elements:

1. The statement or declaration must relate to the main event and must explain, elucidate, or in some manner characterize that event.
2. It must be a natural declaration or statement growing out of the event, and not a mere narrative of a past completed affair.
3. It must be a statement of fact, and not the mere expression of an opinion.
4. It must be a spontaneous or instinctive utterance of thought dominated or evoked by the transaction or occurrence itself and not the product of premeditation, reflection or design.
5. While the declaration or statement need not be coincident or contemporaneous with the occurrence of the event, it must be made at such time and under such circumstances as will exclude the presumption that it is the result of deliberation.
6. It must appear that the declaration or statement was made by one who either participated in the transaction or witnessed the act or fact concerning which the declaration, or statement, was made. 31A C.J.S. Evidence 403 (1).

Res gestae declarations may be admitted only where the circumstances under which the declarations were made afford assurance of sufficient probability of their truth warranting their being received by the jury. Kan.—Pacific Indem. Co. v. Berge, 205 Kan. 755, 473 P.2d 48 (1970); Md.—Cluster v. Cole, 21 Md.App. 242, 319 A.2d 320 (1974).

I like to think of res gestae statements as being hearsay statements which have a presumption against admissibility, but if it can be shown that there is little likelihood of prefabrication or deliberation, and they are relevant to the main issue, they should be admitted.

§ 8.5 MAJOR USE OF RES GESTAE

The major uses of res gestae are as follows:

1. Declarations evidencing a state of mind.
2. Declarations by agents, servants or employees.
3. Declaration by victim of a rape.
4. Spontaneous declaration.
5. Declarations of pain and suffering.
6. Declarations accompanying and explaining a relevant act.
7. Complaint of coerced confession.
8. Declaration of intention.
9. Startled utterance.
10. Declarations of testator.

§ 8.6 RES GESTAE—TIME OF ACT OR STATEMENT

An act or declaration must be substantially contemporaneous with the act of which it is alleged to be a part. If it is otherwise it is nothing more than a narrative of what has been. Ohio—Dugan v. Industrial Commission of Ohio, 135 Ohio St. 652, 22 N.E.2d 132 (1939). The modern tendency seems to treat spontaneity as a substitute for contemporaneousness, i. e., the speaker should not have sufficient time to fabricate an act or a statement. N.J.—Atamanik v. Real Estate Mgmt., 21 N.J.Super. 357, 91 A.2d 268 (1952). The lapse of time between the event and the utterance is important only as it bears upon the question of spontaneity. In Wash.—Britton v. Washington Water Power Co., 59 Wash. 440, 110 Pac. 20, 33 L.R.A.(N.S.) 109 (1910), the injured person who had been unconscious for eight days made a declaration immediately upon regaining consciousness and before he had any opportunity to reflect. The declaration was held admissible.

However, in N.Y.—Greener v. General Electric Co., 209 N.Y. 135, 102 N.E. 527, 46 L.R.A.(N.S.) 975 (1913), a workman stepped upon a ladder which bent under his weight and threw him to the ground causing injuries which later caused his death. The witness testified that when he saw him fall, he ran over to where he lay and asked him what happened. The injured workman replied, "My feet is broke; the ladder bent over." The court held this inadmissible and said "The distinction to be made is in the character of the declaration; whether it be so spontaneous or natural an utterance as to exclude the idea of fabrication, or whether it be in the nature of a narrative of what occurred. In the present case, the declaration of the deceased was not spontaneous; it was called forth by the inquiry as to "what had happened" and was distinctly narrative. Other cases have admitted res gestae in response to inquiry, N.Y.—People v. Del Vermo, 192 N.Y. 470, 85 N.E. 690 (1908). Later cases have indicated that the fact that the statement was in response to an inquiry should be regarded merely as a circumstance in determining spontaneity. N.Y.—People v. Marks, 6 N.Y.2d 67, 188 N.Y.S.2d 465, 160 N.E.2d 26 (1959).

§ 8.7 RES GESTAE STATEMENTS—WHO MAY BE DECLARANT

As a general rule res gestae statements may not be based on hearsay. Tex.—Moore v. Drummet, 478 S.W.2d 177 (Civ.App.1972). In order for a declaration or statement to be admissible as a part of the res gestae it must appear that it was made by one who either participated in the transaction or witnessed the act or fact concerning which the declaration or statement was made. N.J.—Lieberman v. Saley, 94 N.J.Super. 156, 227 A.2d 339 (1967). For example, in an action for damages by one who fell while getting off from a train, testimony of conductor concerning a statement by a bystander to the effect that plaintiff fainted was not admissible as a part of the res gestae where there was no showing that the bystander saw plaintiff faint, or that he was present at the time of the occurrence, since he may have received the information that she fainted from others. Ark.—Hines v. Patterson, 146 Ark. 367, 225 S.W. 642 (1921).

Declarations of a deceased person may be admissible when it is part of the res gestae. Pa.—Curran v. James Regulator Co., 10 Sch. Reg. 62 (Comm.Pl.), affirmed 157 Pa.Super. 44, 41 A.2d 443 (1945).

The fact that a person was dazed or shocked brought on by injury at the time he made the statement does not render his statement inadmissible but bears on the weight and creditability thereof. S.C.—Magill v. Southern R.Co., 95 S.C. 306, 78 S.E. 1033 (1913).

The statement need not have been made by one of the litigants. Del.—Garrod v. Good, 7 Storey 556, 203 A.2d 112 (1964). A res gestae declaration made during the life of a person, who is dead at the time of trial, is admissible. Ind.—Moster v. Bower, 286 N.E.2d 418 (App.1972).

It follows naturally that a declarant of a res gestae statement whose statement is to be admissible must possess sufficient mental condition at the time of making the statement so as to indicate that it has probative value. Minn.—Ammundson v. Tinholt, 228 Minn. 115, 36 N.W.2d 521, 7 A.L.R.2d 1318 (1949). A person need not necessarily be competent to testify in order to have their res gestae statement admitted so long as the party making it had the capacity of recollecting and narrating the facts to which his utterance relates. Wash. —Johnston v. Ohls, 76 Wash.2d 398, 457 P.2d 194 (1969) (infant).

§ 8.8 DECLARATIONS EVIDENCING A STATE OF MIND

Declarations, spontaneously made, which reflect a state of mind of the declarant, are admissible under the res gestae exception. This is closely related to declaration of intention treated later. An example of the state of mind res gestae exception took place in U.S.—Braatelien v. United States, 147 F.2d 888 (8th Cir. 1945), wherein after a conspiracy was established prima facie, everything said or done by any of the conspirators in execution or furtherance of the common purpose is deemed to have been said or done by every one of them and is admissible against each of them, and the declaration of each of the parties was part of the res gestae.

§ 8.9 RES GESTAE—DECLARATION BY AGENTS, SERVANTS OR EMPLOYEES

A spontaneous utterance, arising from the principal fact, made by an agent or employee is admissible the same as that of any other observer. Conn.—Perry v. Haritos, 100 Conn. 476, 124 A. 44 (1924); N.J.—Kelly v. Hicks, 9 N.J.Super. 266, 76 A.2d 23 (1950); N.Y.—Golden v. Horn and Hardart Co., 244 App.Div. 92, 278 N.Y.S. 385, affirmed 270 N.Y. 544, 200 N.E. 309 (1936). However an agent's declaration is receivable even though it is made outside the scope of his authority if, under another rule of evidence, its admissibility is not made dependant upon the fact of agency. Thus a spontaneous declaration made by an agent may be admissible as if it were made by a person not an agent. Let us assume that a driver of a vehicle was not the owner of the vehicle but was an agent of the owner. Assume further that this driver was involved in a collision with another vehicle and, before he had time to think, made the statement "Oh my God. If I had not been looking in back of me this accident would not have taken place." This statement would be admissible in evidence if heard by someone who would testify that the driver made this statement. It could be admitted as an admission and also as part of the res gestae as a spontaneous declaration. It could be admitted in the criminal action, if there be one, for criminally negligent homicide, if death resulted to someone because of the action of this driver. It could also be admitted in an action against the owner of the vehicle who gave the driver permission to use this automobile. This could be admitted against the owner of the vehicle as a spontaneous utterance of an agent or as an admission by an agent.

§ 8.10 RES GESTAE—DECLARATION OF A VICTIM OF A RAPE

In a forcible rape case, the timely complaint of a victim is admissible if it is made promptly or at the first suitable opportunity after the commission of the crime. It may be testified to by the victim herself or by any witness who heard her make the complaint. The testimony must be confined to the fact that the victim made such timely complaint and may not contain any of the particular facts which she stated because this would be hearsay without the probability of reliability so necessary to entitle it to the category of an exception to the hearsay exclusionary rule. N.Y.—Baccio v. People, 41 N.Y. 265 (1896).

If the complainant did not make timely complaint, it is not part of the res gestae (the part of the transaction wherein she had no time to fabricate) and hence her complaint is excluded from the trial record.

The later complaint might also be excluded on the theory that it was a self-serving declaration.

§ 8.11 RES GESTAE—SPONTANEOUS DECLARATION

In order for a res gestae statement to be admissible under the spontaneous declaration exception to the hearsay exclusionary rule, the statement must be so spontaneous as to exclude the possibility of fabrication. Okl.—Gulf Oil Co. v. Harris, supra; Pa.—Eller v. Work, 233 Pa.Super. 186, 336 A.2d 645 (1975). The primary concern in cases dealing with spontaneous declarations is whether there is any likelihood that the declarant has fabricated his statement or that the declarant's recollection has become clouded prior to the time the statement was made. U.S.—Government of Virgin Islands v. Dyches, 507 F.2d 106 (3d Cir. 1975), certiorari denied 421 U.S. 917, 95 S.Ct. 1579, 43 L.Ed.2d 783. The judge who presides has wide latitude in what constitutes a spontaneous utterance but this discretion must be exercised soundly on the facts of each case. This discretion must not be disturbed on appeal unless clearly erroneous. U.S.—Pietrzak v. United States, 188 F.2d 418 (5th Cir. 1951), certiorari denied 342 U.S. 824, 72 S.Ct. 44, 96 L.Ed. 623; Baber v. United States, 324 F.2d 390 (D.C.Cir. 1963), certiorari denied 376 U.S. 972, 84 S.Ct. 1139, 12 L.Ed.2d 86.

§ 8.12 RES GESTAE—DECLARATIONS OF PAIN AND SUFFERING

There can be no definite and fixed limit of time within which statements must be made to become a part of the res gestae, but every case will depend on its own facts, the burden is on the party offering the evidence to show such connection which will make it admissible. Pa.—Curry v. Riggles, 302 Pa. 156, 153 A. 325 (1931). Therefore, acts or statements, although subsequent to the time of the infliction of the personal injury but which follow immediately thereafter and serve to explain the event or which are done or made under such circumstances as to exclude the possibility of premeditation or design and which are so close to the injury as to be a part of the occurrence are admissible as part of the res gestae. N.J.—Demeter v. Rosenberg, 114 N.J.Law 55, 175 A. 621 (1935). Statements made, such as exclamations or complaints of present pain and suffering are admissible. Tex.—Texas Employers' Ins. v. Davidson, 288 S.W. 471 (Civ.App.1927), rehearing denied 290 S.W. 571. Generally one can say that involuntary expressions of pain, such as groans, screams or moans are always admissible, however, declarations of present pain and suffering are not admissible except

1. when the declarant is dead at the time of trial;
2. when the statement is made to a physician in order to aid the physician in his attempt to treat the injured party;

3. when the statement may be classified as a spontaneous declaration.

Statements of present pain are not admissible under this hearsay exception when made to a physician who examined the patient not for the purpose of treatment but only for the purpose to prepare the physician so that he may testify regarding the injuries.

§ 8.13 RES GESTAE—DECLARATIONS ACCOMPANYING AND EXPLAINING A RELEVANT ACT

The declarations accompanying and explaining a relevant act is most often found in civil law situations such as a statement made by a testator simultaneously with the tearing of a will that "From now on my son will have to work for a living," is admissible under this exception. Such a statement may be relevant as to whether the tearing of the will was intentional or unintentional. N.Y.—Waterman v. Whitney, 11 N.Y. (1 Kern) 157 (1891). A criminal law example of the use of this exception might be best illustrated in a situation where a tractor-trailer truck driver says to his helper who is seated next to him in the cab of the tractor "I'll teach that guy in the Chevrolet never to cut off a truck driver again," whereupon he rams the rear of the Chevrolet killing the driver. This last example is very close to declaration of intention previously discussed except that we cannot say that the truck driver intended to kill the person in the Chevrolet but we can say that he intended to teach him a lesson by ramming the rear of the Chevrolet; therefore it was an intentional act and hence a declaration accompanying and elucidating a relevant act.

§ 8.14 RES GESTAE—COMPLAINT OF COERCED CONFESSION

Where a defendant claims that a confession offered against him had been extorted from him, it is error to exclude evidence showing that, at the first suitable opportunity, he had complained of his mistreatment. N.Y.—People v. Alex, 260 N.Y. 425, 183 N.E. 906, 85 A.L.R. 939 (1933).

§ 8.15 RES GESTAE—DECLARATION OF INTENTION

Certain crimes require an element showing that the defendant intended to do the proscribed act. For example, in the crime of murder, in some jurisdictions, it is necessary to show that the defendant intended to do the act. Hence a declaration of intention whereby the defendant is alleged to have stated to a third person "When I see John (the victim) I am going to kill him," is admissible to show that the defendant had the intention to do the act and it was premeditated. Such a statement may also be used by John (the intended victim) if instead of being killed by the declarant, he kills the declarant in self-defense or justifiable homicide. Even if this declaration was not communicated to the intended victim, he may have someone who heard it, testify that the victim had made the statement and this would tend to prove that the intended victim killed the declarant in defense of his own life. N.Y.—Stokes v. People, 53 N.Y. 164 (1898).

§ 8.16 RES GESTAE—STARTLED UTTERANCE

It sometimes occurs that a statement is made by a person while the person is under stress or excitement produced by a startling event and made before the person has had time or opportunity to reflect or contrive. U.S.—United States v. Lehman, 468 F.2d 93 (7th Cir. 1972), certiorari denied 409 U.S. 967, 93 S.Ct. 273, 34 L.Ed.2d 232. There is a shadow of a difference between the startled utterance category and the spontaneous utterance type of exception. The startled utterance is a subdivision of the spontaneous utterance. It therefore would be safe to say that a spontaneous utterance may not be a startled utterance while a startled utterance is always a spontaneous utterance. This might be a brain teaser for you to think about and understand.

§ 8.17 RES GESTAE—DECLARATIONS ELUCIDATING AN ACT

Statements are sometimes made which explain an act. Let us suppose that there was a question in an action on an insurance policy on the life of a deceased. If the insured took his own life, according to the terms of the policy, his estate would not collect on accidental death benefit. Let us further assume that the insured lost his life by means of a discharge of a firearm. If the insured said to his wife immediately after the shot was discharged, "The gun went off accidentally", this statement may, in the court's discretion, be admitted as part of the res gestae of the event to elucidate an act. See Neb.—Falkinburg v. Prudential Ins. Co. of Amer., 132 Neb. 831, 273 N.W. 478 (1937) and Ill.—Grebe v. Vacek & Co., 103 Ill.App.2d 79, 243 N.E.2d 438 (1969) and Mo.—State ex rel. 807, Inc. v. Saitz, 425 S.W.2d 96 (1968) for other examples of this principle.

§ 8.18 RES GESTAE—DECLARATIONS OF A TESTATOR

A testator is a male person who executes a Last Will and Testament in conformity with the statutory requirements of the state in which he is executing this document. He need not be a domiciliary of that jurisdiction to make a valid and enforceable will. However, all states require that a colloquy take place between the testator and the witnesses to the Last Will and Testament prior to the signatures of the testator and the witnesses being affixed thereto. This is done to ascertain whether the testator is competent and that he is aware that he is signing a will. Declarations made at that time by the decedent which are part of the transaction of executing the document come under the same exception to the hearsay exclusionary rule as indicated in Section 8.7, supra. For use of such a statement see N.Y.—Re Walton's Estate, 206 Misc. 908, 135 N.Y.S.2d 690 (1955).

§ 8.19 COMPETENCY OF DECLARANT AS A WITNESS

It may appear as a surprise to some readers that the admissibility of a res gestae statement is not dependent on whether the witness who made the statement would be competent to testify if called to the witness stand. Thus in State v. Lasecki, 90 Ohio S. 10, 106 N.E. 660, L.R.A.1915E 202 (1914), the spontaneous exclamation of a child of four years of age that "the bums killed Pa with a broomstick" made a few seconds after his father had been killed by the assault, was held admissible over the objection that the boy was not old enough to be a witness.

§ 8.20 RES GESTAE—FEDERAL RULE

The Federal Rules of Evidence do not use the words res gestae as one of the exceptions to the hearsay exclusionary rule. However, in Rule 803(2) the rule reads as follows:

803 Hearsay exceptions; Availability of declarant immaterial

The following are not excluded by the hearsay rule, even though the declarant is available as a witness,

1. . . . ..
2. Excited utterance—A statement relating to a startling event or condition caused by the event or condition.
3. . . . through 24 . . . ..

CHAPTER IX

HEARSAY—DYING DECLARATION EXCEPTION

§ 9.1 INTRODUCTION

In the discipline of criminal justice, it frequently becomes necessary for a police officer or a prosecuting official to gather admissible evidence on short notice and with little time for reflection or preparation. The dying declaration is an example of this type of situation. Theoretically there are certain requirements in the law which must be recited to the dying declarant. It appears on the surface, to be a matter of fact inquiry easily accomplished.

However, if one experiences this situation, he normally has to have nerves of steel to carry it through to a successful conclusion. The elements necessary for the admissibility of a dying declaration are as follows:

1. The declarant must be in extremis;
2. The declarant must be under a sense of impending death without any hope of recovery;
3. The declarant, if living, would be a competent witness.
4. Declaration must relate to facts and circumstances surrounding the death of the declarant.

§ 9.2 REASON FOR DYING DECLARATION EXCEPTION

You will remember that if the statement is offered for the truth of the assertion and the declarant is not available for cross-examination, it is a hearsay statement. You will also remember that any exception to the hearsay exclusionary rule is based upon the probability of reliability. In the case of the dying declaration, the presumption is made that the declarant who is certain of impending death wants to make peace with his God and will speak the truth. Hence the probability of reliability. The author has conducted polls of his classes during the past several years with respect to the probability of reliability of a dying declaration and without exception the students have voted against the acceptance of dying declaration in that the students contend that the religious influence which gave rise to this exception is not prevalent as it was in yesteryear. Perhaps an additional element should be added to those indicated above, namely, that the declarant have a reputation in the community of being a religious or God fearing person.

Nevertheless, courts still accept the dying declaration as an exception to the hearsay exclusionary rule. The principle upon which dying declarations are received in evidence is that the mind, impressed with the awful idea of approaching dissolution, acts under a sanction equally powerful with that which it is presumed to feel by a solemn appeal to God upon an oath. N.Y.—People v. Sarzano, 212 N.Y. 231, 234, 106 N.E. 87, 88 (1914).

§ 9.3 DYING DECLARATIONS ADMISSIBLE IN SPECIFIED CASES

It has been generally held that dying declarations are not admissible in civil cases. Miss.—Phillips v. Dow Chemical Co., 151 So.2d 199 (1963). The exception to this is where the declaration is part of the res gestae. Some jurisdictions permit dying declarations in civil actions by statute. Cal.Evidence Code, Section 1242, Colo.—Barsch v. Hammond, 110 Colo. 441, 135 P.2d 519 (1943). The dying declaration is usually admitted in homicide cases and the declaration which is admitted is how the deceased's injuries resulting in his impending death occurred and who was the person who brought about this mortal injury. Certain jurisdictions permit the use of dying declarations in the case of a criminal abortion where the victim dies before trial. This is not universally accepted. It is however safe to say that it is applicable in homicide cases when the victim is not available for the trial. Naturally where the victim believes he is about to die and later recovers, any statement made by him as a dying declaration would not be admissible as a dying declaration. However, it might be admissible as a prior inconsistent statement and may be used for impeachment purposes. In any event, the declaration must relate to the facts and circumstances pertaining to the injury or death. U.S. — Henry H. Cross Co. v. Simmons, 96 F.2d 482 (C.C.A. 8th Cir. 1938).

§ 9.4 DECLARANT IN EXTREMIS

In order for a dying declaration to be admissible it is, as indicated in Section 9.1 (supra) necessary that the declarant be in extremis. This means that he is imminently dying from the injury which he has received and has little time in which to live. There have been cases where the declarant's statement was not admissible because this element of the exception to the hearsay exclusionary rule was absent. For example, where a deceased made statements relating to how he received his injury, and these statements were made while he was a patient in a hospital following an operation for a hernia, where it appeared from medical testimony that at no time while he was in the hospital was he considered to be a dying man, nor was his condition considered to be critical, except that a blood clot in his leg might dislodge, his statements were held to be inadmissible. Or.—Mercep v. State Industrial Accident Comm., 167 Or. 460, 118 P.2d 1061 (1941).

§ 9.5 DECLARANT MUST BE UNDER A SENSE OF IMPENDING DEATH

The declarant must be conscious of impending death and without any hope of recovery or expectation of recovery. Kan.—Ritchie v. Metropolitan Life Ins. Co., 145 Kan. 525, 66 P.2d 622 (1937). Let us assume the following questions being asked of the victim. "Mr. V, I am Officer Law and this is Doctor Medicine. I understand that Doctor Medicine has told you that you are about to die from the injuries that you have just received. Is that true?" After an affirmative answer, the officer continues. "Mr. V, do you have any hope of recovery?" After a negative answer, the officer again continues. "Do you wish to tell us who was the person who caused your injury and the facts surrounding your receiving this injury?" After an affirmative answer, the decedent proceeds to identify the assailant and the circumstances of the infliction of the injury. As Officer Law and Doctor Medicine were about to leave the room the victim then turned to Dr. Medicine and said "Doc, please save me." The last statement indicated that despite what the victim had said earlier, he still had a hope of recovery and hence his dying declaration should not be admitted.

§ 9.6 COMPETENCY OF DECLARANT

The declarant must be competent to testify to the facts which he declares. He must be as competent to testify to these facts as though he were present on the witness stand at the time of trial. Colo.—Barsch v. Hammond, 110 Colo. 441, 135 P.2d 519 (1943). Accordingly, he should know the seriousness of an oath, have knowledge of the facts declared. U.S.—Henry H. Cross Co. v. Simmons, 96 F.2d 482 (C.C.A. 8th 1938), and he must be of sound mind. He may not testify as to an opinion or conclusion unless he was able to do so had he lived, i. e., an expert in the particular discipline of the question. If the declaration is a suspicion or surmise, it is not admissible. N.Y.—People v. Shaw, 63 N.Y. 36 (1900).

§ 9.7 DYING DECLARATION—FORM

A dying declaration may be oral or in writing. There is no precise form and it is discretionary with the trial court as to whether or not it should be admitted. N.Y.—People v. Smith, 104 N.Y. 491, 10 N.E. 873 (1887).

§ 9.8 DYING DECLARATION—WEIGHT

The weight of the evidence which is to be attributed to a dying declaration is determined by the jury. N.Y.—People v. Ludkowitz, 266 N.Y. 233, 194 N.E. 688 (1935). Upon request the trial court is required to instruct the jury that a dying declaration is not to be regarded as having the same value and weight as the sworn testimony of a witness in open court. N.Y.—People v. Mleczko, 298 N.Y. 153, 81 N.E. 2d 65 (1948).

§ 9.9 DYING DECLARATION—NOT A VIOLATION OF CONSTITUTIONAL PROTECTION

The United States Constitution and the constitutions of most states require that in a criminal prosecution, the defendant is entitled to confrontation of witnesses against him with the right of cross-examination. Many cases have attacked the constitutionality of the admission of testimony from a declarant who cannot be cross-examined. The courts have unanimously held that this objection is not tenable on the ground that such a declarant is not a witness within the meaning of such a provision. The concept being that the right accrues to a defendant against any living witness, not a dead one. Pa.—Brown v. Commonwealth, 73 Pa. 321, 13 Am.Rep. 740 (1885); N.Y.—People v. Corey, 157 N.Y. 332, 51 N.E. 1024 (1898). The defendant may still have his right of cross-examination by cross-examining the living witness who is testifying about the statement made by the dying declarant.

CHAPTER X

HEARSAY—BUSINESS RECORDS EXCEPTION

§ 10.1 INTRODUCTION

Few police officers who have testified in court are not asked by an astute defense counsel as to the contents of their memorandum book entries. This is a form of documentary evidence which often changes the outcome of a case. It is therefore very necessary that a police officer make entries in his/her memorandum book which are both accurate and according to the precise rules of his/her department. The officer should always remember that the entries concerning the incident are, in most jurisdictions, available for inspection by defense counsel. N.Y.—People v. Gezzo, 307 N.Y. 385, 121 N.E.2d 380 (1954). Some defense counsel are very cognizant of police department procedure with respect to these entries and a variation from these procedures might be inferred to be at variance with the truth. Improper entries might change the outcome of a case. For example, if a police department requires an entry describing an event to be in longhand, in English, and consecutively on a line after line basis and the officer is to sign his name and shield number at the end of the days entries, an officer's account of the occurrence which included a witness' name and address on the back of the preceding page is highly suspect. It might rightfully be inferred in the defense counsel's summation, that the witness appeared after the officer's days work had been completed.

The student has just learned that this is a form of documentary evidence.

§ 10.2 DOCUMENTARY EVIDENCE

Documentary evidence is evidence in the form of writing. It is that furnished by written instruments, inscriptions and documents of all kinds. N.Y.—Ticknor v. Ticknor, 23 Misc.2d 257, 200 N.Y.S.2d 661 (1960). The admissibility of documentary evidence is subject to the same rules of evidence with respect to relevancy, competency and materiality as is oral testimony (Ind.—State v. Schaller, 111 Ind. App. 128, 40 N.E.2d 976 (1942). The admissibility of documentary evidence rests in the sound discretion of the trial court, C.J.S. Evidence § 624, Or.—Wynn v. Sundquist, 259 Or. 125, 485 P.2d 1085 (1971).

§ 10.3 AUTHENTICATION

In order for documentary evidence to be admissible, it must be authenticated. This may be done by sworn testimony of a witness as to the genuineness of the writing, its authenticity or identity of the document, proof of its execution and of the correctness of the document. Ga.—Weaver v. Georgia Power Co., 134 Ga.App. 696, 215 S.E. 2d 503 (1975). The party offering it is only required to make out a prima facie case to render it admissible. Cal.—Fakhoury v. Magner, 25 Cal.App.3d 58, 101 Cal.Rptr. 473 (1973). The foundation for such a writing might occur in the following manner.

Let us assume that a bank teller is presented with a request by a customer to cash a check on the customer's account. The customer is the person cashing the check. The bank procedure is that the customer is required to endorse the check on the reverse side thereof in the presence of the teller. This is done and the teller compares the signature with the depositor's signature on file in the bank. The teller asks the head cashier to compare the signatures and both agree that it is a valid signature. The check is cashed. After the customer received the monthly statement of his account and saw this check, he claimed that he never drew nor cashed this check. After he received no satisfaction from the bank, he sued the bank for the amount of the check. Prior to the trial, the bank served a notice to produce the original check on the customer who is the plaintiff. At the trial, the check is produced and the bank will place the first teller on the stand to testify that on a particular day the plaintiff presented a check for payment to the witness for "x" number of dollars, that upon request the check was endorsed on the reverse side thereof by the plaintiff, that the witness compared the signature with that on file in the bank and enlisted the aid of the chief cashier to compare the signatures. The foundation then is being laid for the next statement by the bank's attorney, "I offer exhibit A for defendant for identification." After it has been marked by the court stenographer, the bank's attorney will say, "I show you defendant's exhibit A for identification. What is this, if you know?". The witness will say that it is a bank check. The attorney will say, "When, if ever, have you seen this bank check before?" The witness will testify that this is the check that the plaintiff endorsed in the teller's presence and upon which a payment was made by the witness. The check is then offered into evidence as defendant's exhibit A in evidence.

You will note that the foundation was made by placing the events which lead to the execution of the document in proper focus first, to show its relevancy and then the document was placed into evidence to let the trier of the fact make its own conclusion. Naturally, the bank signature card would also have to be placed in evidence for a comparison.

Some documents are self-authenticating by statute in that they prove themselves. In that category are deeds which have been acknowledged before a Notary Public. Ind.—Patterson v. Churchman, 122 Ind. 379, 22 N.E. 662, 23 N.E. 1082 (1890). Public documents like birth certificates, baptism, marriage and death certificates properly sealed with an official pressure seal or certified by an official authorized to certify the document. N.Y.—Woltin v. Metropolitan Life Ins. Co., 167 Misc. 382, 4 N.Y.S.2d 296 (1938).

§ 10.4 ANCIENT DOCUMENTS

Ancient documents are also self-proving. An ancient document is one that is purported to be thirty or more years old, which is found in proper custody and which is unblemished by alterations and is otherwise free from suspicion. It is admissible without direct proof of its execution on the theory that under such circumstances the instrument proves itself, or that its due execution is presumed. Mass.—Puffer v. City of Beverly, 345 Mass. 396, 187 N.E.2d 840 (1963). Federal Rule 901(b) 8 drops the requirement to twenty years.

§ 10.5 NEWS PUBLICATIONS

Newspaper accounts are generally not admissible as documentary evidence because of their general unreliability of trustworthiness. However, there have been some cases that have admitted newspaper accounts of facts where the account was very old. U.S.—Montana Power Co. v. Federal Power Comm., 185 F.2d 491 (D.C.Cir. 1951).

§ 10.6 PRIVATE WRITINGS

Wills, deeds and agreements reduced to writing are admissible under the documentary evidence concept. 32 C.J.S. Evidence § 623. They must be proved by a person who saw the execution of the documents.

§ 10.7 DEATH CERTIFICATES

There is a difference of opinion as to the admissibility of death certificates. Generally, where they are made according to statutory authority and under conditions assuring the accuracy of the information contained therein, they may be admitted under the public records and documents rule. Mass.—Wadsworth v. Boston Gas Co., 352 Mass. 86, 223 N.E.2d 807 (1967); Wash.—Hayden v. Insurance Co. of N. A., 5 Wash.App. 710, 490 P.2d 454 (1971).

§ 10.8 AUTOPSY REPORTS

A report of an autopsy conducted by a duly authorized physician on behalf of the governmental authority empowered to conduct autopsies in the locality where the deceased died is admissible in evidence when relevant and when properly authenticated. They are considered public records and such records are admissible in evidence. N.Y.—Rocco v. Travelers Ins. Co., 38 Misc.2d 311, 238 N.Y.S.2d 43 (1962); Colo.—Michael v. John Hancock Mut. Life Ins. Co., 138 Colo. 450, 334 P.2d 1090 (1972).

§ 10.9 PRIVATE DOCUMENTS

Records of deeds or other private writings have been held admissible for certain purposes. For example, a mechanics lien claim, sufficiently signed to entitle it to be filed, and filed, is admissible in evidence as a "public record" under the rule admitting private writings which may become public records by recording under a statute. Cal.—D.I. Nofsizer Lumber Co. v. Solomon, 13 Cal.App. 621, 110 Pac. 474 (1910). A deed would also fall within this category. Tex.—Woodson Oil Co. v. Pruett, 281 S.W.2d 159 (Civ.App.1955); Wis.—Blaha v. Borgman, 142 Wis. 43, 124 N.W. 1047 (1910).

§ 10.10 MEMORANDUM USED BY WITNESS

A witness who is frequently called to the witness stand or even one who rarely makes such an appearance may make an entry in a book or on a piece of paper or in cement or clay or on a blackboard with chalk or any manner of writing so that when the time comes for the witness to testify in a trial or hearing, s/he may use this writing to revive a recollection. Sometimes a memorandum such as this fails to stimulate the witness' recollection. In such a case the memorandum itself may be accepted into evidence as a past recollection recorded. In New York the Court of Appeals stated in Howard v. McDonough, 77 N.Y. 592, 593, 8 Daly 365 (1879).

1. "A witness may, for the purpose of refreshing his memory, use any memorandum whether made by himself or another, written or printed, and when his memory has thus been refreshed, he must testify to facts of his own knowledge, the memorandum itself not being evidence.
2. When a witness has so far forgotten the facts that he cannot recall them, even after looking at a memorandum of them, and he testifies that he once knew them and made a memorandum of them at the time or soon after they transpired, which he intended to make correctly, and which he believes to be correct, such memorandum, in his own handwriting, may be received as evidence of the facts therein contained, although the witness has no present recollection of them.
3. Memorandum may be used in other cases which do not precisely come under either of the foregoing heads."

From a reading of the Howard v. McDonough case (supra) it is quite apparent that the court in its discretion may permit past recollections recorded into evidence. The rule has been enlarged, perhaps under the instructions of paragraph 3 above, to include that it need not be in the handwriting of the witness as long as the witness saw the memorandum soon after it was made and recognized it at that time as containing a true statement of facts within his own knowledge. N.Y.—Clark v. National Shoe & Leather Bank, 164 N.Y. 498, 58 N.E. 659 (1900). This is the foundation required before a past recollection recorded may be admissible. Naturally, like all evidence, it is subject to cross-examination. Mich.—People v. Hobson, 369 Mich. 189, 119 N.W.2d 581 (1963).

§ 10.11 MEMORANDUM USED BY WITNESS—PROOF OF DUE EXECUTION

The student has just learned that if a memorandum of an event was made either by the witness or another at or soon after the event and the witness fails to refresh his recollection of the event after receiving the writing, the writing itself may be placed in evidence. Remember that the one placing evidence into the record of the trial of proceeding has the burden of proof with respect to the credibility of the evidence. In the case of a past recollection recorded, he has the additional burden to establish the genuineness, authenticity or identity of the document. Minn.—Walker v. Larson, 284 Minn. 99, 169 N.W.2d 737 (1969). This must be done by laying a proper foundation before it is offered as evidence. This simply means that testimony must be elicited to cover that the writing was seen at or shortly after the event; that it was either written by the witness or someone with whom he was acquainted; that it was written at or shortly after the event; that it was the purpose and intent of the writer to make a full and accurate account of the event; that the witness believes that the entry is a true and accurate account of the event, and that he presently has no independent recollection of the event. After these facts are established, the written memorandum may be offered in evidence and is received in the discretion of the court.

§ 10.12 BOOK ENTRIES—THE SHOP BOOK RULE

A general rule sometimes referred to as the shop book rule is that books of account of a party, or entries therein, are admissible in his favor to show the recorded transactions when a proper foundation is laid and the entries are relevant and material to the main issue of the case. These records are received as an exception to the hearsay exclusionary rule because of necessity and because of their probability of reliability. Del.—Edsall v. Rockland Paper Co., 8 W.W.Harr. 495, 194 A. 115 (1937).

Originally, the common law precluded a party from testifying in his own behalf. Accordingly tradesmen were not able to testify in their own claims.

In order to prevent a miscarriage of justice, the common law permitted a tradesman to offer into evidence his own record of the transaction in issue. In New York a foundation had to be laid before the evidence was admissible. The plaintiff had to show

1. That the party kept no clerk.
2. That some of the articles charged had been delivered, or that some of the services charged had been rendered.
3. That the books produced were the account books of the party.

4. That the party kept fair and honest books and this was required to be proved by those who dealt and settled with him on the basis of the books. (Vosburgh v. Thayer, N.Y., 12 Johns 461).

The shop book rule continues to exist but it has been replaced by statute in most jurisdictions. Many states have adopted the Uniform Business Records as Evidence Act abrogating many of the technical common law rules with respect to the admission of business records in evidence. This statute has expanded the operation of the common law rule for the admission of such records as an exception to the hearsay exclusionary rule. The Uniform Evidence Act relating to business records applies to criminal as well as civil procedure. Ohio—State v. Phillips, 103 N.E.2d 14, 90 Ohio App. 44 (1913).

In New York, the Civil Practice Law and Rules section 4518 provides:

> (a) *Generally.* Any writing or record, whether in the form of an entry in a book or otherwise, made as a memorandum or record of any act, transaction, occurrence or event, shall be admissible in evidence in proof of that act, transaction, occurrence or event, if the judge finds that it was made in the regular course of any business and that it was the regular course of such business to make it, at the time of the act, transaction, occurrence or event, or within a reasonable time thereafter. All other circumstances of the making of the memorandum or record, including lack of personal knowledge by the maker, may be proved to affect its weight, but they shall not affect its admissibility. The term business includes a business, profession, occupation and calling of every kind.
>
> (b) *Hospital Bills.* A hospital bill is admissible in evidence under this rule and is prima facie evidence of the facts contained provided it bears a certification by the head of the hospital or by a responsible employee in the controller's or accounting office that the bill is correct, that each of the items was necessarily supplied and that the amount charged is reasonable. This subdivision shall not apply to any proceeding in a surrogate's court nor in any action instituted by or on behalf of a hospital to recover payment for accommodations or supplies furnished or for services rendered by or in such hospital, except that in a proceeding pursuant to section one hundred eighty-nine of the lien law to determine the validity and extent of the lien of a hospital, such certified hospital bills are prima facie evidence of the fact of services and of the reasonableness of any charges which do not exceed the comparable charges made by the hospital in the care of workmen's compensation patients.

(c) *Other Records.* All records, writings and other things referred to in sections 2306 and 2307 are admissible in evidence under this rule and are prima facie evidence of the facts contained, provided they bear a certification or authentication by the head of the hospital, library, department or bureau of a municipal corporation or of the state, or by an employee delegated for that purpose.

§ 10.13 POLICE RECORDS

One of the most often subpoenaed records of a police department is the report of the facts involving an accident which may later evolve into a civil law dispute involving money damages. Most jurisdictions still practice the concept of law that if a man wrongs another man, he should be punished. This concept has been highly successful over the years in preventing wilful wrongs.

There are police records however, other than accident reports, which may be admissible in evidence. For example, a police report of a stolen vehicle is not admissible to show that the car was stolen but it is admissible to show that it had been reported stolen. Missouri and some other states admit police reports under the Uniform Business Records as Evidence Law. A more detailed analysis of police accident reports admissibility follows in the next section.

§ 10.14 ACCIDENT REPORTS

If an officer is called upon to investigate the scene of an auto accident, it is his sworn duty to report the facts as he sees it to the best of his ability. Once this record is made, is it not expected that it should be used in a subsequent civil suit? It is expected, but usually it never actually is admitted into evidence.

If the student constantly remembers that the law of evidence is based on a search for truth, he can easily understand that the facts of most accident reports are given to the officer by others after the officer arrives on the scene. The student must ask himself the question "Can the person who gave the statement to the officer be cross-examined." You will remember that it was previously said in this book, that if you can't cross-examine the person who made the statement and it is offered for the truth of the assertion, it is hearsay and is subject to an exclusionary rule unless there is some compelling reason for its admission.

An accident record, made by a police officer who did not see the facts which he reported on this record is not admissible in evidence. N.Y.—Johnson v. Lutz, 253 N.Y. 124, 170 N.E. 517 (1930), except if certain conditions occur at the trial.

There are however, exceptions to the famous Johnson v. Lutz rule.

1. Where an officer's testimony is assailed as a recent fabrication, the police blotter [1] report, as well as the memorandum book, may be admitted into the evidence to bolster his testimony. N.Y.—Yeargans v. Yeargans, 24 A.D.2d 280, 265 N.Y.S.2d 562, 565 (1966).
2. Those portions of a police report which contain admissions against interest made by a party are admissible as an exception to the hearsay rule. N.Y.—Yeargans v. Yeargans (supra).

Many times, lawyers, judges and police officers misinterpret the Johnson v. Lutz (supra) decision to mean that no police accidents reports are admissible in evidence. This is not the case. As has been shown in the previous paragraph, even if someone else not under a duty to report the accident gave the information to the police officer, it may, nevertheless, be admitted under the circumstances previously described. However, there are other situations where a police accident report has been found to be admissible. For example:

1. The observations made by the police officer of the physical circumstances existing at the time of his arrival at the scene of the accident are admissible. N.Y.—Yeargans v. Yeargans (supra).
2. As to those portions of the report which are based upon the officer's observations, these may be admitted to impeach that portion of his testimony which is inconsistent with the report. Yeargans v. Yeargans (supra).
3. The contents of such reports which reflect the observations of the officer while carrying out his duty are admissible. Yeargans v. Yeargans (supra).

The New York decisions have been codified in CPLR 4518(a) and further clarified in N.Y.—Toll v. State, 32 A.D.2d 47, 299 N.Y.S. 2d 589 (1969), where the Court of Appeals said . . . CPLR 4518 (a) permits a police report to be admitted if

1. the entrant of those facts was the witness
2. the person giving the entrant the information was under a business duty to relate the facts to the entrant.

   If neither of the above conditions are apparent, the report may still be admitted under, N.Y.—Kelly v. Wasserman, 5 N.Y.2d 425, 185 N.Y.S.2d 538, to

3. prove that the statement recorded therein was made by an outsider . . . and then the facts recited in the statement may be proven by the business record if the

1. The police blotter is a term used in law decisions which means all official police records and is not restricted to a police blotter sometimes kept at a police station house which is a chronological record of specified police business occurring in that command. It sometimes does not include all of the police business occurring in that command, some of which is recorded in form reports and filed separately in the ordinary course of police business.

statement qualifies as a hearsay exception e. g., admission.

§ 10.15 TORTS

The law of civil wrong or private wrong, may be referred to as a tort. A tort may be in the nature of an action in negligence; an action in trespass; an action in assault and battery; an action in defamation; an action in slander or libel; and many other private wrong actions.

It is not the intent of this book to make you familiar with the law of tort but just to acquaint you with the fact that it exists.

It is the duty of every police officer to enforce the law. This is often thought to be only the enforcement of the criminal law. However, this is not entirely true. The officer is responsible for the orderly administration of justice and this responsibility includes the administration of civil justice.

§ 10.16 NO FAULT CONCEPT OF LIABILITY

There is a movement away from this theory in the area of automobile negligence liability. The movement is called "no fault insurance." A few states have legislated the no fault insurance concept into law and its full impact is yet to be determined. The author of this book feels that an extensive examination of the advantages and disadvantages of the no fault concept should not be included in this book. Nevertheless, the student should be made aware of the idea that in "no fault" damages are paid to any party whether he was the cause of the injury or not, but the amount received may be substantially less than what the injured person would have received had he not been at fault and the other person was negligent under the tort and damages system of law.

There is usually a threshold amount, which varies in different states. When it is reached or exceeded it entitles the wronged party to institute a suit in negligence. The threshold amount is that sum of money which the injured party expended or owes as a result of services he/she received in the treatment of the injury, plus the loss of earnings occasioned by his/her incapacity caused by his/her injury.

§ 10.17 COMPARATIVE NEGLIGENCE

Again, it is not the intention of the author to include a comprehensive analysis of negligence law. That is a subject unto itself. Nevertheless, it is thought that a book such as this which deals with proof at a trial, should include a reference to negligence actions. In many states a party who fails to exercise due care and injures another is liable to the other person in money damages providing the other person was free from all contributory negligence. This rule created harsh and sometimes inequitable results such that when a defendant in such an action was greatly negligent he would not get a judgment against him if he could show that the plaintiff had contributed to the accident in the slightest degree. Many states and the Federal government have changed this concept by statute to apportion the damages among the parties depending upon the degree of negligence proved to the satisfaction of the trier of the facts. This is known as comparative negligence.

§ 10.18 SELF-SERVING DECLARATIONS

A self-serving declaration is an oral or written statement made, or an act done, by a party to an action, or by one in privity with him, on some prior occasion, which supports a claim of that party at the time of trial. N.Y.—Latimer v. Burrows, 163 N.Y. 7, 57 N.E. 95 (1900). As a general rule, a self-serving declaration or act of a party is inadmissible in his favor; and the death of the declarant does not render his self-serving declarations admissible unless they are admissible by reason of a statute. C.J.S. Evidence § 216. However, when a self-serving declaration is part of the res gestae it may be admitted. Ga.—Tifton Brick & Block Co. v. Meadow, 92 Ga.App. 328, 88 S.E.2d 569 (1955); Md.—Shirks Motor Exp. v. Oxenham, 204 Md. 626, 106 A.2d 46 (1954).

§ 10.19 HOSPITAL RECORDS

The student should now be able to understand why hospital records are admissible in evidence. He should understand that entries made in a hospital record relevant to diagnosis, prognosis and/or treatment qualify for admission under the statutory business records rule because it is the business of the hospital to diagnose and treat people who come to the hospital for assistance.

However, very often, a hospital record of a patient contains entries which are not necessary to diagnosis, prognosis and/or treatment and these entries may not be admissible because of other exclusionary rules.

Self-serving declarations may often appear in a hospital record. An example of this may be as follows:

> "Patient states that she was standing on the sidewalk of 27th Street and Park Avenue South, talking with May Jones when she was struck from behind by vehicle bearing New York registration J.D. 44 for the current year."

It is quite apparent that the only part of this statement which might reasonably be necessary for diagnosis, prognosis and/or treatment is the fact that the patient was struck down by a vehicle. The remainder of the statement is superfluous and indeed may be described as self-serving. Perhaps the patient was crossing the street against the traffic light pattern. There would then be an issue of contributory negligence and in that event, the patient would not be entitled to recovery of any money in most jurisdictions.

Accordingly, the practice is to cover over those portions of the hospital record not relevant to diagnosis, prognosis and/or treatment, before the trier of the facts may see the hospital record.

This is usually accomplished in the trial by the attorney who is offering this record in evidence. He does this by affixing narrow width adhesive tape over the portions of the record which are not admissible in evidence and offering the remainder of the record either under the common law business entries rule or the statutory rule.

§ 10.20 EMPLOYEES TIME CARDS

Shop or time cards showing the time worked by employees during a particular day may be received in evidence. Pa.—Johnson v. Kusminsky, 287 Pa. 425, 135 A. 220 (1926); Wash.—Willett v. Davis, 30 Wash.2d 622, 193 P.2d 321 (1948); Cal.—Katz v. T. I. Butler Co., 81 Cal.App. 747, 254 Pac. 679 (1927).

§ 10.21 AIR LINE TICKETS

Air line tickets are admissible under the business records rule. U.S.—Rotolo v. United States, 404 F.2d 316 (5th Cir. 1968).

§ 10.22 MAGNETIC TAPE RECORDS

There is hardly a large business conducted today that does not rely upon electronic data process. With the computer has come the familiar magnetic tape and the printout sheets. These sheets are a necessary ingredient to the functioning of the business and are now accepted under the business entry exception to the hearsay exclusionary rule. Miss.—King v. State ex rel. Murdock Accept. Co., 222 So.2d 393 (1969).

§ 10.23 SURVEYS

A certified copy of a survey or a map on file in the land office is usually held admissible in evidence. Me.—Jackson v. Burnham, 129 Me. 344, 152 A. 56 (1930); U.S.—Zippo Mfg. Co. v. Rogers Imports Inc., 216 F.Supp. 670 (S.D.N.Y.1963).

§ 10.24 LEARNED TREATISES

There is a divergence of opinion with respect to the admissibility of learned treatises. However, there is a line of cases which permit standard works of recognized authority to be introduced in evidence. Ala.—Berry v. Robertson, 285 Ala. 623, 235 So.2d 657 (1970); Nev.—Foreman v. Ver Brugghen, 81 Nev. 86, 398 P.2d 993 (1965), but in Florida—City of St. Petersburg v. Ferguson, 193 So.2d 648 (App. 1967), it was held that medical or other works of science or learning are inadmissible as independent evidence of the theories and opinions expressed therein or as evidence for any purpose except to some extent in connection with the examination of an expert.

§ 10.25 MARKET REPORTS

The general rule is that standard price lists and market reports which are shown to be in general circulation and relied on by those engaged in the trade may be received as evidence of market value. Iowa—Wilbur v. Buckingham, 153 Iowa 194, 132 N.W. 960 (1911). The value of automobiles which is so necessary in prosecuting larceny cases involving automobiles may be proven by introducing in evidence *The National Automobile Dealer's Association Blue Book* or *Guide Book*. N.M.—Curtis v. Schwartzman Packing Co., 61 N.M. 305, 299 P.2d 776 (1956); Wyo.—O'Brien v. G.M.A.C., 362 P.2d 455 (1961). However, it is not conclusive evidence. N.M.—O'Meara v. Commercial Ins. Co., 71 N.M. 145, 376 P.2d 486 (1963).

§ 10.26 MARRIAGE AND BAPTISMAL CERTIFICATES

Marriage and baptismal certificates are competent evidence of the facts which they recite. Ind.—Blasche v. Himelick, 140 Ind.App. 255, 210 N.E.2d 378 (1965); La.—State ex rel. Lytell v. Louisiana St. Bd. of Health through Rein, 153 So.2d 498 (1963).

§ 10.27 VITAL STATISTICS

Information gathered and recorded for the preservation of health and the prevention of disease which is not always open to public inspection is not admissible as a public document or official statement. Pa.—In re Marks, 121 Pa.Super. 181, 183 A. 432 (1936). But data and records of vital statistics, such as birth, marriage and death, may be admissible as public documents. Pa.—In re Marks, supra.

§ 10.28 FAMILY RECORDS

Records in a family bible is considered inferior or secondary evidence where there is available the testimony of the party who made the entry and it is thus not admissible in this case as independent evidence. Tex.—Jaffe v. Deckard, 261 S.W. 390 (Civ.App.1924). If there is no one able to testify as to the facts related in the family bible, the record of the date of a person's birth or death may be competent evidence. Tex.—Jaffe v. Deckard, supra.

§ 10.29 FEDERAL RULE

The hearsay exceptions covered in this chapter are treated extensively in the Federal Rules of Evidence in Rule 803, Subdivisions 5, 8, 9, 12, 13, 14, 15, 17, 18 and 19. The limitation on the necessity for authentication of certain documents is treated in Rule 902. The reader is referred to those sections in the appendix of this book so as to avoid extensive repetition.

CHAPTER XI

HEARSAY—PERSONAL OR FAMILY HISTORY EXCEPTION

§ 11.1 INTRODUCTION

In every exception to the hearsay exclusionary rule, we must ask ourselves whether there is a necessity for the exception and whether there is great probability of reliability. Personal or family records appear to meet these requirements. It is highly improbable that a record of a birth, death, marriage, adoption, divorce, legitimacy, relationship by blood, adoption, ancestry or other similar fact of personal or family history found in a family bible, geneologies, charts, engravings on rings, inscriptions on family portraits, engravings on urns, crypts or tombstones or the like, would be unreliable. Accordingly, these items are admissible as an exception to the hearsay exclusionary rule when certain criteria are met. A form of this type of evidence is sometimes referred to as pedigree evidence. The Federal Rules of Evidence permit this hearsay evidence in the trial record even though the declarant is available as a witness. Rule 802(19).

§ 11.2 ELEMENTS

Most states require:

1. That the declarant was competent at time of making statement;
2. That the declarant be dead;
3. That the declarant was related by blood or affinity to the family about which he speaks;
4. That the declarations were made ante litem motam.
5. That matters of pedigree must be in issue.

There are some states which permit this information into the trial record even though the declarant is available as a witness. W.Va. —State v. Adkins, 106 W.Va. 658, 146 S.E. 732 (1929). The Federal Rules of Evidence also admit this evidence even though the declarant is available as a witness. Rule 802(19). I believe the better rule which still exists among many states is that if the declarant is available as a witness, s/he is thus available for cross-examination and his/her credibility may be tested. The pedigree exception to the hearsay exclusionary rule is a well established exception. Fla.—Cone v. Benjamin, 157 Fla. 800, 27 So.2d 90 (1946); N.Y.—In re Dowd's Estate, 18 A.D.2d 715, 236 N.Y.S.2d 147 (1963).

§ 11.3 DEATH OF DECLARANT

Declarations of pedigree as an exception to the hearsay exclusionary rule will ordinarily not be received when better evidence is available. Va.—Rawles v. Bazel, 141 Va. 734, 126 S.E. 690 (1962). As a general rule, declarations as to pedigree are not admissible unless declarant is dead. Tex.—Simpson v. Simpson, 380 S.W.2d 855 (Civ.App.1964). However, the rule is sometimes relaxed where declarant is beyond the jurisdiction of the court. Or.—Garvin v. Western Cooperage Co., 94 Or. 487, 184 Pac. 555 (1919), or if he is incapable of testifying. Ala.—Perolio v. Doe, 197 Ala. 560, 73 So. 197 (1954).

§ 11.4 RELATIONSHIP OF DECLARANT

As a general rule for a declaration of pedigree to be admissible, it must have been made by someone related to the family concerned. Del.—Pote v. Farren, 3 W.W.Harr. 1, 129 A. 238 (1925); Tenn.—In re McElroy's Adoption, 522 S.W.2d 345 (App.1975).

§ 11.5 STATEMENT MADE ANTE LITEM MOTAM

In order to get a pedigree declaration admissible, it is necessary that the declarant should be disinterested to the extent of having no motive which would induce him to state the fact otherwise than as he understood it. It must therefore be shown that the statement was made ante litem motam. Hawaii—In re Cunha's Estate, 49 Haw. 273, 414 P.2d 925 (1966); Cal.—Peterson v. Peterson, 121 Cal.App.2d 1, 262 P.2d 613 (1953).

§ 11.6 DECLARATION—FORM

A pedigree declaration is not required to be in a precise form. It is admissible if in any form capable of conveying thought provided the authenticity of the vehicle conveying the statement is established to the satisfaction of the court. N.J.—In re Blau's Estate, 4 N.J. Super. 343, 67 A.2d 316 (1907); Ariz.—In re Wallin's Estate, 16 Ariz.App. 34, 490 P.2d 863 (1971).

§ 11.7 DECLARANT'S LACK OF PERSONAL KNOWLEDGE

There is a conflict of authority with respect to whether declarant is required to have actual knowledge of the contents of the pedigree declaration. In Idaho, a case held that a witness may testify to facts of family history if his knowledge of the subject is derived from intimate acquaintance with the family or families (albeit hearsay upon hearsay). Idaho—In re Stone's Estate, 77 Idaho 63, 286 P.2d 329 (1955). However, another case holds that as to matters of family history, reputation or tradition, the declarations concerning such matters, of one connected with the family, are admissible, notwithstanding declarant did not disclose the source or an authoritive source for such knowledge. Mo.—Gordon v. Metropolitan Life Ins. Co., 238 Mo.App. 46, 176 S.W.2d 506 (1944).

§ 11.8 MATTERS OF PEDIGREE MUST BE IN ISSUE

In order to bring a case within the pedigree exception to the hearsay exclusionary rule, the issue must be geneological in that pedigree must be directly in issue and not merely incidental. In a prosecution for rape in the second degree, the declarations of the deceased mother of the complainant are inadmissible to establish the complainant's age. N.Y.—People v. Lammes, 208 App.Div. 533, 203 N.Y.S. 736 (1924).

§ 11.9 FEDERAL RULE

Rule 803. Hearsay exceptions; availability of declarant immaterial

The following are not excluded by the hearsay rule, even though the declarant is available as a witness:

1. . . . through 18 . . . .

19. Reputation concerning person or family history.—Reputation among members of his family by blood, adoption, or marriage, or among his associates, or in the community, concerning a person's birth, adoption, marriage, divorce, death, legitimacy, relationship by blood, adoption, or marriage, ancestry, or other similar fact of his personal of family history.

20. . . . through 24 . . . .

CHAPTER XII

PRIVILEGED COMMUNICATIONS

§ 12.1 INTRODUCTION

Any student who has watched a television performance of a courtroom trial has probably heard of the phrase "Privileged Communication." If the student substitutes the word "confidential" for the word "privilege" s/he has a better understanding of the meaning of the concept of privileged communication. When one speaks to another in confidence, s/he usually does so with the thought that the contents of the communication will not be divulged by the listener. In certain situations, the law has contended that the best interests of society will be served by prohibiting the listener from divulging the information s/he has received unless the informer has expressly released the listener from this prohibition. The idea of privileged communication originated in the common law by being based on a code of honor that certain categories of persons could not divulge information given to them in confidence. Later, it was enacted into the statutory law to include a minister, priest or rabbi, an attorney, a physician, a psychologist, certain conversations between husband and wife, and compromise offers. The statutes do not give blanket coverage to the above named categories of persons but do include these people in controlled situations which we will now discuss.

§ 12.2 FAILURE TO WAIVE PRIVILEGED COMMUNICATION —INFERENCE

There is conflict of authority with respect to the issue as to whether or not an unfavorable inference may be drawn by the refusal of a party to waive the privilege of a confidential communication. The prevailing view appears to be that no unfavorable inference shall be drawn by the failure of a party to waive the privilege. In N.D.—Meyer v. Russell, 55 N.D. 546, 214 N.W. 857 (1927), it was held that failure to call as witnesses, physicians who first attended the injured plaintiff does not permit a presumption that their testimony would have been unfavorable.

§ 12.3 PRIVILEGED COMMUNICATION—CLERGYMAN

It is well recognized that there was no common law privilege in the case of confidential communications or confessions made to a clergyman. The legislatures of most jurisdictions however, have found it to be in the best interest of the public to enact statutes granting such a privilege to a clergyman or other minister of any religion. The New York Civil Practice Law and Rules provides in Section 4505 "Unless the person confessing or confiding waives the privilege, a clergyman or other minister of any religion or duly accredited Christian Science practitioner shall not be allowed to disclose a confession or confidence made to him in his professional character as spiritual advisor." The student should take particular note of the words in the statute "in his professional character as spiritual advisor." If the penitent or confessor made an inculpatory statement to such a clergyman, not knowing that the listener were a clergyman, it would appear that the clergyman would not be bound by the privilege. On the other hand, it has been held that it is not essential that the penitent be a member of the same church as the clergyman. Minn.—Matter of Swenson, 183 Minn. 602, 237 N.W. 589 (1931). Statutes vary in different jurisdictions with respect to how this privilege is waived. Some require that the waiver only be on the trial, except that a waiver between the attorneys representing adverse interests was also acceptable even though done before the trial. The modern trend is to permit waiver at any time, even before the execution of the contract. For example, a waiver of the privilege in an insurance policy constituted effective waiver. N.Y.—Lynch v. Mutual Life Ins. of N. Y., 55 Misc.2d 179, 284 N.Y.S.2d 768 (1968).

§ 12.4 PRIVILEGED COMMUNICATION—HOSPITAL RECORDS

It has been indicated in Chapter X where business records are discussed, that hospital records are admissible where the entries were necessary for diagnosis, prognosis and/or treatment. This was allowed by the common law business entries rule and by the statutory rule enacted by most states authorizing the use of hospital records in trials. We now have the problem of a head-on collision between rules of law. On the one hand, the statute permits its introduction into evidence and on the other hand, a privileged communication exists between physician and patient. The courts, in some cases have excluded hospital records where they involve a communication between a doctor and a patient and the patient does not waive his privilege. N.Y.—Vanderhule v. Berinstein, 285 App.Div. 290, 136 N.Y.S.2d 95 (1955).

§ 12.5 PRIVILEGED COMMUNICATION—PHYSICIAN

There was no privilege existing at common law between physician and patient. In 1828, New York State was the first state to legislate a law which mandated this privilege into existence. The present statute which embodies and specifies this privilege is found in Section 4504 CPLR of New York State.

. . .

§ 4504. Physician, dentist and nurse

(a) Confidential information privileged. Unless the patient waives the privilege, a person authorized to practice medicine, registered professional nursing, licensed practical nursing or dentistry shall not be allowed to disclose any information which he acquired in attending a patient in a professional capacity, and which was necessary to enable him to act in that capacity. The relationship of a physician and patient shall exist between a medical corporation, as defined in article forty-four of the public health law, a professional service corporation organized under article fifteen of the business corporation law to practice medicine, and the patients to whom they respectively render professional medical services.

. . .

An analysis of CPLR 4504 reveals that four elements must exist in order for it to operate.

1. There must be a relationship of physician and patient, or dentist and patient or registered nurse or registered practical nurse, and patient.
2. The persons named must be duly authorized under the law to practice their respective profession.
3. The information must be acquired while attending the patient.
4. The information must be necessary to enable the professional to act in that capacity.

The student who analyzes the preceding elements can easily imagine many situations wherein a physician/patient relationship may exist and confidences may be expressed by the patient, to the physician, said confidences not coming within the scope of the privilege. It is for this reason that in Section 12.1 supra, a caveat was indicated that the statutes include certain categories of people in controlled situations only. E. g., Examples of lack of privilege are: where physician is a chiropractor, a midwife, an unregistered practical nurse, or where the information given by the patient is not necessary for diagnosis and/or treatment. N.Y.—People v. Decina, 2 N.Y.2d 133, 157 N.Y.S.2d 558, 138 N.E.2d 799 (1957), or where a physician is required by law to report a wound inflicted by a deadly weapon. Ohio—State v. Antill, 26 Ohio Op. 366, 197 N.E.2d 548 (1964).

§ 12.6 PRIVILEGED COMMUNICATION—PSYCHOTHERAPIST-PATIENT

A psychotherapist is a medical physician who is particularly qualified to treat mental and emotional conditions. In this capacity, it sometimes becomes necessary to gain the knowledge of the innermost feelings and thoughts of the patient in order to arrive at a method of treatment. The psychotherapist therefore must, of necessity, be one to whom everything that is told by the patient be kept secret and privileged unless the patient waives this privilege. Therefore, the statutes cover this relationship guardedly.

§ 12.7 PRIVILEGED COMMUNICATION—HUSBAND AND WIFE

Before women's liberation, the common law considered a woman little more than a chattel in many circumstances. For example, in common law a husband or wife of a party to an action was disqualified as a witness. Eng.—Davis v. Dinwoody, 4 T.R. 678, 100 Eng.Rep. 1241. There were some exceptions to this blanket rule but the statutory law of most jurisdictions have removed most uncertainties in this area of privileged communications. New York State has enacted one statute covering this area. It is CPLR 4512.

In summary CPLR 4512 states that in an action founded upon adultery as a ground for divorce neither spouse is competent to testify against the other except

(a) to prove the marriage;

(b) to disprove the adultery;

(c) to disprove a defense after evidence has been introduced tending to prove such defense.

Note that the prohibition only applies to divorce actions founded on adultery and not to other grounds of actions wherein husband and wife might be adversaries, such as one for separation or a divorce based on cruel and inhuman treatment or other statutory reasons.

CPLR 4502 also provides that neither spouse may be required or without the consent of the other if living, allowed, to disclose a confidential communication made by one to the other during marriage.

At common law, in a prosecution of one spouse for an injury inflicted upon the other, the injured spouse was a competent witness. The 1909 Penal Law of New York, § 2445 provided for a prohibition of the revelation of a confidential communication between husband and wife. The 1967 Penal Law of New York omitted this section with the apparent result of a return to the common law.

It should be noted that the reason for invoking the privilege is to protect and strengthen the marital bond. If the spouses are not living together but are married in name only, the privilege does not exist unless it was made as part of an attempted reconciliation. N.Y. —People v. Oyola, 6 N.Y.2d 259, 189 N.Y.S.2d 203, 160 N.E.2d 494 (1959).

The privilege is continued even after divorce in a husband and wife situation or even after death of one of the parties. U.S.— Pereira v. United States, 347 U.S. 1, 74 S.Ct. 358, 98 L.Ed. 435 (1954).

§ 12.8 PRIVILEGED COMMUNICATION—POLICE INFORMANT

It has often been said that the work quality of a detective is no better than his information. In order to operate efficiently a police department requires the information supplied to it by police informants. If the names of these informants were divulged, less persons would either volunteer information or be in the business of supplying information to police authorities. It is apparent, that if these people are identified, they would either bear the scars of their profession or they would have a much shortened life span. Accordingly, it becomes necessary, in the public interest, to protect these people.

Frequently defense attorneys will, in the course of pretrial motions, or even on trial itself, make requests for the identity of the police informant.

There has been some confusion with respect to the discretion of the judge to reveal the identity of the confidential informant of the police. It appears that, for the most part, the state does not have to disclose the name of the informant who gave information to the police to establish probable cause for the issuance of a search warrant. In U.S.—United States v. Ventresca, 380 U.S. 102, 85 S.Ct. 741, 13 L.Ed.2d 684 (1965), the court held " . . . an affidavit may be based upon hearsay information and need not reflect the direct personal observation of the affiant so long as the magistrate is informed of some of the underlying circumstances supporting the affiant's conclusions and his belief that any informant whose identity need not be disclosed . . . was credible and his information reliable."

It therefore can be said that an officer who gets information from an informant who has proven reliable previously, will not be required to divulge the identity of the informant for the purpose of establishing probable cause for the issuance of a search warrant. It might also be further stated that the identity of informants will not be revealed if the information leads to the discovery of the crime.

This privilege however, is not without exception. In U.S.—Roviaro v. United States, 353 U.S. 53, 77 S.Ct. 623, 1 L.Ed.2d 639 (1957), a prosecutor was required to divulge the identity of an informant where the informant had a direct involvement as the sole participant with an accused in the offense for which the accused was being tried.

The privilege runs to the favor of the government in the interest of the public. It does not run to the informant. Hence, if the government wishes to identify the informant, it may do so by waiving the privilege without first getting the permission of the informant.

In a New York case, the People refused to divulge the name of an informer and went one step further in not offering any evidence of his reliability, thereby failing to establish the existence of probable cause to make the arrest and the indictment was dismissed by the New York Court of Appeals. N.Y.—People v. Malinsky et al., 19 N.Y.2d 262, 279 N.Y.S.2d 20, 225 N.E.2d 748 (1967).

However, where observations of two defendants by police officer were sufficient, quite apart from informer's communication, to establish that probable cause existed to support issuance of warrant for search of apartment for policy violations, or, indeed to arrest without a warrant, the People were not under necessity of disclosing the identity of informer or of producing him, on motion of those two defendants to set aside search warrant and suppress evidence seized on search conducted pursuant thereto. N.Y.—People v. Smith, 21 N.Y. 2d 698, 287 N.Y.S.2d 425, 234 N.E.2d 460 (1968).

There is a need to protect the government's privilege of nondisclosure of identity of informant so as to encourage citizens to communicate their knowledge of crime to law enforcement officials.

Government's privilege of nondisclosure of identity of informers of violations of law is limited by the fundamental requirements of fairness and must give way where its assertion would seriously prejudice the defendant by making a fair hearing impossible. Denial of disclosure of identity of informant did not deprive defendant of a fair trial where informant's communication was not essential to establishment of probable cause for issuance of search warrant, since informer's information that defendant was selling narcotics was independently verified and corroborated by observations of detectives during their stakeout of defendant's apartment and building. N.Y.—People v. Cerrato, 24 N.Y.2d 1, 298 N.Y.S.2d 688, 246 N.E.2d 501 (1969), certiorari denied 397 U.S. 940, 90 S.Ct. 951, 25 L.Ed.2d 120 (1970).

It would therefore appear that the courts are reluctant to order the prosecutor to divulge the identity of an informer, but if a fair defense requires the identity of the informer, and there is no other evidence that the prosecution can rely on to substantiate probable cause for the arrest, the court will dismiss the indictment unless the People reveal the identity of the informant to the defendant.

The better practice then for police officers to follow, is to obtain the initial information from informants and then make observations by themselves which may lead them to conclude, by virtue of their training and experience, that criminal activity is occurring, describing the type of criminal activity which they believe is taking place. Suspicion alone will not produce probable cause to obtain a warrant.

§ 12.9 PRIVILEGED COMMUNICATION—ATTORNEY–CLIENT

When a client visits the office of an attorney with the purpose in mind of asking the attorney's assistance for some difficulty that the client finds himself in, the client, must, of necessity, reveal certain facts which he might not wish the whole world to know. In order for the attorney to fully and competently advise the client as to a course of action to be taken, the attorney must know all of the relevant facts about the situation. The law presumes this and protects the client by a privilege. In effect, when the client is talking to the attorney, the client is talking to himself. A different result obtains when there is a third person present during the conversation. The common law permitted an eavesdropper to a confidential communication to disclose the contents of the communication. Today it would be a violation of a constitutional right of counsel. However, if a communication is made in the presence of a third party, who is neither the agent of the attorney nor the client, the privilege does not apply because it is apparent that the communication was not intended to be confidential. Baumann v. Steingester, 213 N.Y. 328, 107 N.E. 578 (1915).

§ 12.10 PRIVILEGED COMMUNICATION—OVERHEARD BY THIRD PERSONS

Ordinarily, privileged communications overheard by third persons lose their status as privileged communication. This may occur in attorney, client relationship, U.S.—Wolfle v. United States, 291 U.S. 7, 54 S.Ct. 279, 78 L.Ed. 617 (1944), or husband, wife situations, N.Y.—People v. McCormack, 278 App.Div. 191, 104 N.Y.S.2d 139 (1951), or in any like situation. The reasoning being, that if it was really a confidential communication the relator would not wish to have a third person share in the secret.

§ 12.11 PRIVILEGED COMMUNICATION—WAIVER

The privileged communication may be waived by the oral or written consent given by the person to whom the privilege runs. If it is orally done, it may be by the failure on the part of the person to whom the privilege runs to object to its admissibility at the time of trial.

A patient waives his privilege when he calls his attending physician to testify in behalf of the patient with respect to the patient's physical or mental condition. N.Y.—Steinberg v. New York Life Ins. Co., 263 N.Y. 45, 188 N.E. 152, 90 A.L.R. 642 (1934).

A peculiar result occurs when a representative of one who has been killed by the negligent act of another, sues the other person in what is known as a wrongful death action. In this type of action it is necessary for the decedent's representative to tender proof of decedent's pecuniary worth to his next of kin, i. e., his health and earning capacity. He must therefore produce evidence of his good health. When he does this, courts have held that he waives the privilege of doctor-patient and the defendant may then validly expect the physician who treated the decedent to testify as to what he found with respect to the quality of decedent's health. N.Y.—Eder v. Cashin, 281 App.Div. 456, 120 N.Y.S.2d 165 (1953).

Once a person waives his privilege in a trial, either by affirmative action or by failing to object to its admission by the other side, the cases have held that the privilege is waived for all time. N.Y.—People v. Bloom, 193 N.Y. 1, 85 N.E. 824, 18 L.R.A.(N.S). 898 (1908). Testimony elicited on cross-examination, however, does not waive the privilege. N.Y.—Vilardi v. Vilardi, 200 Misc. 1043, 107 N.Y.S.2d 342 (1951).

§ 12.12 STATE SECRETS—PRIVILEGE

The student is reminded that the rules of evidence have as their basis, the ascertainment of the truth according to the best ability and the conscience and mind of man. In the area of the state secrets privilege, it is very easy to understand that great injustice could be done to a defendant if the prosecution were to rely unscrupulously on the right to refrain from furnishing certain information on the ground that to do so would reveal state secrets. In most cases involving this point it has been held that the judge ought to have some facts presented to him to base his decision unless there is clear evidence that the disclosure would be dangerous to the government.

In the interest of justice, where the refusal might seriously prevent the defense from presenting its case, the prosecutor may be required to move for a dismissal of charges. U.S.—United States v. Reynolds, 345 U.S. 1, 73 S.Ct. 528, 97 L.Ed. 727 (1953).

Federal Rule 509 deals with a codification of the exclusion from evidence of Secrets of States. Congress failed to enact it however and the common law rule still prevails.

§ 12.13 PRIVILEGED COMMUNICATION—EXECUTIVE PRIVILEGE

Little was known about the term "executive privilege" prior to its being invoked by President Nixon during the "Watergate" controversy of 1974.

The concept was that in the running of the government, the executive had the implied right to keep secret all of the conversations which the President had with others with respect to the administration of his position. The Supreme Court in an 8–0 decision, rejected these claims and this was probably the major reason which caused his resignation on August 9, 1974. U.S.—United States v. Nixon, 418 U.S. 683, 94 S.Ct. 3090, 41 L.Ed.2d 1039 (1974).

§ 12.14 PRIVILEGED COMMUNICATION—NEWSPAPER REPORTER

Great influence has been brought upon state and national legislatures to extend the concept of privileged communications to the sources of information given to newspaper reporters. Frequently reporters have gone to jail because they have refused to divulge the source of their information after being directed to do so by a judge. This area of the law may change but as of this writing a newspaper reporter called as a witness before a grand jury cannot under the common law, lawfully refuse to answer pertinent questions relating to communications made to him on the ground that such communications are privileged. N.Y.—People ex rel. Mooney v. Sheriff of New York County, 269 N.Y. 291, 199 N.E. 415, 102 A.L.R. 769 (1936).

The reason given by the courts and legislatures for not granting this privilege is that there is a superior interest of the public in the due administration of the law over any private considerations that may exist as between journalists and their informants.

There is a conflict of constitutional law in this area with respect to the constitutional protection of the First Amendment (freedom of press . . .) and Fifth Amendment (self-incrimination . . .) It is not completely within the scope of this text to delve deeply into constitutional law problems but suffice it to say that in most jurisdictions a journalist does not enjoy the privilege unless it is expressly provided for by statute. New York and New Jersey are among some of the jurisdictions which have legislation protecting the source of information of journalists but these statutes are being interpreted by the courts and erosions of the privilege have already taken place.

In June of 1972 the Supreme Court of the United States handed down a decision in the Caldwell case involving Earl Caldwell of the New York Times and two other newsmen in which it held that the First Amendment did not give newsmen an automatic right or privilege to refuse to testify before grand juries about their work. However, it did not require the jailing of all newsmen who refuse to testify. It left open the concept that in determining whether to uphold subpoenas of newsmen, the courts must balance the interests of a free press against the interests of the grand jury investigation to which the newsman is being asked to contribute. It also said that Congress was free to create whatever "newsman's privilege" they see fit—including an "absolute privilege."

In New Jersey where a statutory privilege for newsmen exists, a reporter, Peter J. Bridge, was confined to jail for attempting to exercise the privilege. The state courts of New Jersey have held that he waived the privilege when he named one person as having given him information. The student is referred to his own state laws for a more detailed analysis of the law in his jurisdiction.

§ 12.15 PRIVILEGED COMMUNICATION—STATUTORY IMMUNITY

Who has not gone fishing and when he sees a small fish he may throw it back into the water or use it as bait to get a larger fish. So, too, in the law enforcement profession. It sometimes becomes necessary to let a small time "punk" go free in order to get at the higher echelon criminal. The legislatures understand this phenomenon and have enacted statutes giving law enforcement officials, particularly prosecutors, the authority to grant immunity to those who would claim a protection of the Fifth Amendment self-incrimination clause.

The theory is that if immunity is granted, there is no reason for the witness to ask for the privilege. In this fashion, much information can be secured by the government that probably would not have become known but for the granting of the immunity privilege.

§ 12.16 FEDERAL RULE

Rule 501. General rule

> Except as otherwise required by the Constitution of the United States or provided by Act of Congress or in rules prescribed by the Supreme Court pursuant to statutory authority, the privilege of a witness, person, government, State or political subdivision thereof shall be governed by the principles of the common law as they may be interpreted by the courts of the United States in the light of reason and experience. However, in civil actions and proceedings, with respect to an element of a claim or defense as to which State law supplies the rule of decision, the privilege of a witness, person, government, State, or political subdivision thereof shall be determined in accordance with State law.

The Supreme Court prescribed twelve additional rules with respect to privilege but Congress failed to enact them. In essence the Advisary Committees Note explained that the grand design of these provisions does not readily lend itself to codification.

CHAPTER XIII

DECLARATIONS AGAINST INTEREST

§ 13.1 INTRODUCTION

Generally, declarations made by a litigant, which are against his/her interest even though they may be hearsay, are admissible as an exception to the hearsay exclusionary rule under certain conditions and may be admissible as proof both of facts directly asserted and of facts incidental thereto and within the scope of the declaration. As with other exceptions to the hearsay exclusionary rule, here too, there is necessity and a great probability of reliability.

§ 13.2 ELEMENTS OF THE EXCEPTION

A declaration against interest, in order to be admissible must contain the following elements.

1. The declaration when made must be against the pecuniary or proprietary interest and more recently, in New York, the penal interest of the declarant.
2. The declarant is dead at the time of trial (in some states declarant may be unavailable).
3. The declarant had competent knowledge of the facts.
4. There was no probable motive to misrepresent the facts.

§ 13.3 DECLARATION AGAINST PECUNIARY OR PROPRIETARY INTEREST

To bring the statement within the exception, the statement must be a money or property interest of the declarant which prejudices his present contention. Let us assume that a complainant in a criminal action testified at a hearing in a lower court before the case was presented to the grand jury. He then testified before the grand jury and an indictment was found against the defendant for grand larceny of $16,000.00. The defendant was arraigned before the trial court on the grand larceny charge and he plead not guilty and a date was set for trial. Before the date for trial, the complainant made a statement to a third party that he never had $16,000.00 in his possession and he is only making the complaint against the defendant because the defendant had taken away the complainant's lady friend. Prior to the trial, the complainant died and the district attorney attempts to prove the case by reading the testimony of the complainant before the hearing court. Conceivably, the statement made by the complainant relating to the fact that he never had $16,000.00 in his possession and that he was making the complaint against the defendant because the defendant had taken away the deceased's lady friend, although hearsay, may be admitted under the declaration against interest exception because:

1. The statement was against his interest because he could be sued for false arrest and also he would not have a right of recovery in the civil action of conversion.
2. He was dead at the time of trial.
3. He had competent knowledge of the facts.
4. There was no probable motive to misrepresent the facts.

Another example where incidental and collateral facts and circumstances were admitted in a declaration against interest occurred in a leading English case. Higham v. Ridway, 10 East. 109, 103 Eng.Rep. 717. In this case a male widwife made an entry of the delivery of a child on a certain day, and this entry referred to a ledger in which the midwife had entered a charge for her services and which contained a notation of payment at a later date. The entry of birth was held admissible as evidence of the child's age after the midwife had died.

§ 13.4 DECLARATIONS AGAINST PENAL INTEREST

There is movement afoot to make a declaration against penal interest, a declaration against interest which is admissible. However, the prevailing rule is that declaration against penal interest is not admissible. U.S.—Donnelly v. United States, 228 U.S. 243, 33 S.Ct. 449, 57 L.Ed. 820 (1913). Some states permit declaration against penal interest to be received. Minn.—State v. Voges, 197 Minn. 85, 266 N.W. 265 (1936); Md.—Brennan v. State, 151 Md. 265, 134 A. 148, 48 A.L.R. 342 (1926); N.Y.—People v. Brown, 26 N.Y.2d 88, 308 N.Y.S.2d 825, 257 N.E.2d 16 (1970). However, a plea of guilty to a motor vehicle violation was held not to be within the rule. Okl.—Dover v. Smith, 385 P.2d 287 (1963).

The Federal Rules of Evidence Rule 804(b) (3) has further qualified this concept by holding: "A statement tending to expose the declarant to criminal liability and offered to exculpate the accused is not admissible unless corroborating circumstances clearly indicate the trustworthiness of the statement." Therefore, according to the Federal Rule, if "D", a defendant in a murder trial of "V" was able to get "W", a witness, to testify that "A" had confessed to the murder of "V", the confession might be admissible if there was some corroboration to "A's" statement. Fingerprints of "A" on the murder weapon might satisfy this requirement.

The model Code of Evidence would make a declaration admissible where the fact asserted subjects the declarant to civil or criminal liability or even to social disapproval.

If the declaration is contrary to both penal and pecuniary interest there is no question in any jurisdiction but that the statement would be admissible if all other requirements are satisfied.

§ 13.5 UNAVAILABILITY OF DECLARANT

Declarations against interest are admissible only where the declarant is unavailable as a witness. Some authorities contend that the declarant must be dead. Others contend that if the declarant cannot be compelled to testify because he is absent from the jurisdiction of the court, the declaration may be received. Pa.—Alter v. Berghaus, 8 Watts. 77 (1839). In another case, absence from the jurisdiction was not sufficient. N.Y.—Bunge Corp. v. Manufacturers Hanover Trust Co., 65 Misc.2d 829, 318 N.Y.S.2d 819 (1971). The law is not consistent in the declaration against interest exception and the student is referred to his/her own state legal digest to ascertain the law applicable to the student's jurisdiction. However, in all jurisdictions where the declarant is dead and all other necessary elements are present, the exception is admissible. Tenn.—Tom Love Grocery Co. v. Maryland Casualty Co., 166 Tenn. 275, 61 S.W.2d 672 (1933); Ala.—Taylor v. First Nat. Bank of Tuscaloosa, 279 Ala. 624, 189 So.2d 141 (1966).

§ 13.6 DECLARANT'S KNOWLEDGE THAT DECLARATION IS AGAINST HIS INTEREST

The fact that the declarant is aware that at the time he made the statement, it was against his pecuniary or proprietary interest is a necessary component because it furnishes the circumstantial probability of its trustworthiness. However, most of the cases read by the author on this subject do not list the declarant's awareness as a separate element of this exception. Rule 509 of the Model Code of Evidence adopts the reasonable man test wherein a reasonable man must have known that the declaration was against his interest. In a New York case, N.Y.—Ellwanger v. Whiteford, 15 A.D.2d 898, 225 N.Y.S.2d 734 (1962), the court held that the declarant's awareness was an essential requirement of the declaration against interest exception.

§ 13.7 NO PROBABLE MOTIVE TO MISREPRESENT

In order to render a declaration against interest to be admissible, there must be a great probability of reliability and therefore there should be a great probability of the trustworthiness of the declaration, but if a declaration is actually against the interest of the declarant, it is immaterial that the declarant may have had a motive to misrepresent the matter. N.H.—Rau v. First Nat. Stores, 97 N.H. 490, 92 A.2d 921 (1915). Where there exists both a self-serving and a self-disserving interest, the latter must preponderate over the self-serving interest. La.—Demasi v. Whitney Trust & Savings Bank, 176 So. 703 (App.1937).

§ 13.8 FEDERAL RULE

Rule 804. Hearsay exceptions: declarant unavailable

(a) . . . through (b) (2) . . . .

(b) (3) Statement against interest.—A statement which was at the time of its making so far contrary to the declarant's pecuniary or proprietary interest, or so far tended to subject him to civil or criminal liability, or to render invalid a claim by him against another, that a reasonable man in his position would not have made the statement unless he believed it to be true. A statement tending to expose the declarant to criminal liability and offered to exculpate the accused is not admissible unless corroborating circumstances clearly indicate the trustworthiness of the statement.

(4) . . . through (5).

CHAPTER XIV

SELF-SERVING DECLARATION

§ 14.1 INTRODUCTION—SELF-SERVING DECLARATION

Generally, a declaration which is characterized as a self-serving declaration or act of a party, is not admissible in evidence in his favor. Even when the declarant is dead or not available at the time of trial, his previous self-serving declaration or act is not admissible.

To understand the idea of a self-serving declaration it is best to explain it by an example. Let us assume that you are involved in an automobile accident involving a subsequent suit for money damages. Let us further assume that immediately after the collision you jump out of your vehicle and shout at the driver of the other vehicle the words "Why did you pass that red traffic light?"

These words uttered by you, if believed by the trier of the facts would infer that the other driver was at fault and you were not at fault. If you were later testifying at the trial where you were the plaintiff and you were asked "Immediately after the collision of the vehicles, what, if anything, did you say to the defendant and what, if anything did he say to you?" Whereupon you replied "I jumped out of my auto and I shouted at the defendant and asked him why he passed the red traffic light?" This statement should be objected to by opposing counsel in that they infer that the defendant passed the red traffic light. On the other hand the plaintiff may testify that when s/he arrived at the intersection, the traffic light was green for him/her. S/He is then testifying as to a fact which s/he had seen and perceived and not a statement in his/her favor which s/he previously made.

It has been defined as a statement made by a party in his own interest at some time and place out of court, and it does not include testimony which he gives as a witness at the trial. Conn.—Dawson v. Davis, 125 Conn. 330, 5 A.2d 703 (1886); Ga.—Childers v. Ackerman Const. Co., 211 Ga. 350, 86 S.E.2d 227 (1955); Cal.—Weber v. Leuschner, 240 Cal.App.2d 829, 50 Cal.Rptr. 86 (1966).

§ 14.2 EFFECT OF ADMISSION OF SELF-SERVING DECLARATION OVER OBJECTION

If there is direct evidence admitted relating to the same matters which a party had been permitted to testify over objection even though it was self-serving, it has been held that it should not be considered prejudicial error. Pa.—In re O'Keefe's Estate, 27 Leh.L.J. 17 (Orph.Ct.); Tex.—Johnson v. Tunstall, 25 S.W.2d 828 (Com.App. 1930).

§ 14.3 EFFECT OF FAILURE TO OBJECT

If a self-serving declaration is admitted and the opposing counsel fails to object, the evidence cannot later be objected to as being incompetent and therefor inadmissible. N.Y.—Thyll v. New York and L. B. R. Co., 92 App.Div. 513, 87 N.Y.S. 345 (1904).

§ 14.4 ACTS AS SELF–SERVING DECLARATIONS

Acts which are self-serving are a different form of a declaration. They are not admissible. Thus, checks which were indorsed by defendant after the trial in a lower court which were offered to show his customary method of endorsing checks were properly excluded as being self-serving acts. Mass.—Benuliewicz v. Berger, 245 Mass. 137, 139 N.E. 784 (1923).

§ 14.5 SELF–SERVING DECLARATIONS—PART OF RES GESTAE

When considering the general rules of nonadmissibility of self-serving declarations, if we compare it with the hearsay exclusionary rule, we will find great similarities. The student will no doubt remember that we said that hearsay evidence is generally not admissible but there are exceptions to the hearsay exclusionary rule which provide that when there is necessity and a great probability of reliability, we permit this type of evidence into the trial record.

For example, you may recall that res gestae statements are admissible as an exception to the hearsay exclusionary rule. So too, are res gestae self-serving declarations admissible as an exception to the self-serving declaration exclusionary rule. N.J.—Schloss v. Trounstine, 135 N.J.Law 11, 49 A.2d 677 (1946); Ill.—Werdell v. Turzynski, 128 Ill.App.2d 139, 262 N.E.2d 833 (1970). It however, must be noted with great emphasis that a party may not bolster his case by testifying to his own self-serving declaration even if it is part of the res gestae. Minn.—Perkins v. Great Northern Ry. Co., 152 Minn. 226, 188 N.W. 564 (1922).

For example, if a defendant in a homicide trial testified that simultaneously with the defendant shooting the fatal bullet, the defendant said to the deceased "Don't throw that knife at me," the defendant could not testify to that statement, but another who heard the statement might testify to it on the grounds that it was a res gestae statement even though it might be self-serving on the issue of justification.

§ 14.6 SELF–SERVING DECLARATIONS—STATE OF MIND

Self-serving declarations have been admitted to show the state of mind or intention of the declarant and not for the truth of the contents of the statement. Cal.—Ensher, Alexander & Barsoom, Inc. v.

Ensher, 210 Cal.App.2d 184, 26 Cal.Rptr. 381 (1962); Conn.—McDermott v. McDermott, 97 Conn. 31, 115 A. 638 (1922).

§ 14.7 CHARTS OR DRAWINGS—SELF-SERVING DECLARATIONS

Charts or drawings made by a party are admissible to clarify testimony even though it may be self-serving, so too are the use of motion pictures. Tex.—Richardson v. Missouri, K–T. R. Co. of Texas, 205 S.W.2d 819 (Civ.App.1947).

§ 14.8 SELF-SERVING DECLARATIONS—DECLARATIONS OF PAIN

Often, a physician requires a statement from the patient as to what is hurting the patient. This is necessary for the physician to properly diagnose the illness or injury and to assist him/her in the diagnosis, and treatment. It is assumed that the patient is telling the physician the truth becaue if s/he were lying, s/he might receive treatment which might be injurious to the patient. Accordingly statements of pain made by a patient to a physician for the purpose of diagnosis and treatment are admissible even though they may later be self-serving in a trial. U.S.—Hartford Accident & Indemnity Co. v. Baugh, 87 F.2d 240 (5th Cir. 1936), certiorari denied 57 S.Ct. 670, 300 U.S. 679, 81 L.Ed. 883 (1937). If the statement to a physician for a purpose other than treatment, it is hearsay, not an exception to the hearsay exclusionary rule and may be self-serving and therefore not admissible. Ohio—Toledo Rys. & Light Co. v. Prus, 7 Ohio App. 412; Tex.—Gaines v. Stewart, 57 S.W.2d 207 (Civ.App.1933).

Declarations of groans and screams made by a person to another, not an attending physician, however, were found to be admissible on the ground that it is better and clearer and a more vigorous description of the then existing physical condition of the party by the eye witness than could be given in any other way. . . . N.Y.—Roche v. Bklyn. City and Newtown R. R. Co., 105 N.Y. 294, 11 N.E. 630 (1887).

To summarize the area of self-serving declarations which courts have held admissible where pain and suffering are the issue before the court we can say:

1. If the person makes an involuntary expression of pain such as an involuntary scream or groan or a moan, it is admissible.
2. Declarations of pain which the person makes of his/her present condition are not admissible except if the statement is made admissible by some other exception to the hearsay rule or where the declarant is dead or when it is made to a physician for the purpose of treatment.

CHAPTER XV

PUBLIC DOCUMENTS

§ 15.1 INTRODUCTION

It is often necessary for the contents of a public document to be offered in evidence for the truth of the assertion contained therein. As was indicated earlier, a document may be considered as hearsay just as much as an oral statement by one not actually testifying at the time. However, because of the great probability of reliability and further, because of the necessity of introducing the contents of public documents into evidence, the courts have permitted properly authenticated records to be admitted into evidence. It is quite evident that since the public official who has custody of the records has no motive to distort the truth and it was made in the discharge of his/her duty, the record is considered to be received as an exception to the hearsay rule.

If the public official were required to be called in every case where a public record is subpoenaed, it would put a strain on the efficient operation of the office. Hence the courts have permitted public records which are kept in the ordinary course of business to be admissible in evidence.

Each jurisdiction may have its own rules with respect to the admission of public records as an exception to the hearsay exclusionary rule. In New York the CPLR 4520 reads:

> "Where a public officer is required as authorized, by special provision of law, to make a certificate or an affidavit to a fact ascertained, or an act performed, by him in the course of his official duty, and to file or deposit it in a public office of the state, the certificate or affidavit so filed or deposited is prima facie evidence of the facts stated."

§ 15.2 PUBLIC RECORDS—RELEVANCY AND COMPETENCY

Naturally a public record cannot be admitted unless the facts contained therein are relevant, competent and material to the issue before the court. Conn.—City of New London v. Pequot Point Beach Co., 112 Conn. 340, 152 A. 136 (1930). The records which are admissible under this exception to the hearsay exclusionary rule are those to which the public officer would be able to testify to were he called as a witness. They must deal with observed facts. U.S.—Vanadium Corp. of America v. Fidelity & Deposit Co. of Md., 159 F.2d 105 (C.C.A. 2d Cir. 1947).

§ 15.3 PUBLIC RECORDS—PUBLIC CHARACTER

The public record must be essentially public in nature. If they are really private records they may not be admitted into evidence. For example, an entry in the books of a poor person's asylum, made by an unknown person, not in the regular course of entrant's business with respect to the date of a child's birth and the name of the mother was held to be inadmissible to prove pedigree. R.I.—Budlong v. Budlong, 48 R.I. 144, 136 A. 308 (1927).

However, records which a private person is required to make and file with the government may be admissible as public records. C.J.S. Evidence § 626, Pa.—Harrison v. Metropolitan Life Ins. Co., 168 Pa.Super. 474, 79 A.2d 115 (1911).

A statement recorded in a death certificate that a decedent committed suicide, where there was no witness to the occurrence, is a mere opinion and it is not admissible in a trial of a case where the issue was the fact of the suicide. See Carson v. Metropolitan Life Ins. Co., 156 Ohio St. 104, 100 N.E.2d 197 (1951), for a discussion of this rule.

§ 15.4 PUBLIC RECORDS—BIRTH, DEATH AND MARRIAGE CERTIFICATES

In all of the states, birth, death and marriage certificates are required to be filed with the official who has custody of vital statistics. Ordinarily, a physician, a clerk or a clergyman who may not be a public official is the person who prepares these documents. Authorities, however, differ as to the extent to which birth, death and marriage certificates are admissible to prove matters other than the fact of the event and the date thereof. There is authority that these records are not to be used in litigation between private parties of the facts recorded because they are only kept tu assist officials in the conduct of the affairs of their office. Neb.—Sovereign Camp W. W. v. Grandon, 64 Neb. 39, 89 N.W. 448 (1902).

§ 15.5 PUBLIC RECORDS OF A SISTER STATE

Public records of sister states may be admissible in courts of your state but they must be properly authenticated. Even though copies of records of other states are sworn to, they may not be received in evidence until it is demonstrated that these records were kept in accordance with law. Ohio—Richmond v. Patterson, 3 Ohio 368. For example, it has been held that in order to permit the introduction in evidence of a certified copy of the record of the incorporation of a corporation in another state, that the laws of such state authorizes its incorporation. Mont.—Harvey E. Mack Co. v. Ryan, 80 Mont. 524, 261 Pac. 283 (1927).

The records of a sister state must have authentication by the custodian of the record. This must be done by affixing a certification with his signature and seal of his office to the document. In the legal profession, this is commonly referred to as an authentication flag. It has also been held that a copy of a record which is attested by a clerk and which did not have a certificate of the secretary of state, judge or other designated official stating that the attestation of the clerk is in proper form and that he has proper authority, was not received in evidence. Mass.—Bay State Wholesale Drug Co. v. Whitman, 280 Mass. 188, 182 N.E. 361 (1932).

The purpose of the authentication requirements is to guarantee that the original record really exists, as exemplified. This is accomplished by the following:

1. show authority of person certifying record;
2. that s/he is present incumbent and keeper of the record;
3. that the signature is genuine;
4. that the seal is genuine.

The same general rules apply to public records of foreign countries as well as state records in federal courts.

§ 15.6 AUTOPSY REPORTS

As the knowledge of medicine and forensic science increases, it becomes increasingly important to the criminal justice community to have the reports of autopsies included in the trial record to "wrap up" a case against a defendant. These autopsy reports are admissible in evidence under the public documents exception to the hearsay exclusionary rule. They could also find their way into the trial record through the business records exception to the hearsay exclusionary rule. The results of an autopsy have been permitted into evidence in Ala.—Simon v. State, 108 Ala. 27, 18 So. 731 (1896); Tex.—McClelland v. Great Southern Life Ins. Co., 220 S.W.2d 515 (Civ.App.1949).

§ 15.7 JUDICIAL RECORDS

A witness may be asked by the prosecuting officer whether he had ever been convicted of a crime. If s/he answers in the negative, the prosecuting officer has the obligation to produce evidence to the contrary if he is aware of it. The question is asked of the witness for the purpose of inquiring into his/her credibility, not his/her character. In New York, this is accomplished by the offering into evidence of a certificate issued by a criminal court, or the clerk thereof, certifying that a judgment of conviction against a designated defendant has been entered in such court, constitutes presumptive evidence of the facts stated in such certificate. CPL § 60.60(1).

§ 15.8 FINGERPRINT RECORDS

It is not uncommon for fingerprint records to be introduced into evidence in a criminal trial. These are public records even though they are not generally open to the inspection of the public without court order. In New York, the legislature has provided that a report of a public servant charged with the custody of official fingerprint records which contains a certification that the fingerprints of a designated person who has previously been convicted of an offense are identical with those of a defendant in a criminal action, constitutes presumptive evidence of the fact that such defendant has previously been convicted of such offense. CPL § 60.60(2).

§ 15.9 PROOF OF THE EXISTENCE OF A PUBLIC RECORD

Whenever a public record is taken from the office of its custodian, there is great danger that it will be lost, misplaced or destroyed. Accordingly the laws of most jurisdictions provide for proof of the existence of the public record by means of duly authenticated copies. Colo. —Landauer v. Huey, 143 Colo. 76, 352 P.2d 302 (1960); N.Y.—CPLR 4540, 4542 and also by the rules of common law CPLR 4543.

§ 15.10 EXEMPLIFIED COPIES

An exemplified copy of a public record is a copy which is made in the name of the sovereign power. For example:

The People of the State of New York,

TO ALL TO WHOM THESE PRESENTS SHALL COME OR MAY CONCERN,

SEND GREETING:

KNOW YE, That having Inspected the records and proceedings in our Surrogate's Court of our County of Queens, we do there find remaining

(The document exemplified is named here.)

[A7372]

№ 31 SPECIMEN COPY

STATE OF NEW YORK, } ss.:
COUNTY OF QUEENS,

I, CHRISTOPHER J. GORMAN, Clerk of the Surrogate's Court of said County, do hereby certify that I have compared the foregoing copy of

(The document exemplified is named here.)

with the original thereof now remaining in this office, and have found the same to be correct transcript therefrom and of the whole of such original.

IN TESTIMONY WHEREOF, I have hereunto set my hand and affixed the seal of Office of the Surrogate of said County, this day of

(SEAL) , one thousand nine hundred and

Clerk of the Surrogate's Court.

STATE OF NEW YORK, } ss.:
COUNTY OF QUEENS,

I, LOUIS D. LAURINO, Surrogate of said County, and sole presiding Magistrate of the Surrogate's Court, do certify that CHRISTOPHER J. GORMAN, whose name is subscribed to the preceding exemplification, is the Clerk of the said Surrogate's Court of the County of Queens and that full faith and credit are due to his official acts. I further certify that the seal affixed to the exemplification is the seal of our said Surrogate's Court, and that the attestation hereof is in due form and according to the form of attestation used in this state.

WITNESS, my hand and the seal of said Surrogate's Court, this day of , one thousand nine hundred

(SEAL) and

Surrogate.

STATE OF NEW YORK, } ss.:
COUNTY OF QUEENS,

I, CHRISTOPHER J. GORMAN, Clerk of the Surrogate's Court of the County of Queens, do hereby certify that HON. LOUIS D. LAURINO, whose name is subscribed to the preceding Certificate is the sole presiding Magistrate of the Surrogate's Court of the County of Queens, duly elected, sworn and qualified, and that the signature of the said Magistrate to said Certificate is genuine.

IN TESTIMONY WHEREOF, I have hereunto set my hand and affixed the seal of the said Court this day of one thousand nine hundred and

(SEAL)

Clerk of the Surrogate's Court.

[A7373]

§ 15.11 CERTIFIED COPIES

A certified copy is a copy of an official document certified as correct by the person who has legal custody of the record or by any other official who is authorized by a statute to certify said document. This infers that the officer has compared the copy with the original and that it is a correct transcript therefrom and of the whole of the original. In some states the requirement of the authorizing statute requires these words to be spelled out. Particular procedural practices vary in each jurisdiction but usually the authorizing statute requires a certificate to be attached to the document signed by the legal custodian or duly authorized representative with his official seal affixed. In New York, when a certification is made by a county clerk, the county seal must be affixed. CPLR 4540(b).

§ 15.12 EXAMINED OR SWORN COPIES

An examined or sworn copy is a copy which must be proved by testimony of one who is on the stand as a witness in which he testifies that he has compared the copy with the original record, word for word, or who has examined the copy word for word, while another person read the original aloud to him. An examined copy can be authenticated only by proof of comparison with the original and not by proof of comparison with some other copy. 32 C.J.S. Evidence § 650, Tex.—Grimes v. Bastrop, 26 Tex. 310 (1862).

§ 15.13 METHODS TO PROVE A PUBLIC RECORD

At common law, public documents could always be proved by the most simple manner of examined or sworn copies indicated in the preceding paragraph. If the party wished to be more effective before the trier of the facts, he would use, in the alternative, an exemplified copy or a certified copy. As indicated above, New York is among the many states that have simplified the method of proving public records by providing particular methods of proving a public record by statute, CPLR 4540, 4541, 4542 and finally CPLR 4543 which permits proof of a fact or a writing by any other method authorized by any applicable statute or by the rules of evidence at common law. Parol evidence is usually not admissible to prove the contents of a public record but it is generally admissible to prove that the record does not exist or the record is silent as to particular acts or proceedings. Conn.—Mower v. State Department of Health, 108 Conn. 74, 142 A. 473 (1928); Fla.—Kent v. Knowles, 101 Fla. 1375, 133 So. 315 (1931).

§ 15.14 PRIVATE WRITINGS—REVISITED

In § 10.6 we discussed private writings in connection with the business record exception to the hearsay exclusionary rule. Private writings can also be considered when discussing the public documents exception because many writings, although private in nature, may become public. Private writings which might be public or quasi-public in nature may consist of such things as corporate instruments, checks drawn on banks, church registers, baptismal registers and the like.

Writings such as those enumerated above must be proved to be genuine before they are admissible in evidence. The authenticity of the writing may be proved by testimony of anyone who was present when the writing was executed and saw the paper signed by the necessary parties. The proof can also be adduced by circumstantial evidence. Mich.—Champion v. Champion, 368 Mich. 84, 117 N.W.2d 107 (1962); Ga.—Cotton States Mut. Ins. Co. v. Clark, 114 Ga.App. 439, 151 S.E.2d 780 (1967).

§ 15.15 FEDERAL RULE

Rule 803. Hearsay exceptions: Availability declarant immaterial

The following are not excluded by the hearsay rule, even though the declarant is available as a witness:

(1) . . . through (7).

(8) Public records and reports.—Records, reports, statements, or data compilations, in any form, of public offices or agencies, setting forth (A) the activities of the office or agency, or (B) matters observed pursuant to duty imposed by law as to which matters there was a duty to report, excluding, however, in criminal cases matters observed by police officers and other law enforcement personnel, or (C) in civil actions and proceedings and against the Government in criminal cases, factual findings resulting from an investigation made pursuant to authority granted by law, unless the sources of information or other circumstances indicate lack of trustworthiness.

(9) Records of vital statistics.—Records or data compilations, in any form, of births, fetal deaths, deaths or marriages, if the report thereof was made to a public office pursuant to requirements of law.

(10) Absence of public record or entry.—To prove the absence of a record, report, statement, or data compilation, in any form, or the nonoccurrence or nonexistence of a matter of which a record, report, statement, or data compilation, in any form, was regularly made and preserved by a public office or agency, evidence in the form of a certification in accordance with rule 902, or testimony, that diligent search failed to disclose the record, report, statement, or data compilation, or entry.

(11) Records of religious organizations.—Statements of birth, marriages, divorces, deaths, legitimacy, ancestry, relationship by blood or marriage, or other similar facts of personal or family history, contained in a regularly kept record of a religious organization.

(12) Marriage, baptismal, and similar certificates.—Statements of fact contained in a certificate that the maker performed a marriage or other ceremony or administered a sacrament,

made by a clergyman, public official, or other person authorized by the rules or practices of a religious organization or by law to perform the act certified, and purporting to have been issued at the time of the act or within a reasonable time thereafter.

(13) Family records.—Statements of fact concerning personal or family history contained in family Bibles, genealogies, charts, engravings on rings, inscriptions on family portraits, engravings on urns, crypts, or tombstones, or the like.

(14) Records of documents affecting an interest in property.—The record of a document purporting to establish or affect an interest in property, as proof of the content of the original recorded document and its execution and delivery by each person by whom it purports to have been executed, if the record is a record of a public office and an applicable statute authorizes the recording of documents of that kind in that office.

(15) Statements in documents affecting an interest in property.—A statement contained in a document purporting to establish or affect an interest in property if the matter stated was relevant to the purpose of the document, unless dealings with the property since the document was made have been inconsistent with the truth of the statement or the purport of the document.

(16) . . . .

CHAPTER XVI

REAL EVIDENCE

§ 16.1 INTRODUCTION

The student should differentiate between real evidence, circumstantial evidence, rule of evidence, positive and negative evidence, legal evidence, extrinsic evidence, direct evidence and the like. Not all of these terms are treated in this text so that it might be kept to a reasonable and practical size. The terms most often met by a law enforcement officer are, however, included. If the student wishes a definition of the terms indicated above that are not discussed in this book, s/he is referred to *Black's Law Dictionary, 4th Edition*, for further study.

It is thought however, that the student should be particularly familiar with the term "real evidence". This is evidence that can be presented to the trier of the facts to see, touch, smell or is generally perceptible to the senses. A book, a blood stained knife, a revolver, an inscription on a grave stone presented to the court by means of a photograph, or a photograph of a mutilated person, etc. could be characterized as real evidence. The judge has wide discretion in the admission of evidence generally but in particular in the cases where the display of the actual person or the photograph of a person or a scene may be so gruesome as to be prejudicial to any of the litigants s/he has wide discretion. In such cases the judge may require the witness to testify from his/her own mouth instead of exhibiting the gruesome subject to the trier of the facts.

§ 16.2 FOUNDATION FOR INTRODUCTION

It is of paramount importance to show the relevance of every item of evidence before it can be considered for admissibility. To satisfy this requirement, the object must be properly identified and it may also be necessary to show that the object exhibited to the jury is in substantially the same condition as it was at the time of the event in issue. N.Y.—People v. Flanigan, 174 N.Y. 356, 66 N.E. 988 (1903).

Its admission or exclusion rests largely within the discretion of the trial court. Ariz.—Arnold v. Frigid Food Exp. Co., 9 Ariz.App. 472, 453 P.2d 983 (1969); N.Y.—Riddle v. Memorial Hospital, 43 A.D.2d 750, 349 N.Y.S.2d 855 (1973); R.I.—Martin v. Estrella, 107 R.I. 247, 266 A.2d 41 (1970). Thus it is part of the trial judge's function to decide necessary preliminary questions of fact such as the identity of articles offered in evidence. Wyo.—Friesen v. Schmelzel, 78 Wyo. 1, 318 P.2d 368 (1958); U.S.—Walker Drilling Co. v. Phillips Petroleum Co., 417 F.2d 378 (Civ.App.Tex.1969), and having reached the conclusion that the information to be gained by inspection is relevant, the court decides whether the jury shall be granted or refused a view of real or personal property. Ill.—Tudor Iron Works v. Weber, 129 Ill. 538, 21 N.E. 1078 (1889).

§ 16.3 CRIME SCENE

Most law enforcement agencies have prescribed procedures to guide its personnel when a member of the force comes upon the scene of a crime. It is of paramount importance for the solution of the crime and for its ultimate legal prosecution to insure that there is no interference with the real evidence which may be found on the scene which may destroy its usefulness as evidence in a subsequent criminal action. Articles used in the commission of a crime or connected with it are admissible in evidence but the prosecution must show a connection between the article and the accused to show relevance.

Where a defendant was charged with conspiracy to commit a robbery that gave the appearance of involving a weapon, evidence of defendant's relation to guns found inside his automobile and that guns which could be used in the commission of such a crime were available to him, was relevant and admissible. U.S.—United States v. Vosper, 493 F.2d 433 (5th Cir. 1974), and in a United States Court of Appeals in Kansas it was held proof of possession of means or instruments to commit offense charged is probative. United States v. Leaphart, 513 F.2d 747 (10th Cir. 1975).

§ 16.4 EXHIBITION OF PERSONS AND OBJECTS

There is frequently an attempt in paternity proceedings to exhibit the child to the tribunal to show the resemblance between the respondent male and the child. This is an extremely prejudicial practice because if the race of the infant and the father is the same, there are usually some similar characteristics which an advocate can point out to prove his/her case. Some jurisdictions still permit the introduction of this evidence but the better view prevails in New York and most other states to exclude this type of evidence because the subject of human resemblance is deemed largely a matter of fancy and guesswork; and this is especially true concerning very young children. Department of Public Welfare of the City of New York v. Hamilton, 282 App.Div. 1025, 126 N.Y.S.2d 240 (1954).

On the other hand, objects which are relevant to the issues of the trial and are in the same condition as at the time of the occurrence, are admissible in evidence. When a tangible object is offered into evidence to prove its quality, character, or condition at the time of an earlier occurrence in issue, the article is relevant and competent only if its condition is substantially unchanged, so that its present condition fairly represents the past condition, but changes in condition which do not destroy the evidentiary value of the object do not prevent its reception. U.S.—United States v. Skelley, 501 F.2d 447 (7th Cir. 1974), certiorari denied 419 U.S. 1051, 95 S.Ct. 629, 42 L.Ed.2d 647.

§ 16.5 BLOOD STAINS

Forensic scientists have developed tests to identify blood stains to indicate the likelihood that the blood was the blood of a particular individual. Scotland Yard has been in the forefront of this investigation with respect to dried blood stains and further work was done by Professors Alexander Joseph and Jerome Metzner of John Jay College of Criminal Justice in their cooperation with Bryan J. Culliford of the London England Metropolitan Police entitled "Examination and Typing of Blood Stains in the Crime Laboratory". This is available from the United States Printing Office, Superintendent of Documents, Washington, D.C., under Stock Number 2700–0083.

The question is sometimes raised as to whether or not a specimen of blood is human or from some other animal. This can be determined and courts have accepted expert opinions with respect to this. Del.—State v. Miller, 14 Del. 564, 32 A. 137 (1895); Pa.—Commonwealth v. Crossmire, 156 Pa. 304, 27 A. 40 (1893).

Experts can determine by the shape of the blood stain, the circumstances of a murder. If the distance of the fall is short, they appear as round spots. If the fall is from a greater height, the drops have jagged edges. The greater the height the more jagged the blood drops will be. If the blood drops are not at right angles to the surface, forensic scientists can determine the movement of the donor of the blood. These and other facts about blood stains are known by the experts in this discipline. For the purpose of this text, however, it is sufficient to know that blood stains are admissible in evidence and experts can then be called to testify as to the probable significance and origin of these blood stains. See Neb.—Dinsmore v. State, 61 Neb. 418, 85 N.W. 445 (1901), for a discussion relating to expert opinion on the flow of blood.

§ 16.6 GARMENTS

Garments worn by a party to the court action which are logically relevant to the issues, are admissible in evidence. A landmark case, Warden v. Hayden, 387 U.S. 294, 87 S.Ct. 1642, 18 L.Ed.2d 782 (1967), is best illustrative of this point. In this case a suspected robber went into his house after being pursued, he disrobed and placed his outermost garments in a washing machine in the cellar of the premises. A constitutional search and seizure issue was also present in this case but this is not germane to the point illustrated at this juncture in this text. The garments were introduced in evidence after a proper foundation for their relevance was established.

§ 16.7 WEAPONS

If a defendant is accused of a crime of violence where a weapon was used, and he/she is found to possess a weapon at the time of arrest, the weapon is not necessarily admissible in evidence for proof that the defendant committed the crime for which s/he is charged. For example, if the victim was killed by a stab wound, the fact that the alleged perpetrator was found to have a .38 caliber revolver on his person at the time of his arrest, would not be relevant to prove that the defendant had stabbed the decedent to death.

On the other hand, wounds may be examined by experts who may testify to the kind of gun by which the wound was inflicted. Ky.—Franklin v. Commonwealth, 20 Ky.L. 1137, 105 Ky. 237, 48 S.W. 986 (1899). It follows naturally that if the expert can determine that a particular gun was the cause of the injury, the gun found on the accused which matches the description of the expert, would therefore be admissible in evidence because its relevancy is established.

§ 16.8 PHOTOGRAPHS

It has often been said that one picture is worth a thousand words. The admissibility of photographs however, must be very limited or the thousand words may convey incorrect conclusions to the trier of the facts.

A photograph must be properly authenticated before it is admissible. Authentication must be made by testimony of a witness who is well acquainted with the subject of the photograph to the effect that the photograph is a substantially true and faithful representation of the place, object or person sought to be described as it existed at the time pertinent to the inquiry. N.C.—State v. Strickland, 276 N.C. 253, 173 S.E.2d 129 (1970); Mo.—State ex rel. State Highway Commission v. Cone, 338 S.W.2d 22 (1960); Wyo.—Metcalfe v. Winchester, 72 Wyo. 142, 262 P.2d 404 (1953).

Posed photographs may also be admissible if they are properly authenticated. A person who sustains injuries to his body may take photographs of the injured portions of his body to show to the trier of the fact how the injured portion of the body looked after the injury. He, or someone in his behalf, would be required to testify as to when, where and how the photographs were taken to establish the relevancy. If the pictures are too gruesome, the judge may not permit their introduction but, if the photograph is gruesome, this will not, of itself, render it inadmissible. It is subject to judicial discretion. Fla.—Breeding's Dania Drug Co. v. Runyon, 147 Fla. 123, 2 So.2d 376 (1941).

§ 16.9 X-RAYS

An x-ray picture, which is properly authenticated in a similar manner to the way a photograph is authenticated, and shown to be accurate, may be admitted when it may aid the jury to understand the nature and extent of injuries sustained by the party to the action. Cal.—Wilburn v. United States Gypsum Co., 16 Cal.App.2d 111, 60 P.2d 188 (1936); Ill.—Cooney v. Hughes, 310 Ill.App. 371, 34 N.E.2d 566 (1941).

§ 16.10 MOTION PICTURES

How many times have we heard that motion pictures are taken of riot scenes, funerals of leaders of organized crime, and of plaintiffs in personal injury cases who claim total incapacity although they are photographed playing tennis?

Some states are videotaping trials to speed up the judicial process. Testimony is taken outside of the presence of the judge and jury. Objections are made to some of the testimony and the judge rules on the objections after a private viewing. The objectionable matter is deleted and the motion picture of the trial is shown to the jury minus the deleted material. The jury then determines the conclusion of facts. Florida, among other states, is accepting videotape motion pictures of the testimony of an expert witness taken in his/her own office.

All of these motion pictures, unknown at the common law, are admissible in evidence today. There is a great danger however, that cutting out of relevant material will effect the conclusion reached by the trier of the facts and this has to be closely monitored. Kansas—Millers' Nat. Ins. Co., Chicago, Ill. v. Wichita Flour Mills Co., 257 F.2d 93 (10th Cir. 1958). However, the admissibility of motion pictures is left largely to the discretion of the trial judge. Md.—State v. United Railway & Electric Co., 162 Md. 404, 159 A. 916, 83 A.L.R. 1307 (1932).

§ 16.11 ENLARGEMENTS

Enlargements of photographs sometimes become a practical necessity for the proper presentation of evidence. In this way, an enlarged photograph may be placed on an easel in the courtroom and an advocate can by means of a pointer, call the attention of the jury to certain aspects of the enlarged photograph. This can also be accomplished by projection of a negative of the photograph on a screen in the courtroom.

There can be no objection to the admissibility of an enlarged photograph providing it does not have a tendency to mislead. N.Y.—Jarvis v. L. I. Railroad Co., 50 Misc.2d 769, 271 N.Y.S.2d 799 (1966), affirmed 25 A.D.2d 617, 268 N.Y.S.2d 963; Ga.—Western & A.R.R. v. Reed, 35 Ga.App. 538, 134 S.E. 134 (1926). However, when the party who produced the enlargements was not present when the enlargements were made and there were variations not visible in the original, the enlargements were excluded. Pa.—Poelcher v. Zink, 375 Pa. 539, 101 A.2d 628 (1954).

The same rules prevail with respect to other enlargements such as handwriting exemplars, fingerprint pictures or x-ray negative enlargements.

§ 16.12 AERIAL PHOTOGRAPHS

The judge has discretion as to the admissibility of many items of evidence. This discretion however, must not be abused to become arbitrary, unreasonable and capricious. Great discretion is given to the jurist particularly in determining the admissibility of aerial photographs. If other evidence provides the trier of the facts with a sufficiently accurate comprehension of the subject matter, aerial photographs will be excluded. La.—Airway Home, Inc. v. Boe, 140 So.2d 264 (App.1962); Conn.—Trombly v. New York, New Hampshire & H. Ry. Co., 137 Conn. 465, 78 A.2d 689 (1951).

§ 16.13 DOCUMENTS

Naturally, documents are characterized as real evidence and are admissible when relevant and authenticated. For a thorough discussion of the admissibility of documents and case authorities, see Chapter X, supra.

§ 16.14 WRITINGS

Writings, like documents, are characterized as real evidence but it would be redundant to discuss their admissibility when it has been treated in Chapter X, supra. The student is likewise referred to the discussion of private and public writings as contained in that chapter.

§ 16.15 GRUESOME OR PREJUDICIAL

It has been previously stated in § 16.8 that if pictures are too gruesome, the judge may not permit their introduction, but if the photograph is gruesome, this will not, of itself, render it inadmissible. It is subject to judicial discretion. Fla.—Breeding's Dania Drug Co. v. Runyan, 147 Fla. 123, 2 So.2d 376 (1941). It could occur that a gruesome photograph, the subject of which was capable of testamentary exposition, is offered into evidence and the judge over objection permits its introduction. If it is so prejudicial against the party against whom it is offered, some argue that it is sufficiently prejudicial error so as to result in a reversal. However, the overwhelming weight of authority is to affirm the discretion of the trial judge as to the admission of gruesome photographs. Minn.—Hoffman v. Naslund, 274 Minn. 521, 144 N.W.2d 580 (1966); Wash.—Gephart v. Stout, 11 Wash.2d 184, 118 P.2d 801 (1941); N.H.—Zielinski v. Cornwell, 100 N.H. 34, 118 A.2d 734 (1956).

§ 16.16 NON-VISUAL

Real evidence has been defined as meaning a fact, the existence of which is perceptible to the senses. Vt.—McGrath v. Haines, 125 Vt. 49, 209 A.2d 479 (1965). If we then are referring to the senses, we are referring to perception as a result of outside stimuli, commonly referred to as the five senses of touching, hearing, seeing, feeling and tasting. If real evidence which is relevant is admissible in evidence, it therefore logically follows that such stimuli which will make a person perceive without the intervention of oral testimony that something was hot to the touch, or smelled like rotten eggs, or was a screeching sound, or felt like a sponge, or tasted sour, are the results of conclusions of perception and should upon proper foundation be admitted in evidence. Thus records which were played in the presence of a jury in a criminal prosecution were held to be admissible. Pa.—Commonwealth v. Clark, 123 Pa.Super. 277, 187 A. 237 (1936); also see N.Y.—Riddle v. Memorial Hospital, 43 A.D.2d 750, 349 N.Y.S.2d 855 (1973).

§ 16.17 MODELS, DIAGRAMS AND MAPS

Models, diagrams and maps, all of which are real evidence, may also be further subdivided to be defined as demonstrative evidence. Real evidence involves the production in court of some object which has a direct part in the incident and includes the exhibition of injured parts of the body, while demonstrative evidence involves the production in court of such things as models, maps, photographs or x-ray pictures which have no probative value in themselves but serve merely as visual aids to the trier of the facts in comprehending the verbal testimony of the witness. Tex.—Mapco, Inc. v. Holt, 476 S.W.2d 64 (Civ.App.1972).

§ 16.18 HANDWRITING EXEMPLARS

Examples of handwriting of a suspect for comparison with the handwriting of another document in evidence is another form of demonstrative evidence. The genuineness of a standard of comparison must be preliminarily and satisfactorily established and the discretionary action of the trial court in admitting or rejecting the standing will not ordinarily be disturbed. Pa.—Shannon v. Castner, 21 Pa.Super. 294 (1906). There is no violation of Fifth Amendment protection against self-incrimination in requiring a suspect to give handwriting specimens. U.S.—United States v. Mara, 410 U.S. 19, 93 S.Ct. 774, 35 L.Ed.2d 99 (1973).

§ 16.19 PAINT CHIPS OR STAINS

It sometimes becomes of crucial importance to show that a suspect was at the scene of a crime in the face of his denial that s/he was present. If paint chips or stains are detected in his/her clothing or in his/her hair, or other parts of his/her person, these specimens may lead to identification of the paint as being similar to the paint found at the scene of the crime. This can be done by microscopic spectographic diagnosis and microchemical analysis. This can be accomplished even with minute quantities of paint. The paint chip or stain is admissible in evidence subject to the connection of the testimony of the expert witness to explain its relevance to the issues of the case.

For a discussion of this, see Cardwell v. Lewis, 417 U.S. 583, 94 S.Ct. 2464, 41 L.Ed.2d 325 (1974).

§ 16.20 DUST

It may come as somewhat of a shock to the student that even dust could, in a proper case, be the subject of real or demonstrative evidence. Such was the case when in an action against an employer for illness resulting from poisoning, jars of dust collected from the room in which the employee worked were admitted into evidence. N.J.—Davis v. New Jersey Zinc Co., 116 N.J.Law 103, 182 A. 850 (1936).

§ 16.21 BLACKBOARD

Blackboards may be used in the presentation of evidence but under strict restrictions. For example, a witness may not write a copy of a disputed signature on a blackboard and then, by alleged copies of authentic writings institute a comparison between them and the copy of the alleged forged signature. Pa.—Groff v. Groff, 209 Pa. 603, 59 A. 65 (1904).

§ 16.22 ARTICLES USED IN CRIME

An article used in the commission of a crime might be a weapon, an automobile, a boat, an airplane, a disguise, or any number of articles of personal property which directly or indirectly aided the perpetrator in the implementation of the crime. If these articles have a direct part in the incident, they are admitted as real evidence. If they involve something that has no probative value in themselves but serve merely as visual aids to the trier of the facts in comprehending the verbal testimony of a witness, they may also be admitted if it is important for the jury to understand the significance of it and their display is explanatory. Ill.—Smith v. Ohio Oil Co., 10 Ill.App.2d 67, 134 N.E.2d 526, 58 A.L.R.2d 680 (1956).

§ 16.23 INTOXICATION TEST APPARATUS

A defense attorney in an intoxicated driver case may question the results of a drunkometer and may require the prosecution witness to reenact the test in court, subject to the discretion of the judge. However, where there is evidence of scientific tests such as a drunkometer test, for determining the amount of alcohol in the breath of a suspected intoxicated person, it is essential that the reliability of the tests and the results thereof be generally recognized and accepted before evidence thereof is admissible. Ala.—Rivers v. Black, 259 Ala. 528, 68 So.2d 2 (1953).

§ 16.24 EXPERIMENTS

There is the mythical story of a defense attorney who was defending a client accused of poisoning another. The lawyer showed the jury a bottle of the alleged suspected poison and in his attempt to prove that the solution could not kill a human being, he drank the solution in front of the jury, to the utter astonishment of all. A recess was immediately called and the attorney is alleged to have repaired to the men's room where his aide was waiting with an emetic to induce vomiting. Whether this ever happened is highly improbable but it is worth remembering to show that experiments may be conducted in the courtroom, but the situation must be substantially similar to the factual situation of the issue of the trial.

Generally, the result of an experiment or test is admissible on trial to show the nature, quality or tendency of an object, provided the conditions under which the experiment or test was conducted were sufficiently similar to those existing at the time in question. N.Y.—Washington v. Long Island Railroad Co., 13 A.D.2d 710, 214 N.Y.S.2d 115 (1961).

§ 16.25 CONTINUITY OF EVIDENCE

In police science, we know that there must be continuity of evidence or the evidence will not be admitted on trial. There is continuity of evidence if the law enforcement authority can demonstrate that the evidence is in the same condition at the trial as it was at the time the property came into possession of the police authority. Department regulations usually mandate that small articles be scratched with some identification mark such as the number of the officer's shield, or that they be placed in sealed envelopes and the officer write his signature and shield number over the flap so that if it is opened it will be visible to the eye. The officer is also required to testify what hands the evidence passed through. All of this is done to reasonably assure the trier of the facts that the evidence has not been altered in any way. This is also sometimes referred to as a chain of custody. Conn.—State v. Brown, 163 Conn. 52, 301 A.2d 547 (1973).

It can be generally said that the unbroken chain of possession must be demonstrated by calling each person who has had access to or possession of the evidence for the purpose of establishing identity and unchanged conditions, and such is particularly required if the sole proof of guilt rests on chemical analysis of a blood specimen or drug, and if such proof is available, but if circumstances provide reasonable assurances of identity and unchanged conditions and it would be an impossible requirement to produce each physical custodian as a witness, there can be a relaxation of such general rule. N.Y.—People v. Porter, 46 A.D.2d 307, 362 N.Y.S.2d 249 (1974).

§ 16.26 FEDERAL RULE

The Federal Rules of Evidence do not mention the term real evidence by name but in Rule 401 is found a definition of "relevant evidence" as being evidence having any tendency to make the existence of any fact that is of consequence to the determination of the action more probable or less probable than it would be without the evidence. In Rule 402, it is mandated that all relevant evidence is admissible, except as otherwise provided by the Constitution of the United States, by Act of Congress, by these rules, or by other rules prescribed by the Supreme Court pursuant to statutory authority. Evidence which is not relevant is not admissible.

Records, documents and process or system are specifically referred to in Federal Rules of Evidence 901, 902 and recording and photographs are covered in Rule 1001. Public records are found n Rule 1005.

Therefore, while the Federal Rules of Evidence do not specifically include all of the items discussed in this chapter on real evidence, each item is included by inference after reference is made to Rules 401 and 402.

CHAPTER XVII

PRESUMPTIONS

§ 17.1 INTRODUCTION

There is little doubt that anyone reading this page has not heard the much quoted phrase "A defendant in a criminal action is presumed to be innocent and his guilt must be established beyond any reasonable doubt." To state it another way, it means that there is an inference that a defendant is innocent and it is now up to the prosecution to rebut that inference and convince the trier of the facts beyond a reasonable doubt that this inference is not correct. It has been said that a presumption is a rule of evidence but it is also a rule of law as to which party shall first proceed and go forward with the evidence. It is an inference of the existence or non-existence of some fact which courts or juries are required or permitted to draw from the proof of other facts. Fla.—Nationwide Mut. Ins. Co. v. Griffin, 222 So.2d 754 (App.1969); Ill.—Flynn v. Vancil, 41 Ill.2d 236, 242 N.E.2d 237 (1969). Presumptions have been created in the law from motives of public policy and for the sake of greater certainty. Del.—Bailey v. Blodgett, 10 Terry 485, 119 A.2d 756 (1956). The inference is mandatory once the "basic fact" the fact which gives rise to the presumption is established on the trial. Model Code of Evidence Rule 701. This inference ("presumed fact") continues until it is overcome by sufficient evidence to the contrary. N.Y.—St. Andrassy v. Mooney, 262 N.Y. 368, 186 N.E. 867 (1963). Where the evidence rebutting a presumption presents an issue of creditability, it is for the jury to determine whether the rebuttal evidence is to be believed, and consequently for the jury to determine whether the presumption has been destroyed. N.Y.—Bornhurst v. Mass. Bonding & Ins. Co., 21 N.Y.2d 581, 289 N.Y.S.2d 937, 237 N.E.2d 201 (1968).

§ 17.2 CONSTITUTIONALITY OF PRESUMPTIONS

Many of the liberties which we enjoy have been brought about by lawyers who have argued vehemently in favor of their client. Often, their cause seemed to be doomed at the outset but in spite of criticism from the populous at large and also from many of their colleagues at the bar, they continued in their persistence for what they believed was right. Many times this has been done at great financial and physical cost to themselves and their families. These are the unsung heroes of our democracy. They were not always successful.

Statutes sometimes create presumptions unknown to the common law. For example, 18 U.S.C.A. § 545 makes possession of unlawfully imported goods sufficient for conviction of smuggling, unless explained, or in the New York Penal Law § 265.15(5) we find that the possession by any person of a defaced machine gun or firearm is presumptive evidence that such person defaced the same.

At first impression, one may think that statutes such as those indicated above are unconstitutional because they force the defendant to come forth with an explanation and hence might be a violation of the privilege against incrimination and due process of law prescribed in the Fifth Amendment and Fourteenth Amendment of the United States Constitution. The courts have ruled otherwise. Congress has power to provide in a criminal statute that proof of one fact shall constitute presumptive evidence of another fact. U.S.—United States v. Dimario, 473 F.2d 1046 (6th Cir. 1972), certiorari denied 412 U.S. 907, 93 S.Ct. 2298, 36 L.Ed.2d 972. The test of the validity of a presumption created by statute is that there must be a rational connection between the facts proved and the facts presumed. U.S.—United States ex rel. Rogalski v. Jackson, 58 F.Supp. 218 (D.C.N.Y.1944), affirmed 146 F.2d 251, certiorari denied 324 U.S. 873, 65 S.Ct. 1011, 89 L.Ed. 1427.

The New York Statute quoted was tested in People v. Russo, 278 A.D. 98, 103 N.Y.S.2d 603 (1951), affirmed 303 N.Y. 673, 102 N.E.2d 834, and it was found that the statute was rebuttable and was constitutional. There have been some later cases which hold that statutory presumptions which presume a defendant guilty by unexplained behavior, are unconstitutional as a violation of the Fourteenth Amendment Due Process Clause. See United States v. Gainey, 380 U.S. 63, 85 S.Ct. 754, 13 L.Ed.2d 658 (1965); United States v. Romano, 380 U.S. 942, 85 S.Ct. 1530, 15 L.Ed.2d 210 (1965).

§ 17.3 CLASSES OF PRESUMPTIONS

Presumptions have been divided into classes, they are:

a. presumptions of law;

b. presumptions of fact;

c. mixed presumptions;

d. rebuttable presumptions;

e. conclusive presumptions.

§ 17.4 PRESUMPTIONS OF LAW

A presumption of law is an inference, which in absence of direct evidence on the subject, the law requires to be drawn from the existence of certain established facts. 31A C.J.S. Evidence § 210. Generally, the effect of the presumption is to place the burden upon the adversary to come forward with evidence to rebut the presumption. A presumption of law has been said to be the only true presumption. Utah—Wyatt v. Baughman, 121 Utah 98, 239 P.2d 193 (1952). A presumption of law derives its force from law of the jurisdiction, not from logic or probability whereas a presumption of fact is mere inference. Tenn.—Berretta v. American Cas. Co. of Reading, Pennsylvania, 181

Tenn. 118, 178 S.W.2d 753 (1944). The rule that a mere presumption disappears in the face of rebutting evidence has no application where the legislature has directed that the establishment of one fact is prima facie evidence of another fact. Ariz.—Mitchell v. Emblade, 81 Ariz. 121, 301 P.2d 1032 (1956). A presumption of law may be created by statute if there is some justification of public policy. Mo.—Kellogg v. Murphy, 349 Mo. 1165, 164 S.W.2d 285 (1942). For example, the New York Penal Law § 265.15 reads as follows: "(1) The presence in any room, dwelling, structure or vehicle of any machine-gun is presumptive evidence of its unlawful possession by all persons occupying the place where such machine-gun is found." Other examples of presumptions of law in New York are presumption of disqualification under Education Law § 3022(2), presumption of regularity. N.Y.—People v. Langan, 303 N.Y. 474, 104 N.E.2d 861 (1952). We can thus observe that presumptions of law may be presumptions created by statutory law and presumptions created by case law (common law). The presumption is overcome when the adversary produces "substantial" evidence to the contrary. N.Y.—People v. Langan, supra. However, some presumptions require a higher degree of rebuttal evidence. For example, the presumption of legitimacy, the presumption of innocence, the presumption against suicide, the presumption of validity of marriage.

§ 17.5 PRESUMPTION OF FACT

A presumption of fact is that mental process by which the existence of one fact is inferred from proof of some other fact or facts with which experience shows it is usually associated by succession or coexistence. N.C.—In re Wall's Will, 223 N.C. 591, 27 S.E.2d 728 (1943). In one New York case it was held that a presumption of fact is no presumption at all. The court said that it is a term used to describe a logical inference which the trier of the facts is authorized, but not required to draw from the evidence in the case. Justice v. Lang, 52 N.Y. 323 (1873). Disputable presumptions are "rules about evidence" in that an inference is permissible whereas a "presumption" is mandatory and compels finding of a presumed fact in absence of evidence to the contrary. Me.—Hinds v. John Hancock Mut. Life Ins. Co., 155 Me. 349, 155 A.2d 721 (1959). A presumption of fact must be drawn from premises which are uncertain. Conn.—Savin Exp. Co. v. Hanover Fire Ins. Co., 132 Conn. 181, 43 A.2d 69 (1945); Fla.—Atlantic Coast Line R. Co. v. McIntosh, 144 Fla. 356, 198 So. 92 (1940).

An example which has been decided in this area was a case where the defendant was being sued for conversion of property. A suit such as this is the civil law equivalent of a larceny of property found in the criminal law. The distinction in the actions is that in the civil action the plaintiff is looking for a money judgment against the defendant whereas in the criminal action the government is looking for penal sanctions against the defendant. Armed with the above knowledge.

the student will understand the decision in N.M.—Williams v. Sinclair Refining Co., 39 N.M. 388, 47 P.2d 910 (1935), which held in an action for conversion of personalty contained in a gasoline filling station wherein there was no direct testimony showing what personalty was in the station when the defendant took possession thereof, and wherein the trial court found that the defendant converted personalty, the presumption that the property which the plaintiff had left locked in the station remained and continued in the same condition in which he left it is strong enough to warrant accepting as true a presumed fact that the defendant had possession of the property.

§ 17.6 MIXED PRESUMPTIONS

It sometimes becomes difficult to characterize a presumption as one solely of fact or solely of law. This occurs when a presumption of fact from its strength, importance or frequent occurrence becomes a quasi-presumption of law. Scholars have called this a mixed presumption of law and fact because the court lays down the law and the jury acts on it. N.C.—Lee v. Pearce, 68 N.C. 63 (1873).

§ 17.7 REBUTTAL PRESUMPTIONS

A rebuttable presumption is a type of evidence that may be accepted and acted on when there is no other evidence to uphold the contention for which it stands, but one which may be overcome by other evidence. Iowa—In re Weems Estate, 258 Iowa 711, 139 N.W.2d 922 (1966). The jury may determine if the presumption has been destroyed. N.Y.—Bornhurst v. Mass. Ins. Co., 21 N.Y.2d 581, 289 N.Y.S. 2d 937 (1968).

§ 17.8 CONCLUSIVE PRESUMPTIONS

A conclusive presumption, on the other hand, is one which is really a rule of substantive law, rather than an evidentiary rule. Cal. —Hagny v. Flournoy, 19 Cal.App.3d 496, 96 Cal.Rptr. 786 (1971). The rule with respect to conclusive presumptions rests on the ground of policy so compelling in character as to override the generally fundamental requirement of law that fact questions must be resolved according to proof. U.S.—United States v. Provident Trust Co., 291 U.S. 272, 58 S.Ct. 389, 78 L.Ed. 793 (1938). A conclusive presumption cannot be rebutted by other evidence. It is an inference which the law makes so peremptorily that it will not allow (it) to be overturned by contrary proof, however strong. N.Y.—Brandt v. Morning Journal Assn., 81 App.Div. 183, 80 N.Y.S. 1002 (1903), affirmed 177 N.Y. 544, 69 N.E. 1120.

§ 17.9 PRESUMPTION OF LEGITIMACY

The presumption that every person is born in wedlock from parents who were legally married to each other at the time of conception is a strong presumption of law. The presumption of legitimacy is now rebuttable although in early common law, it was not rebuttable.

The presumption may now be rebutted by evidence which establishes illegitimacy by "clear and convincing" evidence. N.Y.—Comm. of Public Welfare v. Ryan, 238 App.Div. 607, 265 N.Y.S. 286 (1933). Proof of a husband's impotency or of his lack of access, or a negative result of a reliable blood grouping test which is properly conducted, which excludes the husband as the father are types of proof which have been held to be clear and convincing. N.Y.—Foglio v. Foglio, 13 Misc.2d 767, 176 N.Y.S.2d 43 (1958).

§ 17.10 PRESUMPTION FAVORING LOVE OF LIFE

There is a presumption that a person wants to live unless there is evidence to the contrary. It is therefore presumed that no one will voluntarily do an act which will endanger his own life or the life of others. Iowa—Schofield v. White, 250 Iowa 571, 95 N.W.2d 40 (1959). Even in civil cases, where a person had been found dead, even with marks of violence, nothing else appearing, presumption is that decedent was not murdered. Tenn.—Nichols v. Mutual Life Insurance of New York, 178 Tenn. 209, 156 S.W.2d 436 (1942). In another case, murder was held not to be presumed from mere fact of killing by a gunshot wound. U.S.—McClure v. N. Y. Life Ins. Co., 50 F.2d 972 (D.C.La.1931). We can therefore say that there is a presumption against a person committing suicide and a presumption against a person wilfully taking the life of another. These presumptions are rebuttable in the same way as other presumptions can be negated.

§ 17.11 PRESUMPTION OF SANITY

Sanity is considered the normal condition of man. Every man is presumed to be sane until the contrary is proved. N.Y.—Jones v. Jones, 137 N.Y. 610, 33 N.E. 479 (1893). If a person is found to have committed suicide, the presumption of sanity is not overcome because the cases have held that sane men have taken their own lives. N.Y.—Weed v. Mutual Benefit Life Ins. Co., 70 N.Y. 561 (1877). In criminal cases, the presumption of sanity should disappear when substantial evidence to the contrary is introduced by the defendant. The burden of coming forward with evidence of insanity is upon the defendant. N.Y.—People v. Egnor, 175 N.Y. 419, 67 N.E. 906 (1903). New York has codified this burden of going forward by making insanity a defense. Penal Law § 30.05. Then the people have the burden of disproving this defense beyond a reasonable doubt—Penal Law § 25.00. However, once insanity has been established, it will be presumed to have continued. Fla.—Stanley v. Campbell, 157 Fla. 891, 27 So.2d 411 (1946); Mass.—Parry v. Parry, 316 Mass. 692, 56 N.E.2d 875 (1944); N.Y.—Rosario v. State, 42 Misc.2d 699, 248 N.Y.S.2d 734 (1964).

§ 17.12 PRESUMPTION OF MARRIAGE

When a marriage ceremony is performed, it is presumed that it was properly and legally performed. N.Y.—Fisher v. Fisher, 250 N.Y. 313, 165 N.E. 460 (1929), and that the marriage is continuing. Ky.—Kentucky Stave Co. v. Page, 125 S.W. 170 (App.1910). A stricter rule is apparent in criminal prosecutions than in civil actions. Accordingly in a prosecution for bigamy, there had to be direct proof of the marriage. N.Y.—Hayes v. People, 25 N.Y. 390 (1906). In New York, a marriage certificate is prima facie evidence of the marriage, CPLR 4526.

§ 17.13 PRESUMPTION OF CHASTITY

There is a presumption that people are moral and that they are chaste and virtuous, notwithstanding the modern concept of many persons, of reverse marriage, namely, the honeymoon, first, the living together, second, and the wedding, third, in order of occurrence. The presumption of chastity, however, may be rebutted by evidence to the contrary. Cal.—People ex rel. Bradford v. Laine, 41 Cal.App. 345, 182 Pac. 986 (1919). For example, Missouri Statute 559.300 provides "If any person over the age of seventeen years shall have carnal knowledge of any unmarried female, of previously chaste character, between the age of sixteen and eighteen years of age, he shall be guilty of a felony . . . ." The prosecutor, relying on the presumption of chastity, does not have to prove the female as being chaste. This is a rebuttal presumption which may be rebutted by the defendant.

§ 17.14 PRESUMPTION OF REGULARITY

There is a presumption in favor of the regularity and validity of private transaction. For example, in the absence of evidence to the contrary, the foreclosure of a mortgage, being shown is presumed to be regular and valid. Ala.—Williams v. Oates, 212 Ala. 396, 102 So. 712 (1925). There is also a presumption of regularity in favor of blood tests in absence of evidence that such tests call for unusual medical skill to make or interpret. U.S.—Wong Fuey Ying v. Dulles, 137 F.Supp. 470 (D.C.Mass.1956).

§ 17.15 PRESUMPTION OF VALIDITY OF JUDICIAL ACTS AND DUTIES

Where a court is one of general jurisdiction there is a presumption that the proceedings are regular and valid. N.Y.—Hiser v. Davis, 234 N.Y. 300, 137 N.E. 596 (1922); Cal.—In re Newman's Estate, 75 Cal. 213, 16 Pac. 887, 7 Am.St.Rep. 146 (1888). This presumption is conclusive unless it is impeached by the record itself, and it does not fall within the rule that presumptions are dissipated by contrary evidence and, hence, it was not affected by constrictive admission by demurrer of a charge in the bill to the contrary. Tenn.—McCartney v. Gamble, 184 Tenn. 243, 198 S.W.2d 552 (1947). No presumptions are permitted against the validity of judgment of a court of record. Tex. —Ex parte Kuehne, 111 Tex.Cr. 363, 12 S.W.2d 790 (1929). It is presumed that a judgment is valid and subsisting and was rendered only after a hearing according to law. Mont.—State v. Broadwater County Fourteenth Judicial District Ct., 51 Mont. 310, 152 Pac. 753 (1915). There is a presumption that a judgment roll was actually filed in the clerk's office, and that it contained the judgment appearing in the judgment book. N.Y.—Burke v. Kaltenbach, 125 App.Div. 261, 109 N.Y.S. 225 (1908).

§ 17.16 PRESUMPTION OF DEATH AFTER ABSENCE

The common law presumed that if a person was absent for more than seven years and has not been heard from in his usual places of contact, he is presumed to have died. This is important to establish civil rights of survivors. For example, an action may then be instituted to have the absentee declared dead so that a spouse may remarry, or his assets distributed to his beneficiaries or devisees, if he has executed a Last Will and Testament or to his distributees if he has never executed such a document. Some jurisdictions have shortened the period of absence to five years. N. Y. Estates, Powers and Trusts Law § 2–1.7. The presumption may be negated by proof showing that the alleged decedent is still alive. In Cal.—People v. Niccoli, 102 Cal. App.2d 814, 228 P.2d 827 (1951), a surety on a defendant's bond attempted to avoid forfeiture of bail and attempted to have the alleged decedent declared judicially dead. The petitioner introduced evidence that defendant had disappeared, after leaving his auto at an airport and that an extensive search had failed to locate him. Other evidence indicated that defendant had been indicted, was a member of a group who had been the subject of a murderous assault and the defendant had good reason to flee. The court upheld the forfeiture on the ground that where a motive or doubt as to the reason exists, the presumption of continued life remains.

The above decision raises a new point to be considered by the student. First, that the presumption of death is not conclusive and secondly, the situation that places one presumption against another. In such a situation, the law of evidence maintains that one presumption is stronger than the other presumption. In the instant case we see that the court held that the presumption of continuance is a stronger presumption than the presumption of death after unexplained absence.

§ 17.17 CONFLICTING PRESUMPTIONS—FIRST IMPRESSION

We have just seen that the presumption of the continuance of life was a stronger presumption than that of death after a period of years of unexplained absence. Rule 301(b) of the Uniform Rules of Evidence provides: "If presumptions are inconsistent, the presumption applies that is founded upon weightier considerations of policy. If considerations of policy are of equal weight neither presumption applies." § 17.32 (infra) explains this concept more fully.

§ 17.18 PRESUMPTION OF CONTINUANCE

The reader has been exposed to several situations supra, wherein the presumption of continuance has been indicated as a strong presumption. To this point, we have not defined what a presumption of continuance is. It is really an inference or a presumption of fact. Proof of the existence of a particular time of a fact of a continuous nature gives rise to an inference within logical limits, that it exists at a subsequent time. Mass.—Malden Trust Co. v. George, 303 Mass. 528, 22 N.E.2d 74 (1939).

Let us assume that four police officers are trailing a suspect and they find that the suspect enters a residential house that is unattached and has four sides to it with two doors leading to the outside. Each of the police officers station themselves in unobstructed view of all sides of the house and the suspect does not come out of the house until one and a half hours have passed. He then comes out the front door and is followed again by all police officers. The time between the hour and one half that he entered the house and the time that he exited from the house might be inferred as the time he remained in the house. The officers observed a known fact—i. e., he entered the house, and they did not see him come out until an hour and a half later. Based upon the presumption of continuance, it would be logical to infer that he remained in the house during this time. However, this is a rebuttable presumption of fact because if a later and recent inspection of the house would reveal a subterranean tunnel in the basement of the house, which leads to a location out of the sight of the officers, the presumption of continuance of a fact is negated.

§ 17.19 PRESUMPTION OF OWNERSHIP FROM POSSESSION

When an officer sees a person wearing an overcoat in a cold climate and there is nothing to make him suspicious of the person, the officer presumes that the wearer has ownership of the coat. However, this type of presumption has been held to be "the lowest species of evidence" in Rawley v. Brown, 71 N.Y. 85 (1877). It is merely presumptive and liable to be overcome by any evidence showing the character of the possession and that it is not necessarily as owner. If the custody and possession is shown to be equally consistent with an outstanding ownership in a third person, as with a title in the one having the possession, no presumption of ownership arises solely from such possession.

§ 17.20 PRESUMPTION OF INNOCENCE

In every criminal trial, the defendant is presumed to be innocent of the offense with which s/he is charged. This is based upon the common law but is reinforced by statute in most jurisdictions. This presumption means that the burden is upon the people to establish the guilt of the defendant beyond all reasonable doubt. This does not mean beyond all doubt for if this were so, it would be highly unlikely that a defendant would ever be convicted.

In Dodson v. United States, 23 F.2d 401 (C.C.A.4th 1928) the court held "that a presumption of innocence is not a mere belief at the beginning of the trial that the accused is probably innocent. It is not a will-o-the-wisp, which appears and disappears as the trial progresses. It is a legal presumption which the jurors must consider along with the evidence and the inferences arising from the evidence, when they come finally to pass upon the case. In this sense, the presumption of innocence does accompany the accused through every stage of the trial."

In some jurisdictions, the presumption of innocence is regarded as a matter of evidence in the case. (See notes 34 A.L.R. 938, 47 A.L.R. 968, 94 A.L.R. 1042, 152 A.L.R. 626.) It is customary to charge the jury concerning the burden of proof, that the defendant is presumed to be innocent.

This presumption of innocence applies to civil as well as criminal cases. Cal.—Guidera v. Lapiana, 52 Cal.App. 460, 199 Pac. 557 (1921); Ariz.—State v. Miranda, 3 Ariz.App. 550, 416 P.2d 444 (1966); N.J.—Michaels v. Michaels, 91 N.J.Eq. 408, 110 A. 573 (1920). The presumption of innocence is not a presumption of law in some jurisdictions but is evidentiary. It regulates the burden of the evidence. Cal.—Alford v. Bello, 130 Cal.App.2d 291, 278 P.2d 962 (1955). It therefore is considered to be a mixed presumption of law and fact. However, many jurisdictions have made this a presumption of law. N.Y.—CPL § 300.10(2). The presumption means that the burden is always on the prosecution to establish the guilt of the accused beyond a reasonable doubt.

The defendant is entitled to rest upon the presumption of innocence in his favor until this presumption is so far outweighed by the evidence offered by the prosecution that the jury is convinced of his guilt beyond a reasonable doubt. He need not take the stand in his own defense and no inference is to be drawn by his failure to take the stand, if so requested by the defendant. N.Y. CPL § 300.10(2).

§ 17.21 PRESUMPTION THAT MAIL DEPOSITED IN POST OFFICE IS RECEIVED BY ADDRESSEE

There is a presumption that mail, properly addressed and placed in a post office collection box with postage prepaid is presumed to have been received by the addressee. There must be satisfactory proof that it was duly mailed. N.Y.—James E. Cashman, Inc. v. Spellman, 233 App.Div. 45, 251 N.Y.S. 240 (1931). This is a rebuttal presumption by evidence that it was not in fact delivered or received. Pa.—Teitelbaum v. Board of Revision of Taxes, 65 Pa.D. & C. 619 (1947). The proof of due mailing need not consist of direct and positive testimony to the fact of mailing. Proof of the existence of an office practice or custom in the mailing of letters, together with proof that the custom was followed in the particular instance may constitute sufficient evidence of mailing to support a presumption of due receipt. 31A C.J.S. Evidence § 136.

§ 17.22 PRESUMPTION OF GUILT FROM POSSESSION OF FRUITS OF CRIME

The recent and exclusive possession of the fruits of a crime, if unexplained, justifies the inference of guilt. This rule is applicable to all crimes. N.Y.—Knickerbocker v. People, 43 N.Y. 177 (1877); People v. Roman, 12 N.Y.2d 220, 238 N.Y.S.2d 665, 188 N.E.2d 904 (1963). This is a presumption of fact and not of law because the jury is permitted to draw the inference. Let us suppose that an automobile is wanted on a stolen vehicle alarm. The police officer on patrol is alerted and he sees an automobile meeting the description of the wanted car. He also observes two young men in the car and it is being operated by one of them. The alarm has been transmitted within 24 hours prior to the officer viewing the vehicle. There is a strong presumption that the occupants of the vehicle stole the automobile. After being apprehended and brought to court, the defendant who was driving the vehicle takes the stand and testifies that he rented the vehicle from a car rental agency and he was of the opinion that he could keep it an additional week without notifying the car rental agency. He also testified that the extra week had not yet passed when he was arrested. He then had no intention of stealing the vehicle and this negates larcenous intent. He did, however, breach a contractual relationship and in New York State, as well as some others, he would be guilty of an offense of unauthorized use of a motor vehicle, a class A misdemeanor punishable, upon conviction by up to $1,000 fine and/or up to one year in prison. His passenger, might testify that he had no knowledge of the unauthorized use but did know that the vehicle was a rented vehicle. The jury might determine that the passenger was not guilty of any crime.

The preceding case probably would never come to trial in a practical situation because after hearing the facts and if believed by the District Attorney or State Attorney, s/he would probably ask the court to dismiss the charges against the passenger on condition that the defendant release civilly all persons who might be responsible for his incarceration. The prosecutor would most likely then recommend the acceptance of a plea to a class B misdemeanor (in New York) for which there might be criminal sanctions of up to three months in jail and/or a fine of $500 as well as other sanctions with a recommendation to the court that the driver be fined. The complainant would still have a civil remedy available for breach of contract. This dual remedy is contrary to the common law, in that in common law, the complainant must select either a civil remedy or the criminal remedy, not both. In New York as well as many other jurisdictions, the legislature has passed statutes in derogation of the common law which makes both civil and criminal remedies available to person aggrieved. N.Y. Penal Law § 5.10(3), N.Y. C.P.L.R. 106.

§ 17.23 PRESUMPTION FROM FLIGHT

When an officer arrives at the scene of a reported crime and s/he observes persons running from the scene, his/her first impulse is that the running persons have committed the crime and are running from the scene. After further reflection one may understand that there may be other reasons for the flight. Perhaps the one who is running is trying to save his/her own physical life, or s/he is trying to save his/her marital life (s/he might have been in the wrong place at the wrong time), or his/her political life for the same preceding reasons. S/He might have run instinctively without realizing why.

All of the above circumstances tend to explain that most states do not consider flight of the accused as a legal presumption of guilt although it may be introduced as evidence of guilt. N.M.—State v. Rodriguez, 23 N.M. 156, 167 Pac. 426 (1917). Some states consider flight or concealment as an admission of guilt but such evidence is very weak and has no weight whatever unless there are facts pointing to the motive which prompted it. N.Y.—People v. Reddy, 261 N.Y. 479, 185 N.E. 705, 87 A.L.R. 763 (1933).

§ 17.24 PRESUMPTION OF CONSTITUTIONALITY OF LEGISLATIVE ACTS

When a legislative body, be it the Congress of the United States, the Legislature of the State, a City Council or Board of Selectmen, enacts a statute, the courts have held that there is a presumption that the statute is constitutional. This, of course, is a rebuttable presumption. It therefore becomes the burden of a person or group of persons who may test the constitutionality of the statute to overcome the presumption by clearly overcoming the evidence sustaining its constitutionality. N.Y.—Wasmuth v. Allen, 14 N.Y.2d 391, 252 N.Y.S.2d 65 (1964).

§ 17.25 PRESUMPTION OF REGULARITY OF OFFICIAL ACTS

Let us assume that a hypothetical law requires that a legislative bill shall be considered for "x" days before it is enacted and then it is sent to the Governor of the state and should be signed by the Governor within "y" days. Once this bill is signed into law and is entered on the laws of the state, there is a presumption that all of the requirements of proper enactment were adhered to. This, again, is a rebuttable presumption. Another way of saying this is that it is presumed that a public official properly and regularly discharges his duties or performs acts required by law in accordance with the law and the authority conferred on him. W.Va.—State ex rel. Smith v. Boles, 150 W.Va. 1, 146 S.E.2d 585 (1966); Vt.—In re Waterhouse, 125 Vt. 202, 212 A.2d 696 (1965). This presumption is a very strong one and prevails until overcome by clear and convincing evidence to the contrary. U.S.—United States v. Chemical Foundations Inc., 272 U.S. 1, 47 S.Ct. 1, 71 L.Ed. 131 (1926).

§ 17.26 PRESUMPTION FROM FAILURE TO CALL A WITNESS

If a material witness is available to be called to testify on behalf of a litigant and this witness is not called, the fact might be called to the attention of the trier of the facts. The trier of the facts might be persuaded that the reason that this witness was not called is that if s/he did testify, his/her testimony would not support the position of the party who failed to call him/her. This is a very dangerous assumption however, because there might have been other reasons to prevent the calling of this witness. The witness might not be articulate; s/he may be mentally unsound; under a legal prohibition, s/he might be extremely nervous; or s/he might be suffering from some disease or impediment which would, when the totality of the circumstances are considered, preclude calling this witness to the stand. Nevertheless, there is a general presumption that in the absence of explanation, the failure to call a witness may create an inference against such party where the witness is available. Conn.—Raia v. Topehius, 165 Conn. 231, 332 A.2d 93 (1973); R.I.—Benevides v. Canario, 111 R.I. 204, 301 A.2d 75 (1973); Wash.—Roghrust v. Seto, 2 Wash.App. 215, 467 P.2d 204 (1970).

§ 17.27 PRESUMPTION FROM WITHHOLDING EVIDENCE

If material evidence is peculiarly in the control of a litigant and that litigant fails to introduce it at trial, or at the very least, fails to attempt its introduction at trial, it is natural for the trier of the facts to conclude that s/he must be hiding something which would cause them to decide the case against the person who acts in this manner. In the absence of an explanation, the failure or refusal of a party to produce evidence may create an adverse inference where such evidence is within his knowledge. Cal.—Am.-Cal. Inv. Co. v. Sharlyn Estates, Inc., 255 Cal.App.2d 526, 63 Cal.Rptr. 518 (1967); Nev.—Ewing v. Sargent, 87 Nev. 74, 482 P.2d 819 (1971).

§ 17.28 PRESUMPTION OF IDENTITY OF PERSON BY IDENTITY OF NAME

In the United States, composed as it is of so many ethnic, religious and racial groups, it is not an unreasonable presumption that a person who has the same name as you, and has the same middle initial, is, in fact, you. This is a rebuttable presumption but nevertheless is a reasonable presumption in this country. I hasten to limit this presumption to this country because many other countries have problems with this because of so many persons who have the same name, residing there.

There are countries in Europe where telephone directories of names are followed by the employment of the individual so as to differentiate the identity of the persons. However, if we carried this concept a little further, we could have a name like Johannes Schmitt, the baker, and we could presume that a certain Johannes Schmitt who is a baker and resides in that town is the person who we think he is.

This presumption is stronger in civil cases than in criminal actions. Identity of name is not always sufficient in criminal prosecutions to show the identity of a person, but it may be accepted as sufficient, if fortified by circumstances. N.Y.—People v. Reese, 258 N.Y. 89, 179 N.E. 305, 79 A.L.R. 1329 (1932).

§ 17.29 PRESUMPTION OF KNOWLEDGE OF THE LAW

As a practical matter if there was no presumption that everyone knew the law, malefactors might violate the law with impunity if they merely indicated that they did not know that their behavior was a breach of the law. Admittedly, this author is hard pressed to explain why the U. S. Supreme Court in Miranda v. Arizona, 384 U.S. 436, 86 S.Ct. 1602, 16 L.Ed.2d 694 (1966), made it mandatory for law enforcement officers to advise every prisoner immediately upon initiating custodial interrogation, about his rights to the retention of a lawyer and to remain silent, etc. if we all are presumed to know the law. Nevertheless, in other areas the courts have held that as a general rule, subject to qualifications, all persons are presumed to know, and are bound to take notice of the general public laws of the country or state in which they have residence or do business. Ga.—Grady County v. Banker, 81 Ga.App. 701, 59 S.E.2d 732 (1950); Mo.—Thies v. St. Louis County, 402 S.W.2d 376 (1966); Minn.—City of Bloomington v. Munson, 300 Minn. 195, 221 N.W.2d 787 (1974).

§ 17.30 PRESUMPTION OF REGULARITY OF ACTS DONE IN THE COURSE OF BUSINESS

Like the presumption explained above with reference to the regularity of official acts (§ 17.25), so too, there is a presumption of regularity of acts done in the regular course of business. Therefore, if a clerk usually completes a sales slip and includes the name of a purchaser on that sales slip, and the name is given to that clerk by the vendee, there is a presumption that the clerk placed the correct name on that sales slip. In the absence of a showing to the contrary, it is presumed that the ordinary course of business or conduct was followed in a particular case. Ark.—Les-Bil, Inc. v. General Waterworks Corp., 511 S.W.2d 166 (1974); Del.—David J. Greene & Co. v. Dunhill Intern., Inc., 249 A.2d 427 (Ch.1969); Fla.—In re Sackett's Estate, 171 So.2d 906 (App.1965).

§ 17.31 PRESUMPTION—RES IPSA LOQUITUR

Res Ipsa Loquitur is a Latin term which may be defined literally as "the thing speaks for itself". It is applied in the negligence aspect of civil law to be a rule of evidence whereby negligence of the alleged wrongdoer may be inferred from the mere fact that the accident happened, that the instrumentality of the accident was under the exclusive control or management of the alleged wrongdoer and that one could reasonably believe that in the absence of negligence, the injury would not have occurred. In effect, then, the doctrine creates a presumption that the alleged wrongdoer was at fault and he has to come forward with evidence to show that he was not at fault. Cal.—Bauhofer v. Crawford, 16 Cal.App. 676, 117 Pac. 931 (1911).

§ 17.32 CONFLICTING PRESUMPTIONS

No general rule can be laid down as to the effect of a particular presumption in the actual trial of a case, since this depends on the rule in the particular jurisdiction and the purpose the presumption is designed to serve. Conn.—O'Dea v. Amodeo, 118 Conn. 58, 170 A. 486 (1934). Where a presumption is a matter of public policy promulgated by a legislature, it disappears when substantial evidence of facts are introduced which rebut the presumption, but where the presumption is founded on the laws of nature it will not be brushed aside by a mere contradiction. Ark.—Union Cent. Life Ins. Co. v. Sims, 208 Ark. 1069, 189 S.W.2d 193 (1945). Where a presumption is of unequal weight, the stronger will prevail. For example, we have already discussed the presumption of continuance. Let us assume that a couple were validly married; there is then a presumption that the marriage has continued. Let us further assume that one of the parties to the first marriage entered into a second marriage with a third person. There is a presumption of validity attaching to the second marriage. We thus have two presumptions in direct conflict with each other. In N.Y.—Apelbaum v. Apelbaum, 7 A.D.2d 911, 183 N.Y.S.2d 54 (1959), it was held, that the presumption of the validity of the later marriage is considered so strong as to place upon the party asserting the invalidity of the second marriage the burden of proving that the first marriage had not ended before the second marriage.

The above example only considered two contradictory presumptions. The student can well understand that there are many presumptions which might come into conflict with each other and a general rule is difficult to arrive at, which will cover all situations.

§ 17.33 EFFECT OF PRESUMPTIONS AS A SUBSTITUTE FOR EVIDENCE

It is quite simple to understand that when one party has a presumption favoring his position s/he does not have to introduce evidence to substantiate his/her position. If there are two persons in an automobile and a gun illegally possessed is found on the floor of this automobile by a policeman, in most states there is a statutory presumption that all persons in the automobile illegally possessed that gun. The prosecutor is not charged with the responsibility of introducing proof at the trial that each of the occupants possessed the gun knowingly that it was illegally possessed. In this hypothetical case, we additionally call upon the common law presumption of knowledge of the law of the state or county by all persons residing or doing business in that place.

We then use presumptions as a substitute for evidence. This shifts the burden of going forward with the evidence to the other litigant. Note, however, that in a criminal trial the burden of proving the defendant guilty beyond any reasonable doubt always remains on the prosecution but the burden of going forward with the evidence may shift to the defendant because of the use of presumptions by the prosecutor. The burden of proof is not affected by a presumption. Fla.—Leonetti v. Boone, 74 So.2d 551 (1954); Ill.—Lucas v. Bowman Dairy Co., 50 Ill.App.2d 413, 200 N.E.2d 374 (1964). The Federal Rules of Procedure provide in Rule 301 that in civil cases a presumption imposes on the other party the burden of going forward. While no federal statutory rule exists at the time of this writing with respect to criminal cases, the common law rule to the same effect is used.

§ 17.34 PRESUMPTION—FEDERAL RULE

The Federal Rules of Evidence have included sections on presumptions after much deliberation. They are as follows:

Rule 301. Presumptions in general in civil actions and proceedings

In all civil actions and proceedings not otherwise provided for by Act of Congress or by these rules, a presumption imposes on the party against whom it is directed the burden of going forward with evidence to rebut or meet the presumption, but does not shift to such party the burden of proof in the sense of the risk of nonpersuasion, which remains throughout the trial upon the party on whom it was originally cast.

Rule 302. Applicability of state law in civil actions and proceedings

In civil actions and proceedings, the effect of a presumption respecting a fact which is an element of a claim or defense as to which State law supplies the rule of decision is determined in accordance with State law.

Originally a proposed Rule 303 was to be adopted to include presumptions in criminal cases. This was not adopted by Congress and the Advisory Committee's notes indicate that there are presumptions spelled out in specific criminal statutes and that differences between the permissible operation of presumptions against the accused in criminal cases and in other situations prevent the formulation of a comprehensive definition of the term presumption and none is attempted . . . common law presumptions continue. This may be changed in the near future by the Committee to revise the Federal Criminal Code.

CHAPTER XVIII

JUDICIAL NOTICE

§ 18.1 INTRODUCTION

In every trial, one of the parties has the burden of proof. In a criminal trial the burden is on the prosecution to prove the defendant's guilt beyond a reasonable doubt. Sometimes the burden shifts to a slight degree. For example, in some jurisdictions if the defendant raises a defense that he/she is an infant and therefore incapable of committing the crime, the prosecution must disprove this defense beyond a reasonable doubt. If the defendant raises the defense of insanity in some jurisdictions it is characterized as a defense and the burden remains with the people to disprove the defense beyond a reasonable doubt. New York Penal Law § 25.00. On the other hand, it is an affirmative defense in any prosecution for coercion committed by instilling in the victim a fear that he/she, or another person would be charged with a crime, if the defendant reasonably believed the threatened charge to be true and that his/her sole purpose was to compel or induce the victim to take reasonable action to make good the wrong which was the subject of such threatened charge. N.Y.P.L. § 135.75. In this case the defendant in New York and many other jurisdictions, would merely have to go forward with the evidence to establish his/her affirmative defense by a preponderance of the evidence. N.Y.P.L. § 25.00.

Let us assume that a home owner looks at his front door and finds drawings in crayon on it. He believes that a certain neighborhood boy did this as a prank and he finds the boy, accuses him of drawing with crayons, forces him bodily to the scene of the alleged crime and compels him to scrub the door until the crayon marks are removed. The boy returns to his home and tells his parents. The parents cause criminal charges to be placed against the home owner. One of the charges is coercion (i. e., compelling the boy to engage in conduct which he has a legal right to abstain from doing). Later investigation by the authorities revealed that another boy committed the act. The home owner could raise the affirmative defense of the fact that he reasonably believed the boy he coerced had committed the act of defacing his property. He need only do this by establishing this by a preponderance of the evidence.

However, since it is basic in a criminal case that the rule that the defendant is entitled to the benefit of a reasonable doubt applies not only to the case as made by the prosecution, but to any defense interposed. N.Y.—People v. Downs, 123 N.Y. 558, 564, 25 N.E. 988, 989 (1891). It therefore seems to be that the true rule is that if the defendant interposes an affirmative defense in some jurisdictions, the burden of coming forward with the evidence is on the defendant but the burden still remains with the prosecution to prove the defendant guilty beyond any reasonable doubt.

There are certain items of evidence which may be introduced into a trial which need not be proved. The reason that these items need not be proved is that it would needlessly prolong the trial and insult the intelligence of all concerned. The following need not be proved.

1. That which is admitted in the pretrial pleadings.
2. That which is agreed to by pretrial proceedings by means of a stipulation.
3. That which is admitted by the lawyer adversaries or their parties in open court.
4. That which is judicially noticed.

§ 18.2 PROOF NOT REQUIRED OF ADMISSIONS IN PRETRIAL PLEADINGS

Before a court case comes to trial, there may be exchanges between the lawyer adversaries of what are termed pretrial pleadings. These are more prevalent in a civil case than in a criminal case. However even in a criminal case, there may be some pretrial pleadings. The pleadings consist of writings which are written by the attorneys and are submitted to the court. For example, in the usual criminal case an affidavit is prepared which is sometimes known as a complaint or an accusatory instrument, charging the defendant with the commission of an offense or crime or other type of infraction of the law. The terms offense, violation, crime, felony, traffic infraction or violation may have a different definition in different jurisdictions and the reader is advised to consult his/her state's criminal laws for precise definitions of these terms in his/her own jurisdiction. However, basically all jurisdictions have formal written accusatory instruments. They may also be termed informations or indictments depending again on the jurisdiction and the severity of the legal infraction.

Sometimes the accusatory instrument is a general statement alleging misconduct by the defendant and indicating that the misconduct was a violation of a designated section of a statute. The defendant's attorney will then serve upon the prosecution what is known as a demand for a bill of particulars. Let us assume that an indictment charges a defendant with the unlawful possession of a firearm on a designated date at a designated place in violation of a section of a state statute.

The defendant's attorney may serve on the prosecutor and the Court Clerk a motion for a bill of particulars returnable at a future session of the court where s/he demands to know more about the allegation of misconduct in order to properly defend the defendant. S/He may ask such questions as follows:

1. The exact location and time of the day that the defendant is alleged to have possessed the firearms.

2. Whether or not defendant was alone or with others at the time of the apprehension?
3. If defendant was with others, the names and addresses of the others.
4. Was defendant in an auto or on foot or in a building at the time of apprehension?
5. If defendant was in an auto, what seat was he in immediately before the apprehension?
6. Whether the weapon was found on the person of the defendant or in some other place?
7. If the weapon was found in some other place, in what place was it found?
8. If the weapon was found in an automobile, was this a vehicle designed to carry merchandise as a public livery or was this a taxicab?
9. Was defendant operating this vehicle for hire or was he operating it not for hire or was he a passenger?

It is quite evident that the above list could be carried on much further but it would serve no useful purpose to the reader of this book for this to be done.

The court determines what it feels is necessary for the defendant to know to provide a defense and what is evidentiary and can only be brought out at the trial. The court will then direct the prosecutor to answer certain of the demands for a bill of particulars. Let us assume that the court directs the District Attorney to answer questions numbered 4, 5, 6, 7 and 9 among others and the prosecutor in writing, answers that the defendant was in an automobile in the driver's seat, that the weapon was found in the rear section of a taxicab where others were seated and that defendant was operating the vehicle for hire. If the prosecutor did not answer with these facts it would have been necessary for the defendant to have either himself/herself or other witness testify as to these facts in order to properly defend his/her claim that she/he was just a taxi driver in the wrong place at the wrong time.

In civil actions, as has been said, the use of admissions in pretrial pleadings is much more widespread. In some jurisdictions the case is begun by the service of a summons upon the defendant, followed by a notice of appearance and demand for a complaint from defendant's counsel to plaintiff's counsel. This is followed by service of a complaint upon the defendant's counsel, which in turn is followed by an answer to the complaint. Here too there may be a demand for a bill of particulars, which if it is not honored by the adversary is followed by a Notice of Motion for a Bill of Particulars returnable in court much the same as the criminal case's Notice of Motion for a Bill of Particulars. This may be followed by an examination before trial. These are all characterized as pretrial pleadings and certain admissions made in these papers need not be proven at the trial by witnesses. This shortens the trial without any injustice being done to either party.

§ 18.3 THAT WHICH IS AGREED TO BY PRETRIAL PLEADINGS BY MEANS OF STIPULATION

Let us return to our taxicab driver who was in the wrong place at the wrong time. It might be possible for the defense counsel to ask the prosecutor to stipulate (agree to a certain fact situation) that the defendant was operating a taxi as a taxi driver for hire at the time of the alleged wrongful possession of the weapon, that others were in the vehicle with him/her at the time, and that the weapon was found in the rear of the vehicle. If the prosecutor agrees to these facts the defense attorney may have this stipulation typed and both the defendant's attorney and the prosecutor will subscribe their names to the document. At the time of the trial, it may be read into evidence so that the trier of the facts will understand that these facts were agreed to and need not be proved by the testimony of witnesses. The reader may wonder why a prosecutor would agree to such a stipulation. The problem is that s/he does not believe s/he needs this to prove his case that the taxi driver was actually in a conspiracy with the passengers and on this point s/he expects to prove the defendant guilty of the offense.

§ 18.4 THAT WHICH IS ADMITTED BY LAWYER ADVERSARIES OR THEIR PARTIES IN OPEN COURT

Let us once again return to our taxi driver. If the defendant's attorney in open court, immediately before the trial, addresses the prosecutor thus: "Will the people stipulate that defendant John Doe at the time of the alleged commission of this offense was a driver of the ABC Taxi Corp.; that s/he was operating an auto owned by the said corporation which was a public taxi cab bearing license registration number 000000 for this state and that s/he was on duty as a public hack, and that other persons were in the rear compartment of the vehicle?" When the prosecutor answers "So stipulated," the result is that there has been a stipulation in open court of facts which need not be proved by the lengthy testimony of witnesses. Sometimes the defendant might stipulate that s/he was at a particular place at a particular time and this too might shorten the trial without any harm being done to the litigants.

§ 18.5 THAT WHICH IS JUDICIALLY NOTICED

When something is judicially noticed it is the same as a judicial shortcut or a doing away with evidence because there is no necessity for it. Cal.—Varcoe v. Lee, 180 Cal. 338, 181 Pac. 223 (1919). It is the cognizance of certain facts which judges and jurors may properly take and act on without proof because they already know them. C.J.S.

Evidence § 822. Judicial notice has been termed judicial knowledge. Wash.—State v. Brooks, 58 Wash. 648, 109 Pac. 211 (1910), or judicial cognizance. Ala.—Teat v. C. D. Chapman & Co., 1 Ala.App. 491, 56 So. 267 (1911). Generally speaking, judicial knowledge is limited to facts evidenced by public records and facts of general notoriety. N.J. —Mancuso v. Rothenberg, 67 N.J.Super. 248, 170 A.2d 482 (1961).

§ 18.6 JUDICIAL NOTICE OF STATUTES

Statutes often delineate matters of which courts may take judicial notice or shall take judicial notice. A close reading of the previous sentence will demonstrate that those statutes which indicate the word "may" leave the taking of judicial notice of their existence to the discretion of the court whereas those which use the word "shall," make it mandatory for the courts to take judicial notice of their existence. There is some divergence of opinion however in this area. Some courts have held that although a statute controls as to the matters of which a court will take judicial notice, its purport is merely that which a court may take judicial notice of those matters and things therein enumerated, it will do so only when requested and when they are relevant to some matter in issue. N.D.—In re McKee's Estate, 67 N.D. 504, 274 N.W. 601 (1937).

§ 18.7 JUDICIAL NOTICE OF MATTERS OF COMMON KNOWLEDGE

Courts may properly take judicial notice of facts that may be regarded as forming part of the common knowledge of every person of ordinary understanding and intelligence. Conn.—Muse v. Page, 125 Conn. 219, 4 A.2d 329 (1939); Fla.—State v. Sarasota County, 118 Fla. 629, 159 So. 797 (1935). For example, there is no person of ordinary understanding and intelligence who does not know that the Statue of Liberty is located in New York City's harbor and is a mecca for tourists visiting New York City. A court could therefore take judicial notice of this. It should be borne in mind that what might be proper subjects of judicial notice at one time may not be at another. Mo.—Calvin F. Feutz Funeral Home, Inc. v. Werner's Estate, 417 S.W.2d 25 (App.1967).

§ 18.8 METHOD OF ASCERTAINING FACTS JUDICIALLY NOTICED

Judicial notice of facts may extend to areas which are beyond the actual knowledge of the judge but he may ascertain these facts by resorting to any source which he feels would be helpful. He may require the assistance of the party to ask him to take judicial notice or he may investigate the matter himself or may use both methods. Ill.—Catlin, Village of v. Tilton, 281 Ill. 601, 117 N.E. 999 (1918).

In the process of judicial notice, a judge may seek sources of information to assist him, and in such process counsel of either side are entitled to offer materials containing the information, even though the judge may or may not rely on them or use them, and the judge may request the assistance from counsel, and for lack of such assistance, he may decline to notice the desired fact. Nev.—Choate v. Ransom, 74 Nev. 100, 323 P.2d 700 (1958).

The judge may refer to properly authenticated public official documents or records of all kinds, to dictionaries or publications or encyclopedias, or other books. N.Y.—Auerbach v. Mr. and Mrs. Foster's Place, 128 Misc. 875, 220 N.Y.S. 281 (1961).

§ 18.9 JUDICIAL NOTICE RESTS ON COURT'S DISCRETION

The power to take judicial notice is to be exercised by courts with caution, care must be taken that the requisite notoriety exists; and every reasonable doubt on the subject should be promptly resolved by the court not taking judicial notice. N.Y.—Berg v. Oriental Consol. Min. Co., 70 N.Y.S.2d 19 (1937); Fla.—Makos v. Prince, 64 So.2d 670 (1953). However, when the matter of judicial recognizance is one of law, the court is bound to take judicial notice of it. Fla.—Atlantic Coast Line R. Co. v. Holliday, 73 Fla. 269, 74 So. 479 (1917).

§ 18.10 FACTS AGREED—ADMITTED OR UNCONTROVERTED

Even though the respective adversaries agree or admit or if one party fails to controvert a fact in a pleading, the court may find the fact to be otherwise by resorting to its judicial knowledge. Wash.—Gottstein v. Lister, 88 Wash. 462, 153 Pac. 595 (1916), however judicial knowledge has been taken of the truth of matters admitted by counsel in his oral arguments. U.S.—Benesch v. Underwood, 132 F.2d 430 (C.C.A.6th 1943).

§ 18.11 JUDICIAL NOTICE OF STATUTES OR OTHER LAW

In general, a court will take judicial notice and apply the law of its own jurisdiction without pleading and proof thereof. Cal.—People by Mosk v. Lynam, 353 Cal.App.2d 959, 61 Cal.Rptr. 800 (1967); N.Y.—Souveran Fabrics Corp. v. Virginia Fibre Corp., 32 A.D.2d 753, 301 N.Y.S.2d 273 (1969). Accordingly, judicial notice is taken of the rules of common law. N.Y.—Stokes v. Macken, 62 Barb. 145 (1875), and the principles of equity. Tex.—Nimmo v. Davis, 7 Tex. 26 (1851). Doctrines established in England since the Declaration of Independence of the United States are not judicially noticed where their existence as constituting the law of England is in question. U.S.—Liverpool and G. W. Steam Co. v. Insurance Co. of North America, 129 U.S. 464, 9 S.Ct. 480, 32 L.Ed. 800 (1889). All laws of every state and territory of the United States and the District of Columbia have been judicially noticed. U.S.—Flanigan v. Security-First Nat. Bank of Los Angeles, 41 F.Supp. 77 (D.C.Cal.1941).

Judicial notice of a statute includes the history of its introduction to the legislature. N.Y.—Dale Engineering Co. v. State, 114 Misc. 233, 186 N.Y.S. 490 (1921), when it was passed and approved. Ind.—State ex rel. Rabb v. Holmes, 196 Ind. 157, 147 N.E. 622 (1925), when it went into effect. Fla.—Gaulden v. Kirk, 47 So.2d 567 (Sup.1950). Judicial notice cannot be taken of a law before the date on which it is to take effect. Mo.—State ex rel. Brunjes v. Bockelman, 240 S.W. 209 (1951).

Courts of equity will judicially notice the doctrines of equity jurisprudence and practice. Tex.—Nimmo v. State, 7 Tex. 26 (1851). Opinions of the attorney general have been judicially noticed. La.—Coco v. Jones, 154 La. 124, 97 So. 337 (1923).

§ 18.12 JUDICIAL NOTICE OF PUBLIC LAW OF SISTER STATES AND TERRITORIES OF THE UNITED STATES

In the absence of a statute to the contrary, courts will not take judicial notice of the laws of other states. Most states however, provide by statute or court rule that judicial notice be taken of the public law of sister states, territory or jurisdiction of the United States. N.Y. Rule 4511(a) CPLR. In the New York rule, the court is required, without request, to take judicial notice of the public laws of the aforementioned governments.

§ 18.13 JUDICIAL NOTICE OF THE LAWS OF FOREIGN COUNTRIES

The problem of judicial notice of the laws of foreign countries is similar to that of the states in that, unless otherwise provided by statute, the courts do not take judicial notice of the laws of foreign countries. The similarity is distinguished however by the states themselves. For example, New York State, by virtue of Rule 4511(b) of the CPLR directs that courts may take judicial notice of the laws of foreign countries or their political subdivisions. In effect, this statute is to give the court discretion even though another part of the same rule seemingly makes it mandatory for a court to take judicial notice of the laws of a foreign country or its political subdivision when a party requests such notice "furnishes the court sufficient information to enable it to comply with the request and has given each adverse party notice of his intention to request it." There are other requirements which are not pertinent to the purposes of this book but the word "sufficient" in the rule is so nebulous as to leave it to the discretion to the court.

§ 18.14 JUDICIAL NOTICE OF PRIVATE STATUTES

Sometimes laws are passed by legislatures which are specifically for the benefit of designated persons. These are not necessarily preferential laws but are usually passed to correct some injustice. For example, if a person is improperly convicted of a crime and incarcerated for a long period, the legislature may pass a specific private law which will in some measure indemnify the person for the injustice perpetrated on him/her. Such a law will be voted on, naming the subject person. Sometimes such a law is appended to some other bill currently before the legislature. These laws are called private statutes. It is however difficult to distinguish between a private and public statute. It may generally be said that a statute which affects the public at large is a public statute, and this is true although the statute is limited in its operation to a particular locality.

There is a general rule that the court may not judicially notice a private statute in the absence of a constitutional or statutory provision to the contrary. Fla.—Trustees of Internal Imp. Fund v. Claughton, 86 So.2d 775 (1956). This general rule is modified by statute in many states. New York State has modified it by CPLR 4511(b) which provides, in part, that the New York court may "take judicial notice without request of private acts and resolutions of the congress of the United States and of the legislature" of New York.

§ 18.15 JUDICIAL NOTICE OF COUNTY, TOWN AND MUNICIPAL LAWS, ORDINANCES, OR BY-LAWS

Generally, judicial notice of county, town or municipal laws, ordinances or by-laws will not be taken by the courts unless there is official sanction from the government. N.Y.—Rule 4511(a) CPLR or where there is an admission of the existence thereof by counsel. Ill.—Weber Co. v. Stevenson Grocery Co., 194 Ill.App. 432 (1895), or where the existence of the ordinance is so generally known that the court may notice it as a matter of common knowledge. R.I.—Town of Lincoln v. Cournoyer, 95 R.I. 280, 186 A.2d 728 (1963). Each jurisdiction may be different in this but the reader must begin with the premise that judicial notice of County, Town and Municipal laws are not taken, in accordance with common law principles, but this concept may be to the contrary if a statute is passed in derogation of the common law. In the case of municipal courts, trying municipal violations, generally judicial notice may be taken of municipal ordinances. Traffic courts involving traffic violations pursuant to municipal traffic regulations will take judicial notice of these regulations. Cal.—People v. Cowles, 142 Cal. App.2d Supp. 865, 298 P.2d 732 (1956).

§ 18.16 JUDICIAL NOTICE OF MATTERS OF FACT

The principals involving the judicial notice of matters of fact are not unlike those of judicial notice of matters of law in that they are judicial shortcuts to the proper administration of justice. Courts have been known to take judicial notice of the principal offices in their own state. 31 C.J.S. Evidence § 37, or official signatures or sales. Conn. —Creer v. Active Automobile Exchange, 99 Conn. 266, 121 A. 888

(1923), or the judicial notice of geographical facts such as the general distance between two cities such as to permit the accused to be at the scene of both the crime and the alibi on the same day. Ill.—People ex rel. Lejcar v. Meyering, 345 Ill. 449, 178 N.E. 80 (1931), or of scientific facts, such as the general reliability of radar speed meter as a mechanism for measuring speed of a moving vehicle thereby eliminating the need in each case, of testimony of an expert to explain the function, or scientific principles upon which the radar instrument relies for its calculation, or the course and laws of nature, such as the alternation of day and night, or the courses of the seasons. Ark. —Floyd v. Ricks, 14 Ark. 286, 58 Am.Dec. 374 (1853).

§ 18.17 JUDICIAL NOTICE OF THE TIME OF THE RISING AND SETTING OF THE SUN

Many times the main issue in a case is whether or not the sun had risen or fallen at a particular time. Statutes requiring a vehicle to be illuminated frequently refer to the terms "sunrise and sunset". Courts will however admit, not strictly as evidence but merely for the ostensible purpose of refreshing the court's recollection, any reputable almanac containing tables giving the periods of the rising and setting of the sun and moon on each day of the year. N.Y.—Montenes v. Metropolitan Street Ry. Co., 77 App.Div. 493, 78 N.Y.S. 1059 (1902). Weather reports issued by the United States Weather Bureau however, are in themselves admissible in evidence in N.Y. CPLR 4528. These reports contain other information besides precipitation and temperature reports. They also include the time of sunrise and sunset and other pertinent information.

§ 18.18 JUDICIAL NOTICE OF ORDINARY AND GENERALLY ACCEPTED MEANING OF ENGLISH WORDS

You will recall at the introduction of the chapter dealing with judicial notice, it was written that there were certain items of evidence which may be introduced into a trial which need not be proved. It was also written that the reason that these items need not be proved is that it would needlessly prolong the trial and insult the intelligence of all concerned (§ 18.1, infra.) Can you imagine to what lengths a trial might go if every word that was used in the testimony required a dictionary definition to cause the trier of the facts to better understand the issues? Naturally, it would be ridiculous to permit this sort of thing in the conduct of a trial. Accordingly it has been held that courts may take judicial notice of the meaning of words and phrases. N.Y.—Turner-Looker Co. v. Aprile, 195 App.Div. 706, 187 N.Y.S. 367 (1921), affirmed 234 N.Y. 517, 138 N.E. 429. When a witness testifies that he saw a railroad train coming along the track at a fast rate of speed, everyone knows that it consisted of a vehicle or vehicles operating on steel tracks restricted to the use of a railroad. Another case presenting this concept is N.Y.—Pearis v. Goldschmidt, 37 A.D.2d

1001, 325 N.Y.S.2d 506 (1971), where the court held that it would take judicial cognizance of the words "sale of whiskey in bond" to mean sale in bonded warehouses.

§ 18.19 JUDICIAL NOTICE OF OTHER FACTS

There are innumerable other facts which courts will take judicial notice of but it is not the function of this text to be exhaustive but to present a general treatment of the subject of the law of evidence.

§ 18.20 CHANGES IN THE LAW OF JUDICIAL NOTICE

The law of judicial notice is the one law in evidence which is constantly changing. Constantly changing conditions of human life, and the boundless variety of facts presented to the courts, cause new applications of the doctrine to take place. A court in 1900 would not be able to take judicial notice that it is possible for man to be placed on the moon nor could it take judicial notice that an airplane could fly across the Atlantic Ocean in less than six hours. Yet today a court would take judicial notice of these facts. The reader can easily comprehend various other changes in the conditions of human life which were unthought of in former years and which are common knowledge today.

§ 18.21 CONCLUSIVENESS OF JUDICIAL NOTICE

Usually what is judicially noticed is not a matter concerning which there is any controversy. If there is a possibility of controversy, the court should not judicially notice the law or the fact. However, there is some disagreement among the authorities as to the effect which should be given to a fact which is judicially noticed. Some courts have held that once the court admits a fact as judicially noticed, the fact should be indisputable and evidence to the contrary should be rejected. N.J.—State v. Cromwell, 6 N.J.Misc.R. 221, 140 A. 429 (1928). Other courts have held that a fact judicially noticed is only a rule of evidence and if the question is disputable, contrary evidence is competent and should be admitted. Mo.—Timson v. Manufacturers' Coal & Coke Co., 220 Mo. 580, 119 S.W. 565 (1909).

§ 18.22 FEDERAL RULE OF JUDICIAL NOTICE

In Thayer's Preliminary Treatise on Evidence (279–280) (1898), we find that he wrote:

> "In conducting a process of judicial reasoning, as of other reasoning, not a step can be taken without assuming something which has not been proved; and the capacity to do this with competent judgment and efficiency, is imputed to judges and juries as part of their necessary mental outfit."

With this definition in mind, the Advisory Committee was instrumental in causing the enactment of Rule 201 of the Federal Rules of Evidence, which reads as follows:

Rule 201. Judicial notice of adjudicative facts

(a) Scope of rule.—This rule governs only judicial notice of adjudicative facts.

(b) Kinds of facts.—A judicially noticed fact must be one not subject to reasonable dispute in that it is either (1) generally known within the territorial jurisdiction of the trial court or (2) capable of accurate and ready determination by resort to sources whose accuracy cannot reasonably be questioned.

(c) When discretionary.—A court may take judicial notice, whether requested or not.

(d) When mandatory.—A court shall take judicial notice if requested by a party and supplied with the necessary information.

(e) Opportunity to be heard.—A party is entitled upon timely request to an opportunity to be heard as to the propriety of taking judicial notice and the tenor of the matter noticed. In the absence of prior notification, the request may be made after judicial notice has been taken.

(f) Time of taking notice.—Judicial notice may be taken at any stage of the proceeding.

(g) Instructing jury.—In a civil action or proceeding, the court shall instruct the jury to accept as conclusive any fact judicially noticed. In a criminal case, the court shall instruct the jury that it may, but is not required to, accept as conclusive any fact judicially noticed.

Adjudicative facts have been defined as those facts which normally go to a jury in a jury case. U.S.—Ikerd v. Lapworth, 435 F.2d 197 (7th Cir. 1970), where distances between two locations was judicially noticed.

Those items of adjudicative facts which a court might take judicial notice of must be facts which are beyond controversy, such as the fact that the City of Miami, Florida is in Dade County, Florida and that it has a higher mean average weather temperature than the City of New York.

The Federal Rules of Evidence omitted a rule regarding judicial notice of law because, according to the note by the Advisory Committee, these matters have traditionally been treated as requiring pleading and proof and are left to the Rules of Civil Procedure and the Rules of Criminal Procedure. The Advisory Committee further added that judicial notice of a rule of law is not a proper concern of the rules of evidence but rather of the rules of procedure. (Rule 44.1 Federal Rules of Civil Practice; Rule 26.1 Federal Rules of Criminal Practice.).

CHAPTER XIX

UNCONSTITUTIONALLY OBTAINED EVIDENCE

§ 19.1 INTRODUCTION—THE EXCLUSIONARY RULE

It is not the function of this book to elucidate in detail about evidence which is subject to an exclusionary rule because of constitutional prohibitions. However, since it is the basic requirement of all law enforcement personnel to be aware of certain limitations in the use of evidence garnered from constitutionally protected areas, a general discussion of this topic follows.

While the general law of evidence is constantly changing, the changes in this area of law have not undergone drastic revision in recent years, except the enactment of the Federal Rules of Evidence effective July 1, 1975. The rules dealing with the exclusion of evidence which has been seized in a manner which violates the constitutional guarantees of the inhabitants of our land, however, have experienced great changes caused by interpretations of the United States Constitution by the United States Supreme Court. This Court considers cases each term where at least four justices consider a substantial federal question is involved in a case that is before it, either on a certified question of law from a lower court, a petition for writ of certiorari, or on appeal.

In order to effectively control excesses by law enforcement officers, the court has devised a procedure which has been called the exclusionary rule. If the court finds that the law enforcement officer violated a basic constitutional right of a defendant, the court orders that all evidence seized by the government which was obtained through violation of the defendant's constitutional rights, not be admitted in evidence at the trial of the defendant.

The trier of the facts therefore is never to consider this evidence in its deliberation as to the guilt or innocence of the defendant. Hence many offenders who are clearly guilty of the crimes with which they are charged, are acquitted or have the charges dropped because of insufficient evidence.

The cry of law enforcement has been that the United States Supreme Court has handcuffed them and yet they are expected to do a job.

A crisis in law enforcement has been taking place because of the stringent limitations placed upon the government in the enforcement of laws. Whenever a crisis develops, whether it be in the family, in business, or in government, it is time to stop to reevaluate goals, procedures and theories to come up with a viable solution. Most often, the solution is found. Law enforcement has been responding to this crisis by professionalization and greater in-depth training.

Lawyers, as legal counsel to police departments were unheard of in small departments until recently. The International Association of Chiefs of Police now has a section consisting solely of legal advisors to law enforcement agencies. There is a common need and the law enforcement community is rising to the occasion.

On the other hand, the strict limitations on law enforcement caused by the "Warren Court" are being eased somewhat by the "Burger Court". It appears that the "Burger Court" is leaning towards the primary issue of the guilt or innocence of the defendant and considering this factor in its decisions where there is no wanton abuse by law enforcement personnel.

As indicated previously, this text is not designed to treat constitutional law in detail but is meant to give the student a general view of the theories so that the student can deal with the problem in a better frame of mind.

§ 19.2 THE CONSTITUTION—A LIVING DOCUMENT

The Constitution of the United States has been described as a living document in that the framers of the Constitution were careful not to define with any degree of specificity many of the terms used. For example, Article I Section 8 Paragraph 3 reads:

> (3) To regulate Commerce with foreign nations, and among the several States, and with the Indian Tribes; . . .

The most ingenious minds of the framers would never think that there would be a day in the future that almost instantaneous communication could be achieved by telephone, telegraph, radio and television. Nor could they be expected to know that some day people could fly in aircraft all over the world. The vague use of the word commerce has been interpreted by the judiciary to include all of the above without any structural change of the wording of the basic document.

Another example of the loose use of language is found in the Fourth Amendment where we find a prohibition against unreasonable search and seizure. The word unreasonable was left for future generations to define pursuant to the customs, mores, and needs of the times. Article III of the Constitution which was interpreted by Chief Justice John Marshall in Marbury v. Madison, 5 U.S. (1 Cranch) 137, 2 L.Ed. 60 (1803), held that the Supreme Court has constitutional powers to strike down statutes, state or federal, that violate commands of the Federal Constitution. In this way as the needs of the nation change and the identities of the Associate Justices of the Supreme Court and the Chief Justice of the United States change, so do the interpretations of the Constitution, adhering however, whenever possible, to the concept of stare decisis.

§ 19.3 THE EARLY FUNCTION OF THE UNITED STATES GOVERNMENT

We must remember that in the latter part of the 18th century, the colonies consisted of scattered settlements with small cities. The population consisted of approximately 75% farmers with the remaining 25% distributed among tradesmen, merchants, craftsmen, seamen and professionals. It was generally considered that the function of government was to maintain law and order and to protect life, liberty and property from internal and external threats. The individual followed his own interests in competition with other individuals without interference from the government. The elderly or sick were cared for by their families or charitable associations. There was no civil police department as we know it today until one was implemented in London, England by Sir Robert Peel in 1829. The citizenry did not expect nor did they wish such benefits as unemployment compensation, old age pensions, consumer protection laws, free health care, free legal services and their concomitant high taxes.

§ 19.4 THE OFFENDER'S RIGHTS UNDER EARLY COMMON LAW

It has taken centuries to evolve the concept of a fair trial as we know it. There was no precedural guarantee in early English history for those accused of crime. They had a system sometimes referred to as the "Hue and Cry". In this system a victim of a crime would raise a hue and cry and all of the inhabitants of the area would arm themselves to seek the felon. If the accused were captured, there would be a hastily convened court to try the defendant. If s/he would resist capture, a member of the community could legally kill the person. Ususally s/he had little chance of getting an impartial jury and the defendant could not testify as a defense witness. S/He was usually executed by being hanged or thrown off a cliff by the victim or a relative of the victim.

If an accusation was made against an alleged perpetrator and s/he escaped, the escapee would be declared an outlaw and was thus not entitled to the protection of the law, whatever that might be. In that case, s/he could be executed without a prior indictment. If an outlaw was apprehended while in the possession of stolen goods, s/he could be executed summarily by a member of the area.

It is easy to see how, under this system of justice, nefarious persons caused the imprisonment and/or death of others who might have been in the way of the accuser in one way or another.

§ 19.5 THE RULE OF LAW

There is a concept known as the rule of law under which Anglo-Saxon law has come to operate. It was enunciated when, in the latter part of the 19th Century, the English Constitutional scholar, Albert V. Dicey, wrote that the rule of law had three distinct parts. The third part does not apply to American law and is not included below. The first two are abbreviated as follows:

1. No man is punishable or can be lawfully made to suffer in body or goods except for a distinct breach of law established in the ordinary legal manner before the ordinary courts of the land . . . .

2. . . . No man is above the law . . . Every man . . . is subject to the ordinary law of the realm.

We have no better example of the operation of this concept than when President Richard Nixon, one of the most powerful persons in the world, was caused to resign from office because of a breach of the law.

§ 19.6 PROCEDURAL SAFEGUARDS OF THE ACCUSED

Fortunately for law abiding persons as well as the criminal, the practices of the ancient common law with respect to the apprehension and trial of one accused of crime, is no longer practiced. Today, in the United States, many safeguards are afforded to the accused to prevent an infringement of constitutional rights in the interest of justice. It was not uncommon, even in recent years, to force confessions from accused persons by third degree methods. The pain and torture, both physical and mental, which was inflicted upon criminal suspects often caused them to admit to the commission of crimes in which they had not been involved. Accordingly, the courts have insured that this type of activity by law enforcement officers would be for naught and the prisoner/defendant would be free. The procedural safeguards are based on the integrity of the individual and government by law rather than by men.

§ 19.7 CONSTITUTIONAL BASIS FOR ARREST

While there was a common law basis for arrest of violators of the common law, prior to the adoption of the Constitution, the Constitution authorizes arrest of malefactors but proscribes certain limitations on this power. We find these limitations outlined in Amendments Fourth, Fifth, Sixth and Eighth of the original document.

Statutory penal codes came later on in our history. The New York Penal Code was enacted in 1881 consisting of 727 sections which proscribed conduct which would be considered as violations of law.

§ 19.8 MOTOR VEHICLES—STATUTORY AUTHORITY TO STOP

The police power, i. e., control over the health, welfare and morals, is one of the powers reserved to the states in the United States Constitution by virtue of the reserve powers clause of the Tenth Amendment of that document. Accordingly, the power to regulate the ownership and movement of motor vehicles is vested in each of the states. The states have legislated licensing statutes whereby an operator of a motor vehicle must first qualify for a license to operate and/or own a motor vehicle. In order for the state to enforce compliance, it is therefore necessary to give power and authority to law enforcement personnel charged with the responsibility of enforcing traffic laws, to stop drivers of motor vehicles and ascertain whether they are properly licensed to operate the vehicle and whether the vehicle is properly registered. Each state has such a statute.

> **Fla.—322.15** (1) Every licensee shall have his operator's or chauffeur's license in his immediate possession at all times when operating a motor vehicle and shall display the same upon demand of a patrol officer, peace officer, or field deputy or inspector of the department.

An officer's motive for checking a driver's license and registration is immaterial. The fact that he was suspicious that a driver of a particular automobile may be committing a crime neither adds to nor detracts from his authority to stop the automobile and check the driver's license. Fla.—Cameron v. State, 112 So.2d 864 (App.1959). A municipal police department could operate a "road block" or similar system for the purpose of checking automobile driver's licenses and such practice did not amount to an illegal search and seizure contrary to State and Federal Constitutions, nor did it amount to an unconstitutional invasion of a motorist's right to use the public ways. Fla.—City of Miami v. Aronowitz, 114 So.2d 784 (1959).

It follows therefore that if an officer has probable cause to check a driver's license, as statutorily authorized, any evidence which s/he observes by virtue of this activity would be admissible into evidence.

§ 19.9 FINGERPRINTS—DETENTION FOR

It is common knowledge that a person may be positively identified by his/her fingerprints and that no two persons have ever been found to have identical fingerprints. The courts have taken judicial notice of this scientific fact. Fingerprint classification was reportedly first developed by the Chinese. They were found to be commonly used for identifications purposes during the Tang Dynasty (618 to 906 A.D.). The most widely used system today is the Galton-Henry system. This science, like so many others, is now computerized but it still requires a fingerprint expert to classify the prints being examined.

As a practical matter it becomes necessary to keep a record of persons who have been arrested and convicted of crime to enable the law enforcement community to detect crime and also to properly charge the defendant. Many statutes carry a higher sanction if the defendant has been previously convicted. Statutes provide that in certain types of arrests, the prisoner is required to be fingerprinted.

Conn.—Gen.Stat.Ann. § 29–11. The bureau in the state police department known as the state bureau of identification, shall be maintained for the purpose of providing an authentic record of each person over sixteen years of age who is charged with the commission of any crime involving moral turpitude and of providing definite information relative to the identity of each person so arrested and of providing a record of the final judgment of the court resulting from such arrest . ..

Many states now have statutes requiring the return of all fingerprints, copies and photos and description and other identification data and all copies and duplicates thereof if the defendant is later acquitted or the charges are dismissed or not prosecuted, see Conn.—Gen.Stat.Ann. § 29.15.

Therefore, it is incumbent upon law enforcement officers to detain arrestees for the purpose of taking their fingerprints.

§ 19.10 CLOSE PURSUIT ARRESTS

Each state has its own criminal procedure law or criminal code. In these statutes is found the grounds upon which a law enforcement officer or citizen may make an arrest of a person who is believed to have committed an offense against society. The law enforcement powers of police officers are applicable within the jurisdiction in which they are appointed. It was not uncommon in the days of the Old West for the malefactor to race the sheriff to the border of the officer's jurisdiction and if the criminal was successful in getting across the border before apprehended, he might find sanctuary because the officer was not authorized to make an arrest beyond his jurisdiction. To avoid this miscarriage of justice, states have adopted what have been termed as close pursuit, hot pursuit or fresh pursuit laws. Del.—11 Del.Code Ann. §§ 1931 and 1932 which reads as follows:

§ 1931. Definitions

As used in this subchapter

"Fresh pursuit" includes fresh pursuit as defined by the common law, and also the pursuit of a person who has committed a felony or a misdemeanor or a violation of the Motor Vehicle Code of this State or who is reasonably suspected of having committed a felony or a misdemeanor or a violation of the Motor Vehicle Code of this State, and also includes the pursuit of a person suspected of having committed a supposed felony or misdemeanor or violation of the Motor Vehicle Code of the State though no violation of the law has actually been committed, if there is reasonable grounds for believing that a violation of the law has been committed; however, fresh pursuit as used in this subchapter does not necessarily imply instant pursuit, but pursuit without reasonable delay. (41 Del.Laws, c. 216 § 5; 11 Del.C. 1953, § 1931; 56 Del.Laws, c. 154 § 1.)

§ 1932. Arrest by out-of-state police

(a) Any member of a duly organized state, county or municipal peace unit of another state of the United States who enters this State in fresh pursuit, and continues within this State in such fresh pursuit, of a person in order to arrest him on the ground that he is believed to have committed a felony, a misdemeanor or a violation of the Motor Vehicle Code in such other state, shall have the same authority to arrest and hold such person in custody, as has any member of any duly organized state, county or municipal peace unit of this State, to arrest and hold in custody a person on the ground that he is believed to have committed a felony, a misdemeanor or a violation of the Motor Vehicle Code in this State.

(b) This section shall not be construed so as to make unlawful any arrest in this State which would otherwise be lawful. (41 Del.Laws, c. 216 §§ 1, 3; 11 Del.C. 1953, § 2.)

§ 19.11 THE FIRST, FOURTH, FIFTH, SIXTH, EIGHTH, TENTH AND FOURTEENTH AMENDMENTS

We speak of the First, Fourth, Fifth, Sixth, Eighth, Tenth and Fourteenth Amendments as amendments to the Constitution which everyone who has completed a high school education in the United States has read and knows by rote memory. Experience, however, has demonstrated to the contrary. In order to facilitate the student to become acquainted with the contents of these amendments which have become so important in the administration of the criminal law, they are reproduced below. These amendments are part of the first ten amendments to the Constitution which are known as the Bill of Rights. They were placed in the Constitution shortly after the adoption of it, in order to comply with the demands of certain states which made their adoption a condition of ratification.

AMENDMENT I (Freedom of religion, speech, press, assemblage and petition)

Congress shall make no law respecting an establishment of religion, or prohibiting the free exercise thereof; or abridging the freedom of speech, or of the press; or the right of the people peaceable to assemble, and to petition the Government for a redress of grievances.

AMENDMENT IV (Searches and seizures)

The right of the people to be secure in their persons, houses, papers, and effects, against unreasonable searches and seizures, shall not be violated, and no warrants shall issue, but upon probable cause, supported by oath or affirmation, and particularly describing the place to be searched, and the persons or things to be seized.

AMENDMENT V (Criminal indictment; double jeopardy; self-incrimination; due process; compenstaion for taking private property)

No person shall be held to answer for a capital, or otherwise infamous crime, unless on a presentment or indictment of a Grand Jury, except in cases arising in the land or naval forces, or in the militia, when in actual service in time of war or public danger; nor shall any person be subject for the same offence to be twice put in jeopardy of life or limb; nor shall be compelled in any criminal case to be a witness against himself, nor be deprived of life, liberty, or property, without due process of law; nor shall private property be taken for public use, without just compensation.

AMENDMENT VI (Rights of defendant in criminal prosecutions)

In all criminal prosecutions, the accused shall enjoy the right to a speedy and public trial, by an impartial jury of the State and district wherein the crime shall have been committed, which district shall have been previously ascertained by law, and to be informed of the nature and cause of the accusation; to be confronted with the witnesses against him; to have compulsory process for obtaining witnesses in his favor, and to have the assistance of counsel for his defence.

AMENDMENT VIII (Excessive bail; cruel and unusual punishments)

Excessive bail shall not be required, nor excessive fines imposed, nor cruel and unusual punishments inflicted.

AMENDMENT X (Powers reserved to the states)

The powers not delegated to the United States by the Constitution, nor prohibited by it to the States, are reserved to the States respectively, or to the people.

AMENDMENT XIV (§ 1. Citizens; privileges and immunities; due process; equal protection)

Section 1. All persons born or naturalized in the United States, and subject to the jurisdiction thereof, are citizens of the United States and of the State wherein they reside. No State shall make or enforce any law which shall abridge the privileges or immunities of citizens of the United States; nor shall any State deprive any person of life, liberty, or property, without due process of law; nor deny to any person within its jurisdiction the equal protection of the laws.

(Sections 2, 3, 4 and 5 are not applicable to this discussion.)

§ 19.12 EVIDENCE OBTAINED BY VIOLATION OF THE FIRST AMENDMENT

You will recall that our founding fathers were interested in making certain that they did not recreate in the new world a system of government which they had fled from in the old world. They were particularly concerned about the right of a person to speak and publish his convictions whether or not those in authority concurred in them. The First Amendment to the Constitution was to guarantee this right for their contemporaries and for their posterity. The law books have been replete with many cases involving a temporary restriction on a person's right to determine his religion, to speak, to publish, to assemble and to petition against the government for redresses.

Fortunately, the courts have righted any persons so wronged. There are many countries that have such provisions in their constitutions but because of a lack of a system of checks and balances whereby the legislative, judicial and executive branch of the government checks and balances the other parts of the government, the words in the constitutions of these other nations have become meaningless. We have had statutes which have been declared unconstitutional and hence unenforceable because of the violation of the First Amendment. U.S.—Shuttlesworth v. Birmingham, 394 U.S. 147, 89 S.Ct. 935, 22 L.Ed.2d 162 (1969).

§ 19.13 EVIDENCE OBTAINED BY VIOLATION OF FOURTH AMENDMENT IN COMBINATION WITH FOURTEENTH AMENDMENT

It was first thought that the proscriptions of the first ten amendments to the United States Constitution were applicable against the Federal government alone in that each citizen of a state retained his state citizenship and was also a citizen of the United States of America. Through painstaking efforts on the part of many attorneys, most of the proscriptions were made applicable against the individual state action by the United States Supreme Court decisions which absorbed the Bill of Rights amendments on a case by case basis after the adoption of the Fourteenth Amendment. A further amplification of this concept is left to a course of study dealing exclusively with Constitutional Law.

§ 19.14 EVIDENCE OBTAINED BY MEANS OF UNREASONABLE SEARCH AND SEIZURE

The United States Supreme Court construes the meaning of the words used in the Constitution by deciding cases which come before the court. Accordingly the law changes based upon the most recent decisions of the Supreme Court. The student is advised to refresh his recollection as to how the common law is changed. This was explained in chapter one of this book exhibit 1.

The Fourth Amendment to the United States Constitution has been interpreted by perhaps more cases than any other constitutional amendment except perhaps the First Amendment.

The Constitution grants power to each of our divisions of government i. e., (Executive, Judicial and Legislative) but through a system of checks and balances, it also places restraints on that power to the end that neither branch of the government is too powerful to the exclusion of the other branches.

The executive power is charged with implementing court orders and the law as enacted by the legislative power. The judicial power is charged with the responsibility of construing the Constitution and statutory law.

The Fourth Amendment does not prohibit all searches. It only prohibits unreasonable searches. What may be considered unreasonable at one stage in our history may not be considered unreasonable at a later point in our history.

For example, during 1960, it would have been considered highly unreasonable for a prospective passenger on a commercial airliner to be searched for weapons. It is submitted that if such a search were conducted at that time and an unlawfully possessed firearm was found on a prospective passenger, the search would be held to be unconstitutional and all such evidence would not be admissible in a trial for the unlawful possession of a firearm.

By 1973, however, the courts had determined that it was not unreasonable to search a prospective passenger of a commercial airliner for weapons because of the high incidence of hijacking of airplanes.

However, it is unreasonable if other contraband such as narcotics were found on such a search because it is not necessary to the efficient operation of the aircraft that persons with narcotics be prohibited from boarding the airplane. An argument to the contrary might be that the initial search was reasonable and that the narcotics found were the result of a search incidental to a lawful arrest, if an arrest were made in this instance for concealed weapons. The United States Constitution prohibition against unreasonable search and seizure has been held to be a prohibition against state action in Mapp v. Ohio, 367 U.S. 643, 81 S.Ct. 1684, 6 L.Ed.2d 1081 (1961).

In order to prevent law enforcement authorities from overreaching their powers, the courts have adopted what has been called an exclusionary rule discussed in § 19.1 (supra). In essence, the courts will not admit evidence into the trial which has been obtained by means of a violation of the defendant's constitutional rights. The procedural methods employed by counsel to implement this exclusion will be discussed later in this book.

As indicated above, in Mapp v. Ohio (supra), the United States Supreme Court interceded in violations of unreasonable search and seizure activities by state law enforcement personnel and applied the exclusionary rules to state action. This opened a Pandora's box and caused many state cases to find their way into the federal courts. The "Burger" United States Supreme Court has begun to qualify and limit some of the decisions of the "Warren" United States Supreme Court. In 1976, for example, in the case of Stone v. Powell, 428 U.S. 465, 96 S.Ct. 3037, 49 L.Ed.2d 1067, 440 U.S.L.W. 5313 (1976), the court held that after a defendant has been afforded an opportunity for the full and fair litigation of Fourth Amendment claims by the state, he may not thereafter obtain habeas corpus relief on the ground that illegally seized evidence was introduced at his trial. The court emphasized that the purpose of the judicially created exclusionary rule is deterrence, and that the policies behind it are not absolute, but relative to the competing public interest in the determination of truth at trial by means of highly probative evidence. Balancing the utility of the exclusionary rule against the cost of extending it to collateral review, therefore, reveals that the costs exceed the marginal benefits. Application of the rule "deflects the truth finding process and often frees the guilty". On the other hand, "There is no reason to believe . . . that the overall educative effect of the exclusionary rule would be appreciably diminished if search and seizure claims could not be raised in federal habeas corpus review of state convictions."

§ 19.15 ARREST WARRANT REQUIREMENTS

We have just read the caveats of the Fourth Amendment with respect to the issuance of warrants. It has been the function of the courts to define what was meant by this direction. The word "particularly" and the phrase "probable cause" have been the subject of much litigation. U.S.—Andresen v. Maryland, 423 U.S. 822, 96 S.Ct. 2737, 46 L.Ed.2d 39 (1976); N.Y.—People v. Malinsky et al., 19 N.Y. 2d 262, 279 N.Y.S.2d 20, 225 N.E.2d 748 (1967).

The usual procedure is for the law enforcement officer to obtain information, either by his own direct observation or through a reliable informant, coupled with the officer's observation, that a crime is being committed at a particular location and/or a particular wanted person may be found at a particular address. The officer will state in affidavit form his/her request and reasons that s/he believes that a warrant will assist the officer in affecting an arrest for violation of law.

The independent judicial officer, will read the affidavit and decide in his/her judgment based on the allegations in the affidavit, whether there is probable cause for the issuance of the warrant and whether there is sufficient particularity. If s/he is so satisfied, a warrant will be signed by the judicial officer directing the law enforcement officer to make the search and/or arrest and bring the results of the search and/or arrest before the judicial officer. When this occurs, many states call this a "return". An inventory is made of all items seized and presented to the court. The law enforcement officer is charged with the responsibility of safeguarding the items seized until such time as they are required by the prosecution for introduction into evidence. Sometimes the officer will scratch his/her initials on the surface of the evidence for identification purposes at a later date. If the evidence is capable of being placed into an envelope or bag or container, some departments require their officers to seal the receptacle and sign their names over the seal to insure continuity of control of the evidence.

Naturally, there will be variations of this procedure in different jurisdictions but mainly the thought is to safeguard the evidence and to insure its reliability when it is offered as real evidence at the trial. The judicial officer is usually a judge or justice of a court but the United States Supreme Court has held in Shadwick v. City of Tampa, 407 U.S. 345, 92 S.Ct. 2119, 32 L.Ed.2d 783 (1972), that a clerk of a court may issue warrants in designated situations.

§ 19.16 EVIDENCE OBTAINED IN VIOLATION OF RIGHT OF PRIVACY BY MEANS OF ILLEGAL WIRETAPS OR EAVESDROPPING

The fathers of our government could not possibly envisage the electronic age of today but because the Constitution is a living document, the Supreme Court finally included wiretapping within the protection of the Fourth Amendment. The case history of this amendment also went a full circle. In the early cases, the court held that the proscription was limited to search and seizure of material things. Olmstead v. United States, 277 U.S. 438, 48 S.Ct. 564, 72 L.Ed. 944 (1928). Later, however, the court held that illegal wiretaps violated the Federal Communication Act of 1934. Still later the Supreme Court held that surveillance without trespass and without seizure of material fell within the protection of the Fourth Amendment of the United States Constitution. Katz v. United States, 389 U.S. 347, 88 S.Ct. 507, 19 L.Ed.2d 576 (1967). Title 3 of the Omnibus Crime Control Act authorizes wiretapping under specified conditions. This act has no effect upon actions by state officials in this area unless a state statute is passed to supplement the federal statute. It is suggested that the student consult the statutory law in his state to determine the admissibility of this type of evidence in his jurisdiction.

§ 19.17 EVIDENCE OBTAINED BY VIRTUE OF A SEARCH WARRANT

Where probable cause is shown, the law enforcement officer obtains a search warrant from a judicial officer. This officer makes an independent assessment of the facts based upon an affidavit signed by a law enforcement officer or others, and if he is convinced, based upon the evidence before him, that probable cause exists for the issuance of the search warrant, the judicial officer issues and signs such a warrant, particularly describing the places to be searched and/or the persons or items to be seized. The officer, armed with a search warrant, may conduct the search or seizure but he must strictly adhere to the directions in the warrant. If he fails in this, all evidence which he brings to the court may later be found to be inadmissible.

There are other situations wherein the courts have held that the evidence obtained was not unreasonable. Some of these are as follows:

1. Evidence seized which was incidental to a lawful arrest.
2. Evidence seized by virtue of the defendant or someone in lawful control of a premises consenting to the search.
3. Evidence seized from the person of a consenting defendant.
4. Evidence obtained from a vehicle where the items seized were in open view.
5. Evidence seized from an area which is not constitutionally protected.
6. Evidence obtained by a private person who has no connection with a law enforcement agency, because the constitution protections have been construed to protect one against official action and not private acts.
7. Weapons found by a police officer as a result of a stop and frisk, when necessary to protect the officer or anyone in the vicinity.
8. Evidence seized from the person of one who has been arrested for a traffic violation.
9. Probable cause arrest.
10. Automobile search.

Not only is evidence which has been obtained by an unreasonable search not admissible in evidence but also any information obtained as a result of the illegal search is excluded under a doctrine which has become known as the "fruit of poison tree" doctrine.

§ 19.18 SEARCH INCIDENTAL TO A LAWFUL ARREST

Once a lawful arrest has been made, the officer is required, in order to safeguard himself/herself, the prisoner and others with whom the prisoner may come in contact, to make a thorough search of the prisoner. Any contraband that is surfaced as a result of this search is admissible under the doctrine that it is admissible as incidental to a lawful arrest. This principle was explained by the court in Agnello v. United States, 269 U.S. 20, 30, 46 S.Ct. 4, 70 L.Ed. 145 (1925), where the court said "the right without a search warrant contemporaneously to search persons lawfully arrested while committing crime and to search the place where the arrest is made in order to find and seize things connected with the crime as well as weapons and other things to effect an escape from custody, is not to be doubted". In Chimel v. California, 395 U.S. 752, 89 S.Ct. 2034, 23 L.Ed.2d 685 (1969), the court again gave full authority to an officer to make a search incidental to a lawful arrest and included area into which arrestee may reach, or area within his immediate control.

§ 19.19 CONSENT SEARCH

The Constitution prohibits unreasonable searches, it does not prohibit consent searches. When a person consents to a search, he/she is in effect waiving any right to contest the search as being unconstitutional. In practice, courts have looked very carefully into the credibility of an officer's testimony that the defendant consented to a search. Assuming that a wife in the absence of her husband may waive his constitutional immunity against search of his dwelling as granted by Article I, § 14 of the Constitution of Ohio, such waiver cannot be said to have occurred where the testimony as to the wife's assent is conflicting, and there is a probability that any assent given was by reason of the coercive influence of an officer, or officers of the law. Ohio—State v. Lindway, 131 Ohio St. 166, 2 N.E.2d 490 (1936).

§ 19.20 PLAIN OR OPEN VIEW DOCTRINE

The plain or open view doctrine can best be explained by an example.

If a police officer were walking on a foot patrol beat and he observed an automobile parked on his post wherein the back seat had several decks of glassine envelopes containing white powder and two hypodermic needles, the officer would have good grounds to arrest the occupant or the person who claims the vehicle.

Objects falling in plain view of an officer who has a right to be in the position to have the view are subject to seizure and may be introduced in evidence. U.S.—Harris v. United States, 390 U.S. 234, 88 S.Ct. 992, 19 L.Ed.2d 1067 (1968).

§ 19.21 NON-CONSTITUTIONALLY PROTECTED AREAS

The Fourth Amendment protects persons and places from unreasonable interference with their privacy by agents of government. It does not protect persons who may be carrying out criminal acts in areas which are public and the officer has probable cause to make the arrest. U.S.—United States v. Watson, 423 U.S. 411, 96 S.Ct. 820, 46 L.Ed.2d 598 (1976).

§ 19.22 PRIVATE PERSON'S ARREST

The individual's protection in the Bill of Rights of the United States Constitution has been construed to be effective against governmental authority and not against the acts of private persons. In Miranda v. Arizona, 384 U.S. 436, 86 S.Ct. 1602, 16 L.Ed.2d 694 (1966), the court specifically pointed out in 384 U.S. 436, 444, that "It was necessary in Escobedo, as here, to insure that what was proclaimed in the Constitution had not become but a 'form of words', Silverthorne Lumber Co. v. United States, 251 U.S. 385, 392, 40 S.Ct. 182, 64 L.Ed. 319 (1920), in the hands of government officials. . . . By custodial interrogation, we mean questioning initiated by law enforcement officers after a person has been taken into custody or otherwise deprived of his freedom of action in any significant way."

Therefore, it may be reasoned that a store detective employed by a private corporation who is not deputized by any governmental authority, need not adhere to the constitutional mandate of Miranda.

§ 19.23 STOP AND FRISK SEARCH

The stop and frisk search is designed to protect a law enforcement officer or anyone in the vicinity from the harmful effects of weapons found on the person of the defendant. To effect this result, the officer is permitted to pat down the outergarments of a suspect to ascertain whether the suspect is carrying a concealed weapon and if so, the officer is authorized to remove the weapon from the suspect and place him/her under arrest. There is a problem if the suspect is of the opposite sex to the searching officer because there is the latent complaint that the officer performed this frisk to fulfill his/her sexual gratification. This might be a cogent argument for the practice of causing men and women police officers to be assigned together either on foot patrol or in cruiser patrol. The leading cases in this area are Ohio—Terry v. Ohio, 392 U.S. 1, 88 S.Ct. 1868, 20 L.Ed.2d 889 (1968), and New York—Peters v. New York, 392 U.S. 40, 88 S.Ct. 1889, 20 L.Ed.2d 917 (1968).

In the former case, there was no statutory authorization for the stop and frisk. In the latter case, there was a statute directing such a search. In both cases the court upheld the validity of the search.

§ 19.24 TRAFFIC VIOLATION—EVIDENCE SEIZED INCIDENTAL TO LAWFUL ARREST

A custodial arrest of a suspect based on probable cause is a reasonable intrusion under the Fourth Amendment; that intrusion being lawful, a search incident to the arrest requires no additional justification. It is the fact of the lawful arrest which establishes the authority to search. Where there is a lawful custodial arrest and a full search of the person, it is a reasonable search requiring no warrant. This principle applies to all lawful arrests including but not limited to an arrest for a traffic offense that carried a mandatory minimum prison sentence or fine, or both, where heroin was found on the person arrested and the heroin was admissible in evidence. U.S.—U. S. v. Willie Robinson, Jr., 414 U.S. 218, 94 S.Ct. 467 (1973). In Gustafson v. State of Florida, 414 U.S. 260, 94 S.Ct. 488, 38 L.Ed.2d 456 (1973), the court held that a person arrested for the offense of driving his automobile without a valid operator's license, may be taken into custody and a police officer was entitled to make a full search of the petitioner's person. All "fruits," instrumentalities or contrabands found on such person, probative of criminal conduct are admissible in evidence as incidental to a lawful arrest. It is not material that the initial offense did not carry a mandatory minimum sentence.

§ 19.25 PROBABLE CAUSE SEARCH

The Fourth Amendment to the United States Constitution provides among other items, that no warrants be issued but upon probable cause. The various state criminal procedure statutes have similarly provided. Arrests and searches however, can be made without a warrant where the officer has probable cause to effect the arrest and the search, and there is insufficient time, as a practical matter, to first obtain a search warrant from a detached magistrate. Although no search warrant has been issued, intoxicating liquor which is discovered in an automobile by an officer who has stopped and searched such automobile in good faith, and relying on bona fide information, may be offered in evidence. Ohio—Houck v. State, 106 Ohio St. 195, 140 N.E. 112 (1922).

§ 19.26 AUTOMOBILE SEARCH

The automobile is particularly vulnerable to lawful search by law enforcement officers. As has been previously noted, the state law enforcement officer has a responsibility to see that the traffic laws are complied with. This gives him/her a wedge to inspect the vehicle. States have given law enforcement officers further authority to inspect the contents of vehicles by other statutes. For example, Pennsylvania authorizes officers whose duty it is to enforce the game laws, to stop and search vehicles. Failure to stop the vehicle makes the malefactor liable to a fine of $25.00 providing the officer was in full uniform. Pa.—34 Pa.Statutes § 1311.73(*o*).

When a vehicle is impounded by the police, an inventory search has been held to be a constitutionally valid search. Neb.—State v. Wallen, 185 Neb. 44, 173 N.W.2d 372 (1970).

In a 1976 case, South Dakota v. Opperman, 428 U.S. 364, 96 S.Ct. 3092, 49 L.Ed.2d 1000, 44 U.S.L.W. 5294 (1976), a defendant's car was impounded by the police for multiple parking violations. Following the police department's standard inventory procedures, the police made an inventory of the contents of the car and discovered marijuana in a closed, unlocked glove compartment. The defendant was convicted of possession of marijuana after his motion to suppress was denied. The court affirmed his conviction, holding that the routine inventory search of the impounded automobile was not an unreasonable search and seizure. The search was primarily for the purpose of safeguarding valuables in plain view inside the car, and there was no indication that the standard procedure followed served as a pretext for a criminal investigation.

Another 1976 auto search case was Texas v. White, 423 U.S. 67, 96 S.Ct. 304, 46 L.Ed.2d 209 (1976), wherein the court held that a warrantless search of an automobile at a police station was permissible if probable cause to search was present at the scene of the arrest.

It should be quite obvious to the student that the "Burger Court" is looking for a way to validate an arrest if reasonably possible, so as to protect the interests of society as well as those rights of the defendant.

§ 19.27 DOG SNIFFING—BLOODHOUND EVIDENCE

It is well known that dogs have been trained to track down suspects by smelling garments of the suspect and by tracing the movements of the suspect until apprehended. Such evidence is not inadmissible on the ground that the dog is the witness and cannot be cross-examined. It is the human testimony which makes the trailing done by the animal competent. Ohio—State v. Dickerson, 77 Ohio St. 34, 82 N.E. 969 (1907). Dogs have also been trained to smell narcotics or gun powder and alert law enforcement officers to locations where these items are located. In order to get this evidence admitted into the trial record, the prosecutor must lay a foundation. S/He is required to show by testimony of the trainer, the qualifications of the trainer and the dog, and no interference with the condition of suspected items found at the scene of the occurrence had been countenanced until the arrival of the dog, and in the case of tracking, the dog had been placed on the suspected trail of the offender, that no interruptions occurred in the tracking and there was other circumstantial evidence linking the suspect with the crime. For an extended discussion of dog sniffing, or what is sometimes referred to as bloodhound evidence, see Pedigo v. Commonwealth, 103 Ky. 41, 44 S.W.2d 143, 42 L.R.A. 432, 19 Ky.L. 1723 (1898); Terrell v. State, 3 Md.App. 340, 239 A.2d 128 (1968); United States v. Bronstein, New York Law Journal (2d Cir. 8/13/75).

§ 19.28 EVIDENCE OF CONFESSION IN VIOLATION OF THE FIFTH AMENDMENT

To understand the Fifth Amendment one must know of the history of government prior to the adoption of the Constitution.

It was not uncommon for those in authority to seize the persons of suspected malefactors and torture them to confess their crimes. It was found that persons so tortured would admit to crimes even though they were not guilty of these crimes, so that their torture might be stopped. There were also incidents wherein a defendant would be successively tried until he was found guilty. Our founding fathers, recognizing the temperament of man and desiring to put an end to such practices, incorporated safeguards in the Constitution to prevent miscarriages of justice.

Accordingly, we often hear that a person "Takes the Fifth." In effect he is exercising his right to refrain from making statements which might incriminate him as having committed a crime.

In the development of American Constitutional Law through decisions of the United States Supreme Court, it became apparent that law enforcement officers were using various methods in contravention of the constitutional rights of both the Fifth and the Sixth Amendments of the United States Constitution to extract confessions from suspected perpetrators. The court finally came to the conclusion in the case of Miranda v. Arizona, 384 U.S. 436, 86 S.Ct. 1602, 16 L.Ed.2d 694 (1966), that when an individual was held for custodial interrogation by law enforcement officers, he must be clearly informed that he has a right to consult with a lawyer and to have the lawyer with him during interrogation. That prior to investigation the person must be warned that he has a right to remain silent, that any statement he does make may be used as evidence against him, and that he has a right to the presence of an attorney either retained or appointed by the court, if he cannot afford to retain an attorney. The defendant may waive these rights provided the waiver is made voluntarily, knowingly and intelligently. If he indicates in any manner, at any stage of the process that he wishes to consult with an attorney before speaking there can be no questioning. If the individual is alone and indicates in any manner that he does not wish to be interrogated, the police may not question him. If he may have answered some questions or volunteered some statements on his own, it does not deprive him of the right to refrain from answering any further questions until he has consulted with an attorney and thereafter consents to be questioned.

If evidence is obtained in violation of these caveats, the evidence is not admissible. However, the Supreme Court commonly referred to as the "Burger Court" has been qualifying the Miranda holding by subsequent decisions. For example, if a defendant has not been given these warnings and makes an inculpatory statement, this statement may not be used on the prosecutions direct case but if the defendant takes the stand to testify and testifies to a contradictory statement to that which he made to the law enforcement officer, the defendant's statement made, without prior Miranda warnings, may be admissible for impeachment purposes. Or.—Oregon v. Hass, 420 U.S. 714, 95 S.Ct. 1215, 43 L.Ed.2d 570 (1976). A further refinement of the Miranda decision is to be found in Mass.—Commonwealth v. Simpson, 345 N.E.2d 899 (1976), where a defendant was invited to come to a police station where the police questioned him without advising him of his Miranda rights. The Supreme Court held that this was not custodial interrogation in that the defendant was there voluntarily and could have left if he so desired. No doubt more decisions whittling away the strictures of Miranda are on the way.

§ 19.29 EVIDENCE OBTAINED IN VIOLATION OF SIXTH AMENDMENT RIGHTS

The Sixth Amendment to the Constitution provides:

> "In all criminal prosecutions, the accused shall enjoy the right to a speedy and public trial, by an impartial jury of the State and district wherein the crime shall have been committed, which district shall have been previously ascertained by law, and to be informed of the nature and cause of the accusation; to be confronted with witnesses against him, to have compulsory process for obtaining witnesses in his favor, and to have the Assistance of Counsel for his defence."

The decisional law dealing with this amendment has been very interesting and has run a full circle. For example, at one time, the states were not required to provide counsel for all defendants. Later they were required to provide counsel for certain types of crimes. Still later, counsel was to be provided in every case where there was a possibility of incarceration. U.S.—Gideon v. Wainwright, 372 U.S. 335, 83 S.Ct. 792, 9 L.Ed.2d 799 (1963); Argersinger v. Hamlin, 407 U.S. 25, 92 S.Ct. 2006, 32 L.Ed.2d 530 (1972).

In 1976, the "Burger Court" handed down a decision in Geders v. United States, 425 U.S. 80, 96 S.Ct. 1330, 47 L.Ed.2d 592, wherein the court held that a defendant was denied his right of counsel when a trial court ordered that the defendant and his counsel were not to confer during an overnight recess of the trial. Defendant had been testifying on direct examination when an overnight recess was called. Cross-examination was to be held shortly thereafter.

A 1977 case, Brewer v. Williams, 45 U.S.L.W. 4287, decided March 23, 1977, held that a defendant was denied his right to counsel when an officer accompanying the defendant on a long auto ride to a place of detention, in an effort to locate the body of a deceased child, inveigled the defendant to tell the officers where the body of the child was by telling the defendant that the child was entitled to a Christian burial. The officer knew that the defendant was Christian and a very religious man. The defendant had already retained counsel and the officer had agreed with counsel that the defendant would not be questioned during the ride to the detention facility. This case went up to the Supreme Court on a writ of habeas corpus, notwithstanding the fact that in Stone v. Powell, 428 U.S. 465, 96 S.Ct. 3037, 49 L.Ed.2d 1067 (1976) the court said that the federal courts should not be available to state prisoners for habeas corpus review of a Fourth Amendment violation where it has been fairly and fully litigated in the state courts. It appears that the court is not precluding habeas corpus relief to state prisoners in alleged Fifth and Sixth Amendment rights questions.

§ 19.30 PROCEDURAL METHOD TO EXCLUDE EVIDENCE UNCONSTITUTIONALLY OBTAINED

It is the function of the defendant's attorney to move to suppress any evidence illegally obtained. This is usually accomplished by making a written motion based on affidavits of the defendant and the attorney explaining to the court the reasons that they believe are good grounds for the exclusion of certain evidence obtained in violation of the defendant's constitutional rights. The moving papers request a hearing before the court to determine whether the items of evidence should be excluded at the trial.

This procedure is called pretrial motion practice. Here too, it is not the intent of this book to make trial lawyers out of the reader but a general knowledge of the pretrial motion practice may be useful to the law enforcement officer to enable him to understand his position more fully.

In the ordinary course of events, the court grants a hearing. The legal profession has given names to certain of these pretrial hearings and motions as follows:

1. Huntley hearing—determine the admissibility of a confession.
2. Wade hearing—determine legality of identification.
3. Controvert a warrant hearing—determine whether probable cause existed for the issuance of a warrant or whether warrant was validly executed.
4. Miranda hearing—determine whether defendant was given proper admonition with respect to his right of counsel.
5. Motion to inspect Grand Jury minutes—determine whether legal evidence sufficient to sustain a conviction was testified to in Grand Jury proceedings.

Upon such hearing in New York and other states, the ordinary exclusionary rules of evidence applicable to trials of criminal actions are inapplicable to the extent that evidence tending to demonstrate that the evidence sought to be suppressed was or was not unlawfully or improperly obtained . . . is admissible even though of a hearsay nature or otherwise incompetent by trial standards. N.Y.—CPL § 375.60(4).

§ 19.31 PLEA BARGAINING

Reference has been made in Section 17.22 as to what would happen in a practical situation. The District Attorney and defense counsel enter into negotiations to permit the defendant to plead guilty to a lesser included offense. This is known as plea bargaining. There has been much discussion of late as to the desirability of accepting pleas from defendants for lesser included offenses than the one with which they are charged. It might be informative to explain the purpose of plea bargaining. Since there are so many safeguards on behalf of a defendant built into a criminal trial, the prosecution reasons that there is a great likelihood of a substantial error being committed which might result in a reversal of a conviction by an appellate court, with the further result that many offenders may not be properly punished. In addition to this problem, the length of time that it takes to try a case before a jury under our present system is of long duration. If every case were tried to its conclusion and every appeal were granted a hearing, the wheels of justice would come to a sudden grinding halt and no justice would be dispensed. Admittedly, plea bargaining is not real justice either but it is an attempt to face the realities of the situation. However, Alaska has discontinued the practice and there is a powerful movement to discontinue it in other jurisdictions. The criminal justice system in the United States has much to be desired but it is attempting to cure some of its ills. Just as no one's body is perfect at all times, so too is our criminal justice system not perfect at all times.

The rules of evidence, however, are used when the case cannot be negotiated for one or more reasons and the trial must run its course to a full conclusion.

§ 19.32 CONCLUSION

The student should understand that if law enforcement officers arrest a perpetrator for a crime and the perpetrator is not given his constitutionally protected rights, the officer is, in effect, laying the ground-work for the subsequent dismissal of the charges against the defendant. Often the prosecutor is unable to continue with the prosecution of the case because the evidence which she/he has left, after the exclusion of the tainted evidence, is insufficient to convict the defendant. Special care on the part of the law enforcement officer is essential, if he/she wants to see justice prevail.

*

PART II

JUDICIAL DECISIONS RELATING TO PART I

The judicial decisions in this section of the book have been edited and reprinted. The reading and analysis of these decisions should make the first section of the book more meaningful. It is suggested that the student brief each case assigned according to a format which the instructor prefers. When a student is able to dissect a case and articulate principles of law which the decision proclaims, he is well on his way to understanding, not only the law of evidence, but the entire study of law.

The facility to be able to extract the principle of law from a decision will not be achieved easily. However, by continued attempts and assistance from the instructor, everyone will be able to do this.

If the reader is desirous of reading the full text of the decision or decisions cited in part I, he may do this by resorting to central city libraries, court house libraries, law school libraries and/or the library of some friendly attorney upon whom he feels he can impose.

DECISIONS RELATING TO CHAPTER I, COMMON LAW AND STATUTORY LAW

FUNK v. UNITED STATES

Supreme Court of the United States, 1933.
290 U.S. 371, 54 S.Ct. 212, 78 L.Ed. 369.

. . .

On Writ of Certiorari to the United States Circuit Court of Appeals for the Fourth Circuit.

John S. Funk was convicted of conspiracy to violate the National Prohibition Act, and to review a judgment of the Circuit Court of Appeals [66 F.2d 70], affirming the judgment of conviction, he brings certiorari.

. . .

Mr. Justice SUTHERLAND delivered the opinion of the Court.

The sole inquiry to be made in this case is whether in a federal court the wife of the defendant on trial for a criminal offense is a competent witness in his behalf. Her competency to testify against him is not involved.

The petitioner was twice tried and convicted in a federal District Court upon an indictment for conspiracy to violate the prohibition law. His conviction on the first trial was reversed by the Circuit Court of Appeals upon a ground not material here. 46 F.2d 417. Upon the second trial, as upon the first, defendant called his wife to testify in his behalf. At both trials she was excluded upon the ground of incompetency. The Circuit Court of Appeals sustained this ruling upon the first appeal, and also upon the appeal which followed the second trial. 66 F.2d 70. We granted certiorari, limited to the question as to what law is applicable to the determination of the competency of the wife of the petitioner as a witness.

Both the petitioner and the government, in presenting the case here, put their chief reliance on prior decisions of this court. The government relies on United States v. Reid, 12 How. 361, 13 L.Ed. 1023 (1851); Logan v. United States, 144 U.S. 263, 12 S.Ct. 617, 36 L.Ed. 429 (1892); Hendrix v. United States, 219 U.S. 79, 31 S.Ct. 193, 196, 55 L.Ed. 102 (1911); and Jin Fuey Moy v. United States, 254 U.S. 189, 41 S.Ct. 98, 65 L.Ed. 214 (1921). Petitioner contends that these cases, if not directly contrary to the decisions in Benson v. United States, 146 U.S. 325, 13 S.Ct. 60, 36 L.Ed. 991 (L.1892), and Rosen v. United States, 245 U.S. 467, 38 S.Ct. 148, 150, 62 L.Ed. 406 (1918), are so in principle. We shall first briefly review these cases, with the exception of the Hendrix Case and the Jin Fuey Moy Case, which we leave for consideration until a later point in this opinion.

In the Reid Case, two persons had been jointly indicted for a murder committed upon the high seas. They were tried separately, and it was held that one of them was not a competent witness in behalf of the other who was first tried. The trial was had in Virginia; and by a statute of that state passed in 1849, if applicable in a federal court, the evidence would have been competent. Section 34 of the Judiciary Act of 1789 (28 U.S.C.A. § 725) declares that the laws of the several states, except where the Constitution, treaties, or statutes of the United States otherwise provide, shall be regarded as rules of decision in trials at common law in the courts of the United States in cases where they apply; but the court said that this referred only to civil cases, and did not apply in the trial of criminal offenses against the United States. It was conceded that there was no act of Congress prescribing in express words the rule by which the federal courts would be governed in the admission of testimony in criminal cases. "But," the court said (page 363 of 12 How.), "we think it may be found with sufficient certainty, not indeed in direct terms, but by necessary implication, in the acts of 1789 and 1790, establishing the courts of the United States, and providing for the punishment of certain offences."

The court pointed out that the Judiciary Act regulated certain proceedings to be had prior to impaneling the jury, but contained no express provision concerning the mode of conducting the trial after the jury was sworn, and prescribed no rule in respect of the testimony to be taken. Obviously, however, it was said, some certain and established rule upon the subject was necessary to enable the courts to administer the criminal jurisprudence of the United States, and Congress must have intended to refer them to some known and established rule "which was supposed to be so familiar and well understood in the trial by jury that legislation upon the subject would be deemed superfluous. This is necessarily to be implied from what these acts of Congress omit, as well as from what they contain." Page 365 of 12 How. The court concluded that this could not be the common law as it existed at the time of the emigration of the colonists or the rule which then prevailed in England, and [therefore] the only known rule which could be supposed to have been in the mind of Congress was that which was in force in the respective states when the federal courts were established by the Judiciary Act of 1789. Applying this rule, it was decided that the witness was incompetent.

In the Logan Case it was held that the competency of a witness to testify in a federal court sitting in one state was not affected by his conviction and sentence for felony in another state; and that the competency of another witness was not affected by his conviction of felony in a Texas state court, where the witness had since been pardoned. The indictment was for an offense committed in Texas and there tried. The decision was based, not upon any statute of the United States, but upon the ground that the subject "is governed by the common law, which, as has been seen, was the law of Texas . . . at the time of the admission of Texas into the Union as a state." Page 303 of 144 U.S., 12 S.Ct. 617, 630.

We next consider the two cases upon which petitioner relies. In the Benson Case two persons were jointly indicted for murder. On motion of the government there was a severance, and Benson was first tried. His codefendant was called as a witness on behalf of the government. The Reid Case had been cited as practically decisive of the question. But the court, after pointing out what it conceived to be distinguishing features in that case, said (page 335 of 146 U.S., 13 S.Ct. 60, 63): "We do not feel ourselves, therefore, precluded by that case from examining this question in the light of general authority and sound reason." The alleged incompetency of the codefendant was rested upon two reasons, first, that he was interested, and, second, that he was a party to the record, the basis for the exclusion at common law being fear of perjury. "Nor," the court said, "were those named the only grounds of exclusion from the witness stand. Conviction of crime, want of religious belief, and other matters were held sufficient. Indeed, the theory of the common law was to admit to the witness stand only those presumably honest, appreciating the sanctity of an oath, unaffected as a party by the result, and free from any of the temptations of interest. The courts were afraid to trust the intelligence of jurors. But the last 50 years have wrought a great change in these respects, and today the tendency is to enlarge the domain of competency, and to submit to the jury for their consideration as to the credibility of the witness those matters which heretofore were ruled sufficient to justify his exclusion. This change has been wrought partially by legislation and partially by judicial construction." Attention then is called to the fact that Congress in 1864 had enacted that no witness should be excluded from testifying in any civil action, with certain exceptions, because he was a party to or interested in the issue tried; and that in 1878 (c. 37, 20 Stat. 30 [28 U.S.C.A. § 632]) Congress made the defendant in any criminal case a competent witness at his own request. The opinion then continues (page 337 of 146 U.S., 13 S.Ct. 60, 64):

> "Legislation of similar import prevails in most of the states. The spirit of this legislation has controlled the decisions of the courts, and steadily, one by one, the merely technical barriers which excluded witnesses from the stand have been removed, till now it is generally, though perhaps not universally, true that no one is excluded therefrom unless the lips of the originally adverse party are closed by death, or unless some one of those peculiarly confidential relations, like that of husband and wife, forbids the breaking of silence.
>
> " . . . If interest and being party to the record do not exclude a defendant on trial from the witness stand, upon what reasoning can a codefendant, not on trial, be adjudged incompetent?"

That case was decided December 5, 1892. Twenty-five years later this court had before it for consideration the case of Rosen v. United States, supra. Rosen had been tried and convicted in a federal District Court for conspiracy. A person jointly indicted with Rosen, who had been convicted upon his plea of guilty, was called as a witness by the government and allowed to testify over Rosen's objection. This court sustained the competency of the witness. After saying that, while the decision, in the Reid Case had not been specifically overruled, its authority was seriously shaken by the decisions in both the Logan and Benson Cases, the court proceeded to dispose of the question, as it had been disposed of in the Benson Case, "in the light of general authority and of sound reason."

> "In the almost twenty [twenty-five] years," the court said, "which have elapsed since the decision of the Benson Case, the disposition of courts and of legislative bodies to remove disabilities from witnesses has continued, as that decision shows it had been going forward before, under dominance of the conviction of our time that the truth is more likely to be arrived at by hearing the testimony of all persons of competent understanding who may seem to have knowledge of the facts involved in a case, leaving the credit and weight of such testimony to be determined by the jury or by the court, rather than by rejecting witnesses as incompetent, with the result that this principle has come to be widely, almost universally, accepted in this country and in Great Britain.
>
> "Since the decision in the Benson Case we have significant evidence of the trend of congressional opinion upon this subject in the removal of the disability of witnesses convicted of perjury. Rev.St. § 5392, by the enactment of the federal Criminal Code in 1909 with this provision omitted and section 5392 repealed. This is significant, because the disability to testify, of persons convicted of perjury, survived in some juris-

dictions much longer than many of the other common-law disabilities, for the reason that the offense concerns directly the giving of testimony in a court of justice, and conviction of it was accepted as showing a greater disregard for the truth than it was thought should be implied from a conviction of other crime.

"Satisfied as we are that the legislation and the very great weight of judicial authority which have developed in support of this modern rule, especially as applied to the competency of witnesses convicted of crime, proceed upon sound principle, we conclude that the dead hand of the common-law rule of 1789 should no longer be applied to such cases as we have here, and that the ruling of the lower courts on this first claim of error should be approved."

. . .

The rules of the common law which disqualified as witnesses persons having an interest long since in the main have been abolished both in England and in this country; and what was once regarded as a sufficient ground for excluding the testimony of such persons altogether has come to be uniformly and more sensibly regarded as affecting the credit of the witness only. Whatever was the danger that an interested witness would not speak the truth—and the danger never was as great as claimed—its effect has been minimized almost to the vanishing point by the test of cross-examination, the increased intelligence of jurors, and perhaps other circumstances. The modern rule which has removed the disqualification from persons accused of crime gradually came into force after the middle of the last century, and is today universally accepted. The exclusion of the husband or wife is said by this court to be based upon his or her interest in the event. Jin Fuey Moy v. United States, supra. And whether by this is meant a practical interest in the result of the prosecution or merely a sentimental interest because of the marital relationship makes little difference. In either case, a refusal to permit the wife upon the ground of interest to testify in behalf of her husband, while permitting him, who has the greater interest, to testify for himself, presents a manifest incongruity.

Nor can the exclusion of the wife's testimony, in the face of the broad and liberal extension of the rules in respect of the competency of witnesses generally, be any longer justified, if it ever was justified, on any ground of public policy. It has been said that to admit such testimony is against public policy because it would endanger the harmony and confidence of marital relations, and, moreover, would subject the witness to the temptation to commit perjury. Modern legislation, in making either spouse competent to testify in behalf of the other in criminal cases, has definitely rejected these notions, and in the light of such legislation and of modern thought they seem to be altogether fanciful. The public policy of one generation may not, under changed conditions, be the public policy of another. Patton v.

United States, 281 U.S. 276, 306, 50 S.Ct. 253, 74 L.Ed. 854, 70 A.L.R. 263 (1930).

The fundamental basis upon which all rules of evidence must rest—if they are to rest upon reason—is their adaptation to the successful development of the truth. And, since experience is of all teachers the most dependable, and since experience also is a continuous process, it follows that a rule of evidence at one time thought necessary to the ascertainment of truth should yield to the experience of a succeeding generation whenever that experience has clearly demonstrated the fallacy or unwisdom of the old rule.

It may be said that the court should continue to enforce the old rule, however contrary to modern experience and thought, and however opposed, in principle, to the general current of legislation and of judicial opinion it may have become, leaving to Congress the responsibility of changing it. Of course, Congress has that power; but, if Congress fail to act, as it has failed in respect of the matter now under review, and the court be called upon to decide the question, is it not the duty of the court, if it possess the power, to decide it in accordance with present-day standards of wisdom and justice rather than in accordance with some outworn and antiquated rule of the past? That this court has the power to do so is necessarily implicit in the opinions delivered in deciding the Benson and Rosen Cases. And that implication, we think, rests upon substantial ground. The rule of the common law which denies the competency of one spouse to testify in behalf of the other in a criminal prosecution has not been modified by congressional legislation; nor has Congress directed the federal courts to follow state law upon that subject, as it has in respect of some other subjects. That this court and the other federal courts, in this situation and by right of their own powers, may decline to enforce the ancient rule of the common law under conditions as they now exist, we think is not fairly open to doubt.

In Hurtado v. California, 110 U.S. 516, 530, 4 S.Ct. 111, 118, 28 L.Ed. 232 (1884), this court, after suggesting that it was better not to go too far back into antiquity for the best securities of our liberties, said:

> "It is more consonant to the true philosophy of our historical legal institutions to say that the spirit of personal liberty and individual right, which they embodied, was preserved and developed by a progressive growth and wise adaptation to new circumstances and situations of the forms and processes found fit to give, from time to time, new expression and greater effect to modern ideas of self-government.
>
> "This flexibility and capacity for growth and adaptation is the peculiar boast and excellence of the common law. . . . And as it was the characteristic principle of the common law to draw its inspiration from every fountain of

> justice, we are not to assume that the sources of its supply have been exhausted. On the contrary, we should expect that the new and various experiences of our own situation and system will mould and shape it into new and not less useful forms."

Compare Holden v. Hardy, 169 U.S. 366, 385–387, 18 S.Ct. 383, 42 L.Ed. 780 (1898).

To concede this capacity for growth and change in the common law by drawing "its inspiration from every fountain of justice," and at the same time to say that the courts of this country are forever bound to perpetuate such of its rules as, by every reasonable test, are found to be neither wise nor just, because we have once adopted them as suited to our situation and institutions at a particular time, is to deny to the common law in the place of its adoption a "flexibility and capacity for growth and adaptation" which was "the peculiar boast and excellence" of the system in the place of its origin.

The final question to which we are thus brought is not that of the power of the federal courts to amend or repeal any given rule or principle of the common law, for they neither have nor claim that power, but it is the question of the power of these courts, in the complete absence of congressional legislation on the subject, to declare and effectuate, upon common-law principles, what is the present rule upon a given subject in the light of fundamentally altered conditions, without regard to what has previously been declared and practiced. It has been said so often as to have become axiomatic that the common law is not immutable but flexible, and by its own principles adapts itself to varying conditions. In Ketelsen v. Stilz, 184 Ind. 702, 111 N.E. 423, L.R.A.1918D, 303, Ann.Cas.1918A, 965 (1916), the Supreme Court of that state, after pointing out that the common law of England was based upon usages, customs, and institutions of the English people as declared from time to time by the courts, said (page 707, of 184 Ind., 111 N.E. 423, 425):

> "The rules so deduced from this system, however, were continually changing and expanding with the progress of society in the application of this system to more diversified circumstances and under more advanced periods. The common law by its own principles adapted itself to varying conditions and modified its own rules so as to serve the ends of justice as prompted by a course of reasoning which was guided by these generally accepted truths. One of its oldest maxims was that where the reason of a rule ceased the rule also ceased, and it logically followed that when it occurred to the courts that a particular rule had never been founded upon reason, and that no reason existed in support thereof, that rule likewise ceased, and perhaps another sprang up in its place which was based upon reason and justice as then conceived. No rule of the common law could survive the

> reason on which it was founded. It needed no statute to change it but abrogated itself."

That court then refers to the settled doctrine that an adoption of the common law in general terms does not require, without regard to local circumstances, an unqualified application of all its rules; that the rules, as declared by the English courts at one period or another, have been controlling in this country only so far as they were suited to and in harmony with the genius, spirit, and objects of American institutions; and that the rules of the common law considered proper in the eighteenth century are not necessarily so considered in the twentieth. "Since courts have had an existence in America," that court said (page 708 of 184 Ind., 111 N.E. 423, 425), "they have never hesitated to take upon themselves the responsibility of saying what are the proper rules of the common law."

. . .

The Supreme Court of Connecticut, in Beardsley v. City of Hartford, 50 Conn. 529, 542, 47 Am.Rep. 677 (1883), after quoting the maxim of the common law, cessante ratione legis, cessat ipsa lex, said:

> "This means that no law can survive the reasons on which it is founded. It needs no statute to change it; it abrogates itself. If the reasons on which a law rests are overborne by opposing reasons, which in the progress of society gain a controlling force, the old law, though still good as an abstract principle, and good in its application to some circumstances, must cease to apply as a controlling principle to the new circumstances."

The same thought is expressed in People v. Randolph, 2 Parker, Cr.R. 174, 177 (N.Y.1855):

> "Its rules [the rules of the common law] are modified upon its own principles and not in violation of them. Those rules being founded in reason, one of its oldest maxims is, that where the reason of the rule ceases the rule also ceases."

It was in virtue of this maxim of the common law that the Supreme Court of Nevada, in Reno Smelting Works v. Stevenson, 20 Nev. 269, 21 Pac. 317, 4 L.R.A. 60, 19 Am.St.Rep. 364 (1889), in a well-reasoned opinion, held that the common-law doctrine of riparian rights was unsuited to conditions prevailing in the arid land states and territories of the West, and therefore was without force in Nevada; and that, in respect of the use of water, the applicable rule was based upon the doctrine of prior appropriation for a beneficial use.

In Illinois it was held at an early day that the rule of the common law which required an owner of cattle to keep them upon his own land was not in force in that state, notwithstanding its adoption of the common law of England, being unsuited to conditions there in view of the extensive areas of land which had been left open and unfenced and devoted to grazing purposes. Seeley v. Peters, 5 Gilman 130 (Ill.1848).

Numerous additional state decisions to the same effect might be cited; but it seems unnecessary to pursue the matter at greater length.

It results from the foregoing that the decision of the court below, in holding the wife incompetent, is erroneous. But that decision was based primarily upon Hendrix v. United States and Jin Fuey Moy v. United States, supra, and in fairness to the lower court it should be said that its decision was fully supported by those cases.

In the Hendrix Case the opinion does not discuss the point; it simply recites the assignment of error to the effect that the wife of Hendrix had not been allowed to testify in his behalf, and dismisses the matter by the laconic statement, "The ruling was not error." In the Jin Fuey Moy Case it was conceded at the bar that the wife was not a competent witness for all purposes, but it was contended that her testimony was admissible in that instance because she was offered, not in behalf of her husband, that is, not to prove his innocence, but simply to contradict the testimony of government witnesses who had testified to certain matters as having transpired in her presence. The court held the distinction to be without substance, as clearly it was, and thereupon disposed of the question by saying that the rule which excludes a wife from testifying for her husband is based upon her interest in the event, and applies without regard to the kind of testimony she might give. The point does not seem to have been considered by the lower court to which the writ of error was addressed ([D.C.] 253 F. 213); nor, as plainly appears, was the real point as it is here involved presented in this court. The matter was disposed of as one "hardly requiring mention." Evidently the point most in the mind of the court was the distinction relied upon, and not the basic rule which was not contested. Both the Hendrix and Jin Fuey Moy Cases are out of harmony with the Rosen and Benson Cases and with the views which we have here expressed. In respect of the question here under review, both are now overruled.

Judgment reversed.

Mr. Justice CARDOZO concurs in the result.

Mr. Justice McREYNOLDS and Mr. Justice BUTLER are of opinion that the judgment of the court below is right and should be affirmed.

FEDERAL TRUST CO. v. EAST HARTFORD FIRE DIST.

United States Circuit Court of Appeals, Second Circuit, 1922.
283 F. 95.

. . .

In Error to the District Court of the United States for the District of Connecticut.

Action by the Federal Trust Company against the East Hartford Fire District. Judgment for defendant on demurrer, and plaintiff brings error. Reversed and remanded, with directions.

The defendant fire district is a minor municipal corporation of Connecticut, created in 1889 (10 Sp.Laws Conn. p. 1316). This act of incorporation was amended from time to time, always by "special laws" duly passed by the Connecticut Legislature, until in 1899 (13 Sp.Laws, p. 492, § 14) the district was given the power and authority to make and maintain waterworks, and to do so by lawfully obtaining "the same rights, powers, and duties as were conferred and imposed upon the East Hartford Water Company by its charter approved May 10, 1887, and the amendments thereto."

Defendant thus became entitled to procure by eminent domain the watersheds necessary for its waterworks in like manner as the East Hartford Water Company had been entitled so to do. That water company had, by virtue of certain "special laws," "full power . . . to take water from any brook in [certain enumerated towns including Glastonbury] or from any other source as said company may desire. . . ."

The method of exercising this right of taking water is prescribed by special law (10 Sp.Laws, p. 729, § 8) thus: "Said corporation [district] shall pay all damages, that shall be sustained by any person or persons or corporation in their property or estate by the taking of any real estate or easement, or by the taking the water from any brook," etc.

The statute then declares that, if the damages shall not be agreed upon, they shall be assessed under the supervision of the superior court, upon an application made to that court either by the condemning corporation or by the person sustaining damages, "which application shall be accompanied by a summons served upon the owner of the property as in the case of civil process before said court."

Another proviso of this series of special laws declares: "Said court may make any order necessary for the protection of the rights of all persons or corporations interested in said property or sustaining such damages: but said property shall not be taken or interfered with by said corporation until the amount of said judgment shall be paid to the person to whom it is due, or deposited for his use with the treasurer of Hartford county." Section 10.

By virtue of this conference of the power of eminent domain the fire district in December, 1916, began proceedings in the superior court against the Glastonbury Power Company et al. to condemn "the waters of Cold brook" in the town of Glastonbury. After appeal to the Supreme Court of the state (East Hartford Fire District v. Glastonbury Power Co., 92 Conn. 217, 102 Atl. 592), the proceeding succeeded, and on December 12, 1918, judgment was entered in said superior court awarding to the Glastonbury Power Company damages for the taking of Cold brook in the sum of $7,500.

In 1904 said power company had duly made a mortgage, affecting all its property including the Cold brook lands. Plaintiff, Federal Trust Company, is the mortgagee as trustee for bondholders. The mortgage was duly recorded and was in full force during the whole of the above referred to condemnation proceeding; but (as averred in the complaint) plaintiff had "no notice of said condemnation proceedings, nor was it cited as a party defendant in" the same. The amount of plaintiff's mortgage was $57,000. The complaint does not aver that it had matured when complaint was filed (December, 1920), or that the mortgagor was down to that date in default. But (continues the complaint) "as such mortgagee plaintiff was entitled to payment of said award to the extent of the amount due upon the mortgage before any sum was paid to the owner of the property. No payment of any amount has been made to the plaintiff on account of said award of damages, although plaintiff requested defendant to pay said sum over to the plaintiff." Complaint concludes with a prayer for general damages, viz. $100,000.

To this complaint defendant demurred, assigning for cause of demurrer that at the time of action begun no "sum of money was due and payable from defendant to plaintiff," and that it was not alleged that "defendant is indebted to plaintiff." This in substance was a general demurrer.

At all times during the pendency of the condemnation proceeding above referred to, and since 1895, there had been and was in force in Connecticut a general statute (Gen. Stat.Conn. Revision of 1918, § 5192), reading as follows: "Whenever any real estate, or any interest in real estate, is taken by right of eminent domain under any statute, notice shall be given to all persons appearing of record to hold any mortgage, lien or other incumbrance on the property to be taken, and the amount due to such mortgagee, lienor or other incumbrancer, not exceeding the amount to be paid for the property taken, shall be paid to them in the order of their respective rights before any sum is paid to the owners of the property."

The trial court sustained the demurrer and gave judgment absolute for defendant, whereupon plaintiff brought this writ.

. . . .

Before HOUGH, MANTON, and MAYER, Circuit Judges.

HOUGH, Circuit Judge (after stating the facts as above). Plaintiff certainly had an interest in the lands condemned, and its action is for damages to that interest. It rests on the alleged unlawful act of defendant in failing to give notice or opportunity to assert its right to the plaintiff pursuant to the statute. The judgment below is in effect a holding that under the allegations made it is impossible, on benevolent reading of the complaint, to discover any recoverable damage.

Yet it is equally plain that, if defendant was bound by the provisions of Gen.Stat. § 5192, it failed in a duty imposed by law, and plaintiff should have opportunity to show a jury that damage to it—i. e., to its interest in the Glastonbury property—was thereby proximately caused. On demurrer we cannot speculate as to whether damages are likely to be provable.

The judgment complained of is sought to be justified by the assertion that the act imposing obligation on one exercising eminent domain to give notice to the mortgagors and lienors of record is a general statute, whereas the defendant possessed and exercised its power of condemning the Cold brook lands wholly by virtue of "special acts," and therefore the general statute has no application.

It is not and cannot be asserted that the Legislature may not affect or modify special acts by general statutes; but this, it is said, requires specific reference to them. The language of the general statute in force when condemnation began is that whoever takes by eminent domain "under any statute of this state" shall do the thing which this defendant did not do; and we are of opinion that the phrase "any statute of this state" covers and includes all statutes of Connecticut, whether denominated general or special, public or private.

A statute or statute law is by long-accepted definition the express written will of the Legislature, rendered authentic by certain prescribed forms and solemnities. Potter's Dwarris, 37. Cf. Lewis' Sutherland on Statutory Construction, § 321 et seq.; Bishop on the Written Law, § 42a et seq., and Bouvier, tit. "Statutes."

A "statute of a state" is any law directly passed by the Legislature of that state (Cumberland, etc., Co. v. Memphis, 198 F. 955, 957 (D.C.Tenn.1912)); and any enactment to which a state gives the force of law is a statute of the state (Atlantic, etc., Co. v. Goldsboro, 232 U.S. 548, 34 S.Ct. 364, 58 L.Ed. 721 (1914)).

Historically the phrases "special act" and "private act" mean the same thing; and in Unity v. Burrage, 103 U.S. 447, 455 (26 L.Ed. 405 (1880)) it was pointed out that such acts or statutes as those incorporating counties, establishing courthouses and the like "all operate upon local subjects, [but] they are not for that reason special or private acts. In this country the disposition has been, on the whole to enlarge the limits of this class of public acts, and to bring within it all enactments of a general character, or which in any way affect the community at large."

Nor does the fact that a given statute affects only a portion of the territory under the Legislature's dominion influence the matter at all, if the statute affects all of the population within the limited area. Lewis' Sutherland, supra, and cases cited. Finally, whether a law be local, or otherwise entitled to some peculiar appellation, is a question of fact, and not of form. Gray v. Taylor, 227 U.S. 51, 33 S.Ct. 199, 57 L.Ed. 413 (1913).

For these reasons, while inclined to think that the special acts giving to defendant the power of eminent domain are public acts in fact, we hold that they are plainly statutes of Connecticut, and therefore within the phrase "any statute of this state."

It appears to have been held below as another reason for sustaining demurrer that there was nothing "due" to this plaintiff at the time of condemnation. But the word "due," as applied to debts, is sometimes used to express the mere state of indebtedness, and it is then equivalent to "owed" or "owing" (United States v. State Bank, 6 Pet. 29, 8 L.Ed. 308 (1803)); and the word in its larger and general sense signifies that which is owed, that which one contracts to pay to or perform to another (Wyman v. Kimberly-Clark Co., 93 Wis. 554, 556, 67 N.W. 932 (1896), with full citation of authorities).

We are clear that the word "due," as used in this statute, imports existing obligations or indebtednesses of record, without regard to maturity; if it were otherwise, the statute would wholly fail of its obvious purpose, which is to prevent exactly the condition of affairs that here exists. For these reasons, the judgment must be reversed, and the defendant required to answer over on payment of costs and within a time to be fixed by the lower court.

For the sake of accuracy it should be pointed out that, while defendant's whole case has hitherto rested upon the assertion of rights under private acts or special acts, the case has been treated as though the acts in question were general and public, for the court has taken cognizance of them on demurrer without pleading or proof. Observance of the fundamental rule that acts, if really private, must be pleaded, would have prevented a journey to this court on general demurrer.

As trial before a jury would be the natural result of this decision, we point out again that the action is for damages to the plaintiff's estate or interest by the appropriation of certain mortgaged lands without compensation to it. Like all damages, they must be proved, and not presumed. This is not an action for debt. Non constat but that the remaining lands are amply sufficient to satisfy plaintiff's mortgage lien.

Judgment reversed, with costs, and case remanded, with directions to proceed in a manner not inconsistent with this opinion.

PEOPLE v. NITZBERG

Court of Appeals of New York, 1941.
287 N.Y. 183, 38 N.E.2d 490.

LOUGHRAN, Judge. The defendant stands convicted of murder in the first degree. One Shuman was the victim of the homicide. On January 10, 1939, his slain body was found in an automobile that was parked on a street in Brooklyn.

(1) Abraham Reles—a self-confessed accomplice in the crime—was the chief witness for the People. Put into direct discourse his story in substance was this: My business was murder in Brooklyn. Lepke was one of my bosses. In December, 1938, Mendy Weiss and I visited Lepke at his hideout apartment where Mendy "told Lep that Pug Shuman was speaking to Inspector McDermott, giving him information against him." Lepke said, "If he is giving information against me go out and take him." After that, I got from the defendant—who knew the man—a promise to lure Shuman into the hallway of a building near the intersection of Eastern parkway and Buffalo avenue in Brooklyn so that we could kill him there. Later on I thought less of that plan when I recalled that a traffic policeman was usually on duty at that street intersection. I told this to the defendant and gave him another plan which was carried out on the night of January 9, 1939. The defendant at that time got Shuman to go riding with him in a stolen automobile I had supplied and shot him to death while I followed in another automobile in which the defendant and I drove away.

Reles having given this testimony, the prosecution in its direct case brought Dorothy Walker, Philip J. Bang, Herman Breitman, Michael F. McDermott, Bernard Moskowitz and Bernard Freundlich to the witness stand. Walker—the housekeeper for Lepke at his so-called hideout apartment—testified that Reles and others (of whom the defendant was not one) had visited Lepke there in the latter part of 1938. Bang testified that, as a member of the police department assigned to traffic patrol on Eastern parkway throughout December, 1938, he had during that month spent some time at the corner of Eastern parkway and Buffalo avenue, because accidents frequently happened at that spot. McDermott is the police inspector to whom Reles referred in his testimony. McDermott's evidence was that from time to time in December, 1938, he had had conversations with Shuman at police headquarters in Brooklyn and at the office of the District Attorney of the county of New York. Breitman was the owner of the automobile in which Shuman's body was found. He testified that the vehicle had been stolen from a garage in Long Island City in September, 1938. Moskowitz was the keeper of that garage. He gave similar testimony. Freundlich testified that the license plates that were on the car in which Shuman's body was found had been stolen in December, 1938, from another automobile owned by himself.

For convenience we shall here and there refer to Walker, Bang, McDermott, Breitman, Moskowitz and Freundlich as the nonaccomplice witnesses.

After the trial judge had delivered his charge to the jury he was requested by counsel for the defendant to instruct them that the facts sworn to by the non-accomplice witnesses were "insufficient evidence to corroborate the accomplice." The judge responded: "That is right, and I so charge, that those facts which you have just stated are not intended to connect the defendant with the commission of the crime, but they are intended to corroborate the witness as to whether or not he is telling the truth as to credibility." Counsel for the defendant thereupon made this protest: "I say that that evidence cannot tend to connect the defendant with the commission of the crime." Again the judge rejoined: "I so charge, but it does tend to show, or prove or disprove the credibility of a witness." To these rulings, and to the refusal of the trial judge to strike out the testimony of some of the non-accomplice witnesses, counsel for the defendant took exceptions which are now pressed upon us.

Each and every of the matters sworn to by the non-accomplice witnesses was undisputed by the defendant. Not a single item of the testimony of any of them had any applicability whatsoever to his identity as a participator in this crime. So, indeed, the trial judge ruled. In that state of the case the question is whether we can sustain the further ruling that such independent testimony was none the less to be used by the jury in constructing for the accomplice-witness Reles a general credibility that would perhaps amount to a sanction for his narration of the vital and controverted particulars of his story against the defendant.

Was the fact that Walker (in the defendant's absence) saw Reles in Lepke's apartment relevant to show that Reles was truthful in his testimony that he and the defendant planned this crime? Was the fact that Officer Bang patrolled Eastern parkway relevant to show that Reles was truthful in his testimony that he told the defendant an officer was on duty there? Was the fact that Shuman was in communication with Inspector McDermott relevant to show that Reles was truthful in his testimony that he had prevailed on the defendant to kill Shuman? Was the fact of the theft of the automobile in which Shuman's body was found relevant to show that Reles was truthful in his testimony that he procured that stolen vehicle for the defendant? There is no element of novelty in any of these queries, save as they bring to the top of our minds one or two rules of ordinary human thought that have seldom called for explicit statement in the case law.

"There is a principle—not so much a rule of evidence as a presupposition involved in the very conception of a rational system of evidence . . . —which forbids receiving anything irrelevant, not logically probative." Thayer, Preliminary Treatise on Evidence, 264, 265. "It is not the law which furnishes the test of relevancy, but logic. Probative value, or capability of supporting an inference, is a matter of reasoning . . . and the rules of relevancy aim only to determine whether a given fact is of sufficient probative value to be admissible at all." 1 Greenleaf on The Law of Evidence, Wigmore's 16th Ed., § 14. For the purposes of the present case it is enough in the way of a definition of relevancy to say that a fact is relevant to another fact when the existence of the one renders the existence of the other highly probable, according to the common course of events. See Sir James Stephen, Digest of the Law of Evidence, Chase's 2d Ed., Introduction XVIII. Cf. Platner v. Platner, 78 N.Y. 90, 94 (1879).

The fact sworn to by Walker—the presence of Reles in the Lepke apartment—was a criminal fact. On the say-so of Reles that fact initiated the killing of Shuman. The fact sworn to by Breitman, Moskowitz and Freundlich—the theft of the vehicle in which Shuman's body was found—was on the face of it a criminal fact. On his own say-so, too, Reles was closely tied to that fact. Now it was precisely because he was attainted in that way that Reles as a witness stood in need of support from a purer source to show that he was not doing a bad turn by putting the defendant in his place in the disputed accusatory parts of his story. In other words, Reles' self-confessed connection with those criminal facts put him outside the limit of the presumption that witnesses ordinarily are honest up to their lights. In the face of all this the trial judge, nevertheless, told the jury in respect of Reles that the independent evidence of those very criminal facts "does tend to show, or prove or disprove the credibility of a witness."

We think it unnecessary to probe this idea that a strong implication of the non-credibility of a witness may be rebutted by independent evidence which confirms him in his confession of the very criminality which gives rise to that implication. Whatever its merits, such a process, we believe, is not fit for the trial of issues on which life and liberty depend. To our minds it appears safe enough to say at once that the testimony of Walker, Breitman, Moskowitz and Freundlich did not indicate with any fair degree of probability that Reles might here be taken in the light of common experience to have been over all a truthful witness. We do not mean, however, that their testimony was not receivable as evidence of a part of the principal occurrence in issue. Cf. People v. Sherman, 103 N.Y. 513, 9 N.E. 178 (1886).

The testimony of Officer Bang has a somewhat different aspect. The location of his post of duty was a fact that had no necessary connection with Reles. Indeed, it was a fact that was known to everybody. But if an accomplice-witness could be supported at large by independent evidence that he told the truth in matters of that sort, then every accomplice (not incompetent for want of understanding) could always rake into his story materials for such confirmation of it. See Commonwealth v. Bosworth, 22 Mass. (Pick.) 397, 399 (1839). It has been a long time since an accomplice-witness has been suffered so to lift himself by his own bootstraps. Cf. People v. Katz, 209 N.Y. 311, 342, 103 N.E. 305 (1913). We are not persuaded that the location of the post of Officer Bang on Eastern parkway made it highly probable in point of reason that Reles was truthful in his testimony that he told the defendant an officer was usually on duty there.

So with the testimony of Inspector McDermott that Shuman (the victim of this crime) had been in communication with him. We will make the good-sized assumption that this testimony was well enough as evidence that Reles had reported the same fact to Lepke. This report of Reles (as he said) had been made in a secret conference among him, Lepke and Weiss when they were privately assembled for the sake of their common protection from interference by the police. To us it seems that the results of ordinary human experience do not countenance the notion that the testimony of Inspector McDermott was proximately probative of the fact that the truth was in Reles once more when (after his arrest and with the promise that the District Attorney "would speak to the court for me") he testified that the major part in the commission of this crime had been taken over by this defendant.

In a word, all the testimony of the non-accomplice witnesses was, in our judgment, inadmissible as evidence of the credibility of the accomplice witness Reles, because it was of merely slight, remote or conjectural significance in respect of that issue—to say nothing for the moment of the fact that such a use of that testimony inevitably tended unnecessarily to confuse the real issues and unfairly to surprise the defendant to his prejudice. See People v. Harris, 209 N.Y. 70, 102 N.E. 546 (1913).

Perhaps it should be added at this point that there was in this case no question of restoring the credit of Reles after his impeachment as a witness. The facts that discredited him came out on his direct examination and, as we have noticed, the non-accomplice witnesses were called by the prosecution in its direct case. See People v. Edwards, 282 N.Y. 413, 26 N.E.2d 957 (1940).

. . .

(4) We come now to an often burdensome question. May the error be regarded as technical and insufficient to require a reversal? See People v. Marendi, 213 N.Y. 600, 618, 620, 107 N.E. 1058 (1915). This defendant took the stand. His guilt is far from being clearly exhibited by the record. Of the three witnesses for the People who gave evidence sufficient to satisfy the statutory requirement of corroboration of Reles two had been prisoners in a jail where the defendant had been confined. Their testimony was that the defendant admitted his guilt to them or in their hearing to persons who visited

him there. The third of these witnesses was a thrice-convicted criminal.

In that state of the record we cannot say that the inadmissible use made of the testimony of the non-accomplice witnesses did not affect the result. It is quite manifest that their testimony was adduced in the apprehension that without such use thereof it was not unlikely that the verdict would be not guilty.

The judgment of conviction should be reversed and a new trial ordered.

TESTIMONY AND EVIDENCE

EX PARTE JACKSON

Court of Criminal Appeals of Texas, 1971.
470 S.W.2d 679.

OPINION

ONION, Presiding Judge. This is an appeal from an order entered in a habeas corpus proceeding in the 59th District Court of Grayson County remanding appellant to custody for extradition to the State of Arizona to answer the charge of robbery.

. . .

A formal order of the court entered later reflects the court had heard "evidence and argument of counsel" and the order concludes:

> "It is ordered, adjudged and decreed that extradition be granted and relator be placed in custody of Jack Bowen for removal to the State of Arizona *ad* directed in Governor's Warrant."

The Executive Warrant of the Governor of Texas and the supporting papers from the demanding state are in the record before us. The Executive Warrant appears regular on its face. Appellant's brief acknowledges that he received copies of the same on the date of the hearing, and that he was responsible for filing the same with the clerk on November 26, 1970.

There does appear in the record two agreed "statement of facts." One filed on January 14, 1971, bearing the approval of both counsel and the Judge, reads as follows:

> "The State of Texas called Jack Bowen to the stand as a witness, and he testified as follows:
>
> "That he was a deputy sheriff in Tucson, Arizona. That he had seen Martin Arnold Jackson one time in his life and that was at a barbeque party, and this was a week or so before the alleged offense occurred in 1968. That he had not seen him since and that he had not seen him on the date the alleged offense was committed. He identified Martin Arnold Jackson as being the same person wanted by the State of

> Arizona. There was no other testimony presented by the State.
>
> "Martin Arnold Jackson testified that he was not in Arizona at the time of the alleged offense, but that he was living in New Orleans, Louisiana, at the time of the alleged offense. He denied being at any barbeque party or ever having seen Deputy Jack Bowen. There was no other testimony presented on behalf of Martin Arnold Jackson.
>
> "This, in substance, truly and accurately sets out all the testimony at said hearing."

Another instrument (entitled "Statements of Facts") bearing the date of January 21, 1971, but reflecting no file mark is found in the record. Such statement shows the following:

> "On behalf of the State of Texas Jack Bowen testified as follows:
>
> "That he is a deputy sheriff in and for Pima County, Arizona and is acquainted with Martin Arnold Jackson who is also known as Jack Alvin Cage. That he was acquainted with the said Martin Arnold Jackson on and before the 27th day of November, 1968. That he did not see Martin Arnold Jackson in Tucson, Arizona on the 27th day of November, 1968, but that he did see him about a week prior to that time in Tucson which is in Pima County.
>
> "Martin Arnold Jackson testified on behalf of himself that on the 27th day of November, 1968, he was in New Orleans, Louisiana which was his residence. He testified that he had lived in Pima County, Arizona prior to November 27th, 1968, but that he had not been in such county for several weeks prior to the date of the alleged offense.
>
> "The foregoing represents in substance the testimony adduced at said hearing."

It is appellant's contention the evidence offered was insufficient to justify extradition.

> "In proceedings to challenge the legality of the arrest and detention of an accused under an executive warrant for his extradition, the state has the initial burden of showing that the arrest and detention are lawful." 25 Tex.Jur.2d, Extradition, Sec. 3, p. 180, citing Ex parte Hagler [161 Tex. Cr.R. 387], 278 S.W.2d 143.

The Executive Warrant of the Governor of the asylum state would appear to be an indispensable part of the evidence in any such proceeding. Ex parte Hagler, supra. If such warrant is in the courtroom at the habeas corpus hearing, it should be introduced in evidence by the State. If it is not introduced, it must be presumed that it does not authorize extradition. Ex parte Hagler, supra.

It is well established that when the Executive Warrant, regular on its face, is introduced into evidence, a prima facie case authorizing extradition is made out. By the same token, such prima facie case is not established until the Executive Warrant is introduced. Ex parte Hagler, supra.

In Ex parte Sykes, 400 S.W.2d 568 (Tex.Cr.App.1966), the order remanding Sykes for extradition was reversed. There the court said:

> "The statement of facts agreed to be a true and correct statement of all the evidence introduced in the case consists only of the testimony of appellant elicited by his counsel.
>
> "The Executive Warrant of the Governor of Texas is not found in the record, though the order appealed from recites that it was considered. The same is true as to the Requisition of the Governor of Arizona, and supporting documents.
>
> "In the absence of the Executive Warrant or other evidence offered by the state, there was no showing that appellant was lawfully restrained."

Sykes is distinguished from the instant case in two respects. First, the Executive Warrant, regular on its face, is in the record before us. Second, the agreed "Statement or Statements of Facts" relate only to the testimony given and do not purport to include all the evidence presented as in Sykes.

"Testimony" is evidence given by a competent witness under oath or affirmation as distinguished from evidence derived from writing and other sources. See Black's Law Dictionary, DeLuxe Fourth Ed.; Cauble v. Key, 256 S.W. 654, 655 (Tex.Civ.App.1924). Although "testimony" and "evidence" are frequently used synonymously, Superior Lloyds of America v. Foxworth, 178 S.W.2d 724, 726 (Tex.Civ.App.1944), the terms are not synonymous. Bednarik v. Bednarik, 18 N.J.Misc. 633, 16 A.2d 80, 89 (1940). Evidence is the broader term and includes all testimony which is one species of evidence. Bednarik v. Bednarik, supra. It is clear that the "agreed Statement or Statements of Facts" applied only to the testimony found in the spoken words of the witnesses and did not attempt to encompass all the evidence introduced at the habeas hearing.

Since the Texas Governor's Warrant, regular on its face, is in the record before us, and the trial judge's order clearly indicated it was before him when he entered his order, we deem the record sufficient to reflect its introduction and to establish a prima facie case authorizing extradition.

Once the Executive or Governor's Warrant is in evidence, then the burden is upon the person named therein to overcome the prima facie proof of the existence of every fact which the Texas Governor was obliged to determine before issuing the extradition warrant, including the fact that the person named in the warrant was in the demanding state at the time of the commission of the offense charged.

See Ex parte Mach, 448 S.W.2d 126 (Tex.Cr.App.1970). See also 25 Tex.Jur.2d, Extradition, Sec. 31, pp. 182–183.

In addition to the warrant, the State offered the testimony of an Arizona deputy sheriff that the petitioner had been in Arizona "about a week prior" to the date of the alleged offense. Appellant admitted he had lived in Arizona prior to the date in question but had not been in the county where alleged offense occurred for several weeks prior to the date of the alleged offense, claiming he was living in New Orleans, Louisiana on that date.

It should be noted that testimony of the appellant standing alone is insufficient to require a finding that he was not in the demanding state at the time the offense was alleged to have been committed. Ex parte Martin, 374 S.W.2d 436 (Tex.Cr.App.1964); Ex parte Overaker, 404 S.W.2d 595 (Tex.Cr.App.1966); Ex parte Gibson, 149 Tex.Cr.App. 543, 197 S.W.2d 109 (1946); Ex parte Moore, 436 S.W. 2d 901 (Tex.Cr.App.1969). See also 25 Tex.Jur.2d, Extradition, Sec. 12, p. 140.

The judgment is affirmed.

DOCUMENTARY EVIDENCE

TICKNOR v. TICKNOR

Supreme Court, Special Term, Nassau County, Part I, 1960.
23 Misc.2d 257, 200 N.Y.S.2d 661.

FRANK A. GULOTTA, Justice. This is a motion for alimony pendente lite and counsel fee in a separation action which includes general allegations of cruel and inhuman treatment, conduct on the part of the defendant which has made it unsafe for plaintiff to cohabit with him, abandonment, refusal and neglect of the defendant to provide for plaintiff, and adultery.

The defendant has made a cross-motion for summary judgment, pursuant to Rule 113 of the Rules of Civil Practice, asking that the complaint be dismissed on the ground that the parties were divorced in the State of Alabama by decree dated June 16, 1958, issued by the Circuit Court of that State in the Tenth Judicial District. In support of his contention defendant has submitted documentary evidence consisting of a power of attorney executed by the plaintiff on May 31, 1958, authorizing one William L. Allison to appear for her in the action commenced by this defendant against her in the State of Alabama, an Answer and Waiver signed by her and the Final Decree of Divorce.

Plaintiff counters by saying she did not know what she was signing and that defendant "(threatened) the plaintiff with bodily harm unless she executed some documents which were thrust under her nose."

It appears that the parties were married on July 18, 1952. There is no issue of this union although plaintiff has a daughter by a prior marriage. On April 18, 1958, the parties separated, plaintiff returning with her daughter to the family home in Sunbury, Pennsylvania, and the defendant remaining in Mount Vernon, New York, where they then lived.

Plaintiff contends that the reason for the separation was that defendant no longer desired to live with her. On the other hand, defendant says that plaintiff just packed her belongings and with her daughter went to reside in Sunbury, Pennsylvania, because she couldn't live in New York and got too homesick and lonesome. Defendant's version seems to be substantiated by a letter postmarked May 8, 1958, sent by plaintiff from Sunbury, Pennsylvania, to defendant at Mount Vernon, New York, wherein she says, in part:

> " . . . as I told you don't think I'll ever live in N. Y. again. I get too homesick & lonesome . . . . Maybe it is best we call it quits as I don't feel you could settle here ever & you have a good job so please keep it. In time I feel you will probably find a nice girl. There is no one else I want & probably never will marry again. If I ever do it will be a surprise to me. So if you want to go out go. Also in time you can get a divorce if you want as I won't stop you."

The letter is very solicitous and written in a very friendly and understanding tone. It ends as follows:

> "Be good & take care of yourself. May God Bless You. Love, Loretta."

The Alabama documents above referred to were signed by her on May 31, 1958, some three weeks later, when defendant visited her in Pennsylvania. The power of attorney was executed before a Notary Public in Sunbury and her signature to the Answer and Waiver was witnessed by the same Notary.

Apparently both parties felt that a divorce was the only solution because on May 20, 1958, defendant wrote to plaintiff:

> "If you feel that divorce is our solution, why don't you see about obtaining one in Sunbury there. You have established a residence there and know a great many people. I would be more than willing to shoulder whatever expense would be incurred in such action."

Plaintiff could not have been surprised by being given the Alabama papers to sign for the correspondence on both sides was leading to just that. On May 26, 1958, she received a letter from defendant stating:

> "I cannot see much practical sense in us being married when you are out there in Sunbury and I am working and trying to get along up here alone. My lawyer is a very nice

> man and he feels that a clean break is the best thing for both of us under the circumstances.
>
> "I do want you and Phyllis to have all your personal belongings and things that you might want. That is why I am coming out and I can bring the papers for you to sign in order to make the necessary preparations for divorce."

For two years plaintiff did nothing and has now suddenly brought this action on very tenuous allegations, with no facts.

There is no need to discuss the lack of probability of success in the plaintiff's matrimonial action, since the only point involved is the validity of the Alabama decree. Concededly the defendant has not supported the plaintiff since it was obtained and that decree must be the justification for not having done so, or there is none.

Insofar as the foreign decree is attacked because the plaintiff was not a bona fide resident, that avenue is no longer open, since it cannot now be questioned in Alabama on that ground, neither can it be collaterally attacked in New York, and it must be accorded full faith and credit here. Boxer v. Boxer, 7 A.D.2d 1001, 184 N.Y.S.2d 303 (1959); Sherrer v. Sherrer, 334 U.S. 343, 68 S.Ct. 1087, 1097, 92 L.Ed. 1429 (1948).

The question of alleged duress presents a different problem. Were we to have a case of true duress, i. e. coercion in forcing defendant to sign an authorization of appearance so overwhelming that the act would not represent a voluntary act of the defendant at all, it may be assumed that such facts could form the basis for a direct attack in the forum of the decree or for an oblique attack here. Finan v. Finan, 47 N.Y.S.2d 429 (Sup.1944).

The facts here do not support such a conclusion; in fact they point the opposite way.

However, to bring this case within the new Rule 113 which permits a defendant in a matrimonial action to move for summary judgment when his defense is based on documentary evidence or official records it is necessary to consider whether the plaintiff's letter of May 8, 1958, fits into the first category.

The divorce decree is undoubtedly an official record, but the letter is needed to prove the absence of duress. I think a letter may properly be considered a document. Richardson on Evidence, 8th Edition, § 2, states:

> "Documentary evidence is evidence in the form of a writing or writings. White v. Merchants Despatch Co., 256 App.Div. 1044, 10 N.Y.S.[2d] 962; Schusterman v. C. & F. Caterers, 192 Misc. 564, 566, 77 N.Y.S.[2d] 718. It has been more elaborately defined as follows: a document is 'any substance having any matter expressed or described upon it by marks capable of being read', and when 'produced for the inspection of the court . . . such documents are called

documentary evidence.' Chase's Stephen's Digest of the Law of Evidence, pp. 3, 4."

Tripps' Guide to Motion Practice, cp. 289, states:

> "The documentary proof contemplated by the rule is not defined or limited. Any document which meets a dictionary definition of that term is a document within the meaning of Rule 113, R.C.P., as it need not 'completely and conclusively establish the defense, without resort to extrinsic or fragmentary connecting links of proof supplied by affidavit or scattered entries or memoranda.' (Chance v. Guaranty Trust Co. of New York, 173 Misc. 754, 20 N.Y.S.[2d] 635, aff'd 257 App.Div. 1006, 13 N.Y.S.[2d] 785, 285 N.Y. 802; . . ."

Black's Law Dictionary defines documentary evidence as:

> "Evidence supplied by writings and documents of every kind in the widest sense of the term; evidence derived from conventional symbols (such as letters) by which ideas are represented on material substances. Such evidence as is furnished by written instruments, inscriptions, documents of all kinds, and also any inanimate objects admissible for the purpose, as distinguished from 'oral' evidence, or that delivered by human beings viva voce. People v. Purcell, 22 Cal.App.2d 126, 70 P.2d 706, 709."

The doctrine of "divisible divorce" does not obtain where there was in personam jurisdiction to support the foreign decree and thus the determination of the duress issue likewise disposes of the applicability of § 1170–b of the Civil Practice Act.

The plaintiff's motion is denied and the defendant's cross-motion is granted.

Short form order signed.

DECISIONS RELATING TO CHAPTER II, EXAMINATION OF WITNESS AND TRIAL PROCEDURES

ALFORD v. UNITED STATES

Supreme Court of the United States, 1931.
282 U.S. 687, 51 S.Ct. 218, 75 L.Ed. 624.

. . .

On Writ of Certiorari to the United States Circuit Court of Appeals for the Ninth Circuit.

J. W. Alford was convicted of using the mails to defraud, the conviction being affirmed by the Circuit Court of Appeals [41 F.2d 157], and he brings certiorari.

. . .

Mr. Justice STONE delivered the opinion of the Court.

Petitioner was convicted in the District Court for southern California of using the mails to defraud in violation of section 215 of the Criminal Code (18 U.S.C.A. § 338). This Court granted certiorari, 282 U.S. 826, 51 S.Ct. 77, 75 L.Ed. 624, October 20, 1930, to review a judgment of affirmance by the Court of Appeals for the Ninth Circuit, which upheld certain rulings of the trial court upon the evidence. 41 F.2d 157.

In the course of the trial the government called as a witness a former employee of petitioner. On direct examination he gave damaging testimony with respect to various transactions of accused, including conversations with the witness when others were not present, and statements of accused to salesmen under his direction, whom the witness did not identify. Upon cross-examination questions seeking to elicit the witness's place of residence were excluded on the government's objection that they were immaterial and not proper cross-examination. Counsel for the defense insisted that the questions were proper cross-examination, and that the jury was entitled to know "who the witness is, where he lives and what his business is." Relevant excerpts of the record are printed in the margin.[1]

1. Q. Where do you live, Mr. Bradley?

Mr. Armstrong: That is objected to as immaterial and not proper cross-examination.

The Court: I cannot see the materiality.

Mr. Friedman: Why, I think the jury has a perfect right to know who the witness is, where he lives and what his business is, and we have the right to elicit that on cross-examination. I may say that this is the first witness the Government had called that they have not elicited the address from.

The Court: I will sustain the objection.

Q. By Mr. Friedman: What is your business, Mr. Bradley? A. My profession is an accountant, public accountant.

Q. What is your occupation now? A. I am not doing anything at the present time on account of this case.

Q. On account of this case? A. Yes.

Later, the jury having been excused, counsel for the defense urged, as an "additional" ground for asking the excluded questions, that he had been informed that the witness was then in the custody of the federal authorities, and that such fact might be brought out on cross-examination "for the the purpose of showing whatever bias or prejudice he may have." But the court adhered to its previous rulings, saying that if the witness had been convicted of a felony that fact might be proved, but not that he was detained in custody.

The Court of Appeals, after stating that it is customary to allow cross-examination of a witness with reference to his place of residence, upheld the trial court, saying, page 160 of 41 F.2d:

> "The purpose of such evidence is to identify the witness and to some extent give proper background for the interpretation of his testimony. In this case, however, the counsel indicated his purpose to use the information for the purpose of discrediting the witness. It is part of the obligation of a trial judge to protect witnesses against evidence tending to discredit the witness unless such evidence is reasonably call-

Q. Do you live in Los Angeles?

Mr. Armstrong: That is objected to as immaterial and invading the Court's ruling.

The Court: I have ruled on that question.

Mr. Friedman: I will temporarily pass on to something else. I would like leave to submit authorities on my right to develop that on cross-examination. I haven't them with me.

The Court: All right. . . .

The jury were thereupon excused by the court until 9:30 o'clock on the morning of July 24, 1929, whereupon the jury retired after which the following proceedings were had relative to the materiality of the testimony, as to the residence and place thereof of Cameron Bradley.

The Court: So ordered. In what particular do you think that evidence is material?

Mr. Friedman: I think it is material for this purpose, first, not only on the general grounds I urged in asking the question, but on the additional grounds that I have been informed and caused to believe that this witness himself is now in the custody of the Federal authorities.

Mr. Armstrong: You mean Mr. Bradley? You mean by the Federal authorities here?

Mr. Friedman: I don't know by what authorities, but that is my impression, that he is here in the custody of the Federal authorities. If that is so, I have a right to show that for the purpose of showing whatever bias or prejudice he may have.

The Court: No; I don't think so. If you can prove he has ever been convicted of a felony, that is a different thing.

Mr. Friedman: I realize that is the rule. I may impeach him if he has been convicted of a felony.

The Court: No. You may prove that fact as going to his credibility, but you can't merely show that he is detained or in charge of somebody. Everybody is presumed to be innocent until proven guilty.

Mr. Friedman: It is a violent presumption sometimes, I know.

The Court: Your defendant is certainly to be given the benefit of that presumption.

Mr. Friedman: I have no doubt of that.

The Court: If that is all you have, I will have to stand on the ruling. . . .

Mr. Friedman: I would like, if the Court please, our exception noted to the Court's ruling made yesterday after the jury retired to the effect that we could not inquire as to the present address and residence of the witness.

The Court: Very well.

ed for by exigencies of the case. A witness is not on trial and has no means of protecting himself. Here it was evident that the counsel for the appellant desired to discredit the witness, without, so far as is shown, in any way connecting the expected answer with a matter on trial. If it had been contended that the witness was in custody because of his participation in the transaction with which the appellant was charged, and if it was sought to show that he was testifying under some promise of immunity, it would undoubtedly have been prejudicial error to have excluded such testimony; but counsel avowed no such purpose, and indicated that the proposed question was merely in pursuit of a fishing expedition by which he hoped to discredit the witness. The witness was examined at great length concerning his relation to the appellant and great latitude was accorded in that examination."

Cross-examination of a witness is a matter of right. The Ottawa, 3 Wall. 268, 271, 18 L.Ed. 165 (1859). Its permissible purposes, among others, are that the witness may be identified with his community so that independent testimony may be sought and offered of his reputation for veracity in his own neighborhood, cf. Khan v. Zemansky, 59 Cal.App. 324, 327ff, 210 Pac. 529 (1923); 3 Wigmore, Evidence (2d Ed.) § 1368, I. (1) (b); that the jury may interpret his testimony in the light reflected upon it by knowledge of his environment, Kirschner v. State, 9 Wis. 140 (1859); Wilbur v. Flood, 16 Mich. 40, 93 Am.Dec. 203 (1867); Hollingsworth v. State, 53 Ark. 387, 14 S.W. 41 (1890); People v. White, 251 Ill. 67, 72ff., 95 N.E. 1036 (1911); Wallace v. State, 41 Fla. 547, 574ff., 26 So. 713 (1900); and that facts may be brought out tending to discredit the witness by showing that his testimony in chief was untrue or biased, Tla-koo-yel-lee v. United States, 167 U.S. 274, 17 S.Ct. 855, 42 L.Ed. 166 (1897); King v. United States, 112 F. 988 (C.C.A.1902); Farkas v. United States, 2 F.2d 644 (C.C.A.1925); see Furlong v. United States, 10 F. 2d 492, 494 (C.C.A.1926).

Counsel often cannot know in advance what pertinent facts may be elicited on cross-examination. For that reason it is necessarily exploratory; and the rule that the examiner must indicate the purpose of his inquiry does not, in general, apply. Knapp v. Wing, 72 Vt. 334, 340, 47 A. 1075 (1901); Martin v. Elden, 32 Ohio St. 282, 289 (1877). It is the essence of a fair trial that reasonable latitude be given the cross-examiner, even though he is unable to state to the court what facts a reasonable cross-examination might develop. Prejudice ensues from a denial of the opportunity to place the witness in his proper setting and put the weight of his testimony and his credibility to a test, without which the jury cannot fairly appraise them. Tla-koo-yel-lee v. United States, supra; King v. United States, supra; People v. Moore, 96 App.Div. 56, 89 N.Y.S. 83 (1949), affirmed without opinion, 181 N.Y. 524, 73 N.E. 1129 (1905); cf. People v. Becker, 210 N.Y. 274, 104 N.E. 396 (1914). To say that prejudice can be established only by showing that the cross-examination, if pursued, would necessarily have brought out facts tending to discredit the testimony in chief, is to deny a substantial right and withdraw one of the safeguards essential to a fair trial. Nailor v. Williams, 8 Wall. 107, 109, 19 L.Ed. 348 (1868); see People v. Stevenson, 284 Pac. 491 (Cal.Sup.1930); cf. Brasfield v. United States, 272 U.S. 448, 47 S.Ct. 135, 71 L.Ed. 345 (1926). In this respect a summary denial of the right of cross-examination is distinguishable from the erroneous admission of harmless testimony. Nailor v. Williams, supra.

The present case, after the witness for the prosecution had testified to uncorroborated conversations of the defendant of a damaging character, was a proper one for searching cross-examination. The question, "Where do you live?" was not only an appropriate preliminary to the cross-examination of the witness, but on its face, without any such declaration of purpose as was made by counsel here, was an essential step in identifying the witness with his environment, to which cross-examination may always be directed. State v. Pugsley, 75 Iowa 742, 38 N.W. 498 (1888); State v. Fong Loon, 29 Idaho 248, 255ff., 158 Pac. 233, L.R.A.1916F, 1198 (1916); Wallace v. State, supra; Wilbur v. Flood, supra; 5 Jones, Evidence (2d Ed.) § 2366.

But counsel for the defense went further, and in the ensuing colloquy with the court urged, as an additional reason why the question should be allowed, not a substitute reason, as the court below assumed, that he was informed that the witness was then in court in custody of the federal authorities, and that that fact could be brought out on cross-examination to show whatever bias or prejudice the witness might have. The purpose obviously was not, as the trial court seemed to think, to discredit the witness by showing that he was charged with crime, but to show by such facts as proper cross-examination might develop, that his testimony was biased because given under promise or expectation of immunity, or under the coercive effect of his detention by officers of the United States, which was conducting the present prosecution. King v. United States, supra; Farkas v. United States, supra, and cases cited; People v. Becker, supra; State v. Ritz, 65 Mont. 180, 211 P. 298 (1923), and cases cited on page 188, 211 Pac. 298; Rex v. Watson, 32 How.St.Tr. 284. Nor is it material, as the Court of Appeals said, whether the witness was in custody because of his participation in the transactions for which petitioner was indicted. Even if the witness were charged with some other offense by the prosecuting authorities, petitioner was entitled to show by cross examination that his testimony was affected by fear or favor growing out of his detention. See Farkas v. United States, supra; People v. Dillwood, 4 Cal.Unrep. 973, 39 Pac. 438 (1895).

The extent of cross-examination with respect to an appropriate subject of inquiry is within the sound discretion of the trial court. It may exercise a reasonable judgment in determining when the subject is exhausted. Storm v. United States, 94 U.S. 76, 85, 24 L.Ed.

42 (1876); Rea v. Missouri, 17 Wall. 532, 542–543, 21 L.Ed. 707 (1873); Blitz v. United States, 153 U.S. 308, 312, 14 S.Ct. 924, 38 L.Ed. 725 (1894). But no obligation is imposed on the court, such as that suggested below, to protect a witness from being discredited on cross-examination, short of an attempted invasion of his constitutional protection from self incrimination, properly invoked. There is a duty to protect him from questions which go beyond the bonds of proper cross-examination merely to harass, annoy or humiliate him. President, etc., of Third Great Western Turnpike Road Co. v. Loomis, 32 N.Y. 127, 132, 88 Am.Dec. 311 (1865); Wallace v. State, supra; 5 Jones, Evidence (2d Ed.) § 2316. But no such case is presented here. The trial court cut off in limine all inquiry on a subject with respect to which the defense was entitled to a reasonable cross examination. This was an abuse of discretion and prejudicial error. Tla-koo-yel-lee v. United States, supra; Nailor v. Williams, supra; King v. United States, supra; People v. Moore, supra; cf. People v. Becker, supra. Other grounds for reversal were set up in the petition for certiorari, but we do not find it necessary to pass upon them.

Reversed.

CROSS EXAMINATION

UNITED STATES v. PALERMO

United States Court of Appeals, Seventh Circuit, 1969.
410 F.2d 468.

KERNER, Circuit Judge. Defendants were indicted for conspiring to violate the Hobbs Act, 18 U.S.C.A. § 1951, by interfering with commerce by extorting money from a builder and in so doing, interfering with interstate shipments of construction materials. The jury found all defendants guilty and from these convictions they appeal.

From 1962 to 1965 Riley Management Company, with William G. Riley as president, was building various apartment building complexes in suburbs surrounding Chicago. Melrose Park Plumbing was a subcontractor on Riley's first construction project in Addison, Illinois, in 1962. Nick Palermo, a defendant and the owner of Melrose Park Plumbing, wanted to be sure that Riley would use his company on all of Riley's building projects. To accomplish this, Palermo and defendant Joseph Amabile, also known as Joe Shine, conspired together with others to force Riley into using Melrose Park Plumbing as a subcontractor and at the same time having Riley pay them extra money for their work. See United States v. Battaglia, 394 F.2d 304 (7th Cir. 1968). In essence, Amabile, Palermo and others agreed to obtain as much money as possible from Riley by threatening him with work stoppages and physical violence.

Early in 1962, Riley became interested in building another apartment complex in Northlake, Illinois. In April of 1962, defendant

Henry Ed Neri, Mayor of Northlake, and Wayne Seidler, an unindicted co-conspirator, met with Riley's attorney at which time Mayor Neri told him it would cost $100 per unit or $70,000 in order to build the project in Northlake. Without this money, required zoning changes would not be made nor would building permits be issued. A few days later Amabile told Neri that he and Nick Palermo were taking over the project in Northlake and could obtain at least $40,000 for Neri's people. Neri then asked Amabile for $10,000 before the next meeting of the Zoning Board.

Defendants Leo Shababy and Joseph Drozd were aldermen in Northlake. They and some members of the Zoning Board received various monies from Amabile for rezoning the area. When the money demanded was not being paid on time, Shababy, Drozd, Seidler and Neri put pressures on Amabile including withholding approval of the zoning change and refusing to issue building permits. In turn, Amabile and Palermo pressured Riley into paying them $64,000 by threatening him both with work stoppage at the Addison project and physical violence to himself and his family. Riley testified that Palermo hit him in the face and threatened to make him understand with a baseball bat. See United States v. Battaglia, 394 F.2d 304, 308 (7th Cir. 1968).

. . .

CROSS-EXAMINATION

Alford v. United States, 282 U.S. 687, 51 S.Ct. 218, 75 L.Ed. 624 (1931), and Smith v. Illinois, 390 U.S. 129, 88 S.Ct. 748, 19 L.Ed.2d 956 (1968), require reversal where the district judge refuses to allow questions as to a witness' address and present employment since they are threshold questions of cross-examination. "The purpose of the inquiry is to make known to the jury the setting in which to judge the character, veracity or bias of the witness. . . . Since there is no requirement of materiality, it is not necessary to show the possibility of the witness being in custody in order to make such inquiry." United States v. Varelli, 407 F.2d 735, p. 749 (7th Cir. 1969).

However, the decision to disclose a witness' address or place of employment cannot be made in a vacuum. This Court is not unaware of the problem that the government has in obtaining witnesses in cases where a witness' life may be in jeopardy if he testifies. As Justice White said in his concurrence in Smith v. Illinois, 390 U.S. 129, 133–134, 88 S.Ct. 748, 751 (1968), "In Alford v. United States, 282 U.S. 687, 694, 51 S.Ct. 218, 220, 75 L.Ed. 624 (1931), the Court recognized that questions which tend merely to harass, annoy, or humiliate a witness may go beyond the bounds of proper cross-examination. I would place in the same category those inquiries which tend to endanger the personal safety of the witness."

This Court agrees with Justice White that where there is a threat to the life of the witness, the right of the defendant to have the witness' true name, address and place of employment is not absolute. United

States v. Varelli, 407 F.2d 735 (7th Cir. 1969). However, the threat to the witness must be actual and not a result of conjecture. Shaw v. Illinois, 394 U.S. 214, 89 S.Ct. 1016, 22 L.Ed.2d 211 (1969). The government bears the burden of proving to the district judge the existence of such a threat.

An actual threat being shown, the government must also disclose to the district judge *in camera* the relevant information. United States v. Varelli, 407 F.2d 735 (7th Cir. 1969). Knowing of the existence of an actual threat and the witness' location, the district judge must determine whether the information must be disclosed in order not to deny effective cross-examination. "The trial judge can then ascertain the interest of the defendant in the answer and exercise an informed discretion in making his ruling." (White, J. concurring) Smith v. Illinois, 390 U.S. 129, 134, 88 S.Ct. 751 (1968). Such decision is reviewable on appeal. Under almost all circumstances, the true name of the witness must be disclosed. Smith v. Illinois, 390 U.S. 129, 88 S.Ct. 748 (1968). If the witness is located in a penal institution, this, too, must be disclosed. Alford v. United States, 282 U.S. 687, 51 S.Ct. 218 (1931). A witness' prior address must also be disclosed if the witness does not intend to return to this location. United States v. Varelli, 407 F.2d 735 (7th Cir. 1969). If the trial judge concludes that the defendant does not have a right to the exact address of the witness and his place of employment, the defendant is entitled to ask any other relevant questions which may aid the jury in weighing the witness' credibility.

Here, the trial judge, having been requested to order Seidler and Riley to disclose their addresses and present employment, refused to order them to answer. While there was an adequate showing of a threat to the life of Riley, there was no showing as to Seidler. In neither case was the relevant information disclosed to the trial judge in order that he could make an informed decision. On remand the government must comply with the standards set out above.

Remanded with directions.

POINTER v. STATE OF TEXAS

Supreme Court of the United States, 1965.
380 U.S. 400, 85 S.Ct. 1065, 13 L.Ed.2d 923.

Mr. Justice BLACK delivered the opinion of the Court.

The Sixth Amendment provides in part that:

> "In all criminal prosecutions, the accused shall enjoy the right . . . to be confronted with the witnesses against him . . . and to have the Assistance of Counsel for his defence."

Two years ago in Gideon v. Wainwright, 372 U.S. 335, 83 S.Ct. 792, 9 L.Ed.2d 799 (1963), we held that the Fourteenth Amendment makes the Sixth Amendment's guarantee of right to counsel obligatory upon the States. The question we find necessary to decide in this case is whether the Amendment's guarantee of a defendant's right "to be confronted with the witnesses against him," which has been held to include the right to cross-examine those witnesses, is also made applicable to the States by the Fourteenth Amendment.

The petitioner Pointer and one Dillard were arrested in Texas and taken before a state judge for a preliminary hearing (in Texas called the "examining trial") on a charge of having robbed Kenneth W. Phillips of $375 "by assault, or violence, or by putting in fear of life or bodily injury," in violation of Texas Penal Code Art. 1408. At this hearing an Assistant District Attorney conducted the prosecution and examined witnesses, but neither of the defendants, both of whom were laymen, had a lawyer. Phillips as chief witness for the State gave his version of the alleged robbery in detail, identifying petitioner as the man who had robbed him at gunpoint. Apparently Dillard tried to cross-examine Phillips but Pointer did not, although Pointer was said to have tried to cross-examine some other witnesses at the hearing. Petitioner was subsequently indicted on a charge of having committed the robbery. Some time before the trial was held, Phillips moved to California. After putting in evidence to show that Phillips had moved and did not intend to return to Texas, the State at the trial offered the transcript of Phillips' testimony given at the preliminary hearing as evidence against petitioner. Petitioner's counsel immediately objected to introduction of the transcript, stating, "Your Honor, we will object to that, as it is a denial of the confrontment of the witnesses against the Defendant." Similar objections were repeatedly made by petitioner's counsel but were overruled by the trial judge, apparently in part because, as the judge viewed it, petitioner had been present at the preliminary hearing and therefore had been "accorded the opportunity of cross examining the witnesses there against him." The Texas Court of Criminal Appeals, the highest state court to which the case could be taken, affirmed petitioner's conviction, rejecting his contention that use of the transcript to convict him denied him rights guaranteed by the Sixth and Fourteenth Amendments. 375 S.W.2d 293. We granted certiorari to consider the important constitutional question the case involves. 379 U.S. 815, 85 S.Ct. 88, 13 L.Ed.2d 28.

. . .

. . . In this case the objections and arguments in the trial court as well as the arguments in the Court of Criminal Appeals and before us make it clear that petitioner's objection is based not so much on the fact that he had no lawyer when Phillips made his statement at the preliminary hearing, as on the fact that use of the transcript of that statement at the trial denied petitioner any opportunity to have the benefit of counsel's cross-examination of the principal witness against him. It is that latter question which we decide here.

I.

The Sixth Amendment is a part of what is called our Bill of Rights. In Gideon v. Wainwright, supra, in which this Court held that the Sixth Amendment's right to the assistance of counsel is obligatory upon the States, we did so on the ground that "a provision of the Bill of Rights which is 'fundamental and essential to a fair trial' is made obligatory upon the States by the Fourteenth Amendment." 372 U.S., at 342, 83 S.Ct., at 795. And last Term in Malloy v. Hogan, 378 U.S. 1, 84 S.Ct. 1489, 12 L.Ed.2d 653 (1964), in holding that the Fifth Amendment's guarantee against self-incrimination was made applicable to the States by the Fourteenth, we reiterated the holding of Gideon that the Sixth Amendment's right-to-counsel guarantee is " 'a fundamental right, essential to a fair trial,' " and "thus was made obligatory on the States by the Fourteenth Amendment." 378 U.S., at 6, 84 S.Ct., at 1492. See also Murphy v. Waterfront Comm'n, 378 U.S. 52, 84 S.Ct. 1594, 12 L.Ed.2d 678 (1964). We hold today that the Sixth Amendment's right of an accused to confront the witnesses against him is likewise a fundamental right and is made obligatory on the States by the Fourteenth Amendment.

It cannot seriously be doubted at this late date that the right of cross-examination is included in the right of an accused in a criminal case to confront the witnesses against him. And probably no one, certainly no one experienced in the trial of lawsuits, would deny the value of cross-examination in exposing falsehood and bringing out the truth in the trial of a criminal case. See, e. g., 5 Wigmore, Evidence § 1367 (3d ed. 1940). The fact that this right appears in the Sixth Amendment of our Bill of Rights reflects the belief of the Framers of those liberties and safeguards that confrontation was a fundamental right essential to a fair trial in a criminal prosecution. Moreover, the decisions of this Court and other courts throughout the years have constantly emphasized the necessity for cross-examination as a protection for defendants in criminal cases. This Court in Kirby v. United States, 174 U.S. 47, 55, 56, 19 S.Ct. 574, 577, 43 L.Ed. 890 (1899), referred to the right of confrontation as "[o]ne of the fundamental guaranties of life and liberty," and "a right long deemed so essential for the due protection of life and liberty that it is guarded against legislative and judicial action by provisions in the constitution of the United States and in the constitutions of most, if not of all, the states composing the Union." Mr. Justice Stone, writing for the Court in Alford v. United States, 282 U.S. 687, 692, 51 S.Ct. 218, 219, 75 L.Ed. 624 (1931), declared that the right of cross-examination is "one of the safeguards essential to a fair trial." And in speaking of confrontation and cross-examination this Court said in Greene v. McElroy, 360 U.S. 474, 79 S.Ct. 1400, 3 L.Ed.2d 1377 (1959):

> "They have ancient roots. They find expression in the Sixth Amendment which provides that in all criminal cases the accused shall enjoy the right 'to be confronted with the witnesses against him.' This Court has been zealous to protect these rights from erosion." 360 U.S., at 496–497, 79 S.Ct., at 1413 (footnote omitted).

There are few subjects, perhaps, upon which this Court and other courts have been more nearly unanimous than in their expressions of belief that the right of confrontation and cross-examination is an essential and fundamental requirement for the kind of fair trial which is this country's constitutional goal. Indeed, we have expressly declared that to deprive an accused of the right to cross-examine the witnesses against him is a denial of the Fourteenth Amendment's guarantee of due process of law. In In re Oliver, 333 U.S. 257, 68 S.Ct. 499, 92 L.Ed. 682 (1948), this Court said:

> "A person's right to reasonable notice of a charge against him, and an opportunity to be heard in his defense—a right to his day in court—are basic in our system of jurisprudence; and these rights include, as a minimum, a right to examine the witnesses against him, to offer testimony, and to be represented by counsel." 333 U.S., at 273, 68 S.Ct., at 507 (footnote omitted).

And earlier this Term in Turner v. State of Louisiana, 379 U.S. 466, 472–473, 85 S.Ct. 546, 550, 13 L.Ed.2d 424 (1965), we held:

> "In the constitutional sense, trial by jury in a criminal case necessarily implies at the very least that the 'evidence developed' against a defendant shall come from the witness stand in a public courtroom where there is full judicial protection of the defendant's right of confrontation, of cross-examination, and of counsel."

Compare Willner v. Committee on Character & Fitness, 373 U.S. 96, 103–104, 83 S.Ct. 1175, 1180–1181, 10 L.Ed.2d 224 (1963).

We are aware that some cases, particularly West v. State of Louisiana, 194 U.S. 258, 264, 24 S.Ct. 650, 652, 48 L.Ed. 965 (1904), have stated that the Sixth Amendment's right of confrontation does not apply to trials in state courts, on the ground that the entire Sixth Amendment does not so apply. See also Stein v. People of State of New York, 346 U.S. 156, 195–196, 73 S.Ct. 1077, 1098–1099, 97 L.Ed. 1522 (1953). But of course since Gideon v. Wainwright, supra, it no longer can broadly be said that the Sixth Amendment does not apply to state courts. And as this Court said in Malloy v. Hogan, supra, "The Court has not hesitated to re-examine past decisions according the Fourteenth Amendment a less central role in the preservation of basic liberties than that which was contemplated by its Framers when they added the Amendment to our constitutional scheme." 378 U.S., at 5, 84 S.Ct., at 1492. In the light of Gideon, Malloy, and other cases cited in those opinions holding various provisions of the Bill of Rights applicable to the States by virtue of the Fourteenth Amendment, the statements made in West and similar cases generally declaring that the Sixth Amendment does not apply to the States can no longer be regarded as the law. We hold that petitioner was entitled to be tried in accordance with the protection of the confrontation guarantee of the Sixth Amendment, and that that guarantee, like the right against compelled self-incrimination, is "to be enforced against the States under the Fourteenth Amendment according to the same standards that protect those personal rights against federal encroachment." Malloy v. Hogan, supra, 378 U.S., at 10, 84 S.Ct., at 1495.

II.

Under this Court's prior decisions, the Sixth Amendment's guarantee of confrontation and cross-examination was unquestionably denied petitioner in this case. As has been pointed out, a major reason underlying the constitutional confrontation rule is to give a defendant charged wtih crime an opportunity to cross-examine the witnesses against him. See, e. g., Dowdell v. United States, 221 U.S. 325, 330, 31 S.Ct. 590, 592, 55 L.Ed. 753 (1911); Motes v. United States, 178 U.S. 458, 474, 20 S.Ct. 993, 999, 44 L.Ed. 1150 (1900); Kirby v. United States, 174 U.S. 47, 55–56, 19 S.Ct. 574, 577, 43 L.Ed. 890 (1899); . . . Nothing we hold here is to the contrary. The case before us would be quite a different one had Phillips' statement been taken at a full-fledged hearing at which petitioner had been represented by counsel who had been given a complete and adequate opportunity to cross-examine. Compare Motes v. United States, supra, 178 U.S., at 474, 20 S.Ct., at 999. There are other analogous situations which might not fall within the scope of the constitutional rule requiring confrontation of witnesses. The case before us, however, does not present any situation like those mentioned above or others analogous to them. Because the transcript of Phillips' statement offered against petitioner at his trial had not been taken at a time and under circumstances affording petitioner through counsel an adequate opportunity to cross-examine Phillips, its introduction in a federal court in a criminal case against Pointer would have amounted to denial of the privilege of confrontation guaranteed by the Sixth Amendment. Since we hold that the right of an accused to be confronted with the witnesses against him must be determined by the same standards whether the right is denied in a federal or state proceeding, it follows that use of the transcript to convict petitioner denied him a constitutional right, and that his conviction must be reversed.

Reversed and remanded.

PEOPLE OF THE STATE OF NEW YORK v. BENJAMIN OYOLA

Court of Appeals of New York, 1959.
6 N.Y.2d 259, 189 N.Y.S.2d 203, 160 N.E.2d 494.

. . .

VAN VOORHIS, Judge. Appellant has been convicted in the New York City Court of Special Sessions of causing the morals of a child under 16 years of age to become depraved in violation of subdivision 1 of section 483 of the Penal Law, and of assault in the third degree in violation of subdivision 1 of section 244. Both of these misdemeanors are claimed to have been perpetrated on the daughter of appellant and his wife. Matrimonial differences had arisen which culminated in appellant's removal from the home when his wife had him arrested following the alleged incident on which these criminal charges depend. The evidence against him consists of testimony by Nancy, their 10-year-old daughter, and an admission which his wife testified that he subsequently made to her on the telephone. We are satisfied that this conversation was erroneously admitted into evidence for reasons hereinafter stated.

The police were in the Oyola home within four hours and Mrs. Oyola was there within two hours of the earliest possible happening of this alleged sexual assault. The child testified to all the particulars of a completed act of intercourse upon her by her father, soon after she had retired for the night. She said that she had on her nightgown, and that he was clothed. In spite of the early arrival of both mother and the police, no evidence was offered by the People of any examination of the child's body, nor the finding of any residual evidence of a seminal emission in or about the child's sex organs, adjacent area nor on any other portion of her body, bedclothes or nightgown nor upon appellant's clothing or anywhere else. No evidence was introduced of any cutaneous, structural or tissue injury or disturbance of this girl's private parts, such as abrasions, lacerations, discoloration, redness, swelling or the like. No circumstantial evidence supports the child's version of what occurred, all of which appellant has denied. In answer to questions from the Presiding Judge at Special Sessions, Nancy said that her mother had rehearsed her story privately with her five times before the daughter told it to anyone else. Appellant had no previous criminal record. His good character was attested by his employer and another witness, and was recognized by Special Sessions when he was sentenced to an indefinite term in the New York City Penitentiary. Nancy testified that he had done the same thing to her and to her playmate each on one prior occasion, but that this was the first time when she told her mother. This disclosure coincided in time with her mother's lawyer's instruction to Nancy to remember that she would have to repeat the same testimony in a matrimonial action against her father.

The question is whether this evidence against appellant was sufficient to prove him guilty beyond a reasonable doubt. In People v. Ledwon, 153 N.Y. 10, 46 N.E. 1046 (1897), it was held that the burden being upon the People of establishing the guilt of the accused beyond a reasonable doubt, a mere scintilla or even some proof is not enough to create an issue of fact. In the exercise of their judicial function, courts have often held that in certain situations as matter of law the evidence must be more than usually clear and convincing. The degree of proof required may be affected by whether the testimony is contradicted by other evidence, whether it is consistent, credible or contains elements of suspicion. Moreover all evidence is to be weighed according to the proof which it was in the power of the party to have produced, as Lord Mansfield observed (2 Wigmore, Evidence, § 285, p. 163). Upon the record in this case including the omission of any circumstantial evidence lending credibility to the testimony of this child, we have concluded that appellant has not been proved guilty beyond a reasonable doubt.

Our attention has been directed to the circumstance that in the instance of this and certain other sexual offenses no statute specifically requires corroboration of the testimony of the complainant, like the statutes in the cases of abduction (Penal Law, § 71), adultery (id., § 103), compulsory prostitution (id., §§ 1091, 2460), compulsory marriage (id., § 1455), rape (id., § 2013), and until the crime was abolished, seduction under promise of marriage (id., § 2177). It is not altogether clear on what principle the Legislature adopted separate statutes in regard to these crimes. If appellant had been indicted under section 483–a of the Penal Law (carnal abuse of a child) he would have been charged with a felony punishable on conviction by imprisonment for not more than 10 years. That is exactly the same punishment prescribed for rape in the second degree (Penal Law, § 2010), yet in the latter instance there is a statute expressly requiring corroboration of the testimony of the complainant (§ 2013) whereas in case of the former there is no such statute. The absence of legislation requiring other evidence to support the testimony of the complainant extending to every material fact essential to constitute the crime, as in case of rape (People v. Downs, 236 N.Y. 306, 140 N.E. 706 (1923); People v. Page, 162 N.Y. 272, 274, 56 N.E. 750, 751 (1900)), does not signify that courts fail to scrutinize with special care the same type of testimony in view of the case with which crimes of this nature are charged and the difficulty of disproving them, and in view of the instinctive horror with which they are regarded by mankind (People v. Friedman, 139 App.Div. 795, 124 N.Y.S. 521 (1910); People v. Donohue, 114 App.Div. 830, 100 N.Y.S. 202 (1906)).

Attention is called to the provision in Section 392 of the Code of Criminal Procedure that when in criminal proceedings a child under 12 years of age does not in the opinion of the court or magistrate understand the nature of an oath, the unsworn statement of the child may be received "But no person shall be held or convicted of an offence upon such testimony unsupported by other evidence." Corroboration would have been required of every material fact essential to constitute the crime if Nancy Oyola had not been sworn (People v. Meeks, 283 N.Y. 694, 28 N.E.2d 413 (1940); People v. Dutton, 305 N.Y. 632, 111 N.E.2d 889 (1953)). In a series of decisions, however, where the infant complainant was sworn, this court has reversed convictions on charges of this nature and dismissed the indictments or informations as not proved beyond a reasonable doubt on the records before the court which depended upon the testimony of the complaining witness alone (People v. Churgin, 261 N.Y. 661, 185 N.E. 782 (1933) [9 years old]; People v. Slaughter, 278 N.Y. 479, 15 N.E.2d 70 (1938) [15 years old]; People v. Derner, 288 N.Y. 599, 42 N.E.2d 605 (1942) [10 years old and 12 years old]; People v. Rosen, 293

N.Y. 683, 56 N.E.2d 297 (1944) [8 years old]; People v. Meyers, 309 N.Y. 837, 130 N.E.2d 622 (1956) [9 years old]). A child under 12 years of age is presumed to be incompetent to be sworn as a witness in a criminal trial, and this presumption must be overcome by proper preliminary examination (People v. Klein, 266 N.Y. 188, 194 N.E. 402 (1935)). Olshansky v. Prensky, 185 App.Div. 469, 172 N.Y.S. 856 (1919), indicates the nature of such preliminary examination. The records of the preliminary examinations in the cases cited lead to the conclusion that the application of this test is necessarily superficial and inconclusive in most instances. Some children were sworn who were younger than in other cases where unsworn statements were taken. The difficulty in applying the test of the understanding of an oath is illustrated by the preliminary examination of the 10-year-old girl upon whose testimony appellant's fate depends, in which she repeated five times to the Presiding Judge of Special Sessions that she had never told a lie, but added, on reconsideration, that she had lied about 20 times during the previous year. She stated that she believed that, although one may sin by lying, nobody can do anything to you if you do lie. Can it be, in cases of this nature, that the need to have some verification of the testimony of the child depends altogether upon such collateral factors as whether, for example, this child had said in her preliminary examination that she had told 30 lies instead of 20 lies during the year before, or to whom she told the lies, or when she stopped lying? Mention of this is not frivolous, since this is the kind of thing in preliminary examinations of children under Section 392 of the Code of Criminal Procedure which would determine the guilt or innocence of defendants unless the courts required some objective earmarks of truth even in cases where the child witness has been sworn. Where the witness has been sworn, it may not be necessary to have supporting evidence of every material fact essential to constitute the crime but the courts are not automatons of the Legislature to such a degree as to make patchwork of the law by being obliged to require full corroboration in instances where the trial court has taken the unsworn statement of the witness, but at the same time being compelled to dispense with all objective verification where an oath has been administered. To draw this sharp distinction would be as unreal today as the older law preventing atheists from testifying in court on the basis that they do not appreciate the nature of an oath (Jackson ex dem. Tuttle v. Gridley, 18 Johns. 98, 104 (1920)). This can hardly have been intended by the Legislature. Whether a child eight years old is sworn as in People v. Rosen, supra, or a child of nine years has an unsworn statement taken as in People v. Dutton, supra, is largely fortuitous. Causing the criminal liability of a defendant to depend entirely upon this collateral and largely accidental circumstance would have almost as little to do with deliberative justice as trial by ordeal where, under a practice now happily extinct, the guilt or innocence of a defendant was determined by whether his hand was burned when he thrust it into boiling water or fire.

It is said that the acts charged against this appellant are usually performed in secret, out of the view of corroborating witnesses. That does not signify that some circumstantial evidence cannot be obtained lending veracity to the complainant's narrative where the charge is true. Moreover the same criticism would be applicable to the other sexual offenses to which reference has been made where specific statutes require corroborative evidence. Our liberties are based upon the idea that it is better for some of the guilty to go free than for any who are innocent to be convicted. In the extensive discussion of this subject by Professor Wigmore, to which the dissenting opinion in People v. Porcaro, 6 N.Y.2d 248, 253, 189 N.Y.S.2d 194 (1959), refers, it is recognized that the general rule is to require corroboration of charges of all offenses against the chastity of women (Vol. III, p. 467; Vol. VII, p. 342 et seq.). His recommendation of changes in the law relate to the extension of existing rules to require in addition the psychiatric examination of complaining witnesses. It is noteworthy that a recommendation of such examinations was contained in the 1937–1938 Report of the American Bar Association's Committee on the Improvement of the Law of Evidence (3 Wigmore, Evidence, p. 466), and that out of the fullness of his experience Professor Wigmore distrusted testimony by complainants in these cases advising the retention of whatever rules of corroboration exist under statute or case law, and reminded the bench and bar that errant young girls and women are given to "contriving false charges of sexual offenses by men" (p. 459) concerning which he observed (p. 460) that "It is time that the Courts awakened to the sinister possibilities of injustice that lurk in believing such a witness without careful psychiatric scrutiny." Psychiatric scrutiny goes beyond anything at issue on this appeal. The subject is mentioned only on account of the attention which has been given to it in the dissenting opinion in People v. Porcaro, supra, decided herewith.

The alleged admission against interest which appellant's wife testified that he made to her consisted in a telephone call to her about two weeks after she had brought about his arrest, during which interval they had been separated. She testified that he said over the telephone "that it was true what he done" and that "he was sorry for what he did to his daughter, and then I told him that I couldn't forgive him for what he had done to her" and "that he violated his rights as a father, and then he told me about this other woman that he had." If this statement, which appellant denied having made, could amount to an admission of a sexual assault upon his daughter, which is not altogether clear, we consider that the objection to its introduction into evidence should have been sustained on the ground that it was a confidential communication between husband and wife induced by the marriage relation. It is true that they had been living separately for a short time after appellant's arrest, but the circumstances indicate that (if spoken at all) this statement was part of an attempted reconciliation between husband and wife (People v. Daghita, 299 N.Y. 194, 198–199, 86 N.E.2d 172, 173–174, 10 A.L.R.2d 1385

(1908); Warner v. Press Pub. Co., 132 N.Y. 181, 185–186, 30 N.E. 393, 394–395 (1892); Parkhurst v. Berdell, 110 N.Y. 386, 393, 18 N.E. 123, 126 (1888)). The presumption of confidentiality has not been rebutted as was held in Poppe v. Poppe, 3 N.Y.2d 312, 165 N.Y. S.2d 99 (1957). The Appellate Division held that this conversation was erroneously admitted.

The conviction appealed from should be reversed upon the ground that appellant has not been proved guilty of the offenses charged beyond a reasonable doubt.

. . .

CONWAY, C. J., and FROESSEL, J., concur with VAN VOORHIS, J.

FULD, J., concurs in his separate concurring opinion in People v. Porcaro, 6 N.Y.2d 248, 252, 189 N.Y.S.2d 194 (1959), decided herewith.

BURKE, J., dissents in an opinion in which DYE, J., concurs and in which DESMOND, J., concurs in a separate opinion.

Judgments reversed and information dismissed.

DECISIONS RELATING TO CHAPTER III, CIRCUMSTANTIAL EVIDENCE

WILKERSON v. CLARK

Supreme Court of North Carolina, 1965.
264 N.C. 439, 141 S.E.2d 884.

BOBBITT, Justice. Clark, 34 or 35, and Wilkerson, 29, were frequent associates and close friends. Clark was the manager of Clark Chevrolet Company of Apex, N.C., a business owned solely by his father, defendant David Judson Clark. On occasions, Wilkerson did part time work for Clark Chevrolet Company.

Clark Chevrolet Company sold Corvairs. The Corvair involved in the wreck on March 31, 1962 "was a brand new Corvair demonstrator."

On March 31, 1962, the "Beltline," now U.S. 1, was under construction. It had not been "opened for traffic." However, certain lanes thereof had been paved. It was not "opened for traffic" until September 19, 1962.

U.S. 1, a primary north-south highway, runs generally east-west in the area where the wreck occurred. However, the lanes for traffic from Raleigh toward Apex are referred to as lanes for southbound traffic and those for traffic toward Raleigh as lanes for northbound traffic.

U.S. 1, between where it overpasses Western Boulevard and where it underpasses the Cary-Macedonia Road, is a four-lane highway, the two 12-foot lanes for southbound traffic being separated by a median strip from the two lanes for northbound traffic. Southbound traffic, before reaching the Cary-Macedonia underpass, comes to an exit ramp which extends obliquely to the right from U.S. 1 and provides access to the Cary-Macedonia Road. An additional traffic lane is provided for approaching motorists who plan to leave U.S. 1 and enter said exit ramp. Where the highway lanes and the ramp converge, the total width of the pavement is 56 feet. The exit ramp itself is 20 feet wide at said point of convergence and 16 feet wide beyond that point.

The portions of highway referred to above had been paved. The shoulders, consisting of red clay, were under construction.

There was evidence tending to show the following facts: The Clark Corvair, although the "Beltline" had not been "opened for traffic," was proceeding thereon from Raleigh toward Apex. Approaching the Cary-Macedonia exit ramp, it did not travel in the additional lane providing access thereto but traveled in the right lane of said two 12-foot lanes for southbound traffic. It passed a short distance beyond the point of entry to the exit ramp, cut to its right across the "V" dirt median between said lane and said ramp, crossed the ramp and the dirt shoulder thereof, went down the shoulder embankment into a 40-foot deep ravine and finally stopped some sixty feet beyond said embankment. The wrecked Corvair, with Wilkerson's body and Clark *therein*, was discovered prior to 2:45 a. m.

There was sufficient admitted evidence to support a finding that Clark was the driver and that his actionable negligence proximately caused the wreck and Wilkerson's death. A review of this evidence is unnecessary to decision on this appeal. The court properly overruled defendants' motion(s) for judgment of nonsuit.

There was evidence tending to show the "Beltline," then under construction, underpassed the Jones-Franklin Road; and that the Jones-Franklin Road is "almost parallel" with the Cary-Macedonia Road and is "about a half a mile towards Raleigh from the Cary-Macedonia Road."

Freeman, plaintiff's witness, testified in substance, except when quoted, as follows: On Friday night, March 30, 1962, he was visiting on Dillard Drive. He left "around 12:00, five minutes after or something like that," to go to Mebane where he then lived. Traveling along the Jones-Franklin Road, he stopped his car on the bridge over the "Beltline" to determine whether the "Beltline" was then open for traffic. While stopped there, he saw only one car. This car approached on the "Beltline" from his right (from the direction of Raleigh) and traveled to his left after passing under the Jones-Franklin bridge. He saw this car as it traveled three-tenths of a mile approaching the underpass and as it traveled three-tenths of a mile beyond the underpass. When he last saw it, this car was headed toward and lacked "approximately two-tenths of a mile" of reaching "the Cary-Macedonia exit." He saw only the headlights, taillights and top of this car. He is familiar with Corvair cars and could and did identify this car as a Corvair. During the time he saw it, this Corvair, in his opinion, "was traveling in excess of 80 miles an hour."

Freeman testified he told Cecil Wilkerson, brother of plaintiff's intestate, substantially what he had testified at the trial, and Cecil Wilkerson so testified.

After plaintiff had offered his evidence and rested, the judge instructed the jury he had come to the conclusion that said testimony of Freeman and of Cecil Wilkerson had been improperly admitted in evidence, and that defendants' objections thereto should have been and were now sustained. Thereupon, the court instructed the jury "not to consider that testimony at all in the trial of this case," and to dismiss it from their minds completely "just as if it were never spoken in this court by anybody." Plaintiff excepted and assigns as error the exclusion of said testimony and the court's said instructions in relation thereto.

If Freeman saw the Clark Corvair, and if the wreck occurred after its uninterrupted travel from where it was when Freeman last saw it to the scene of the wreck, the testimony of Freeman is not inadmissible on account of remoteness or otherwise. Under the facts here, the distance between the point when last observed by Freeman and the scene of the wreck would bear on the weight rather than the competency of Freeman's testimony. Honeycutt v. Strube, 261 N.C. 59, 64, 134 S.E.2d 110 (1964), and cases cited.

"Circumstantial evidence is evidence which, without going directly to prove the existence of a fact, gives rise to a logical inference that such fact does exist." C.J.S. Evidence § 161.

Under our decisions, actionable negligence may be established by circumstantial evidence; and where there is evidence of facts and circumstances from which it may be inferred that actionable negligence is the more reasonable probability, the issue is for jury determination. Frazier v. Gas Company, 247 N.C. 256, 100 S.E.2d 501 (1957); Drum v. Bisaner, 252 N.C. 305, 113 S.E.2d 560 (1960); Patton v. Dail, 252 N.C. 425, 114 S.E.2d 87 (1960).

In State v. Johnson, 199 N.C. 429, 154 S.E. 730 (1930), Stacy, C. J., referring to circumstantial evidence in criminal cases, said: "The general rule is that, if there be any evidence tending to prove the fact in issue, or which reasonably conduces to its conclusion as a fairly logical and legitimate deduction, and not merely such as raises a suspicion or conjecture in regard to it, the case should be submitted to the jury." Since State v. Stephens, 244 N.C. 380, 93 S.E.2d 431 (1956), to which reference is made for a full discussion by Higgins, J., this Court has approved the quoted statement as the established rule in this jurisdiction.

The question here is whether there was evidence of facts and circumstances from which *it may be* inferred as the more reasonable probability (1) that Freeman saw the Clark Corvair *and* (2) that the wreck occurred after its uninterrupted travel from where it was when Freeman last saw it to the scene of the wreck. If so, it was for the jury to determine whether the evidence is sufficient to establish such facts and circumstances *and* to warrant findings in plaintiff's favor as to both propositions. In this connection, see Morgan v. Bell Bakeries, Inc., 426 N.C. 429, 98 S.E.2d 464 (1957), where circumstantial evidence was held admissible and sufficient to support a finding that a particular bread truck was in fact the motor vehicle involved in the accident; also, see Annotation, "Proof, in absence of direct testimony, of identity of motor vehicle involved in accident." 81 A.L.R.2d 861–888.

There was evidence tending to show the following facts: In the late afternoon of Friday, May 30, 1962, Clark asked Wilkerson to come by the place of business of Clark Chevrolet Company at or about 9:00 p. m., closing time, just to ride around with him. The car in which they were riding was "a brand new Corvair demonstrator." Clark and Wilkerson "left Raleigh about midnight," Clark driving. They traveled "out of Raleigh on the Western Boulevard and onto the new Beltline," headed back toward Apex. The paved roadway on which they traveled had not been "opened for traffic." At 2:45 a. m., when a Cary police officer arrived, Wilkerson was dead. His neck was broken and his body "felt clammy, cold, or cool." Clark was seriously injured. The Corvair was on its right side. Clark's back was against the top. His feet and legs extended over the legs of Wilkerson. Clark did not know what occurred after the wreck until he heard a car stop and voices of investigating officers.

In addition to the foregoing: When and by whom the wrecked Corvair was discovered does not appear. There is no evidence the "Beltline," then under construction and not "opened for traffic," had been or was being used by unauthorized persons other than Clark. Testimony as to tire marks, course of travel, damage to the Corvair and tragic consequences to the occupants, are consistent with Freeman's testimony as to speed.

Delay in the discovery of the wrecked Corvair, notwithstanding evidence the lights thereon were burning, is consistent with non-use of the "Beltline" by the traveling public. If Clark "left Raleigh about midnight," it may be reasonably inferred that he passed under the Jones-Franklin bridge approximately at the time referred to in Freeman's testimony; and, then headed for Apex, it would seem reasonable to infer it would be improbable he would be traveling the same course at a later hour.

Further discussion of the evidence is deemed inappropriate. In our view, the circumstantial evidence was sufficient *to permit* the jury to find that Freeman saw the Clark Corvair and that the wreck occurred after its uninterrupted travel from where it was when Freeman last saw it to the scene of the collision. If the jury should so find by the greater weight of the evidence, Freeman's testimony as to speed was competent. Hence, Freeman's testimony should have been admitted and the jury should have been instructed as indicated with reference to the findings prerequisite to its consideration as evidence relating to the speed of the Clark Corvair.

Defendants contend the court's exclusion of Freeman's testimony and of said portion of Cecil Wilkerson's testimony, if error, was not prejudicial to plaintiff. They contend this evidence was first admitted and was before the jury "over a day" before excluded by the court's ruling. However, the court, in substance, instructed the jury there was no evidence Freeman saw the Clark Corvair. We must assume the jury acted in compliance with the court's ruling and positive direction. Thereafter, the evidence for jury consideration as to what occurred in respect of speed and other alleged negligence prior to and at the time of the wreck related solely to physical facts observed at the scene after the wreck occurred. Under the circumstances, we cannot say the erroneous ruling did not substantially prejudice plaintiff.

For the error indicated, a new trial is awarded. Discussion of other assignments of error, relating to matters which may not recur at the next trial, is deemed unnecessary.

New trial.

BYRD v. LORD BROTHERS CONTRACTORS, INC.

Supreme Court of Oregon, 1970.
256 Or. 421, 473 P.2d 1018.

HOLMAN, Justice. Plaintiff brought an action to recover damages for personal injuries occasioned when he was hit by a piece of concrete. Plaintiff appealed from a judgment entered on a jury verdict for defendant. The only issues relate to the admissibility of evidence.

At about ten o'clock in the evening, plaintiff was operating his motor vehicle on Lombard Street under the 33rd Street overpass in the city of Portland, when a piece of concrete came through his windshield and injured him. Defendant was engaged in the remodeling of the overpass, which involved removing a concrete walk and railing along one side. A bulkhead had been constructed for the purpose of confining debris. The testimony was in dispute as to its efficiency. Concrete had previously been broken away below the bulkhead for the purpose of inserting beams for its support. No work was being done at the time of the accident, but work had been performed that day. The overpass was open to pedestrians and vehicular traffic at the time of the accident. There was no direct evidence concerning the cause of the falling concrete.

Defendant introduced evidence, to which plaintiff objected, that at approximately the time of the accident, four or five boys around junior high school age were seen running west on Columbia Boulevard at its intersection with 27th Street. The intersection where the boys were seen is six blocks west and one block north of where the accident occurred. However, the north end of the overpass is approximately at the intersection of 33rd Street and Columbia Boulevard, six blocks from where the boys were seen. There was no other evidence to connect the boys to the chunk of concrete which struck plaintiff.

The problem is one of relevancy. The conclusion sought to be drawn is that the boys threw the concrete from the overpass. The fact from which this conclusion is to be inferred is that they were seen six blocks away running in a direction away from the north end of the overpass at about the time of the accident. The question is whether this fact has sufficient probative bearing on the issue to make it relevant and thus admissible. McCormick says as follows:

> "What is the standard of relevance or probative quality which evidence must meet if it is to be admitted? We have said that it must 'tend to establish' the inference for which it is offered. How strong must this tendency be? Some courts have announced tests, variously phrased, which seem to require that the evidence offered must render the inference for which it is offered more probable than the other possible inferences or hypotheses, that is, the chances must appear to preponderate that the inference claimed is the

> true one. It is believed, however, that while this might be a reasonable standard by which to judge the sufficiency of all of a party's proof to enable him to get to the jury on the issue, it makes too heavy a demand upon a given item of proof at the admissibility stage, when we are gathering our bits of information piece by piece. And, in fact, much circumstantial evidence is commonly received which does not meet so stringent a test . . . . It is believed that a more modest standard would better reflect the actual practice of the courts, and that the most acceptable test of relevancy is the question, does the evidence offered render the desired inference *more probable than it would be without the evidence?* . . . .." (footnotes omitted; emphasis his.) McCormick, Evidence 317–18, § 152 (1954).

The jury, of course, realized that there was the possibility that the concrete was thrown from the overpass by someone, because the public had access to the overpass. From the jury's knowledge of everyday life, it could have legitimately concluded that boys are inclined to run away from the scene of a wrong. From the same knowledge, they could believe that children are more likely to throw things from an overpass than are adults. Under these circumstances, we cannot say that the admitted testimony had no probative value.

Admittedly, the boys could have come from numerous other places than the overpass and could have been running for any one of the various reasons that boys run. The relation between the boys and the overpass six blocks away is an attenuated one, but we believe that, after the introduction of the evidence in question, there was a greater possibility that the concrete was thrown from the overpass than would have so appeared in the absence of such evidence. Had the boys been seen running from the end of the overpass, no one would have any difficulty in concluding that the evidence was highly relevant. When the same thing occurs six blocks away, its probative value is very greatly lessened. However, we cannot say it has none. We do not mean that it was probable that the boys threw the concrete or that the evidence would justify the submission of a case to the jury if they were being sued for having caused the injury. Wigmore has the following to say:

> "On the other hand, the judges constantly find it necessary to warn us that their function, in determining Relevancy, is not that of final arbiters, but merely of preliminary testers, i. e., that the evidentiary fact offered does not need to have strong, full, superlative, probative value, *does not need to involve demonstration* or to produce persuasion by its sole and intrinsic force, but merely to be *worth consideration by the jury.* It is for the jury to give it the appropriate weight in effecting persuasion. The rule of law which the judge employs is concerned merely with admitting the fact through the evidentiary portal. The judge thus

> warns the opponent of the evidence that he is not entitled to complain of its lack of absolute demonstrative power; a mere capacity to help in demonstration is enough for its admission:" (footnote omitted; emphasis his.) 1 Wigmore on Evidence 411, § 29 (3d ed. 1940).

The plaintiff had the burden of persuading the jury that the defendant was negligent. The defendant is entitled to make this burden as heavy as possible by calling to the jury's attention any fact which would raise a not completely unreasonable *possibility* that the untoward occurrence happened in a manner inconsistent with its negligence.

When the offered testimony gets to the outer fringes of relevancy, courts allow the trial judge a certain amount of leeway in evaluating its admissibility. 1 Conrad, Modern Trial Evidence 53, § 37 (1956) expresses it this way:

> ". . . Before evidence can be excluded on the ground of irrelevancy, it is essential that it appear so beyond doubt. If the question is doubtful, the settled rule is that the evidence should go to the jury for evaluation by it . . . ." (footnote omitted.)

Plaintiff also contends that the trial court erred in admitting the following testimony over objection because it called for a conclusion which was the ultimate question to be decided by the jury:

> "Q. State whether or not, Mr. Percival, there was any way for debris to come down, and if so, explain how it could come down.
>
> " . . . .
>
> "A. The only way it would have to come over the top of the bulkhead."

Even if the evidence was conclusory and therefore not admissible, no prejudicial error was involved. Substantially, the same evidence came in without objection from another witness.

> "Q. Were there in fact any breaks in that bulkhead or holes in it that would have permitted debris to pass through?
>
> "A. No."

The judgment of the trial court is affirmed.

PEOPLE v. FELDMAN

Court of Appeals of New York, 1949.
299 N.Y. 153, 85 N.E.2d 913.

CONWAY, Judge. Proof of guilt of administering poison to another, resulting in death, is always difficult and the instant case constitutes no exception. Unless there be a confession or direct testimony by observers of the act, dependence must be upon circumstances attending the event and then the question, in a capital case, which is presented to us for our consideration is whether the guilt of the accused has been established to a moral certainty by circumstances which not only point to the guilt of the accused but are inconsistent with his innocence. People v. Fitzgerald, 156 N.Y. 253, 258, 50 N.E. 846, 849 (1898); People v. Razezicz, 206 N.Y. 249, 273, 99 N.E. 557, 556 (1919); People v. May, 290 N.Y. 369, 49 N.E.2d 486 (1898).

One of the difficulties here is that there is no direct proof that the defendant had anything to do with the strychnine which it is alleged was administered to his wife, the deceased. There was no proof that he ever purchased or possessed any. As a substitute for such proof it is pointed out that the defendant was a licensed employed pharmacist and thus had access to the poison. The bottle alleged to have contained it was discarded as refuse in the hospital (contrary to good practice) by the nurse in attendance on the deceased after her death. Thus no one can say with certainty that the bottle contained strychnine. The toxicologist, who was not a physician, testified to the presence of strychnine in the organs of the deceased, other than intestines, when he performed an autopsy and analyses some five months after burial. He also testified that in discovering it, all of the organs supplied him consisting of the brain, lungs, liver, spleen, heart, kidneys, blood, empty stomach, two pieces of rib and a male foetus, were used up and that no material is left. There is thus in existence no tangible evidence which others may check and test which would show the presence or amount of strychnine at any time in the body of the deceased. The "very few notes" made on pieces of paper from time to time during the tests which took about a week, were destroyed after being typed by the toxicologist personally, after he had completed his examination and tests. We must proceed, of course, upon the assumption, for the purpose of this opinion, that the toxicologist made no error in *estimate of quantity* of strychnine in the body of deceased and the matter is adverted to only for the purpose of indicating that the entire proof of guilt here depends on oral testimony and not upon articles or objects which can now be touched or viewed. To put it succinctly, the opinion testimony revolved about the estimate of "the total amount of strychnine in the entire body, exclusive of the gastro-intestinal tract and exclusive of the urine" and was calculated upon a body weight of 132 pounds or approximately "60 kilos". Moreover, the stomach showed too small a trace of strychnine to estimate it. The case against the defendant hung upon the correctness of the estimate and calculation plus the opinion testimony. It is rare when a charge in a capital case may depend upon such an "estimate" and conviction should follow only upon the clearest and unconfused proof.

In addition to the toxicologist, four experts or opinion witnesses were called upon to give testimony. No one of the five had seen Mrs. Feldman in life. The doctors who had seen and attended her at home on December 7th and in the hospital on December 8th, before her death in the early morning hours of December 9th, diagnosed her case as one of tetany accompanying pregnancy. That indicated a calcium deficiency. The five opinion witnesses called upon the trial all agreed that on December 7th, the deceased had ingested strychnine. There is no contention by the People that the accused had anything to do with that. The two opinion witnesses for the defendant gave it as their opinion that the deceased died from the December 7th ingestion. The three opinion witnesses called by the People gave it as their opinion that she did not, but died from the ingestion of strychnine in the early hours of December 9th at the hospital. There was no strychnine found at either hospital or home. If the deceased died from the ingestion of strychnine in her home on December 7th, the accused was entitled to acquittal of the charge made. If she died from the ingestion of strychnine in the hospital on December 9th, the guilt of the accused depended on whether he had put strychnine in one of the bottles which he brought to the hospital and delivered to the nurse in attendance upon his wife and no part of the contents of which was analyzed because of the conduct of the nurse in disposing of it, to which reference has already been made.

In a case as close as this one, it is clear that it was essential for the trial court to make certain that no error in the admission or exclusion of evidence occurred and that there was no confusion as to facts. Concededly that was not an easy task. It is against the background outlined that we consider some of the facts and some of the rulings made.

. . .

On the night of December 7, 1943, the deceased was visited by her sister about 9 o'clock. She was alone while her husband, the defendant, was on duty at the drugstore in which he was employed. Following her sister's visit, she became ill and suffered convulsions. Her condition was diagnosed as a calcium deficiency by two physicians and she was removed before midnight to a hospital. The defendant had requested the first doctor called to engage a consultant. At the hospital Mrs. Feldman had a convulsion at 9 o'clock in the morning of December 8th, and then improved. Shortly after noon of that day a third physician, a specialist in "tetany and calcium metabolism" was engaged at defendant's insistence. The defendant on December 8th had suggested that it might be well to get a doctor from Johns-Hopkins Hospital but was told that the first two doctors consulted had selected for further consultation the specialist in tetany to whom reference has been made. That specialist reached the hospital at 6 o'clock in the evening and found Mrs. Feldman comfortable. The only troublesome symptom was that Mrs. Feldman complained of some tenderness in her feet. The doctor though her condition was "strongly suggestive of hypocalcemic tetany of pregnancy" and finding the prognosis good he dictated a prescription consisting of "60 grains of calcium chloride in 150 c.c. of elixir lactate of pepsin" to be administered every four hours. That prescription would be contained in six bottles. It was designed to build up calcium content of the blood. He also prescribed a patented medicine known as hytakerol to be given once a day. That consisted of highly concentrated vitamin D.

One of the doctors met defendant in the corridor, told him his wife might be suffering from tetany "and if so the patient would be very much better by tomorrow, and from all indications she ought to do very well." Defendant was then given the two prescriptions which had been written on a prescription pad. He was told that he could get the hytakerol at the pharmacy of one Jacoff and while there he might as well have the other prescription filled.

The defendant went to Jacoff's pharmacy and obtained the hytakerol. He was driven there by the husband of his wife's sister, one Kushner. Then Kushner drove him to the drugstore of Ruvinsky where the defendant was employed. There defendant asked one Rothbaum to help him make up the prescription. The defendant prepared the bottles individually, weighing out each quantity prescribed separately and putting it into the bottle then under preparation. Ruvinsky and Rothbaum said that there was nothing unusual about the method of preparation. The largest graduate measure used in the store held but thirty-two ounces. To put thirty ounces as required by the prescription for the five-ounce bottles into the quart measure would render it difficult to stir the compound without spilling it. Rothbaum helped defendant get out the calcium chloride and lactate of pepsin. After the preparation of the first two bottles was completed, Rothbaum left for his home. Ruvinsky was busy waiting on customers but could see the defendant if he looked toward him. There was a cabinet of poisonous drugs near the defendant but no proof that he opened it. After preparing the six bottles containing the medicine he was driven with them, again by Kushner, at about 10:30 in the evening to the hospital where he knocked on his wife's door and placed them and the bottle of hytakerol in the hands of nurse Bierle. Shortly thereafter contents of one of the six bottles was administered to Mrs. Feldman. At 2:30 on the morning of December 9th, nurse Worrell, who had succeeded as the attending special nurse, administered the second bottle. One-half hour later the deceased was seized with a convulsion. She died one hour later at 4:00 o'clock. The nurse thereafter threw out all of the six bottles. The cause of death certified was "tetany with convulsions; cause unknown, associated with pregnancy".

. . .

Moreover, we think the judgment of conviction must be reversed because of the ruling of the court upon the right of the defendant to cross-examine the expert or opinion witnesses. When the toxicologist was being cross-examined, the following questions were asked of him:

> "Q. Now, you said that you got part of your information or knowledge about toxicology from literature; is that right? A. That's right.
>
> "Q. Did you ever read 'Textbook of Physiology' by Howell? A. I've glanced at it."

The court, without more, then ruled that if counsel wished to refer to any textbook or literature he must show it to the witness and that if the witness agreed with it and adopted it, the witness might then be questioned about it. The court said, ". . . I shall not permit you to read from that book or any other book. If you wish to question this witness regarding any material, any writing, any dissertation or questions or statements contained in that book, you will first refer to the witness; let him read it and if the witness replies that he is in agreement with it or that he adopts that argument as his own, then I will allow you to make reference to it. Otherwise, not."

During the same discussion the court repeated the ruling as follows: " . . . you will first refer the book to this witness and if the witness tells the Court that he is in agreement with that statement or that writing and adopts that argument as his own, you may then question him regarding such statement or such argument. Otherwise I shall exclude it."

In this State when an expert witness has given opinion testimony and on cross-examination has testified that a book called to his attention is recognized by him as an authority upon the subject as to which he has given an opinion, he may be confronted with a passage from the book which conflicts with the opinion he has expressed. This is permitted for the purpose of discrediting or weakening his testimony. Egan v. Dry Dock, East Broadway & Battery R. Co., 12 App.Div. 556, 42 N.Y.S. 188 (1897); Hastings v. Chrysler Corp., 273 App.Div. 292, 77 N.Y.S.2d 524 (1902). In the Egan case, supra, it was said: " . . . it has been the custom, in this state at least, to call the attention of expert witnesses, upon cross-examination, to books upon the subject, and ask whether or not authors whom he admitted to be good authority had not expressed opinions different from that which was given by him upon the stand. The reference to books in such cases is not made for the purpose of making the statements in the books evidence before a jury, but solely for the purpose of ascertaining the weight to be given to the testimony of the witness." 12 App.Div. at page 571, 42 N.Y.S. at page 200.

. . .

The judgment of conviction should be reversed and a new trial ordered.

OTHER SEX CRIMES

HUBER v. STATE OF MARYLAND

Court of Special Appeals of Maryland, 1967.
2 Md.App. 245, 234 A.2d 264.

GEORGE L. RUSSELL, Special Judge.

Paul E. Huber was indicted by the Grand Jury of Baltimore City for kidnapping and rape. Upon request by the Appellant, the case was removed to the Circuit Court for Howard County. A Motion to Dismiss the first count of the rape indictment was granted, and the other indictments were consolidated and tried before a jury. The Appellant was convicted of common law assault and kidnapping on May 25, 1966. After a Motion For New Trial was heard and denied, the Appellant was sentenced to fifteen years for kidnapping and five years for assault in the Maryland Penitentiary, the sentences to be served consecutively.

The Appellant raises the following contentions in his appeal from the above judgments:

> 1. That the use of the Appellant's military records were improper:
>
> > (a) The Appellant's military court-martial convictions were not admissible for the purposes of impeachment.
> >
> > (b) The State was not entitled to show the details of the court-martial convictions and to introduce the records into evidence.
> >
> > (c) The Court did not adequately instruct the jury on the evidential use of the Appellant's military records.

. . .

The Appellant met the prosecuting witness after she finished work at 1 a. m. on the morning of March 4, 1964. After stopping at a restaurant and a night spot, the Appellant drove to a place several blocks from the prosecutrix's home, where he left the car. After returning, he drove the car around the corner and stopped, claiming that he had to wait for his brother to bring some money. The prosecuting witness testified that after ten minutes, the Appellant suddenly grabbed her arms, gagged her with a handkerchief and Kleenex, and tied her arms with ropes procured from the glove compartment. The Appellant pushed the victim down in the seat and drove to a secluded area where they remained until dawn. The Appellant alternately tied and untied the prosecutrix, but made no advances. He then drove to a motel, rented a cabin, and once inside, resumed his procedure of tying and untying the prosecutrix. During this time, he removed all of the prosecutrix's clothing, but left her feet tied, and made an unsuccessful attempt to have sexual intercourse with her. Some time in the late morning, the Appellant helped the prosecutrix to dress and they left the motel. Upon reaching the residence of the prosecutrix, the Appellant unbound her arms, and, after warning her not to report the incident, allowed her to leave.

The uncle of the prosecutrix testified that she came to his home about 12 noon on the day the alleged offense occurred, and that she related the episode at that time. The prosecutrix went to work on the night of March 4, 1964, and did not report the incident until the next day, some thirty hours after its occurrence.

I.

In regard to that part of the Appellant's first contention which concerns the admissibility of the Appellant's court-martial convictions, the Court finds that such evidence, within the guidelines set down by this opinion, is admissible. The Appellant argues that the fact of convictions is not admissible, as the Appellant was convicted by a military tribunal, and there was no showing of whether or not the conduct of the court-martial provided due process of law to the Appellant. This particular issue is a point of first impression in Maryland, and the Court has reviewed the pertinent decisions of other jurisdictions in arriving at its conclusion.

Wharton's Criminal Evidence, 12th Ed., Vol. 3, Sec. 939, p. 375, states that:

> "Conviction by court-martial of a military offense or imprisonment for breach of military discipline involve no moral turpitude and cannot be shown to affect a witness's credibility."

Wharton cites People v. Joyce, 233 N.Y. 61, 134 N.E. 836, where the district attorney was permitted to inquire over objection and exception for two pages of the record as to whether the defendant was imprisoned while in the army in World War I and as to whether he did anything there for which he was imprisoned. The Court said:

> "The objection to that class of evidence was well taken. Assume that defendant had omitted to salute his superior officer and the latter ordered him to the guard house for a few hours, such omission might be considered a breach of military discipline rather than a crime and his brief detention in the guard house would scarely be held equivalent to a conviction of a crime." (233 N.Y. at 71, 134 N.E. at 840)

In Midkiff v. State, 29 Ariz. 523, 243 P. 601 (1926), also cited by Wharton, the defendant tried to impeach a witness by proving that the witness had been convicted by a court-martial for desertion. The Court, in ruling that such evidence was properly refused admission, stated:

> "Desertion is purely a military offense; it is not a crime under the general law; its character is such as not to involve moral turpitude or to indicate a disposition or trait that would make the witness's testimony questionable." (29 Ariz. at 537, 243 P. at 606)

The rule of law applied in the above authorities can be stated in more concise form by reference to three cases cited by Appellant. Henderson v. United States, 202 F.2d 400, at 405–406 (6th Circuit Court of Appeals), held that cross-examination for impeachment purposes should be limited to showing convictions for felonies or crimes involving moral turpitude, and that the lower court erred in admitting evidence of court-martial convictions for absent without leave (AWOL) offenses. The Second Circuit held in United States v. Tomaiolo, 249 F.2d 683, at 692 (1958) that a court-martial conviction for an AWOL offense was a breach of military discipline, and as such, was neither a felony or a crime involving moral turpitude. Rhea v. State, 208 Tenn. 559, 347 S.W.2d 486 (1961) citing Henderson v. United States, supra, and United States v. Tomaiolo, supra, held that:

> " . . . the rule seems to be that for the purpose of impeachment of a witness a bad conduct or a dishonorable discharge is not admissible unless it is shown that the breach of military discipline involved acts of moral turpitude." (347 S.W.2d at 487)

It seems, then, that in order for evidence of prior court-martial convictions of a witness to be admitted for the purpose of impeaching the witness's credibility, the conviction must involve an act of moral turpitude, which is not purely a matter of military discipline, and which is a crime under the general law.

The Court finds that Huber's convictions were admissible for the purposes of impeachment because a conviction for assault involves an act of moral turpitude; an "assault on a German national" is not purely a matter of military discipline, and assault is clearly a crime under the law of Maryland. See Miller v. State, 1 Md.App. 653, 232 A.2d 548 (1967).

The Appellant contends further that the details of the court-martial convictions are inadmissible, even if the fact of these convictions is to be admitted.

The record shows that the Appellant was asked on cross-examination whether or not he had ever been convicted of larceny. He answered that he had been convicted, that his conviction was reversed, and the State then confessed not guilty. . . .

At the conclusion of the court's charge to the jury, the Appellant requested the following instruction which the Court denied:

> "Secondly, I would request the Court on behalf of the defendant to advise the jury that the past convictions and the Court Martials, which the Court admitted into evidence, was merely as—can merely be applied against the credibility of defendant's testimony, and is not substantive evidence that the defendant was a person—a sick and dangerous person. I say this, particularly now, after hearing the summation by the State's Attorney, because the State's Attorney—in his parting words to the jury . . . —very clearly was urging the jury to find on the basis of the facts of his past convictions, particularly the Court Martials, that he did commit this crime, in other words, the using not as evidence against his credibility but as evidence that he is the kind of a person who would commit these types of crimes and should there-

fore be convicted in order to prevent further such activities."

It is established in this state that in criminal cases, where the defendant is a witness in his own behalf, he thereby puts his character in issue, and may be asked on cross-examination if he has been convicted of crime. Taylor v. State, 226 Md. 561, at 567, 174 A.2d 573 (1961). Article 35, Section 10, Annotated Code of Maryland, provides that in any proceeding, a party may prove by legal evidence any facts showing the conviction of the witness of an infamous crime. M.L.E., Witnesses §§ 143–144. While evidence of a defendant's prior convictions of crimes, other than that charged, need not be restricted to infamous crimes or crimes involving moral turpitude in order to be admissible, such convictions should be for violations which may have some tendency to impeach the defendant's credibility as a witness. Linkins v. State, 202 Md. 212, at 220, 96 A.2d 246 (1953). As no rigid classification of crimes is possible, the court must exercise its discretion in admitting the fact of a criminal conviction, and its decision will not be interfered with on appeal, except where the evidence is so clearly irrelevant that its admission could not be said to be within the discretion of the trial court. Linkins v. State, supra; Taylor v. State, supra.

Article 35, Section 10, further provides that in order to prove a criminal conviction of a witness, it shall not be necessary to produce the record of the proceedings pertaining thereto, but a sealed certificate of the clerk of the proper court, stating the fact of conviction and for what crime, shall suffice. We find that the proper interpretation of Article 35, Section 10, would permit only the fact of conviction for a specific crime to be permitted into evidence, and not the details of the commission of the crime.

When the details of the commission of a prior crime by a witness are introduced into evidence, there is a danger that the jury may be misled into a conviction by evidence of an offense for which the defendant is not indicted, Wentz v. State, 159 Md. 161, at 165, 150 A. 278 (1930), and hence the introduction of such evidence should be subjected to rigid scrutiny by the court, Berger v. State, 179 Md. 410, at 414, 20 A.2d 146 (1941). To come within the exception to the rule that evidence of previous offenses is irrelevant, there must appear some real connection between the previous offense and that with which the defendant is charged other than the allegation that the offenses have sprung from the same disposition. The exception does not go to the extent of sanctioning the admission of evidence of the "propensity" of the accused to commit crimes similar to that for which he has been indicted. Berger v. State, supra; Gorski v. State, 1 Md.App. 200, at 202–203, 228 A.2d 835 (1967).

When only the fact of a prior conviction of a criminal defendant is introduced into evidence when he is a witness in his own behalf, there exists a similar, albeit somewhat lesser danger than that outlined above, of the jury drawing an improper inference that the defendant may have a tendency to commit crimes similar to that for which he is being tried. In such a situation, the trial court should, upon proper request by the defendant, advise the jury that such evidence is to be considered only for the purposes of evaluating the defendant's credibility as a witness.

In the instant case, the prosecuting witness testified that the Appellant tied and untied her with ropes innumerable times; the State introduced tracing made by the Appellant of pictures portraying women bound and gagged, and the State was permitted, over objection, to introduce the details of the Appellant's court-martial conviction. The latter evidence revealed that the Appellant, while serving in the Army in Germany, was accused of tying up one woman and tearing the clothes off another woman. The admission into evidence of these facts, when considered by the jury with the other contested evidence showing the defendant's preoccupation with women in bondage, could only serve, at least in the absence of a proper cautionary instruction from the court to prejudice the jury unfairly against the Appellant and permit them to draw an inference that he did tie up the prosecuting witness.

It is incumbent upon the court, when requested in a criminal case, to give an advisory instruction on every essential question or point of law supported by the evidence. Bruce v. State, 218 Md. 87, at 97, 145 A.2d 428 (1958). The court finds that the trial court should have instructed the jury on the effect of the prior convictions of the Appellant as requested, and the failure of the lower court to so advise the jury constituted reversible error.

. . . .

. . . Arresting officers, being neither lawyers nor judges, cannot be expected to make subtle distinctions between the degrees of relevancy of any evidentiary item which is not clearly irrelevant to the issue of the guilt of the accused. This is a problem capable of taxing the minds of the most experienced and learned jurists, and the remedy, if any, to be afforded a defendant in such circumstances is by way of suppression of such evidence before or during trial.

In all cases, civil or criminal, the evidence must be confined to the point in issue. MacEwen v. State, 194 Md. 492, 71 A.2d 464 (1950). The Court of Appeals stated in that case:

> "The application of the rule results in the exclusion of all evidence of collateral facts or of those which are incapable of affording any reasonable presumption or inference as to the principal fact or matter in dispute; the reason being that such evidence tends to divert the minds of the jury from the real point in issue, and arouse their prejudices." (194 Md. at 501, 71 A.2d at 468.)

The tracings of women in various states of bondage can only show that the defendant liked to trace and draw pictures of women in bondage. This fact was admitted by the Appellant in his direct examination; however, one cannot rationally infer from these tracings that the Appellant did in fact bind and tie the prosecutrix, or even that he had a tendency to bind women with ropes. The admission of this evidence could only serve to arouse the prejudice of the jury against the Appellant by allowing them to draw such an improper inference. This evidence in no way tends to establish the facts at issue (the assault and kidnapping of the prosecutrix), and its admission constitutes reversible error.

Judgments reversed; case remanded for new trial.

HEARSAY—OTHER SIMILAR ACTS

UNITED STATES v. BRETTHOLZ

United States Court of Appeals, Second Circuit, 1973.
485 F.2d 483.

MOORE, Circuit Judge. James Brettholz and Milton Santiago appeal from judgments of conviction entered after trial by jury in the United States District Court for the Eastern District of New York. The indictment charged appellants and three other persons, Jerry A. Rosenblum, Jory Ira Prince, and Lon M. Posner, in three counts with violations of the federal narcotics laws: Count I charged defendants with knowingly and unlawfully possessing with intent to distribute one quarter kilogram of cocaine, in violation of 21 U.S.C.A. § 841(a)(1); Count II charged defendants with attempted distribution of cocaine, in violation of 21 U.S.C.A. §§ 841(a)(1), 846; Count III charged defendants with conspiring to conceal, possess, and distribute cocaine, in violation of 21 U.S.C.A. § 841(a)(1). A fourth count, naming appellant Santiago only, charged him with forcibly assaulting, impeding, and intimidating a federal narcotics agent engaged in the performance of his official duties, in violation of 18 U.S.C.A. §§ 111 and 1114.

Prior to trial, defendants Rosenblum, Prince, and Posner pleaded guilty to Count III, the conspiracy count, and appeared as government witnesses against appellants Brettholz and Santiago. Both appellants were found guilt as charged on the first three counts of the indictment; Santiago was also found guilty on Count IV. Brettholz was sentenced to a term of five years on each of the first three counts, the sentences to run concurrently, plus a parole term of three years, plus a fine of $1,000 on each count, for a total of $3,000. Santiago was sentenced to a term of five years on each of the first three counts, the sentences to run concurrently, plus a special parole term of three years; he was sentenced on Count IV to a term of imprisonment of three years, the sentence to run concurrently with those imposed under the first three counts of the indictment.

On appeal appellants raise no material issues of fact but argue (1) that reversible error occurred when the trial court permitted the introduction of testimony by co-defendant Posner that Brettholz had sold cocaine to Posner on ten prior occasions; . . .

A brief recital of the facts concerning this attempted sale of cocaine is necessary to a determination of the issues raised by appellants.

At trial the government's evidence established that during the last week of July, 1972, after he had been contacted by government informer Gary Kaplan, co-defendant Jerry Rosenblum telephoned co-defendant Jory Prince for the purpose of securing one-half pound of cocaine. Prince in turn telephoned co-defendant Posner, who indicated that he would see whether he could find a source for the narcotic. Several days thereafter Posner contacted appellant Brettholz, informed the latter that he had a prospective purchaser of cocaine, and asked whether Brettholz could supply the drug. Brettholz told Posner to call back later that week; Posner did so and on that occasion Brettholz indicated that he could supply the half-pound of cocaine, and that he would meet with Posner the following day, August 5, 1972. (Trial Transcript, hereinafter "Tr.", at 326–27).

The next day Brettholz met with Posner at the latter's place of business, a car wash located in Far Rockaway, New York, which was co-managed by co-defendant Prince. Brettholz gave Posner a small sample of cocaine for the latter's customer to "taste", indicating that he would be able to supply only seven, and not eight, ounces of the drug. (Tr. 328–31). Posner then gave Brettholz the telephone number at co-defendant Prince's home in Far Rockaway, instructing Brettholz to telephone him there at 7:30 that evening. (Tr. 331–32). After Prince himself had "tasted" the cocaine sample, he and Posner telephoned Rosenblum, who in turn contacted government informer Kaplan, with the information that the deal would be consummated that evening at the home of Jory Prince. (Tr. 152, 332). Kaplan quickly contacted the federal narcotics agent to whom he informed, Agent Hall, who made plans to be present with other agents and Kaplan in the vicinity of Prince's home that evening.

At approximately 7:30 that night, the various characters in this narrative began to arrive at Prince's house. First to arrive were Posner and Rosenblum, who went up to Prince's upstairs bedroom for conversation. Posner had brought with him a brown shopping bag containing a scale with which to weigh the cocaine to be brought to the house by appellants Brettholz and Santiago; at trial Posner testified that the shopping bag had contained nothing but the scale. (Tr. 400, 433). In addition to the scale, Posner had brought the cocaine sample supplied earlier that day at the car wash by appellant Brettholz. (Tr. 336–37). Next to arrive at the house was government informer Kaplan, who secretly had been waiting in a parked auto with two federal undercover narcotics agents; Rosenblum went to the parked auto and accompanied Kaplan to the Prince house. All persons again convened in Prince's upstairs bedroom. Kaplan "tasted" the cocaine, expressed approval, and was told to go back to his auto until the full supply of the drug had arrived. (Tr. 165, 178–79). At this same time the pre-arranged telephone call from Brettholz was received at the Prince residence. (Tr. 179, 340). Posner told Brettholz that "everything seemed to be all right, everything looked cool and he should come by." (Tr. 340). Brettholz announced that he would do so after finishing his dinner.

At approximately 9:00 p. m. that evening appellants Brettholz and Santiago arrived at the house. The two men immediately went to the upstairs bedroom to confer with co-defendants Rosenblum, Posner, and Prince. (Tr. 341–43). After expressing concern at the number of autos parked outside, announcing that the cocaine was still in their auto, and looking around the house to chart an escape route just in case something went wrong (Tr. 185, 189), Brettholz, accompanied by Santiago, went back to their auto, to return to the house a few minutes later with the cocaine. Upon their return, Santiago positioned himself downstairs at the front door while Brettholz took the cocaine to the upstairs bedroom. (Tr. 190–91). Brettholz asked Rosenblum if he was the buyer; answering in the negative, Rosenblum then went outside to get the "purchaser," government informer Kaplan. Rosenblum and Kaplan re-entered the house and were promptly searched for weapons by appellant Santiago, who was still keeping his vigil at the front door. (Tr. 127–28). Once upstairs Kaplan "snorted" or sampled the cocaine which Brettholz had brought, expressed satisfaction with the deal, and left the house, ostensibly to go to his auto for the purchase money. (Tr. 464).

Back at the auto, Kaplan informed the agents that the cocaine had arrived. At this point Kaplan and agents Hall and Lightcap went to the house. Lightcap waited outside. Santiago, still standing watch at the front door, latched the door after Kaplan and Agent Hall had entered, and admonished Kaplan for bringing others to the house against orders. (Tr. 467). Santiago, using colorful expletives to make his point, further warned Kaplan and Hall that nothing had better go wrong because "We f___ people that f___ us." (Tr. 467). While Santiago was searching Hall for weapons, the latter unlatched the door to allow Agent Lightcap to enter; thereupon, Hall took out his badge, identified himself to Santiago as a federal agent (a fact which appellant Santiago disputes), and announced an arrest. (Tr. 469–70). Santiago responded by throwing a punch at Agent Hall and screaming, "Jimmy, Jimmy," appellant Brettholz's nickname. (Tr. 505). Other agents quickly entered the house and ran to the upstairs bedroom. Having heard all the commotion, defendants Prince, Posner, Rosenblum, and Brettholz went into action upstairs; Brettholz grabbed the cocaine and was seen by Agent Hall to be leaving out of a bathroom window. In the ensuing chaos, Brettholz escaped, only to turn himself in several days later. The other defendants were arrested on the spot.

After the arrests the agents conducted a search of the premises and the surrounding vicinity. A small plastic bag containing seven ounces of cocaine was found on the roof of a garage located directly behind the Prince house. (Tr. 528). The agents also found three small bags of marijuana in a shopping bag stuffed into a drawer of a bureau in Prince's bedroom. (Tr. 537).

At trial both Brettholz and Santiago testified in their own defense, and each supported the other's testimony. In essence, their defense was that they had gone to the Prince house not with the intention of selling cocaine, but for the purpose of buying marijuana from Posner for their personal use. The jury returned a guilty verdict on all counts of the indictment.

Appellants' first argument on appeal is that the trial court committed reversible error by permitting a government witness, co-defendant Posner, to testify that he had bought cocaine from appellant Brettholz on ten occasions within a year prior to the transaction in question. Prior to Posner's testimony the Assistant United States Attorney made an offer of proof to the trial court as to what Posner would testify, i. e., that Brettholz had sold cocaine to him on ten prior occasions. The prosecutor asked that the testimony be admitted on the theory that the ten prior sales "show[ed] that there was intent to distribute on the part of defendant [Brettholz] as opposed to being used for his own personal use." (Tr. 136). The trial court ruled that the offered testimony would be admitted, as it later was over defense objection, on the ground that:

> [I]t is pretty well established that proof of each commission of acts of a similar nature previously and not too remotely, of course, is some evidence of intent in a crime where intent is a necessary factor as it is in this case. (Tr. 137).
>
> . . . .
>
> I think the testimony would be admissible for the purpose I have stated a moment ago, that is, to show intent on the part of the defendant Brettholz. (Tr. 138).

Appellants contend that the admission of Posner's testimony was reversible error since, they argue, "there was not and could not be any real issue of intent in the case." (Brief, hereinafter "Br.", at 13). We disagree.

The law in this Circuit is that evidence of prior similar acts is admissible "for all purposes except to show the criminal character or disposition of the defendant." United States v. Warren, 453 F.2d 738, 745 (2d Cir. 1972), certiorari denied, 406 U.S. 944, 92 S.Ct. 2040, 32 L.Ed.2d 331. See also, United States v. Deaton, 381 F.2d 114, 117 (2d Cir. 1967); United States v. Knohl, 379 F.2d 427, 438 (2d Cir. 1967); United States v. Bozza, 365 F.2d 206, 213 (2d Cir. 1966); McCormick, Evidence § 190, at 447 et seq. (2d ed. 1972). The case law and the legal scholars uniformly indicate that such evidence is admissible if offered to prove knowledge, intent, or design on the part of the defendant; 2 Wigmore, Evidence § 300, at 192–93 (3d ed. 1940); McCormick, supra, Evidence § 190 at 449; United States v. DeCicco, 435 F.2d 478, 483 (2d Cir. 1970). In ruling on the admissibility of such evidence, the trial judge is required to balance all of the relevant factors to determine whether the probative value of the evidence outweighs its prejudicial character. Spencer v. State of Texas, 385 U.S. 554, 561, 87 S.Ct. 648, 17 L.Ed.2d 606 (1967); United States v. Deaton, supra, 381 F.2d at 117. As summarized by one scholar,

> the problem is not merely one of pigeonholing, but one of balancing, on the one side, the actual need for the other-crimes evidence in the light of the issues and the other evidence available to the prosecution, the convincingness of the evidence that the other crimes were committed and that the accused was the actor, and the strength or weakness of the other-crimes evidence in supporting the issue, and on the other, the degree to which the jury will probably be roused by the evidence to overmastering hostility.

McCormick, supra, Evidence § 190 at 453. See United States v. Byrd, 352 F.2d 570, 574 (2d Cir. 1965).

Appellants place great reliance upon the concurring opinion of Judge Lumbard in United States v. DeCicco, supra, and upon opinions from other circuits, for the proposition that evidence of similar prior acts is not admissible unless the defendant himself has first raised the issues of motive or intent. See 435 F.2d at 486. Appellants' reliance is misplaced, however, since the cases in this Circuit provide otherwise. See, e. g., United States v. Freedman, 445 F.2d 1220, 1224 (2d Cir. 1971), where we held:

> Evidence of similar acts by a defendant is admissible to prove his knowledge, intent, or design if knowledge, intent, or design "is placed in issue in the case at trial, either by the nature of the facts sought to be proved by the prosecution or the nature of the facts sought to be established by the defense." United States v. DeCicco, 435 F.2d 478, 483 (2 Cir. 1970).

See also, United States v. Birrell, 447 F.2d 1168, 1172 (2d Cir. 1971), certiorari denied 404 U.S. 1025, 92 S.Ct. 675, 30 L.Ed.2d 675 (1972); United States v. Egenberg, 441 F.2d 441, 443–44 (2d Cir.), certiorari denied 404 U.S. 994, 92 S.Ct. 530, 30 L.Ed.2d 546 (1971); United States v. Klein, 340 F.2d 547, 549 (2d Cir.), certiorari denied 382 U.S. 850, 86 S.Ct. 97, 15 L.Ed.2d 89 (1965).

In the case before us, intent was placed in issue by the defendants themselves in maintaining that they had gone to the Prince house not with the intention of selling cocaine (although the proof overwhelmingly showed otherwise), but with the intention of purchasing marijuana for their own use. Under the circumstances, it cannot be said that the trial court abused its discretion in determining that the probative value of Posner's testimony as to the ten prior cocaine transactions outweighed its prejudicial effect. Inasmuch as the prior acts of Brettholz involved a situation virtually identical to the transaction for which appellants were indicted, and inasmuch as intent was an element of the defense case, there was no error in the admission of Posner's testimony.

The judgments of conviction are affirmed.

DECISIONS RELATING TO CHAPTER IV, OPINION EVIDENCE

STAFFORD v. MUSSERS POTATO CHIPS, INC.

Supreme Court, Appellate Division, Fourth Department, 1972.
39 A.D.2d 831, 333 N.Y.S.2d 139.

Before DEL VECCHIO, J. P., and WITMER, MOULE, CARDAMONE and HENRY, JJ.

MEMORANDUM:

On April 17, 1966 at about 8:20 p. m. decedent's pickup truck was proceeding northerly on a two lane macadam highway when it collided with defendant's southbound tractor trailer at a point where there was a slight incline proceeding south. Decedent and his passenger were killed. There was no eyewitness to the accident. It was dark at the time. Skid marks from the southbound vehicle veered across into the northbound lane and debris was scattered all around. Photographs showing the conditions immediately after the accident were received in evidence. Although parts of defendant's examination before trial were read into evidence, no explanation for the accident was offered by defendant. At the close of plaintiff's proof the court granted defendant's motion for a nonsuit, severed defendant's counterclaim and continued the trial on the counterclaim. In our opinion upon all the proof a prima facie case was made out sufficient to go to the jury to determine liability in plaintiff's action. (Pfaffenbach v. White Plains Express Corp., 17 N.Y.2d 132, 269 N.Y.S.2d 115, 216 N.E.2d 324 (1940)).

The trial court based its dismissal on the testimony of the State Trooper who investigated the accident. He was permitted upon cross examination to fix the point of impact in the southbound or defendant's lane of travel. We have previously held that the receipt into evidence of such testimony is error, since the Trooper was not qualified as an expert, and, even had he been, the conclusion he drew as to the point of impact was within the competence of the jury (Sacco v. Bodwitch, 34 A.D.2d 885, 312 N.Y.S.2d 259 (1971)). The right to have a jury pass on questions of fact may be taken from them only when "by no rational process could the trier of the facts base a finding in favor of the defendant upon the evidence here presented" (Blum v. Fresh Grown Preserve Corp., 292 N.Y. 241, 245, 54 N.E.2d 809, 811 (1944)). The Court should take that view of the evidence most favorable to the non-moving party and from the inferences reasonably to be drawn therefrom determine whether a verdict might properly and lawfully be found for the nonmoving party (Wessel v. Krop, 30 A.D.2d 764, 291 N.Y.S.2d 986 (1937)). We are persuaded from a review of the facts and exhibits in this case that a verdict in favor of the plaintiff would not have to be set aside as legally insufficient. We note further that where plaintiff is dead and there is no eyewitness, the plaintiff is not held to as high a degree of proof of the cause of action as where an injured plaintiff can himself describe the occurrence (Noseworthy v. City of New York, 298 N.Y. 76, 80, 80 N.E.2d 744, 745 (1948)). Finally, although plaintiff's attorney's objections were not made as timely as they should have been, the record makes clear that he did object to the Trooper's conclusions and took an appropriate exception to the judge's order granting the motion of dismissal. We deem this sufficient to preserve the point for appeal and even were it not, we should reverse in the interest of justice (Van v. Clayburn, 21 A.D.2d 144, 249 N.Y.S.2d 310 (1964)). Judgment reversed on the law and facts and a new trial granted with costs to abide the event.

All concur, except MOULE, J., who dissents and votes to affirm, in the following Memorandum:

I dissent and vote to affirm. At the time of the accident, plaintiff's decedent's vehicle was traveling northbound and defendants' vehicle southbound. Plaintiff alleges that defendants' vehicle crossed the center line into the northbound lane causing the accident. Defendants' attorney asked a trooper, called by plaintiff, if defendants' vehicle had been traveling in the southbound lane and the court sustained an objection to the question. However, plaintiff's attorney did not object when the trooper testified that the point of impact was in the southbound lane and stated that he had no objection to the introduction into evidence of a picture on which the trooper had marked the point of impact as being in the southbound lane.

This evidence tended to prove negligence on the part of the plaintiff's decedent and lack of negligence on the part of defendants and in the absence of an objection the question of its admissibility was not preserved for review (People v. Vidal, 26 N.Y.2d 249, 309 N.Y.S.2d 336, 257 N.E.2d 886 (1970); Brady v. Nally, 151 N.Y. 258, 264, 45 N.E. 547, 549 (1897)). However, even if this evidence were disregarded, there was no proof in the record that defendants were negligent and there is no rational basis on which a jury could find a verdict for the plaintiff (Blum v. Fresh Grown Preserve Corp., 292 N.Y. 241, 54 N.E.2d 809 (1944); Greenberg v. Bar Steel Constr., 37 A.D.2d 162, 323 N.Y.S.2d 193 (1971)).

TURBERT v. MATHER MOTORS, INC.

Supreme Court of Connecticut, 1973.
165 Conn. 422, 334 A.2d 903.

. . .

The defendant Smith had been driving his car south on Windsor Avenue at about 10 p. m. on the evening of the collision; directly after the accident the Smith car was located on the east side of the northbound lanes heading in a northeasterly direction, north of the Daley car which also came to rest in the northbound lanes partly in the driveway leading into the supermarket, facing in a northeasterly direction.

The defendant Smith had stopped at the traffic light with his left blinker on, intending to make a left-hand turn into the driveway. A car was stopped in the left-hand northbound lane, and when the light turned green for him, Smith waited for that car to move northerly, which it failed to do. Smith proceeded to make a left-hand turn and as he did so he was struck by the Daley car which was in the right-hand northbound lane.

The posted speed limit in the vicinity of the collision was thirty-five miles per hour in both directions; the portion of Windsor Avenue from 200 yards to the south of the opening in the esplanade in front of the twenty-four foot wide supermarket driveway to a point approximately 200 yards to the north of that opening was generally level and substantially straight.

When the vehicles stopped immediately after the collision, the right rear portion of the Daley car was approximately six and one-half feet from the east curb line of Windsor Avenue, on the traveled portion of the northbound lanes adjacent to the supermarket driveway entrance, and the rear portion of the Smith car also came to rest on the traveled portion of Windsor Avenue.

The defendant Daley claims that the trial court erred in instructing the jury under General Statutes § 14–299(b) which he argues is inapplicable to the facts of this case so that the instructions imposed inconsistent duties upon the drivers and confused the jury; and that the trial court erred in limiting the cross-examination of a police officer and excluding an exhibit offered by the defendant.

The determinative issue in this case is whether, as the defendant Daley contends, the trial court erred when it charged the jury pursuant to General Statutes § 14–299(b), which regulates the right-of-way at intersections when traffic is directed by traffic control signals exhibiting colored lights. The crux of the defendant's argument is that the rules prescribed by § 14–299(b) apply, by its specific terms, only to intersections as defined by General Statutes § 14–1(18) which states that an intersection "means the area embraced within the prolongation of the lateral curb lines of two or more highways which join one another at an angle, whether or not one such highway crosses the other." The defendant Daley claims that the area in question does not fall within the statutory definition because, as he argues, there is only one highway as defined by General Statutes § 14–1(16), despite the existence of traffic control signals suspended over the highway and at the supermarket entrance, a one-hundred-foot break in the esplanade, a five-second lead green light to allow southbound cars to turn left into the parking area, a pedestrian crosswalk enclosed by painted lines, and "trip" mechanisms at the entrance to control the light.

Section 14–299(b) of the General Statutes is the only section which governs motor vehicle operational conduct at areas controlled by signals exhibiting colored lights and which, at the time of the collision, mandated rules applicable to drivers facing green lights at intersections. There was no statute which specifically governed the conduct of drivers at traffic control signals exhibiting colored lights at areas other than "intersections." The trial court did not instruct the jury that the site of the accident was an intersection as the word is commonly used or an "intersection" within the meaning of the term as defined by § 14–1(18). Rather, the court charged that there was a statute which applied when a light changed from green to red and which defined the meaning of the green light. The court then quoted portions of the statute, including that language which required that traffic facing a green signal must yield to traffic lawfully within the intersection. The issue presented, therefore, assuming arguendo that the area controlled by the traffic light was not an intersection within the definition of § 14–1(18), is whether the trial court's statement defining the legal duties of drivers confronting a green light at an intersection was correct as applied to operators facing the green light controlling traffic on the four-lane highway, the cross-over area and the supermarket drive-in.

Other jurisdictions have resolved the enigma wherein the legislature did not in statutory language specifically provide rules for particular factual situations involving traffic lights e. g., the Supreme Court of Nebraska has held, where there was no statute relating to left turns at a traffic light, that "[i]n the absence of a statute or ordinance, the meaning to be given to a traffic control signal is that which a reasonably prudent motorist would understand and apply." Heavican v. Holbrook, 187 Neb. 814, 818, 194 N.W.2d 208, 211 (1972); Galloway v. Hartman, 271 N.C. 372, 377, 156 S.E.2d 727 (1967); C.J.S. Motor Vehicles § 360(1), p. 536. Furthermore, some jurisdictions have held that statutes governing intersections applied to areas which appeared to be intersections but were not technically intersections because private roads were abutting public roads. Grulich v. Paine, 231 N.Y. 311, 132 N.E. 100 (1921); Perry v. Carter, 14 La. App. 102, 129 So. 388 (1930). The rationale of these cases was stated succinctly by the New York Court of Appeals in the *Grulich* case, supra, 231 N.Y. 316, 132 N.E. 102 (1921), wherein a railroad depot driveway abutted a public road:

> "The statutes are intended to promote safety, order and convenience. The same reasons why drivers of motor vehicles should observe the rules that are generally accepted and enforced in crossing streets where another street intersects or abuts, exist at the entrance of the driveway in question as if it had been dedicated to and accepted by the public."

References in a charge to the jury concerning the rights and duties of motorists in intersections have been held not erroneous in a case involving a collision which occurred when an automobile was making a left turn into a shopping center parking lot on a divided four-lane highway. The court reasoned that regardless of whether the area in question was an intersection, the trial court's charge was not prejudicial because it correctly stated the applicable law. Gilmore v. Marsh, 424 Pa. 361, 227 A.2d 881 (1967).

A driver when faced with a green light at an intersection must act as a reasonably prudent person with a knowledge that he cannot proceed in disregard of other vehicles in the intersection. General Statutes § 14–299(b); Gorman v. American Sumatra Tobacco Corporation, 146 Conn. 383, 386, 151 A.2d 341 (1959); Rose v. Campitello, 114 Conn. 637, 640, 159 A. 887 (1932). We have also said that in determining what is reasonable care under all the circumstances and what rules of the road are applicable, the conduct of the parties should be judged from the viewpoint of the reasonably prudent person. Although an area may not fall within the prescribed definition of an intersection, we have held that a pedestrian was justified in assuming that a driver was subject to the usual intersection rules and, therefore, that he would keep to the right of the center of the highway in turning to his left into a private entrance. McInerney v. New England Transportation Co., 131 Conn. 633, 635, 41 A.2d 764 (1945); Heavican v. Holbrook, supra. In the *McInerney* case, supra, the plaintiff was struck by a bus at an area where a private way intersected a public street. The defendant maintained that there was no requirement, as in the case of public street intersections, to keep to the right of center of such an intersection. This court rejected this contention and stated (131 Conn. pp. 634–635, 41 A.2d p. 764): "The jury were bound to consider the conduct of the plaintiff from the viewpoint of the reasonably prudent person and might well have found that to such a person the private way would have appeared to have been part of the city highway system subject to the rules of the road relating to public ways."

Automatic traffic control systems are intended to minimize the dangers inherent at the locations where they are installed and it is the duty of motor vehicle operators to obey and observe traffic signals. Drivers, passengers and pedestrians, for instance, have a right to assume that an apparently legal traffic light was placed by legal authority, which is not disputed in the case before us, that the parties act accordingly as reasonably prudent persons under the circumstances, and that the signal is still effective to control the question of negligence of one who disregards it, at least to the extent that such disregard may be taken into consideration as one of the circumstances to be passed upon. Geisking v. Sheimo, 252 Iowa 37, 41, 105 N.W.2d 599 (1960); note, 164 A.L.R. 8, 216; Blashfield, Automobile Law & Practice (Perm.Ed.) §§ 686.5, 998, 1040.

Regardless of whether the area in question be considered an intersection within the meaning of General Statutes § 14–1(18), the trial court did not erroneously impose legal burdens upon the drivers at the area in question which reasonably prudent drivers should not have assumed. Application of different standards to drivers facing green lights at divided highways with enclosed crosswalks and cross-vehicular traffic but not a statutory "intersection" would be contrary to the interests of safety and good order by contravening the normal expectations of reasonably prudent drivers, and a statutory definition is not always applicable to a complicated traffic pattern. Baird v. Gaer Bros., Inc., 152 Conn. 219, 223, 205 A.2d 490 (1965); Mathis v. Bzdula, 122 Conn. 202, 206, 188 A. 264 (1937). Statutory rules of the road are to be interpreted in light of their purpose to prevent collisions, "and, if their meaning is not definitely settled by the language used, they are to be interpreted in the light of their application to traffic moving over the highways." Mathis v. Bzdula, supra, 205, 188 A. 265 (1937). Constructions are to be avoided which are impractical and undesirably rigid. Baird v. Baer Bros., Inc., supra, 152 Conn. 223, 205 A.2d 490 (1965).

Not to utilize the statute, § 14–299(b), in instructing the jury under the circumstances of this case would lead to absurd consequences or to "possible bizarre results"; Bridgeport v. Stratford, 142 Conn. 634, 641, 642, 116 A.2d 508 (1955); since operators of motor vehicles might otherwise justifiably disregard such traffic control signals with impunity.

The defendant Daley claims not only that § 14–299(b) was inapplicable but also that it prescribed a different right-of-way than the statute under which he requested the trial court to charge, General Statutes § 14–242(a). The court instructed the jury pursuant to both statutes paraphrasing § 14–242(a). Immediately following this recitation, the court specifically told the jury, clearly applying § 14–242(a) to the southbound defendant that unless the jury found that the defendant Smith made a left turn to enter the supermarket parking lot at a time when it could not be done with reasonable safety, the jury must find that defendant negligent.

Although § 14–242(a) does embody a standard for vehicles turning left into a private alleyway, it has often been applied to left turns at intersections. Ramonas v. Zucker, 163 Conn. 142, 147, 302 A.2d 242 (1973); Michaud v. Gagne, 155 Conn. 406, 409, 232 A.2d 326 (1967); Kronish v. Provasoli, 149 Conn. 368, 371, 179 A.2d 823 (1962). The legislature has recognized that a standard of reasonable safety applies both to left turns into private alleys and left turns within intersections with its recent repeal of § 14–246 (Public Acts 1971, No. 66) and enactment of § 14–242(e), which in specific terms imposes the same duties upon drivers intending to turn left in either case. This duty is the same upon a driver facing a green light, intending to turn left; § 14–299(b); except to the degree that it may impose a higher standard of care in requiring the driver to yield not only to vehicles within the intersection or extended lateral lines but also to those so close as to constitute an imminent hazard. Yet a driver facing a green light must operate his vehicle with reasonable safety and cannot disregard the presence of other vehicles which might be approaching the intersection. Pinto v. Spigner, 163 Conn. 191, 196, 302 A.2d 266 (1973); Rose v. Campitello, 114 Conn. 637, 640, 159 A. 887 (1932).

The evidence at the trial was in sharp conflict as to the relevant and material facts surrounding the collision and the jury could properly conclude that the negligence of either Daley or Smith or of both, caused the collision and the resultant injuries to the plaintiff. The question was one of fact and was resolved by the verdict.

. . .

Finally, the defendant Daley contends that the trial court improperly rejected cross-examination of a police officer, not an eyewitness, which attempted to elicit from the officer his understanding of what the defendant Daley meant when Daley told the officer that the southbound car turned "behind" the third unidentified vehicle in the left northbound lane. The court also rejected the officer's report because it contained the officer's conclusion as to the cause of the accident. The officer was allowed to read portions of his report and testify from it concerning what the defendant told him. Both defendant and plaintiff testified and submitted to cross-examination.

The admissibility of lay opinions is within the trial court's discretion and its decision will not be reversed unless that discretion is abused. State v. Orsini, 155 Conn. 367, 372, 232 A.2d 907 (1967). The trial court could reasonably conclude that a police officer, not a witness to the accident, was being asked to give his opinion as to what in fact happened at the time of the collision. When questioned concerning his intent in writing a certain paragraph of his report, he stated: "I drew a conclusion what caused the accident." The court did not abuse its discretion in refusing to admit the testimony or the report. As we said in Mucci v. LeMonte, 157 Conn. 566, 569, 254 A.2d 879, 881 (1969): "Moreover, a police officer's conclusion about the cause of or responsibility for an injury is merely an opinion which the officer would not be permitted to give if he was on the witness stand. Giamattei v. DiCerbo, 135 Conn. 159, 163, 62 A.2d 519 (1949)." See McCormick, Law of Evidence § 56.

There is no error.

In this opinion the other judges concurred.

TREBOTICH v. BROGLIO

Supreme Court of Ohio, 1973.
33 Ohio St.2d 57, 294 N.E.2d 669.

CELEBREZZE, Justice. This case turns upon the proposition of the extent to which an expert witness may go in giving an opinion upon an ultimate issue.

In this highly technical age, the use of specialized testimony seems to be an ever-present question. There are even those in our society who say that the use of a specialist is no longer a solution to the dilemma of the day but a part of the problem.

The use of expert opinion testimony is perhaps best stated in paragraph one of the syllabus of McKay Machine Co. v. Rodman, 11 Ohio St.2d 77, 228 N.E.2d 304 (1967), which reads as follows:

> "In all proceedings involving matters of a scientific, mechanical, professional, or other like nature, requiring special study, experience or observation not within the common knowledge of laymen in general, expert opinion testimony is admissible to aid the court or the jury in arriving at a correct determination of the litigated issue."

That quotation was later referred to in Huffman v. Stone, 26 Ohio St.2d 159, 270 N.E.2d 347 (1971), wherein the trial court permitted a duly qualified traffic engineer to testify ". . . that in braking a car in an emergency, the wheels are almost certain to lock; that if that happens all directional control force is transferred to stopping the forward motion of the car . . . *making it impossible to control the car's direction*." (Emphasis added.)

2 Jones on Evidence (6 Ed.), 578, lists some 22 sections setting out various subjects of expert testimony. Although the tendency is in the direction of expanding this field, the admissibility of expert testimony is based upon established or generally recognized scientific principles or discoveries which are sufficiently established so as to have gained general exceptance in a particular field. The testimony of such witnesses is subject to the rules of evidence governing admissibility of opinions of experts on the ultimate issue of fact to be determined by the jury.

This rule seems to be most clearly set forth in the first two paragraphs of the syllabus in Shepherd v. Midland Mutual Life Ins. Co., 152 Ohio St. 6, 87 N.E.2d 156 (1949), a case involving the duty to pay a double indemnity in a contract of life insurance, which read as follows:

> "1. Although a witness may be qualified to give an opinion concerning a matter upon which opinion evidence may be admissible in and pertinent to the determination of an issue, as a general rule such an opinion, whether expert or otherwise, may not be admitted when it, in effect, answers the very question as to the existence or nonexistence of an ultimate fact to be determined by the jury.
>
> "2. Where an ultimate fact to be determined by the jury is one depending upon the interpretation of certain scientific facts which are beyond the experience, knowledge or comprehension of the jury, a witness qualified to speak as to the subject matter involved may express an opinion as to the probability or actuality of a fact pertinent to an issue in the case, and the admission of such opinion in evidence does not constitute an invasion or usurpation of the province or function of the jury,

> even though such opinion is on the ultimate fact which the jury must determine."

In the instant case, the threshold question the trier of the facts, the jury, had to resolve, before it could even consider any other issue, was "who negligently crossed the center line?" We acknowledge that under certain circumstances this may become a highly technical problem, but in this case it was reduced to "where was the point of impact?" And there was eyewitnesses' testimony on both sides of this issue. The most elemental function of the jury under our system of jurisprudence is its exclusive privilege as judge of the disputed facts and of the credibility of the witnesses and their testimony. The question here is not a complex one nor is it beyond the comprehension of the average juror, but, rather, it is one we find a jury in this state would be qualified to determine.

"In many cases it is asserted as a broad general rule, often assumed to be an inflexible rule of law, that while an expert may be permitted to express his opinion, or even his belief, he cannot give his opinion upon the precise or ultimate fact in issue before the jury, which must be determined by them." 21 Ohio Jurisprudence 2d 422, Section 414; Ohio & Indiana Torpedo Co. v. Fishburn, 61 Ohio St. 608, 56 N.E. 457 (1900); Fowler v. Delaplain, 79 Ohio St. 279, 87 N.E. 260 (1909); Mitchell v. Indus. Comm., 135 Ohio St. 110, 19 N.E. 2d 769 (1939).

We find that in this case permitting an expert witness to give his opinion on the *point of impact,* in view of the testimony of the eyewitnesses, did not serve to enlighten the jury with respect to a matter outside its competence but rather was a clear invasion of the jury's province on the precise ultimate fact in issue.

The judgment of the Court of Appeals is affirmed and the cause is remanded to the Court of Common Pleas for further proceedings according to law.

Judgment affirmed.

ROBERTS v. STATE OF FLORIDA

Supreme Court of Florida, 1964.
164 So.2d 817.

THORNAL, Justice. John Henry Roberts and John Alfred Adderley seek reversal of verdicts and judgments convicting them of first degree murder without recommendation of mercy.

We have for consideration numerous alleged errors in the trial proceeding.

At approximately 11:30 A.M., Friday, May 12, 1961, Benjamin Franklin Campbell, Jr., was shot while tending his grocery store. A customer, standing across the store, heard one shot and also heard a voice announce "You shot me." The customer ran to an adjoining kitchen area where Mrs. Campbell was preparing her husband's dinner.

Mrs. Campbell also heard a statement, "I am shot." Upon entering the store proper, she found her husband lying on the floor mortally wounded. The drawer of the cash register was open and she noted that certain ten and twenty dollar bills which were previously in the drawer had disappeared. Before entering the store from the kitchen Mrs. Campbell dialed the telephone operator to call for an ambulance and the police. While on the phone she saw the heads of two people as they were leaving the front of the store. At about 6:00 P.M., May 12, 1961, John Henry Roberts was taken into custody. He was arrested initially for "investigation of the homicide." At about 11:30 P.M., May 12, 1961, John Alfred Adderley was similarly arrested. From about 6:30 P.M. until about 1:30 A.M., Roberts was interrogated by law enforcement officers. He denied any connection with the crime. Shortly after midnight May 13, and within approximately one hour after his arrest, Adderley made a full confession of his participation in the robbery and murder. He implicated Roberts. At about 11:45 A.M., May 13, 1961, Adderley was brought face to face with Roberts. Adderley stated, "It was a terrible thing we did. They have caught us . . . the only thing . . . to do . . . (is) . . . to tell the truth." Thereupon, around noon on Saturday, May 13, Roberts likewise gave a full confession, the essential aspects of which were factually corroborative of the confession made by Adderley. At the trial the defendants repudiated their confessions and undertook to establish alibis. They were found guilty of first degree murder by separate verdicts. There were no mercy recommendations. The death sentences ensued. The appellants have filed separate briefs. They seek reversal on numerous grounds which we shall discuss.

Roberts assaults the validity of his confession with the claim that it was obtained by prolonged and excessive interrogation which overcame his capacity to resist. It will be recalled that he was arrested at approximately 6:00 P.M., May 12. The interrogation started at about 6:30 P.M. and continued intermittently until 1:30 A.M. the next morning. The interrogation was not constant. There were periodic breaks. The significant fact is that at the end of this period of questioning Roberts continued to maintain his innocence. No confession was obtained during this initial interrogation. He went to bed around 1:30 A.M. He was not questioned again until after 9:30 A.M. on Saturday, May 13. In the meantime, Adderley had confessed. It is clear from the record that Roberts showed no inclination to confess until he was confronted by his accomplice. In fact, Adderley does not question the voluntariness of his confession by his brief in this Court. This, of course, does not affect Roberts.

We have held that a confession freely and voluntarily given while one is in custody for investigation of a crime is admissible at his subsequent trial. Williams v. State, 143 Fla. 826, 197 So. 562 (1941). The test of admissibility is whether the confession was voluntary. It must be shown that it was given without fear, hope of reward, or some other illegal influence or inordinate mental or physical pressures. It is true that Roberts was arrested at 6:00 P.M., Friday, May 12, and before being presented to a magistrate, his confession was obtained approximately sixteen hours later. This fact, however, would not destroy the validity of the confession if it was otherwise freely and voluntarily given. Dawson v. State, 139 So.2d 408 (Fla.1962); Singer v. State, Fla., 109 So.2d 7 (Fla.1959). There is no evidence to indicate either mental or physical abuse of the accused. Out of the presence of the jury, the trial judge correctly investigated the voluntariness of the confessions as a condition to their admissibility. In the presence of the jury, the defendants were permitted to offer evidence to support their view that the confessions were not freely given. This evidence went to their credibility. The jury evidently accepted the confessions. We find no basis for reversal on this point.

The state placed in evidence a .25 caliber pistol which was shown to have belonged to Roberts. Also in evidence was a shell case found at the scene of the crime and a slug removed from the body of the victim. The state then called Ed Bigler, a ballistics expert, who testified that he had test-fired the pistol and had compared the markings on the test bullet with those from the evidence bullet removed from the victim. This he did under a comparison microscope. On the basis of this experiment he submitted the opinion that the bullet which resulted in Campbell's death had been fired from the gun belonging to Roberts. The test bullet was not placed in evidence. Both Adderley and Roberts contend that the test bullet should also have been filed in evidence so that the jury could compare it with the evidence bullet which had caused the death. It is clear that the markings on the bullets could not be identified with the naked eye. Additionally, they could be interpreted only by one trained in the science or experience of ballistics.

Thompson v. Freeman, 111 Fla. 433, 149 So. 740 (1933), cited by appellants, does not support their position. It involved the authenticity of a document and was governed by a statute. We have no such situation in the instant case.

It is now well established that a witness, who qualifies as an expert in the science of ballistics, may identify a gun from which a particular bullet was fired by comparing the markings on that bullet with those on a test bullet fired by the witness through the suspect gun. An expert will be permitted to submit his opinion based on such an experiment conducted by him. The details of the experiment should be described to the jury. Riner v. State, 128 Fla. 848, 176 So. 38 (1937), rehearing denied 131 Fla. 243, 179 So. 404; State v. Vuckovich, 61 Mont. 480, 203 Pac. 491 (1922); Edwards v. State, 198 Md. 132, 81 A.2d 631, 83 A.2d 578, 26 A.L.R.2d 874 (1951).

In McKenna v. People, 124 Colo. 112, 235 P.2d 351 (1951), it was held that the opinion of an expert based on the test firing of a gun could be offered in evidence without the necessity of submitting a corroborating microphotograph for inspection by the jurors. In McKenna the expert relied upon a comparison of the test bullet with the evidence bullet under a comparison microscope. This was the identical procedure followed in the case at bar. In State v. Wojculewicz, 140 Conn. 487, 101 A.2d 495 (1954), the Court held that it was unnecessary to place the test bullet in evidence to sustain the admissibility of the expert's opinion based upon an experiment in which the test bullet was fired.

In cases such as these the opinion of the witness is allowed under the rules which govern other forms of expert testimony. He will be permitted to submit his conclusions where it is shown that by training and experience he is qualified to give an expert opinion on the basis of the ballistic tests which he himself conducted. It is not necessary that the test be conducted in the presence of the jury nor is it required that the expert submit to the jury the actual test materials. It was not error to refuse to compel the state to produce the test bullet.

When the jury was being qualified on voir dire the trial judge explained to them that it would be their function to determine the facts on the basis of the evidence. He told them that it was his duty to explain the law and their duty to apply the law to the facts. He informed them that even though they disagree with him on some statement of law, nevertheless, it was their responsibility to accept the law as he announced it. In the course of these remarks the judge stated, "If the court is mistaken as to what the law is it is not the duty of the jury to correct him, but there is a way that it can be corrected through appellate procedure." Both appellants contend that this statement constituted reversible error. They base their contention on Pait v. State, 112 So.2d 380 (Fla.1959) and Blackwell v. State, 76 Fla. 124, 79 So. 731, 1 A.L.R. 502 (1918). In the cited cases the state attorney argued to the jury that if they committed any error it could be corrected in the Supreme Court. We held that in effect these remarks merely suggest to the jury that they need not be too greatly concerned about the results of their deliberations because there would be an appellate court to review them. Such was not the effect of the statement of the trial judge in the instant case. He impressed the jurors with the importance of their responsibility regarding factual determinations. He correctly informed them that they had no responsibility in deciding the law of the case. The power of an appellate court to review his decisions on the law did not in any particular relieve the jurors of any aspect of their vital responsibility in settling the facts. Overstreet v. State, 143 Fla. 794, 197 So. 516 (1940).

The state produced a witness, Boswell, who testified that on Monday, May 8, 1961, he accompanied Roberts to the establishment of one Livingston for the purpose of pawning Roberts' pistol. Boswell handled the negotiations with Livingston. Other testimony revealed that Roberts had redeemed his pistol from Livingston on the morning of the homicide. This was the pistol which was identified as the murder weapon. Cross-examination of Boswell indicated that he too had been taken into custody on the day the murder was committed. He was then asked "Were you a suspect?" The state's objection to the question was sustained. The defendants then made a proffer to show that if they were permitted to continue this line of questioning they could prove that Boswell had spent some five hours in jail under "suspicion" for the same crime and that "by virtue of being accused of this crime himself that he was likely to have given evidence in favor of the City [Sic] in order to get himself off the hook . . . ." The judge refused the proffer.

A defendant is permitted wide latitude in the cross-examination of a state witness to show the motive of the witness in giving testimony for the state. It is permissible to interrogate the witness on the subject of any agreement to grant him leniency or immunity from prosecution in exchange for his testimony. Henderson v. State, 135 Fla. 548, 185 So. 625, 120 A.L.R. 742 (1939); Spaeth v. United States, 232 F.2d 776, 62 A.L.R.2d 606 (6th Cir. 1956).

The proffer in the instant case did not include a showing that the witness was still suspected of the crime nor did it include a tender of proof that the state had made any concessions to him in exchange for his testimony. The proffer merely submitted a conclusion that the witness "was likely to have given evidence" in favor of the state's position. Moreover, if Boswell had been completely discredited, there was other reliable testimony regarding the pawning of the pistol. In fact, Roberts himself testified to the pawning of the pistol on May 8 and its redemption on May 12. There was no question but that the gun belonged to Roberts, that he pawned it on May 8th and retrieved it on May 12. The ruling of the trial judge on the attempted cross-examination of Boswell was not reversible error.

Prior to and during the trial Adderley repeatedly sought a severance. We have held that the allowance of a severance rests within the sound discretion of the trial judge. His decision will not be disturbed absent a showing of abuse of discretion or some significant resultant damage to the defendant who seeks a separate trial. Sawyer v. State, 100 Fla. 1603, 132 So. 188 (1931); Manson v. State, 88 So.2d 272 (Fla.1956); Samuels v. State, 123 Fla. 280, 166 So. 743 (1936). In the instant case, there was no antagonism between the defenses of the two defendants. They both sought to establish alibis. Their attorneys collaborated constantly during the trial. In those instances where evidence was admissible against one but not against the other, the trial judge carefully instructed the jury to this effect. We do not find that the judge abused his discretion in denying the motion for severance.

Adderley further contends that the indictment against him should have been quashed because of a claimed systematic exclusion of Negroes from the grand jury. The record is devoid of any evidence to support this claim. The mere fact that in this instance only one Negro was called to serve on the petit jury does not support the claim of systematic exclusion from the grand jury. Porter v. State, 160 So.2d 104 (Fla.1964). Adderley also contends that the grand jury which indicted him consisted of only 18 persons, rather than 23 as provided by Chapter 25554, Laws of 1949. Without exploring the constitutionality of the cited statute, it appears from the record that the 18-man grand jury was properly constituted as of the time the indictment was presented.

It is further pointed out that the indictment charged an unlawful homicide with a premeditated design. By its evidence, the state undertook to prove a homicide committed in the perpetration of a robbery. We are requested to recede from our previous holdings to the effect that an indictment generally charging an unlawful homicide with a premeditated design can be proven by evidence of a homicide committed in the perpetration of a robbery. Section 782.04, Florida Statutes, F.S.A. We see no reason to recede from our prior decisions on this point. Blake v. State, 156 So.2d 511 (Fla.1963).

We have examined the several other points assigned for reversal. We find them to be without merit and insufficient to justify an extensive discussion.

In addition to the contentions made by the appellants, we have reviewed the evidence in detail as required by Section 924.32, Florida Statutes, F.S.A. On the basis of this examination we fail to find that the interests of justice require a new trial.

The judgments are affirmed.

It is so ordered.

DECISIONS RELATING TO CHAPTER V, BEST EVIDENCE RULE

PERRY v. RYBACK

Supreme Court of Pennsylvania, 1931.
302 Pa. 559, 153 A. 770.

. . .

Appeal from Court of Common Pleas, Erie County; J. W. Bouton, President Judge, specially presiding.

Action by Eugenia C. Perry against Bernie Ryback. Judgment for plaintiff, and defendant appeals.

. . .

KEPHART, J. Lytle Perry, Bernie Ryback, and another, members of a hunting party, were driving along the Roosevelt Highway in Ryback's car shortly after noon on November 30, 1927. Ryback, who was driving from fifty to sixty miles an hour in a very hard rain, attempted to go around an "S" curve. The car slid off the road, broke a telephone pole in half, turned over and killed Perry. Deceased's widow brought this action, for herself, and children, against Ryback, and recovered a verdict. On judgment in her favor, this appeal followed.

Appellant contends that his negligence should be imputed to Perry, since they were engaged in a joint enterprise. Whether or not the journey was a joint enterprise is immaterial to the determination of this case. That doctrine is applicable only where one of the parties to the enterprise sues a third party. "Where the action is brought against a third party, the rule is that the negligence of one member of the joint enterprise within the scope of that enterprise will be imputed to the other. . . . When the action is brought by one member of the enterprise against another, there is no place to apply the doctrine of imputed negligence. . . . The situation when the action is brought by one member of the enterprise against the other is entirely different from that when recovery is sought against a third person." Johnson v. Hetrick, 300 Pa. 225, 233, 150 A. 477, 479 (1930).

Where the action between parties to a joint enterprise is for injuries from a negligent act, it will be treated as an ordinary action for injuries as a result of negligence. The general rule may be stated as follows: When two or more persons are engaged in any pursuit, whether it is pleasure, business, mutual convenience, or fellowship, each owes to the other the duty to exercise due care in their relation that no injury shall happen through a neglect of that duty. The care required in such relation is what men of ordinary prudence would use in similar circumstances. The fact that the mutual safety of the persons in the relation depends on the exercise of care by all does not enlarge or emphasize the duty. It is ordinary care under the circumstances. Where one in that relation fails to perform that duty, he is responsible for the resultant injury. The rights of the parties as to each other, with regard to the duty enjoined, are separate and distinct, even though one of the parties in the relation is dependent. What constitutes a failure of duty is a relative term, and must depend on the facts of each case. The owner of an automobile is liable to his guest or passenger if he negligently operates his car to the injury of his guest or passenger. We do not here determine liability if the car is driven other than by the owner.

While this liability is thus fixed on one of the parties of the enterprise through his negligent acts, there is a duty imposed on the other party, the deceased in this case. It has been stated in many of our cases that, where the action is against third persons, the duty thus resting on the other party is to caution, warn, remonstrate, or protest to the driver as to his fast or careless driving. Curran v. Lehigh Valley R. R., 299 Pa. 584, 591, 149 A. 885 (1930). See Kilpatrick v. P. R. T. Co., 290 Pa. 288, 294, pars. 2, 3, and page 295, 138 A. 830 (1927). Also Campagna v. Lyles, 298 Pa. 352, 357, 148 A. 527 (1930), and cases there cited. The same rule applies where the action is between the parties of a mutual venture. It was the duty of the deceased, when he noticed Perry [Ryback] driving at the rate of speed as here testified, to protest or warn him against it. If he failed to perform this duty, he was guilty of contributory negligence; the law would assume under such circumstances that he was satisfied with the operation of the car, and that he was willing to join Perry [Ryback] in the hazard or in taking a chance on the result of fast driving.

But, as appellee's husband is dead, the law presumes that he used due care, that is, that he did protest or remonstrate with Perry [Ryback] as to his driving. Johnson v. Hetrick, supra. The presumption of due care on the part of the deceased may be rebutted, in appellee's case, by incontrovertible, physical facts, that is, such facts as a court will take judicial notice of (Patterson v. Pittsburgh, etc., Ry. Co., 210 Pa. 47, 59 A. 318 (1904); Unger v. P., B. & W. R. Co., 217 Pa. 106, 66 A. 235 (1907); Hartig v. American Ice Co., 290 Pa. 21, 30, 31, 137 A. 867 (1927)), or by evidence as indicated in Hartig v. American Ice Co., supra. Where any such facts are present, or such evidence is presented, and plaintiff's case depends solely on the presumption, it must fail for want of sufficient evidence. Where the effort to rebut the presumption is by other evidence, the credibility of the witnesses is necessarily for the jury. Where there is an uncertainty as to the facts or the inferences to be drawn from them the case is necessarily for the jury. Hartig v. American Ice Co., et al., supra.

There are neither admitted nor incontrovertible physical facts nor uncontroverted oral and written testimony of disinterested witnesses here to rebut the presumption. There may be some inferences, but these are not sufficient, as a matter of law, to overcome the presumption. What evidence there was on the subject, and it was all negative, was properly submitted to the jury.

Appellant contends that there are a number of alleged trial errors sufficient to cause a reversal. They are as follows: (1) The court below permitted evidence to be introduced showing deceased's habits and ability as a lawyer. (2) The stenographer was erroneously allowed to refresh her recollection of his earnings from the income tax return and ledger which she had kept. (3) That it was impossible to distinguish from plaintiff's testimony between the personal earnings of the deceased and the return from capital invested. (4) The court did not charge fully on contributory negligence.

As to the question stated in 1 and 3, the rule as to the measure of damages is fully stated in Gaydos et al. v. Domabyl (Pa.) 152 A. 549, 552, an opinion handed down November 24, 1930. We there said that the jury may take into consideration deceased's "age, ability and disposition to labor, and his habits of living and expenditure." Pennsylvania R. Co. v. Butler, 57 Pa. 335, 338 (1868); Mansfield Coal & Coke Co. v. McEnery, 91 Pa. 185, 189, 36 Am.Rep. 662 (1879); McHugh v. Schlosser, 159 Pa. 480, 486, 28 A. 291, 23 L.R.A. 574, 39 Am.St.Rep. 699 (1894); Burns v. P. R. Co., 219 Pa. 225, 228, 68 A. 704 (1908). Appellant argues that evidence of character and reputation was offered and admitted. Neither the assignments of error nor the record disclose any such condition. There was no effort to prove character or reputation. It is common knowledge that a lawyer of outstanding ability or of average capacity and good habits will possess a larger clientele and will receive a greater remuneration than the lawyer of limited ability.

Where it is impossible to distinguish between personal earnings of the individual and the return from capital invested in the labor of others the net income or net results from such business should not be considered in determining the amount of damages to which the claimant is entitled. Baxter v. Phila. & R. Ry. Co., 264 Pa. 467, 107 A. 881, 9 A.L.R. 504 (1919). But there is no such impossibility in the evidence in this case. Appellee's husband was a lawyer, and also published the Erie County Law Journal. The net income from the law practice and the journal were given, and there was testimony that more than half the income came from the law practice. Appellant had every opportunity to check the reliability of this testimony. The books, with these charges entered, were in court. The witness testified from them, and, when appellant was asked if he wished to have the items read, he specifically declined to have this done. The evidence was only important to show that his earnings were sufficient each year to give to his wife and children what, as was testified to, they received before his death. Such contributions are the basis for the measure of damages, as will be seen later. They did not comprise all his earnings and were a few hundred dollars over one-half of his net income. The verdict of $8,000 shows that the jury was very considerate in its conclusion. The charge of the court was full and explicit on the question of damages, following closely the opinion of Mr. Justice Walling in Glasco v. Green, 273 Pa. 353, 117 A. 79 (1922), and the charge was fully supported by the evidence.

While defendant's assignments of error do not cover the second question, we will consider the use of the ledger by the witness to refresh her recollection; she having made the entries of charges and being familiar with the facts. It is argued that such evidence was insufficient for the court to base any charge as to the measure of damages, relying on Muncey v. Pull. Taxi Serv. Co., 269 Pa. 97, 112 A. 30 (1921), since the evidence was not the best evidence to prove the fact at issue.

There is no general rule that the best evidence must be introduced or that better evidence must be introduced before inferior evidence. Wigmore on Evidence, vol. 2, §§ 1173, 1174. The application of the best evidence rule is ordinarily confined to primary and secondary evidence, and relates largely to the production of documents, as where one desires to prove the terms of a writing. Production of the original or an exact duplicate, must be made, unless its absence is satisfactorily explained. Here there is no attempt to prove the contents of a writing but to show the amounts of deceased's earnings. For this purpose, written or oral testimony is clearly admissible. Books of original entry are not necessarily the only evidence nor the best evidence of a given state of facts, but a party may make out his case as to such facts by the testimony of a witness. See Wigmore on Evidence, supra; also Henry's Pa. Trial Evidence, § 97, and authorities cited. Books of account are always competent to refresh the memory of a witness who had personal knowledge of a transaction. Nichols v. Haynes, 78 Pa. 174, 176 (1875); Hottle v. Weaver, 206 Pa. 87, 89, 55 A. 838 (1903). See Croushore's Estate, 79 Pa.Super.Ct. 286, 289. The fact that the latter may be more accurate is a matter for the jury.

Defendant relies on Muncey v. Pull. Taxi Serv. Co., supra, but the case does not control the instant one. Plaintiff there, who conducted a detective agency, merely stated he made $10,000 a year. This was an approximation of his earnings. We held that, as no effort was made to give any detailed account or description of his business or gross receipts and expenses, or in any manner to depict what he was doing, the evidence was not sufficient; it was merely a guess at earnings, insufficient on which to base a claim for damages. The court distinctly held that it was not always necessary to produce books to prove damages in a personal injury case.

The stenographer, testifying from the ledger, stated that she took the accounts she received from each person and kept them in the ledger and added them up. There were receipts from deceased's law and publishing business. With the book before her, she stated his net income per year was $5,700. All the evidence was admitted without objection. She stated that the receipts from the legal journal were nearly half of the net receipts. The evidence was sufficient for the jury to find deceased's earning power as it related to the contribution made to his family. Even if an objection had been made, we would not regard it as serious.

The learned trial judge endeavored to charge the jury on the question of contributory negligence as fully as it was possible for him to do, requesting appellant to point out in what respect his charge was insufficient. As we read the charge, it more than protected appellant's rights. The verdict was reasonable; the case was free from error.

The judgment of the court below is affirmed.

CHAGNON LUMBER CO., INC. v. PATENAUDE

Supreme Court of New Hampshire, 1961.
103 N.H. 448, 174 A.2d 415.

BLANDIN, Justice. The plaintiff's claim, in brief, is that the defendant as an independent contractor signed a contract with a John R. Contrell to build a house for him in Lexington, Massachusetts, and that the plaintiff sold the defendant lumber and materials for the house, for which the defendant is liable.

The defendant denied these allegations and testified that he was an employee carpenter working by the day for Contrell, that he never bought the supplies himself, but told the plaintiff to charge them to Contrell.

An examination of the entire record convinces us that the sharply conflicting claims of the parties were for the jury to resolve. Hiltz v. Gould, 99 N.H. 85, 87, 105 A.2d 48 (1954). If the jury believed the defendant's evidence that the plaintiff agreed to charge the supplies to Contrell the defendant would not be liable. Restatement, Second, Agency, § 320. It follows that the plaintiff's exception to the denial of its motion to set aside the verdict must be overruled.

In regard to the alleged contract between Contrell and the defendant, it appears that the original was never produced and that the Court in excluding the copy offered by the plaintiff found that no satisfactory excuse was given for the nonproduction. It has long been the established law that a copy of a private document (containing here merely the typed signatures of the parties) is inadmissible unless the absence of the original is satisfactorily accounted for. Wallace v. Goodall, 18 N.H. 439, 451, 455 (1846); C.J.S. Evidence §§ 813, 823, 826; see Skaling v. Remick, 97 N.H. 106, 108, 82 A.2d 81 (1951). The principle upon which the rule rests is that the original is the best evidence of the facts to be proved and that "it is to be procured and offered *if it can be had.*" IV Wigmore on Evidence (3d Ed.) § 1192(1).

Each case must rest upon its own facts and it was for the Trial Court to determine, within its discretion, whether the plaintiff had made reasonable efforts to procure the original of the alleged contract. IV Wigmore, supra, § 1194, pp. 339–340. The record convinces us that there was no abuse of discretion in the Court's finding that the absence of the original was not properly accounted for (cf. Skaling v. Remick, supra) and that the exclusion of the copy is sustainable. The order is

Judgment on the verdict.

All concurred.

STATE OF OHIO v. JAMES

Court of Appeals of Ohio, 1974.
41 Ohio App.2d 248, 325 N.E.2d 267.

CRAWFORD, Presiding Judge. The defendant, Frank James, and the decedent, Lula Frey, lived at 713 Westwood Avenue in Dayton. They had an argument there on April 15, 1969. Lula Frey then called the police, who arrived at about 12:45 a. m., and left with them.

The next day, April 16, 1969, decedent was in the house at 713 Westwood talking on the telephone to the police dispatcher and, while she was holding the telephone, defendant, the appellant, came into the house and fired four shots into her and her death ensued.

Defendant claimed self-defense on the basis that he believed deceased was bringing a gun out of her bra. Such gun was never found. During this episode, the telephone was still open and connected with the police department, where the sounds transmitted by the telephone were recorded on tape. This tape recorded the shots and conversation. Defendant was convicted of the second-degree murder of Lula Frey. The tape was introduced in evidence at defendant's trial as part of the *res gestae.*

On defendant's present appeal from that conviction, his single assignment of error is the introduction into evidence of the tape recording of the conversation and other sounds received over the telephone in the office of the police dispatcher. He contended that the tape is not the best evidence, but that the best evidence would be the testimony of the police dispatcher.

Janet Welz, the police dispatcher, was called by the state to testify. She verified the accuracy of a typewritten transcript of the conversation taken from the tape. The transcript was introduced in evidence. She was not asked either on direct or cross-examination about hearing the shots recorded on the tape, which were not reflected in the typewritten transcript.

Defendant's argument that the testimony of the dispatcher would be the best evidence, so as to render the tape inadmissible is not supported by his citations.

In People v. Kulwin, 102 Cal.App.2d 104, 226 P.2d 672 (1951), the defendant objected to the testimony of a witness to a conversation which had been recorded, contending that the recordings were the best evidence. The court held that the testimony of a witness testifying from memory is not rendered inadmissible by the existence of a record of what was heard.

Both mechanical recordings and the testimony of a witness whose memory was refreshed thereby were held properly admitted in Kilpatrick v. Kilpatrick, 123 Conn. 218, 193 A. 765 (1937). Both mechanical recording and personal testimony were held admissible in Thompson v. State, 298 P.2d 464 (Okl.Cr.1956).

None of these cases holds that the taped record is inadmissible. On the contrary, as set forth in 29 American Jurisprudence 2d 496, Evidence, Section 436, both the tape and the oral testimony are admissible.

"Where proof of a conversation has been of two different kinds, namely, a recording thereof and testimony by witnesses who overheard it, it has been argued that both the recording and the testimony were the best evidence; however, the courts have not relegated either to a secondary position, but have held that both types of evidence are equally competent primary evidence, and that one is not to be excluded because of the existence of the other."

Also, see annotation, 10 L.Ed.2d 1169, at 1175, entitled "Admissibility of sound recordings as evidence in Federal criminal trial." More than one witness may testify to the same facts or conversation, and the same fact may be proved by different types of proof as, for example, direct and circumstantial evidence. Where both are introduced, the one may corroborate the other, or, if they are contradictory, a question is presented for the jury.

Counsel for the state make the valid comparison between a photograph and the photographer's description of the thing or scene photographed. The photograph, if properly authenticated, as the tape was here, is clearly admissible. In fact, the photograph and the recorded tape here are much more likely to be free from error than the words of a witness testifying from memory.

The rules of evidence regarding admission and exclusion, including the rule requiring the production of the best evidence, are founded basically upon considerations of truth and reliability. A mechanical record, if audible or legible, and not tampered with, is likely to be much more accurate and dependable than oral testimony. The taped record was properly admitted and the judgment will be affirmed.

Judgment affirmed.

KERNS and SHERER, JJ., concur.

BAITCHER v. LOUIS R. CLERICO ASSOCIATES, INC.

Court of Appeals of Georgia, 1974.
132 Ga.App. 219, 207 S.E.2d 698.

PANNELL, Judge. Plaintiff sued for the balance due on a contract entered March 26, 1969 for the interior design of a restaurant and the furnishing of lighting fixtures and furniture for it. Defendant denied any indebtedness existed and raised the defense of accord and satisfaction. The defendant also claimed that he had to employ others to repair work improperly performed by plaintiff and to complete certain other work not performed as agreed.

. . .

4. Appellant complains that the court erroneously admitted certain of plaintiff's exhibits in violation of the best evidence rule. The exhibits were carbon copies of documents purportedly mailed to defendant, who denied having received the originals. Assuming, arguendo, that proper objections to these exhibits were made at proffer the enumeration is without merit. "[A]ll papers executed by the same stroke upon a typewriter—those written by carbon impressions, as well as the sheet which receives the stroke of the letter from the typewriter—are alike originals . . ." Carmichael Tile Co. v. McClelland et al., 213 Ga. 656, 659, 100 S.E.2d 902, 905 (1958). "[D]uplicate or triplicate originals, made with the same stroke of pen or typewriter as the original are admissible as primary evidence." Campbell v. Pure Oil Co. et al., 92 Ga.App. 523, 524, 88 S.E.2d 630, 631 (1955).

5. The remaining enumerations of error have been considered and are found to lack merit.

Judgment affirmed.

BELL, C. J., EBERHARDT, P. J., and DEEN, QUILLIAN, CLARK, STOLZ and WEBB, JJ., concur.

EVANS, J., dissents.

DECISIONS RELATING TO CHAPTER VI, HEARSAY AND CHARACTER EVIDENCE

JORDAN v. COPELAND

Supreme Court of Alabama, 1961.
272 Ala. 336, 131 So.2d 696.

COLEMAN, Justice. This is an appeal from a decree denying a petition to remove the administration of an estate from the probate court to the circuit court in equity.

The petitioner for removal, Fred Jordan, the appellant, asserts that he is the husband of Armina Jordan, deceased; that her will has been admitted to probate; and that appellee, Monette Copeland, has applied for letters testamentary as executrix of the will.

The appellee asserts that testatrix was the wife of Arthur Stevens at the time of her purported marriage to appellant and that the prior marriage of Stevens to testatrix had not been dissolved at the time of her death. Appellee concludes, therefore, that appellant was not the husband of testatrix and has no such interest in her estate as would entitle him to remove the administration to the circuit court under § 139, Title 13, Code 1940.

After hearing testimony ore tenus, the court found that appellant was not the husband of testatrix, because her marriage to Stevens had not been dissolved, and denied the removal petition.

Appellant insists that the court erred in finding from the evidence that appellee had sustained the burden of proof that rested on her to show that the marriage of testatrix to Arthur Stevens had not been dissolved.

The evidence shows a ceremonial marriage of testatrix to appellant in Washington County on May 24, 1944. This is the last marriage of testatrix shown by the evidence. The evidence also showed a prior marriage of testatrix to Arthur Stevens and that he was living after the death of testatrix. He testified as a witness. The appellee asserts the invalidity of the last marriage of testatrix, that is, her marriage to appellant. The presumption is that the prior marriage has been dissolved by divorce, and the burden to show that it has not been dissolved rests upon the person seeking to impeach the last marriage, notwithstanding he is thereby required to prove a negative. Ex parte Young, 211 Ala. 508, 101 So. 51 (1924); Sloss-Sheffield Steel & Iron Co. v. Alexander, 241 Ala. 476, 3 So.2d 46 (1941); Freed v. Sallade, 245 Ala. 505, 17 So.2d 868 (1944); Jordan v. Courtney, 248 Ala. 390, 27 So.2d 783 (1946). So, the question presented on this appeal is whether or not the evidence is sufficient to support the finding that the marriage of testatrix and Arthur Stevens had not been dissolved by divorce.

The presumption of an innocent second marriage is overcome when the circumstances require a reasonable inference to the contrary. Freed v. Sallade, supra.

The circumstances shown by the evidence are as follows: Arthur Stevens testified that he married testatrix in Waynesboro, Mississippi, but had forgotten the date. A marriage certificate purporting to have been executed by the clerk of the Circuit Court of Wayne County, Mississippi, was admitted in evidence over appellant's objection. The certificate states that Stevens and "Miss Areminer Phillips" were married March 26, 1916. Stevens testified that he and testatrix had three children; that they separated in 1931 or 1932; that they were never divorced; that in 1936 he, Stevens, filed suit in Memphis, Tennessee, for a divorce but "left it" with his lawyer, "Charlie," who sent Stevens "an affidavit" when he "came back to Mississippi"; and that he never got a divorce in that proceeding and never filed any other proceeding for divorce. Stevens further said the contents of the affidavit were "The same as a divorce as I understand it," and that he lost the affidavit when he left it in Vicksburg in 1938. Stevens said also that he had not lived with testatrix since 1936, and that he now has a wife in Florida where he was living at the time of the trial. A certificate by the ordinary of Lowndes County, Georgia, showing the marriage of "Arthur Stevens" to Callie Guynn on March 7, 1948, was received in evidence without objection. Stevens further said he did not know whether testatrix had ever obtained a divorce from him or not, that he did not know where she had lived, and that he "would hear from her along from the children." Stevens testified that he was served with process in a divorce proceeding instituted by testatrix in Waynesboro, Mississippi. It is not clear whether he was served with that process in Waynesboro or elsewhere. He said he was living in Alabama at that time and that he did not know the disposition of that case. Stevens said he did not know whether testatrix had ever obtained a divorce from him or not, and that when he married Callie Guynn "I believed I was free to marry, yes, or I would not have married."

A certificate, by the Judge of Probate of Washington County, stating that the records of his office show that Walter Wright and "Armenta" Phillips were married May 30, 1936, was introduced in evidence. A showing was admitted that Walter Wright would testify that he was married to testatrix, that he knew nothing of any divorce that she got from Stevens, and that as far as Wright knew she never had a divorce from Stevens. It was stipulated that Walter Wright was married to testatrix and divorced from her by decree of the Circuit Court of Washington County, but the validity of the marriage was not admitted.

Fred Jordan, the appellant, testified that he married testatrix in Washington County on May 24, 1944, and certificate to that effect is in evidence. He testified that after their marriage they lived together until the death of testatrix in 1958; that they had lived in

Chickasaw; Chatom; Palestine, Texas; Chatom; Mizell, Mississippi; near Wagarville, Alabama; and then in Chatom until death of testatrix; that he had seen Arthur Stevens one time since 1944; that appellee, daughter of testatrix, had been in the home of appellant and testatrix "Lots of times"; and that he, appellant, had first heard the accusation that he and testatrix were not married on the day the will was supposed to be probated. With reference to records of a divorce of testatrix and Stevens, appellant testified as follows:

> "Q. Have you ever seen a divorce decree between Armina Stevens and Arthur Stevens? A. No, sir.
>
> "Q. Have you made diligent search for one? A. No, I didn't. I have since this trial started.
>
> "Q. You have investigated in almost all the counties in which Armina has lived? Yes. Since I knew her, yes.
>
> "Q. And you do not find in any of those counties a divorce proceeding between Armina and Arthur Stevens; a decree of divorce divorcing them? A. No, sir.
>
> "Redirect examination by Mr. Turner:
>
> "Q. Mr. Hurst is putting words in your mouth, isn't he?
>
> "Judge Pelham: I strike that remark.
>
> "Q. Did you make these investigations yourself? A. No, I didn't.
>
> "Q. You are not trained in searching the records to determine whether or not there have been any divorce proceedings, is that right? A. I looked for some in different places.
>
> "Q. Do you know how to search the records for a divorce? A. No, sir, I had to get somebody at the courthouses to do it for me.
>
> "Q. You have done none of it yourself? A. No, sir."

Monette Copeland, appellee, testified that she was born in 1925, that her parents, Arthur Stevens and the testatrix, separated when appellee was nine or ten years old; that she, the appellee, until her own marriage in 1941, lived with the testatrix, and thereafter visited her "every three or four weeks"; that appellee had no knowledge of her mother's ever getting a divorce from Stevens, but "knew all along that she wasn't divorced from him." Appellee admitted that she filed a sworn petition to probate the will of testatrix. The petition is dated July 28, 1958, and recites in pertinent part as follows:

> "Your petitioner herewith propounds said will in which she believes that she is named as legatee and devisee and as executrix. Your petitioner further represents that the names, ages, and residences of the next of kin are as follows:
>
> "1. Fred J. Jordan, husband of deceased, over the age of 21 years, and a resident of Washington County, Alabama."

In answer to a question whether or not testatrix could have gotten a divorce from Stevens without appellee's knowing about it, appellee replied:

> "A. While ago I explained to you I don't know. She could have or she could not."

This court has refused to accept the uncorroborated testimony of one of the parties to the prior marriage, to the effect that the prior marriage had never been dissolved by divorce, as being sufficient proof to establish the dissolution of the prior marriage when the evidence did not show an examination of the records of the divorce courts of the counties in which the parties had lived. Freed v. Sallade, supra; Dorsey v. Dorsey, 256 Ala. 137, 53 So.2d 601 (1951). On the second appeal in Dorsey v. Dorsey, 259 Ala. 220, 66 So.2d 135 (1953), however, the court held that the corroborating evidence was sufficient where the other party to the undissolved marriage refused to testify and the evidence showed that the divorce records in the counties where the parties had lived disclosed no divorce. In Bell v. Tennessee Coal, Iron & R. Co., 240 Ala. 422, 199 So. 813 (1941), the testimony of the wife in the prior marriage was corroborated by evidence that the records in Jefferson County, where the husband had lived, showed no divorce, and this was held to be sufficient to support a finding that the prior marriage had not been dissolved by divorce. In Sloss-Sheffield Steel & Iron Co. v. Watford, 245 Ala. 425, 17 So.2d 166 (1944), the testimony of the prior wife that the prior marriage had never been dissolved by divorce was corroborated by evidence that the records of four counties where the husband had lived did not show a divorce, and this evidence was held sufficient to rebut the presumption in favor of the subsequent marriage.

The law casts a strict burden on appellee to prove a negative, that is, that testatrix and Arthur Stevens had not been divorced. Dorsey v. Dorsey, 259 Ala. 220, 66 So.2d 135 (1953), supra; Vinson v. Vinson, 260 Ala. 254, 258, 69 So.2d 431 (1954). The testimony of the parties, not properly supported by evidence as to the divorce records in the various jurisdictions in which a decree could be rendered, is usually treated as not sufficient to overcome the presumption. Ashley v. Ashley, 255 Ala. 313, 319, 51 So.2d 239 (1951). However, such record evidence of non-divorce has not been regarded as an indispensable element of such proof in every case. Jones v. Case, 266 Ala. 498, 97 So.2d 816 (1957). The situation in Whitman v. Whitman, 253 Ala. 643, 46 So.2d 422 (1950), was like the situation here. The wife of the prior marriage, like Arthur Stevens here, testified that she knew of no divorce proceedings, but there was no evidence offered as to the status of the divorce records in Jefferson, one of the counties where the husband had lived, and the offered evidence as to the other county, Dallas, was held inadmissible. This court held there was no error in the decree denying relief to the first wife. Denial of relief was based on insufficiency of the evidence to overcome the presumption that the last marriage was valid. As to the testimony of the first wife that the prior marriage had not been dissolved this court said:

> " . . . . Her own testimony to that effect must be supported by legal evidence that the divorce courts of all the counties in the State, which would have jurisdiction of such a suit, did not have a record of a decree of divorce. . . . ." 253 Ala. 643, 645, 46 So.2d 422, 424.

Appellee argues that the testimony of four witnesses (Arthur Stevens, Walter Wright, and appellee and appellant) is sufficient to sustain the finding that the marriage of testatrix and Stevens had never been dissolved by divorce. We do not agree.

Arthur Stevens' testimony is to the effect that he never obtained a divorce and does not know whether testatrix obtained one or not. Even if the testimony of Stevens be considered as positive that no divorce was obtained by either himself or testatrix, it would not, standing alone, be sufficient under Freed v. Sallade, supra, and the first appeal in Dorsey v. Dorsey, supra. Moreover, the action of Arthur Stevens in marrying his present wife, Callie Guynn, is not consistent with his testimony that he had never been divorced from testatrix. By his subsequent marriage, he solemnly declared that he was then free to marry again. Freed v. Sallade, 245 Ala. at page 508, 17 So.2d 868.

At best, the testimony of appellee and Walter Wright shows merely that these witnesses had no knowledge of a divorce. As appellee admitted, testatrix could have gotten a divorce without appellee knowing about it. After the death of testatrix, appellee had stated under oath in the petition to probate the will that appellant was the surviving husband of testatrix. After Stevens and testatrix separated, Walter Wright married her and later obtained a divorce in the court of Washington County. The actions of appellee and Wright are based on the proposition that Stevens and testatrix had been divorced and are diametrically opposed to the contrary inference which appellee draws from their testimony.

The testimony of appellant concerning his investigation of records falls short of establishing the fact that no divorce is shown by the records of the several counties in which testatrix and Stevens are shown to have lived after they separated. Appellant admitted he did not in his own person make the search and that he was not qualified to do so. We are of opinion that the testimony of appellant is not sufficient to establish as a fact that the records in all the counties where the parties had lived do not show a divorce of testatrix from Stevens. The testimony of appellant is that he had to get some one else at the courthouse to make the search and did none of it himself. All his testimony that the records do not show a divorce is hearsay and is not competent to show the absence of a divorce decree. Smith v. Smith, 268 Ala. 348, 106 So.2d 260 (1958). Act No. 101, General Acts 1943, page 105; Pocket Parts, Code 1940, Title 7, § 372(1).

Moreover, the testimony is that he investigated "almost all," and not all, the counties involved.

We do not wish to be misunderstood on the holding that appellant's testimony with respect to his investigation is hearsay. This testimony is hearsay because he is repeating the statement of some one else who had told him that the records contained no divorce decree. His testimony is not hearsay for the reason that it is an attempt to prove the contents of a decree by parol. Hereafter in this opinion we express the view that appellant cannot, by parol, prove the existence or contents of a decree until proper predicate for secondary evidence has been laid. Parol testimony of the existence or contents of a decree is not the best evidence of its existence or contents. The fact that a decree does not exist is a different matter. Parol testimony to the effect that a decree does not appear in a record is not parol evidence of something a record contains. Such parol testimony is evidence that a record does not contain something, to wit, a divorce decree. In a strict sense, the record is the best evidence of what it does not contain, but it is manifestly impractical to require a party to introduce in evidence all the records of a court, or certified copies thereof. Competent, legal testimony given in answer to interrogatories by the register, custodian of the records of Barbour County, that a certain divorce decree did not appear in his records, was admitted to prove that fact on the second trial in Dorsey v. Dorsey, supra, 259 Ala. at page 223, 66 So.2d 135. The reason for allowing parol testimony to prove that records do not contain a divorce decree has been stated as follows:

> " . . . 'The law requires the best proof the case is susceptible of. It does not require impossibilities, and therefore did not require the production in our courts of the records of the courts of a sister state. Where there is a mass of records to examine, the law does not require the production of certified copies of all of them to prove the negative fact that a certain decree cannot be found. Such proof may rest in parol ex necessitate rei. But there should and could have been furnished the testimony of the custodian of those records, or of other persons who qualified as familiar with them and all of them, in order that the negative fact might be clearly shown. . . . ' " Note in 34 A.L.R. 495, quoting from Nelson v. Jones, 245 Mo. 579, 151 S.W. 80.

The testimony relating to the suits begun by appellant in Memphis and by testatrix in Waynesboro certainly fails to establish the fact that a divorce was granted, but it strongly supports an inference that divorce proceedings were instituted. A satisfactory conclusion as to whether those suits were actually instituted and, if so, as to their result, can hardly be reached on the record before us. We are clear to the conclusion that appellee has not proved that a divorce was not granted in either suit.

We will summarize the pertinent facts appearing from the record. Testatrix and Stevens married each other in 1916; they had six children of whom three were still living; they lived together until 1931 or 1932 when they permanently separated. Stevens made some move to initiate a suit for divorce in Memphis and testatrix did the same thing in Waynesboro, but the result of neither suit is shown. In 1936 testatrix married Arthur Wright and they were later divorced. In 1944 testatrix married appellant and lived with him until her death in 1958. Arthur Stevens married Callie Guynn in 1948 and was living with her in Florida at the time of the trial. Stevens, Wright, and appellee testified that they did not know of any divorce between Stevens and testatrix, and appellee emphatically states that she knows they were not divorced.

If their testimony be taken as positive to the effect there was no such divorce, it is nevertheless contradicted by their several actions, i. e., by Stevens in marrying Guynn, by Wright in marrying and divorcing testatrix, and by appellee in swearing that appellant was the surviving husband.

It may be that the records of all the counties concerned do not show a divorce of testatrix from Stevens, but we are of opinion that the evidence now before us is insufficient to establish that fact. Consequently, we are of opinion that appellee has failed to support the burden that rested on her to prove that the prior marriage had not been dissolved, and that the decree finding to the contrary is in error, for which it must be reversed and the cause remanded in order that the parties may present further proof as they may be advised.

Appellee cites Darrow v. Darrow, 201 Ala. 477, 78 So. 383 (1918), which appears to hold that evidence of a prior marriage and testimony by a party thereto that no notice of divorce had been served on such party prima facie, negatives a dissolution of the prior marriage; and, further casts on the opposite party seeking to sustain the later marriage the burden to show a record of a decree dissolving the prior marriage. We have not found where this holding in the Darrow case has been cited or followed. It appears to be in conflict with Freed v. Sallade, Ashley v. Ashley, the first appeal in Dorsey v. Dorsey, and Vinson v. Vinson, all supra; and to the extent that it is in conflict with the later cases, the Darrow case is overruled.

As we understand appellee's brief, she concedes that appellant's objection to introduction in evidence of the Mississippi certificate of the marriage of testatrix to Stevens is well taken, but says it is error without injury. Because it thus appears that on another trial appellee will remove the grounds of this objection we forego its further consideration.

Appellant offered to prove by himself that testatrix, in her lifetime, had told appellant that she had a divorce from Stevens. The court sustained objection to this evidence and that ruling is assigned as error.

A party who is to prove a fact must do it by the highest evidence of which the nature of the thing is capable, and which it is within his power to produce. Although the court of a justice of the peace is not a court of record, our court has held that a party could not prove by the justice himself the result of a suit in his court, where the proceedings had been reduced to writing, without first laying a predicate for the introduction of secondary evidence; Bullock v. Ogburn, 13 Ala. 346 (1848). Even a judgment certificate made by the clerk for registration in the office of the judge of probate cannot be substituted for the judgment itself where the issues call for proof of the fact of an existing judgment; Boasberg v. Cooke, 223 Ala. 389, 136 So. 797 (1931). In the absence of a predicate for secondary evidence, as was the case here, testimony of testatrix herself would not have been admissible to prove a decree dissolving her marriage to Stevens. See Cotton v. Cotton, 213 Ala. 336, 104 So. 650 (1925). Therefore, the court did not err in refusing to allow appellant to testify that testatrix had said she had a divorce from Stevens. For cases supporting this view, see McDonald v. McDonald, 180 Ga. 771, 180 S.E. 815 (1935); Trimble v. Wells, 314 Ky. 206, 234 S.W.2d 683 (1951); Weaver v. Patterson, 92 N.J.Eq. 170, 111 A. 506 (1920); Moore v. Follett, Tex.Civ.App., 11 S.W.2d 662 (Tex.Civ.App.1929); Hupp v. Hupp, 235 S.W.2d 753. Two California cases, In re Smith's Estate, 193 P.2d 90 (Cal.App.1920), and 33 Cal.2d 279, 201 P.2d 539 (1949), appear to be contrary to our conclusion here, but we are persuaded that the California rule is not the better one.

Reversed and remanded.

All the Justices concur.

KAPLAN v. CITY OF NEW YORK

Supreme Court, Appellate Division, First Department, 1960.
10 A.D.2d 319, 200 N.Y.S.2d 261.

STEVENS, Justice. The plaintiffs were passengers in a private taxicab owned and operated by one Lomio. The taxicab collided with a pillar supporting an elevated transit railroad overpass on Baychester Avenue in The Bronx, causing certain injuries to the plaintiffs. Suit was instituted against Lomio, the driver of the cab, and the City. Judgment was rendered against both defendants. Lomio did not appeal. The City appealed, and the matter was reversed as to it (Kaplan v. City of New York, 6 A.D.2d 489, 179 N.Y.S.2d 885 (1920)), because of the receipt of improper testimony of prior accidents. The court said "[i]t is not proper, however, to offer such testimony unless it is first shown that the circumstances attending the earlier accidents were sufficiently similar to the relevant conditions prevailing at the time of the later accident." 6 A.D.2d at page 491, 179 N.Y.S.2d 888. On the retrial, judgment was rendered against the City, and it is from that judgment that the defendant now appeals.

The defendant contends that the plaintiffs failed to prove the existence of a dangerous condition, and that the trial court committed error by (a) admitting evidence concerning unrelated dissimilar accidents which happened at the scene; (b) permitting the reading of testimony of a witness at the first trial; and (c) permitting into evidence a notice of claim, a complaint and a bill of particulars in totally unrelated actions. It contends also that the verdicts are excessive.

. . .

The plaintiffs then introduced and were permitted to read into evidence, portions of a notice of claim and complaint of one Anna E. Wagner, dated May 21, 1951, on the theory of notice to the City of an alleged dangerous and hazardous condition. The fact that a notice of claim had been sent and received and that a complaint was served, might well be relevant and properly admissible, but only after the dangerous condition to which it relates has been shown. However, the plaintiffs were permitted to read the descriptive and conclusory allegations contained therein that the area "is in an unsafe, dangerous, obstructive and impassable condition. The most westerly post pillar and supporting column of the superstructure then and there present is in such a manner and position that it constituted a nuisance of vehicular traffic; that this is an improperly lighted elevator pillar, and it constitutes a dangerous, unsafe, unlighted and unguarded position—it occupies a dangerous, unsafe, and unguarded position in said public highway; that it constitutes a menace to vehicular traffic"; was not properly marked, roadway unsafe, etc.

A like ruling was made as to certain papers in a prior accident, the Moore case, and a portion of the documents read to the jury. No attempt was made in either case to offer independent proof of what caused the accidents, whether human frailty, mechanical defect, or physical obstructions. (In fact an offer of proof by the defendant that 3-plus alcohol was found in the brain of Moore was excluded.) Nor were Wagner or Moore produced to testify or be subjected to cross-examination. The contents of the documents beyond title, proof of service, etc., in such circumstances were hearsay evidence, and the admission thereof was clearly prejudicial. Its effect, despite disclaimer, was to go far beyond proof of notice and tended to establish the existence of a claimed dangerous condition. The mere happening of an accident is not in and of itself proof of negligence, nor proof of freedom from contributory negligence. Proof of similar dangerous conditions attending or proximately causing prior accidents upon which plaintiff seeks to rely may be by testimonial or documentary means or a combination of both. But when testimonial in the sense that descriptive allegations of the parties are relied upon, or the natural result of their introduction in evidence is to prove both a dangerous condition and proximate cause, the parties claimant in such cases should be produced and available for cross-examination. There was no preliminary proof of similar circumstances attending the Wagner and Moore accidents.

In our view the admission into evidence of the contents of the papers, as distinguished from proof of the fact of filing and service thereof, constituted prejudicial error requiring reversal and a new trial. Again we point out that even the proof of notice would be immaterial unless it first had been established by competent evidence that a dangerous condition existed.

In Parks v. City of New York, 111 App.Div. 836, 98 N.Y.S. 94 (1906), on a retrial additional evidence of notice to the City of a defective sidewalk condition was offered by a policeman, Baxter, who testified from his personal observation of the shaky condition of the bridge or temporary sidewalk. He testified also that one Hess called his attention to the condition and that he made an oral report and a written report. Hess testified that he called Baxter's attention to the condition. The court held "[n]otice to Baxter—a police officer—was notice to the city" (111 App.Div. at page 839, 98 N.Y.S. at page 95), and that the verdict was not against the weight of the evidence, either as to the defective condition or as to notice. It appeared from a former trial (Coolidge v. City of New York, 99 App.Div. 175, 90 N.Y.S. 1078 (1905)), that a city inspector, Hamel, had made several inspections of the bridge and knew its condition. There was no question but that the collapse of the bridge caused the death of plaintiff's intestate.

. . .

The judgment appealed from should be reversed, on the law and in the exercise of discretion, and a new trial ordered, with costs to abide the event.

Judgment unanimously reversed upon the law and in the exercise of discretion and a new trial ordered, with costs to abide the event. All concur.

PEOPLE v. HELMBRECHT

Court of Appeals of New York, 1948.
297 N.Y. 789, 77 N.E.2d 798.

DESMOND, Judge (dissenting). Defendant, tried on an assault charge, admitted "grabbing" the complainant, but denied striking him and attempted to justify the battery by testimony that the complainant had used improper language to defendant's wife. Four witnesses testified to defendant's good character. The Trial Justice, in charging the jury, discussed this character evidence to some extent, informing the jurors that it was to be considered solely "upon the question of whether or not he would be likely to commit the crime with which he is charged here." Defendant's counsel thereupon asked for an instruction to the jury "that if the jury believes the evidence of good character introduced here, that that evidence alone is sufficient to create a reasonable doubt." The trial court declined so to charge, stating that he would stand on his original charge which, it is plain, contained no discussion at all as to the effect which the character evidence could or should have in bringing into existence a reasonable doubt of defendant's guilt.

As we understand it, it is now argued that, even if defendant had a right to have the jury instructed as to the relationship between credible evidence of good repute and reasonable doubt, the requested charge, it is said, was not correctly phrased.

It has been the New York law for at least a century that character evidence, if believed by a jury, "will sometimes of itself create a doubt when without it none would exist". Remsen v. People, 43 N.Y. 6, 9 (1870); Stephens v. People, 4 Parker Cr.R. 396 (1859). It follows that this "was an important item of evidence, and the defendant was entitled to the full benefit of it". People v. Lamb, 2 Keyes 360, 377 (1866). As Judge Crane wrote in People v. Colantone, 243 N.Y. 134, 136, 152 N.E. 700, 701 (1926): "Evidence of good character is a matter of substance, not of form, in criminal cases, and must be considered by the jury as bearing upon the issue of guilt, even when the evidence against the defendant may be very convincing." It is no matter of verbiage, and no defendant should lose the benefit of his good character witnesses, merely because his lawyer uses one form of words rather than another. And failure to charge correctly and fully on this subject is not such an error as may be overlooked under Section 542 of the Code of Criminal Procedure. People v. Bonier, 179 N.Y. 315, 324, 72 N.E. 226, 229, 103 Am.St.Rep. 880 (1904).

Many convictions have been reversed in this and other courts because of the trial judges' refusals to tell the jury that doubt of guilt is no less a reasonable doubt because it is produced by character evidence, rather than by proof directly bearing on the issues. In none of those reversals was it said, or suggested, that a particular formula must be employed by counsel in making a request. The idea is the thing, and the idea that should go to the jury is that a showing of fair repute is in itself justification for a juror's reasonable doubt. Was that not the idea simply and briefly stated by counsel here, when he requested a charge that character evidence alone "is sufficient to create a reasonable doubt"? Any difference between that and the statements in the cases that character evidence "may create a reasonable doubt" or "can create a reasonable doubt" or "will sometimes create a reasonable doubt" is verbal only. For instance, there was a unanimous reversal in People v. D'Anna, 243 App.Div. 259, 277 N.Y. S. 279 (1935), because the court declined to tell the jury that, if they believed the evidence produced as to good character, they might "base a reasonable doubt on that alone". All these expressions mean the same thing.

People v. Trimarchi, 231 N.Y. 263, 266, 131 N.E. 910, 911 (1921), is not to the contrary. There defendant's counsel omitted from his requested instruction any reference to the necessary condition that the jury must credit the character evidence. "Such evidence," this court pointed out, "in order to raise a reasonable doubt, must be believed by the jury." Indeed, Judge McLaughlin's opinion in the Trimarchi case, supra, impliedly approves the exact form of charge requested by defendant's counsel in the present case. Counsel for Trimarchi had asked for an instruction: "That evidence of good character is sufficient to raise a question of reasonable doubt." Judge McLaughlin said that request was defective in that it did not include the thought that the evidence had to be believed by the jury. The discussion in this court's opinion, in the second paragraph on page 266 of 231 N.Y., on page 911 of 131 N.E., shows that if Trimarchi's counsel had included that absent element, the request would have had to be granted as matter of law. With that missing part added, the Trimarchi request is identical with that in this case, except that Trimarchi's counsel said "raise" a reasonable doubt, while appellant Helmbrecht's counsel used the word "create".

Finally, let us assume, for argument, that the instruction prayed for in this case, was elliptical, or lacking a word or two. "The defendant was entitled to have the jury charged, substantially as requested by his counsel" (People v. Conrow, 200 N.Y. 356, 362, 93 N.E. 943, 945 (1911)), and, even if the request was inartistically framed, "yet its obvious intention was plain, and the court should have instructed the jury adequately as to the legal bearing of the question which it raised" People v. Buccufurri, 158 App.Div. 186, 192, 143 N.Y.S. 62, 67 (1913).

The judgment should be reversed and a new trial ordered.

PEOPLE v. MALLARD

Supreme Court, Criminal Term, Queens County, Part III, 1974.
78 Misc.2d 858, 358 N.Y.S.2d 913.

Abraham Werfel, Jamaica, for defendant.

Nicholas Ferraro, Dist. Atty. (Robert Cox McGann, Maspeth, of counsel), for plaintiff.

LEONARD L. FINZ, Justice. On this motion, the defendant seeks a prospective ruling to limit the District Attorney in utilizing the prior conviction record of the defendant for impeachment purposes during the trial. The troublesome and pressing issue that emerges is the extent to which the past criminal transgressions of a defendant can be revived and presented to a jury should the defendant elect to defend himself against the current charges by testifying on his own behalf.

The procedure, inspired by the recent pronouncement of the Court of Appeals in People v. Sandoval, 34 N.Y.2d 371, 357 N.Y.S.2d 849, 314 N.E.2d 413 (1974), must, therefore, be analyzed to determine the ultimate decision to be reached—what prior crimes, if any, could properly be surfaced to attack the credibility of the defendant.

As a pretrial procedure designed to protect the constitutional rights of a defendant, the name of a *Sandoval* Hearing, it would appear, can now be added to the illustrious list of constitutional safeguards joining such company as *Miranda*, *Wade*, *Huntley* and others.

In the instant matter, the defendant faces trial for robbery in the first degree, a Class B felony, conviction of which would subject him to a mandatory term of imprisonment with a possible maximum of 25 years. He has nine prior convictions, four of which are drug convictions and three gambling convictions included in that total.

What then is the special formula to be employed by a trial judge in resolving an issue that has plagued and is continuing to plague judicial discretion in order to determine its proper direction?

An examination of some of the major cases on the subject is necessary toward an ultimate decision that would be consistent with justice.

In *Sandoval* the Court of Appeals, after much discussion of the cases on the subject, concluded that the resolution of this issue must rest with the trial judge preferably for a determination in a pretrial procedure such as the one before this Court. In attempting to set forth criteria and guidelines for the proper exercise of discretion in such instances, the Court stated the following:

> "From the standpoint of the prosecution, then, the evidence *should be admitted if it will have material probative value on the issue of defendant's credibility, veracity or honesty* on the witness stand. From the standpoint of the defendant it should not be admitted unless it will have such probative worth, or, even though it has such worth, if to lay it before the jury or court would otherwise be so highly prejudicial as to call for its exclusion. The standard—whether the prejudicial effect of impeachment testimony far outweighs the probative worth of the evidence on the issue of credibility—is easy of articulation but troublesome in many cases of application." (Emphasis supplied.)

Hence, two countervailing forces, each exerting its influence on the conscience of the Court, come forward in its quest for a sound base in determining the exercise of proper discretion. On one side is the desirability of admitting prior convictions so that the jury will be able to assess the degree of credence to be given to the testimony of the defendant, and on the other, the firm recognition by the Court that to permit the impeachment of the credibility of the defendant by such device is to invite undesirable prejudice in the minds of the jury.

An uncomfortable ambivalence is created, as the Court well recognized in its succeeding statement:

> "At the threshold it must be recognized as inevitable, and thus not determinative, that evidence of prior criminal, vicious or immoral conduct will always be detrimental to the defendant. . . . Will the testimony to be elicited *in cross-examination have a disproportionate and improper impact*

> *on the triers of fact? Will the apprehension of its introduction undesirably deter the defendant from taking the stand and thereby deny the jury or court significant material evidence?*" (Emphasis supplied.)

One of the most significant aspects of *Sandoval* is eloquently expressed in the "recognition of the principles underlying broadened discovery in criminal procedure and a growing awareness that there may be undue prejudice to a defendant from unnecessary and immaterial development of previous misconduct."

"Trial Court discretion" becomes the common thread joining all cases on the subject of the instant application. In this regard, it is interesting to observe how attitudes in this area have changed through the years. In an early case decided in 1893, dealing with the introduction of evidence that the defendant was guilty of adulterous conduct, the Court pronounced the exercise of discretion thusly:

> "It is urged that this evidence should have been excluded because it tended to implicate the defendant's wife, who was a witness for him, and thus to impeach her, in an unauthorized way, before the jury. But any apprehended misuse of this species of evidence may always be avoided by asking and obtaining an instruction to the jury that it is only to be considered in determining the credibility of the witness who makes the confession." (People v. Webster, 139 N.Y. 73, 84, 34 N.E. 730, 733.)

In view of the anticipated caveat to the jury, the impeachment evidence was held to be admissible. It is interesting to note that at the turn of the century adultery was considered so heinous as to bear on the credibility of the defendant while he was on trial for murder. Today, such conduct, although still considered immoral, would scarcely cause the lifting of an eyebrow.

Realistically, however, to suggest that an instruction to a jury, despite its articulate quality, would result, without risk, in a juror drawing a mental curtain on the fine line segregating impeachment testimony from the possible prejudice it could produce, is a nuance of human nature that eludes this Court.

This theme of avoidance of undue prejudice is not novel. The subject was, indeed, treated in length in Luck v. United States, 348 F.2d 763 (D.C.Cir. 1965). There, Circuit Judge McGowan, writing for the majority, stated (p. 769):

> "In exercising discretion in this respect, a number of factors might be relevant, . . . above all, the extent to which it is more important to the search for truth in a particular case for the jury to hear the defendant's story than to know of a prior conviction. The goal of a criminal trial is the disposition of the charge in accordance with the truth. The possibility of a rehearsal of the defendant's criminal

record in a given case, especially if it means that the jury will be left without one version of the truth, may or may not contribute to that objective."

Continuing in this vein in Gordon v. United States, 383 F.2d 936, 939 (D.C.Cir. 1967), Circuit Judge, and now Chief Justice, Warren Burger stated:

> "The standard to be applied by the District Judge was stated in terms of whether he 'believes the prejudicial effect of impeachment far outweighs the probative relevance of the prior conviction to the issue of credibility.' The impact of criminal convictions will often be damaging to an accused and it is admittedly difficult to restrict its impact, by cautionary instructions, to the issue of credibility. The test of *Luck*, however, is that to bar them as impeachment the court must find that the prejudice must '*far outweigh*' [emphasis supplied] the probative relevance to credibility, or that even if relevant the 'cause of truth would be helped more by letting the jury hear the defendant's story than by the defendant's foregoing that opportunity because of the fear of prejudice founded upon a prior conviction.' "

Further in the same case (p. 940):

> "Even though a judge might find that the prior convictions are relevant to credibility and the risk of prejudice to the defendant does not warrant their exclusion, he may nevertheless conclude *that it is more important that the jury have the benefit of the defendant's version of the case than to have the defendant remain silent out of fear of impeachment*." [Emphasis supplied.]

The concern of the Court (p. 941) in the foregoing cases is the same as that of the Court of Appeals in *Sandoval*:

> "We are well aware that these are not firm guidelines which can be applied readily as though they were part of the structure of the Federal Rules of Criminal Procedure; the very nature of judicial discretion precludes rigid standards for its exercise; we seek to give some assistance to the trial judge to whom we have assigned the extremely difficult task of weighing and balancing these elusive concepts. Surely, it would be much simpler if prior convictions of an accused were *totally admissible or totally excludable as impeachment;* but in the face of an *explicit, unambiguous statute* allowing use of prior convictions and the holding in *Luck* we have little choice. The lesser step has been taken in *Luck* saying that the statute is to be read as permitting a discretion in the trial judge." (Emphasis supplied.)

Having in mind the list of cases issuing out of the Supreme Court of the United States, some under Chief Justice Burger, expressing a philosophy greatly protective of the rights of defendants in this regard, can it be said that there are no signposts indicating the direction in which the Court should move on this issue?

Since there appears to be reluctance to part with this rule of evidence, the Courts have sought to find a rationale which will permit its continuance where directly relevant, namely, on the issue of credibility. In United States v. Palumbo, 401 F.2d 270, 274 (2 Cir. 1968), it was said: "More recently, *Luck* has been construed to allow impeachment of a defendant by convictions involving fraud or stealing, which 'are universally regarded as conduct which reflects adversely on a man's honesty and integrity.' Gordon v. United States, 127 U.S.App.D.C. 343, 383 F.2d 936, 940 (1967)."

It is noteworthy and significant that Palumbo never took the stand. Is it too much to speculate that the Court's decision to permit cross-examination at least as to some of Palumbo's past record may have inhibited his appearance as a witness in his own behalf, thereby depriving him *de facto* of the constitutional right to relate to the jury exculpatory conduct on his part?

Following in the track of *Luck* and *Gordon* is United States v. Puco, 453 F.2d 539, 542, 543 (2 Cir. 1971), where the Court stated:

> "Reference to a defendant's criminal record *is always highly prejudicial. The average jury is unable, despite curative instructions, to limit the influence of a defendant's criminal record to the issue of credibility.* . . . While there is considerable uncertainty as to what crimes, by reason of their nature, may be considered to be highly probative of lack of veracity, we believe that a narcotics conviction has little necessary bearing on the veracity of the accused as a witness." (But see United States v. McIntosh, 138 U.S.App. D.C. 237, 426 F.2d 1231.) (Emphasis supplied.)

The scarcity of cases on the Appellate level in New York was pointed out by Mr. Justice Shapiro in People v. Duffy, 44 A.D.2d 298, 354 N.Y.S.2d 672 (1974), a case of very recent origin, although it predates *Sandoval* by several months. In *Duffy* the Court makes a scholarly review of the cases on this subject, pointing first of all to the statute (CPL 60.40, subd. 1), which allows a prosecutor to ask, if he does so "properly" if he, the defendant, has been convicted of a "specific offense". On reviewing the cases and quoting from them at length, mainly from the *Luck* and *Gordon* opinions, the Appellate Division stated the following (p. 305, 354 N.Y.S.2d p. 678):

> "On appropriate application, made either at or prior to trial, and in the exercise of a sound discretion, the trial court should determine whether an applying defendant has sustained the burden, which should be his, of demonstrating that the prejudice involved in permitting into evidence proof of prior convictions or criminal acts so far outweighs the probative value of such proof for impeachment purposes that

the proof should not be received. *Hence, we today announce that to be the applicable law.*" (Emphasis supplied.)

And again, we are left with the dilemma created by a statute that permits the use of prior convictions for cross-examination against the backdrop of lofty decisional law highly suggestive of proceeding to its application with measured caution—all in the stricture of "judicial discretion". Unfortunately, however, little relief is provided the trial judge, to whom the application is addressed and who must weigh in the two pans of the scale the pressures exerted by credibility on the one hand and prejudice on the other. If one were to construct such a scale, with the lowliest offense on the one end and murder most foul on the other, where would one place the fulcrum, the point of balance, which is the present alleged crime of the defendant? And how does one, in truth, assess the weight to be placed on each side of the scale?

Once again, we observe that the "balance" issue is the overriding theme in determining the proper application of judicial discretion. So, too, in People v. Schwartzman, 24 N.Y.2d 241, 299 N.Y.S.2d 817, 247 N.E.2d 642 (1969), does the Court of Appeals proclaim its "balance" position:

> "The rules governing the admissibility of evidence of other crimes represent a balance between the probative value of such proof and the danger of prejudice which it presents to an accused. When evidence of other crimes has no purpose other than to show that a defendant is of a *criminal bent or character* and thus likely to have committed the crime charged, it should be excluded." (Emphasis supplied.)

Again, we must return to *Sandoval,* and its pronouncement of "undue prejudice to a defendant from unnecessary and immaterial development of previous misconduct".

As such, we now focus upon this defendant, whose prior criminal record consists for the most part of narcotics and gambling convictions. Would not the knowledge gained by a jury that the defendant has trafficked in narcotics be sufficient to create in the mind of a juror a prejudice, or even a fury which would eliminate for him any possibility of fair consideration—or a fair trial? In a time when such a crime is considered so serious as to be punishable by a sentence of life imprisonment, how can a judge instruct a jury, with any degree of assurance that his direction will be adhered to, that the evidence that this man was formerly convicted of selling narcotics or gambling is only to be considered as bearing on his credibility?

This, it appears to this Court, is the threshold theme, especially in the light of all constitutional safeguards that have evolved toward the protection of the basic rights of all defendants. It is in furtherance of a conscious effort on the part of those whose duty it is to administer justice to weigh the factors involved in the protection of society and the preservation of the rights of the individual, knowing full well that society as a whole can survive the impact of many calamities but that the individual is, at best, but a frail mortal, easily destroyed and impossible of resurrection, that energizes this thrust toward justice.

This Court, in its search for fairness, reaches the conclusion that only those prior convictions that bear *directly* upon the issue of the defendant's credibility be admitted into evidence. The prior crimes fitting this narrow description should be limited to perjury, fraud and deceit, larceny by misrepresentation and other closely related crimes which have at their very core *the prior dishonest or untruthful quality of the defendant.* The danger of prejudice and the fear by the defendant that he might have to remain silent in his own defense are so great as to warrant no other just determination than the total and absolute exclusion of his prior criminal record short of that which focuses precisely upon his credibility, veracity or honesty.

The gravamen of this decision rests with the resolving of all doubts in favor of the individual defendant. As such, should the trial court's decision to exclude prior convictions be incorrect, the defendant, at best, receives but a small measure of assistance in resisting the present charges against him. Conversely, however, should the decision to admit prior convictions be an improvident one, the damage wrought could be crushing and irreversible in the minds of a jury. The alternatives leave but one conclusion—that is, that society can better withstand the result of a "close" decision against it than can the "frail mortal" defendant.

Justice, in this context, can neither be computerized, nor punched out by some mechanical brain in calibrating the exact balance which could be determined solely on the basis of raw data derived from general guidelines. This being so, and recognizing candidly the impossibility of any specific judicial criteria that could chart wisely the proper path in the pursuit of judicial discretion, the offered alternative, while not the panacea, more closely parallels the spirit of justice than its present counterpart. To this extent, *Sandoval* meets this issue brilliantly when it states that prior convictions "should not be admitted unless it will have . . . probative worth" (on the issue of defendant's credibility, veracity, or honesty).

In *Sandoval* the theme of weighing and balancing is constant. In that atmosphere, the instant decision falls squarely upon the *Sandoval* scales and is consistent with the sound tone and humane philosophy expounded therein.

Additionally, the major constitutional issue raised by the gagging of the defendant, who otherwise would speak out in his own defense, but for fear of prosecutorial cross-examination of prior crimes, is so offensive to our basic sensitivity for fairness as to warrant immediate redress and correction.

In an evolutionary sense, the former harsh common law doctrine, now codified, is eroding through judicial interpretation, approaching its inevitable demise, and leaving in its wake a residue of fairness. Stated another way: *Luck* has turned the key. *Duffy* has opened the door. *Sandoval* has invited you in, and *Mallard,* in the light of the foregoing, may permit you to stay.

Accordingly, it is the judgment of this Court, in the posture of this opinion, that the entire prior conviction record of the defendant is suppressed for purposes of cross-examination should he choose to speak out in defense of the crime for which he is *now* charged.

WERDELL v. TURZYNSKI

Appellate Court of Illinois, First District, Second Division, 1970.
128 Ill.App.2d 139, 262 N.E.2d 833.

Attorney's action against former client for balance of attorney's fees. A jury in the Circuit Court, Cook County, Russell J. Dolce, J., returned a verdict for the attorney and a posttrial motion was overruled. The former client appealed. . . .

LEIGHTON, Justice. This appeal arises from a bitter dispute between the plaintiff, a lawyer, and the defendant, a former client, concerning fees. The cause was heard by a jury that returned a verdict for the plaintiff. After overruling a post-trial motion, the trial court entered judgment on the verdict.

In urging us to reverse, defendant contends that (1), he was not given an opportunity to present his meritorious defense; (2), evidence, misleading to the jury and prejudicial to him, was erroneously admitted; (3), plaintiff's conduct at the trial and that of his counsel while arguing to the jury, were prejudicial, misled the jury and prevented a fair and impartial verdict; (4), the trial judge gave the jury two erroneous instructions; and (5), the verdict of the jury was against the law and the evidence. The facts are before us in a voluminous record.

On May 4, 1961 the defendant, Doctor Stanley Turzynski, agreed to buy from a Doctor Samuel A. Libert his medical practice, a medical center and real estate at 6165 and 6169 Archer Avenue in the City of Chicago. A consideration for the sale was a restrictive covenant, without time limitation, that prohibited Doctor Libert from engaging in the practice of medicine, directly or indirectly, within a radius of 15 miles of the medical center he sold. In April 1963, Doctor Libert announced his return to medical and surgical practice in the same block on which the medical center was situated. Doctor Turzynski filed suit to restrain breach of the covenant. Doctor Libert's defense was that on December 1, 1961, the restrictive covenant was canceled by a document which amended the 1961 sales agreement. Doctor Turzynski countered this defense with the claim that the document was obtained by fraud. The cause was referred to a Master who conducted hearings and filed his report.

Plaintiff, Mr. Stanley Werdell, has been a lawyer since 1930. His practice is restricted to chancery, probate and appeals. Ninety-five percent of his cases are referred to him by other members of the bar. On April 17, 1965, on the advice of his lawyer, Doctor Turzynski consulted Mr. Werdell. On April 21, 1965 Doctor Turzynski signed a written agreement to employ Mr. Werdell "[a]s my attorney to prosecute or settle the . . . case: Stanley Turzynski v. Samuel A. Libert, . . . " According to the document he and Mr. Werdell signed, Doctor Turzynski agreed to pay as a retainer $1500.00 within five days, an additional $1500.00 on or before June 9, 1965; "[a]nd the following additional amount: (a) the sum of $35.00 per hour for whatever time he devotes to the above matter. . . ." By the terms of the retainer agreement, Doctor Turzynski consented to pay all court costs, court reporter charges, master's fees, documentary fees and title charges. If there was an appeal, the parties were to enter into a new agreement. The last paragraph provided "[i]t is further understood that the $3,000.00 above mentioned shall be applied to the amount of time that the said attorney shall devote to this cause."

April 26, 1967 Mr. Werdell filed the suit involved in this appeal. To the complaint, as exhibits, were attached the retainer agreement of April 21, 1965 and a statement to Doctor Turzynski, which acknowledged receipts totaling $6,248.00 and showed 361 hours and 5 minutes of work devoted by Mr. Werdell to Turzynski v. Libert, at $35.00 per hour, making the sum of $12,635.00 for attorney fees. The statement showed disbursements of $48.00 for costs and $6,200.00 received and applied to fees. The statement claimed there was due a balance of $6,435.00. A judgment in this amount was prayed.

Doctor Turzynski appeared by counsel, asked for a jury trial and pleaded to the complaint with a "Separate Affirmative Answer" containing eight paragraphs. In these, Doctor Turzynski alleged he retained Mr. Werdell as his attorney on April 21, 1965 "[t]o represent him in the preparation and presentation of Objections to the Master's Report in the case of TURZYNSKI vs. LIBERT, Case No. 63 S. 8949, and for no other purpose; . . . [and that] STANLEY WERDELL orally represented to STANLEY TURZYNSKI that the estimated number of hours for this task would not exceed 60." One paragraph of the "affirmative answer" alleged that because Mr. Werdell failed to perform his duties, he was discharged by Doctor Turzynski "[f]or good cause . . . on December 14, 1966." The remainder of the "affirmative answer" contended that as a matter of law, an attorney who is discharged for good cause cannot enforce a written contract for fees "[b]ut may maintain such an action only on Quantum Meruit (sic), if at all, and further that the amounts charged by STANLEY WERDELL are not fair and reasonable and that the total number of hours claimed are unnecessary and not reasonable or justified." Defendant alleged that the sum he paid Mr. Werdell was $6,700.00; that he was not indebted to the plaintiff in the amount claimed. On the contrary, it was alleged, Mr. Werdell owed Doctor Turzynski a refund in at least the amount of $2,000.00.

Doctor Turzynski filed a counter-complaint against Mr. Werdell. In it he alleged that from April 21, 1965 to December 14, 1966 he paid Mr. Werdell $6,700.00 for legal services; that Mr. Werdell had the duty to represent him "with all due and reasonable care and diligence such as is required of an attorney . . . ;" that notwithstanding this duty, Mr. Werdell "[n]egligently pursued his client's cause and, in particular, negligently prepared the plaintiff's Objections to the Master's Report, . . . " Ten subparagraphs alleged the manner by which, according to Doctor Turzynski, Mr. Werdell failed or willfully and negligently did acts which were either opposed by Doctor Turzynski or which were to his detriment in Turzynski v. Libert. The counter-complaint then alleged, in three consecutive paragraphs, that on and after December 19, 1966, Mr. Werdell, "[w]illfully and negligently and unethically . . . " injured the cause of his former client, Doctor Turzynski. The concluding paragraphs of the counter-complaint prayed for damages in the sum of $750,000.00.

In a trial that lasted from May 31 to June 7, 1968, Doctor Turzynski was called and examined as an adverse witness. He was asked whether when he signed the retainer agreement it contained the last paragraph that provided for application of the $3,000.00 retainer to the amount of time Mr. Werdell devoted to the case. Doctor Turzynski said, "No, was not (sic)". He then added, "[h]e introduced himself as a very qualified lawyer and as a very honest lawyer. I didn't know that I have to deal with a dishonest, corrupt man, and let's state this corrupt and dishonest. I am able to prove this (sic)." Thereafter, over defendant's objections, interspersed in other testimony, plaintiff called five character witnesses: a magistrate, an associate judge, a circuit court judge, a justice of the Appellate Court of Illinois and a justice of the Illinois Supreme Court. The lawyer who referred Doctor Turzynski to Mr. Werdell appeared as plaintiff's occurrence and character witness. Then Mr. Werdell testified to the circumstances under which he was retained by Doctor Turzynski, the way he kept a record of the time he worked on Turzynski v. Libert and the way he discharged his professional responsibility to his client. Mr. Werdell's secretary testified to the way she recorded the time spent by Mr. Werdell in Doctor Turzynski's case and the way she prepared and mailed letters which Mr. Werdell testified were sent to the client. These letters, and other exhibits totaling twenty-four in number, were admitted as plaintiff's evidence. Doctor Turzynski then testified as the only witness for the defense. He described how Mr. Werdell told him the preparation of the objections to the Master's report would not take much time and that the unused portion of the $3,000.00 retainer would be returned. Doctor Turzynski was shown the retainer agreement and he told the jury his understanding of its terms. He described his experiences with Mr. Werdell and their disagreements concerning the case.

When he was cross-examined, defendant was asked if he was the same Stanley Turzynski who on July 31, 1967 was found guilty of the offense of filing a false and fraudulent income tax return in violation of Section 7201, Title 26, United States Code. After objections to these questions were overruled, Doctor Turzynski admitted he was the defendant named. A certified copy of the record was admitted in evidence. At the conclusion of Doctor Turzynski's testimony, the cause was argued and the jury instructed. After deliberation, the jury returned a verdict against Doctor Turzynski in the sum of $5,-935.00. He appeals.

. . .

A self-serving declaration is a statement, oral or written, or an equivalent act, by or on behalf of a party which if admitted would constitute evidence in his favor. Lord v. Reed, 254 Ill. 350, 98 N.E. 553. The exhibits about which complaint is made were prepared by Mr. Werdell contemporaneous with his claimed discharge of professional responsibilities to Doctor Turzynski. They were not offered to prove the truth of statements they contained. These exhibits were a part of the *res gestae*. "To be a part of the *res gestae*, a declaration, whether verbal or written, must affect the act which is the subject of inquiry and explain, illustrate, qualify, limit, or characterize it, and must not be narrative of a past transaction." Cooke Co. v. Miller Brewing Co., 316 Ill. 46, 51, 146 N.E. 459, 460 (1925). The nine exhibits were documents plaintiff offered to prove that he did the work he alleged in his suit. Mr. Werdell was allowed to explain their content so that the jury could have an intelligent understanding of them. Therefore, we conclude that no prejudicial error was committed by admission in evidence of plaintiff's exhibits 15 to 23.

. . .

Vehemence is a poor substitute for credence. No matter how much denunciation is exuded, it will not hide Doctor Turzynski's failure to convince the jury that what he said was true. The jury, after hearing both sides, returned a verdict consistent with law and the evidence.

Mindful that Doctor Turzynski is before us *pro se*, we have carefully examined each claim of error he has urged in this appeal. We find no reason to disturb the judgment. It is affirmed.

Judgment affirmed.

DECISIONS RELATING TO CHAPTER VII, HEARSAY—ADMISSION EXCEPTION

MAYHOOD v. LA ROSA

Supreme Court of California, 1962.
58 Cal.2d 498, 24 Cal.Rptr. 837, 374 P.2d 805.

Action by husband to quiet title to land against devisee of wife and personal representative of wife's estate. The Superior Court, Solano County, Harlow V. Greenwood, J., rendered judgment for husband and defendants appealed.

. . .

TRAYNOR, Justice. Plaintiff brought this action to quiet title to 47 acres of land against Nanette La Rosa, the granddaughter and sole devisee of Hattie Mayhood, and against the personal representative of Mrs. Mayhood's estate. Plaintiff acquired the land before his marriage to Mrs. Mayhood in 1915. Mrs. Mayhood died in 1959. During the 44 years of the marriage, the land was used to grow fruit trees and grape vines. Until he became incapacitated by illness in 1957, plaintiff devoted most of his working time and energy to managing and cultivating the orchard and vineyard. All receipts therefrom were placed in a single bank account, and all expenditures were made from this account. One such expenditure, in the amount of $12,000, was for a residence constructed on the land in 1928. Defendants offered but were not allowed to introduce evidence that another expenditure of $14,300 was made in 1939 to replant the land with trees and grape vines. The trial court, sitting without a jury, entered judgment quieting plaintiff's title and denying the relief sought in defendants' cross-complaint. Defendants appeal.

Defendants contend that the land was community property to the extent that plaintiff's efforts increased its value and funds used to improve it are attributable to his efforts and that half of such community property therefore passed to Mrs. La Rosa under the will. The trial court rejected this contention on the authority of Estate of Pepper, 158 Cal. 619, 623–624, 112 Pac. 62, 31 L.R.A.,N.S., 1092 (1911).

In Estate of Neilson, 57 Cal.2d 733, 22 Cal.Rptr. 1, 371 P.2d 745 (1962), we overruled the Pepper case and held that the part of the profits of a separate property enterprise attributable to the husband's efforts are community property, whether the enterprise be classified as "commercial" or "agricultural." The funds in plaintiff's bank account were derived primarily from profits of the enterprise. These funds, which were used to pay for the improvements in 1928 and 1939, must therefore be apportioned between plaintiff's separate property and the community property. Any increase in the value of the land attributable to plaintiff's efforts was also community property. Estate of Neilson, supra, 57 Cal.2d 733 at pp. 737, 738, 22 Cal.Rptr. 1, 371 P. 2d 745 (1962).

Defendants also contend that the trial court erred in ruling that they could not introduce into evidence plaintiff's deposition and certain answers he gave to interrogatories except to impeach his testimony. Code of Civil Procedure Section 2030, subdivision (b), provides that answers to interrogatories "may be used to the same extent as provided in subdivision (d) of Section 2016 of this code for the use of the deposition of a party." Section 2016, subdivision (d), paragraph (2), provides that, "so far as admissible under the rules of evidence," any part or all of the deposition of a party "may be used by an adverse party for any purpose." Thus, insofar as plaintiff's deposition and answers to interrogatories contained admissions, they should have been admitted in evidence. (Dini v. Dini, 188 Cal.App.2d 506, 512, 10 Cal.Rptr. 570, 574 (1961); Murray v. Manley, 170 Cal.App.2d 364, 367, 338 P.2d 976, 978 (1959).) As stated in the two cited cases, an adverse party's deposition "may be used to establish any material fact, a prima facie case, or even to prove the whole case." Consequently, a party is not limited to using an adverse party's deposition or answers to interrogatories for the purpose of impeaching his testimony.

The judgment is reversed.

GIBSON, C. J., and SCHAUER, McCOMB, PETERS, WHITE and TOBRINER, JJ., concur.

ANDO v. WOODBERRY

Court of Appeals of New York, 1960.
8 N.Y.2d 165, 203 N.Y.S.2d 74.

Action by motorcycle policeman for injuries sustained in collision of motorcycle and an automobile. The Supreme Court, Trial Term, Bronx County, James E. Mulcahy, J., 15 Misc.2d 774, 181 N.Y.S.2d 905, rendered judgment on verdict for defendant, and plaintiff appealed. The Supreme Court, Appellate Division, First Judicial Department, 9 A.D.2d 125, 192 N.Y.S.2d 414, entered a judgment December 4, 1959 as resettled by an order entered December 16, 1959, affirming the judgment by a divided court. Plaintiff appealed.

. . .

FULD, Judge. This appeal calls upon us to decide a question of first impression in this court: May a defendant's prior plea of guilt to a traffic offense be introduced as evidence of his carelessness in a civil action for damages?

The relevant facts are simple and undisputed. Robert Ando, a police officer, driving a motorcycle, and Edward Nichols, driving an automobile owned by Essie Woodberry, were both proceeding north on Fifth Avenue, New York City, on the afternoon of December 28, 1955. Car and motorcycle collided when Mr. Nichols attempted to make a left turn at 110th Street, and Officer Ando was injured as a result of the collision. Mr. Nichols was given a summons which charged him with failing to make a proper turn and failing to signal before turning, and he subsequently appeared in the Manhattan Traffic Division of Magistrates' Court and pleaded guilty to both charges.

Upon the negligence trial, held in the Supreme Court, the only witnesses to the occurrence of the accident were the plaintiff and the defendant Nichols who drove the car. According to the plaintiff, Mr. Nichols, after first pulling over to the right, made a left turn without prior warning or signal and struck his motorcycle. Mr. Nichols not only denied that he had moved to the right, but asserted that he had given a signal upon making the turn. In order to strengthen his case, the plaintiff attempted to prove Mr. Nichols' plea of guilt in Traffic Court on the theory that it constituted an admission, but, upon the defendants' objection, the trial court excluded the proffered evidence. The jury returned a verdict in favor of the defendants and the Appellate Division, two Justices dissenting, affirmed the judgment subsequently rendered.

In deciding whether proof of a plea of guilty to a traffic violation should be received as evidence in chief in a subsequent civil action, it is well to recall the principle, basic to our law of evidence, that "All facts having rational probative value are admissible" unless there is sound reason to exclude them, unless, that is, "some specific rule forbids" (1 Wigmore, Evidence [3d ed., 1940], p. 293). It is this general principle which gives rationality, coherence and justification to our system of evidence and we may neglect it only at the risk of turning that system into a trackless morass of arbitrary and artificial rules.

In view of the fact that Mr. Nichols' plea of guilty to the charges leveled against him—failing to signal and making an improper turn—is relevant to the issue of his negligence in turning off Fifth Avenue, we must simply decide whether there is any justification for excluding it. Two possible grounds of exclusion suggest themselves; the first, that such testimony is hearsay and, the second, that its introduction violates public policy.

Since a prior plea of guilt represents an admission, it is not obnoxious to the hearsay rule. See 4 Wigmore, op. cit., §§ 1048, 1049, pp. 2–7. Accordingly, the courts of this State, as well as of other jurisdictions, have generally sanctioned the receipt in evidence in a negligence action of a prior plea of guilty to a traffic violation. See People v. Formato, 286 App.Div. 357, 363–364, 143 N.Y.S.2d 205, 211–212, 64 A.L.R.2d 812 (1955); Walther v. News Syndicate Co., 276 App.Div. 169, 176, 93 N.Y.S.2d 537, 544 (1950); Stanton v. Major, 274 App.Div. 864, 82 N.Y.S.2d 134 (1948); Same v. Davison, 253 App.Div. 123, 124, 1 N.Y.S.2d 374, 375 ( ); Barnum v. Morresey, 245 App. Div. 798, 280 N.Y.S. 899 (1935); Rednall v. Thompson, 108 Cal.App. 2d 662, 666, 239 P.2d 693 (1952); Koch v. Elkins, 71 Idaho 50, 54, 225 P.2d 457 (1924); Dimmick v. Follis, 123 Ind.App. 701, 703, 111 N.E. 2d 486 (1953); Race v. Chappell, 304 Ky. 788, 792, 202 S.W.2d 626 (1947); Morrissey v. Powell, 304 Mass. 268, 271, 23 N.E.2d 411, 124

A.L.R. 1522 (1939); Remmenga v. Selk, 150 Neb. 401, 415, 34 N.W.2d 757 (1949); Public Serv. Co. of New Hampshire v. Chancey, 94 N.H. 259, 261, 51 A.2d 845 (1947); Freas v. Sullivan, 130 Ohio St. 486, 491, 200 N.E. 639 (1936); Olk v. Marquardt, 203 Wis. 479, 485, 234 N.W. 723 (1931). Thus, when Mr. Nichols pleaded guilty to the traffic infractions charged against him, his plea of guilty amounted to a statement or admission by him that he did the act charged. As such, it should be treated like any other admission or confession, and subject to the same rules relating to its weight and effect.

The defendants insist, however, that there is a public policy which requires us to treat the admission implicit in pleading guilty to a traffic offense differently from others. It is the policy of this State, they urge, that a traffic infraction be distinguished from a crime and that it be recognized that a plea of guilt is entered in traffic court for numerous reasons unrelated to actual guilt. To support their contention, they point to subdivision 29 of Section 2 of the Vehicle and Traffic Law, Consol.Laws, c. 40, Hart v. Mealey, 287 N.Y. 39, 38 N.E.2d 121 (1942) and Walther v. News Syndicate Co., 276 App.Div. 169, 93 N.Y.S.2d 537 (1950), supra.

The portion of the Vehicle and Traffic Law relied upon provides that "a traffic infraction is not a crime, and the penalty or punishment imposed therefor . . . shall not affect or impair the credibility as a witness, or otherwise, of any person convicted thereof." (Vehicle and Traffic Law § 2, subd. 29; see, also, Civil Practice Act, § 355). Whatever else this provision may mean, it is clear that it is directed solely against the use of a conviction of a traffic infraction to "affect or impair . . . credibility as a witness" of the person convicted and not against the use of a plea as evidence in chief. The statute does no more than restate the rule of the common law that a prior conviction may be shown to attack the credibility of a witness only if it was a conviction of a *crime*. See People v. Joyce, 233 N.Y. 61, 71, 134 N.E. 836, 840 (1922); People v. Brown, 2 A.D.2d 202, 203, 153 N.Y.S.2d 744, 746 (1956); see, also, Civ.Prac.Act, § 350.

Since a traffic infraction was declared not to be a crime, it was but natural for the Legislature to, in effect, codify the settled rule prohibiting the use of a conviction of such an offense to impeach the offender when called to testify as a witness. Had more than this been intended, had it been the legislative design to render evidence of a traffic infraction unavailable for *any* purpose in a subsequent civil action, it could easily have so provided. See, e. g., Minn.Stats.Ann. § 169.94, subd. 1; Colo.Rev.Stat., 13–4–140.[1] The Legislature of this State having written a clearly limited rule of exclusion, we may not apply it beyond its terms to exclude the use of a guilty plea as evidence in chief.

1. The Minnesota statute declares that "No record of the conviction of any person for any violation of [the Highway Traffic Regulation Act] shall be admissible as evidence in any court in any civil action" (Minn.Stats.Ann. § 169.94, subd. 1).

Nor may legislative policy be taken to justify its exclusion. Certain violations of the Vehicle and Traffic Law were denominated traffic infractions and distinguished from crimes in order to establish a new type of offense, one "with the stigma of criminality removed." Squadrito v. Griebsch, 1 N.Y.2d 471, 476, 154 N.Y.S.2d 37, 41 (1956). The legislation simply represented a recognition of the fact that most traffic violations do not involve the degree of moral turpitude associated with crime.

Our case law, likewise, offers no support for the defendants' position. It is quite true that in Hart v. Mealey, 287 N.Y. 39, 38 N.E.2d 121 (1942), supra, where the issue was whether there was sufficient evidence to justify a determination by the Commissioner of Motor Vehicles that a driver's license be revoked on account of reckless driving, this court remarked on the "weakness" of evidence of a conviction after trial—not of a plea of guilt, as was inadvertently assumed by the Appellate Division—as proof of the facts involved. The Hart case, however, did not involve any issue of admissibility and, therefore, has no bearing on the issues before us. The case of Walther v. News Syndicate Co., 276 App.Div. 169, 93 N.Y.S.2d 537 (1950), supra, did hold that a judgment of conviction of a traffic infraction after trial was inadmissible in a subsequent civil action, but it recognized that its decision represented a limited exception to the general rule announced by this court in Schindler v. Royal Ins. Co., 258 N.Y. 310, 179 N.E. 711, 80 A.L.R. 1142 (1932); see, also, Matter of Rechtschaffen's Estate, 278 N.Y. 336, 16 N.E.2d 357 (1938), and, even more significant, it expressly distinguished the case before it from those in which a plea of guilty is involved. "In such cases," wrote the court, "the record or proof of the defendant's guilty plea is received . . . as a declaration or admission against interest". Walther v. News Syndicate Co., 276 App.Div. 169, 176, 93 N.Y.S.2d 537, 544 (1950), supra. Consequently, even if we were to assume that the Appellate Division was correct in its conclusion in the Walther case—and we observe that we have never had occasion to consider the question there presented—the opinion supports, rather than detracts from, the conclusion that a guilty plea deliberately recorded by the defendant is admissible against him on the issue of his negligence in a subsequent civil action.

In addition to their reliance on policy and precedent, the defendants also offer an argument based on what they label "experience". They contend that one charged with a traffic violation pleads guilty, even though he believes himself innocent, in order to avoid the expenditure of time and money which would be involved if guilt were denied and the charge contested. Based on this assumption, they suggest that the plea of guilt must be looked upon as one of *nolo contendere*. The contention has no merit. In the first place, the plea of *nolo contendere* has long been abolished in this State (see People v. Daiboch, 265 N.Y. 125, 128, 191 N.E. 859, 860 (1934)) and may not be resurrected without legislative sanction. In the second place, while we are willing to assume that pleas to traffic charges are not infrequently prompted by considerations of expediency, we have no reliable means of judging how significant a portion of all guilty pleas to traffic charges are of this character. But, quite apart from this, there is no basis for the defendants' unverified generalization or "hunch" in cases where, as here, the alleged violation was attended with injury to the person or property of a third party and the plea carries with it serious consequences to the offender's future status as a motor vehicle operator (Vehicle and Traffic Law § 71).[2]

What the defendant Nichols is actually arguing is that, when he pleaded guilty, he "really didn't mean what he said." This claim, however, goes to the weight of evidence and entitles the defendant not to exclusion of the plea, but to an "opportunity to explain" it. Chamberlain v. Iba, 181 N.Y. 486, 490, 74 N.E. 481, 482 (1905); see, also, Wachtel v. Equitable Life Assur. Soc., 266 N.Y. 345, 351, 194 N.E. 850, 852 (1935); Gangi v. Fradus, 227 N.Y. 452, 125 N.E. 677 (1920); Hirsch v. New York Life Ins. Co., 267 App.Div. 404, 406, 45 N.Y.S.2d 892, 894 (1944); 4 Wigmore, op. cit., pp. 23–24. After the defendant has given his explanation, his reasons for pleading guilty, it is for the jurors to evaluate his testimony and decide whether the plea is entitled to any weight. As this court wrote some years ago with respect to extra-judicial admissions, it is for the jury, noting "the conditions and circumstances under which [such admissions] were made", to determine their "effect . . . and their probative weight and value, which may range from the lowest, or none at all, to conclusiveness." Gangi v. Fradus, 227 N.Y. 452, 457, 125 N.E. 677, 679 (1920), supra. The traditional treatment accorded to admissions by our courts takes account of the very claim here made, namely, that the defendant's guilty plea was not an admission that he committed the acts charged against him.

To the claim that the jury will be unduly prejudiced by the introduction of a plea of guilt despite the opportunity to explain it away, we content ourselves with the statement that he underestimates the intelligence of jurors and overlooks their awareness of those very circumstances said to destroy the meaning and significance of the plea. If voluntarily and deliberately made, the plea was a statement of guilt, an admission by the defendant that he committed the acts charged, and it should be accorded no less force or effect than if made outside of court to a stranger.

The judgment of the Appellate Division should be reversed and a new trial granted, with costs to abide the event.

VAN VOORHIS, Judge (dissenting).

The law of evidence has its roots in experience, and in common experience men and women charged with minor traffic violations

2. Under the so-called "point system," in effect in New York, a plea of guilt, for instance, to the charge of failing to signal or of making an improper turn, is taken into account in determining whether the offender's license should be suspended or revoked. (See pamphlet issued by the Commissioner of Motor Vehicles, entitled, "What You Need to Know About New York State's Point System for Persistent Traffic Law Violators".)

plead guilty to avoid inconvenience whether they are innocent or guilty. In the Federal courts it is possible for a defendant in a criminal action to plead *nolo contendere*, the accepted meaning of which is that the defendant chooses not to contest and takes the consequences of conviction but without admitting the truth of the charge against him. Such a plea could not be received in evidence as a voluntary admission against interest under the reasoning of the opinion by Judge FULD in this case. The State procedure does not give opportunity to plead *nolo contendere* but that is exactly what persons accused of minor traffic violations generally mean to do and are understood to have done when they enter guilty pleas in such instances. They are subject to the punishment provided by law for the offenses to which they have pleaded guilty, but the criminal statutes do not impose the additional burden of having the conviction used in a civil action as a factual admission by the person charged that he or she did or omitted the act on which the traffic infraction depends. It is irrelevant that *nolo contendere* is not a form of plea that is used in the State courts, inasmuch as we are not confronted in this case with any of the consequences of conviction under the criminal law. We have before us merely the collateral effect of such a plea as bearing upon the civil rights of the party in an action for damages. It is contrary to ordinary experience to give that effect to this plea of guilty in the Magistrates' Court, as the Appellate Division has correctly held. When Mr. Nichols pleaded guilty in the Manhattan Traffic Division of Magistrates' Court to failure to make a proper turn or to signal, he rendered himself liable to whatever penalties were involved but in my view it cannot be said with justice or a sense of reality that he conceded whatever facts he was accused of by the arresting officer. I think that it was not intended that the first steps in the enforcement or defense of damage claims in automobile negligence accident cases should be taken in traffic courts or police courts, nor does it aid their most effective functioning if that is so (contrast Walther v. News Syndicate Co., 276 App.Div. 169, 93 N.Y.S.2d 537 (1905), with Schindler v. Royal Ins. Co., 258 N.Y. 310, 179 N.E. 711, 80 A.L.R. 1142 (1932)).

DESMOND, C. J., and DYE, FROESSEL, BURKE and FOSTER, JJ., concur with FULD, J.

VAN VOORHIS, J., dissents in an opinion.

Judgment reversed, etc.

STATE OF MISSOURI v. THOMPSON

Supreme Court of Missouri, En Banc, 1965.
396 S.W.2d 697.

EAGER, Judge. This defendant was convicted in December, 1961, of first degree murder and, upon a finding making our Second

Offender Act applicable, he was sentenced by the court to be executed. At the trial he was represented by counsel of his own choice. Upon appeal, the judgment and sentence were affirmed. 363 S.W.2d 711. Generally, the points involved upon the appeal did not include those which confront us now. The crime of which defendant was convicted occurred in Cape Girardeau County; he was tried in Bollinger County on a change of venue. The essential facts are stated in our former opinion. By sundry intermediate proceedings the execution of the sentence has been stayed.

On January 13, 1964, defendant filed in the trial court, acting through new counsel, his motion to vacate the judgment under our Rule 27.26, V.A.M.R. The court denied the motion without a hearing from an examination of the files and record. On appeal this court, acting on its own motion, reversed the judgment and order and remanded the cause for a hearing upon specifically designated questions of fact raised in the motion. Upon disqualification of the regular judge, the Honorable Marshall Craig was designated to hear the matter. He has done so in a lengthy and meticulously conducted hearing, has entered his findings, and has denied the motion. The matter is now here for a determination de novo on the merits upon the voluminous evidence presented.

. . .

As stated, the facts are rather fully set out at 363 S.W.2d 711. On the evening of March 10, 1961, two police cars had been pursuing a 1956 Oldsmobile driven by Sammy Aire Tucker with the defendant riding as a passenger, in the north part of Cape Girardeau; they stopped it on the shoulder. One police car stopped a few feet behind the Oldsmobile, the other turned around and stopped on the opposite shoulder. From the first car Officer Crittendon walked up beside the driver and began to question him, Officer Goss walked to a position opposite the rear window on the right side. Tucker, without warning, shot Officer Crittendon fatally in the stomach, and immediately began firing at the officers across the road; at almost the same instant shots were heard on the right side of the Oldsmobile, resulting in the death of Officer Goss whose gun was still in its holster. One shot went through both of his legs near the knees, severing arteries in both legs, and he died that evening from loss of blood. The present defendant was standing beside the passenger's seat of the Oldsmobile at the time. Another officer, Lang, was somewhat to the rear. As indicated in our former opinion, there was ample evidence to support the conviction of this defendant for the murder of Officer Goss.

It is generally both difficult and disagreeable for a court to "rehash" the events of a criminal trial and conviction after such a lapse of time, particularly in collateral proceedings, as here. And, certainly, the prolonging of such proceedings over a period of years usually works no good, either to our processes of justice, or to the regard in which those processes are held in the minds of the lay public or the Bar. Yet, so long as this mode of review is permissible, it is our solemn duty to consider and enforce it. In this background we have given this record a somewhat unusual amount of study.

We agree with the findings of the trial judge in all particulars but one. That, of course, proves vital. This point of disagreement is expressed in defendant's brief in part as follows: ". . . that the prosecutor at the appellant's trial deliberately suppressed and failed to disclose to the court or defense counsel material ballistic evidence in the possession of the state consisting of cartridge cases found at the scene of the shooting and in the appellant's automobile." In the argument which follows counsel emphasizes the misleading effect of the Prosecutor's oral arguments to the jury. Various courts have held that the suppression of (or failure to disclose) evidence in the possession or control of the prosecution which is favorable to defendant and which might be persuasive to a jury, constitutes such a fundamental unfairness as to invalidate a conviction because violative of due process. Ashley v. State of Texas, 319 F.2d 80 (5th Cir. 1963) (withholding of report of doctors that defendant was incompetent); . . . .

. . .

The foregoing point more or less merges into the contention that defendant was denied the effective assistance of counsel in that his counsel failed to require a determination of the voluntary or involuntary nature of the statements. Actually, neither the oral nor the written statement constituted a confession, for neither contained an admission of the *crime* charged. C.J.S. Evidence § 270, p. 696. They were introduced as admissions against interest. Defendant did not admit in either statement that he had fired a shot on the occasion in question. Counsel (and defendant) apparently determined as a matter of trial strategy that the statements were as likely, or more likely, to be helpful than harmful. These are matters normally within the realm of counsel's judgment and do not constitute acts of ineffectiveness entitling defendant to relief under Rule 27.26. It is hardly possible that this matter will arise again in any similar form, but we agree entirely with the detailed finding of the trial court that defendant was not thus denied the effective assistance of counsel.

. . . The court remands the case with great reluctance. We note here that the defendant is now under life sentence upon conviction of murder in Butler County; the appeal taken from that judgment was dismissed on February 11, 1963.

The judgment of the trial court denying defendant's motion to vacate is reversed for the reasons specifically stated herein; the original judgment of conviction and sentence are vacated and set aside, and the cause is remanded to the Circuit Court of Bollinger County for a new trial. Defendant will remain in the custody of the Department of Corrections until taken under appropriate process for retrial.

LAN-CHILE AIRLINES, INC. v. RODRIGUEZ

District Court of Appeal of Florida, Third District, 1974.
296 So.2d 498.

HENDRY, Judge. This is a consolidated appeal from two adverse judgments entered upon jury verdicts in favor of the two appellees, Manuel Rodriguez and Juan Jane.

The appellees each were awarded $2,500 in compensatory damages and $110,000 in punitive damages as a result of a physical beating they received on January 5, 1971 by five assailants in the appellant's VIP room at the Miami International Airport.

The evidence elicited at the trial indicated that the assailants were hired by agents of Lan-Chile Airlines, Inc. to commit an assault and battery upon Rodriguez and Jane in order to discourage their activities on behalf of a labor union.

In their main brief, the appellants have raised four points; and in the reply brief, a fifth point has been asserted challenging the excessiveness of the damages.

Appellant's first point on appeal presents a question as to whether or not the doctrine of sovereign immunity is a bar to recovery on the record of this case. Appellant argues that although it did not raise sovereign immunity as a defense in the pleadings, the appellees introduced the issue by comments during trial at voir dire of the jury, during opening and closing statements and by the testimony adduced during the proceeding.

Generally, it was shown during the trial that Lan-Chile Airlines was owned by the Chilean State and run as an independent business in the United States. In addition, there was testimony that one Osvaldo Moremans was designated by the Marxist Government in power in Chile at the time as a "super-boss" to oversee the airline's executives in this country.

The first time sovereign immunity was directly raised as an issue before the trial court was by the appellant's motion for a new trial. In our view, the fact of state ownership which appears in the record does not signify that the legal issue of sovereign immunity was tried effectively by consent either expressly or impliedly. See Worth Insurance Co. v. Gammons, 228 So.2d 127 (Fla.App.1969); Langlois v. Oriole Land & Development Corp., 283 So.2d 143 (Fla.App.1973); RCP 1.190(b), 30 F.S.A.

In addition, we do not think that the doctrine of sovereign immunity operates as a bar to a cause of action arising out of a purely commercial operation by a foreign government in the United States. Harris & Company Advertising, Inc. v. Republic of Cuba, Fla.App.1961, 127 So.2d 687.

Appellant next attacks certain admissions against interest made by the alleged assailants to the appellees which were introduced into evidence on the basis that their agency was established by extra judicial statements. This point is devoid of substantial merit.

The record demonstrates that the trial judge made a specific finding that a prima facie case of agency had been proven prior to permitting testimony regarding statements made by the assailants. We think that the record amply supports the finding. The fact of agency may be demonstrated by inference from facts and circumstances and the conduct of the parties involved in a particular case. 29 Am.Jur.2d Evidence § 663.

. . .

Therefore, for the reasons stated and upon the authorities cited and discussed, it is ordered as to each of the appellees, that unless he shall, within thirty days after the filing of our mandate, file in the circuit court a remittitur of $85,000 of the punitive damages (thereby making the amount of the judgment in his favor to be for $2,500 compensatory damages plus $25,000 punitive damages) the judgment as to him will hereby be reversed with directions for a new trial on punitive damages. Upon the timely filing by an appellee of a remittitur as herein provided for, the judgment in his favor, as so reduced by such remittitur, shall stand affirmed.

It is so ordered.

CITY OF LOUISVILLE v. PADGETT

Court of Appeals of Kentucky, 1970.
457 S.W.2d 485.

EDWARD P. HILL, JR., Chief Justice.

In her original and amended complaints, Marsha L. Padgett sued the City of Louisville (the City), Ruby Construction Company (Ruby), Louisville and Jefferson County Metropolitan Sewer District (Metropolitan), and Perry M. Adams for damages for injuries sustained when the automobile in which she was riding as a passenger and which was being operated by Perry M. Adams ran into a pool of water on River Road and wrecked. She alleged negligence on the part of the City, Ruby, and Metropolitan in the construction and maintenance of the drainage system of the road in question.

The City filed cross-claim against Ruby for indemnity. It also filed cross-claim against Adams for indemnity or contribution.

The City also filed cross-claim for indemnity against Metropolitan, claiming that under KRS Chapter 76 Metropolitan had the sole responsibility for the drainage of the streets of the City, including River Road at the place of the accident, and that if there was liability anywhere it was on Metropolitan. In the alternative the City asked for contribution against Metropolitan.

Metropolitan filed cross-claim against the City, Ruby, and Adams.

At the conclusion of plaintiff's case, the circuit court sustained Ruby's motion for a directed verdict.

At the close of the entire case, the circuit court sustained Metropolitan's motion for a directed verdict and overruled plaintiff's motion for a directed verdict as to the City and Adams.

The jury returned a joint verdict against the City and Adams for $28,357.86. Later a separate judgment was entered in favor of the City against Adams for $14,178.93. Adams and his insurance carrier paid into court $10,000 (its limit of liability). This amount was accepted by plaintiff in full satisfaction of her claim against Adams under a previous agreement that Adams, then in Korea, would not demand a continuance providing plaintiff would not claim from Adams a greater amount than the limit of liability under his insurance policy. All of this was with court approval.

The City has appealed. Plaintiff filed cross-appeal against Ruby and Metropolitan. Metropolitan cross-appeals from that part of the judgment which dismissed its cross-claim against Ruby.

The facts are as follows. On November 5, 1966, at about 7:14 p. m., the car in which appellee Marsha L. Padgett was a passenger and which was being driven eastwardly on River Road in the City of Louisville by Perry Morrison Adams, after rounding a slight curve, ran into a pond or accumulation of water. The splashing water covered the windshield blinding the driver, causing him to lose control of the car. The car left the road and struck a utility pole causing serious injuries to appellee Marsha L. Padgett. The pond of water was about 200 feet long and ranged in depth up to six inches next to the curb. It was dark at the time.

Four or five days prior to the accident, an officer of the Louisville Police Department observed the accumulation of water at the place of the accident and telephoned a report thereof to police headquarters. He told the "complaint desk" something should be done to the puddle, that it was in the lane of traffic.

During or prior to 1965, Ruby contracted with the State Highway Department to construct a portion of I–64, known as Riverside Expressway, from east of the interchange at the North-South Expressway to near Washington Street.

On November 3, 1966, a city policeman notified Metropolitan of the flooding on River Road. Metropolitan placed barricades about the place and pumped the water off. On November 7, 1966, Metropolitan notified the State Highway Department of the flooding of the road, but this was after the accident. Ruby used a backhoe to dig a temporary ditch which stopped the flooding. Only one or two hours was required to do this.

On this appeal the City presents these three arguments: "(1) The negligence of the appellant, City of Louisville, if any there was, was not the proximate cause of appellee Padgett's injuries, but the independent intervening negligence of the defendant, Perry Adams, was the sole proximate cause of appellee's injuries as a matter of law; (2) appellant was, as a matter of law, entitled to judgment for indemnity on its cross-claim against Ruby, or at least a jury issue was raised on said cross-claim"; and "(3) appellant was, as a matter of law, entitled to judgment for indemnity, or in the alternative, contribution, on its cross-claim against Metropolitan Sewer District, or at least a jury issue was raised on said cross-claim."

Turning to the City's first argument, the City contends that appellee Padgett is bound under rules pertaining to judicial admissions by her notice of the accident given to the City under KRS 411.110. The City reasons that Adams, the driver, had from 321 to 375 feet after discovering the water in which to "attempt to stop the auto," apply his brakes, or turn on his windshield wipers. By all the evidence, Adams was not traveling at an excessive speed. He stated he was traveling at about 30 miles per hour. There was no evidence of drinking. Street lighting in the vicinity of the water was not good. At least two of the investigating officers used flashlights at the scene of the wreck. We have some reservations as to whether Adams was guilty of negligence, but the jury found that he was. He or his insurance carrier has satisfied the judgment, and neither has cross-appealed. So that question is not before us unless it can be said that Adams' negligence was the sole cause of the accident, and that we certainly cannot say. The City had notice of the condition from observations of two of its police officials and actually caused Metropolitan to pump the water off the road once before the accident. We think, as did the jury, that the City was guilty of negligence by failing to keep the water from accumulating or by failing to place barricades up to notify the public of the obvious hazard.

Taking Padgett's notice to the City as true, it does not admit negligence on the part of Adams and did not amount to a judicial admission.

We agree with the jury that Adams' negligence was not the sole or primary cause of the accident.

The negligence of Adams must have been the "primary and active" cause of the accident in order for the City to be entitled to indemnity. See Ambrosius Industries v. Adams, 293 S.W.2d 230 (Ky. 1956); Mackey v. Allen, 396 S.W.2d 55 (Ky.1966); and Seelbach v. Cadick, 405 S.W.2d 745 (Ky.1966).

. . .

The judgment is affirmed on both the direct and cross-appeals.

All concur.

DECISIONS RELATING TO CHAPTER VIII HEARSAY—RES GESTAE EXCEPTIONS

GREENER v. GENERAL ELECTRIC CO.

Court of Appeals of New York, 1913.
209 N.Y. 135, 102 N.E. 527.

. . .

Action by Mary Greener, as administratrix, against the General Electric Company. A judgment for plaintiff and an order denying a new trial were affirmed by the Appellate Division, Third Department (153 App.Div. 439, 138 N.Y.Supp. 273 (1912)), and defendant appeals.

GRAY, J. This action was brought to recover damages of the defendant for being the cause of the death of the plaintiff's intestate, an employé. In substance, the alleged negligence was that the defendant had provided for the use of its workmen a defective and insecure ladder, in connection with an overhead crane erected in its works, from which the deceased fell, or was thrown, to the floor of the building. The facts disclosed by the evidence were such as to warrant the jurors in finding that the deceased, who was employed as a "rigger," upon the day in question was standing on top of the carriage of the crane, when he was called to by the crane repairman, from the floor, to come down and to assist in hoisting up a piece of machinery; that, in attempting to comply with the order and to descend from his position, he stepped upon an iron ladder, extending from a crane cage, which depended from the cross-girders on which the crane carriage moved, for the purpose of reaching the lateral girders and of thus using another ladder to get to the floor; that this mode of ascending, or descending, from floor to crane was not prohibited, nor unusual; that the crane ladder, which was bolted to the floor and to the top of the crane carriage, and extended some three or four feet above it, unattached, was inadequate to the strain of the weight of the deceased, when subjected to it on this occasion; that it had bent under him, throwing him to the floor; and that, as the result of injuries then received, he had subsequently died.

Without otherwise referring to the evidence, we think that the judgment appealed from might stand, were it not for a serious error committed by the trial court in the reception in evidence of a declaration of the deceased, made to a fellow workman after his fall, and which may have influenced the decision by the jurors of the question of fact. Whatever we may consider to have been the sufficiency of the other evidence, we could, and should, not assume that a declaration, made under such circumstances, may not have had its effect upon the jurors' minds. A witness, also employed as a "rigger," and who was standing a few feet away from where the deceased had fallen, went over to him, and, as he lay there, "asked him what had happened." Over the objection of the defendant, he was then allowed to state what the deceased said, and an exception was taken to the ruling. The witness testified: "When I asked him what had happened, he said: 'My feet is broke; the ladder bent over.'" The admission in evidence of the declarations of an injured person constitutes an exception to the general rule that excludes hearsay evidence, and is only justified when the declarations are spontaneous utterances, or exclamations. There is no confusion in the decisions of this court upon this question. Waldele v. N. Y. C. & H. R. R. R. Co., 95 N.Y. 274, 47 Am.Rep. 41 (1884); Martin v. N. Y., N. H. & H. R. R. Co., 103 N.Y. 626, 9 N.E. 505 (1887); People v. Del Vermo, 192 N.Y. 470, 85 N. E. 690 (1908). In Waldele v. N. Y. C. & H. R. R. R. Co., the question was carefully considered, and the authorities were reviewed. There, the testimony of a witness as to what the injured person had declared, a few minutes after the accident, as to how it happened, was admitted, and, for the error in the admission, the plaintiff's judgment was reversed. The vice of the evidence was held to be in the declaration being narrative of the past transaction, and thus depending for its truth upon the reliability of the statements of the deceased and the veracity of the witness. The decision was followed in Martin v. N. Y., N. H. & H. R. R. Co. In People v. Del Vermo, the witness was walking with the deceased and the defendant, when the former fell upon the sidewalk. The witness asked him "What is the matter?" and the deceased answered, "Del Vermo stabbed me with a knife." The admission of the witness' evidence as to this declaration was held proper "as a part of the res gestae, in the broadest sense of the term." Judge Willard Bartlett again considered the question with much care, in the light of our and of other decisions, and held that the testimony was properly received. The declaration so accompanied the occurrence of the assault as to come within the exception to the general rule.

The distinction to be made is in the character of the declaration, whether it be so spontaneous, or natural, an utterance as to exclude the idea of fabrication, or whether it be in the nature of a narrative of what had occurred. In the present case, the declaration of the deceased was not spontaneous; it was called forth by the inquiry as to "what had happened" and was distinctly narrative. As it was observed in the dissenting opinion below, "it was, in effect, a statement that the falling was not accidental, nor due to the negligence of the plaintiff's intestate, but was due to an occurrence upon which might be predicated negligence upon the part of the defendant."

For the error pointed out, the judgment must be reversed and a new trial had; costs to abide the event.

CULLEN, C. J., and WERNER, HISCOCK, COLLIN, CUDDEBACK and MILLER, JJ., concur.

Judgment reversed, etc.

MAGILL v. SOUTHERN RY. CO. ET AL.

Supreme Court of South Carolina, 1913.
95 S.C. 306, 78 S.E. 1033.

. . .

Appeal from Common Pleas Circuit Court of York County; T. S. Sease, Judge.

Action by Samuel T. Magill against the Southern Railway Company and another. Judgment for the plaintiff, and defendants appeal.

WATTS, J. This was an action in the court of common pleas for York county for $20,000 damages for alleged personal injuries to the plaintiff, received while on or near the track of the defendant Southern Railway Company. The case was heard by Judge Sease and a jury at the November term of the court, for said county, in 1912, and resulted in favor of the plaintiff for $8,000. At the close of plaintiff's testimony a motion was made and granted by the court to direct a verdict for the defendant as to the cause of action for punitive damages set out in the complaint. At the close of all testimony, the defendants asked the court to direct a verdict in their favor on two grounds: (1) That there was no evidence tending to show a breach of any duty that the defendants owed to the plaintiff, and that there was therefore no evidence of negligence on their part which was the proximate cause of his injuries; (2) upon the ground that the plaintiff was a trespasser upon one of the cars of the defendant, and that there was no evidence of a breach of any duty on the part of the defendants, owed to the plaintiff. This motion was refused. After verdict was rendered a motion for a new trial was made and refused. Defendants, after entry of judgment, appeal and allege error by 12 exceptions. At the hearing in this court appellants' counsel announced that they abandoned exceptions 2 and 3.

Exceptions 1, 4, and 5 allege that his honor was in error in admitting, over defendant's objection, in permitting plaintiff's witnesses to testify as to certain matters; exception 1, in permitting witness McNinch to testify as to statements made by plaintiff as to how he received the injuries, as such statements were not part of the res gestae, and the plaintiff was not at that time in a condition to make an intelligent statement, being dazed and shocked. As to exception 1, in allowing McNinch, the uncle of the plaintiff, to detail the statement, made by the plaintiff, immediately after he received the injury, we see no error in this, as we think it was admissible as part of the res gestae. As was said in the case (State v. Arnold, 47 S.C. 9, 24 S.E. 926, 58 Am.St.Rep. 867 (1896)), the court held admissible as res gestae the statement: " 'Charlie shot me to death,' made by a man shot in a doorway of a house, from which he staggered some 30 yards and fell; the utterances being made a few minutes after the shooting, to the first person who reached him in response to his cries for help. The declarations here in question were made probably . . . within 200 or 300 feet of the place of the shooting. These circumstances of time and place do not alone necessarily prevent a declaration from being part of the res gestae, but they are factors, with other circumstances, in determining whether the declarations were the spontaneous utterances of the mind under the immediate influences of the transaction." The court, in the same case, further says: "Questions of this kind must be very largely left to the sound judicial discretion of the trial judge, who is compelled to view all of the circumstances in reaching his conclusion, and this court will not reverse his ruling, unless it clearly appears, from undisputed circumstances in evidence, that the testimony ought to have been admitted or rejected, as the case may be." "In the nature of the case, there can be no hard and fast rule as to the precise time near an occurrence within which declarations explanatory thereof must be made, in order to be admissible. The general rule is that the declarations must be substantially contemporaneous with the litigated transaction, and be the instinctive, spontaneous utterances of the mind under the active influences of the transaction, the circumstances precluding the idea that the utterances are the result of reflection, or designed to make false or self-serving declarations." State v. McDaniel, 68 S.C. 310, 311, 47 S.E. 386, 102 Am.St.Rep. 661 (1948). "This court has several times held that the declaration need not be made coincident with the injury, but near about it, so nearly that it is not likely that the declaration could be manufactured." Williams v. Southern Railway Co., 68 S.C. 373, 47 S.E. 707 (1904). See, also, Shelton v. Southern Railway Co., 86 S.C. 102, 103, 67 S.E. 899, 901 (1910), wherein the court says: "The testimony on the part of the plaintiff was that the second car from the engine was the first to jump the track, and that the engine ran on about three-quarters of a mile before it stopped; the engineer said he stopped within 150 or 200 yards, and when the engineer ran his engine back to the wreck, he said to the conductor: 'Cap, we have played hell.' Error is imputed to the judge in admitting the declaration of the engineer, on the ground that it was too long after the accident to be admitted as part of the res gestae." The court quotes from the case of State v. McDaniel, and says: "While the length of the time between the wreck and the making of the declaration in this case was such as to raise some doubt as to its admissibility, it was not such a clear case as would warrant the holding that the testimony was not within the rule."

When this evidence was admitted McNinch, the witness, testified that he had been in his office looking after some business, had changed his clothes, put on overalls, and was standing in the porch of the store, and was hailed, turned and saw a brakeman, of the railroad of this train, running, and the brakeman hollered: " 'Captain, for God's sake get a doctor here quick! We have killed a man, or cut a man's leg off.' I followed in a moment after sending to Ft. Mill for a doctor." In answer to the question, "You got up there as quickly as you could?" he said, "Yes, sir; I was there inside a half a minute. I couldn't have been longer; as soon as I could run there, as hard as I could go." "Did he make a statement as soon as you got there? Yes, sir; just as soon as I got down on my knees by him. Oh, I guess it was a few seconds." As to that part, which complains that when statement was made by plaintiff he was dazed and shocked, the evidence was admissible, and what force and effect and credence the jury gave to it was for the jury alone, but in answer to a question by his honor, as to whether the statement made by plaintiff was sensible and coherent, or rambling, the witness's answer was: "It was as intelligent as could be. There is no question about it." This exception is overruled.

Exceptions 2 and 3 were abandoned at the hearing of the case. Exception 4 alleges error in allowing plaintiff's witness Berry Hill to testify as to the existence of a rule of the company, forbidding employés to place obstructions near the track. This exception is overruled for the reason that later in the trial the rule was brought out in examination of one of the defendant's witnesses, E. L. Hughes, and for this reason the exception cannot be sustained. Hyland v. Telephone Co., 70 S.C. 315, 49 S.E. 879 (1905); Young v. McNeil, 78 S.C. 143, 59 S.E. 986 (1908).

Exception 5 is as follows: "Because his honor erred in permitting the plaintiff, over the objection of defendants, to prove by their witness W. H. Howard that freight cars, other than those that are alleged to have injured the plaintiff, projected out over the ends of the cross-ties; the error being that it was incompetent to prove what the size or length of other cars might have been, or how far their ends would project over the ends of cross-ties, as it was not shown that they were of the same width or size as the one that injured the plaintiff, as alleged in the complaint." By reference to the testimony of Howard it will be seen that he had run as a train hand, and on switch engine, and witness had made experiments on the morning that the injuries occurred; that he was called as an expert witness, and testified sufficiently to show that he was an expert, and was entitled to give an opinion, and his testimony was not contradicted by any of the train crew, who were on the train at the time of plaintiff's injury, and who were present at the trial of this case. This exception is overruled.

. . .

Judgment affirmed.

GARY, C. J., and HYDRICK and FRASER, JJ., concur.

GULF OIL CORPORATION v. HARRIS

Supreme Court of Oklahoma, 1967.
425 P.2d 957.

WILLIAMS, Justice. Under review in this original action is the State Industrial Court's award of death benefits to the widow of a deceased workman.

The record shows that decedent, a pumper serving employer near Meeker, had under his charge approximately twenty-seven oil wells; that he worked five days a week, approximately eight hours a day; a co-pumper had an additional 30 or so wells to pump; that when his co-pumper would have a day off decedent took charge of the additional thirty wells regularly assigned to that co-worker; that on Saturday, December 13, 1958, because of the co-pumper having his customary day off duty, decedent was responsible for all fifty-seven wells; that such day was very cold; that there was an appreciable accumulation of ice and snow; that about 8:00 or 8:30 A.M. decedent left his home in his pick-up truck to service the wells; that he took his lunch this day; that such truck was equipped with an engine-starter operated by car battery which was used to start the engines of the several wells; that he returned home about 12:30 P.M. complaining of severe pain in his chest; and that he died a few minutes later as a result of a coronary occlusion.

The cause of decedent's cardiac episode formed the principal issue before the trial tribunal. Claimant, decedent's widow, sought to attribute the fatal attack to strain and physical exertion from cranking an engine by hand on the morning in question at one of employer's well sites. She testified that decedent returned to their home on the day here involved after being away at work for four and one-half hours and further testified as follows: [That at that time]

> "A: He was cold, and he was blue around the eyes, and around the mouth.
>
> "Q: Did you learn from him there that there was anything wrong with him?
>
> "A: Yes.
>
> "Q: Did he make gestures or demonstrate to you anything?
>
> "A: He said he had a sharp pain in his chest.
>
> "Q: Did he inform you anything about where he had had this trouble?
>
> "A: Yes, he said while he was working."
>
> . . . .
>
> "Q: Did you call the doctor?
>
> "A: Yes.
>
> . . . .
>
> "Q: And by the time he [doctor] got there, was Mr. Harris dead?
>
> "A: Yes, sir, I think he was."
>
> . . . .
>
> "Q: Mrs. Harris, you testified a little bit ago that Mr. Harris came, and you testified that he was purple, blue

around the mouth. Did he make any statement right then to you as to what he had been doing?

. . . .

"A: Yes.

"Q: What did he say he had been doing?

"A: He said he had been cranking on this motor. First, he said he had been working. I said, 'What do you mean working?' He said 'I have been cranking this motor.' I said, 'How come you didn't use the starter?' He said, 'They were all frozen up and the starter would not do any good.'

"Q: Mrs. Harris, did he tell you how long?

"A: He said forty-five minutes. It would have been more or it could have been less. He said forty-five minutes. I don't know if he meant he cranked forty-five minutes, or he cranked and worked altogether forty-five minutes."

This testimony was admitted over the employer's objection.

Mr. Cooke, employer's production foreman, testified that he visited Mrs. Harris within two or three hours of the death of her husband and discussed the matter with her. Her testimony continued, as follows, to-wit:

"Q: And did she give you any narrative relation, such as she has recited here, about what he had related to her about the well?

"A: Yes, uh-huh."

. . . .

"Q: Why do you provide a starter?

"A: Too many back injuries and hernias and things you get with starting engines, they claim.

"Q: Do you think that is because of the unusual exertion that is required [by cranking] to start them?

"A: That's possibly true."

Dr. B testified of effect that Mr. Harris had reported that he had cranked one of the motors and that a sacroiliac lesion the doctor found was by Mr. Harris ascribed as to causation thereof to such activity.

Mr. Polk, decedent's co-worker, testified that after decedent's death he checked the wells he and decedent serviced; that two or three of the wells were not operating; that "There was two wells in particular. One of them was the Henthorne Estate No. 1, and there was a lot of tracks in the snow there, and there was also on the Calvin Hill, I don't remember that well number, it was either 1 or 2, but there was a lot of tracks and snow was all tracked down around the well, the engine, and both wells was down and I started them both." In answer to the question, "But if you can't start them with your starter or your starter doesn't work, then it is necessary to use the crank?", he stated, "Yeah, in some occasions". He further testified that:

> " . . . It was down and I started it and went on and made my rounds and also started that Henthorne well and made my rounds, and came back and the Calvin Hill was down again and I started it again."

. . . .

> "Q: And do you know that you saw evidence of where Mr. Harris had been attempting to start some of the motors there that morning?
>
> "A: That's right.
>
> "Q: Now whether he started them or not, you don't know?
>
> "A: I do not know.
>
> "Q: But you are positive about the fact that he is the only one that was out there that day?
>
> "A: That's right.
>
> "Q: And the tracks and the evidence that you saw around those motors were indicative to you that he had had some kind of trouble at least at one of the wells?
>
> "A: That's right.

. . . .

> "Q: And all of you have, even though the company didn't want you to do that, you do have a crank there for the purpose of starting it if your starter won't work or when you are unable to start it with the self-starter, isn't that correct?
>
> "A: Yes. Well, the cranks come with the engines before we got the starters, electric starters."

Mr. Harris's son testified that on occasion he had seen the deceased crank different ones of the various motors.

As shown in the foregoing recitation and from other facts in evidence, we have the following facts and circumstances in this case, to-wit: (1), According to claimant, the deceased, over a period of 1½ or 2 years, had been going to doctors with chest pains; (2), on the day in question the decedent ostensibly had more than twice as much work to do (some 57 wells to get and/or keep going as against his usual 27), and that, without any help from other workmen; (3), he had to work outside in the accumulated ice and snow, where it was very cold; (4), decedent was the only person who had been out on the lease that day (working and making tracks around) until Polk, after decedent's death was reported, was sent to finish decedent's assignment for the day; (5), the deceased apparently had made a lot of tracks around at least two, possibly three, of the stationary engines; (6), these facts indicated considerable physical activity and movement around the wells by decedent; (7), the employer thought it better for the workmen to use battery-operated starters, then to crank them by hand; (8), according to its production foreman, the employer furnishes battery-operated starters to the men who start and tend its pump-engines to save them from the unusual exertion that is required to crank them and to prevent the men having back injuries, hernias "and things you get with starting engines"; (9), decedent had been provided with such a starter; (10), the gasoline motors were more difficult to start on a cold day; Mr. Sowers, a former Seminole County Sheriff, being a graduate engineer with many years oil-field experience and then Assistant State Labor Commissioner, employer's Superintendent Cooke, Dr. B, Mr. Harris's son and his co-worker, Polk, all testified of effect that cranking such a pump-engine, more especially on a cold day, was strenuous work; (11), even after being started, the engines on occasion would quit and have to be started again (e. g., the Calvin Hill well 1 or 2, that being one of the very wells around which witness Polk found decedent evidently had worked and made a lot of tracks); (12), when the pump-engines could not be started with a battery-operated starter, a workman would have to crank them by hand; (13), that, when he deemed it necessary, deceased would not refrain from cranking the motors out of deference to his condition of health; (14), the cranks were inserted into the motors at about elbow height; (15), this cranking process included removing the spark-plug from the motor, pouring some gasoline into the firing-chamber, replacing the spark-plug, inserting the crank and quickly turning the full weight of the motor by hand with the crank; (16), this would entail having to move and twist and strain and struggle, about, (giving one explanation for all the tracks Polk found when he went on duty); (17), the concern which supplied the employer with the pump-engines furnished cranks with the individual motors, which cranks were stored for use "next time" underneath the respective motors; (18), the decedent experienced the beginning of his cardiac episode between the time he left for work and his return, some 4 hours later; (19), he came home some 5 hours earlier than usual, (under circumstances warranting the State Industrial Court in determining a recognition on his part of some abnormality in his physical condition); (20), decedent's wife found decedent, upon his early arrival home, to be cold, blue and purple around the eyes and around the mouth, complaining of a sharp pain in his chest; (21), acting as a normal wife, concerned for her husband's welfare and based upon her observation of him and his statements, the wife called a physician; (22), Mr. Harris died before the physician arrived; (23), based upon his assumption that decedent had strained himself out in the cold by cranking pump-engines, the physician gave his opinion in evidence that the workman died as a result of his cardiac episode, induced by strain and exertion caused by his unusual activity in conjunction with the elements (severe weather).

The question is, (1), whether the wife in her proof showed enough circumstantial evidence by way of facts and circumstances together with the physician's opinion to demonstrate reasonably to the Industrial Court that claimant's decedent had his coronary attack as a result of his strenuous work, or, if not, (2), whether the wife may lawfully be heard to report to the trial court as a part of the res gestae that her husband, soon after his cardiac episode had commenced but also shortly before his death, then said he had this pain (which he had already reported to her that he had) "while he was working" and, by way of accounting for his blue and purple appearance about the mouth and eyes, further said that "they [the motors] were all frozen up and the starter wouldn't do any good," and that he had "been cranking on this motor," "forty-five minutes", all as a basis for the expression of medical opinion as to cause of deceased's death, or, (3), whether based upon all the foregoing facts and circumstances and alleged "res gestae" evidence claimant may be permitted to recover.

We here note that in our opinion in Young v. Neely, 353 P.2d 111, 113 (Okl.1960), wherein was involved the situation of a workman being discovered lying dead, across the lower wire of a fence located on the lease where he had worked and between an operating motor he apparently had just started and one not operating but toward which he apparently had turned, this Court in sustaining an award in favor of decedent's widow, stated:

> "Strain and exertion arising out of and in the course of employment constitutes ipso facto an accidental injury. Choctaw County v. Bateman, supra [208 Okl. 16, 252 P.2d 465]. It may be proved either by direct or circumstantial evidence alone. In Marby Construction Co. v. Mitchell, Okl., 288 P.2d 1108, 1110, it is stated:
>
> " 'In a workmen's compensation case, it is not required that the claimant shall establish his right to an award by direct evidence alone, or that he produce an eyewitness to the accident. Circumstantial evidence may be used to establish the claim, and it is not necessary that the circumstantial evidence should rise to that degree of certainty as to exclude every reasonable conclusion other than that found by the trial court.' "

From a consideration of all of the facts and circumstances in this case, including but not limited to those heretofore enumerated, we are of the opinion that the award made to the claimant has been reasonably established by direct and circumstantial evidence.

An issue presented by the argument of the parties is whether there was competent evidence that decedent had tried to start a pump engine by hand-cranking which could form the basis for the hypothetical question presented to claimant's expert medical witness that assumed that decedent had made such effort. The employer contends that the activity so described and included in the hypothetical question did not stand established as a fact by competent evidence, direct or circumstantial. The claimant contends that the statements made to her by decedent immediately prior to his death from a coronary occlusion which related the circumstances surrounding the onset of his pain were properly admitted as a part of the res gestae and therefore competent evidence. We agree with the claimant's contention.

In Sand Springs Ry. Co. v. Piggee, 196 Okl. 136, 163 P.2d 545, 547 (1945), we stated:

> "It is sometimes difficult to determine as to whether certain statements which would be otherwise inadmissible under the hearsay rule are admissible as part of res gestae. It may be said generally that in order for such statements to be admissible they must be made at or near the time of the occurrence of the accident, they must have been spontaneously made, they must have been provoked or influenced by the happening of the accident itself so as to become a part thereof; if made in relating a past occurrence or event they are inadmissible. Missouri O. & G.R. Co. v. Adams, 52 Okl. 557, 153 P. 200; Chicago, R.I., & P. R. Co. v. Foltz, 54 Okl. 556, 154 P. 519; Schaff v. Coyle, 121 Okl. 228, 249 P. 947; Sears, Roebuck & Co. v. Robinson, 183 Okl. 253, 80 P.2d 938."

In Henry Chevrolet Co. v. Taylor, 188 Okl. 380, 108 P.2d 1024, 1027 (1941), this Court, in discussing res gestae, stated:

> ". . . It seems clear that the statement was admitted upon the theory that it is a part of the res gestae, and we will confine our discussion to the question of whether the statement was properly admitted under the res gestae rule. This rule has been the subject of much discussion by this and other courts. In some jurisdictions the rule has been given a most strict construction, while in others, of which Oklahoma is one, a more liberal view is taken with regard to the application of the rule. In Margay Oil Corp. v. Jamison, supra [177 Okl. 433, 59 P.2d 790], it was said: 'The question of the admissibility of statements as a part of the res gestae is largely determined by the facts and circumstances of each case, and should in a great measure be left to the determination of the trial court.'
>
> "In view of our numerous decisions upon the question, it is not deemed necessary to enter upon a lengthy discussion of the rule. It is sufficient to say that admission of such statements is justified by the spontaneous nature of the statement, which is in itself a sufficient guarantee of the trustworthiness of such declarations to render them admissible, if they are made under the immediate influence of the occurrence to which they relate, and it is not necessary that the declarations be so strictly contemporaneous with the occurrence to which they relate as to be admissible under the so-called 'verbal act' doctrine, the element of time

> being important only for the purpose of determining whether the declaration was made when the speaker was under the stress of nervous excitement as a result of the occurrence to the extent that the reflective faculties were stilled and the utterance therefore a sincere expression of his actual impressions and belief. See Wigmore on Evidence (2d Ed.) § 1750. This has been the tenor of numerous Oklahoma decisions upon the question. See Gibson Oil Co., et al. v. Westbrooke, 160 Okl. 26, 16 P.2d 127, 129; . . .

. . .

It is clear from the above cited reasoning that this Court through a period of years has approved the admission of statements sought to be introduced as part of the res gestae though not occurring contemporaneously with the main or principal fact. In following this reasoning, we have held that a statement made as much as 1 hour after the act it referred to was admissible as long as the evidence indicated the statement "was provoked and influenced by the happening of the event itself and therefore a part thereof." Huffman v. Gaylor, 267 P.2d 564, 567 (Okl.1954).

. . .

We are of the opinion that the reasoning of the above cited decisions is correct and is controlling in the instant case. Considering the circumstances under which decedent uttered the statements related by claimant concerning the difficulty he experienced in attempting to start an engine at one of the wells and the onset of his pain, we determine that such statements were admissible in evidence. These statements appear to have been made spontaneously in that they were provoked by pain and suffering and made while decedent was in a state of shock immediately prior to his death.

When the claimant saw her husband, who had taken his lunch with him, come home from work at noon, being about five hours before the time he usually returned home, and obviously ill and in pain, her natural reaction would be to inquire as to what was the matter with her husband and what had precipitated such an outwardly manifested condition. The statements of decedent in response thereto appear to have been the usual and natural expressions and exclamations of such person and spontaneous manifestations of his bodily condition naturally flowing from such condition as opposed to being deliberate, narrative descriptions of past events. Such statements were seemingly induced by the occurrence of the events surrounding the occasion and spoken while decedent was under the influence of pain, shock and excitement and at the point of death.

In view of the above cited decisions, we hold that the testimony of the claimant was properly received.

As this testimony was the basis of the hypothetical question propounded to Dr. B, the employer's contention that such question was based on facts not properly in evidence cannot be sustained.

Further, as above intimated, it is clear that claimant's evidence was sufficient to sustain the award of the Industrial Court. . . .

Award sustained.

PEOPLE OF THE STATE OF NEW YORK v. MARKS

Court of Appeals of New York, 1959.
6 N.Y.2d 67, 160 N.E.2d 26.

VAN VOORHIS, Judge. Appellant has been convicted of murder in the second degree for having shot and killed one Pickens on June 16, 1955, in the basement of 254–256 West 146th Street, New York City. The Appellate Division has affirmed. The verdict of the jury is supported by evidence. Appellant advances two points (1) that the trial court erroneously excluded evidence of a declaration by the victim exculpating appellant, and (2) that the prosecutor made prejudicial statements in his summary to the jury. These points are discussed in the order named.

Patrolman Muldoon testified that at 10:30 a. m. on the day of the homicide he was directed by radio to drive his patrol car immediately to 260 West 146th Street, where the wounded man had been seen by a person who notified the police. On his way to that address, Muldoon observed that a crowd had gathered around 2742 Eighth Avenue, where he stopped his car and found Pickens lying in the vestibule. He was suffering from a gunshot wound in his left chest which was bleeding. Muldoon had a conversation with Pickens and then took him to the Harlem Hospital where they arrived at 10:40 a. m. There is evidence that the shooting occurred at 10:25 a. m. which was five minutes before the notification of Muldoon, who testified that he talked to Pickens within a minute afterward. According to this evidence, Pickens' statement to Officer Muldoon was made six minutes after he had been shot. Muldoon testified that he asked Pickens by whom he had been shot, and wrote the answer on a card which became part of the records of the Police Department. He was interrogated upon the witness stand by defense counsel: "Q. Did you write on that aided card that the deceased was shot by one Edward Small?" An objection to this question was sustained. The officer testified that Pickens gave no indication that he was in fear of death at the time. Defense counsel offered the card in evidence, which was deemed marked for identification. This offer was made as a business record of the Police Department under Section 374–a of the Civil Practice Act, but objections to the offer and to oral testimony of Pickens' declaration were sustained. No question has been raised concerning the form of the proof and the ruling of the court was based on the inadmissibility of any statement by Pickens under these circumstances. It is assumed that Pickens told Officer Muldoon that he had been shot by Edward Small.

Appellant's first point is that this declaration by the deceased apparently exculpating defendant should have been received in evidence as a spontaneous declaration under People v. Del Vermo, 192 N.Y. 470, 85 N.E. 690, 692 (1908). There the defendant was charged with having fatally stabbed one Tony Page in the abdomen. According to the testimony of the principal witness, they were walking on Dominick Street in Rome, New York, three abreast, Tony Page being between defendant and the witness. Defendant told Tony Page, according to this witness, that he had had connection with Page's wife and was going to have connection again. "If you want to come and see," said the defendant, "I will go just right now." Tony Page responded with an epithet at which the defendant laughed, they walked together a further distance of about two blocks, when the witness saw defendant run and exclaimed: "What is the matter with that fellow?" Page walked forward four or five steps and dropped to the sidewalk. The witness inquired, "What is the matter?" and Page answered, "Del Vermo stabbed me with a knife." The witness helped him to his home where Page's wife met him, and there Page repeated in response to her inquiry: "Del Vermo stabbed me with a knife", stating that he had been killed. Page died as the result of the wound within several hours. The witness had not seen him stabbed. At the trial the first declaration made to the witness immediately after the stabbing, when Page dropped to the sidewalk, was admitted into evidence as a spontaneous declaration. The later declaration made in the presence of his wife in the house, accompanied by the exclamation "Oh! my poor children! I am going to die. What are my children going to do after this?" was admitted as a dying declaration. Later, statements to others were admitted as dying declarations.

It is not contended that appellant's exculpation by the victim was admissible as a dying declaration. Officer Muldoon testified that Pickens did not indicate that he thought that he was going to die. The holding in the Del Vermo case, supra, about spontaneous declarations is addressed to our attention.

Professor Wigmore has analyzed this subject with his usual clarity, distinguishing spontaneous declarations from the doctrine of *res gestae*. The latter refers to verbal acts, forming part of the transaction itself. A spontaneous declaration, upon the other hand, is a true exception to the hearsay rule (Wigmore, Evidence, § 1745). It is a narrative of a past transaction, although usually of a transaction occurring immediately before. The basis of this exception to the hearsay rule is that the spontaneity of declarations of this kind gives more assurance of veracity than is true of the usual hearsay declaration. Wigmore says (§ 1747, subd. [I]): "This general principle is based on the experience that, under certain circumstances of physical shock, a stress of nervous excitement may be produced which stills the reflective faculties and removes their control . . .. Since this utterance is made under the immediate and uncontrolled domination of the senses, and during the brief period when considerations of self-interest could not have been brought fully to bear by reasoned reflection, the utterance may be taken as particularly trustworthy (or, at least, as lacking the usual grounds of untrustworthiness), and thus as expressing the real tenor of the speaker's belief as to the facts just observed by him; and may therefore be received as testimony to those facts. The ordinary situation presenting these conditions is an affray or a railroad accident. But the principle itself is a broad one."

It was tersely stated by Bleckley, C. J., in Travelers' Ins. Co. v. Sheppard, 85 Ga. 751, 775–776, 12 S.E. 18, 26 (1890), that "What the law altogether distrusts is not after-speech, but after-thought . . . That [the declarations] shall be or appear to be spontaneous is indispensable, and it is for this reason alone that they are required to be speedy."

Wigmore says that there can be no definite or fixed limit of time within which the declaration shall have been made, that each case must depend upon its own circumstances (§ 1750), adding that the utterance must have been before there has been time to contrive and misrepresent, i. e., while the nervous excitement may be supposed still to dominate and the reflective powers to be yet in abeyance. In this context, it may be appropriate to cite the often repeated language of Judge Vann, speaking for the unanimous court in People v. Gilbert, 199 N.Y. 10, 24, 92 N.E. 85, 89 (1910), concerning what constitutes premeditation and deliberation: "While the time for reflection is not measured in minutes or seconds, it is measured by facts. The time must be long enough to make a choice, as the result of thought and reflection, and to act upon the choice thus made. It is obviously impossible to measure this period by the ordinary method of measuring time and, hence, it is necessary to measure it by what must be done". Many cases are cited by Wigmore, in some of which the time interval is shorter and in others longer than in the case at bar. The passage which has been quoted from Wigmore is important not only on account of his authority and clarity, but also for the reason that it was followed in People v. Del Vermo, supra. Wigmore's distinction is recognized in Del Vermo between spontaneous declarations and the narrower meaning of *res gestae*, and the first declaration by Page but not the later ones was held to have been properly admitted on account of its spontaneity, immediately after Page fell to the sidewalk.

. . .

The Court of General Sessions gave this reason for excluding the declaration by Pickens in the instant case: "As I understand the theory, a declaration of a decedent, even if made in response to an inquiry, would be admissible, provided the element of spontaneity was present; that the statement is made so impulsively as to exclude the element of reflected fabrication. On the present state of the record, however, there has necessarily been such a lapse of time as to permit, on the part of the now deceased, a period within which he had an opportunity to reflect and to contrive, and this necessarily destroys the basic ground upon which such a statement might be conceivably introduced under the theory of the Del Vermo case, and I want the record clearly to show the grounds for the Court's rulings with respect to these alleged statements by the deceased."

According to appellant, Pickens was still subject to the nervous excitement and physical shock of having been shot, which is claimed to have stilled his reflective faculties and removed their control. In support of this view is evidence that Pickens was interrogated by Officer Muldoon six minutes after he had been shot. Assuming the time interval to have been as brief as this, a number of events occurred before decedent's conversation with Officer Muldoon. After having been shot in the basement of 254–256 West 146th Street, he was seen in the hallway of the adjacent building, 260 West 146th Street; to have reached there he must have climbed down a 3-foot ledge, mounted a flight of 15 steps, and walked, in all, about 100 feet. In the hallway, he spoke to a woman, but what he said was stricken from the record on motion of counsel for defendant. He was later seen lying in the vestibule of 2742 Eighth Avenue, where he was interrogated by Officer Muldoon. To have arrived at that location, he must have walked down the steps at 260 West 146th Street, about 45 feet westward on 146th Street, and then gone 50 feet southward on Eighth Avenue. There he was able to talk to the officer.

The People argue that his statement to Officer Muldoon implicating another man than defendant was the product of reflection. The decedent had reason to fabricate a story. He was a narcotic addict recently released from prison. Several days before the shooting he had robbed defendant of several packages of heroin. It is quite possible that in view of defendant's pugnacity, his possession of a gun and his well-merited grievance, Pickens may have feared future violence at defendant's hands. Pickens was not then anticipating death as a result of his wounds, and may have been wary of what defendant might do to him afterward if he were publicly to have charged him with armed assault.

Appellant's brief appears to concede that the circumstances under which this declaration was made are open to different interpretations concerning its spontaneity. It is urged that the declaration should have been received in evidence in any event, and the question of its spontaneity submitted to the jury like the voluntariness of a confession under Section 395 of the Code of Criminal Procedure (People v. Kennedy, 159 N.Y. 346, 54 N.E. 51 (1899); People v. Cassidy, 133 N.Y. 612, 30 N.E. 1003 (1892); People v. Fernandez, 301 N.Y. 302, 93 N.E.2d 859 (1950)). A decision is cited in the intermediate appellate court in California (People v. Keelin, 136 Cal.App.2d 860, 289 P.2d 520 (1972); Annotation 56 A.L.R.2d 372) where the spontaneity of a declaration was held to have been correctly submitted to a jury, under instructions that they were to disregard it if found not to have been spontaneous.

That California decision is contrary to the practice in New York State, where the established rule is that it is for the court and not the jury to decide questions of fact preliminary to determining the admissibility of evidence (Harris v. Wilson, 7 Wend. 57 (1831); Jones v. Hurlburt, 39 Barb. 403, 410 (1863); Roberge v. Winne, 144 N.Y. 709, 715, 39 N.E. 631, 633 (1895); Richardson, Evidence, § 195). In Roberge v. Winne, this court was confronted with conflicting testimony concerning whether a document offered in evidence was proper to be received. The opinion of the General Term is printed in the Court of Appeals Reports, where the affirmance was without majority opinion, stating: "It is apparent, therefore, that, before the paper offered could have been admitted the court had to decide a preliminary question of fact whether the plaintiff had such knowledge of the contents of the unsigned paper as to make it binding upon him as evidence; and, in deciding this question against the defendant, we cannot say, as matter of law, that the learned judge was in error."

. . .

This New York rule is not only well grounded in practice but is also sound in principle. The admissibility of evidence may depend upon complicated, collateral fact issues, which would be confusing in jury trials. If, in addition to the questions of fact which are directly involved, any number of collateral issues must be tried in order to determine the admissibility of evidence upon the principal issue, it would obstruct rather than facilitate the administration of justice.

Submission to juries of the voluntariness of confessions by defendants in criminal cases is an exception to this general rule. The reason for making the exception is apparent. In such instances the confession or admission relates to the subject matter of the criminal action being tried, and the only collateral question is whether it was coerced by force or fear. That, in itself, has a bearing on the guilt or innocence of a defendant. An alleged confession or admission represents an endeavor to prove the charge at issue out of a defendant's mouth. It is advanced to prove recognition by the person charged with the crime that he himself did all or some of the things which constitute the crime charged. The voluntariness of such an admission or confession by a defendant is so intimately related to the merits of the controversy that it has become natural to submit to juries, along with the other issues on trial, whether defendants actually did say or write the damaging material which is ascribed to them. That is different from submitting to juries collateral issues of fact on which depend the admissibility of declarations by third parties.

In the case of dying declarations, it is held that "Whether the declarations were made in apprehension of death, and after the declarant had lost all hope of recovery, is to be determined by the judge" (Follett, J., People v. Kraft, 91 Hun 474, 475, 36 N.Y.S. 1034, 1035 (1896), affirmed 148 N.Y. 631, 43 N.E. 80). "The trial judge must determine, not only from the conversation of the declarant, but from the surrounding circumstances, that there is clear proof showing the certainty of speedy death and that the declarant had no hope of recovery. People v. Ludkowitz, 266 N.Y. 233, 239, 194 N.E. 688, [690] (1935)." (People v. Smith, 245 App.Div. 69, 71, 281 N.Y.S. 294, 299 (1935)). In Ludkowitz this court said (266 N.Y. 239, 194 N.E. 690 (1935)): "Whether the preliminary proof advanced is sufficient to admit the receipt in evidence of a dying declaration presents in each case a question which must be determined by the trial judge." Kraft and Del Vermo, supra, are cited as authority for this conclusion, along with People v. Smith, 104 N.Y. 491, 10 N.E. 873 (1887), in which it was held on the principal point of law in the case that it is the function of the court, and not of the jury, to rule upon preliminary questions of fact affecting the admissibility of dying declarations.

Although we are not here dealing with a dying declaration, the same principle applies that it is in the province of the court and not of the jury (as contended by appellant) to decide preliminary questions of fact on which the admissibility of the declaration depends. That applies in the case of alleged spontaneous declarations as it does to dying declarations. The law would be inconsistent if in the one kind of declaration preliminary fact questions were to be decided by the judge and in the other by the jury. On the record in this case it cannot be held that the Trial Judge erred as matter of law in finding the preliminary fact to be that the declaration of this homicidal victim lacked spontaneity, and that sufficient time had elapsed under the circumstances so that it could have been a reflective fabrication. The Trial Judge found that Pickens had opportunity to reflect and to contrive, which destroys the foundation upon which such declaration could be introduced under the Del Vermo decision.

It is argued for respondent that the evidence establishes as matter of law that Pickens had opportunity to reflect and to contrive before making this declaration, so that no preliminary question of fact was presented for the trial court to decide in ruling on the People's objection to the introduction of this declaration. We do not need to decide on that aspect, inasmuch as even if a preliminary question of fact was presented, it was resolved against appellant by the trial court.

. . .

The judgment of conviction should be affirmed.

. . .

Judgment affirmed.

DECISIONS RELATING TO CHAPTER IX, HEARSAY—DYING DECLARATION EXCEPTION

THRASHER v. BOARD OF MEDICAL EXAMINERS OF STATE OF CALIFORNIA

District Court of Appeal, First District, Division 1, California, 1919.
44 Cal.App. 26, 185 P. 1006.

. . .

Appeal from Superior Court, City and County of San Francisco; Thomas F. Graham, Judge.

. . .

RICHARDS, J. This is an appeal from a judgment of the superior court made and entered upon the hearing of a writ of review, setting aside and annulling an order of the board of medical examiners of the state of California purporting to find and adjudge the respondent guilty of unprofessional conduct, and to revoke his license to practice medicine in this state.

The respondent was charged before said board of medical examiners with unprofessional conduct under the first subdivision of section 14 of the Medical Practice Act, which provides that such unprofessional conduct shall consist in "the procuring or aiding or abetting or attempting or agreeing or offering to procure a criminal abortion." The respondent appeared before said board upon said charge and a hearing was had, during the course of which certain essential evidence in support of said charge was admitted over the objection of respondent as to its competency. At the conclusion of the hearing the said board adjudged the respondent guilty of the said charge, and ordered his license to practice medicine revoked. Thereupon the respondent applied for a writ of review to the superior court which, upon the hearing on said writ, annulled the said judgment and order of the board of medical examiners, whereupon the latter have prosecuted this appeal.

The chief contention of the respondent at the hearing upon said writ and also upon this appeal is that the board of medical examiners received in evidence over his objection certain hearsay evidence which was not admissible under the rules with regard to the admission of evidence by which said board of medical examiners must be governed in proceedings before it. Section 14 of the Medical Practice Act, as amended in 1915 (Stats.1915, pp. 196, 197), provides in respect to such cases that "if the charges on their face be deemed sufficient by the board, and issue be joined thereon by answer, the board shall proceed to determine the matter, and to that end shall hear such proper evidence as may be adduced before it." In the case of Englebretson v. Industrial Accident Commission, 170 Cal. 793, 151 Pac. 421 (1915), the

Supreme Court of this state, in construing the terms of the statute then in force in relation to the rules of evidence governing hearings before said commission (which was much more broad and liberal than the terms of the Medical Practice Act above quoted), held that hearsay evidence was inadmissible upon hearings before tribunals of that character, and annulled the award of said commission because of its error in the admission of such evidence. In the later case of Connolly v. Industrial Accident Commission, 173 Cal. 405, 160 Pac. 239 (1916), this ruling was affirmed.

We have no doubt that the principle enunciated in these cases is to be given full application to hearings before the board of medical examiners, in view of the language of the statute above quoted, which limits the power of said board to the hearing only of "such proper evidence as may be adduced before it." In the case of Englebretson v. Industrial Accident Com., supra, it was further held that where the ruling of the inferior tribunal upon an essential element in the case was based solely upon the hearsay evidence which had been thus improperly admitted, the judgment of such tribunal would be annulled upon a writ of review. In the instant case it is admitted that an essential element in the case necessary to be established by competent evidence was the fact of the pregnancy of the woman upon whom the respondent performed the operation. It is the contention of the respondent herein that the only substantial evidence upon this essential element in the case was wholly hearsay, and particularly that the chief evidence upon this point consisted in a written statement in the nature of a dying declaration made and signed by the patient a short while before her death. We have examined carefully the record before us, and find that this contention of the respondent as to the state of the evidence must be sustained, and that aside from said written statement of the woman there is not only a dearth of evidence of her pregnancy in the record, but that upon that feature of the case the testimony of the autopsy surgeon strongly supports the respondent's claim that the woman was not in fact pregnant when the operation, which was in the nature of a curettement, was performed.

The question then remains as to whether the written but unsworn statement of the deceased woman was admissible upon the hearing before the board of medical examiners, either as a dying declaration or upon any other theory which would take it out of the objection to it as hearsay. That it was not admissible in this particular proceeding as a dying declaration the authorities seem uniform and clear, holding that such declarations are inadmissible except in criminal cases of homicide, and never in civil actions or proceedings. Code Civ.Proc. § 1870, subd. 4; Jones on Evidence, § 330, 2; 21 Cyc. 981, and cases cited; People v. Hall, 94 Cal. 595, 30 Pac. 7 (1892). It is in fact conceded by the appellants herein that the statement in question was not admissible as a dying declaration, but it is insisted by the appellants that it was admissible upon another ground and under subdivision 3 of Section 1870, Code of Civil Procedure, as "the act or declaration of another, in the presence and within the observation of a party, and his conduct in relation thereto." The record of the proceedings had before the board of medical examiners does in fact disclose that the written statement of the respondent's patient was read in the respondent's presence and hearing while she was in the hospital and near to death, but it also discloses that while said statement was being read the respondent interrupted it several times with questions and assertions amounting to denials of its truth, and also produced a statement of his own regarding the case which the woman had already signed as correct, in which it was asserted by him that the patient had already had a miscarriage before coming to him for treatment. To such a state of the record the language of the Supreme Court in the case of People v. Teshara, 134 Cal. 542, 66 Pac. 798 (1901), has exact and special application. The court there says:

> "The court also erred in refusing to strike out the evidence of Patton and Mullen as to the accusation made by Loucks, when Amaya and defendant were brought to his bedside. The statement made by Loucks at that time was hearsay, and Teshara made no admission of its truth, either expressly or tacitly. He expressly denied it. The court and the district attorney seem to have lost sight of the fact that it is not the accusation, but the conduct of the accused, that is evidence in such cases, and that the only reason for admitting the accusation is to explain the conduct. The district attorney should not have offered this evidence, knowing, as he did, that Teshara had not remained silent under the accusation, but had repelled it at the time it was made."

See, also, People v. Ah Yute, 54 Cal. 89 (1880); People v. Hartwell, 175 Pac. 21 (1918).

It will thus be seen that the unsworn statement of the woman as to her state of pregnancy at the time of the respondent's treatment of her case was not competent evidence of the fact of such pregnancy, and that the respondent's acts and conduct in respect thereto cannot be held to amount to an admission of the truth of her statement in that regard. It follows that there was no sufficient evidence before the board of medical examiners upon that essential feature of the case to justify it in finding the respondent guilty upon the charge before it and in making its order revoking his license to practice medicine. The trial court was therefore correct in its ruling that such finding and order were unsupported by evidence, and hence beyond the jurisdiction of said board.

Judgment affirmed.

We concur: KERRIGAN, J.; BEASLY, Presiding Judge pro tem.

PEOPLE v. SARZANO

Court of Appeals of New York, 1914.
212 N.Y. 231, 100 N.E. 87.

PER CURIAM. The appellant was convicted of the crime of murder in the first degree in Erie county, on February 28, 1913. He shot Saverio Gragnanello November 17, 1912, at Buffalo. Gragnanello died January 22, 1913, as the result of the shooting, as the jury found.

The trial court erred in receiving in evidence as a dying declaration the statement made by the deceased on November 17, 1912, after he had been taken to the hospital. The statement was made to Dr. George B. Stocker, who was the deputy medical examiner for Erie county. Dr. Stocker told the deceased "that his condition was critical, and we expected he would die from the way he was, and we wanted his statement for use later." "I talked to him and told him the condition he was in and that he was going to die, and I wanted an ante mortem statement for purposes that might arise later." The deceased said, "All right," he would give it, and made statements, which were written down and read to him by Dr. Stocker. The written statement was:

> "Dying declaration of Salvita Greniera made on the 17th day of November, 1912, at Emergency Hospital in the city of Buffalo, county of Erie, to Geo. B. Stocker, deputy medical examiner of said county.
>
> "He says: I consider my condition critical, and am under the influence of an impression that I am about to die, and have no hopes of my recovery from the effects of my wound. I make this statement under that impression.
>
> "I live at 164–8 Erie street and am a saloonkeeper by occupation. My wife was in back room of saloon and this man Mike by name and I do not know his last name went back to this room and I went back there and asked him what he wanted and told him to go out. He drew a gun and said he would shoot me. I asked him what he wanted to shoot for and again told him to go out. He immediately shot me five times. Then he ran out of the back door. I never had any trouble with him before. He was not drunk. This was between seven and eight o'clock to-night.
>
> his
> "Salvitas X Greniera."
> mark

The objection to its admission, "on the ground there is nothing in evidence except the statement which the doctor wrote that showed he thought he was going to die, and that his death was to be speedy," was overruled with an exception.

The learned district attorney seems confident that the statement was admissible. He points out the three wounds; that the deceased was about to undergo an operation; that a doctor told him he was in a critical condition, and they did not expect him to live; and that he stated he was under the influence of an impression or under an impression that he was about to die. The statements of the district attorney must, however, be modified in these particulars: There is no proof that the deceased knew that he was about to undergo an operation, or that the person talking to him was a doctor, or that he stated that he was under the impression that he was about to die. The statement was upon a printed blank, and the only affirmative statements of the deceased it contains are those including and following the words "I live at 164–8 Erie street." Above those the blanks of the printed form were properly filled, and the entire statement read to him, and he said it was true.

The principle upon which dying declarations are received in evidence is that the mind, impressed with the awful idea of approaching dissolution, acts under a sanction equally powerful with that which it is presumed to feel by a solemn appeal to God upon an oath. The declarations, therefore, of a person dying under such circumstances are considered as equivalent to the evidence of the living witness upon oath. Commonwealth v. Roberts, 108 Mass. 296 (1871). Safety in receiving such declarations lies only in the fact that the declarant is so controlled by a belief that his death is certain and imminent that malice, hatred, passion, and other feelings of like nature are overwhelmed and banished by it. The evidence should be clear that the declarations were made under a sense of impending death without any hope of recovery. People v. Conklin, 175 N.Y. 333, 67 N.E. 624 (1903). Statements made by a doctor to and accepted by a declarant that there was no chance of his recovering are admissible. Commonwealth v. Brewer, 164 Mass. 577, 42 N.E. 92 (1895); Brotherton v. People, 75 N.Y. 159 (1878). If the declarant thinks there is a slight chance of living, the declarations are inadmissible. Commonwealth v. Roberts, 108 Mass. 296 (1871); Commonwealth v. Haney, 127 Mass. 455 (1879). The mere fact that the doctor told declarant that recovery was impossible is insufficient. There must be proof that the declarant believed it and had no hope of recovery. Peak v. State, 50 N.J.Law, 179, 12 Atl. 701 (1888); People v. Chase, 79 Hun, 296, 29 N.Y.Supp. 376 (1894), affirmed 143 N.Y. 669, 39 N.E. 21; People v. Evans, 40 Hun, 492 (1886). Declarant's certainty that he is about to die and lack of all hope of recovery may be proven by his express language or conduct, or inferred from his physical condition and obvious danger, or evidence of his acquiescence in the opinions of doctors or others stated to him, or other adequate circumstances. Williams v. State, 168 Ind. 87, 79 N.E. 1079 (1907); State v. Sullivan, 20 R.I. 114, 37 Atl. 673 (1897).

In the present case the preliminary proof was too slight and indefinite to justify the admission of the statement. The transaction, apart from the wounds, was this: A strange man said to the deceased when received at the hospital that his condition was critical and he was going to die, and they wanted an ante mortem statement for purposes that might arise later, and the deceased said "All right," he would give it, and the statement that he made the statement under "the influence of an impression that I am about to die, and have no hopes of my recovery from the effects of my wounds. I make this statement under that impression"—was read over to him with the other parts of the statement, and said by him to be true. The declarant did not ask for wife, children, friends, or priest or by word or act indicate that he believed his death certain and imminent. He did not say or show that he believed he would not recover and was without any hope whatsoever of living. It would be extending the rule beyond the decision in any case we have read or found, and we think beyond safety, to approve the reception in evidence of the statement. But we do not think we should reverse the judgment because of its reception. The guilt of the defendant was fully proven without it. It, in fact, added nothing to the case. The facts stated in it were proven aliunde and with great fullness and detail. It is inconceivable that the verdict of the jury would have been different had it been rejected.

The judgment of conviction should be affirmed.

. . .

Judgment of conviction affirmed.

BROWN v. THE COMMONWEALTH

Supreme Court of Pennsylvania, 1873.
73 Pa. 321, 13 Am.Rep. 740.

. . .

March 7th 1873. Before READ, C. J., AGNEW, SHARSWOOD and MERCUR, JJ. WILLIAMS, J., at Nisi Prius.

Error to the Criminal Court of Schuylkill county: No. 78, to January Term 1873.

. . .

The opinion of the court was delivered, April 5th 1873, by

READ, C. J. This is a writ of error to the Criminal Court of Schuylkill county, sued out under the Act of the 15th February 1870, upon the oath of the defendant, and brings up the whole record.

The constitutionality and jurisdiction of this court have been finally settled in Commonwealth v. Green, 8 P. F. Smith 226, and in Commonwealth v. Hipple, 19 Id. 9, and its concurrent jurisdiction with the Courts of Quarter Sessions of the Peace and Oyer and Terminer and General Jail Delivery of the County of Schuylkill, is fully recognised and established by the Act of 22d April 1870 (Pamph. L. 1254), and the court below were therefore right on overruling the plea to the jurisdiction, entered by the defendant.

On the preliminary hearing before the committing magistrate, the defendant and his counsel being present, a witness was examined whose testimony was taken down by defendant's counsel, and the witness having died before the trial, the notes of his evidence proved by the counsel under oath, were offered in evidence, objected to and admitted. It was objected that by the Constitution of the state, the defendant was entitled to meet the witnesses face to face.

The doctrine on this subject is thus laid down in the 3d volume of Russell on Crimes, by Greaves, 4th edition, 1865, page 249. "If there has been a previous criminal prosecution between the same parties, and the point in issue was the same, the testimony of a deceased witness, given upon oath at the former trial, is admissible on the subsequent trial, and may be proved by any one who heard him give evidence," and the same is repeated at page 424, in the note. We find the same rule in 1 Phillips & Arnold's Evidence, pp. 306–7, and in 1 Pitt Taylor on Evidence, 4th edition, 1864, pp. 445, 447. Dr. Wharton, in his valuable Treatise on Criminal Law in the United States, vol. 1, p. 667, says: "The testimony of a deceased witness given at a former trial or examination may be proved at a subsequent trial by persons who heard him testify. Even the notes of counsel of the testimony of such witness on a former trial between the same parties, touching the same subject-matter, are evidence when proved to be correct in substance, although the counsel does not recollect the testimony independently of his notes. The better opinion seems to be that it is sufficient to prove the substance of what the deceased witness said, provided the material particulars are stated, though it has been sometimes held, that unless the precise words could be given, the testimony would be rejected."

In The Commonwealth v. Richards, 18 Pick. 434 (1836), it was held that the 12th article of the Declaration of Rights, which provides that in criminal cases the accused shall have the right "to meet the witnesses against him face to face," is not violated by the admission of testimony in a criminal trial before a jury to prove what a deceased witness testified at the preliminary examination of the accused before a justice of the peace."

This case was affirmed seven years afterwards in Warren v. Nichols, in 6 Metc. 261 (1843), and the further ruling in that case "that the whole of the testimony of the deceased witness upon the point in question, and the *precise words used by him* must be proved," was substantially affirmed. Hubbard, Justice, dissented from this ruling and assigned very cogent reasons against it. "As the decision now stands," says this able judge, "it prescribes a rule for the admission of testimony, which the imperfection of our nature, in the construction of our memories, will not warrant. It in truth excludes the thing it proposes to admit, and at the same time opens a door for knaves to enter, where honest men cannot approach." "Other learned judges have maintained, that a rule so rigid was unwise, and I confess, I prefer the reasoning of Gibson, J., in the case of Cornell v.

Green, 10 S. & R. 16, to that of the learned judge in Commonwealth v. Richards, and with him agrees also the learned author of the Treatise on the Law of Evidence." 1 Greenl. § 165.

Upon this subject the ablest discussion of the whole question is to be found in the opinion of Judge Drummond, in The United States v. Macomb, 5 McLane's Rep. 286, delivered in the Circuit Court of the United States for the District of Illinois, at July Term 1851. At the preliminary examination, a witness, since deceased, testified in relation to the offence, which was robbing the mail. The accused was present and his counsel cross-examined the witness. Witnesses were permitted on a trial before a jury, under an indictment found for the same offence, to prove what the deceased witness testified to at the preliminary examination. It is sufficient in such case to prove substantially, all that the deceased witness testified upon the particular subject of inquiry. A decision upon the same point is to be found in United States v. White, 5 Cranch's Circuit Court Rep. 460.

The 6th article of the amendments to the Constitution of the United States provides that in all criminal prosecutions the accused shall enjoy the right "to be confronted with the witnesses against him."

The Constitution of Pennsylvania of 1776, provided "that in all prosecutions for criminal offences, a man hath a right to be confronted with the witnesses." The Declaration of Rights, in the Constitution of 1790, changed the phraseology from confronting, to "to meet the witnesses face to face."

The doctrine enunciated by Judge Drummond in 1851, was followed by the Supreme Court of Missouri, after a very exhaustive argument on the constitutional question, in The State v. McO'Blenis, in 24 Missouri (3 Jones) 402, and The State v. Baker, Id. 437, in 1857, and in The State v. Houser, 26 Missouri (5 Jones 431), in 1858, and by the Supreme Court of Ohio in Summons v. The State, in 5 Ohio (N.S.) 325, in 1856.

In this state the most liberal rule has been adopted, in relation to the evidence of what was testified to by a deceased witness on a former trial or examination, as will be seen by referring to Cornell v. Green, 10 S. & R. 14; Chess v. Chess, 17 Id. 409; Moore v. Pearson, 6 W. & S. 50, and Rhine v. Robinson, 3 Casey 30, in which case Chief Justice Lewis said: "The notes of counsel, showing what a deceased witness testified to on a former trial between the same parties touching the same subject-matter, are evidence when proved to be correct in substance, although the counsel did not recollect the testimony independent of his notes, and although he did not recollect the cross-examination." To which may be added the decision in Phila. & Reading R. R. v. Spearen, 11 Wright 306 (1849), the opinion being delivered by my brother Agnew.

There was, therefore, no error in the court admitting the notes of Mr. McCool of the testimony of Ewing, a deceased witness, in the examination before the committing magistrate, or the notes of any other counsel, or those of the committing magistrate himself.

"Upon the trial of any indictment for murder, or voluntary manslaughter, it shall and may be lawful for the defendant or defendants to except to any decision of the court, upon any point of evidence or law, which exception shall be noted by the court, and filed of record as in civil cases, and a writ of error to the Supreme Court may be taken by the defendant or defendants after conviction and sentence." "If, during the trial upon any indictment for murder or voluntary manslaughter, the court shall be required by the defendant or defendants to give an opinion upon any point submitted and stated in writing, it shall be the duty of the court to answer the same fully and file the point and answer, with the records of the case:" Criminal Procedure Act of 31st March 1860, §§ 57, 58, Pamph.L. 444.

Under this head is ranged the reception under objection of the dying declarations of Mrs. Kraemer, the wife of the murdered man. "The dying declarations of a person who expects to die, respecting the circumstances under which he received a mortal injury, are constantly admitted in criminal prosecutions, where the death is the subject of criminal inquiry, though the prosecution be for manslaughter; though the accused was not present when they were made, and had no opportunity for cross-examination, and against or in favor of the party charged with the death." "When every hope of this world is gone, when every motive to falsehood is silenced, and the mind is induced by the most powerful considerations to speak the truth, a situation so solemn and awful is considered by the law as creating the most impressive of sanctions." 1 Wharton's Criminal Law, § 669; 3 Russell by Greaves 250; 1 Greenleaf, §§ 156, 162, 346; 1 Taylor on Evidence 616.

"The constitutional provision," says Dr. Wharton, "that the accused shall be confronted by the witnesses against him does not *abrogate* the common law principle, that the declarations *in extremis* of the murdered person in such cases are admissible in evidence:" Id.

In Woodsides v. The State, 2 Howard 655 (Miss.1837), the court, at p. 665, in answer to the constitutional objection that the prisoner had a right to be confronted with the witness against him, say: "But it is upon the ground alone, that the murdered individual is not a witness, that his declarations made *in extremis* can be offered in evidence upon the trial of the accused. If he were or could be a witness, his declaration upon the clearest principle would be inadmissible. His declarations are regarded as facts or circumstances connected with the murder, which, when they are established by oral testimony, the law has declared to be evidence. It is the individual who swears to the statements of the deceased that is the witness, not the deceased." In Anthony v. The State of Tennessee, 1 Meigs 277 (1838), the court say, upon the first ground of objection, "We are all of opinion that the Bill of Rights cannot be construed to prevent declarations properly made *in articulo mortis* from being given in evidence against defendants in cases of homicide."

The same doctrine is to be found in The State of Iowa v. Nash, 7 Iowa 347 (1859), and in Robbins v. State of Ohio, 8 Ohio St.R. (N.S.) 131 (1857); Com. v. Casey, 11 Cushing 417 (1853), and very directly in Com. v. Carey, 12 Id. 246. There are also various statements to the same effect in most of the decisions cited above in relation to the admission of evidence of the testimony of a deceased witness.

All these cases are confined to the dying declarations of the murdered person upon the trial of the individual accused of the murder. At the York assizes on the 17th July 1837, in Rex v. Baker, 2 Moo. & Rob. 53, it was held, on an indictment against a prisoner for the murder of A. by poison, which was also taken by B., who died in consequence, that B.'s dying declarations were admissible. Coltman, J., after consulting Parke, B., expressed himself of opinion that as it was all one transaction, the declarations were admissible, and accordingly allowed them to go to the jury, but he said he would reserve the point for the opinion of the judges. The prisoner was acquitted. This case is entitled to greater weight, as Baron Parke, the year before, in Stobart v. Dryden, 1 Mees. & Welsby 615, had been considering the question of dying declarations, after full argument, and delivered the opinion of the court. This case is mentioned in 1 Phillips and Arnold 243, in 3 Russell 268; 1 Taylor on Evidence 618.

In The State v. Terrell, 12 Richardson 321 (S.C.1866), it was held upon the trial of an indictment for the murder of A. by poison, which was taken at the same time by B. and C., both of whom as well as A. died from its effects, the dying declarations of B. are admissible against the prisoner, although the general rule seems to be, that dying declarations are admissible only, where the indictment is for the murder of the party making the declarations. The murder was effected by putting strychnine in a bottle of whiskey, administered by the defendant, at the same time, to three persons, and caused the deaths of the grandfather and uncle of the prisoner, and of a third person, whose dying declarations were received in evidence upon the trial of the accused for the murder of his grandfather.

Upon the authority of these cases the learned judge admitted the dying declarations of the wife, upon the trial of the defendant for the murder of her husband. In this there was error, for the husband was found dead on Monday morning 26th Feb. 1872, three hundred yards from his dwelling, and his wife was discovered on the same morning lying across her bed in the house in an insensible condition and with her face and head terribly beaten and disfigured. Kraemer and his wife were both advanced in years and there was no doubt that robbery of gold and silver which was known to be in the house led to their murder, but we do not see any facts that would bring these dying declarations of Mrs. Kraemer within those two authorities, supposing them to be good law.

If the prisoner had been tried upon the indictment for the murder of Mrs. Kraemer, her dying declarations would have been strictly legal evidence against him.

The array of grand and petit jurors was challenged from their being drawn from a jury-wheel not secured according to law. By the existing law two jury commissioners are elected triennially, who are substituted for the county commissioners, and who with the law judges and the sheriff perform the duties prescribed by the 2d section of the Act of 10th April 1867 (Pamph.L. 62), who shall "place the names of the persons so selected in the proper jury-wheel, and the said *jury-wheel, locked as now required by law,* shall remain in the custody of the said *jury commissioners* and *the keys thereof* in the custody of the *sheriff* of the said county."

The mode of drawing the jurors is prescribed by the 3d section, and the 4th section, after repeating certain acts, provides "that all acts and parts of Acts of Assembly now in force in relation to the custody, sealing and unsealing, locking and opening of the jury-wheel of the respective county, and all Acts and parts of Acts of Assembly now in force imposing any penalty or punishment on the sheriff and county commissioners or either of them for anything done or omitted by them or either of them, in relation to the keeping, locking, opening, sealing or breaking the seal of any jury-wheel, or in relation to the selecting or drawing of jurors shall be taken, deemed and held to apply to the said jury commissioners and sheriff." The duties of the sheriff and commissioners, now jury commissioners, are distinctly prescribed, as may be seen by reference to 1 Brightly's Digest 830, 831.

The 16th paragraph, which is sec. 90 of the Act of 14th April 1834, expressly provides, "as soon as the selection of jurors and the depositing of their names in the wheel as aforesaid shall be completed, the sheriff shall cause the same to be locked and secured by sealing-wax, and thereon the said sheriff and (jury) commissioners shall impress distinctly their respective seals." It is the *jury-wheel* that is to be locked and sealed.

It is clear that only one seal was used, and that it was not sealed with the respective seals of the two jury commissioners and sheriff, making three seals. Of course this was error, and the array so challenged should have been set aside and the indictment for the murder of Kraemer should have been quashed. The same objection will apply to the indictment for the murder of Mrs. Kraemer. New bills therefore should be presented to a new grand jury.

Strict attention should be paid to the execution of the jury law, so as to avoid these technical objections, which if not made at the time, are cured by the 53d section of the Criminal Procedure Act of 31st March 1860.

The judgment is reversed and the record remanded, with this opinion, setting forth the causes of reversal to the court below for further proceeding.

MERCEP v. STATE INDUSTRIAL ACCIDENT COMMISSION

Supreme Court of Oregon, 1941.
167 Or. 460, 118 P.2d 1061.

LUSK, Justice. This appeal is prosecuted by the defendant, State Industrial Accident Commission, from a judgment in favor of the plaintiff, Matilda Mercep, based on the verdict of a jury awarding the plaintiff compensation on account of the death of her husband, Matt Mercep.

The defendant assigns error in the admission into evidence of certain statements made by the deceased a short time before his death. They were admitted as dying declarations. The defendant contended in the court below, and contends here, that the evidence was hearsay. The question was raised on the trial by objections to the evidence, motion to strike the testimony from the record, and motion for a directed verdict.

Mercep died on July 4, 1939. The alleged dying declarations were made while he was sick in a hospital in Hillsboro following an operation for hernia. Two or three days before his death he made the following statement to a friend, John Sarabacha:

"He cleaned up a place for cutting for falling timber, that is all he said. There was a limb on the way and he picked that limb and threw it to one side; he says he stepped, when he grabbed that limb, and he stepped on a windfall and his foot slipped; as quick as his foot slipped and threw the limb, just like a pain, pain him right in his stomach."

He told his wife while in the hospital: "He clean out brush and lift a chunk and slipped to the side, he got the pain."

The precise date of this statement is not shown. Mrs. Mercep saw her husband four times while he was in the hospital, the first time on June 21, the last on June 29. It was on one of these occasions that the statement was made.

Apart from one contention of the defendant, which we find it unnecessary to pass upon, it was a legitimate deduction from this evidence and other facts disclosed that the accident described, which arose out of and in the course of Mercep's employment, was the proximate cause of hernia and subsequently of his death. On the other hand, plaintiff concedes that without the statements in question there is no proof of accidental injury and her case fails.

Decision of the question requires examination of the whole of the testimony.

Matt Mercep was a logger employed by Alder Creek Lumber Co. in Washington County. Prior to June 7, 1939, he had no disability. On that day he complained to a fellow worker of pain in the lower right side. On June 9 he consulted a physician to whom he made the same complaint. On June 19 he was admitted to Jones Hospital in Hillsboro, and the next day was operated on for hernia. He ran a fairly normal course until about the eleventh day after the operation when he developed a thrombophlebitis in the iliac vein on the left side, which caused severe pain. On July 4 he left the hospital against the advice of the attending physician and the manager of the hospital, having first signed a writing relieving them of responsibility for his act. He was taken to his home, a distance of about nine miles, in an automobile. As he entered the house he collapsed, and ten minutes later died. The undisputed immediate cause of death was a blood clot or clots which lodged in the pulmonary artery and blocked the circulation of the lungs. It is explained in the medical testimony that a thrombus is a clot of blood which forms in a vessel during life, while an embolus is that same clot of blood, or a portion of it, which becomes detached and is carried through the circulatory system to some point where its caliber or diameter is greater than the vessel in which it finds itself and where it lodges. If that is a vital spot death ensues. The cause of death in this case is known as pulmonary embolism.

The medical testimony is further agreed that the embolism which caused death had its origin in the thrombus or blood clot which had formed before death in the decedent's iliac veins, the region in which phlebitis or inflammation of the veins had developed.

There is no testimony that a thrombus, located as this one was, could in and of itself cause death. It has in it the potentialities of death on account of the danger that it may break loose and start on its journey through the blood stream.

Dr. Warren C. Hunter a pathologist who performed the autopsy, was of the opinion that Mercep's getting up was "a most potent factor in the cause of death". As to whether pulmonary emboli would have resulted had he remained in bed, he said that he did not know.

Dr. Louis K. Poyntz, who assisted at the autopsy as the representative of the plaintiff, conceded that where a man has thrombosis the medical profession recognizes that rest is the cure since there is danger that activity may cause the blood clot to become detached. He also conceded that the thrombus usually absorbs if the patient remains quietly in bed. But he insisted that in this case the clot probably would have broken loose whether Mercep remained in bed or not, explaining that the microscopic examination showed that the clot had softened and that no one could say whether embolism was caused by movement or by the softening process. He thought that a purely speculative question. Dr. Hunter testified that the thrombus had developed before the patient left the hospital, and it was his opinion that the "whole process (i. e., of the embolism) may have occurred in a few minutes time or it could have been a few hours". Dr. Poyntz testified that there is no way of telling how long it would take the clot to work its way through the vessels and through the blood stream to the pulmonary artery where it lodged.

The medical testimony is further in agreement that enforced rest following the operation for hernia was the probable cause of the thrombus.

Mercep's attending physician was Dr. Archie Pitman, who performed the operation. It was his testimony that the patient ran a normal course until the eleventh day after the operation, which would be July 1, when phlebitis set in, and that he was at no time in a critical condition while in the hospital save that the phlebitis was a potent source of danger without quiet and rest.

The hospital chart fails to disclose that Mercep was either in a serious or critical condition while in the hospital. There is a record of gas distress for four days following the operation, and of pain in the chest which Dr. Pitman diagnosed as a mild attack of pleurisy. This subsided, and there was no more pain apparently until the patient began to suffer pain in his left leg, caused by phlebitis, on the eleventh hospital day, which was June 30. In the cross-examination of Dr. Pitman it was brought out by counsel for plaintiff that Mercep was emotional and a hard patient to control. He answered the following question on cross-examination in the affirmative:

> "And a person of that nature and temperament suffering from these gas pains and the tightening of the bandages might be driven to the point where you might say he was just crazy, isn't that true?"

Dr. F. J. Kabbeisman, the physician whom Mercep consulted on June 9, testified as a witness for the defendant that he saw Mercep in the hospital on July 3 and that Mercep complained of pain on the inner side of the left leg and had considerable tenderness over the iliac vein. He diagnosed the ailment as thrombophlebitis, and advised absolute quiet and rest, no exercise or motion. He gave no other testimony respecting the patient's condition.

Mrs. Minnie Jones Coy, the manager of the hospital, testified that Mercep was a nervous man who didn't mind very well but did whatever he wanted to do, and that he insisted upon leaving the hospital and going home because there would be so much noise on the Fourth of July.

Near the beginning of the trial the court, without the presence of the jury, conducted a preliminary inquiry at which evidence was introduced by the plaintiff designed to lay a foundation for receiving evidence of the alleged dying declarations. At this preliminary inquiry six witnesses testified, three of whom were later recalled and repeated their testimony before the jury. The essential portions of the preliminary testimony follow:

Joe Mercep saw the decedent on June 25 and 30. He testified concerning his visit of June 25:

> "A. When I ask him 'How you feel', he told me he didn't feel so hot. I said 'What is the matter, can't you take it'? He said 'That gas, that thing', he said, 'fill me up: I feel just like I am going to blow up;' he said 'I believe that kill me, that gas'.

> "Q. Is that all he said to you? A. That is all; I didn't bother him much, because he wasn't feeling good, so I just quit talking with him, he don't feel so hot."

He visited the decedent on June 30 with three other men when the following occurred: "Well, I don't have a very long talk with him; I just asked him 'how you feel'. He said 'I don't feel any better'. He said 'I believe I am worse now than the first time you saw him', so another fellow started to talk to him, that is all I talked to him."

Sam Sugura saw Mercep two or three days before his death. He testified: "A. I walked right into his beside, asked him how he feel, then he tell me, he says, 'I feel awful bad, and I am going to die'. I tried right away to cheer him up, I tell him right back, I says 'That operation don't mean death, that is just the same as operating the death out, I had one of those operations myself, Matt, don't get scared, you ain't going to die'. He kept on saying 'Yes, I am going to die'.

> "Q. Did he at that time make a statement as to the manner in which he was injured on June 7, 1939?
>
> "A. Well, then he was talking to John Sarabacha, I walked away, talking to another patient because he called me to come over to see him."

Peter Simondich was one of those who accompanied Joe Mercep on the visit of June 30. His testimony as to his conversation with Mercep was as follows:

> "When I came and shook hands with him, and I says 'Matt, how do you get along'? He says 'Not so good'. I says 'What is the matter'? 'Well,' he says 'it seems to me my day is over, and kind of—you know'. I says 'What is the trouble'? Well, he mentioned something—doctor, like he mentioned that he killed him. I says 'Matt, you know you can get better doctors to went to Portland'. 'Well,' he says 'yes, I should, but' he says 'I was hurt alongside'—on his cheek here—'this doctor fixed me fine.' So he says—this is the first doctor—I show the doctor the rupture, and he says, so he told me this doctor is going to get a report from the state, he is going to operate on me, so he is a friend of mine, coming from California. I said they may come any day. He says 'Please bring him over'. I says 'As soon as I get the chance I will bring him over.' So the rest started to talk to him, that is all there was."

Mary Mercep, wife of Joe Mercep, testified that she saw the decedent on the afternoon of June 30 when the following conversation took place: "He told me—I says 'How you feel'. He said 'No good, I can't breathe', so I says 'What is the matter'. 'I got too much gas'. Then I asked him,—he says 'No, freeze them before you get operation; then they start to cut and I start to scream, then I start to holler, and they give me gas, and they give me lots of it'; then he opened his shirt to show me, he got a belt all around about two inches wide. He says that he no feel good,—'I going to die'."

As already stated, Mrs. Matilda Mercep, widow of the decedent, saw her husband four times while he was in the hospital, the first time on June 21, the last on June 29. On the latter occasion, according to her testimony, "he told me the doctor give him a freeze and cut him open, then he started bawling, and he give him gas, he said the gas kill him." She testified that on each occasion when she visited him he said that he expected to die—"He tell everybody he die". On one of these occasions there were three other persons visiting Mercep whom she did not know.

Pete Matiaco saw Mercep four days before he died. He testified: "He said 'I feel worse, Pete, every day'. 'That may be', I says 'might be all right after that'. 'No', he said, 'they kill me here, worse every day, don't expect to live'."

He went again to the hospital on the Fourth of July and took Mercep home. He testified: "All right, Matt says 'I go home before I die; I going to die'. I think it is funny anyway,—'better die here than in the hospital'."

On cross-examination he said that he heard the nurse tell Mercep that he would die if he left the hospital and that Mercep said that he would like to die at home and not in the hospital.

In this state evidence may be given in both civil and criminal cases of the declarations of a dying person made under a sense of impending death respecting the cause of his death. 1 O.C.L.A. § 2–228 (4); McCredie v. Commercial Casualty Insurance Co., 142 Or. 229, 20 P.2d 232, 91 A.L.R. 557 (1889); McCarty v. Sirianni, 132 Or. 290, 285 P. 825 (1930). Two conditions must exist to render a dying declaration admissible: (1) The declarant must have been in extremis and (2) it must have been made in the conscious belief that death was impending and without hope or expectation of recovery. State v. Gray, 43 Or. 446, 450, 74 P. 927 (1904); 1 Jones on Ev.Civ.Cas. 611, § 332a. As to the second point, see State v. Fuller, 52 Or. 42, 96 P. 456 (1908); State v. Thompson, 49 Or. 46, 48, 88 P. 583, 124 Am.St.Rep. 1015 (1907); State v. Fletcher, 24 Or. 295, 33 P. 575 (1893); State v. Shaffer, 23 Or. 555, 557, 32 P. 545 (1893); 5 Wigmore on Ev., 3d Ed., 233, § 1440. We think that neither condition existed at the times that Matt Mercep described the accident which led up to his death.

He was not in extremis. That is demonstrated both by the evidence of his condition, which has been summarized, and by the total lack of evidence that he was then suffering from a mortal illness. At the time that the trial judge ruled the declarations admissible there was no evidence whatever before the court respecting the nature or gravity of his ailment, nothing, save his own statements and the fact that he was in a hospital, to indicate even that he was sick. The plaintiff, though charged with the duty of laying the foundation for the admission of evidence which otherwise would be inadmissible as hearsay, did not see fit to call to the witness stand Dr. Pitman, the attending physician, surely the best qualified person on the subject of Mercep's condition. When his testimony was finally adduced as a witness for the defendant, it showed that at no time while in the hospital was Mercep a dying man and that his condition was not critical except for the danger that the blood clot in his leg might be dislodged. Nothing in the testimony of the other physicians conflicts with Dr. Pitman's testimony.

Even more eloquent is the absence of evidence. The physical phenomena ordinarily attendant upon approaching dissolution are not here. Neither Mrs. Mercep nor Mercep's friends speak of any. Were death impending the manager of the hospital, the nurses, would know of it. Something would have been recorded on the hospital chart concerning it. There is nothing of the kind from any of these sources.

The cases upon this subject are almost without number. See note, 56 L.R.A. 356, 457. It would be useless to analyze precedents because they all vary so in their facts; but it may be observed that a rather extensive investigation has failed to reveal any case in which admissibility was even claimed for dying declarations under circumstances similar to those disclosed by this record. The cases all deal with mortal illnesses and mortal wounds, the very descriptions of which on the printed pages of the reports are pictures of impending death. See, for example, State v. Fuller, supra, 52 Or. at page 45, 96 P. 456 (1908). The decedent's illness did not take on that character until a few hours, at most, before the end came. Until the blood clot was dislodged there was only a threat of disaster which might have been averted had Mercep been guided by the advice of his physician and nurse and submitted to the treatment which all the medical testimony agrees was indicated.

The second condition for the admissibility of a dying declaration has thus been delineated with his usual felicity of phrase by Mr. Justice Cardozo in Shepard v. United States, 290 U.S. 96, 100, 54 S.Ct. 22, 24, 78 L.Ed. 196 (1933):

> "Fear or even belief that illness will end in death will not avail of itself to make a dying declaration. There must be 'a settled hopeless expectation' (Willes, J. in Reg. v. Peel, 2 F. & F. 21, 22) that death is near at hand, and what is said must have been spoken in the hush of its impending presence. . . . The patient must have spoken with the consciousness of a swift and certain doom."

The evidence fails to meet that test. If the repeated statements of Matt Mercep that he was going to die are more than the excited, exaggerated utterances of an unruly, emotional patient, critical of his doctors, suffering pain, yet the circumstances make it manifest that the words were not "spoken in the hush of death's impending presence". A setting which would befit such a solemn moment is wholly lacking. Rather, there is almost an air of casualness. Though, as we are asked to believe, her husband had given up all hope of life and so told her every time she saw him, Mrs. Mercep, in the period from

June 21 to June 29, visited him in the hospital but four times, and after June 29 she did not see him again until July 4 when he came home to die. It neither appears that she felt impelled to remain with him, to comfort and solace him while the sands of life were running out, nor that he asked her to do so. See People v. Sarzano, 212 N.Y. 231, 106 N.E. 87, 88 (1914), where the court in ruling the declaration inadmissible, said:

> "The declarant did not ask for wife, children, friends, or priest or by word or act indicate that he believed his death certain and imminent." See, also, Rex v. Spilsbury, 7 C. & P. 187.

Pertinent is the following language from State v. Simon, 50 Mo. 370, 375 (1872), quoted in State v. Johnson, 118 Mo. 491, 503, 24 S.W. 229, 232, 40 Am.St.Rep. 405 (1894): "Any person who has been accustomed to attend on those who are injured, or are very ill, knows how common it is for them to say that they will never recover, or that they will die, when there is no good or sufficient reason for the apprehension, and they are not conscious themselves that they are in any real danger. Such expressions are often the result of impatience, restlessness, or great suffering. But at the same time let the attending physician inform them that there is no hope, and that they must die, and they will be perfectly startled."

It is a case where the declarant's conduct, considered in the light of the circumstances, "precludes the idea that his alleged dying declarations were made with a solemn conviction of approaching death." Tibbs v. Commonwealth, 138 Ky. 558, 564, 128 S.W. 871, 873, 28 L.R.A.,N.S., 665 (1910). See, 26 Am.Jur. Homicide, 446, § 417. They may well have been the declarations of a man who, as counsel for the plaintiff suggested on the trial, was "driven to the point where he is just crazy", but not of a dying man conscious of "a swift and certain doom".

We do not base our decision on the length of time that elapsed between the declarations and death. Nor have we overlooked the rule that the discretion of the trial court in passing upon the admissibility of this species of evidence is not lightly to be disturbed. State v. Doris, 51 Or. 136, 147, 94 P. 44, 16 L.R.A.,N.S., 660 (1908). But "the hearsay character of dying declarations necessitates the use of care and caution in admitting them in evidence". 26 Am.Jur. Homicide, 426, § 384; State v. Johnson, supra; Smith v. State, 9 Humph., Tenn., 9 (1848); Reg. v. Jenkins, L.R., 1 C.C.R. 191. The principle on which such evidence is admitted, as stated by Lord Chief Baron Eyre in Woodcock's case, 2 Leach 563, is "that they are declarations made in extremity, when the party is at the point of death, and when every hope of this world is gone; when every motive to falsehood is silenced, and the mind is induced by the most powerful considerations to speak the truth; a situation so solemn, and so awful, is considered by the law as creating an obligation equal to that which is imposed by a positive oath administered in a court of justice."

The evidence in this case, which has been examined with the utmost care and the substance of which has been stated, wholly fails, in our opinion, to reveal that "solemn" and "awful" situation which would justify a court in dispensing with the necessity of sworn testimony upon the crucial question for determination.

We think that the evidence objected to was erroneously admitted, and, as there was no other proof of accidental injury, the motion for a directed verdict should have been granted.

The judgment is, therefore, reversed.

BARSCH v. HAMMOND

Supreme Court of Colorado, 1943.
110 Colo. 441, 135 P.2d 519.

BAKKE, Justice. This is an automobile accident case in which plaintiff in error seeks to reverse a judgment for $2,500 and costs entered in accordance with the verdict of a jury in favor of Louise B. Hammond, to whom we hereinafter refer as Mrs. Hammond, defendant in error, whose husband died as a result of injuries sustained in the accident. A default judgment for $5,000 had been entered prior to this one, but due to a deficiency in the service of process, counsel for Mrs. Hammond confessed error; the default judgment was set aside and a trial had on the merits. Plaintiff in error, Barsch, was the owner of the truck which was being driven by his brother, his admitted agent, at the time of the accident.

The accident occurred about 3:45 a. m., October 18, 1937, near a filling station in the little town of Pinon about thirty miles south of Colorado Springs on U. S. Highway 85, where a family by the name of Holcomb operates a restaurant and service station. The place served as a "truck stop" for a number of truck drivers using the highway. The highway—an eighteen foot wide cement road—at this point is fairly level for quite a distance in each direction, although there is a curve to the left in the road towards Colorado Springs about fifteen hundred feet from the scene of the accident. There was a driveway leading off the highway to the Holcomb buildings on the west side of the road. The morning of the accident Hammond was driving south alone in a 1937 Ford sedan on this road from Colorado Springs to Pueblo, and Barsch was driving north in a thirty-two foot long tractor-trailer. Upon reaching the driveway to the filling station, Barsch turned his truck to the left without making a left hand signal, and the Hammond car crashed into it with such force that the front of his car was smashed in pinning him, Hammond, under the steering wheel, and causing injuries from which he died the next day. Since there were no eyewitnesses to the accident, other than Barsch, it is difficult to ascertain from the testimony the relative speed of each vehicle as it approached the point of collision, although Barsch admits seeing the Hammond car when it came around the curve on the north, about a quarter of a mile north of Pinon. Barsch apparently thought he had enough time to make the turn into the driveway ahead of the Hammond car.

The night was clear and the Holcomb buildings were well lighted. That Hammond saw the truck making the turn is a fair surmise because there were tire skid marks for about thirty feet ahead of the point of impact, indicating that Hammond tried to stop his car, although Barsch testified that he did not hear any screeching of brakes; that when he saw that a crash was imminent, he stopped his truck just off the pavement at an angle to it, facing into the Holcomb driveway. From the tire marks of Hammond's car, it was apparent that he had driven off the pavement on his right in an attempt to avoid a collision. Following the accident, most of the Hammond car was on the pavement, crosswise thereof, with the front part of it against the right front part of the tractor.

Hammond was taken to a hospital in Pueblo. His wife and children arrived there about 7:45 a. m. Mrs. Hammond testified: "As we came up to him, the children and I, he put his arm around the children, kissed each one of us, and said, "Mother dear, I won't ever be home with you and the babies again; I am done for . . . .. He said he saw this other car coming, and it made no indication of turning, and he supposed it was going to continue on its course north, or in the direction in which it was going. . . . But all of a sudden, quite suddenly, this man turned directly in front of him, which would have been to his left, got directly in front of him, giving no intimation he was turning or going into this place . . .. When he struck the car that he was yet on the highway, partly in the highway when he struck it."

(1) This statement was admitted in evidence as a dying declaration, and its admission as such is the principal ground for reversal in this case. Other matters urged are: (2) That Hammond was intoxicated. (3) That the court should have directed a verdict for defendant. (4) That the court erred in giving instruction No. 4. (5) That there was a variance between pleading and proof. (6) That the court erred in denying motion for a new trial.

1. Counsel for plaintiff in error objected to the introduction of the above testimony upon the ground that it was hearsay, but when opposing counsel called attention to Chapter 145, Session Laws 1937, which permits such declarations to be introduced, objection was that no proper foundation had been laid, which objection was cured by a proper foundation being laid. This statute reads, in part: "To render the declarations of the deceased competent evidence, it must be satisfactorily proved: 1, that at the time of the making of such declaration he was conscious of approaching death and believed there was no hope of recovery; 2, that such declaration was voluntarily made, and not through the persuasion of any person; 3, that such declaration was not made in answer to interrogatories calculated to lead the

deceased to make any particular statement; 4, that he was of sound mind at the time of making the declaration." All of these elements were positively established by Mrs. Hammond on both direct and cross examination, and several defense witnesses corroborated Hammond's rationality.

. . .

We think there is no prejudicial error in this record.

The judgment is affirmed.

BURKE, HILLIARD and JACKSON, JJ., concur.

DECISIONS RELATING TO CHAPTER X, HEARSAY—BUSINESS RECORDS EXCEPTION

HOWARD v. McDONOUGH

Court of Appeals of New York, 1879.
77 N.Y. 592.

(Argued March 27, 1879; decided April 8, 1879.)

This action was brought to recover for the alleged unlawful taking of the materials and fixtures of a job printing office, which were seized by defendant McDonough as city marshal, under an execution against a third person.

Upon the trial a witness for plaintiff testified that shortly after the seizure he made a list or schedule of the articles which he knew to have been taken and of their values, which he testified he knew; the articles were very numerous. The witness was allowed under objection and exception to use the list in testifying to the articles and their value, and after he had gone through the list it was offered and received in evidence under objection and exception. *Held,* no error.

The court laid down the rule as to the use of memoranda as follows:

> "The law as to the use of memoranda by witnesses while testifying is quite well settled in this State. 1. A witness may, for the purpose of refreshing his memory, use any memorandum, whether made by himself or another, written or printed, and when his memory has thus been refreshed, he must testify to facts of his own knowledge, the memorandum itself not being evidence. 2. When a witness has so far forgotten the facts that he can not recall them, even after looking at a memorandum of them, and he testifies that he once knew them and made a memorandum of them at the time or soon after they transpired, which he intended to make correctly, and which he believes to be correct, such memorandum, in his own handwriting, may be received as evidence of the facts therein contained, although the witness has no present recollection of them. 3. Memoranda may be used in other cases which do not precisely come under either of the foregoing heads. A store of goods is wrongfully seized, and an action is brought to recover for the conversion. There are thousands of items. No witness could carry in his mind all the items and the values to be attached to them. In such a case, a witness may make a list of all the items and their values, and he may aid his memory while testifying by such list. He must be able to state that all the articles named in the list were

seized, and that they were of the values therein stated, and he may use the list to enable him to state the items. After the witness has testified, the memorandum which he has used may be put in evidence, not as proving anything of itself, but as a detailed statement of the items testified to by the witness. The manner in which the memorandum, in such a case, may be used is very much in the discretion of the trial judge. He may require the witness to testify to each item separately, and have his evidence recorded in the minutes of the trial, and then the introduction of the memorandum will not be important; or he may allow the witness to testify quite generally to the items and their values; and receive the memorandum as the detailed result of his examination, leaving to the adverse party a more minute cross-examination. Without the use of a memorandum in such cases, it would be difficult, if not impossible, to conduct a trial involving the examination of a large number of items. (Driggs v. Smith, 36 N.Y.Superior Ct. 283, affirmed in this court; McCormick v. Penn. Central R. R. Co., 49 N.Y. 303.)"

. . .

EARL, J., reads for affirmance.

All concur.

Judgment affirmed.

JOHNSON v. LUTZ ET AL.

Court of Appeals of New York, 1930.
253 N.Y. 124, 170 N.E. 517.

Action by Irene Johnson, as administratrix of the goods, chattels, and credits of John S. Johnson, deceased, against Frederick Lutz and another, copartners doing business as Chas. Lutz & Sons. From a judgment of the Appellate Division (226 App.Div. 772, 234 N.Y.S. 328 (1929)), affirming a judgment entered upon the verdict of a jury in favor of plaintiff, defendants appeal by permission.

Affirmed.

HUBBS, J. This action is to recover damages for the wrongful death of the plaintiff's intestate, who was killed when his motorcycle came into collision with the defendants' truck at a street intersection. There was a sharp conflict in the testimony in regard to the circumstances under which the collision took place. A policeman's report of the accident filed by him in the station house was offered in evidence by the defendants under Section 374–a of the Civil Practice Act, and was excluded. The sole ground for reversal urged by the appellants is that said report was erroneously excluded. That section reads: "Any writing or record, whether in the form of an entry in a book or otherwise, made as a memorandum or record of any act, transaction, occurrence or event, shall be admissible in evidence in proof of said act, transaction, occurrence or event, if the trial judge shall find that it was made in the regular course of any business, and that it was the regular course of such business to make such memorandum or record at the time of such act, transaction, occurrence or event, or within a reasonable time thereafter. All other circumstances of the making of such writing or record, including lack of personal knowledge by the entrant or maker, may be shown to affect its weight, but they shall not affect its admissibility. The term business shall include business, profession, occupation and calling of every kind."

Prior to the decision in the well-known case of Vosburgh v. Thayer, 12 Johns. 461, decided in 1815, shopbooks could not be introduced in evidence to prove an account. The decision in that case established that they were admissible where preliminary proof could be made that there were regular dealings between the parties; that the plaintiff kept honest and fair books; that some of the articles charged had been delivered; and that the plaintiff kept no clerk. At that time it might not have been a hardship to require a shopkeeper who sued to recover an account to furnish the preliminary proof required by that decision. Business was transacted in a comparatively small way, with few, if any, clerks. Since the decision in that case, it has remained the substantial basis of all decisions upon the question in this jurisdiction prior to the enactment in 1928 of Section 374–a, Civil Practice Act.

Under modern conditions, the limitations upon the right to use books of account, memoranda, or records, made in the regular course of business, often resulted in a denial of justice, and usually in annoyance, expense, and waste of time and energy. A rule of evidence that was practical a century ago had become obsolete. The situation was appreciated, and attention was called to it by the courts and text-writers. Woods Practice Evidence (2d Ed.) 377; 3 Wigmore on Evidence (1923) § 1530.

The report of the Legal Research Committee of the Commonwealth Fund, published in 1927, by the Yale University Press, under the title, "The Law of Evidence—Some Proposals for Its Reform," dealt with the question in chapter 5, under the heading, "Proof of Business Transactions to Harmonize with Current Business Practice." That report, based upon extensive research, pointed out the confusion existing in decisions in different jurisdictions. It explained and illustrated the great need of a more practical, workable, and uniform rule, adapted to modern business conditions and practices. The chapter is devoted to a discussion of the pressing need of a rule of evidence which would "give evidential credit to the books upon which the mercantile and industrial world relies in the conduct of business." At the close of the chapter, the committee proposed a statute to be enacted in all jurisdictions. In compliance with such proposal, the

Legislature enacted Section 374–a of the Civil Practice Act in the very words used by the committee.

It is apparent that the Legislature enacted Section 374–a to carry out the purpose announced in the report of the committee. That purpose was to secure the enactment of a statute which would afford a more workable rule of evidence in the proof of business transactions under existing business conditions.

In view of the history of Section 374–a and the purpose for which it was enacted, it is apparent that it was never intended to apply to a situation like that in the case at bar. The memorandum in question was not made in the regular course of any business, profession, occupation, or calling. The policeman who made it was not present at the time of the accident. The memorandum was made from hearsay statements of third persons who happened to be present at the scene of the accident when he arrived. It does not appear whether they saw the accident and stated to him what they knew, or stated what some other persons had told them.

The purpose of the Legislature in enacting Section 374–a was to permit a writing or record, made in the regular course of business, to be received in evidence, without the necessity of calling as witnesses all of the persons who had any part in making it provided the record was made as a part of the duty of the person making it, or on information imparted by persons who were under a duty to impart such information. The amendment permits the introduction of shopbooks without the necessity of calling all clerks who may have sold different items of account. It was not intended to permit the receipt in evidence of entries based upon voluntary hearsay statements made by third parties not engaged in the business or under any duty in relation thereto. It was said, in Mayor, etc., of New York City v. Second Ave. R. Co., 102 N.Y. 572, at page 581, 7 N.E. 905, 909, 55 Am.Rep. 839 (1886): "It is a proper qualification of the rule admitting such evidence that the account must have been made in the ordinary course of business, and that it should not be extended so as to admit a mere private memorandum, not made in pursuance of any duty owing by the person making it, or when made upon information derived from another who made the communication casually and voluntarily, and not under the sanction of duty or other obligation."

An important consideration leading to the amendment was the fact that in the business world credit is given to records made in the course of business by persons who are engaged in the business upon information given by others engaged in the same business as part of their duty.

"Such entries are dealt with in that way in the most important undertakings of mercantile and industrial life. They are the ultimate basis of calculation, investment, and general confidence in every business enterprise. Nor does the practical impossibility of obtaining constantly and permanently the verification of every employee affect the trust that is given to such books. It would seem that expedients which the entire commercial world recognizes as safe could be sanctioned, and not discredited, by courts of justice. When it is a mere question of whether provisional confidence can be placed in a certain class of statements, there cannot profitably and sensibly be one rule for the business world and another for the court-room. The merchant and the manufacturer must not be turned away remediless because the methods in which the entire community places a just confidence are a little difficult to reconcile with technical judicial scruples on the part of the same persons who as attorneys have already employed and relied upon the same methods. In short, courts must here cease to be pedantic and endeavor to be practical." 3 Wigmore on Evidence (1923) § 1530, p. 278.

The Legislature has sought by the amendment to make the courts practical. It would be unfortunate not to give the amendment a construction which will enable it to cure the evil complained of and accomplish the purpose for which it was enacted. In construing it, we should not, however, permit it to be applied in a case for which it was never intended.

The judgment should be affirmed, with costs.

CARDOZO, C. J., and POUND, CRANE, LEHMAN, KELLOGG, and O'BRIEN, JJ., concur.

Judgment affirmed.

YEARGANS v. YEARGANS

Supreme Court of New York, Appellate Division, First Department, 1965.
265 N.Y.S.2d 562, 24 A.D.2d 280.

. . .

Before BOTEIN, P. J., and RABIN, McNALLY, STEVENS and STEUER, JJ.

PER CURIAM: In this action for damages for personal injuries received August 12, 1961 by plaintiff, a passenger, when a car owned and operated by the defendant ran off the road and struck a tree, reversal is directed and a new trial ordered. The charge presented to the jury a theory contrary to that advanced by plaintiff in his bill of particulars and similarly advanced at the trial, in addition to the one so advanced. That was error. The verdict being a general one, it is impossible to determine upon what theory recovery was actually allowed. Clark v. Board of Education, 304 N.Y. 488, 490, 109 N.E.2d 73 (1953); Fein v. Board of Education, 305 N.Y. 611, 613, 11 N.E.2d 732 (1938). It was also prejudicial error to exclude the motor vehicle report offered by the defendant when the report tended to contradict the version of the accident given by the defendant in a deposition before trial. CPLR 3117(d) specifically provides "[a]t the trial, any party may rebut any relevant evidence contained in a deposition, whether introduced by him or by any other party." It may be noted that the deposition was first used by the plaintiff in his case in chief and was not used to contradict or impeach the defendant-deponent who had not yet testified. See CPLR 3117(d). The motor vehicle report filed August 14, 1961 by defendant contained a version as to the cause of the accident which differed from that given by defendant in her examination before trial. When injuries are suffered in an automobile accident in the State of New York, or the property damage exceeds a specified amount, a report is required to be filed with the Motor Vehicle Commissioner (Vehicle & Traffic Law, § 605). This report becomes a public document (Public Officers Law, § 66–a). Under certain circumstances it could be received in evidence as a public document and used to impeach the witness. While the Motor Vehicle report offered was one filed in Vermont, there was no evidence to indicate that it should be regarded other than as a public document. Moreover, the trial court was empowered to take judicial notice of applicable Vermont law (CPLR 4511).

It was also prejudical error under the circumstances of this case to receive the police report in evidence. The police officer, John J. Ryan, a member of the Bennington, Vermont Police Department, was never called to testify and there is no indication in the report save by possible inference as to his source or sources for the information recorded. Moreover, the report was admitted before that portion of defendant's deposition was read, in which defendant stated she had given the information appearing in such report.

Of course reports of police officers made upon their own observation and while carrying out their police duties are generally admissible in evidence. Trbovich v. Burke, 234 App.Div. 384, 255 N.Y.S. 100 (1932). In that case the police blotter was admitted in evidence, the court finding proof that the entries were made on the basis of the officer's communications. The court also pointed out, however, that the jury should have been instructed that the only value of the entries "was in showing what officer Ciulis reported shortly after the accident, and that, if the entries were not found to have been based on officer Ciulis' communication, the entries were pure hearsay and entitled to no weight" (p. 385, 255 N.Y.S. p. 102). Police reports have consistently been held inadmissible to establish the main fact where the information contained in the police blotter came from witnesses not engaged in the police business in the course of which the memorandum was made (Johnson v. Lutz, 226 App.Div. 772, 234 N.Y.S. 328, aff'd 253 N.Y. 124, 170 N.E. 517 (1930)), or where the employee giving the information (in addition to the bystander witnesses) "had every reason to give a biased and false report" (Needle v. New York Railways Corporation, 227 App.Div. 276, at 278, 237 N.Y.S. 547, at 549). In that case the information had been obtained from the defendant motorman. In Zaulich v. Thompkins Square Co., 10 A.D.2d 492, 200 N.Y.S.2d 550 (1930), the officer testified to what the plaintiff had told him and also to his own physical observations made upon arrival at the scene. He testified also that he had made an entry in the memorandum book which he was required by the rules of the police department to carry on his person, thereafter telephoning such information to the station house and at the end of his tour of duty examined and signed the report made from the information given. Both the report and the memorandum were excluded. This court in reversing said "it seems clear that the police report was admissible as a record made in the regular course of business pursuant to Section 374–a of the Civil Practice Act" (p. 496, 200 N.Y.S.2d p. 555). (Now CPLR 4518.) The court also observed that since the record supported an inference that the testimony was assailed as a possible recent fabrication the exclusion from evidence of the police officer's report and memorandum book to bolster the officer's testimony constituted prejudicial error (p. 497, 200 N.Y.S. p. 555). In this case the officer did not testify, nor did he witness the accident. For a discussion as to the purpose of Section 374–a of the Civil Practice Act see Williams v. Alexander, 309 N.Y. 283 at 286–287, 129 N.E.2d 417 at 419 (Fuld, J.); see also Mtr. of City of N. Y. (5th Ave. Coach), 42 Misc.2d 319, 247 N.Y.S.2d 933 (1931), discussing CPLR 4518 as a restatement, in substance, of 374–a Civil Practice Act. (Cf. Kelly v. Wasserman, 5 N.Y.2d 425, 185 N.Y.S.2d 538, 158 N.E.2d 241 (1959), where Department of Welfare records consisting of a memorandum of conversations with the defendant were admissible to impeach the defendant even though he was the plaintiff's witness. Cf. Coppola v. Melvin, 241 App.Div. 611, at 612, 268 N.Y.S. 736 (1934); Matter of Roge v. Valentine, 280 N.Y. 268, at 278, 20 N.E.2d 751, at 756 (1939). See generally, 5 Wigmore on Evidence, 3d ed., § 1530 et seq.; 5 Bender's New York Evidence, § 375. But in Wilson v. Bungalow Bar Corp. of America, 285 App.Div. 1191, 141 N.Y.S.2d 106 (1955), where the report was not based upon the police officer's own knowledge but upon information obtained from the driver of the truck involved in the accident, there was a limitation on the use of the police report to impeach the officer's testimony.) In the case before us the plaintiff simply offered a certified copy of the police report of an officer of a foreign state and the court received it. The court put no limitations in its charge upon the use or purpose for which the report was received. No exception was taken to the charge by the defendant except as to a portion referring to contributory negligence of the plaintiff.

On this record and in the interest of justice, the judgment appealed from should be reversed on the law and a new trial ordered, with costs to abide the event.

Judgment reversed on the law, and a new trial ordered, with $50 costs to abide the event. All concur except BOTEIN, P. J., who votes to affirm and RABIN, J., who concurs in the result.

TOLL v. STATE OF NEW YORK

Supreme Court, Appellate Division, Third Department, 1969.
32 A.D.2d 47, 299 N.Y.S.2d 589.

COOKE, Justice. This is an appeal from a judgment entered May 13, 1968, upon a decision of the Court of Claims, dismissing appellant's claim for personal injuries, following a trial on the issue of liability.

While it was snowing heavily and when visibility was poor, claimant, operating his automobile in the third or inside lane of the westbound portion of the six-lane Cross-Westchester Expressway, came in contact with the State's truck, in the same lane and on a snow plowing mission, shortly after midnight on March 7, 1967. Sharp issues arose on trial, claimant testifying that the truck was stationary and without lights when hit, with the State's driver swearing it was moving at 20–25 miles per hour with two headlights, a revolving amber dome light, two regular taillights and two red flashers all operating.

The report of the State trooper, who investigated but did not witness the accident, and the accident report of the snow plow operator, made 15 days after the event and filed with the Department of Public Works, were admitted over objections. Appellant contends that the former was improperly received because of its conclusional content and its authorship by an officer who did not witness the accident, and the latter because of not being prepared within a reasonable time after the occurrence.

Subdivision (a) of CPLR 4518 provides for the introduction into evidence of a record made in the regular course of any business, where it was the regular course of such business to make it, and it was made at the time of the act, transaction, occurrence or event, or within a reasonable time thereafter. In Johnson v. Lutz, 253 N.Y. 124, 170 N.E. 517 (1930), the exclusion of a police report was upheld and the Court of Appeals read into the then existing statute a requirement, not expressly found in it, that, to be admissible, the person making the police report be the witness or that the person supplying the information to the entrant be under a business duty to do so (p. 128). (Cf. Cox v. State of New York, 3 N.Y.2d 693, 699, 171 N.Y.S.2d 818, 822, 148 N.E.2d 879, 882 (1958); Trbovich v. Burke, 234 App.Div. 384, 255 N.Y.S. 100 (1932)). Then, in Kelly v. Wasserman, 5 N.Y.2d 425, 185 N.Y.S.2d 538, 158 N.E.2d 241 (1959), in allowing the receipt of a record of the Welfare Department reciting statements of defendant, it appeared that the requirement that the informant be under a business duty to impart the information was abandoned. (Cf. Gutin v. Frank Mascali & Sons, 11 N.Y.2d 97, 99, 226 N.Y.S.2d 434, 435, 181 N.E.2d 449, 450 (1962)). In Zaulich v. Thompkins Sq. Holding Co., 10 A.D.2d 492, 200 N.Y.S.2d 550 (1st Dept. 1960), where plaintiff's at trial version of an accident was at variance with that given by him at the scene to a policeman and then recorded in the police report, the report was held to be admissible as a record made in the regular course of business and that it was, in any event, competent evidence to rebut the inference by plaintiff's counsel that the patrolman's testimony was a recent fabrication. In Chemical Leaman Tank Lines v. Stevens, 21 A.D.2d 556, 251 N.Y.S.2d 240 (3d Dept. 1964), a Deputy Sheriff's report containing defendant's description of an accident, which was at variance with that related by her on trial, was received, it being held that the report was admissible as a business record and that the statements to the Deputy were admissible as admissions of a party.

It is important that these decisions be reconciled and we adopt the following as a workable guide regarding the admission of police officer reports in accident cases. CPLR 4518(a) permits a police report to be admitted as proof of the facts recorded therein if (1) the entrant of those facts was the witness, or (2) the person giving the entrant the information was under a business duty to relate the facts to the entrant (Johnson v. Lutz, supra). If neither of these two requisites is satisfied but the report recites a statement of an outsider, the record may be admitted (under Kelly v. Wasserman, supra), to prove that the statement recorded therein was made by the outsider (even though the main facts set forth in the business record are hearsay and excludable pursuant to *Johnson*) and, then, the facts recited in the statement may be proven by the business record if the statement qualifies as a hearsay exception, e. g., an admission, as in *Kelly* and *Chemical Leaman.* (Barker, Admissibility of Investigational Reports Under Business Records Statutes, 33 Albany L.Rev. 251; Prince, Evidence, 16 Syracuse L.Rev. 459–460; Prince, The Hearsay Rule, Practising Law Institute, Litigation Series, Trial Evidence, pp. 18–7 to 18–11; Supplementary Practice Commentary by Joseph M. McLaughlin, McKinney's Cons.Laws of N.Y., Book 7B, CPLR 4518, Supp., pp. 87–89; cf. Mahon v. Giordano, 30 A.D.2d 792, 291 N.Y.S.2d 854 (1968); Yeargans v. Yeargans, 24 A.D.2d 280, 265 N.Y.S.2d 562 (1966)). Here, the collision not having been witnessed by the State trooper and there being no proof that whoever gave him the facts had a business duty to do so, the report is not admissible to prove the main facts; and, since no other hearsay exception applies to the information from outsiders to the trooper, *Kelly* does not apply and the admission of the report was error.

The police report having contained the conclusion of the officer as to the factors contributing to the impact and it being impermissible for the officer to testify to his conclusions, his written conclusions should have been excluded, if the report had been otherwise acceptable (Albert v. Stumpf, 30 A.D.2d 686, 291 N.Y.S.2d 887 (1968); Bothner v. Keegan, 275 App.Div. 470, 472, 89 N.Y.S.2d 288, 289 (1949)). The business entry statute lifts the barrier of the hearsay objection; it does not overcome any other exclusionary rule which might properly be invoked (Richardson, Evidence [9th ed.], § 235; 5 Weinstein-Korn-Miller, N.Y.Civ.Prac., par. 4518.18).

The statutory requirement that the business record be prepared within a reasonable time after the occurrence, i. e., while the memory of the event was still fresh enough to be fairly reliable, should not be too rigidly applied and did not prevent the introduction of the accident report of the truck driver (5 Weinstein-Korn-Miller, N.Y.Civ. Prac., pars. 4518.02, 4518.17; McCormick, Evidence, p. 601). The self-serving aspect of this report did not preclude its admissibility under the statute, it being merely a consideration affecting its weight (Bromberg v. City of New York, 25 A.D.2d 885, 270 N.Y.S.2d 425 (1966); Bishin v. New York Cent. R. R. Co., 20 A.D.2d 921, 249 N.Y.S. 2d 778 (1964)).

The trial court's decision states that the Cross-Westchester Expressway contains a center mall dividing "two-lane pavements" on each side of the mall and that claimant "was not observing the posted regulation requiring travel in the right or driving lane but was driving in the mall or passing lane". Respondent's brief, however, concedes that each pavement consisted of three lanes and that there was no proof of "posted regulations". The consideration of an inapplicable statute and regulation on such a vital facet of the issue of liability also requires reversal (cf. Morse v. Buffalo Tank Corp., 280 N.Y. 110, 119, 19 N.E.2d 981, 985 (1939); Sarconi v. 122 West 26th St. Corp., 241 N.Y. 340, 150 N.E. 137 (1926); Uliaszek v. Buczkowski, 259 App.Div. 967, 19 N.Y.S.2d 912 (1940); Flaherty v. Metro Stations, 202 App.Div. 583, 587, 196 N.Y.S. 2, 6, affirmed 235 N.Y. 605, 139 N.E. 753 (1923)).

The judgment should be reversed, on the law and the facts, and a new trial ordered, with costs.

Judgment reversed, on the law and the facts, and a new trial ordered, with costs.

GIBSON, P. J., and REYNOLDS, AULISI and STALEY, JJ., concur.

ROCCO v. TRAVELERS INSURANCE COMPANY

Supreme Court, Special Term, Oneida County, 1963.
38 Misc.2d 311, 238 N.Y.S.2d 43.

FRANK DEL VECCHIO, Justice. This is a motion by the plaintiff in the three above entitled actions for an order suppressing and excluding upon the trial any evidence obtained by means of an autopsy alleged to have been unlawfully performed upon the body of plaintiff's deceased husband in violation of § 2214 of the Penal Law. That section, designed to prevent *unlawful* dissection of the body of a human being, provides:

> "A person who makes, or causes or procures to be made, any dissection of the body of a human being, except by *authority of law,* or in pursuance of a permission given by the *deceased,* is guilty of a misdemeanor."

The facts which give rise to the motion are as follows: On August 20, 1960 at about 5:30 P.M. while plaintiff's husband was operating a motor vehicle in the City of Utica with his wife and her mother as passengers, the vehicle struck a parked car, he then lost control of it and went over the curb, struck a telephone pole and proceeded on to strike head-on another car which was parked on the opposite side of the street. Police were called to investigate at the scene and the driver was removed by ambulance to a hospital where he was pronounced dead upon arrival. There is no claim that decedent was medically attended when death occurred.

The following day the Oneida County coroner directed a pathologist to perform an autopsy on the deceased, without having asked plaintiff for her permission or consent. Based on the autopsy report, a death certificate *signed by the coroner* was duly filed, stating as the cause of death: (1) Acute pulmonary edema, (2) Acute coronary heart disease, (3) Chronic coronary artery sclerosis.

The above defendants paid plaintiff, the named beneficiary, a total of $12,500, the face value of the insurance policies issued by them on the life of the deceased. Each defendant refused to pay additional benefits under the double indemnity provisions of the policies, on the ground that death was not caused directly and independently of all other causes through accidental means, or as a result solely and exclusively of accidental means and without disease contributing thereto.

These actions were brought to recover the amounts claimed to be due under the double indemnity provisions, plaintiff alleging that her husband's death occurred as the result of injuries received in the accident described above.

The group policy issued by the defendant The Travelers Insurance Company provides that the company shall have the right and opportunity to make an autopsy where it is not forbidden by law. The policies issued by the other two defendants do not contain any provision relative to an autopsy.

Plaintiff claims that the post mortem examination was unauthorized and constituted an unreasonable search and seizure, depriving her of property without due process of law, and that the evidence obtained thereby and any public records made upon the basis thereof are therefore inadmissible in evidence upon the trial of these actions.

Defendants, on the other hand, take the position that, assuming the autopsy was unlawfully performed, plaintiff's only remedy would be a cause of action for damages against those responsible for it (Darcy v. Presbyterian Hospital, 202 N.Y. 259, 95 N.E. 695 (1911)); that the results of such an examination, even though illegally obtained, would be admissible on the trial of these actions upon the authority of Bloodgood v. Lynch, 293 N.Y. 308, 56 N.E.2d 718 (1944), and Sackler v. Sackler, 16 A.D.2d 423, 229 N.Y.S.2d 61 (1928). In the Bloodgood case (a civil action) the court held that § 270–b of the Penal Law did not apply to a police officer and that it was therefore not unlawful for him to obtain in a hospital after an accident the statement offered in evidence, but by way of dictum said that, even if the statement had been illegally obtained, it would not be incompetent or inadmissible in evidence. In the Sackler case the Second Department, in a 3–2 decision, held that the new rule excluding in criminal cases evidence illegally obtained does not apply (a) to evidence gathered by private persons or (b) to civil actions. Defendants also claim that the coroner's decision represents a judicial determination which cannot be collaterally attacked since the findings are a public record which, by statute, is admissible in evidence. (Civil Practice Act, §§ 367, 374–a.)

Plaintiff recognizes that the question of admissibility of illegally obtained evidence in a civil action has not been passed upon by the Court of Appeals or the Appellate Division of the Fourth Department since the decisions of Mapp v. Ohio, 367 U.S. 643, 81 S.Ct. 1684, 6 L. Ed.2d 1081 (1961), and People v. Loria, 10 N.Y.2d 368, 223 N.Y.S.2d 462, 179 N.E.2d 478 (1962), criminal cases in which it was held that evidence so obtained is inadmissible on trial. She claims however that the rule of inadmissibility laid down in these cases applies to both criminal and civil litigation, that the dictum in the Bloodgood case has been overruled by Mapp and Loria, and that the dissenting opinions in the Sackler case are more logical and persuasive in asserting that exclusionary rules concerning illegally obtained evidence should apply equally in civil as well as in criminal cases.

Prior to Mapp v. Ohio, supra, illegally obtained evidence was admissible in criminal as well as in civil cases in New York state (People v. Richter's Jewelers, Inc., 291 N.Y. 161, 51 N.E.2d 690, 150 A.L.R. 560 (1943); People v. Defore, 242 N.Y. 13, 150 N.E. 585 (1926); Bloodgood v. Lynch, supra) contrary to the long established Federal rule. (Weeks v. United States, 232 U.S. 383, 34 S.Ct. 341, 58 L.Ed. 652 (1914).) It might be noted that Bloodgood (which laid down the rule as to civil actions) was based upon Defore (a criminal case), the effect of which has been destroyed by Mapp and Loria.

In Mapp v. Ohio, supra, the court said, 367 U.S. at page 655, 81 S.Ct. at page 1691: "We hold that all evidence obtained by searches and seizures in violation of the Constitution is, by that same authority, inadmissible in a state court".

In People v. Loria, supra, 10 N.Y.2d 368, at page 370, 223 N.Y.S. 2d 462, 464, at page 179 N.E.2d 478, at page 480 (1962), the Court of Appeals said that the U. S. Supreme Court had held in Mapp "that evidence obtained by search and seizure in violation of the Fourth Amendment, made applicable to the States through the due process clause of the Fourteenth, is inadmissible *in a State court*. There can be no doubt that it is the duty of State courts to follow the Mapp holding *in all trials* taking place after June 19, 1961." (Emphasis supplied.) It is significant that the court did *not* insert the word "criminal" before "trials".

Many states have held that evidence illegally obtained is inadmissible not only in criminal trials but also in civil actions. See Lebel v. Swincicki, 354 Mich. 427, 93 N.W.2d 281 (1959); Hartman v. Hartman, 253 Wis. 389, 34 N.W.2d 137 (1948); People v. Frangadakis, 184 Cal.App.2d 540, 7 Cal.Rptr. 776 (1960); Hair v. McGuire, 188 Cal.App.2d 348, 10 Cal.Rptr. 414 (1961).

This Court is of the opinion that there is merit to plaintiff's position concerning the effect of Mapp and Loria on the Bloodgood dicta. The language of the Court of Appeals enjoining State courts to follow Mapp "in all trials" is unequivocal. Furthermore, it would seem that there is no valid basis for different rules of admissibility of illegally obtained evidence in criminal and civil litigation; evidence obtained by search and seizure in violation of the constitution should be excluded in both types of actions.

However, it is not necessary to pass upon the question which has been discussed above on the present motion, for the Court is satisfied that the autopsy report challenged by plaintiff was not obtained by unlawful search or seizure and that the public records of findings obtained from the autopsy performed by a pathologist at the direction of the coroner under the circumstances present in these cases are admissible in evidence upon the trial of the actions.

Plaintiff points to Section 4210 of the Public Health Law and Code of Criminal Procedure, Section 773 and asserts that, in view of these sections, a coroner is authorized to perform or direct an autopsy only when he has been informed that a person has been killed by another or has suddenly died under such circumstances as to afford a reasonable ground to suspect that his death has been occasioned by the act of another by criminal means, or has committed suicide. Since her husband's death falls within none of these categories, she asserts that the coroner was without power to direct the post mortem examination.

The Court is not satisfied however that the coroner's authority is so limited. (See 13 N.Y.Jur. Counties, § 100.) Certain it is that he may direct an autopsy when circumstances are as described in these sections. Other sections of the laws of this state, not mentioned by plaintiff or defendants, make it clear that, at least by implication, the Legislature has empowered him, in other circumstances also, to perform his general duty to "make inquiry into unnatural deaths within his county" (County Law, § 662) and as an incident thereto to direct post mortem examinations.

Section 603 (formerly Section 75) of the Vehicle and Traffic Law requires the coroner to make a report to the commissioner of motor vehicles with respect to all deaths found to have been the result of motor vehicle or motorcycle accidents. In view of the circumstances surrounding decedent's death, this section might well be relevant to such death.

Section 4143, subd. 2 of the Public Health Law provides that when death occurs without medical attendance the local health officer shall investigate and certify as to the cause of death and in certain circumstances (which are different from those set forth in Public Health Law, § 4210 and Code of Criminal Procedure, § 773) shall refer the case to the coroner for the latter's investigation and certification. By subdivision 3 of Section 4143 the coroner is thereupon charged with the responsibility of stating on the certificate of death the "name of the disease causing death, or if from external causes, the means of death".

Section 4144, subd. 2 of the Public Health Law provides that no burial permit shall be issued by the registrar of vital statistics until a complete and satisfactory certificate of death has been filed with him. When no physician was in attendance on the deceased, such certificate must be issued either by the local health officer or by the coroner, as provided in Section 4143, and must certify as to the *cause* of death.

The sections of the Vehicle and Traffic Law and of the Public Health Law discussed above charge the coroner with a duty of making a determination as to the cause of death and of reporting or certifying the same, without expressly granting him the power to perform an autopsy in these circumstances. It is inconceivable to this Court however that the Legislature would impose a duty to make such a technical and scientific determination—many times impossible without a post mortem examination—without by implication conferring the authority to perform the necessary analytical procedure to make such determination.

Code of Criminal Procedure, § 778a, cited by plaintiff, merely refers to the right of a representative of the deceased to be present at an autopsy. It does not require the person performing the same to notify such representative nor does it affect the validity of the examination.

Plaintiff relies chiefly on Penal Law, § 2214 as prohibiting the autopsy here performed. That section however only prohibits such procedures which are not carried on "by authority of law" or which are not "in pursuance of a permission given by the deceased". This Court is of the opinion that the section referred to does not apply to a coroner acting in the performance of his official duty, anymore than Section 270–b of the Penal Law prohibiting the taking of statements in a hospital applied to a police officer in the Bloodgood case. In any event, as indicated above, the Court is satisfied that the autopsy in question was performed "by authority of law" so as to be removed from the bar of Penal Law, § 2214, and that it was also carried out with the permission given by the deceased, a second basis for its exclusion from the prohibition of the Penal Law section.

It should be recalled that the policy of insurance issued by The Travelers Insurance Company specifically authorized the performance of an autopsy on the body of the insured. This requirement is a condition precedent to recovery on the policy and the deceased, by entering into the contract of insurance, thereby gave his consent to a post mortem examination. In this circumstance, it cannot be said that the autopsy was unauthorized; on the contrary, the procedure was expressly authorized by the deceased. Had not the coroner decided to perform the examination, the insurance company itself could have requested it. Once the coroner had acted however, and had made an official record of the findings of the autopsy, there was of course no purpose to be served by the company's pursuing a second autopsy. It was entitled to rely upon the act of the coroner—over whom neither party had control—and to accept his report in lieu of the examination to which it was entitled by the terms of the policy under which plaintiff now seeks to recover. A public official is presumed to act honestly and in accordance with law and to do nothing contrary to official duty nor omit anything which official duty requires to be done. (Matter of Marcellus, 165 N.Y. 70, 58 N.E. 796 (1900); Matter of Whitman, 225 N.Y. 1, 121 N.E. 479 (1919).) Furthermore, there can be no doubt that an official autopsy report duly filed as a public record is admissible in evidence. (People v. Nisonoff, 293 N.Y. 597, 59 N.E.2d 420 (1945); Iovino v. Green Bus Lines, Inc., 277 App.Div. 1002, 100 N.Y.S.2d 148 (1950).)

Since the Court has determined as a matter of law that the autopsy was not unauthorized, no hearing is required for a determination of the motion. For the reasons given above, the motion to suppress is denied.

CONE v. BENJAMIN

Supreme Court of Florida, Division B, 1946.
157 Fla. 800, 27 So.2d 90.

Appeal from Circuit Court, Pinellas County; T. Frank Hobson, Judge.

. . .

BROWN, Justice. On January 28, 1931, Harrison J. Stewart and Ada Cone Stewart, his wife, an aged and childless couple, who had been residents of St. Petersburg, Florida, for some twenty years, lost their lives in that city as a result of a collision between an automobile in which they were riding and a train. Both died on the day of the collision, but the husband died about an hour prior to the death of his wife. Each of them left a will giving to the other all of his or her estate. Both wills were duly probated.

Soon thereafter the County Judge of Pinellas County appointed Roy L. Benjamin as administrator with the will annexed of the estates of each of the deceased persons, and he duly qualified as such. The estate of Harrison J. Stewart consisted mostly of personal property, stocks, bonds, mortgages, etc., which the administrator's inventory showed amounted to $47,803.13, and some real estate of the value of $10,000, or more. The inventory of Ada Cone Stewart's estate showed no assets discovered. Notice to creditors, legatees, distributees, etc., was duly published for eight weeks, and proof of publication filed, as required by Sections 5597, 5598, C.G.L. of 1927.

On February 15, 1932, Roy L. Benjamin, as administrator c. t. a. of the estate of Harrison J. Stewart, filed a bill of complaint in the Circuit Court of Pinellas County, entitled "A bill for instructions to administrator," against himself, as administrator of Ada Cone Stewart's estate, the New England Life Insurance Company, and unknown heirs of Ada Cone Stewart. The purpose of the bill was to determine which of the decedents died first, and who were the proper heirs and beneficiaries to receive the assets of the two estates. . .

. . .

We come now to the evidence relied on by appellants to prove heirship. None of the twenty two persons, whom the appellants' bill alleged to be the heirs of Ada Cone Stewart, appeared in court or testified in this case. Nine of them declined to join as plaintiffs in the suit, and were made defendants. Counsel for appellants sought to prove such heirship by offering in evidence a book, written and published by one William Whitney Cone of Brandsville, Mo., in 1903, which purported to give a history of the Cone family in America, wherein the names of Ada Cone Stewart, and some 6,567 other persons, appears, and by offering the testimony of several witnesses in an effort to prove that Mrs. Stewart was a cousin of, or related to, the author, the theory being that this rendered the book admissible in evidence as a written declaration made by "a member of the family."

"The rule is that declarations of deceased persons who were de jure related by blood or marriage to the family in question may be given in evidence in matters of pedigree. (Citing authorities.) A qualification of the rule is that before a declaration can be admitted in evidence the relationship of the declarant with the family must be established by some proof independent of the declaration itself." Fulkerson v. Holmes, 117 U.S. 389, 6 S.Ct. 780, 784, 29 L.Ed. 915 (1886). The opinion in this leading case also says: "This exception (to the rule against hearsay) has been recognized on the ground of necessity; for as in inquires respecting relationship or descent facts must often be proved which occurred many years before the trial, and were known to but few persons, it is obvious that the strict enforcement in such cases of the rules against hearsay evidence would frequently occasion a failure of justice. Tayl.Ev. § 635. Traditional evidence is therefore admissible."

"The rule of admission is accordingly restricted to the declarations of deceased persons who were related by blood or marriage to the person whose pedigree is in issue and therefore to the declarations of declarants interested in the succession in question. . . . The declaration of friends, servants and neighbors might not be received, but the rule is now declared by nearly all the authorities that the declarations are confined to those made by legal relatives. So far as blood relatives are concerned, the law does not seem to have limited the inquiry within any particular degree of relationship, although the declarations of very remote relatives might be entitled to very little weight." Jones on Evidence, 2d Ed., Section 1132.

. . .

Generally speaking, the theory underlying the acceptance of the declarations as to pedigree made by deceased persons who were members of or intimately connected with the family is based upon the theory that such persons were familiar with those matters of family history, tradition and repute with which the members of most families are familiar, although based upon hearsay within the family, and that, having been made before any controversy had arisen, there was no motive to speak other than the truth. As was said by Justice Paxson in the old case of Sitler v. Gehr, supra: "Indeed we scarcely realize how little we actually know from our own observation and investigation. We learn the truths of history, the secrets of science and our knowledge of the world generally, from what we have read, or from what others have told us. What does a man know of his own deceased ancestors but what he has learned from his immediate relatives? How was the plaintiff, who had never seen Balser Behr, of

Berks County, to know that the latter was his uncle except from his mother? It is in just such cases that the strict rules of evidence are relaxed as regards hearsay. If it were otherwise pedigree could not be proved at all in many cases, and in one sense it is primary not secondary evidence. The law upon this point is clearly stated in 1 Wharton's Evidence, Sec. 201: 'Pedigree, from the nature of things, is open to proof by hearsay in respect to all family incidents, as to which no living witness can be found. If what has been handed down in families cannot be in this way proved, pedigree could not, in most cases, be proved at all.' " See also C.J.S., Evidence, § 226, p. 970 et seq.; 1 Greenleaf on Evidence, 3rd Ed., Sec. 114 et seq.; 20 Am.Jur. 409 et seq., and other authorities already cited.

It is also well settled that entries as to births, deaths, and marriages shown by family Bibles, Church registers and certificates and inscriptions on monuments; hospital records and hotel registers (under certain circumstances and for certain purposes); letters of deceased relatives containing statements as to family matters, although entitled to different degrees of credibility; recitals in wills, deeds of conveyance, and in marriage settlements and certificates; inscriptions on family portraits, rings, and other family memorials; school censuses and other books and public records which mention births, marriages and deaths, are admissible under certain circumstances. All these, and other matters, are treated in the books.

The book here in question, entitled "Some Account of the Cone Family in America," was written over a period of years by William Whitney Cone and published by him in 1903. This was abundantly proven by his daughter, Mrs. Isabelle C. Harvey, a resident of Topeka, Kansas. The book is more than a mere declaration by a member of a family of matters of family history and repute which would ordinarily be known by any member of any particular family. It is a history and genealogy of the Cone family in America, replete with personal sketches of the careers of many members of that family. It deals primarily with the descendants of Daniel Cone, progenitor in America of the most numerous branch of the Cone family, who settled in Haddam, Connecticut, in 1662, when he appears as one of twenty-eight persons who received from the Connecticut Colony a grant of a considerable body of land situated on both sides of the Connecticut River. The first mention of Daniel Cone, which the author was able to find, was a requisition, signed by Governor John Winthrop, of the Connecticut Colony, to Peter Stuyvesant, Governor of New Netherlands, dated March 2, 1657, and contained in the Massachusetts Historical Collection. The requisition, in the form of a letter, begins: "Honored Sir: Complaint being made to me by Daniel Cone that one James Parker," etc.

In C.J.S., Evidence, § 717, p. 626, it is said: "As a general rule a book or other publication printed by a private person and not shown to be approved by any public authority is not competent evidence of the facts therein state, at least if it does not appear to be in general use among the class of persons interested in the matters of which it treats, and if on account of the recent occurrence of the facts or for other reasons they may be proved by living witnesses or other better evidence. Books and other printed publications shown to be in general use among the class of persons interested in the matters which they contain have, however, been held admissible."

This is indeed a remarkable book; handsomely published and skillfully arranged. The evidence shows that the author carried on an enormous correspondence and also made a trip East, especially to Connecticut, to check over the records and to obtain information. He was born in Monroe County, N. Y., December 18, 1836. He moved from New York to Kansas in 1869, where he engaged in newspaper work and was also clerk in the State Historical Society. He moved to Brandsville, Missouri, in 1896 and lived there until his death, in 1924. He was interested in historical matters and wrote a History of Shawnee County, and contributed to historical magazines. This we get from the book itself and from the testimony of his daughter, Mrs. Harvey. The book is a combination of genealogy and history, and consists of 547 pages including the index. Five hundred copies were published and all but about six volumes, which the author and his family retained, were distributed mostly among the numerous members of the Cone family in thirty-one states. Several copies were deposited in public libraries. Former Governor of Florida, Hon. Frederick P. Cone, obtained a copy. These books were sold at $5 per volume, which was very small compensation indeed to the author for his many years of painstaking work and investigation. Independently of the book, the relationship of the author to the Cone family, whose history he gives, is established by the testimony of his daughter, his grandson, Randal C. Harvey, and to some extent by George A. Root, coworker with the author of another genealogy, "The Bishop Family."

There was ample evidence that this book was well received and regarded as authoritative by many members of the Cone family, including Florida's recent Governor, Frederick P. Cone, whose name is included in the book, Serial No. 6522, and his ancestorship shown. It is true that Governor Cone belonged to a different branch of the family from that of these appellants, but his testimony was that from information he had received from his father and uncles he was quite familiar with his family history for several generations back, and said that he had checked the book with his own knowledge of the history of his branch of the Cone family, and found that it was correct with the exception of a few immaterial errors as to dates and initials. Otherwise the book was correct for four generations back, which was as far as his information went. That he had discussed the book with some of his own family at Statesboro, Georgia, where his great-grandfather lived during the Revolutionary War, and that they stated practically the same facts as those set forth in the book and he considered it an authentic history of the Cone family. He also said that he had met many members of the Cone family from Ohio and practically all of the northeastern states and some of the western states and had discussed the Cone family book with some two dozen of them. He had no interest in this litigation and knew nothing about it until shortly before he was called to testify. The author of the book, who was at that time State Librarian of Missouri, wrote him about it when he was getting it up and later wrote to Governor Cone's brother, who gave the author some information about his immediate family and their ancestors.

The author expresses his appreciation to a long list of persons who have assisted him in assembling available data, and in furnishing family records. He makes no claims to infallibility. But the modesty of his preface tends to increase one's confidence in the author and compiler.

Appellees contend that the book referred to is a mere private writing of William Whitney Cone, and nothing more than a written declaration by him printed in book form. And there being no proof aliunde that the writer was related to Ada Cone Stewart, it was not admissible evidence.

If appellees' premises were correct, we could readily agree, but for the reasons above stated we think that the book is more than a mere declaration of the author, and it having been proven by several witnesses who were members of the Cone family that they had found it to be authentic, we have reached the conclusion that the book constituted at least prima facie evidence of the genealogy of the Cone family and that the chancellor below was not in error when he admitted it in evidence. We find no precedent directly in point which sustains our conclusion, but we are convinced of its soundness. The chancellor did not pass directly upon its evidentiary value, however, as he decided the case against these appellants on other grounds. We have examined this book sufficiently to find that it shows prima facie that Ada Cone Stewart was a fifth cousin of the author of the book, both being direct descendants of the progenitor of the main branch of the Cone family in America, Daniel Cone. Appellants contend that this book clearly shows that all the plaintiffs and nine defendants are relations and heirs of Ada C. Stewart, most of them being second cousins.

. . .

The decree is reversed and the cause remanded, with directions to enter a decree for appellants and such of appellees as are found to be heirs of Ada Cone Stewart. If the chancellor becomes convinced that it is necessary to take further testimony on the issue of this relationship, then nothing in this opinion shall be construed as restricting his power to do that.

Reversed and remanded.

CHAPMAN, C. J., and THOMAS and SEBRING, JJ., concur.

PETERSON v. PETERSON

District Court of Appeal, First District, Division 1, California, 1953.
121 Cal.App.2d 1, 262 P.2d 613.

Paternity proceeding. The Superior Court, County of Marin, Jordan L. Martinelli, J., entered judgment on verdict for alleged father and child appealed.

PETERS, Presiding Justice. This action was instituted by a child through his mother, Anne Kinney, against defendant to have it determined that defendant is the father of plaintiff, and to secure support, counsel fees and costs. At the trial the only witnesses produced were defendant and plaintiff's mother. The jury brought in a verdict for defendant. From the judgment entered on that verdict plaintiff appeals.

The child was born July 26, 1948. The complaint was not filed until July 10, 1951. The cause was tried in March, 1952. The evidence was directly conflicting. Anne testified to meeting respondent on an army transport upon her return to this country from Germany; that upon his promise to get a divorce and to marry her she spent two nights, October 17 and 18, 1947, in two designated hotels in New York City with respondent; that she had sexual intercourse with him on those occasions; that she was then 32 years of age; that prior and subsequent to those two nights she had never had intercourse with any other man; that just before embarking on the transport she had her regular menstrual period.

Respondent, who had been married for ten years at the time of trial, denied these accusations. He admitted meeting Anne on the transport; denied any romantic overtures while on shipboard; admitted that he took Anne to dinner twice in New York but differed from Anne as to the dates, he claiming the two dates were October 16, and 17, 1947. He admitted that, on October 17th, after both had had considerable to drink, he propositioned Anne to spend the night with him at a hotel, and she agreed, but claimed that they were unable to find a hotel that was not full, and so he returned her to her hotel, where men were not admitted, without having accomplished his purpose, and returned to the ship where he was employed. He denied that then, or at any other time, he had had intercourse with Anne.

Anne testified that defendant had registered the first night at Hotel Walcott, and the second night she, at defendant's suggestion, had registered as "Mr. and Mrs. A. Kinney" at the Breslin Hotel. Letters from both hotels were admitted in evidence. The Breslin's records failed to show that a Kinney or a Peterson had registered there on any of the critical nights. The Walcott's records showed a "Mr. and Mrs. A. Peterson and party" had registered on October 15, 1947, and had checked out on October 17, 1947. No other record was found of a Kinney or Peterson registration for the nights in question.

It is not necessary to recount the evidence on these matters in further detail. It is obvious that on the critical issue of whether respondent had intercourse with Anne in October of 1947 there was a direct conflict. The burden rested on appellant to prove his [her] case by a preponderance of the evidence. It was the jury's function to pass on the credibility of the two witnesses. It obviously was not convinced by Anne's story. Moreover, no contention is made that the evidence does not support the verdict and judgment.

The major contention of appellant is that error of a most prejudicial nature was committed on the cross-examination of Anne, in that respondent was then permitted to bring out her general relationships with other men over a period of about six years, and long prior to the period of possible conception. This, it is contended, was prejudicial error even though appellant's counsel at the trial (new counsel have been secured to handle this appeal) made no objection of any kind to the testimony in question.

On this issue the record shows the following: On direct examination by counsel for plaintiff Anne testified that she had been in the Women's Army Corps for three years, and had worked overseas as a civilian for about two years; that she was in Europe, either in the military service or as a civilian, from 1945 to September or October, 1947; that she met respondent on shipboard, and that it was upon their arrival in New York that the events above mentioned occurred. She also, on direct, testified that she never had had intercourse with any other man before or subsequent to October of 1947.

On the cross-examination of Anne respondent elaborated on these matters first brought out on direct. Not one objection was made to this cross-examination. Thus, Anne testified that she was 32 in October of 1947; that she had been born in a small town in Alabama; that after the death of her father she lived for about a year in Birmingham, Alabama, with her sister; that both joined the service in 1941, her sister as a nurse, and she as a WAC; that she spent three years in the WACs, mostly in this country, but a short time in France and Germany. Respondent's counsel had her describe the various military establishments where she had been stationed. She testified that she had spent 2½ years at Mitchell Field, New York, as an aircraft dispatcher; that in these various camps she frequently saw and came in contact with many men, and was under the command of male personnel. It was brought out that Mitchell Field was close to New York City, but she denied making frequent visits to the metropolitan area. She then testified that she was sent overseas and spent several months in France and Germany; that in August of 1945 her enlistment expired, and she elected to stay in Germany on a civilian job; that she lived at Hertz, Germany, near Frankfurt; that she was so employed until September of 1947, when she returned to the United States; that during her stay at Hertz she first lived in an apartment and later in a commandeered house. She admitted that during this period she was in constant contact with male civilian and military personnel. It was brought out that Anne frequently ate and danced with military and civilian personnel, but she denied any steady romances with any particular individual.

In his argument to the jury counsel for respondent, without objection, was permitted to refer to the above evidence and to argue that it indicated Anne's lack of moral home ties during the five plus years she was in government service, and that this background rendered it highly unlikely that she would suddenly surrender her virtue at age 32, but rather indicated that she had lived a life where many men had the opportunity of being the father of the child.

It is urged that this line of questioning and argument was undertaken for the sole purpose of besmirching Anne's reputation and prejudicing her before the jury, and constituted serious and prejudicial error. It is undoubtedly the law that, in such actions, evidence of immorality of the mother prior to the period of possible conception, or questions designed to bring out or imply acts of immorality for the purpose of showing bad character, or for impeachment, are inadmissible, and that it is error to even ask such questions. People v. Crandall, 125 Cal. 129, 57 Pac. 785 (1899) . . . But there are authorities which hold that the trial court may permit questions about general background which, while incidentally or inferentially degrading, may serve to test the credibility and memory of a witness. People v. Le Baron, 92 Cal.App. 550, 268 P. 651, 269 Pac. 476 (1928) . . .

. . .

The last contention that need be mentioned is that the trial court improperly excluded evidence claimed to be admissible under the pedigree exception to the hearsay rule. This contention is predicated upon the fact that on the direct examination of Anne she was prevented from testifying that at birth she had the appellant christened "Clifford Anthony Peterson." Later on cross-examination she testified that she had not told respondent that she intended to name the child after him until some time after the child had been so christened.

It is of course true that declarations of pedigree by those in the family group are generally admissible to prove facts of family history. But there are limitations on this exception to the hearsay rule. If a controversy or a motive to deceive exists when such declarations are made they are then inadmissible. They are then self-serving hearsay. Wigmore, Evidence, Vol. V, pp. 298–302, §§ 1483 and 1484; see, generally, In re Estate of Walden, 166 Cal. 446, 137 Pac. 35 (1914); In re Jessup, 81 Cal. 408, 21 P. 976, 22 Pac. 742, 1028, 6 L.R.A. 594 (1890).

We do not find it necessary to pass on the question as to whether this evidence was admissible or inadmissible. Even if admissible it would only have tended to show that when the child was born his mother claimed or believed that respondent was the father. That fact was already before the jury, particularly by the testimony of Anne that she never had intercourse during her life with any one but respondent. It is also obvious that the jury knew that the child was named Clifford Anthony Peterson because the complaint so names the appellant, and also names Clifford A. Peterson as defendant. Thus, even if such evidence should have been admitted, its exclusion could not have been prejudicial.

The judgment appealed from is affirmed.

PEOPLE v. LAMMES

Supreme Court, Appellate Division, Fourth Department, 1924.
208 App.Div. 533, 203 N.Y.S. 736.

CLARK, J. The defendant was convicted in Monroe county of the crime of rape in the second degree. Defendant formerly resided with his wife in the village of Spencerport, N.Y., where he conducted a bakery. In the year 1922 the complainant, Gertrude Scharn, went to work for defendant in his bakery, and they became intimate friends; she residing with defendant and his wife while she worked for them.

In the fall of 1922 complainant went to Ogden, Utah, to live with her father, and in December, 1922, defendant went to Utah and saw the complaining witness. He returned to Spencerport in January or February, 1923, and continued to live with his wife in that village. The complaining witness, Miss Scharn, returned to Rochester April 30, 1923; defendant having furnished her money to defray her traveling expenses. When she arrived in Rochester, in response to her request over the telephone, defendant went to the New York Central station and met her, and they went to a room on Chatham street, and it is claimed by the people that on the morning of May 1, 1923, at said room, defendant had sexual intercourse with the complainant, Gertrude Scharn.

On the trial she testified that said intercourse took place at that time, and there was sufficient evidence corroborating the prosecutrix as to the act of sexual intercourse with defendant, but she was not sufficiently corroborated as to her age. She testified that she became 18 years of age on the 17th day of May, 1923, and that the act of sexual intercourse charged against defendant was committed on the 1st day of May 1923, only 16 days before she became 18 years of age, according to her own testimony.

The law requires that, in a case of this character, the prosecutrix must be corroborated, and that such corroboration must extend to every material fact essential to constitute the crime charged, and in this case that rule would apply to the fact of the age of the prosecutrix, as well as to each of the material facts essential to constitute the crime. People v. Plath, 100 N.Y. 590, 3 N.E. 790, 53 Am.Rep. 236 (1886); People v. Page, 162 N.Y. 272, 56 N.E. 750 (1900).

The only corroboration of the prosecutrix on the question of her age is an affidavit made by her mother (deceased) on a school census blank, and sworn to before a police officer of the city of Rochester as a commissioner of deeds. According to that affidavit, the prosecutrix was under the age of 18 years at the time she claimed to have had intercourse with the defendant. I think the admission of this affidavit of the mother, purporting to state the date of birth of the prosecutrix, was improper, and that it constituted such a substantial error as to require the reversal of the judgment. This affidavit was hearsay evidence pure and simple. It was received on the theory that it established the pedigree of the complainant. It could not be properly received for any such purpose for age is not essential to establish pedigree, and the question of pedigree was not necessarily involved in this case. Bowen v. Preferred Accident Ins. Co., 68 App.Div. 342, 74 N.Y.Supp. 101 (1902); Bowen v. Preferred Accident Ins. Co., 82 App.Div. 458, 81 N.Y.Supp. 840 (1903) . . .

One of the facts that the people were obliged to establish in order to convict this defendant was that the complainant was under the age of 18 years at the time he had intercourse with her. Penal Law, § 2010. No conviction could properly be had upon the testimony of the prosecutrix, unsupported by other evidence. Penal Law, § 2013. The only other evidence in this case on the question of the age of the prosecutrix was the affidavit of her mother above referred to.

Under the circumstances as disclosed by the evidence, an inspection of the complaining witness would not aid the jury in determining her age at the time she alleges the crime was committed. People v. Todoro, 160 N.Y.Supp. 352 (Sup.1916); People v. Marks, 146 App. Div. 11, 13, 130 N.Y.Supp. 524 (1911). The judgment of conviction should be reversed, and a new trial granted.

Judgment of conviction reversed, upon questions of law and fact, and new trial granted. All concur, except DAVIS and CROUCH, JJ., who dissent, and vote for affirmance, in an opinion by DAVIS, J.

DAVIS, J. (dissenting). The crime is alleged to have occurred on May 1, 1923. The main facts are well established. Gertrude Scharn, the complaining witness, testified that she became 18 years of age on May 17, 1923. This evidence must be corroborated, because it constitutes one of the material facts essential for a legal conviction. Penal Law, § 2013; People v. Todoro, 224 N.Y. 129, 120 N.E. 135 (1918); People v. Harrison, 63 Misc.Rep. 18, 117 N.Y.Supp. 477 (1909).

There was no direct testimony corroborating Gertrude as to her age. She was born in Holland. Her father and mother came with her to this country in 1916, and resided in Rochester. Evidently the parents separated for some reason. The father went to live in Utah. The mother and daughter remained in Rochester, residing on Berkley street, and Gertrude went to school. Testimony of witnesses called by defendant, who knew them both, together with complainant's evidence, established the fact of such residence.

To this home on November 8, 1920, came one Carroll, a policeman, taking the school census. This was apparently shortly before the mother's death, for Gertrude's testimony is that her mother died during that month. The usual school census blank was made out, and Alida Scharn, the mother, signed it and made oath as to the truth of the statements therein contained before the police officer, who was also a commissioner of deeds. The father was not within the jurisdiction of the court at the time of the trial. That sworn statement of the deceased mother was produced, identified, and received in evidence over the objection of the defendant's counsel. It stated that Gertrude Scharn was born in Holland on May 17, 1905.

I think this evidence competent on the question of complainant's age. It is, of course, hearsay. So, also, was the testimony of Gertrude herself on that subject. Declarations in regard to pedigree, though hearsay, are admissible, where made before a controversy arose or action brought and the declarant is a deceased relative. . . . Aalholm v. People, 211 N.Y. 406, 416, 105 N.E. 647, L.R.A. 1915D, 215, Ann.Cas.1915C, 1039 (1914). It is admitted on the theory that it is the best evidence that can be then obtained. People v. Koerner, 154 N.Y. 355, 370, 48 N.E. 730 (1897). Matters of pedigree include such facts as those concerning birth (Eisenlord v. Clum, 126 N.Y. 552, 27 N.E. 1024, 12 L.R.A. 836) (1891), and the time when such event happened (Washington v. Bank for Savings in City of New York, 171 N.Y. 166, 173, 63 N.E. 831, 89 Am.St.Rep. 800) (1902). Age may not of itself be an element of pedigree (People v. Sheppard, 44 Hun, 565 (1887); Bowen v. Preferred Accident Ins. Co., 68 App.Div. 342, 344, 74 N.Y.Supp. 101 (1902)); but, if the date of birth may be proved, the question of the person's age is merely a matter of computation. There is no sound reason why age, when an issue, may not be proved in the same manner as any question of pedigree. I do not regard the rule fixed in this state that declarations of such a genealogical fact as the date of birth are inadmissible. Certainly the weight of modern authority supports the rule favoring admission, when better evidence may not be obtained, whether the issue is strictly one of pedigree or otherwise. Chamberlayne's Modern Law of Evidence, §§ 2923, 2929; Wigmore on Evidence (2d Ed.) § 1503.

The number of persons having actual knowledge of the date of birth is always limited—generally, at the most, to the mother, father, physician, and midwife or nurse. There are times when such witnesses cannot be called to make proof of this essential fact, so the law of necessity accepts records or declarations made by such persons when there was no object to deceive rather than concede that proof of a patent fact is impossible. Washington v. Bank for Savings, supra, page 175 (63 N.E. 834 (1902)); Griffin v. Train, 90 App.Div. 16, 20, 85 N.Y.S. 686; 22 C.J. 216, 234 (1904). So a record made in the family Bible may be admitted to prove the date of birth, and thereby the age of a person (Penal Law, § 817; People v. Slater, 119 Cal. 620, 51 Pac. 957 (1898); 33 Cyc. 1473) no matter by whom the entry is made (Union Central Life Ins. Co. v. Pollard, 94 Va. 146,

26 S.E. 421, 36 L.R.A. 271, 64 Am.St.Rep. 715 (1897); Jones v. Jones, 45 Md. 144, 160 (1876); Wigmore on Evidence [2d Ed.] § 1496); and direct testimony may be given by a physician, based on a record he made at the time of the birth of a child, or by the father concerning an entry in the family Bible, as showing the age of a prosecutrix in such an action as this (James v. State, 125 Ark. 269, 188 S.W. 806 (1916)).

Records of such facts as the age of a person must have recognized reliability and authenticity, or they will be excluded. Penal Law, § 817; . . . Buffalo Loan, Trust & Safe-Deposit Co. v. Knights Templar & Masonic Ass'n, 126 N.Y. 450, 27 N.E. 942, 22 Am.St.Rep. 839 (1891). The evidence offered in this case may not be so impeached. The record offered was made pursuant to a provision of law. Education Law, § 650, and section 651, as amended by Laws 1917, c. 567. It was intended to secure accuracy. Id. § 653. Very likely the records made in its books by the census board would have been competent under the circumstances. Richards v. Robin, 178 App.Div. 535, 165 N.Y.Supp. 780 (1917); Swift & Co. v. Rennard, 119 Ill.App. 173; Armstrong v. Modern Woodmen, 93 Wash. 352, 160 Pac. 946, Ann.Cas.1918E, 263 (1916). But we do not need to determine that question. The original affidavit of the mother was produced. That sworn statement would seem to be as reliable as would be her unverified entry in a family Bible. Russell v. Jackson, 22 Wend. 277, 280 (1839). While not made admissible by statute, as are records of birth and baptism, or entries in the family Bible, if the evidence was admissible in a civil case, it was admissible here. Code Cr.Proc. § 392. The mother possessed peculiar knowledge on the subject. To her the birth of her daughter must always have been a significant event. When she made the affidavit, there was no reason for making a false statement. The mother cannot now give testimony, and the law must be content with the best available evidence. If the jury were convinced of its truth and reliability, it constituted the necessary corroboration.

In such cases, the appearance of the complaining witness on the stand may be considered by the jury in reaching a conclusion as to her age. Penal Law, § 817; . . . State v. Davis, 237 Mo. 237, 140 S.W. 902 (1911); Wigmore on Evidence, §§ 222, 1154 (subd. 3). In this case such evidence might be of slight value, because the complainant lacked but 16 days of being 18 years of age when the act was perpetrated, and she was 14 days past 18 when the trial began. It would obviously be difficult by ordinary observation to make such fine discriminations. People v. Marks, 146 App.Div. 11, 130 N.Y.S. 524 (1911); People v. Todoro, 160 N.Y.S. 352 (1916). But I think we may not hold as a matter of law that the jury could not have taken her appearance into consideration. People v. Justices of Court of Special Sessions of County of New York, 10 Hun. 224, 226 (1877).

I vote for affirmance of the judgment of conviction.

CROUCH, J., concurs.

IN THE MATTER OF THE ESTATE OF WALLIN v. STATE OF ARIZONA EX REL. SWIFT

Court of Appeals of Arizona, 1971.
16 Ariz.App. 34, 490 P.2d 863.

HOWARD, Judge. Hugo A. Wallin died intestate in 1968 and Letters of Administration were issued to one Forest V. Bender. In December, 1969, the appellant filed a petition to determine heirship. The petition alleged that the appellant's ward, Beda Wallin, an incompetent, was the decedent's sister and his only surviving heir at law.

An answer was filed by the administrator denying Beda Wallin's relationship to the decedent and the State of Arizona filed a notice of appearance and concurred in the administrator's answer. Subsequently, the State filed a complaint seeking an order of escheat. Both matters were consolidated for trial which resulted in the court denying appellant's petition to have Beda Wallin declared an heir of the decedent. The court found that the decedent died intestate and without heirs and ordered his estate escheated to the State of Arizona. This appeal followed attacking the correctness of both determinations.

Since reversal of the ruling in the heirship proceeding is dispositive of this appeal, we address ourselves to that aspect of the appeal.

The burden of establishing a claim of heirship is on the alleged heir. Edgar v. Dickens, 230 Ark. 7, 320 S.W.2d 761 (1959); In re Hobart's Estate, 82 Cal.App.2d 502, 187 P.2d 105 (1947). On the other hand escheats are not favored and it is presumed that a decedent left heirs or next of kin capable of inheriting property. Risbry v. Swan, 124 Colo. 567, 239 P.2d 600 (1951); In re Holmlund's Estate, 232 Or. 49, 374 P.2d 393 (1962).

The thrust of appellant's attack on appeal is the exclusion of certain documentary evidence offered to prove the relationship between the decedent and Beda Wallin. These documents consisted of the following:

1. A certified copy of the marriage record of one Carl A. Wallen and Matilda Nordien showing that their marriage took place in LaMoure County, North Dakota, on June 16, 1900, indicating that both were of LaMoure County and their ages were 38 and 28 respectively.
2. A "registration of death record" showing Karl August Wallen died on January 14, 1916 in the province of Saskatchewan, Canada, at the age of 53 years 5 months and 2 days. It indicated that he was a widower at the time of death.
3. A "registration of death" showing that Matilda Wallen [1] died on October 12, 1910 in the province of Saskatchewan,

1. The decedent's name is handwritten and it is difficult to determine whether the surname is Wallen or Waleen. However the signature of the informant contains two l's. (Karl Wallen or Karl Wallin.)

Canada, at the age of 41. It indicated that she was married at the time of death.

4. Letters of guardianship issued to Grace J. Daugherty by the county court of LaMoure County, North Dakota, evidencing her appointment as guardian of the person and Estate of Peter Nordin filed in LaMoure County, North
5. A copy of a petition for letters of administration for the estate of Beda Wallin, an incompetent person.
Dakota, county court. The petition, filed by Carrie Nordin and verified by her, dated October 3, 1934 contains the following caption:

"In the Matter of the Estate of Peter Nordin, deceased
Carrie Nordin,

Petitioner,

v.

Charles Nordin, Emma Johanson, Mathilda Wallin (deceased), Beda Wallin and Hugo Wallin, children of Mathilda Wallin, deceased,

Respondents."

The petition alleged that the decedent Peter Nordin died intestate and that the next of kin and the heirs at law under the law of succession were: Carrie Nordin, widow of decedent, residence being Gladstone Township, Marion, North Dakota, age 69; Charles Nordin, brother of decedent, age 62, address Litchville, North Dakota; Emma Johanson, sister, age 60, address Angelstad, Sweden; Beda Wallin, niece, address, Marion, N. D., age 30; Hugo Wallin, nephew, age 33, address Washington, Mo., both children of Mathilda Wallin, deceased, sister of said decedent; and Lina Magnuson, Hallarp, Annerstad, Sweden. It further alleged:

> "That your petitioner is the widow of said deceased, and therefore, as your petitioner is advised and believes, is entitled to a letter of administration of the estate of said deceased but request [sic] that her niece Beda Wallin be appointed as the administratrix of the estate of said decedent."

6. A copy of a final decree of distribution in the Estate of Peter Nordin (LaMoure County, North Dakota). The caption of this document reads as follows:

"Beda Wallin,

Petitioner,

v.

Charles Nordin, Emma
Johanson, Lina Magnuson,
Hugo Wallin and Carrie
Nordin,

Respondents."

It directed distribution of the decedent's estate to his surviving widow, Carrie Nordin, and that Beda Wallin, administratrix, upon filing satisfactory evidence of distribution, would be finally discharged from her trust as administratrix. This decree was dated July 26, 1935.

Admitted into evidence was the death certificate of Hugo August Wallin indicating that he died on February 16, 1968 in Tuscon, Arizona, at the age of 66 and that he was born in North Dakota.

Various objections were made to the introduction of the excluded documents, primarily on the grounds that they were hearsay and lacked relevance. The trial court, in sustaining the objections, was of the opinion that there was no showing of relevancy and that there was a great deal of hearsay in the documents.

A well-recognized exception to the hearsay rules exists in respect of proof of matters of family history, relationships and pedigree and subject to certain limitations and restrictions, hearsay evidence is admissible to prove such matters. 29 Am.Jur.2d, Evidence § 508. As stated in the foregoing text:

> "Such evidence is held admissible not only because of the extreme difficulty of producing any better evidence—that is, because it is the best evidence of which the nature of the matter admits—but also because of its general reliability. Indeed, it has been held that evidence in respect of pedigree, or ancestral lineage, does not stand upon the footing of secondary evidence, to be excluded if some other witness can be produced who speaks upon the subject from his own knowledge."

No particular form of statement is required to render a declaration as to pedigree admissible in evidence. It may be oral or written, such as a letter, descriptions in wills and in Bibles—these are admitted upon the principle that they are the natural effusions of a person who must know the truth and who speaks upon an occasion when his mind stands in an even position, without any temptation to exceed or fall short of the truth.

Examination of the petition for letters of administration filed in North Dakota in 1934 reveals that it contains a recitation concerning Beda Wallin and Hugo Wallin as to their relationship inter se and to the decedent. It refers to the age of Hugo Wallin at that time which ties in with his age at the date of his death.

Although an allegation with respect to heirship in one proceeding may not be conclusive in a subsequent one, Behan v. Treasurer & Receiver General, 276 Mass. 502, 177 N.E. 654 (1931), a statement as to pedigree in a foreign probate petition and the proceedings thereon is competent evidence as to relationship. In re Weis' Estate, 224 Cal.App.2d 19, 36 Cal.Rptr. 266 (1964); Melton v. Anderson, 32 Tenn. App. 335, 222 S.W.2d 666 (1948); Burrell v. Westbrook, 163 S.W.2d 695 (Tex.Civ.App.1942); See C.J.S. Evidence § 232.

Generally speaking, written declarations are admissible when it appears the declarant is dead or unavailable and is a member of the family. In re Weis' Estate, supra; 2 Jones on Evidence § 286. The 1934 petition for letters of administration reflects that the petitioner,

Carrie Nordin, was then 69 years of age. Under these circumstances, it would not be inappropriate to indulge in the presumption that she was unavailable to testify. We may also presume from the fact that letters issued to Beda Wallin pursuant to Carrie Nordin's request, that the probate court found that they were related. Since written declarations made by a member of the family concerning pedigree are admissible, we believe that it was improper to exclude the documents pertaining to the North Dakota probate.

In the case of In re Weis' Estate, supra, the probate court found that the putative heir was the decedent's half sister. This finding was challenged on the ground that the evidence was insufficient to support it. The claimant, just as in the case at bench, because of her incompetency, was unable to offer any testimony or evidence bearing upon her relationship to the decedent. In attempting to prove family relationship between the decedent and the claimant, certified copies of various documents such as death certificates, a marriage certificate, divorce complaints and copies of documents relating to the insanity proceedings of the claimant were introduced. Also, certified copies of documents relating to the administration of the estate of a sister in law of the decedent were introduced. On appeal, it was contended that these documents were all hearsay, hence inadmissible. The California Appellate Court did not pass upon the admissibility of documents other than those relating to the probate proceedings and held that the assertions made therein as to relationships, although hearsay, were admissible within the "family history" exception to the hearsay rule and were sufficient to support the finding that the claimant was the decedent's half sister.

As to the other documents which were refused admission, it would appear that they become relevant once the record in the North Dakota probate proceeding is admitted into evidence. The certified copies of the marriage certificate and death certificate are admissible as prima facie evidence of the facts therein stated, A.R.S. §§ 12–2264 and 2265; Ranger Insurance Co. v. Industrial Commission, 15 Ariz.App. 45, 485 P.2d 869 (1971). Examination of the various documents reveal that LaMoure County, North Dakota, was where the Nordin probate took place, where Carl A. Wallen and Mathilda Nordien were married, and where a guardian was appointd for Beda Wallin. Also, the ages set forth in the various documents are corroborative of identity, as are the similarity of names. It is not inappropriate, in determining a claim of heirship, to consider these circumstances. In re Lipovsky's Estate, 238 Cal.App.2d 604, 48 Cal.Rptr. 41 (1966); In re Hooper's Estate, 53 Wash.2d 262, 332 P.2d 1077 (1958).

We hold that the trial court erroneously excluded the documentary exhibits in the heirship proceeding. As a consequence thereof, the judgment of escheat must be reversed and the cause remanded for a new trial.

KRUCKER, C. J., and HATHAWAY, J., concur.

DECISIONS RELATING TO CHAPTER XII, PRIVILEGED COMMUNICATIONS

VANDERHULE v. BERINSTEIN

Supreme Court, Appellate Division, Third Department, 1954.
285 App.Div. 290, 136 N.Y.S.2d 95.

HALPERN, Justice. The plaintiffs appeal from an order setting aside a verdict in their favor and dismissing the complaint in an action to recover damages for an assault committed by an employee of the defendants, and from the judgment entered pursuant to the order.

The first four defendants named in the title are copartners owning and operating a bowling alley in the City of Binghamton, New York, known as the State Bowling Center. The defendant Randall is the general manager of the Bowling Center. The Bowling Center has twenty bowling alleys at which 200 people bowl in an evening in two shifts. Immediately adjacent to the alleys, there are benches upon which the bowlers sit between games. Behind the benches are several rows of seats for spectators. In an adjoining room, there is a luncheonette where food and beer are served.

Overlooking the bowling alleys is a desk at which a supervisory employee known as a "desk man" is stationed. He collects the money from the team captains and designates the alleys at which the teams are to bowl. He also makes announcements over the public address system, and generally is in charge of the Bowling Center when the manager is not present. The desk man serves as the assistant manager and is sometimes referred to by that title.

On September 20, 1952, three weeks before the occurrence of the assault which gave rise to this action, a man named Finkle applied to the defendant Randall for a job. He had just come to the city and had no permanent place of residence and he had no funds. Randall admitted that Finkle had all the characteristics of a "floater" except that he was "a little bit better dressed than a floater".

Finkle did not have any letter of reference from any former employer; in fact, he evaded the question and did not give the name of any former employer when Randall asked him about it. Randall made no other inquiries except a request for Finkle's social security number. Finkle was hired as a pin setter. After being so employed for a week, he was promoted to desk man and assistant manager, next in command to Randall, the general manager. No inquiry was made as to his history or background prior to his promotion to desk man and assistant manager. There was some evidence that during the period of his employment, Finkle had told a fellow employee that he had "had trouble with the police agencies in Albany" and that this information had been reported to the general manager.

Randall had rented a room in his own apartment to Finkle and, on October 12, 1952, while they were riding home together, Finkle made some statements, which were obviously irrational or confused, to the effect that "the Democrat organization" was "holding his wife in Albany" and "wouldn't let him get to see her". Randall heard this statement but "took it as a joke"; he did not pursue the matter with Finkle and he made no further inquiry of anyone.

The next evening, October 13, 1952, the plaintiffs, Mr. and Mrs. Vanderhule, went to the Bowling Center shortly before nine o'clock for a game in a league in which Mr. Vanderhule was a member. Upon their arrival, Fingle was acting as the desk man, during the first series of games. During the second series, he was replaced by another man at the desk and Finkle temporarily served as a pin setter, because of an emergency which had arisen due to the absence of one of the pin boys. About half past ten o'clock, while Mrs. Vanderhule was keeping score for her husband's team, Finkle approached her and struck her in the face, without any provocation and without any apparent reason. She had seen Finkle the week before when she had been at the Bowling Center, bowling on a girls' team, but there was no evidence of the occurrence of any altercation that night or of any other incident which might account for the assault. When Mr. Vanderhule observed the assault upon his wife, he engaged in a tussle with Finkle and in the course of it, he fell and fractured his knee.

The defendant Randall was in his office at the time. When he was told of the assault, his immediate response was that Finkle "must have gone off his rocker".

Subsequently, Finkle was confined to the Binghamton State Hospital and was not available upon the trial as a witness for either side.

An action was brought for the assault upon the wife and for the injury suffered by the husband. The complaint alleged several causes of action, two principal grounds of recovery being advanced. One was that the defendants knew or, in the exercise of care, should have known of Finkle's "paranoid and psychopathic tendencies" and that the defendants were negligent in employing and retaining him. The other ground of recovery was that the defendants, in consideration of a fee paid them, "promised and agreed to treat plaintiffs properly and carefully and to protect them at all times while they were at said State Bowling Center", and that the defendants had breached the agreement.

The Trial Court dismissed the so-called contract cause of action at the close of the case but submitted the negligence cause of action to the jury. The jury reported a verdict in favor of the plaintiffs. The court thereafter set the verdict aside and granted the motion made by the defendants at the close of the case to dismiss the complaint. The dismissal was based upon the ground that the plaintiffs had failed to establish that the negligence of the defendants was the proximate cause of the plaintiffs' injuries. The court reasoned that the defendants were under a duty to make inquiry before hiring an employee and that they had breached that duty in employing Finkle without any "inquiry or investigation as to his character or past", but that this negligence was not the proximate cause of the injury because there was no proof of "any fact concerning Finkle or his past, which any inquiry, however extensive and thorough, would have disclosed indicating that his employment would be a potential danger to others".

A more conventional way of expressing the trial court's conclusion would be to say that the defendants had not been guilty of any negligence. The trial court conceived of the defendants' duty as a duty in the abstract to make inquiry but that is not a duty for the breach of which an action could be maintained. " 'Proof of negligence in the air, so to speak, will not do.' " Palsgraf v. Long Island R. Co., 248 N.Y. 339, 341, 162 N.E. 99, 59 A.L.R. 1253 (1928). The ultimate duty of the defendants, for a breach of which the defendants could be held liable, was the duty to refrain from hiring or retaining anyone whom they knew or, in the exercise of reasonable care, they should have known was potentially dangerous. If, as the court concluded, there was no evidence which warranted the inference that the defendants knew or should have known that Finkle was potentially dangerous, there was no negligence on their part in selecting and retaining Finkle as an employee. The question of proximate cause would arise only if it were found that the defendants had been guilty of negligence in retaining Finkle and the question would then be whether the negligence was causally connected with the assault. On that issue there could be little doubt. The risk of assault upon a patron was well within the range of the foreseeable consequences of retaining a potentially dangerous employee.

The troublesome question here is not the question of proximate cause but of negligence. Partly because of the reliance of the plaintiffs' counsel upon incompetent methods of proving the character and prior conduct of Finkle, to which reference is made below, evidence of negligence at the conclusion of the case was very thin. However for the purpose of determining whether a sufficient case had been made out for submission to the jury, the plaintiffs were entitled, under the elementary rule, to that view of the evidence which was most favorable to their claim.

> "The question of negligence is for a jury when there is a conflict in the evidence or when, though there is no such conflict, fair-minded men can draw more than one inference from the undisputed facts. Mead v. Parker, 111 N.Y. 259, 262, 18 N.E. 727, 728; Salt Springs Nat. Bank v. Sloan, 135 N.Y. 371, 384, 32 N.E. 231, 235. In our judgment, fair-minded jurors could here reasonably have inferred from the undisputed facts a failure of the defendant to exercise . . . the due care and caution that were required". Veihelmann v. Manufacturers Safe Deposit Co., 303 N.Y. 526, 530, 104 N.E.2d 888, 890.

Looking at the evidence, which we have summarized above, in the light most favorable to the plaintiffs, we think there was sufficient evidence to make the question of the defendants' negligence a question of fact for the jury. The irrational remarks by Finkle the evening before the assault, coupled with the peculiar circumstances under which he had been employed and promoted, permitted a finding by fair-minded jurors that the general manager should have realized that Finkle was mentally unstable and that it was dangerous to retain him. Furthermore, even if the circumstances were not sufficient of themselves to charge the defendants with notice of Finkle's condition, they were sufficient, when combined with the further fact that Finkle was confined to a mental institution shortly after the assault, to warrant a finding by a jury that, if diligent inquiry had been made before the assault, a history of prior mental instability would have been uncovered.

We therefore cannot accept the trial court's conclusion that the defendants were free from negligence as a matter of law, cf. McCrink v. City of New York, 296 N.Y. 99, 71 N.E.2d 419 (1950); Fleming v. Bronfin, 80 A.2d 915 (D.C.Mun.App.1951).

However, we are of the opinion that the verdict in favor of the plaintiffs was against the weight of the evidence. The distinction between a case insufficient in law and a case not supported by the weight of the evidence is a well-settled one and we believe that this is an appropriate case in which to apply the distinction, see § 457–a, Civil Practice Act; Fifteenth Annual Report of the N.Y. Judicial Council, 1949, p. 241. We therefore sustain so much of the order as sets the verdict aside but we modify the order by granting a new trial instead of dismissing the complaint.

As has been noted above, the plaintiffs sought to prove prior assaults by Finkle by introducing into evidence a memorandum made by a police officer purporting to contain an admission by Finkle that "he had been arrested in Albany in 1950 for the same thing". Any admission by Finkle, even if proved by the testimony of the police officer to whom he had made it, was not admissible in evidence against the defendants. In any event, the memorandum of the alleged conversation was not admissible under Section 374–a of the Civil Practice Act as a record made in the regular course of business. Johnson v. Lutz, 253 N.Y. 124, 170 N.E. 517 (1930). The trial court correctly excluded this proof. It also correctly excluded the records of the Binghamton State Hospital containing statements by Finkle as to his prior history, which the plaintiffs offered to show prior irrational conduct. This proof was inadmissible both upon the ground that the statements were privileged communications and upon the ground that they were not made in the regular course of business. Civil Practice Act, §§ 352, 374–a; Matter of Warrington, 303 N.Y. 129, 100 N.E.2d 170 (1951); Matter of Coddington's Will, 307 N.Y. 181, 120 N.E.2d 777 (1954).

As we have indicated, even without this proof, we believe that there was sufficient evidence to warrant submission of the case to the jury but we point out that the case is so thin that a resubmission of the case upon the same proof may well result in requiring the court again to set aside any verdict in favor of the plaintiffs. The lines of inquiry suggested by the excluded proof should therefore be fully explored prior to the new trial.

. . .

Judgment appealed from reversed, on the law and the facts, and the order setting aside the verdict of the jury is modified by eliminating the provision for the dismissal of the complaint and by substituting therefor a direction that a new trial be ordered, and, as so modified, the order is affirmed, on the law and facts, with costs to abide the event.

BERGAN, J. P., and COON, IMRIE and ZELLER, JJ., concur.

STATE OF OHIO v. ANTILL

Supreme Court of Ohio, 1964.
176 Ohio St. 61, 197 N.E.2d 548.

MATTHIAS, Judge. This case presents two questions for determination by the court:

1. Is a wife a competent witness and can she be compelled to testify against her husband under an indictment charging that he "did unlawfully assault . . . [his wife] with a dangerous weapon or instrument likely to produce great bodily harm," where a personal injury to the wife resulted therefrom?
2. Is the physician who treats a person who has suffered a wound inflicted by a deadly weapon permitted to testify as to the condition of the victim, in a criminal prosecution therefor?

At common law, there are certain exceptions to the general rule excluding a husband and wife from testifying for or against each other. In actions involving a personal injury of one committed by the other, the injured spouse is permitted to testify. This exception was said to be based on "necessity." As a general rule, no outsider is present when a person injures his spouse. If the injured person were not permitted to testify, the law would be powerless to redress the wrong. The guilty party would be able to injure his spouse in the privacy of their home with complete immunity. An exception was therefore necessary in order to prevent injustice. 8 Wigmore, Evidence (1961), 242, Section 2239.

This court in Whipp v. State, 34 Ohio St. 87 (1877), permitted a husband to testify against his wife. The wife had been indicted for assault with intent to kill her husband. The court recognized the general exclusionary rule but held that the husband was a competent witness since his wife had inflicted a personal injury on him.

The Whipp case was cited and approved in State v. Orth, 79 Ohio St. 130, 86 N.E. 476, 22 L.R.A.,N.S., 240 (1908).

The exception in case of personal injury by the husband or wife to the other was codified in Ohio. 86 Ohio Laws, p. 161 (1889). Section 2945.42, Revised Code, authorizes a husband and wife to testify against each other in a prosecution for personal injury of either by the other. In the instant case, the husband was indicted for assault with a dangerous weapon. He allegedly struck his wife and stabbed her with a butcher knife. To hold that the wife is not a competent witness under such circumstances places a strained interpretation on the language of Section 2945.42, Revised Code, and ignores its common-law background.

The injured spouse is permitted to testify in order that he or she will not be exposed to personal injury without having a remedy. However, where, as here, the facts constitute a crime, his or her right to testify also ensures that the public will not suffer an offense without a remedy. The wrongdoer not only injures his spouse but he also injures the public, and it is for his offense against the public that he is subject to criminal prosecution. When the injured spouse is a witness for the state his competency cannot be affected by his desires or fears. He must testify to protect the public. Turner v. State, 60 Miss. 351, 45 Am.Rep. 412 (1882).

The demand for the testimony of the injured spouse comes not from him alone but from the community as a whole. Every member of the community has a duty to give whatever testimony he is capable of giving. The truth must be known, as far as possible, to enable the law to provide justice in each case. See 8 Wigmore, Evidence (1961), 70, Section 2192; and In re Story, 159 Ohio St. 144, 148, 149, 111 N.E.2d 385, 36 A.L.R.2d 1312 (1953).

In some instances, the law feels that another interest is sufficiently important to warrant an exception to this duty to give testimony. Thus, to promote marital peace there is a privilege not to disclose in court confidential communications between husband and wife. However, the basis for this privilege is lacking where a person is tried for assaulting his spouse.

". . . it is an overgenerous assumption that the wife who has been beaten, poisoned or deserted is still on such terms of delicate good feeling with her spouse that her testimony must not be enforced lest the iridescent halo of peace be dispelled by the breath of disparaging testimony. And if there were, conceivably, any such peace, would it be a peace such as the law could desire to protect? Could it be any other peace than that which the tyrant secures for himself by oppression?" 8 Wigmore, Evidence (1961), 242, 243, Section 2239.

Under the circumstances involved in the instant case, the wife is competent and like any other witness can be compelled to testify.

If she refuses she can be found in contempt and imprisoned until she agrees to testify. See Sections 2705.02(C) and 2705.06, Revised Code.

No violation of the physician-patient privilege (Section 2317.02, Revised Code) occurred in allowing the physician who treated the victim to testify. The purpose of this privilege is to encourage patients to make a full disclosure of their symptoms and condition to their physicians without fear that such matters will later become public. Against the interest of the patient in having his condition remain confidential must be balanced the interest of the public in detecting crimes in order to protect society.

To accomplish this end, the General Assembly, in 1961, enacted Section 2917.44, Revised Code (129 Ohio Laws, p. 1034), which reads, in part, as follows:

> ". . . any physician who treats, or is called upon to treat, any such wound [gunshot wound or wound inflicted by a deadly weapon] shall make a report setting forth a description of the wounded person, his name and address, if known, and a description of the nature and location of such wound.
>
> "No person who makes a report in good faith with a view of complying with the requirements of this section shall, by reason thereof, have violated any confidential relationship . . . ."

It is, therefore, proper for the physician who treats a person wounded by a deadly weapon to testify in court as to the nature of the wound. The publicity against which the privilege is supposed to protect has already taken place. The details of the wound must have been reported by the physician to a law-enforcement officer. The only purpose that sustaining the privilege can now serve is to obstruct the course of justice.

The function of this court in reviewing a conviction is limited to the question of whether there was sufficient evidence to warrant the submission of the case to the jury and to support the verdict returned. State v. Sheppard (1956), 165 Ohio St. 293, paragraph five of the syllabus, 135 N.E.2d 340.

If there is evidence from which reasonable minds can reach different conclusions on the issue of whether the defendant is guilty beyond a reasonable doubt, the case should be submitted to the jury for its determination.

. . .

Dr. Christman, who was called to treat Mrs. Antill's wounds, testified as follows:

> "Q. Did he [the defendant] make any statements to you while Esther was there or you and he when he came?
>
> ". . .

"A. He stated *he would not use a squad car* [to send Mrs. Antill to a hospital] *and he said he would see her fall off the chair and bleed to death without calling an ambulance.*

". . .

"Q. I will ask you also, Doctor, whether or not it could have happened—that wound you examined—whether that could have happened by a person just walking, say, into a sharp instrument?

". . .

"A. I would expect a person a recoil as quickly as possible." (Emphasis added.)

Mrs. Antill testified as follows:

"Q. How did you receive that wound? A. Well, I was very much irritated at him and I pushed the chair toward him and he whirled around and *he had a dish and knife in his hand, so I came against it.*

. . .

The jury is the sole judge of the weight of the evidence and the credibility of witnesses. It may believe or disbelieve any witness or accept part of what a witness says and reject the rest. In reaching its verdict, the jury should consider the demeanor of the witness and the manner in which he testifies, his connection or relationship with the prosecution or the defendant, and his interest, if any, in the outcome. The jury may also consider the failure of the defendant to take the stand in his own behalf.

We, therefore, find that there was sufficient evidence in this cause to warrant its submission to the jury and to support the verdict rendered.

Judgment affirmed.

. . .

BAUMANN v. STEINGESTER

Court of Appeals of New York, 1915.
213 N.Y. 328, 107 N.E. 578.

Appeal from Supreme Court, Appellate Division, Second Department.

Action by Lena Baumann against Henry C. Steingester, Magdalena Fuhge, and others, to construe a will. A judgment in favor of the plaintiff was affirmed by the Appellate Division (159 App.Div. 923, 144 N.Y.Supp. 1105), and the defendant Magdalena Fuhge appeals. . . .

SEABURY, J. This action was commenced to obtain a construction of the last will of Maria Schadrack, deceased, and to have it adjudged that the plaintiff is the legatee described in subdivision 1 of paragraph "third" of said will, and that she is one of the three residuary legatees referred to in paragraph "sixth" of said will. The appellant, Magdalena Fuhge, answered, and asked to have it adjudged that she is the legatee described in the two paragraphs of the will referred to above.

The question at issue upon the trial related to the identity of the legatee referred to as "Lena Baumann" in the following paragraphs of the will. Subdivision 1 of paragraph third provides that the testatrix gives "the sum of $1,000 to my niece Lena Baumann of Richmond Hill in the county and borough of Queens," paragraph sixth provides that the testatrix gives "all the rest and residue of my essate to my three nieces, Helene Bang, Katherine Hainer, and Lena Baumann, to be divided among them share and share alike." The plaintiff is a grandniece of the testatrix, and at the time the will was made resided at Richmond Hill. The appellant is a niece of the testatrix, and her maiden name was Magdalena Baumann. There was evidence received upon the trial to show that the testatrix was accustomed to speak of her as "Lena Baumann," and that while she resided at the time the will was made at a place about one mile from Richmond Hill, the testatrix was also accustomed to refer to this place as "Richmond Hill." It thus appears that the language used in these two paragraphs of the will does not accurately designate either the plaintiff or the appellant. It does not accurately designate the plaintiff because the reference in the will is to a niece of the testatrix, and the plaintiff is a grandniece. It does not accurately designate the appellant because while her maiden name was Magdalena Baumann her name at the time the will was made was Magdalena Fuhge, and she did not reside at Richmond Hill. These facts appearing by extrinsic evidence, there was a latent ambiguity in the will. Parol evidence was properly receivable in the effort to dissolve this ambiguity. Lefevre v. Lefevre, 59 N.Y. 434 (1875); Matter of Taylor, Cloak v. Hammond, L.R. 34 Ch. Div. 255; Henderson v. Henderson, 1 Ir.Rep. 353 [1905].

In view of the unanimous affirmance by the Appellate Division of the judgment appealed from, the single question which survives for consideration in this court relates to the rulings of the Special Term excluding the evidence of the witness Kellar. Mr. Kellar was the attorney for the testatrix, and was the draftsman of and a subscribing witness to her will. The testatrix, a woman about 70 years of age, called upon Mr. Kellar and gave him instructions as to the drawing of her will. With her on this occasion and present at the office of Mr. Kellar at the time was Mrs. Stiefhold. Mrs. Stiefhold lived with the testatrix and acted as companion and housekeeper. The instructions as to her will were given to Mr. Kellar in the presence of Mrs. Stiefhold, who, while within hearing, testified that she "did not pay very much attention." When Mr. Kellar was called as a witness he was asked as to the instructions he had received from the testatrix as to the legacies and the provisions for the residuary estate. The question was excluded under objection of the plaintiff and subject to the exception of the appellant. It thus becomes necessary to determine whether Mr. Kellar, the attorney, should have been permitted to testify to communications which took place between himself and his client, the testatrix, in the presence of Mrs. Stiefhold. This evidence should have been received and considered by the court below. Doheny v. Lacy, 168 N.Y. 213, 223, 61 N.E. 255 (1901) . . . Mrs. Stiefhold was not present and acting in the character of a confidential agent of the testatrix, nor was her presence necessary to enable the parties to communicate with each other. No attempt was made by the testatrix to prevent her hearing the communication which she made to her attorney. The fact that Mrs. Stiefhold did "not pay very much attention" to what was said does not alter the situation. She was within hearing and, so far as the testatrix knew, heard all that was said. If the testatrix had desired her communication with her attorney to be confidential, she could have asked Mrs. Stiefhold to withdraw from the room or have communicated with her attorney when Mrs. Stiefhold was not present. She did not do either of these things, but on the contrary, gave her instructions to her attorney as to the manner in which she wished to have her will drawn, in the presence of Mrs. Stiefhold. The fact that these instructions were given in the presence and in the hearing of Mrs. Stiefhold is a circumstance indicative of the fact that the communication was not made in confidence. A third person even though a mere stranger or bystander, in whose hearing communications are made by a client to an attorney, may testify to such communications. Jackson v. French, 3 Wend. 337, 20 Am.Dec. 699 (1829); People v. Buchanan, supra. To allow a stranger or bystander who overhears such a conversation to testify to what he heard and at the same time preclude the attorney of the client from giving his testimony as to what occurred might often result unfairly to the client for whose protection the privilege is designed. The communication not being confidential the attorney is not privileged from disclosing it. Where there is no confidence reposed, no privilege can be asserted. In such cases the attorney is permitted to testify not because the privilege has been waived, but because the communication, not having been made in confidence, was not privileged. The privilege which exempts one from giving testimony, except in so far as it is embodied in statutory provisions, cannot be extended to cover cases not within the reason upon which the privilege rests.

. . .

The judgment should be reversed and a new trial granted, with costs to abide the event.

UNITED STATES v. REYNOLDS

Supreme Court of the United States, 1953.
345 U.S. 1, 73 S.Ct. 528, 97 L.Ed. 727.

Three separate actions under Federal Tort Claims Act by widows of civilians killed in crash of an Air Force plane. The United States District Court for the Eastern District of Pennsylvania, 10 F.R.D. 468, rendered judgments for plaintiffs, and the United States appealed. The Court of Appeals, 192 F.2d 987, affirmed, and the Supreme Court granted certiorari. . . .

Mr. Chief Justice VINSON delivered the opinion of the Court.

These suits under the Tort Claims Act arise from the death of three civilians in the crash of a B–29 aircraft at Waycross, Georgia, on October 6, 1948. Because an important question of the Government's privilege to resist discovery is involved, we granted certiorari. 343 U.S. 918, 72 S.Ct. 678, 96 L.Ed. 1332 (1952).

The aircraft had taken flight for the purpose of testing secret electronic equipment, with four civilian observers aboard. While aloft, fire broke out in one of the bomber's engines. Six of the nine crew members, and three of the four civilian observers were killed in the crash.

The widows of the three deceased civilian observers brought consolidated suits against the United States. In the pretrial stages the plaintiffs moved, under Rule 34 of the Federal Rules of Civil Procedure, for production of the Air Force's official accident investigation report and the statements of the three surviving crew members, taken in connection with the official investigation. The Government moved to quash the motion, claiming that these matters were privileged against disclosure pursuant to Air Force regulations promulgated under R.S. § 161. The District Judge sustained plaintiffs' motion, holding that good cause for production had been shown. The claim of privilege under R.S. § 161 was rejected on the premise that the Tort Claims Act, in making the Government liable "in the same manner" as a private individual had waived any privilege based upon executive control over governmental documents.

Shortly after this decision, the District Court received a letter from the Secretary of the Air Force, stating that "it has been determined that it would not be in the public interest to furnish this report. . . ." The court allowed a rehearing on its earlier order, and at the rehearing the Secretary of the Air Force filed a formal "Claim of Privilege." This document repeated the prior claim based generally on R.S. § 161, and then stated that the Government further objected to production of the documents "for the reason that the aircraft in question, together with the personnel on board, were engaged in a highly secret mission of the Air Force." An affidavit of the Judge Advocate General, United States Air Force, was also filed with the court, which asserted that the demanded material could not be furnished "without seriously hampering national security, flying safety and the development of highly technical and secret military equipment." The same affidavit offered to produce the three surviving crew members, without cost, for examination by the plaintiffs. The witnesses would be allowed to refresh their memories from any statement made by them to the Air Force, and authorized to testify as to all matters except those of a "classified nature."

The District Court ordered the Government to produce the documents in order that the court might determine whether they contained privileged matter. The Government declined, so the court entered an order, under Rule 37(b)(2)(i), that the facts on the issue of negligence would be taken as established in plaintiffs' favor. After a hearing to determine damages, final judgment was entered for the plaintiffs. The Court of Appeals affirmed, both as to the showing of good cause for production of the documents, and as to the ultimate disposition of the case as a consequence of the Government's refusal to produce the documents.

We have had broad propositions pressed upon us for decision. On behalf of the Government it has been urged that the executive department heads have power to withhold any documents in their custody from judicial view if they deem it to be in the public interest. Respondents have asserted that the executive's power to withhold documents was waived by the Tort Claims Act. Both positions have constitutional overtones which we find it unnecessary to pass upon, there being a narrower ground for decision. Touhy v. Ragen, 340 U.S. 462, 71 S.Ct. 416, 95 L.Ed. 417 (1951); Rescue Army v. Municipal Court of Los Angeles, 331 U.S. 549, 574–585, 67 S.Ct. 1409, 1422–1427, 91 L.Ed. 1666 (1947).

The Tort Claims Act expressly makes the Federal Rules of Civil Procedure applicable to suits against the United States. The judgment in this case imposed liability upon the Government by operation of Rule 37, for refusal to produce documents under Rule 34. Since Rule 34 compels production only of matters "not privileged," the essential question is whether there was a valid claim of privilege under the Rule. We hold that there was, and that, therefore, the judgment below subjected the United States to liability on terms to which Congress did not consent by the Tort Claims Act.

We think it should be clear that the term "not privileged" as used in Rule 34, refers to "privileges" as that term is understood in the law of evidence. When the Secretary of the Air Force lodged his formal "Claim of Privilege," he attempted therein to invoke the privilege against revealing military secrets, a privilege which is well established in the law of evidence. The existence of the privilege is conceded by the court below, and, indeed, by the most outspoken critics of governmental claims to privilege.

Judicial experience with the privilege which protects military and state secrets has been limited in this country. English experience has been more extensive, but still relatively slight compared with other evidentiary privileges. Nevertheless, the principles which control the application of the privilege emerge quite clearly from the available precedents. The privilege belongs to the Government and must be asserted by it; it can neither be claimed nor waived by a private party. It is not to be lightly invoked. There must be a formal claim of privilege, lodged by the head of the department which has control over the matter, after actual personal consideration by that officer. The court itself must determine whether the circumstances are appropriate for the claim of privilege, and yet do so without forcing a disclosure of the very thing the privilege is designed to protect. The latter requirement is the only one which presents real difficulty. As to it, we find it helpful to draw upon judicial experience in dealing with an analogous privilege, the privilege against self-incrimination.

The privilege against self-incrimination presented the courts with a similar sort of problem. Too much judicial inquiry into the claim of privilege would force disclosure of the thing the privilege was meant to protect, while a complete abandonment of judicial control would lead to intolerable abuses. Indeed, in the earlier stages of judicial experience with the problem, both extremes were advocated, some saying that the bare assertion by the witness must be taken as conclusive, and others saying that the witness should be required to reveal the matter behind his claim of privilege to the judge for verification. Neither extreme prevailed, and a sound formula of compromise was developed. This formula received authoritative expression in this country as early as the Burr trial. There are differences in phraseology, but in substance it is agreed that the court must be satisfied from all the evidence and circumstances, and "from the implications of the question, in the setting in which it is asked, that a responsive answer to the question or an explanation of why it cannot be answered might be dangerous because injurious exposure could result." Hoffman v. United States, 341 U.S. 479, 486–487, 71 S.Ct. 814, 818, 95 L.Ed. 1118 (1951). If the court is so satisfied, the claim of the privilege will be accepted without requiring further disclosure.

Regardless of how it is articulated, some like formula of compromise must be applied here. Judicial control over the evidence in a case cannot be abdicated to the caprice of executive officers. Yet we will not go so far as to say that the court may automatically require a complete disclosure to the judge before the claim of privilege will be accepted in any case. It may be possible to satisfy the court, from all the circumstances of the case, that there is a reasonable danger that compulsion of the evidence will expose military matters which, in the interest of national security, should not be divulged. When this is the case, the occasion for the privilege is appropriate, and the court should not jeopardize the security which the privilege is meant to protect by insisting upon an examination of the evidence, even by the judge alone, in chambers.

In the instant case we cannot escape judicial notice that this is a time of vigorous preparation for national defense. Experience in the past war has made it common knowledge that air power is one of the most potent weapons in our scheme of defense, and that newly developing electronic devices have greatly enhanced the effective use of air power. It is equally apparent that these electronic devices must be kept secret if their full military advantage is to be exploited in the national interests. On the record before the trial court it appeared that this accident occurred to a military plane which had gone aloft to test secret electronic equipment. Certainly there was a reasonable danger that the accident investigation report would contain references to the secret electronic equipment which was the primary concern of the mission.

Of course, even with this information before him, the trial judge was in no position to decide that the report was privileged until there had been a formal claim of privilege. Thus it was entirely proper to rule initially that petitioner had shown probable cause for discovery of the documents. Thereafter, when the formal claim of privilege was filed by the Secretary of the Air Force, under circumstances indicating a reasonable possibility that military secrets were involved, there was certainly a sufficient showing of privilege to cut off further demand for the document on the showing of necessity for its compulsion that had then been made.

In each case, the showing of necessity which is made will determine how far the court should probe in satisfying itself that the occasion for invoking the privilege is appropriate. Where there is a strong showing of necessity, the claim of privilege should not be lightly accepted, but even the most compelling necessity cannot overcome the claim of privilege if the court is ultimately satisfied that military secrets are at stake. *A fortiori*, where necessity is dubious, a formal claim of privilege, made under the circumstances of this case, will have to prevail. Here, necessity was greatly minimized by an available alternative, which might have given respondents the evidence to make out their case without forcing a showdown on the claim of privilege. By their failure to pursue that alternative, respondents have posed the privilege question for decision with the formal claim of privilege set against a dubious showing of necessity.

There is nothing to suggest that the electronic equipment, in this case, had any causal connection with the accident. Therefore, it should be possible for respondents to adduce the essential facts as to causation without resort to material touching upon military secrets. Respondents were given a reasonable opportunity to do just that, when petitioner formally offered to make the surviving crew members available for examination. We think that offer should have been accepted.

. . .

The decision of the Court of Appeals is reversed and the case will be remanded to the District Court for further proceedings consistent with the views expressed in this opinion.

Reversed and remanded.

Mr. Justice BLACK, Mr. Justice FRANKFURTER, and Mr. Justice JACKSON dissent substantially for the reasons set forth in the opinion of Judge Maris below. 192 F.2d 987.

JENCKS v. UNITED STATES

Supreme Court of the United States, 1956.
353 U.S. 657, 77 S.Ct. 1007, 1 L.Ed.2d 1103.

. . .

Mr. Justice BRENNAN delivered the opinion of the Court.

On April 28, 1950, the petitioner, as president of Amalgamated Bayard District Union, Local 890, International Union of Mine, Mill & Smelter Workers, filed an "Affidavit of Non-Communist Union Officer" with the National Labor Relations Board, pursuant to § 9(h) of the National Labor Relations Act.[1] He has been convicted under a two-count indictment charging that he violated 18 U.S.C. § 1001, 18 U.S.C.A. § 1001[2] by falsely swearing in that affidavit that he was not on April 28, 1950, a member of the Communist Party or affiliated with such Party. The Court of Appeals for the Fifth Circuit affirmed the conviction,[3] and also an order of the District Court denying the petitioner's motion for a new trial.[4] This Court granted certiorari.[5]

Two alleged trial errors are presented for our review. Harvey F. Matusow and J. W. Ford, the Government's principal witnesses, were Communist Party members paid by the Federal Bureau of Investigation contemporaneously to make oral or written reports of Communist Party activities in which they participated. They made such reports to the F.B.I. of activities allegedly participated in by the petitioner, about which they testified at the trial. Error is asserted in the denial by the trial judge of the petitioner's motions to direct the Government to produce these reports for inspection and use in cross-examining Matusow and Ford. Error is also alleged in the instructions given to the jury on membership, affiliation, and the credibility of informers.[6]

Former Party members testified that they and the petitioner, as members of the Communist Party of New Mexico, had been expressly instructed to conceal their membership and not to carry membership cards. They also testified that the Party kept no membership records or minutes of membership meetings, and that such meetings were secretly arranged and clandestinely held. One of the witnesses

1. 61 Stat. 143, 146, as amended, 65 Stat. 602, 29 U.S.C. § 159(h), 29 U.S.C.A. § 159(h).

Section 9(h) provides that processes of the National Labor Relations Board will be unavailable to a labor organization ". . . unless there is on file with the Board an affidavit executed . . . by each officer of such labor organization . . . that he is not a member of the Communist Party or affiliated with such party, and that he does not believe in, and is not a member of or supports any organization that believes in or teaches, the overthrow of the United States Government by force or by any illegal or unconstitutional methods . . . ."

2. 62 Stat. 749.

3. 226 F.2d 540 (5th Cir. 1955).

4. 226 F.2d 553 (5th Cir. 1955).

5. 350 U.S. 980, 76 S.Ct. 467, 100 L.Ed. 849 (1956).

6. Because of our disposition of this case, it is unnecessary to consider the alleged errors in these instructions.

said that special care was taken to conceal the Party membership of members, like the petitioner, "occupying strategic and important positions in labor unions and other organizations where public knowledge of their membership to non-Communists would jeopardize their position in the organization." Accordingly, the Government did not attempt to prove the petitioner's alleged membership in the Communist Party on April 28, 1950, with any direct admissions by the petitioner of membership, by proof of his compliance with Party membership requirements, or that his name appeared upon a membership roster, or that he carried a membership card.

The evidence relied upon by the Government was entirely circumstantial. It consisted of testimony of conduct of the petitioner from early 1946 through October 15, 1949, and of Matusow's testimony concerning alleged conversations between him and the petitioner at a vacation ranch in July or August 1950, and concerning a lecture delivered by the petitioner at the ranch. The Government also attached probative weight to the action of the petitioner in executing and filing an Affidavit of Non-Communist Union Officer on October 15, 1949, because of the events surrounding the filing of that affidavit. The Government bridged the gap between October 15, 1949, and July or August 1950 with the testimony of Ford that, during that period, the Party took no disciplinary action against the petitioner for defection or deviation, and did not replace the petitioner in the Party office which Ford testified the petitioner held as a member of the Party State Board.

The first alleged Party activity of the petitioner preceded his union employment. A witness, who was a Party member in the spring of 1946, testified that, at that time, he and the petitioner were present at a closed Party meeting at the home of the Party chairman for Colorado, where the petitioner, a veteran of World War II, led in urging that veterans who were Party members spread out into several veterans' organizations and not all join the same one, the better to further Party work.

Later in 1946 the petitioner was employed by the International Union of Mine, Mill & Smelter Workers as business agent for several local unions in the Silver City-Bayard, New Mexico, area. It was testified that one of the petitioner's first acts was to meet with the International Union's then Regional Director for the Southwest, a Communist Party member, and with the Communist Party organizer for the area, to develop plans for organizing a Party group within each of those locals, which later merged to form Amalgamated Local 890 under the petitioner's presidency.

J. W. Ford was a member of the Communist Party of New Mexico from 1946 to September 1950 and, from 1948, was a member of the State Board and a Party security officer. He said that in 1948 he became a paid undercover agent for the F.B.I.[7] and reported regu-

7. From 1948 through 1953, Ford was paid $7,025 for his services. Of that sum, approximately $3,325 covered the period to which his testimony related.

larly upon Party activities and meetings. He testified that the petitioner was also a Party and a State Board member, and he related in detail occurrences at five closed Party meetings which he said the petitioner attended.

At the first meeting, in August 1948, Ford said the Party members worked out a plan to support the petitioner's candidacy for Congress on the ticket of the Progressive Party. At the second meeting, in February 1949, Ford said that the petitioner and other Communist Party members were appointed delegates to a meeting of the Mexican-American Association in Phoenix, Arizona, to further a Party plan to infiltrate that organization and to use it for the Party's purposes. At the third meeting, in April 1949, Ford said that the Party's state organization was completed, and the petitioner was appointed to the State Board and the Party leader in the southern half of the State. At the fourth meeting, in May 1949, Ford said that the petitioner gave a progress report upon his success in recruiting Party members among labor groups, and offered to use Local 890's newspaper, "The Union Worker," which he edited, to support issues of Party interest. At the fifth meeting, in August 1949, Ford said that preparations were made for another meeting later in that month of the Mexican-American Association in Albuquerque, and that the delegates, including the petitioner, were instucted to give vigorous support to the meeting but to take care not to make themselves conspicuous in the proceedings.

Ford's duties as a Party security officer were to keep watch on all Party members and to report "any particular defections from the Communist philosophy or any peculiar actions, statements or associations, which would endanger the security of the Communist Party of the state." If any defection reported by a security officer were considered important, the member "would be called in and would be either severely reprimanded or criticized, or disciplined. If he refused to accept such discipline he would either be suspended or expelled." Ford testified that, between August 1949 and September 1950, when Ford ceased his activities with the New Mexico Party, there was no disciplinary action taken against the petitioner and, to his knowledge, the petitioner was not replaced in his position on the State Board of the Communist Party.

The events leading up to the petitioner's execution and filing, on October 15, 1949, of an Affidavit of Non-Communist Union Officer were testified to by a former International Union representative, a Communist Party member during 1947 to 1949. He said that, about 17 months before, in May or June 1948, a meeting of Party members, holding offices in locals of the International Union of Mine, Mill & Smelter Workers, was held in Denver to formulate plans for combatting a movement, led by non-Communists, to secede from the International Union. He said that the Party members, including the petitioner, were informed of Party policy not to sign affidavits required by § 9(h) of the then recently enacted Taft-Hartley Act. There was no testimony that that policy changed before October 15, 1949.

The affidavit was filed shortly before a C.I.O. convention was scheduled to expel the Mine-Mill International and other unions from its membership. After filing the affidavit, the petitioner and other Local 890 officers published an article in "The Union Worker" charging that the contemplated C.I.O. action was part of a program of "right-wing unions . . . gobbling up chunks of militant unions. . . . Our International Union and its officers have swallowed a lot of guff, a lot of insults. But that is not the point. . . . Now that our Union has signed the phony affidavits we can defend ourselves . . . in case of raids. We do not fear attack from that quarter any longer."

Matusow was a member of the Communist Party of New York and was a paid undercover agent for the F.B.I. before he went to New Mexico.[8] In July or August 1950, he spent a 10-day vacation on a ranch near Taos, New Mexico, with the petitioner and a number of other people. He testified to several conversations with the petitioner there. He said he twice told the petitioner of his desire to transfer his membership from the New York to the New Mexico Party, and that on both occasions the petitioner applauded the idea and told him, "we can use you out here, we need more active Party members." On one of these occasions, Matusow said, the petitioner asked him for suggestions for a lecture the petitioner was preparing for delivery at the ranch, particularly as to what the New York Communists were doing about the Stockholm Peace Appeal. Matusow described to the petitioner a "do-day" program adopted in New York when the Party members were doers, not talkers, and performed some activity, such as painting signs around a baseball stadium urging support for the Peace Appeal. He testified that the petitioner showed great interest in the idea and said he might bring it back to his fellow Party members in Silver City.

Matusow testified that the petitioner delivered his planned lecture, informed his audience of the "do-day" idea, praised the Soviet Union's disarmament plan, referred to the United States as the aggressor in Korea, and urged all to read the "Daily People's World," identified by Matusow as the "West Coast Communist Party newspaper." Another witness, an expelled member of Amalgamated Local 890, testified that petitioner, during 1950, 1951 and 1952, repeatedly urged at union meetings that the union members read that paper.

Matusow also testified that, in one of their conversations, the petitioner told him of a program he was developing with leaders of the Mexican Miners Union to negotiate simultaneous expiration dates of collective bargaining agreements, to further a joint action of Mexican and American workers to cut off production to slow down the Korean War effort. Matusow also testified that when he told the petitioner that he had joined the Taos Chapter of the Mexican-Amer-

8. Other activities of Matusow are described in Communist Party of the United States v. Subversive Activities Control Board, 351 U.S. 115, 76 S.Ct. 663, 100 L.Ed. 1003 (1956), and United States v. Flynn, 130 F.Supp. 412 (S.D. N.Y.1955).

ican Association, the petitioner told him that this was proper Communist work because the Association was a key organization, controlled by the Party, for Communist activities in New Mexico and that he, the petitioner, was active in the Association in the Silver City area.[9]

Ford and Matusow were subjected to vigorous cross-examination about their employment as informers for the F.B.I. Ford testified that in 1948 he went to the F.B.I. and offered his services, which were accepted. He thereafter regularly submitted reports to the F.B.I., "sometimes once a week, sometimes once a month, and at various other times; maybe three or four times a week, depending on the number of meetings . . . [he] attended and the distance between the meetings." He said that his reports were made immediately following each meeting, while the events were still fresh in his memory. He could not recall, however, which reports were oral and which in writing.

The petitioner moved "for an order directing an inspection of reports of the witness Ford to the Federal Bureau of Investigation dealing with each of the meetings which he said that he attended with the defendant Jencks in the years 1948 and 1949." The trial judge, without stating reasons, denied the motion.

Matusow, on his cross-examination, testified that he made both oral and written reports to the F.B.I. on events at the ranch, including his conversations with the petitioner. The trial judge, again without reasons, denied the motion to require "the prosecution to produce in Court the reports submitted to the F.B.I. by this witness [Matusow] concerning matters which he saw or heard at the . . . Ranch during the period that he was a guest there . . . ."[10]

The Government opposed petitioner's motions at the trial upon the sole ground that a preliminary foundation was not laid of inconsistency between the contents of the reports and the testimony of Matusow and Ford. The Court of Appeals rested the affirmance primarily upon that ground.[11]

Both the trial court and the Court of Appeals erred. We hold that the petitioner was not required to lay a preliminary foundation

9. Matusow recanted as deliberately false the testimony given by him at the trial. On the basis of this recantation, the petitioner moved for a new trial, while his appeal from the conviction was pending, on grounds of newly discovered evidence. After extended hearings, the District Court denied the motion.

10. During the hearings on the motion for a new trial, the petitioner made several requests for the production of documents in the possession of the Government, relating to the testimony given. These motions were denied. Because of our disposition of this case, it was unnecessary to consider these rulings.

11. In upholding the refusal to require the production of the reports, the Court of Appeals said:

". . . Upon a proper showing that the Government has possession of such inconsistent statements and the presence of the other requisite conditions, a person charged with crime would be permitted to examine and use them. But no such showing was made here . . . ." 226 F.2d at page 552.

of inconsistency, because a sufficient foundation was established by the testimony of Matusow and Ford that their reports were of the events and activities related in their testimony.

The reliance of the Court of Appeals upon Gordon v. United States, 344 U.S. 414, 73 S.Ct. 369, 97 L.Ed. 447 (1953), is misplaced. It is true that one fact mentioned in this Court's opinion was that the witness admitted that the documents involved contradicted his testimony. However, to say that Gordon held a preliminary showing of inconsistency a prerequisite to an accused's right to the production for inspection of documents in the Government's possession, is to misinterpret the Court's opinion. The necessary essentials of a foundation, emphasized in that opinion, and present here, are that "[t]he demand was for production of . . . *specific documents and did not propose any broad or blind fishing expedition* among documents possessed by the Government on the chance that something impeaching might turn up. Nor was this a demand for statements taken from persons or informants not offered as witnesses." (Emphasis added.) 344 U.S. at page 419, 73 S.Ct. at page 373. We reaffirm and re-emphasize these essentials. "For production purposes, it need only appear that the evidence is relevant, competent, and outside of any exclusionary rule . . . ." 344 U.S. at page 420, 73 S.Ct. at page 373.

The crucial nature of the testimony of Ford and Matusow to the Government's case is conspicuously apparent. The impeachment of that testimony was singularly important to the petitioner. The value of the reports for impeachment purposes was highlighted by the admissions of both witnesses that they could not remember what reports were oral and what written, and by Matusow's admission: "I don't recall what I put in my reports two or three years ago, written or oral, I don't know what they were."

Every experienced trial judge and trial lawyer knows the value for impeaching purposes of statements of the witness recording the events before time dulls treacherous memory. Flat contradiction between the witness' testimony and the version of the events given in his reports is not the only test of inconsistency. The omission from the reports of facts related at the trial, or a contrast in emphasis upon the same facts, even a different order of treatment, are also relevant to the cross-examining process of testing the credibility of a witness' trial testimony.

Requiring the accused first to show conflict between the reports and the testimony is actually to deny the accused evidence relevant and material to his defense. The occasion for determining a conflict cannot arise until after the witness has testified and unless he admits conflict, as in Gordon, the accused is helpless to know or discover conflict without inspecting the reports.[12] A requirement of a showing of

12. Cf. United States v. Burr, 25 Fed. Cas. page 187, No. 14,694, wherein Chief Justice Marshall, when confronted with a request for the inspection of a letter addressed to the President and in the possession of the attorney for the United States, stated:

"Now, if a paper be in possession of the opposite party, what statement of its

conflict would be clearly incompatible with our standards for the administration of criminal justice in the federal courts and must therefore be rejected. For the interest of the United States in a criminal prosecution ". . . is not that it shall win a case, but that justice shall be done . . .." Berger v. United States, 295 U.S. 78, 88, 55 S.Ct. 629, 633, 79 L.Ed. 1314 (1935).[13]

This Court held in Goldman v. United States, 316 U.S. 129, 132, 62 S.Ct. 993, 995, 86 L.Ed. 1322 (1942), that the trial judge had discretion to deny inspection when the witness ". . . does not use his notes or memoranda [relating to his testimony] in court . . .." We now hold that the petitioner was entitled to an order directing the Government to produce for inspection all reports of Matusow and Ford in its possession, written and, when orally made, as recorded by the F.B.I., touching the events and activities as to which they testified at the trial. We hold, further, that the petitioner is entitled to inspect the reports to decide whether to use them in his defense. Because only the defense is adequately equipped to determine the effective use for purpose of discrediting the Government's witness and thereby furthering the accused's defense, the defense must initially be entitled to see them to determine what use may be made of them. Justice requires no less.[14]

The practice of producing government documents to the trial judge for his determination of relevancy and materiality, without hearing the accused, is disapproved.[15] Relevancy and materiality for the purposes of production and inspection, with a view to use on cross-examination, are established when the reports are shown to relate to the testimony of the witness. Only after inspection of the reports

contents or applicability can be expected from the person who claims its production, he not precisely knowing its contents? . . .

". . . It is objected that the particular passages of the letter which are required are not pointed out. But how can this be done while the letter itself is withheld? . . ." 25 Fed.Cas. at page 191.

13. United States v. Schneiderman, 106 F.Supp. 731 (S.D.Cal.1952); People v. Dellabonda, 265 Mich. 486, 251 N.W. 594 (1934); see Canon 5, American Bar Association, Canons of Professional Ethics (1947).

14. Chief Justice Marshall also said in United States v. Burr, 25 Fed.Cas. page 187, No. 14,694:

"Let it be supposed that the letter may not contain anything respecting the person now before the court. Still it may respect a witness material in the case, and become important by bearing on his testimony. Different representations may have been made by that witness, or his conduct may have been such as to affect his testimony. In various modes a paper may bear upon the case, although before the case be opened its particular application cannot be perceived by the judge . . . ." 25 Fed.Cas. at page 191.

What is true before the case is opened is equally true as the case unfolds. The trial judge cannot perceive or determine the relevancy and materiality of the documents to the defense without hearing defense argument, after inspection, as to its bearing upon the case.

15. See, e. g., United States v. Grayson, 166 F.2d 863, 869 (2d Cir. 1948); United States v. Beekman, 155 F.2d 580, 584 (2d Cir. 1946); United States v. Ebeling, 146 F.2d 254, 256 (2d Cir. 1945); United States v. Cohen, 145 F.2d 82, 92 (2d Cir. 1944); United States v. Krulewitch, 145 F.2d 76, 78, 156 A.L.R. 337 (2d Cir. 1944).

by the accused, must the trial judge determine admissibility—e. g., evidentiary questions of inconsistency, materiality and relevancy—of the contents and the method to be employed for the elimination of parts immaterial or irrelevant. See Gordon v. United States, 344 U.S. at page 418, 73 S.Ct. at page 372.

In the courts below the Government did not assert that the reports were privileged against disclosure on grounds of national security, confidential character of the reports, public interest or otherwise. In its brief in this Court, however, the Government argues that, absent a showing of contradiction, "[t]he rule urged by petitioner . . . disregards the legitimate interest that each party—including the Government—has in safeguarding the privacy of its files, particularly where the documents in question were obtained in confidence. Production of such documents, even to a court, should not be compelled in the absence of a preliminary showing by the party making the request." The petitioner's counsel, believing that Court of Appeals' decisions imposed such a qualification, restricted his motions to a request for production of the reports to the trial judge for the judge's inspection and determination whether and to what extent the reports should be made available to the petitioner.

It is unquestionably true that the protection of vital national interests may militate against public disclosure of documents in the Government's possession. This has been recognized in decisions of this Court in civil causes where the Court has considered the statutory authority conferred upon the departments of government to adopt regulations "not inconsistent with law, for . . . use . . . of the records, papers . . . appertaining" to his department.[16] The Attorney General has adopted regulations pursuant to this authority declaring all Justice Department records confidential and that no disclosure, including disclosure in response to subpoena, may be made without his permission.[17]

But this Court has noticed, in United States v. Reynolds, 345 U.S. 1, 73 S.Ct. 528, 97 L.Ed. 727 (1953), the holdings of the Court of Appeals for the Second Circuit [18] that, in criminal causes ". . . the Government can invoke its evidentiary privileges only at the price of letting the defendant go free. The rationale of the criminal cases is that, since the Government which prosecutes an accused also has the duty to see that justice is done, it is unconscionable to allow it to undertake prosecution and then invoke its governmental privileges to deprive the accused of anything which might be material to his defense . . . ." 345 U.S. at page 12, 73 S.Ct. at page 534.

16. R.S. § 161, 5 U.S.C. § 22, 5 U.S.C.A. § 22; United States v. Reynolds, 345 U.S. 1, 73 S.Ct. 528, 97 L.Ed. 727 (1953); cf. Totten v. United States, 92 U.S. 105, 23 L.Ed. 605 (1875).

17. Atty.Gen.Order No. 3229, 28 CFR, 1946 Supp. § 51.71 (1939); Atty.Gen. Order No. 3229, Supp. 2, Pike & Fischer Admin.Law (2d), Dept. of Justice 1 (1947); Atty.Gen.Order No. 3229, Rev., 18 Fed.Reg. 1368 (1953).

18. United States v. Beekman, 155 F.2d 580 (2d Cir. 1946); United States v. Andolschek, 142 F.2d 503 (2d Cir. 1944).

In United States v. Andolschek, 142 F.2d 503, 506 (2d Cir. 1944), Judge Learned Hand said:

> ". . . While we must accept it as lawful for a department of the government to suppress documents, even when they will help determine controversies between third persons, we cannot agree that this should include their suppression in a criminal prosecution, founded upon those very dealings to which the documents relate, and whose criminality they will, or may, tend to exculpate. So far as they directly touch the criminal dealings, the prosecution necessarily ends any confidential character the documents may possess; it must be conducted in the open, and will lay bare their subject matter. The government must choose; either it must leave the transactions in the obscurity from which a trial will draw them, or it must expose them fully. Nor does it seem to us possible to draw any line between documents whose contents bear directly upon the criminal transactions, and those which may be only indirectly relevant. Not only would such a distinction be extremely difficult to apply in practice, but the same reasons which forbid suppression in one case forbid it in the other, though not, perhaps, quite so imperatively . . . ."

We hold that the criminal action must be dismissed when the Government, on the ground of privilege, elects not to comply with an order to produce, for the accused's inspection and for admission in evidence, relevant statements or reports in its possession of government witnesses touching the subject matter of their testimony at the trial. Accord, Roviaro v. United States, 353 U.S. 53, 60–61, 77 S.Ct. 623, 627–628, 1 L.Ed.2d 639 (1957). The burden is the Government's, not to be shifted to the trial judge, to decide whether the public prejudice of allowing the crime to go unpunished is greater than that attendant upon the possible disclosure of state secrets and other confidential information in the Government's possession.

Reversed.

Mr. Justice FRANKFURTER joins the opinion of the Court, but deeming that the questions relating to the instructions to the jury should be dealt with, since a new trial has been directed, he agrees with the respects in which, and the reasons for which, Mr. Justice BURTON finds them erroneous.

Mr. Justice WHITTAKER took no part in the consideration or decision of this case.

Mr. Justice BURTON, whom Mr. Justice HARLAN joins, concurring in the result.

Separate concurring decision of Mr. Justice BURTON and Mr. Justice HARLAN, deleted. Dissent of Mr. Justice CLARK, omitted.

DECISIONS RELATING TO CHAPTER XIII, DECLARATIONS AGAINST INTEREST

TOM LOVE GROCERY CO. v. MARYLAND CASUALTY CO.

Supreme Court of Tennessee, 1933.
166 Tenn. 275, 61 S.W.2d 672.

. . .

Appeal from Chancery Court, Shelby County; M. C. Ketchum, Chancellor.

Suit by the Tom Love Grocery Company against the Maryland Casualty Company. From a judgment of the Court of Appeals affirming a judgment for plaintiff, the defendant appeals.

. . .

COOK, Justice. The complainant sued to recover upon a policy of indemnity against burglary of merchandise. The sharply controverted question of fact was whether the goods were taken by entry through force and violence evidenced by visible marks on the premises. The issues, submitted to the jury, were whether or not complainant's warehouse was burglarized, and, if so, what goods were taken.

Under the charge, in which we find no prejudicial error, the jury found that the house was burglarized through forcible entry evidenced by visible marks of violence, and goods of the value of $63 carried away. The chancellor rendered a decree upon the verdict, which the Court of Appeals affirmed.

Before the trial, Fred M. Stubblefield was arrested for the burglary and made a written confession to Inspector Griffin, and an oral statement to Mr. Tom Love, disclosing with particularity all the facts attending the burglary. He was convicted of burglary, and as a result was disqualified as a witness by the judgment of infamy. The chancellor admitted Stubblefield's extrajudicial statement to Inspector Griffin and Mr. Tom Love disclosing the facts of the burglary over the objection of the defendant. The Court of Appeals held the statements admissible as a declaration against interest because they subjected Stubblefield to both civil and criminal liability by statute (Code, §§ 10913–11795) and the common-law (Scruggs v. Davis, 5 Sneed 261), and because Stubblefield was unavailable as a witness by reason of the judgment of infamy.

No rule is more familiar than that which requires the exclusion of unsworn statements or hearsay offered as evidence. Such statements are excluded, because they have not borne the test of cross-examination and are given without the sanction of an oath. There is no opportunity of inquiry into the character of the declarant and his motives for making the statement. Those who repeat such declarations to the court stand upon the simple assertion that the statements were made, and are not obliged to enter into particulars or explain ambiguities in the declarant's statement. If called upon to do so, they could satisfy the inquiry by repeating what they heard.

There are, however, exceptions to the hearsay rule which authorize the reception of admissions and declarations against interest. Declarations, to be distinguished from admissions, as to facts relevant to the matter of inquiry, are admissible in evidence when it appears that the declarant is dead, that the declaration was against his pecuniary or proprietary interest, and that he had no probable motive to falsify the fact declared.

Text-writers, asserting that a litigant has a substantive right to prove his case whether he has one or not, criticize the courts for excluding certain declarations, and insist that administrative necessity requires the admission of extrajudicial assertion of an unavailable witness when the case is absolutely dependent upon his unsworn statement, regardless of the cause of his unavailability. In a few cases, appellate courts, apparently wincing under the prod of criticism, have relaxed the rule and extended the exception beyond declarants whose evidence became unavailable by death. For instance, in Weber v. Railway Co., 175 Iowa 368, 151 N.W. 852, 864, L.R.A.1918A, 626 (1915), a divided court held insanity, calling it mental death, a ground of unavailability, and admitted the declaration. But the majority said: "We do not want to be understood here as extending the rule, in the exception to hearsay evidence, heretofore referred to, beyond the record in this case."

In Griffith v. Sauls, 77 Tex. 630, 14 S.W. 230 (1892), the declaration of a witness unavailable because of his physical condition was held admissible.

Beyond these we find no cases directly in point, and find no authority for extending the rule beyond unavailability by death.

Cases involving the admissibility of declarations by parties and others identified in interest with them are not in point. In our case of Overton v. Hardin, 6 Cold. 375 (1869), the inclusion rested upon the rule that the declaration of parties identified in interest is admissible as primary evidence.

In Harton v. Lyons, 97 Tenn. 180, 36 S.W. 851 (1896), and Brooks v. Lowenstein, 95 Tenn. 262, 35 S.W. 89 (1896), the statements attending the transaction were admissible as part of the res gestae.

Another class of cases hold declarations against title by an owner in possession against those claiming under him admissible as primary evidence. For the distinction, see 22 C.J. 232, 2 Jones on Evidence, § 327, and 4 Chamberlayne, § 2770. Neither are cases in point that involve the reception of secondary proof of evidence given at a former trial, for that character of evidence is beyond the scope of the hearsay rule, being unaffected by the mischiefs against which the rule is directed.

The distinction between the reception of admissions, the reception of evidence given upon a former trial, and the reception of declarations by parties and their privies or agents, and the reception of declarations against interest, cannot be fused by any sort of intellectual metabolism as is attempted in some instances, so as to interchangeably use the several rules to let in hearsay.

The weight of authority is against the unreasonable extension of the exceptions to the rule, and most of the cases held that it is only when the declarant is dead that his declaration against interest will be received. Reasoning and authority support the conclusion that the exception should not be extended to include infamy along with insanity and death as another ground of unavailability authorizing the reception as evidence of the statement of a witness subsequently adjudged infamous.

The parties to this litigation are the insured and the insurer. Stubblefield, the burglar, was not a party to the contract of insurance nor a representative of the parties. It was error to admit his unsworn statement as evidence. For a discussion of the principles underlying the rule applied, in addition to the authorities already mentioned, we refer to 4 Chamberlayne, § 2780; Smith v. Hanson, 34 Utah 171, 96 Pac. 1087, 18 L.R.A.(N.S.) 520 (1908); Penner v. Cooper, 4 Munf. (18 Va.) 458 (1815); Ibbitson v. Brown, 5 Iowa 532 (1858); Mahaska County v. Ingalls, 16 Iowa 81 (1864); United States v. Mulholland, 50 F. 413, 419 (D.C.1892), and our own cases of Peck v. State, 86 Tenn. 267, 6 S.W. 389 (1888); Rhea v. State, 10 Yerg. 258 (1837); Draper v. Stanley, 1 Heisk. 432 (1870); Middle Tennessee Railroad Co. v. McMillan, 134 Tenn. 490, 184 S.W. 20 (1916); Adcock v. Simon, 2 Tenn.App. 617; Brier Hill Collieries v. Pile, 4 Tenn.App. 468; Harton v. Lyons, 97 Tenn. 180, 36 S.W. 851 (1896); Nichol v. Ridley, 5 Yerg. 63, 26 Am.Dec. 254 (1833); Wright v. State, 9 Yerg. 342 (1836); Cox v. State, 160 Tenn. 221, 22 S.W.2d 225 (1893).

Other assignments of error directed to the charge and to the refusal of the court to direct a verdict are without merit. For error in admitting the confession and statement of Stubblefield as evidence in the cause, the judgment of the Court of Appeals is reversed, and the cause remanded to the chancery court of Shelby county for another trial.

PEOPLE OF THE STATE OF NEW YORK v. ONEAL BROWN

Court of Appeals of New York, 1970.
26 N.Y.2d 88, 308 N.Y.S.2d 825, 257 N.E.2d 16.

Defendant was convicted before the Onondaga County Court, Albert Orenstein, J., of murder in the second degree and of carrying a dangerous weapon and he appealed. The Supreme Court, Appellate Division, 28 A.D.2d 646, 282 N.Y.S.2d 215, affirmed and permission to appeal was granted.

. . .

BERGAN, Judge. The main issue in this case, where appellant has been convicted of murder in the second degree, is whether he acted in self-defense. In turn this depends on the proof of appellant's contention that the deceased had a pistol drawn when appellant shot him.

One witness for appellant testified to this effect; but several prosecution witnesses testified decedent did not have a pistol in hand when defendant shot him and the police found no pistol on decedent's clothes or on the floor of the premises where the shooting occurred.

This brings into focus the importance of an admission made both to the police and to appellant's lawyer by one Shelton Seals, who at the time of trial was being held in jail on a charge of robbery, that he had "picked up the gun" apparently which he used in the robbery "immediately after the shooting" for which appellant has been convicted. This admission was made in a conversation at the jail with appellant's counsel; another and similar admission was made by Seals in a confession to the police.

If it had been true that Seals picked up a gun from the floor of the premises immediately after the shooting for which defendant has been convicted, this could have a significant bearing on defendant's contention that decedent was armed and that defendant acted in his own defense.

Seals was called as a defense witness. He refused to answer questions on constitutional grounds. Appellant then offered proof of his admissions. The court sustained objections to them. The ruling was clearly proper upon settled authority in this State. Thus the important question presented by this appeal is whether the existing rule should be continued or abandoned in favor of a more rational view of admissibility of declarations against interest.

In discussing the admissibility of such declarations against interest as an exception to the hearsay rule, Richardson makes the categorical statement that "The fact that the declaration alleged to have been made would subject the declarant to criminal liability is held not to be sufficient to bring it within the declaration against interest exception to the rule against hearsay evidence" (Richardson, Evidence [9th ed.], § 241, pp. 232, 233).

This, as it has been noted, has undoubtedly been the rule in New York (Kittredge v. Grannis, 244 N.Y. 168, 175, 176, 155 N.E. 88, 90 (1927); Ellwanger v. Whiteford, 15 A.D.2d 898, 225 N.Y.S.2d 734 (1962), affirmed 12 N.Y.2d 1037, 239 N.Y.S.2d 680, 190 N.E.2d 24); in the Federal Courts (Donnelly v. United States, 228 U.S. 243, 33 S.Ct. 449, 57 L.Ed. 820 (1913)); and in a majority of the States (C.J. S. Evidence § 219, pp. 608–609).

Yet the distinction which would authorize a court to receive proof that a man admitted he never had title to an Elgin watch, but not to receive proof that he had admitted striking Jones over the head with a club, assuming equal relevancy of both statements, does not readily withstand analysis.

Holmes attacked the distinction in his notable dissent in *Donnelly* (supra, 228 U.S. pp. 277–278, 33 S.Ct. p. 461) in which, among other things, he said: "The rules of evidence in the main are based on experience, logic, and common sense, less hampered by history than some parts of the substantive law. There is no decision by this court against the admissibility of such a confession; the English cases since the separation of the two countries do not bind us; the exception to the hearsay rule in the case of declarations against interest is well known; no other statement is so much against interest as a confession of murder; it is far more calculated to convince than dying declarations, which would be let in to hang a man (Mattox v. United States, 146 U.S. 140, 13 S.Ct. 50, 36 L.Ed. 917 (1892)); and when we surround the accused with so many safeguards, some of which seem to me excessive; I think we ought to give him the benefit of a fact that, if proved, commonly would have such weight. The history of the law and the arguments against the English doctrine are so well and fully stated by Mr. Wigmore that there is no need to set them forth at greater length. 2 Wigmore, Ev. §§ 1476, 1477."

Wigmore, as Holmes notes, developed the argument against the distinction, not only on the basis of sheer logic, but on the historical ground that the English cases which created the distinction, particularly the Sussex Peerage Case (11 Cl. & Fin. 85, 109) were a departure from the basic rule of long standing that admissions against interest generally were received, where relevant, and the declarant dead. The *Peerage* decision was regarded by Wigmore as "not strongly argued and not considered by the judges in the light of the precedents" (5 Wigmore, Evidence, [3d ed.], § 1476, p. 283). Wigmore concludes his comprehensive analysis of the problem with the statement: "It is therefore not too late to retrace our steps, and to discard this barbarous doctrine." (op. cit., p. 290).

There seems to be developing in this country a gradual change of viewpoint which would abolish the distinction. In 1964 the Supreme Court of California decided People v. Spriggs, 60 Cal.2d 868, 36 Cal.Rptr. 841, 389 P.2d 377, opn. per Traynor, J. This held that proof defendant's companion admitted to the police that the heroin found on the ground was hers was admissible.

Justice Traynor, discussing the usual rule that admission against pecuniary interest was admissible, said: "A declaration against penal interest is no less trustworthy. As we pointed out in People v. One 1948 Chevrolet Conv. Coupe, 45 Cal.2d 613, 622, 290 P.2d 538, 55 A.L.R.2d 1272 (1956), a person's interest against being criminally implicated gives reasonable assurance of the veracity of his statement made against that interest. Moreover, since the conviction of a crime ordinarily entails economic loss, the traditional concept of a 'pecuniary interest' could logically include one's 'penal interest.'" (60 Cal.2d pp. 874–875, 36 Cal.Rptr. p. 845, 389 P.2d p. 381 (1964)).

In the same direction in Missouri, see Moore v. Metropolitan Life Ins. Co., 237 S.W.2d 210 (Mo.App.1951), and Sutter v. Easterly (354 Mo. 282, 189 S.W.2d 284 (1945)) where there is a good discussion of Wigmore's analysis; and in Arizona, Deike v. Great Atlantic & Pacific Tea Co., 3 Ariz.App. 430, 415 P.2d 145 (1966).

If, as it is argued, Seals picked up a gun on the floor after the shooting (a gun with which he subsequently committed a robbery) it would be a matter of importance in reaching the truth as to whether or not decedent was armed and it would tend to substantiate defendant's self-defense argument. This kind of admission might well be more important and reliable than the testimony of defendant's witness that decedent had a gun in hand.

There is another facet. The rule on admissions against interest was based on the absence of the witness; and usually this meant that he was dead. But whether the person is dead, or beyond the jurisdiction, or will not testify, and cannot be compelled to testify because of a constitutional privilege, all equally spell out unavailability of trial testimony. If the rule is to be changed to include penal admissions against interest, it ought to embrace unavailability because of the assertion of constitutional right which might be fairly common in the area of penal admissions.

This is the way the St. Louis Court of Appeals approached the question in Moore v. Metropolitan Life Ins. Co., 237 S.W.2d 210, 212 (Mo.App.1951), supra: "In other words, having regard for the principle of necessity which justifies resort to secondary evidence, a witness who stands upon his constitutional rights is, as a practical proposition, just as fully unavailable as though he were insane or dead or prevented from testifying because of some other acceptable reason. Sutter v. Easterly, 354 Mo. 282, 189 S.W.2d 284, 162 A.L.R. 437."

In People v. Spriggs, 60 Cal.2d 868, 36 Cal.Rptr. 841, 389 P.2d 377 (1964), supra, the California Supreme Court held the admission against penal interest admissible without reaching, on that record, the kind of lack of availability which would become a basis for taking the admission. The record of that trial did not show whether she was available.

But Judge Traynor's footnote 3 (p. 875, 36 Cal.Rptr. p. 845, 389 P.2d p. 381) was to the effect that "If Mrs. Roland had taken the witness stand, but refused to testify regarding possession of narcotics, invoking her constitutional right not to incriminate herself, she would not have been available as a witness."

The rule in New York should be modernized to hold that an admission against penal interest will be received where material and where the person making the admission is dead, beyond the jurisdiction and thus not available; or where he is in court and refuses to testify as to the fact of the admission on the ground of self incrimination.

Since there is to be a new trial two other points raised by appellant require discussion. The first is that the People were permitted excessive cross-examination of defendant when he took the stand as a witness in his own behalf. One line of questions related to his participation in a fight in which the victim was cut with a knife. Another concerned his paternity of a child, and his relationship with Pamela Sargent, one of the prosecution witnesses. This included inquiry concerning a paternity action in the Family Court.

The District Attorney contends that the questions relating to the assault and other matters were in good faith which is supported by files in his office. Some of this cross-examination was improper, especially the references to the paternity proceedings and perhaps also the incidents of relationships. But if the questions about the assault were asked in good faith they would be proper (see, e. g., People v. Alamo, 23 N.Y.2d 630, 298 N.Y.S.2d 681, 246 N.E.2d 496 (1969); People v. Van Gaasbeck, 189 N.Y. 408, 82 N.E. 718, 22 L.R.A.,N.S., 650 (1907)).

Appellant also argues he should have been allowed to examine a witness who testified for the defense concerning an attempt by that witness' wife to influence his testimony and to influence him not to testify. The witness' wife, who was a sister of decedent, had been an important prosecution witness. One of the questions excluded was her conversation with her husband (the defense witness) on "whether or not you should testify in this lawsuit".

The sister was, as it has been noted, an important prosecution witness, and her interest or bias would have been relevant. And it would not have been necessary to ask her about the conversation to lay a foundation for showing her bias or interest (People v. Brooks, 131 N.Y. 321, 30 N.E. 189 (1892); People v. Lustig, 206 N.Y. 162, 99 N.E. 183 (1912); People v. Michalow, 229 N.Y. 325, 128 N.E. 228 (1920)). The inquiry should have been allowed.

The judgment should be reversed and a new trial ordered.

FULD, C. J., and BURKE, SCILEPPI, BREITEL, JASEN and GIBSON, JJ., concur.

Judgment reversed, etc.

SCHINDLER v. ROYAL INS. CO.

Court of Appeals of New York, 1932.
258 N.Y. 310, 179 N.E. 711.

Appeal from Supreme Court, Appellate Division, Second Department.

Action by Rose Schindler against the Royal Insurance Company. From an order of the Appellate Division (233 App.Div. 765, 250 N.Y.S. 805) affirming an order of the Special Term granting motion to strike out second affirmative defense in defendant's answer, defendant, by permission (233 App.Div. 849, 250 N.Y.S. 879), appeals on certified question.

The following question was certified: "Do the allegations stated and contained in the paragraphs of the amended answer numbered '9th,' '10th,' '11th,' '12th' and '13th' thereof set forth facts sufficient to constitute a defense?"

POUND, J. Plaintiff sues on an insurance policy for a fire loss. Defendant sets up as a defense that by its terms the policy shall be void in case of any fraud of the insured touching the subject of the insurance; that plaintiff made to it a false and fraudulent statement of loss and damage; that thereafter plaintiff was convicted in the County Court of Nassau of the crime of presenting to defendant such false and fraudulent proof of loss and that such judgment of conviction is a bar to the maintenance of this action by the plaintiff and the issue of plaintiff's fraud is res adjudicata. The defense has been stricken out as bad and a question certified as to its sufficiency.

Appellant does not question the existence of a general rule that conviction in a criminal action is not conclusive proof in a civil action of the facts on which the judgment of conviction rests, but challenges the application of the rule in its extreme form to this case as absurd, unjust, and unsound in principle.

The source of this rule dates back towards the beginning of the common law. The King v. The Warden of the Fleet, 12 Mod. 337. In the Duchess of Kingston's Case (2 Smith's Leading Cases [13th Ed.], 644) the Lord Chief Justice of the Court of Common Pleas, after conference with the judges, answered certain questions of the House of Lords to the effect that a transaction between two parties in a judicial proceeding ought not to be binding on a third; "or it would be unjust to bind any person who could not be admitted to make a defence, or to examine witnesses, or to appeal from a judgment he might think erroneous." It may be thus stated: Any judgment of conviction or acquittal is a decision in rem which estops the whole world from attacking the fact of conviction but estops only the parties, unless the Legislature has otherwise provided, from afterwards raising the question whether the accused was in fact guilty or innocent of the offence of which he was convicted or acquitted. In any civil proceeding to which the people are not parties, one may, after having been convicted of a crime, assert his innocence and put his opponent to his proof of guilt, or, after having been acquitted on a criminal charge, may himself be subjected to a trial anew of the issue of fact.

The reasons given for the rule are that dissimilarity of object, procedure, and degree and elements of proof in the two trials forbid that the criminal judgment should be held to be decisive of the facts on which it is based. 6 North Car. Law Review, 333; . . . While a judgment of acquittal is only a determination that guilt has not been established beyond a reasonable doubt, although a preponderance of evidence might point thereto, a valid judgment of conviction in a court of competent jurisdiction with all the safeguards thrown about a person accused of crime which enable him to make his defense, to examine witnesses and to testify in his own behalf, might be held free from collateral attack without exposing the law to the jibes and jests of the critics of our present system of administering justice. As said Prentis, P., in Eagle, Star & British Dominions Ins. Co. v. Heller, 149 Va. 82, 111, 140 S.E. 314, 323, 57 A. L.R. 490 (1927), in which the rule of conclusiveness is applied in its entirety: "To permit a recovery under a policy of fire insurance by one who has been convicted of burning the property insured, would be to disregard the contract, be illogical, would discredit the administration of justice, defy public policy and shock the most unenlightened conscience."

The rule in New York from an early day (Maybee v. Avery, 18 Johns. 352 (1820)) has relaxed the strict rule of complete exclusion. It permits proof of the conviction as prima facie evidence of the facts involved. The same rule has been stated in England (Matter of Crippen's Estate, L.R. [1911] Prob. 108, 115), where Evans, P., said: "In my opinion, where a convicted felon, or the personal representative of a convicted murderer who has been executed, brings any civil proceeding to establish claims, or to enforce rights, which result to the felon, or to the convicted testator from his own crime, the conviction is admissible in evidence, not merely as proof of the conviction, but also as presumptive proof of the commission of the crime."

It would be an unedifying spectacle if the courts should now apply the strict rule which excluded all reference to the judgment of conviction in the civil action as evidence tending to establish the material facts. We shall, however, continue to hold that it is not effective as a plea in bar.

The order should be affirmed, with costs, and the question certified answered in the negative.

CARDOZO, C. J., and CRANE, LEHMAN, KELLOGG, and O'BRIEN, JJ., concur.

HUBBS, J., dissents for the reasons stated in Eagle, Star & British Dominions Ins. Co. v. Heller, 149 Va. 82, 140 S.E. 314, 57 A.L.R. 490 (1927).

Order affirmed, etc.

TAYLOR v. FIRST NATIONAL BANK OF TUSCALOOSA

Supreme Court of Alabama, 1966.
279 Ala. 624, 189 So.2d 141.

Bill in equity by executor of estate of father against daughter to establish resulting trust in house and lot father had conveyed to daughter in return for her assumption of mortgage thereon, on which he subsequently in effect made a $6,000 payment. The Circuit Court, Tuscaloosa County, W. C. Warren, J., entered decree for the executor and the daughter appealed.

COLEMAN, Justice.

. . .

Complainant, a corporation, is a bank and is the executor of the will of I. N. Schofield, deceased. Respondent is a daughter of the testator. His will is dated October 18, 1952. He died May 22, 1961. The will was admitted to probate a short time after his death.

By the will, testator gave to his wife a life estate in all of his estate, real, personal, and mixed, and the remainder to his children in equal shares. He appointed complainant executor of the will. He was survived by his widow and eight children who were living at the time of the trial.

The court overruled respondent's demurrer to the bill of complaint and this ruling is assigned and argued for error, but we reverse for insufficiency of the evidence to sustain the finding and do not consider the ruling on demurrer.

On July 11, 1958, for a recited consideration of $13,252.00, testator bought a house and lot in a subdivision in Northport. Testator is the grantee named in the deed.

On the same day, testator and wife executed to complainant a mortgage to secure a loan of $13,500.00, payable in monthly installments of $150.00 each. In the mortgage, as security, testator conveyed the Northport property which is described in the above-mentioned deed, and also a tract of land which is referred to in the testimony as 35 acres and is described in the mortgage as being a part of the Wash Christian farm.

Also on the same day, for a recited consideration of $10.00, love and affection, and respondent's assumption of and agreement to pay the above-mentioned mortgage, testator and wife, by warranty deed, conveyed the Northport property to respondent.

The mortgage and both deeds were all recorded in the office of the Judge of Probate on the same day, July 11, 1958.

Thereafter, it seems, respondent executed a paper whereby she acknowledged that, as part of the consideration for the deed to her, she assumed and agreed to pay the debt secured by the mortgage at the rate of $150.00 per month as is provided in the mortgage. This exhibit is dated July 30, 1958, sworn to July 30, 1958, and filed for record in the office of the Judge of Probate July 25, 1961, which was subsequent to testator's death.

By warranty deed dated and acknowledged September 10, 1958, testator and wife, for a recited consideration of $12,000.00, conveyed the 35-acre Wash Christian farm tract to Ernest Morgan and Hugh Bridges. Morgan and Bridges have no other connection with this case.

By instrument dated September 23, 1958, complainant released the 35-acre tract from the lien and operation of the mortgage. The recited consideration for the release is the payment of $6,000.00 to complainant by Morgan and Bridges. It seems to be agreed as a fact that the $6,000.00 paid to complainant for the release was part of the $12,000.00 paid by Morgan and Bridges as the purchase price for the Wash Christian farm land, and, in effect was paid to the complainant by testator. The $6,000.00 payment was the consideration for the release. The intention of testator with regard to respondent's obligation to pay or repay this $6,000.00 to him or to his executor is a contested question in this case.

The trial court found that the $6,000.00 payment was not intended as a gift to respondent and that "it was the intention and judgment of the said I. N. Schofield, Deceased, that she owed him said Six Thousand and No/100 ($6,000.00) Dollars . . . ." The court decreed that respondent pay $6,000.00 to complainant at the rate of $150.00 per month and fastened a lien on the Northport property to secure payment. Respondent appealed.

Respondent testified that she was divorced from her husband by decree granted May 22, 1961, the date her father died. She had three children. Her father arranged for her to get her home by means of the instruments introduced in evidence. At that time she had no home or other property. Her husband was not supporting her and the children at the time of divorce. Her father was sick at the time.

Respondent testified as to a conversation with her father concerning the $6,000.00 payment on the mortgage, but we do not think she is competent to testify against complainant as to that conversation because respondent has a pecuniary interest in the result of this suit, her father's estate is also interested in the result of the suit, and the interest of respondent is diametrically opposed to the interest of complainant. § 433, Title 7, Code 1940. If respondent wins, the estate will be smaller, and if respondent loses the estate will be larger by at least $6,000.00.

A few days after this conversation, respondent took her book, which we understand to be a record of payments on the mortgage, to the Northport branch office of complainant bank and Mrs. Ford, an employee of the bank, marked in the book a credit of $6,000.00 on the mortgage debt. We do not think there can be any well-founded objection by complainant to the testimony proving the fact that this credit entry was made because testator's making of the payment for the credit is the foundation of complainant's lawsuit.

Respondent testified to further conversations with her father, but we think she is also incompetent to testify as to statements made by testator in those conversations.

Complainant offered the testimony of testator's widow and two of his daughters, Mrs. Nelson and Mrs. Hagler, which is to the effect that testator stated that he intended for respondent to pay him the

$6,000.00 he paid on the mortgage debt. We are of the opinion, however, that the testimony of the widow and these two daughters is not to be considered for two reasons, to wit:

1. Because the widow and two daughters are incompetent under the dead man's statute.
2. Because the statements to which they testify are not contemporaneous with the payment but were all made afterwards.

We have already said that we think that the estate is interested in the result of this suit. We think that the widow and daughters also have a pecuniary interest in that result. If the complainant is successful, the estate will be larger. By the will, the widow takes a life interest in that estate and will have a pecuniary gain if the estate is larger. The daughters have a remainder interest in the estate and a pecuniary advantage if the estate is increased by the result of this suit.

The interest of respondent in this suit is squarely opposed to the interest of the other children and widow of testator. If the complainant is successful, respondent will be required to pay $6,000.00, or more, to complainant. After costs of administration and debts of testator have been paid, the widow will have a life estate in whatever is left of the $6,000.00 and the daughters will have a right to the remainder of the $6,000.00 after the life estate is terminated. We think it is an inescapable conclusion that the interest of respondent and the interest of the other daughters and widow are opposed within the meaning of the dead man's statute, § 433, Title 7, Code 1940.

The statute provides:

> ". . . . no person having a pecuniary interest in the result of the suit . . . . shall be allowed to testify against the party to whom his interest is opposed, as to any transaction with, or statement by, the deceased person whose estate is interested in the result of the suit . . . ."

The widow and two daughters testified that testator made certain statements concerning his payment of $6,000.00 on the mortgage and respondent's obligation to repay this amount to testator. The alleged statements made by testator show that he intended that respondent be obligated to repay the $6,000.00 to the estate. We must decide, however, whether the widow and two daughters were competent to testify against respondent that testator made such statements.

The statute seems to require three conditions to exist in order to make the witness incompetent to testify as to statements by the dead man, to wit:

1. The witness must have a pecuniary interest in the result of the suit.
2. His interest must be opposed to the interest of the party against whom he is called to testify.

3. The estate of the deceased person who made the statement must be interested in the result of the suit.

We think all three conditions exist here.

It is a mistaken construction of the statute to assume that it does not prohibit the testimony if it is favorable to the interest of the estate, and the witness is called in behalf of such interest. Pfingstl v. Solomon, 240 Ala. 58, 63, 197 So. 12 (1940).

The competency of the witness is dependent upon the nature of the suit and whether the estate of deceased is interested. If the estate is not interested, there is no incompetency under the statute. If the estate is interested, the witness is incompetent if he has a pecuniary interest in result of the suit at the time of trial, or if his status is such that he would be so interested if he had not transferred his interest. The widow and children of testator having such an interest in the result of the suit, and testator's estate being interested in that result, the widow and children are incompetent to testify as to any transaction with or statement by the testator unless he or she ". . . . '. . . . is called to testify thereto by the party to whom such interest is opposed.' " Niehuss v. Ford, 251 Ala. 529, 532, 38 So.2d 484, 487 (1949).

We are, therefore, of opinion that the widow and two daughters, Mrs. Nelson and Mrs. Hagler, were incompetent to testify against respondent as to statements made by testator which tend to show that respondent is indebted to testator for the $6,000.00 payment made by testator on the mortgage. It follows that such testimony should not have been considered by the trial court and should not be considered by this court under the lazy lawyer's statute. Act No. 101, 1943 Acts, page 105; 1958 Recompilation Code 1940, Title 7, § 372(1); Redwine v. Jackson, 254 Ala. 564, 49 So.2d 115 (1951).

. . .

While the facts in East v. Karter are not the same as in the case at bar, the following statement in the opinion seems to fit here:

> "We cannot permit what may turn out to be an inequality in the distribution of the estate, to prevent the legal consequences of a clearly defined state of circumstances. We must allow legal principles to govern the situation, whatever the result. . . . ." (225 Ala. at page 558, 144 So. at page 27)

We are of opinion that complainant is not entitled to relief and that its bill of complaint should be dismissed. The decree is reversed and the cause remanded so that a decree in accordance with this view may be entered.

Reversed and remanded with directions.

DECISIONS RELATING TO CHAPTER XIV, SELF-SERVING DECLARATION

McDERMOTT v. McDERMOTT

Supreme Court of Errors of Connecticut, 1921.
97 Conn. 31, 115 A. 638.

Appeal from Superior Court, New Haven County; Isaac Wolfe, Judge.

Suit by Michael McDermott against Mary McDermott to compel defendant to cause an alleged undelivered deed of real estate owned by the plaintiff to be erased from the land records, and requiring the premises to be conveyed to the plaintiff. Judgment for the plaintiff, with appeal by defendant.

. . .

WHEELER, C. J. The defendant submits her appeal upon the single point as to whether or not the plaintiff, by his acts and conduct, ratified the act of the defendant in placing the deed on record of the premises which the plaintiff seeks, by this action, to have conveyed to him. The defendant's counsel rightly says that the corrections of the finding are not indispensable to the success of her claim of ratification, except the correction of paragraph 43, and all of the motion to correct may well be disregarded, as either not well taken or as immaterial, except as to this paragraph, and this we propose considering at a later stage of the case.

The finding relates that the plaintiff executed a deed of certain premises, made to the defendant as grantee, but never delivered the same, and placed it among his private papers in a bureau drawer and locked the drawer. Afterward, in September, 1919, plaintiff learned that the defendant had taken the deed and placed it on the land records, without the knowledge or consent of the plaintiff. Immediately upon learning of this, the plaintiff made demand upon the defendant for the return of the deed; but defendant said she purposed holding this property. Prior to this time the plaintiff and defendant had been living together in these premises, and, upon defendant's refusal of plaintiff's demand, he moved from these premises, and has not since lived with the defendant. On October 3, 1919, the plaintiff caused a lis pendens to be placed on the land records, giving notice that he claimed title to the property. On October 23, 1919, he caused the present action to be instituted. In December, 1919, he filed his application in the superior court for the appointment of a receiver of the rents of the premises; but, at the suggestion of the court, a bond in lieu thereof was given by the defendant. On March 30, 1921, the plaintiff again brought his application for the appointment of a receiver for the rents, and on March 31, 1921, the court passed an order appointing such receiver. Since its institution the plaintiff has duly pressed this action clear up to the trial.

The defendant relies for her conclusion of ratification upon the acts and statements of the plaintiff in telling a painter who had presented a bill for work done prior to the taking of this deed by the defendant that he should collect it of the defendant as she was the owner of this property; in telling the savings bank, about October 29, 1919, to send its bill for interest which it had sent to the plaintiff, to the defendant; and in telling the water company, and an insurance firm, to send their bills to the defendant. The defendant subsequently paid each of these bills. The trial court also found, in paragraph 43, that—

> "All of said statements aforesaid concerning the sending of the bills to defendant and the ownership of the property were made by plaintiff because defendant had recorded said deed and the premises stood in her name upon the record, and as she was in possession of said property and was receiving the full benefit thereof, the charges against the property should be paid by her. Plaintiff in making such statements did not intend to and did not in fact ratify, confirm, or adopt the act of defendant in taking said deed into her possession and recording the same, nor intend that title to said premises should be and remain in defendant."

The defendant assigns as error this finding that the plaintiff did not intend to, and did not in fact, ratify the taking of the deed in making these statements to the painter, the water company, the savings bank, and the insurance firm; and the defendant insists that the finding, thus corrected, will present a clear case of ratification of the possession by the defendant of this deed and of these premises.

Whether a grantor intended to make delivery of a deed is a question of fact; intention is a mental process, and of necessity it must be proved by the statement or acts of the person whose act is being scrutinized. When the question at issue was whether one had turned over his salary to his wife as a gift, we said:

> "The question, then, is whether, in a situation where the intent of the witness is material, he may testify directly as to his intent at the time of the transaction under investigation. We think he may, since intent is a mental fact requisite to create a gift." Fox v. Shanley, 94 Conn. 350, 362, 109 A. 249, 254 (1920).

And in Meriden Trust & Safe Deposit Co. v. Miller, 88 Conn. 157, 162, 90 A. 228, 229 (1914), we said:

> "We think the finding of the intent to make present gifts was an inference of fact open to the trial court to draw. . . . A question of intent is a question of fact, the determination of which is not reviewable, unless the conclusion drawn by the trier is one which cannot reasonably be made."

And in Humiston v. Preston, 66 Conn. 579, 34 A. 544 (1896), we held—where the question of the delivery of a deed depended upon the intent with which an act was performed—that the question was one of fact, and the decision of the trial court thereon was not subject to review on appeal. Wiley v. London & Lancashire Fire Ins. Co., 89 Conn. 35, 39, 92 A. 678 (1915); Kronfeld v. Missal, 87 Conn. 491, 493, 494, 89 A. 95 (1914); Saltzsieder v. Saltzsieder, 219 N.Y. 523, 530, 114 N.E. 856 (1917).

The intention with which these statements were made by the plaintiff, whether intending to ratify the conveyance to the defendant or not, was a question of fact, and the evidence amply justified the trial court in finding that the plaintiff did not intend to ratify this conveyance.

If the case were to be disposed of without the further finding of that part of paragraph 43 which recites that in these statements the plaintiff did not in fact ratify the conveyance to defendant, the facts found would lead to the conclusion that the plaintiff did not ratify, whether the conclusion be regarded as one of law or fact, or of mixed law and fact. If ratification be regarded as a question of fact, as our decisions hold, the finding that plaintiff did not intend to ratify of necessity would compel the inference that no ratification then occurred. But if ratification be regarded as a question of law, where the facts are undisputed, the only conclusion which these facts permit is that no ratification took place when these statements were made. Whether there has been a delivery of a deed, or a ratification of a deed, are questions alike in character. Some authorities say the question of delivery is one of law upon the facts. Lee v. Parker, 171 N.C. 144, 151, 88 S.E. 217 (1916); Saltzsieder v. Saltzsieder, 219 N.Y. 523, 530, 114 N.E. 856 (1917); Earle v. Earle, 20 N.J.Law, 347. Others say it is one of law and fact, upon a given set of facts. Johnston v. Kramer Bros. & Co., 203 F. 733, 736 (D.C.1913); Midkiff v. Colton, 155 C.C.A. 149, 242 F. 373, 379 (1917). Others hold it to be a question of fact. Bishop v. Burke, 207 Mass. 133, 140, 93 N.E. 254 (1911); Cook v. Lee, 72 N.H. 569, 572, 58 A. 511 (1904). And a few hold it to be ordinarily a question of fact, or a mixed question of law and fact. Wood v. Montpelier, 85 Vt. 467, 82 A. 671, 677, Ann.Cas.1914D, 500 (1912).

In Humiston v. Preston, 66 Conn. 579, 34 A. 544 (1896), we said that, where the delivery depends upon the intent with which a certain act is performed, the question is one of fact; and similarly we held the question of waiver and abandonment one of fact, Chatfield Co. v. O'Neill, 89 Conn. 172, 175, 93 A. 133 (1915); also acceptance and acquiescence, Evarts v. Johnson, 88 Conn. 683, 686, 92 A. 434 (1914); and whether a contract had been repudiated, McLaughlin v. Thomas, 86 Conn. 252, 258, 85 A. 370 (1913). In Home Banking & Realty Co. v. Baum, 85 Conn. 383, 389, 82 A. 970 (1912), and Curnane v. Scheidel, 70 Conn. 13, 17, 38 A. 875 (1897), the trial court found the ratification as a question of fact. While in Gallup v. Fox, 64 Conn. 491, 495, 30 A. 756 (1895), the charge of the trial court, that ratification was a fact for the jury to find from the evidence, was not held to be error. Devlin on Deeds, vol. 1, (3d Ed.) p. 411, § 268, states the rule to be:

> "The question whether the grantor ratified the delivery, as against a mortgagee from the grantee relying upon the deed, is one that may be submitted to a jury."

Since ratification in a given case depends ultimately upon the intention with which the act or acts, from which ratification is claimed, were done, and since intention is a mental fact, and its finding clearly one of fact, the finding in a given case of ratification is one of fact, and not reviewable, unless the conclusion of ratification, drawn from the facts, is plainly erroneous. Nolan v. New York, N. H. & H. R. Co., 70 Conn. 159, 174, 39 A. 115, 43 L.R.A. 305 (1898). In other words, unless the conclusion drawn be one which men reasoning in a reasonable way would not draw, the finding of ratification must stand, and, except for this limited purpose it is not reviewable.

The exception to a single ruling on evidence is assigned as error. The plaintiff testified in his own behalf, and on cross-examination was asked if he had not gone to the savings bank, the water company, the insurance firm, and the painter, and told them to send their bills to defendant, as she owned the property, and, having answered these questions in the affirmative on redirect he testified that he had, upon learning of the recording of the deed, consulted a lawyer, and caused to be drawn and recorded a lis pendens or caveat. This instrument contained a declaration of ownership of these premises by the plaintiff. The defendant objected to the offer in evidence of this lis pendens, upon the ground that it was a self-serving declaration, made after the fact. It was claimed in explanation of plaintiff's conduct and of his claim that he never intended to convey these premises to defendant. The court admitted the offer, and we think properly. The recording of this instrument was an act indicative of plaintiff's intention, and the fact that it contained declarations in support of plaintiff's claim did not make the act and the instrument inadmissible. Both were inseparable, and unless admitted the truth would have been shut out. We repeat what we said of the rule against the admission of hearsay evidence in Engel v. Conti, 78 Conn. 351, 354, 62 A. 210, 211 ( ):

> "It is not one that can be safely strained beyond its established limits."

Other assignments of error we find no occasion to consider.

There is no error.

The other Judges concurred.

GAINES v. STEWART

Court of Civil Appeals of Texas, 1933.
57 S.W.2d 207.

. . .

Appeal from District Court, Tom Green County; John F. Sutton, Judge.

Suit by J. C. Stewart against C. I. Gaines. Judgment for plaintiff, and defendant appeals.

. . .

BAUGH, Justice. Suit by Stewart against Gaines for damages to his car and for personal injuries resulting from a collision between his car and a truck owned by Gaines and being operated over a public highway in Tom Green county. Upon the jury's answers to special issues, judgment was rendered in favor of Stewart for $3,604; hence this appeal.

Appellant's first proposition is that it was error to permit Dr. Nibling, who treated Stewart in May, 1929, for his injuries at the time same were received, to testify as to what Stewart told him in May, 1930, approximately one year thereafter, about pains he was then suffering in his knees and legs; because such examination and statements so made in 1930 were not for purposes of treatment, but for the purpose of enabling Dr. Nibling to testify in this suit concerning the injuries theretofore received, the continuing nature of same, and the probable future disability of Stewart resulting therefrom.

We think this contention should be sustained. Dr. Nibling testified that he did not examine Stewart in May, 1930, for purposes of treatment, but to enable him to testify as a witness; and that he had discharged Stewart from treatment for his injuries nearly a year before. It does not appear that Dr. Nibling attempted to discover whether such pains existed in Stewart's legs other than by Stewart's own statements to that effect. These facts and circumstances we think bring such testimony under condemnation of the rule against hearsay and self-serving declarations. T. & N. O. Ry. v. Stephens, 198 S.W. 396 (Tex.Civ.App.1917) (writ dismissed) is a case directly in point. In Wheeler v. Ry. Co., 91 Tex. 356, 43 S.W. 876 (1898), the same issue was raised, and, though the Supreme Court declined to pass upon it because not properly presented, the court did intimate that such testimony was inadmissible. And in M., K. & T. Ry. Co. v. Johnson, 95 Tex. 411, 67 S.W. 768 (1902), a state of facts substantially identical with the instant case, the writ was granted upon the exact question here presented. While the court held in that case that the issue was not properly raised, it clearly committed itself to the view that such declarations under such circumstances are not admissible. A very complete and exhaustive set of annotations from numerous state and federal decisions on this question is to be found in 67 A.L.R. 10. See, also, 17 Tex.Jur., §§ 245 and 272, pp. 589 and 649.

The test in such case appears to be whether the motive and opportunity to fabricate without detection the symptoms complained of is presented. Undoubtedly a qualified physician can testify as to symptoms and conditions of injury or disease made known to or discovered by him in his treatment of his patient. Or to such conditions as he finds in the patient from his own independent examination of him. But where an injured party, for the express purpose of qualifying a physician to testify in his behalf about matters on which such party seeks a recovery, makes statements as to subjective matters of pain, suffering, etc., not disclosed to the physician by other and independent means, there exists both motive and opportunity for the patient to magnify or feign injuries. Under such circumstances his statements become clearly self-serving and hearsay, and should not be admitted.

The next proposition complains that it was error to render judgment against appellant because the issue of ownership of the truck was not submitted to the jury. There was no error in this. It was not a disputed issue. The evidence is uncontradicted that appellant owned the truck in question and that Stayton, the driver at the time of the collision, was his servant acting within the scope of his employment. It was not necessary, therefore, to submit such issue to the jury. Livezey v. Putnam Supply Co., 30 S.W.2d 902 (Tex.Civ.App.1930) (writ ref.); Emergency Clinic v. Continental Inv. Co., 41 S.W.2d 640, 641 (Tex.Civ.App.1931); Berryman v. Norfleet, 41 S.W.2d 722 (Tex.Civ.App.1931); Stedman Fruit Co. v. Smith, 45 S.W.2d 804 (Tex.Civ.App.1932); Article 2190, Rev.St.1925, as amended by chapter 78, p. 120, Acts Reg.Sess. 42d Leg. (1931), Vernon's Ann.Civ. St. art. 2190. This was not an independent ground of recovery, but merely one of the elements in plaintiff's cause of action. No request was made that it be submitted. See Ormsby v. Ratcliffe, 117 Tex. 242, 1 S.W.2d 1084 (1928); I. T. A. v. Bettis, 52 S.W.2d 1059, 1061 (Tex. Civ.App.1932) (writ ref.).

Appellant's next proposition raises the issue of misconduct of the jury, in that one juror informed the others that under the law Gaines had to carry insurance on his truck, and that the insurance company, and not Gaines, would have to pay whatever judgment Stewart recovered. This statement was also reaffirmed as true by another juror. Three jurors testified on motion for rehearing that the matter of Gaines having insurance was discussed in the jury room. Two of these jurors, Rice and Key, denied that it in any manner influenced their verdict. The juror Schrum, while he testified on cross-examination that he would not render a larger verdict against an insurance company than he would against an individual, also testified, among other things, with reference to the matter of insurance discussed in the jury room, as follows:

> "Q. Is it not a fact you were influenced in how you would answer those questions by considering whether or not Mr. Gaines had insurance? A. To be plain, I hung the

jury for awhile on account they were giving him more than I thought we had evidence to justify.

"Q. Why did you agree to the sum you did agree to? A. The main thing was, they were all against me on it.

"Q. What other reason? A. I thought, and knowing they always carried insurance—I knew according to law he had to carry insurance—and at the start nobody seemed to know whether they did or not, and I had in my mind that they did."

And on cross-examination further:

"Q. You gave in because there were eleven against you? A. I gave in to that and what I had in mind too.

"Q. You would not go into the jury box and willingly render judgment against one party more than you would another? A. No, sir.

"Q. In agreeing to the sum you did agree upon, were you or not influenced by your belief that Mr. Gaines had insurance? A. I knew it was the law for them to have it.

"Q. In agreeing to that sum did you or not consider that fact? A. I cannot say positively, but it is bound to have had a little influence on me."

It has been repeatedly held that injection into the jury's deliberations of extraneous matters not in evidence and prejudicial in character is ground for reversal, unless it appears that no injury to the losing party resulted. And this is particularly true where the jury is informed that some insurance company, and not the defendant named, is to bear the loss, and such information, not in evidence, influenced the jury's verdict. See D. & H. Truck Line v. Lavallee, 7 S.W.2d 661, 663 (Tex.Civ.App.1928), and cases there cited and discussed; Moore v. Ivey, 277 S.W. 106 (Tex.Com.App.1926); Great West Mill & El. Co. v. Hess, 281 S.W. 234 (Tex.Civ.App.1926); Red Star Coaches v. Lamb, 41 S.W.2d 523 (Tex.Civ.App.1897); S. H. Kress & Co. v. Dyer, 49 S.W.2d 986, 989 (Tex.Civ.App.1899).

Injection of such extraneous matters, prejudicial in nature, by one or more of the jurors, clearly constitutes misconduct; and where there is any reasonable doubt as to its injurious effect the verdict should be set aside. Casstevens v. T. & P. Ry. Co., 119 Tex. 456, 32 S.W.2d 637, 73 A.L.R. 89 (1930); Moore v. Ivey, supra; Small v. Taylor, 54 S.W.2d 151, 153 (Tex.Civ.App.1932). Not only was a doubt raised as to other jurors, but we think it clearly appears from the above-quoted testimony of the juror Schrum that his verdict was influenced by the purported information that insurance protected the defendant against liability.

Appellee contends that, since the evidence showed that appellant operated three trucks under a permit, he was required by law to carry liability insurance under Acts 42d Leg. (1931) p. 480, c.

277, § 13 of amendments to article 911b, Vernon's Ann.Civ.St.; that the jurors were presumed to know the law; and that, therefore, no misconduct should result from their discussion of what the law requires. Numerous cases are cited holding that in such cases, where insurance is carried, the insurance company is a proper party to the suit.

However, the record does not sustain appellee's contention. The act cited applies to "motor carriers" and "contract carriers" for hire over the public highways. The evidence in this case shows that Gaines was in the produce business, owned the trucks in question, and hauled his own produce over the highways. There was no evidence that he hauled anything for others for hire. If not, then the requirement of the statute cited that he carry insurance did not apply to him. Under such circumstances and the settled line of decisions, we think the trial court abused his discretion in overruling appellant's motion for a rehearing.

For the errors pointed out, the judgment must be reversed and the cause remanded. The other error complained of by appellant need not occur upon another trial.

Reversed and remanded.

PERKINS v. GREAT NORTHERN RY. CO.

Supreme Court of Minnesota, 1922.
152 Minn. 226, 188 N.W. 564.

Appeal from District Court, Douglas County; Carroll A. Nye, Judge.

Action by J. F. Perkins against the Great Northern Railway Company. Judgment for plaintiff, and motion for new trial was granted, unless plaintiff consent to a reduction in the verdict, which he did, and the defendant appeals from an order denying a new trial. . . .

LEES, C. Plaintiff was head brakeman on one of defendant's freight trains. On September 16, 1920, he was injured when he fell from the train while it was running between Cokato and Smith Lake in this state. He brought this action under the federal Employers' Liability Act (U.S.Comp.St. §§ 8657–8665), charging defendant with negligence in the following particulars: (1) In permitting the handhold on top of a refrigerator car next to the engine to become so insecure that it pulled out as plaintiff was descending from the car to the tender; (2) in operating the engine with a "Johnson bar" or reverse lever, which was so defective that the engineer was unable to control the movements of the train, and, as a consequence, the train was jerked and the refrigerator car suddenly and violently thrown against the engine.

The jury were instructed not to consider the evidence relating to the alleged defective condition of the reverse lever, but that plaintiff was entitled to a verdict if the handhold was defective or if the motion of the train was suddenly and violently checked without warning to plaintiff, and his injury resulted proximately from either cause. A verdict was returned in plaintiff's favor for $31,000. Defendant moved for judgment notwithstanding or for a new trial. The motion for judgment was denied. The motion for a new trial was granted, unless plaintiff consented to accept a reduction of the verdict to $24,000. He consented to the reduction, and defendant appealed.

1. There was evidence tending to show that the handle of the hatch cover on the refrigerator car next to the engine was missing. It was attached to a block of wood fastened by screws to the roof of the car near the handhold alleged to have been defective. The federal Safety Appliance Act (U.S.Comp.St. § 8605 et seq.) does not extend to hatch handles on refrigerator cars. The accident happened at about 1 o'clock in the morning. Seven or eight hours later, a section man found a hatch handle on the ground beside the track at the place where plaintiff fell from the train. The screws were still in the block of wood, and showed that they had been pulled out of the roof of the car. Defendant's inspectors who examined the car soon after the accident testified that they found the handhold firmly bolted to the roof of the car; that there was rust on the thread of the bolts, indicating that they had not been recently disturbed; and that the hatch handle was not to be found. Defendant contends that it was conclusively shown that plaintiff grasped the hatch handle instead of the handhold when he attempted to descend from the car; that it gave way and as a result he fell. Plaintiff testified that as he started to go over the end of the car the "grabiron fell loose," and he lost his balance; that he knew it gave way because he felt it pull through his hand; that he did not know whether it broke away from the car, but did know that the end next to the running board pulled loose. He also testified that he went down the ladder at the end of the car next to the engine earlier in the night, and noticed nothing wrong with the handhold at that time. All the physical facts tend to show that plaintiff was mistaken, and that in fact he grasped the hatch handle instead of the handhold when he started to go down the car, but it is unnecessary to decide whether a verdict based on the charge that the handhold was defective should be allowed to stand, for there must be a new trial for another reason.

. . .

3. When plaintiff was missed, George A. Coppersmith, one of defendant's conductors, took an engine and caboose and went back to look for him. He arrived at the place of the accident at the same time as a farmer named Preus. When plaintiff was giving his testimony in chief, and after he had stated how he was hurt, he was asked this question:

> "Q. Was there any talk between you and him [Coppersmith] in regard to the happening of the accident? A. Yes, sir.

> "Q. This talk . . . was about an hour and a half after you were hurt, was it? A. Yes, sir; something like that.
>
> "Q. Now I wish you would tell the jury what you said to Mr. Coppersmith regarding how the accident happened and what he said to you."

Objection was made on the ground that the question called for hearsay testimony and a self-serving declaration, and that there was no foundation for the admission of a res gestæ statement. The objection was overruled, and plaintiff answered:

> "He says, 'How did it happen, Buddy?' and I said, 'The engineer jerked the cars, the handhold gave way, and I fell.' "

Subsequently and without objection testimony to the same effect was given by Mr. Preus. In view of this, if it was error to receive plaintiff's testimony, it is doubtful whether the error was prejudicial. But since there is to be a new trial, it is proper to indicate our views respecting the admissibility of the testimony objected to. In harmony with the decided weight of authority, this court has adopted the rule that in general the testimony of a party may not be confirmed by proving previous declarations in his own favor consonant with his testimony. Fredin v. Richards, 66 Minn. 46, 68 N.W. 402 (1896); State v. La Bar, 131 Minn. 432, 155 N.W. 211 (1916); Barrett v. Van Duzee, 139 Minn. 351, 166 N.W. 407 (1918). The exception to the rule mentioned in State v. La Bar was elaborately considered in Lyke v. Lehigh Valley Rd. Co., 236 Pa. 38, 84 A. 595 (1912). See, also, 2 Wigmore, Evid. § 1124; Jones, Evid. § 870. It is clear that the general rule and not the exception is applicable to the testimony in question.

It is suggested that plaintiff's declaration, though self-serving, was so closely connected with the accident that it must be regarded as a spontaneous utterance, and hence was properly received in evidence as part of the res gestæ. To say the least, this is doubtful. A considerable period of time intervened between the accident and the declaration—enough to permit of afterthought, which the law distrusts. There was a longer interval of time than in any case where the admission of declarations has been sustained. . . . Lambrecht v. Schreyer, 129 Minn. 271, 152 N.W. 645, L.R.A.1915E, 812 (1915); . . . State v. Rothi, 188 N.W. 50 (Minn.1922). Conceding for the purpose of this discussion that, in the exercise of the broad discretion possessed by the trial court, it was not required to reject the testimony for this reason, another difficulty is encountered. Plaintiff had testified fully to the circumstances under which he was injured. The jury had his sworn statement. He was not impeached by proof of contrary statements out of court. In effect he was permitted to give in evidence his unsworn self-serving declaration otherwise clearly inadmissible on the theory that because the declaration was part of the res gestae he might testify that he had made it, and that, if made, it tended to prove that the facts were as he had related them from the witness stand. In support of this theory, it may be argued that the law permits one who heard the spontaneous utterance of a party to testify to it and hence there is no good reason why the party himself may not testify to his own exclamations. In Lambrecht v. Schreyer, supra, it was said that the testimony might come from the person who made the declaration, but this was said with reference to testimony given by a witness for the plaintiff, and not by the plaintiff himself. So far as we have discovered, it has never been held that a party may bolster up his case by testimony that he made a self-serving declaration so closely connected with an injury he received as to be part of the res gestæ, and a court should be reluctant to adopt a rule of evidence which would tempt a party accidently injured to make evidence for himself. Plaintiff's testimony was not made competent because Preus and Coppersmith heard his statement. It would have been just as competent if heard by some one he did not know and could not procure as a witness. In no state has the res gestæ doctrine been extended farther than in Minnesota. The extension now proposed would not serve the purpose of getting at the truth, which is the sole end towards which all rules of evidence should be directed. For these reasons we are of the opinion that plaintiff should not have been allowed to give the testimony in question.

The order denying a new trial is reversed, and a new trial granted.

RICHARDSON v. MISSOURI–K.–T. R. CO. OF TEXAS

Court of Civil Appeals of Texas, Fort Worth, 1947.
205 S.W.2d 819.

HALL, Justice. This is a well developed case, the record consisting of a 756-page statement of facts, a transcript of 148 pages, plus a motion picture film and other photographs. The suit was filed by appellant, S. A. Richardson, in the District Court of Grayson County, Texas for personal injury damages under the Federal Employers' Liability Act, 45 U.S.C.A. § 51, against appellee, Missouri-Kansas-Texas Railroad Company of Texas. Appellant Richardson, while operating a shaper machine in a planing mill of appellee's machine shop in Denison, Texas, received an injury which cut his three middle fingers off of his right hand and sustained permanent injury to his right thumb. The trial was to a jury, which found appellant was damaged in the sum of $6,000 but because of his contributory negligence he was only entitled to recover $3,000, and he, being dissatisfied with such finding, perfects this appeal, predicated upon six points of error, to-wit: The trial court erred in allowing the introduction of appellee's exhibit No. 19, the same being a technicolor motion picture, for the reasons,—(1) the same was self-serving; (2) the same was hearsay; (3) because no proper predicate for the introduction thereof was laid; (4) because the picture was repetitious; (5) because the same was irrelevant, highly prejudicial, and inflammatory.

His sixth point was leveled at the trial court's refusal to submit to the jury the definition of circumstantial evidence.

The facts show that appellant Richardson had been working for the appellee in its planing mills as a machine carpenter since 1922. His job at the time of the injury included the work on all power-driven woodwork machines in the mill, including the sharper machine, the one on which he was injured. He testified that this machine was the fastest running machine in the mill, that it was composed of an iron table top approximately 3½ feet above the floor and approximately 3½ feet wide and 6 feet long. On top of the table are two heads, located approximately 2 feet from each end of the same. The shaper head is approximately 5 inches across, into which various sizes of knives are fitted; that it makes around 7,000 revolutions per minute. On top of the table and running diagonally across the same is an adjustable wooden gauge, which extends on each side of the cutting head, is approximately 2½ inches thick and 4 inches wide. This gauge is adjusted so that when lumber is held firmly against the table and wooden gauge while being pushed past the revolving shaper head, the desired groove or cut is made in the timber. The machine would do better work when the lumber was held either mechanically or by hand down against the table and pushed over against the gauge as it passed the cutting head. The machine was also equipped with a lumber block or guard, which was to protect the worker from the saws. The shaper head revolved in a clockwise direction with the clock facing up, so that when the lumber is pushed past it, it tends to push the lumber back toward the operator. He further testified that the operator in order to cut small pieces of lumber would have to use his right hand on the front of the piece of timber to be worked and his left hand behind it, thereby holding the lumber down on the table against the gauge and pushing it past the cutting gauge and that the guard on the machine was made for large pieces of timber. At the instance in which plaintiff received his injury, he had picked up a piece of lumber which was 13/16th of an inch thick and 1¾ inches or 2 inches wide and practically 2 feet long. He turned on the machine, placed his right hand at the front of the lumber and his left hand about 6 inches from the back of it and after his right hand had passed the shaper head, the machine made an awful noise and popped and when it did it caught the piece of material in it, hand and all. The lumber broke and jerked his hand into the head. The piece of lumber on which appellant was working at the time of the injury was never found. He was in the process of testing the machine with such small piece of lumber.

. . .

The appellant's theory advanced in point one, leveled against the introduction of the picture because the same was self-serving, is based on the assumption that the picture shows a scene of the foreman of the shop demonstrating how the appellant's hand could be caught and run through the blades. This objection is not well taken, because even though it was detrimental to the theory of appellant's case, yet it demonstrates by experiment appellee's affirmative defenses to the effect that the appellant was negligent in placing his hand in front of the machine and in the way and manner he operated the same. Experiments have been held by our state courts to be admissible. In the case of Houston, E. & W. T. Ry. Co. v. Sherman et al., 42 S.W.2d 241, 245 (Tex.Com.App.1931), it is stated: "It is permissible to prove the existence or nonexistence of a fact by experiments made for that purpose, under circumstances substantially the same as those existing at the time of the occurrence or nonoccurrence of the alleged fact." See also Panhandle & S. F. Ry. Co. et al. v. Haywood, 227 S.W. 347 (Tex.Civ.App.1921), writ refused; Jewel Tea Co., Inc. et al. v. McCrary, 197 Ark. 294, 122 S.W.2d 534 (1939); James v. Bailey Reynolds Chandelier Co., 325 Mo. 1054, 30 S.W.2d 118 (1930); Potts v. People, 114 Colo. 253, 158 P.2d 739, 159 A.L.R. 1410 (1945); Lynch v. Missouri-Kansas-Texas R. Co., 333 Mo. 89, 61 S.W.2d 918, 921 (1945).

In the case last cited above, it is stated:

> "The admission or exclusion of experimental evidence rests largely in the discretion of the trial court. The rule, supported by authorities from many jurisdictions, is thus stated in Jones' Commentaries on the Law of Evidence (2d Ed.) Vol. II, § 740, p. 1376: 'The appellate courts have quite uniformly maintained a very common-sense attitude with regard to the admission or rejection of experimental evidence in the court below. Admission of evidence of experiments, or permitting them to be performed in court, is a matter peculiarly within the discretion of the trial judge. His discretion in this regard should not be interfered with on appeal unless it is manifest that it has been abused. One reason for the rule leaving the admission or rejection of experimental evidence to the discretion of the trial court is that such a court is in a better position than the appellate court to judge of the similarity of conditions. But a much stronger reason is that the trial judge should not be hampered by arbitrary rules which, if drawn in detail as to this class of evidence, would obviously be so technical as to be difficult of application and productive of appeals.' "

This contention of appellant is therefore overruled.

. . .

We are convinced that the case was fairly tried; therefore, we overrule all of appellant's assignments of error and affirm the judgment of the trial court.

On Motion for Rehearing

Our holding that the trial court did not commit reversible error in refusing the requested charge on circumstantial evidence appears to be in harmony with the decision of the Supreme Court in Johnson v. Zurich Gen. Acc. & Lia. Ins. Co., 205 S.W.2d 353 (1947), not yet reported [in State Reports].

We have carefully considered all assignments of error in the motion for rehearing, and are of opinion that the motion should be overruled.

DECISIONS RELATING TO CHAPTER XV, PUBLIC DOCUMENTS

PEOPLE OF THE STATE OF NEW YORK v. JOSEPH H. FRANKLIN

Supreme Court of New York, Appellate Division, Fourth Department, 1961.
14 A.D.2d 985, 222 N.Y.S.2d 173.

. . .

Before WILLIAMS, P. J., and GOLDMAN, McCLUSKY and HENRY, JJ.

MEMORANDUM. Defendant appeals from his conviction of grand larceny, second degree and from the determination that he was a fourth felony offender. The record amply supports his larceny conviction and this is affirmed. Upon arraignment on the information charging him with having been convicted of prior felonies defendant stood mute. Upon the prior felonies hearing the trial court received in evidence certain exhibits purporting to show convictions of felonies in North Carolina. These documents do not conform to the requisites of Sec. 482–a of the Code of Criminal Procedure. There was no certification of the clerk that the records of conviction had been signed or filed. Furthermore, these exhibits were improperly received for they did not comply with Section 395 of the Civil Practice Act (proof of foreign court records, and proceedings) and section 398–b (authentication of copy). See Martens v. Martens, 284 N.Y. 363, 365, 31 N.E.2d 489 (1941). The County Court did not properly have all the facts before it and could not determine under established rules the question of recognition or nonrecognition when the statutory mandate for qualifying the records of the judgments of conviction was disregarded and where there was admittedly no formal common-law proof to support the introduction of these documents into evidence. The district attorney's contention that a court may take judicial notice of any official seal or signature does not cure the error in the receipt of these exhibits. The limitations upon the availability of judicial notice in such circumstances are pointed out by Judge Cardozo in People v. Reese, 258 N.Y. 89, at p. 98, 179 N.E. 305, at p. 307, 79 A.L.R. 1329 (1932). The prior convictions must be proved beyond a reasonable doubt. (2 Wharton's Criminal Evidence, Sec. 645, p. 539.) The conviction on the prior felonies hearing must be reversed and a new trial had.

Judgment of conviction of grand larceny second degree unanimously affirmed and judgment of conviction of prior felonies unanimously reversed on the law and facts and new trial granted as to prior felonies.

PEOPLE v. REESE

Court of Appeals of New York, 1932.
258 N.Y. 89, 179 N.E. 305.

. . .

CARDOZO, C. J. Upon a plea of guilty, the defendant was convicted in the Court of General Sessions, county of New York, of attempted forgery in the third degree. Thereafter, before sentence was imposed, the district attorney filed an information, in accordance with Penal Law (Consol.Laws, c. 40) § 1943, accusing him of having been convicted of three crimes which would have been felonies if committed in New York. He was accused of having been convicted of forgery under the name of E. F. Lathrop in Spokane County, Wash., of having been convicted of the crime of false pretenses under the name of E. E. Lewiston in Larimer County, Colo., and of having been convicted of forgery under the name of Earl Freeman Lathrop in Multnomah County, Oregon.

Arraigned in response to this information, and cautioned as to his rights, the defendant stood mute. A jury, which was thereupon impaneled to determine his identity, found him to be the same person previously convicted. He was sentenced as a fourth offender to imprisonment for life.

1. The defendant makes the claim that the evidence offered by the people to establish his identity is insufficient and incompetent.

The form of proof was the same as to each of the three felonies. The conviction of forgery in Oregon will illustrate them all. A police officer who had taken the defendant's fingerprints after his conviction in the Court of General Sessions in this state, produced the prints then made. There was then produced an exemplified copy of an indictment of Earl Freeman Lathrop for forgery, and of the conviction and sentence thereunder in a court of competent jurisdiction in Multnomah County, Or., with the warrant of commitment. Next there was received a certificate signed, or purporting to be signed, by the custodian of fingerprint records in the Oregon state penitentiary, certifying that the records in his custody show "a previous conviction of a person whose fingerprints are identical with those hereto attached," adding a description of the crime and the sentence. Two sets of fingerprints were attached: one a set of fingerprints displayed upon a sheet of paper with the printed heading of the bureau of criminal identification of the city of New York; the other a set of prints purporting to have been made at the state penitentiary in Oregon. On the production of this certificate, a member of the police force of the city of New York, who qualified as an expert, testified that the defendant's fingerprints taken in this state and the fingerprints attached to the certificate from Oregon were those of the same person.

Code Criminal Procedure, § 482–b, enacted in 1927 (Laws 1927, c. 356), provides as follows: "The report of a person charged with the custody of finger print records of persons convicted of crime, who shall certify in writing that the records in his custody show certain previous convictions of persons whose finger prints are identical with those of a defendant shall be presumptive evidence of the fact of such previous convictions of such defendant."

The defendant argues, and we think correctly, that this statute does not apply to a certificate by a custodian of fingerprints in a state other than our own. No doubt a foreign custodian, annexing fingerprints to his certificate, would be competent to certify without the aid of any statute that they were prints or copies of prints kept upon his files in conformity with law, and to state, after comparison with the warrant of commitment, the name of the prisoner whose prints were so recorded. 3 Wigmore on Evidence, § 1677, p. 552. There would be a presumption in such circumstances that the prisoner fingerprinted was the prisoner committed; the presumption being merely an instance of the more general presumption of official regularity. 3 Wigmore on Evidence, § 1635, p. 401; § 1636, pp. 402, 403; Chesapeake & Delaware Canal Co. v. United States, 240 F. 903, 907 (C.C.A.1917); Gaines v. Relf, 12 How. 472, 570, 13 L.Ed. 1071 (1851); Evanston v. Gunn, 99 U.S. 660, 25 L.Ed. 306 (1878); Commonwealth v. Slavski, 245 Mass. 405, 415, 140 N.E. 465, 29 A.L.R. 281 (1923), and cases there cited. People v. Bromwich, 200 N.Y. 385, 93 N.E. 933 (1911), is not a decision to the contrary. It rests upon the ground that the so-called rule of confrontation forbids the introduction of a certificate by a foreign officer that a record does not exist, a certificate wholly negative. Cf. 3 Wigmore on Evidence, § 1678, p. 560. The decision goes to an extreme limit of strictness, but it does not touch the admissibility of a certificate, affirmative in tenor, annexing copies of the records and attesting their correctness. The rule of confrontation which in this state is purely statutory (Civil Rights Law [Consol.Laws, c. 6], § 12; Code Cr.Proc. § 8) has never been deemed to require the exclusion of certificates or records made by a public officer in the course of his official duty. 3 Wigmore on Evidence, § 1398, p. 109; Commonwealth v. Slavski, 245 Mass. 405, 414, 415, 417, 140 N.E. 465, 29 A.L.R. 281 (1924); Heike v. United States, 192 F. 83 (C.C.A.1912). If the certificate under the Code were merely one attesting the identity of records in the custody of the certifying officer, there would be little difficulty in applying the Code provisions to officers in other states. Upon proof that a person bearing the same name (5 Wigmore on Evidence, § 2529, p. 531; R. v. Levy, 8 Cox Cr. 73; Bayha v. Mumford, 58 Kan. 445, 49 Pac. 601 (1897); Ayers v. Ratshesky, 213 Mass. 589, 101 N.E. 78 (1913)) had been convicted by a court of competent jurisdiction, a certificate, so framed, would be admissible in evidence, if properly authenticated. Identity of name is not always sufficient in a criminal prosecution to show identity of person (Ayers v. Ratshesky, supra), but it may be accepted as sufficient if fortified by circumstances, as, for example, by reasonable coincidence of time between the conviction and the prints, and by the duty of the officer, presumably discharged, to ascertain that the person fingerprinted is the one described in the commitment. The certificate being received, comparison of the prints annexed with the prints of the defendant on file in this state could then be made in open court by a witness qualified to testify. People v. Roach, 215 N.Y. 592, 604, 109 N.E. 618, Ann.Cas.1917A, 410 (1915).

The difficulty in this case has its origin chiefly in the fact that Section 482–b of the Code of Criminal Procedure does not limit the custodian to a certificate as to the genuineness of the prints and a statement from the warrant of commitment of the name of the prisoner whose prints have been recorded. He is to certify to much besides. He is to certify to his opinion that the prints which he attaches to his certificate are identical with those of the defendant, and the opinion is to be taken as presumptively correct. Plainly a custodian of foreign records is in no position to make the comparison or to venture the opinion which the statute has in view. The data necessary to the formation of a judgment are not in his possession. If the certificate sanctioned by the Code is confined to fingerprints taken in this state, the statute becomes workable. The domestic custodian has upon the files of his bureau the prints of defendants convicted in our courts, prints presumably taken in conformity with law. Cf. Code Cr.Proc. §§ 940–949, as amended by Laws of 1928, c. 875. He is thus in a position to make the comparison permitted by the statute and to express an opinion that the prints are the same. If the defendant challenges the opinion, the maker of the certificate is here, and can be produced and cross-examined. None of these tests is available in the case of a custodian absent from the state. Such a custodian when he expresses an opinion that two sets of prints are those of the defendant is making a comparison without knowledge of one of the two things which he is expected to compare. He knows something about the prints of a convict imprisoned in his state. He knows nothing about any others except that a group of prints, bearing a heading which indicates that they have been transmitted to him by the police department of New York, but not otherwise authenticated, are in his hands for comparison. He does not know when or where or by whom they were made or whether they are genuine or fictitious. How is it possible for him to certify in the language of the statute "that the records in his custody show certain previous convictions of persons whose fingerprints are identical with those of a defendant" ?

The argument may be made that so much of the foreign certificate as expresses a comparison between the foreign prints and others may be rejected as surplusage, and the certificate accepted as identifying the foreign ones only. In that view, the effective comparison would be the one made upon the witness stand. At this point, however, another difficulty confronts us. The foreign certificate is not so authenticated as to be evidence of anything. All that is given us is a document signed by a person who describes himself as the custodian of the fingerprint records of persons convicted of crime. Neither the official character of the signer nor the genuineness of his seal and signature nor the regularity of his certificate is vouched for or attested by any one. We take judicial notice of the authority, and at times even of the signatures, of public officers acting in this state in accordance with our laws. The boundaries of judicial notice are narrower when the officer who certifies is acting under the laws of another state or country. 3 Wigmore on Evidence, § 1679, p. 563. We assume that a custodian of a record has authority, by implication of his office, to certify a copy. 3 Wigmore on Evidence, § 1677, p. 552; United States v. Percheman, 7 Pet. 51, 86, 8 L.Ed. 604 (1833). Whether there is such a custodian is, however, the pivotal fact upon which implication is dependent. 3 Wigmore on Evidence, § 1677, p. 553. There is nothing in this record to inform us whether any such office as that of custodian of fingerprints exists in the state where the certificate was given. There is nothing to inform us whether the person whose name is affixed to the certificate is the incumbent of such an office. There is nothing to inform us (if he is the incumbent) whether his signature is genuine. Authentication is not merely defective. It is lacking altogether. 3 Wigmore on Evidence, § 1679, pp. 561, 563; cf. U.S.Code, tit. 28, § 688 (28 U.S. C.A. § 688); Civil Practice Act, § 344.

. . .

The judgment of the Appellate Division and that of the Court of General Sessions should be reversed and a new trial ordered.

POUND, CRANE, LEHMAN, KELLOGG, O'BRIEN, and HUBBS, JJ., concur.

Judgments reversed, etc.

HARRISON v. METROPOLITAN LIFE INS. CO.

Superior Court of Pennsylvania, 1951.
168 Pa.Super. 474, 79 A.2d 115.

RHODES, President Judge. This is an action in assumpsit by the beneficiary in seven life insurance policies issued by defendant. Plaintiff was the widow of the insured, Tom Harrison, to whom the policies were issued upon his written applications, copies of which were attached to the policies and made part thereof. The policies aggregated $43,000, and each policy contained a clause which provided: "If the age of the insured has been misstated, the amount payable hereunder shall be such as the premium paid would have purchased at the correct age." The insured's applications stated that he was born on December 4, 1886. Defendant, in its answer and new matter, alleged that the correct date of insured's birth was October 3,

1883, admitted liability in the sum of $39,094.06, being the amount of insurance which it was agreed the premiums paid would have purchased if October 3, 1883, was the correct date of birth, and denied liability for the difference between this amount and the total face value of the policies, which difference amounted to $3,905.94. Plaintiff filed an answer to new matter. Defendant paid the amount admitted to be due, and the case proceeded to trial, before a judge and jury, for the amount deducted, to wit, $3,905.94.

At the trial plaintiff offered in evidence the policies which included the applications attached thereto, and the admissions in the pleadings; plaintiff then rested.

Defendant introduced in evidence as one exhibit authenticated copies under the seal of the Department of Justice comprising insured's certificate of naturalization, petition for naturalization, and declaration of intention to become a citizen. In the petition and the declaration, which were signed and sworn to, insured stated that he was born on October 3, 1883, in Lithuania. Included in the records of the Immigration and Naturalization Service, and a part of the exhibit offered in evidence, was a manifest purporting to show insured's arrival in the United States on the S. S. Rhynland in the year 1903 at the age of twenty-one.

Plaintiff did not rely solely upon the presumption that the date of insured's birth (December 4, 1886), as stated in the applications, was correct, cf. Hervitz v. New York Life Insurance Co., 160 Pa. Super. 496, 498, 499, 52 A.2d 368 (1947), but after the defense closed she went on to offer in evidence insured's application for a marriage license in which insured, under oath, gave the date of his birth as October 28, 1886. In her own behalf plaintiff also testified that when she married insured in 1913 he was twenty-seven years old in November of that year, thus making his birth some time in November of 1886. Plaintiff's son, Sigmund, also fixed the year of insured's birth as 1886. He was indefinite as to the exact date of birth. Both he and plaintiff named Thanksgiving Day as the time insured's birthday was usually celebrated.

Plaintiff's counsel requested the trial judge to instruct the jury to make a special finding: "Was Tom Harrison born on October 3, 1883?" The trial judge modified plaintiff's request for the special finding and submitted to the jury the question: "On what date was Tom Harrison born?" The jury found that the insured was born on the date stated in the naturalization papers, October 3, 1883. Accordingly, on this finding the trial judge directed a verdict for the defendant, a point having been reserved as to the sum of $499, with interest, which amount defendant claimed it had a right to deduct from the accidental death benefits payable under a supplementary contract. Plaintiff filed motions for judgment n. o. v. and for a new trial. The court in banc dismissed plaintiff's motion for a new trial and, upon the point reserved, entered judgment for plaintiff in the sum of $571.52, being $499 principal and $72.52 interest. Except as to this plaintiff's motion for judgment was overruled. Plaintiff has appealed to this Court.

Appellant contends that the trial judge submitted the case to the jury on an issue not raised by the pleadings when he asked them to find on what date Tom Harrison was born. Appellant asserts that the issue in the case was much narrower, that is, "was insured born on December 4, 1886," as stated in the applications, or "was insured born on October 3, 1883," as alleged by the defendant. It is true that the trial judge in his charge asked the jury to find "On what date was Tom Harrison born?" Appellant took no exception to this statement and made no suggestion that it be changed. The charge must be considered in the light of the evidence presented which included appellant's evidence, in addition to the date set forth in the applications, that insured was born on October 28, 1886, or some date in November of 1886. Appellant's evidence was not confined to the issue as defined by the pleadings, and under these circumstances appellant's request for a special finding invited the trial judge to modify the question to conform with such evidence. Considered in the light of the evidence presented the charge was correct in substance and contained no fundamental error. In this respect we think the charge favored the appellant. The jury could have found that the date of insured's birth on the evidence submitted by the appellant was one of several dates other than October 3, 1883, which defendant sought to establish as the date of his birth.

. . .

There was no error in the admission in evidence of the records in the naturalization proceedings. These documents were photostatic copies of the original records of the Immigration and Naturalization Service of the Department of Justice and were offered as a whole. They were properly authenticated under the seal of the Department and clearly admissible. 28 U.S.C.A. § 661 [now 28 U.S.C.A. § 1733]; Hervitz v. New York Life Insurance Co., supra, 160 Pa. Super. 496, 500, 52 A.2d 368 (1947). The manifest of the S. S. Rhynland to which appellant especially objects showed insured's arrival in this country in 1903 at the age of twenty-one years, which would make his date of birth at least as early as 1883. This document was part of the official records of the Immigration and Naturalization Service, made in the regular course of business, and properly authenticated. As a part of defendant's exhibit it was not inadmissible.

There is no merit in appellant's argument that the trial judge improperly excluded pedigree evidence or family reputation as to the date of insured's birth. Such evidence is an established exception to the hearsay rule, Simon v. New York Life Insurance Company, 70 Pa.Super. 408 (1918); District of Columbia's Appeal, 343 Pa. 65,

69, 21 A.2d 883 (1941), and appellant and her son were permitted to offer such testimony at length.

. . . The sole issue in this case as limited by the evidence presented, was the date of insured's birth. That issue, under the evidence and in the charge of the court, was clearly submitted to the jury; and the jury made a responsive finding. We find no error in the conduct of the trial or in the charge of the court sufficient to justify a new trial.

Judgment is affirmed.

DECISIONS RELATING TO CHAPTER XVI, REAL EVIDENCE

UNITED STATES v. SKELLEY

United States Court of Appeals, Seventh Circuit, 1974.
501 F.2d 447.

JULIUS J. HOFFMAN, Senior District Judge.

Defendant appeals from a judgment of conviction for unlawful possession of counterfeit obligations of the United States, 18 U.S.C.A. § 472. Finding no prejudicial error, we affirm.

Through his court-appointed counsel, defendant relies upon six asserted errors of the district court: (1) a 72-day delay between issuance of the federal warrant for defendant's arrest and his subsequent arrest and arraignment, during which period he was jailed on a related state charge; (2) the admission into evidence of the counterfeit money, allegedly without a proper foundation that the bills were in the same condition—and of the same color—as when seized from defendant; (3) a claimed variance caused by the transposition of two digits in the serial numbers of the counterfeit bills; (4) allegedly prejudicial argument by the United States attorney inviting the jury, without a foundation in expert testimony, to appraise the probability of obtaining fingerprints from a leather wallet; (5) additional allegedly prejudicial argument by the prosecutor, urging the credibility of a witness' prior inconsistent statement which had been admitted to impeach his current testimony and not to prove the truth of the matter asserted; and (6) allegedly improper comment in the prosecutor's summation upon defendant's refusal to answer certain questions without consulting his attorney.

Delay in Arraignment. Defendant's argument concerning the alleged delay in "arraignment" does not involve the familiar principle that a confession is inadmissible if obtained during detention for an unreasonable period of time between the arrest and the prisoner's appearance before a magistrate. See Mallory v. United States, 354 U.S. 449, 77 S.Ct. 1356, 1 L.Ed.2d 1479 (1957); McNabb v. United States, 318 U.S. 332, 63 S.Ct. 608, 87 L.Ed. 819 (1943); 18 U.S.C.A. § 3501 (1968). Here no confession was made.

Nor does the case present the question of what remedy, if any, beyond exclusion of confessions, might be appropriate for unreasonable federal detention prior to appearance before a magistrate, in violation of the command of Rule 5(a), Fed.R.Crim.Pro., directing the arresting officer to "take the arrested person without unnecessary delay" before a magistrate. The detention here was by the state, upon charges arising wholly under state law, for driving while under the influence of drugs, unlawful possession of drugs, and possession of hypodermic syringes. After hearing, the district judge found nothing to suggest that this imprisonment was in any way attributable to federal authority, through collusion or otherwise. See United States v. Romano, 482 F.2d 1183, 1190–1191 (5th Cir. 1973); United States v. Moriarty, 375 F.2d 901 (7th Cir. 1967), certiorari denied 388 U.S. 911, 87 S.Ct. 2116, 18 L.Ed.2d 1350 (1967). The defendant would not have gained his liberty by being admitted to bail by a magistrate upon the federal charge, and the supposed delay did nothing to prolong his detention.

The arrest on state charges was made by state officers on January 21, 1973 (a Sunday), and defendant was arraigned the next day on those state charges before the Circuit Court of Effingham County, Illinois, and was detained for want of bail in the county jail. The counterfeit Federal Reserve notes found in defendant's car were delivered to an agent of the United States Secret Service, who swore out a federal complaint on January 29, 1973. A warrant for defendant's arrest on this charge was issued the same day, and a federal detainer was lodged with the state officials. When defendant was released from state custody on April 11, 1973, upon dismissal or imminent dismissal of the state charges, he was immediately arrested on the outstanding federal warrant and taken before a federal magistrate who appointed counsel to represent him.

Nothing in this course of events violates either of the objectives of the prohibition against unreasonable delay between the arrest and the appearance before a magistrate. No confession was elicited during a period of coercive detention, and the detention itself was a result of pending state charges. Even if the detention were somehow attributable to the pendency of federal charges, on a supposition finding no support in the facts, defendant does not argue that he was thereby unlawfully deprived of his liberty in view of his inability to make bail, or that the necessary remedy for prolonged pre-hearing detention is dismissal of the substantive charge even though no prejudice appears. His argument is rather that he was prejudiced because the delay in arresting him under the federal warrant operated to delay the appointment of counsel to defend against the federal charge, and allowed the federal authorities to complete their investigation before defendant's counsel could begin. In this interim, the federal officers obtained a statement, incriminating defendant, from one of his associates.

On analysis, defendant is complaining not about any delay between arrest and the magistrate appearance, but about delay in the arrest itself, which would have set the wheels in motion to provide him with defense counsel for the federal charge. A similar claim was rejected by the Supreme Court in United States v. Hoffa, 385 U.S. 293, 310, 87 S.Ct. 408, 17 L.Ed.2d 374 (1966). There defendant complained that the federal authorities' delay in arresting him impaired his right to counsel under the Fifth Amendment, since it permitted the officers to interrogate the defendant without the presence of his lawyer, and that the defendant's statements thus procured were inadmissible. The Court declared: "There is no constitutional right to be arrested. . . . Law enforcement officers are under no constitutional duty to call a halt to a criminal investigation the moment they have the minimum evidence to establish probable cause, a quantum of evidence which may fall far short of the amount necessary to support a criminal conviction." 385 U.S. 310. For the same reasons, in this case the government had no duty to arrest defendant, and provide him with counsel, before continuing its investigation. See United States v. Palazzo, 488 F.2d 942, 948 (5th Cir. 1974); Koran v. United States, 469 F.2d 1071 (5th Cir. 1972). The fact that he was otherwise in custody did not curtail the investigatory power. "When an individual is in custody on probable cause, the police may, of course, seek out evidence in the field to be used at trial against him." Miranda v. Arizona, 384 U.S. 436, 477, 86 S.Ct. 1602, 1629, 16 L.Ed.2d 694 (1966).

Condition of the $20 Bills. In his second assignment of error, defendant claims that the twenty-seven counterfeit $20 bills were improperly admitted into evidence over his objection that no proper foundation had been laid in the absence of evidence that the bills were in substantially the same condition when offered as when they were first seized. Of course, when a tangible object is offered into evidence to prove its quality, character, or condition at the time of an earlier occurrence in issue, the article is relevant and competent only if its condition is substantially unchanged, so that its present condition fairly represents the past condition. See McCormick, Evidence, § 212 (2d ed. 1972); 7 Wigmore, Evidence § 2129 (3d ed. 1940). But changes in condition which "do not destroy the evidentiary value of the object" do not prevent its reception. Comment, Preconditions for Admission of Demonstrative Evidence, 61 Nw.U.L.Rev. 472, 484 (1966). Here the $20 bills partook of the nature of written documents, since their written content was itself evidence of their counterfeit character: the fact that multiple bills bore identical serial numbers established their lack of genuineness. They were adequately identified by government witnesses as the bills found in defendant's automobile. When a written document is properly identified as the same document previously examined, it is implicit in the identification that the content is the same, and nothing would be added by a direct negative answer to the question where its written contents have been altered or changed.

Apart from their written content, defendant asserts that the bills when offered were blue in color, unlike genuine green currency, and argues that the jury might have considered this peculiar color as evidence that the defendant must have known that the bills were not genuine, and thus had the requisite guilty knowledge to make his possession a crime. For this purpose, he urges, the evidence was improper and prejudicial in the absence of a foundation showing that the bills were the same color as when they were seized. While a possible change in color would affect the probative value of the bills on this issue of intent, no change in color could destroy the relevance of the bills to show their counterfeit character from the identity of serial numbers, and their competence as evidence for this purpose is unimpaired by the unexcluded possibility of a change in color. In such a situation, when offered evidence bears on two issues, and a proper foundation has been laid as to one of those issues, the evidence is admissible over a general objection. See McCormick, Evidence, § 59 2d ed. 1972). Here the evidence disclosed that the bills had been subjected to tests and analysis in the process of examining them for fingerprints. Upon appropriate and specific request, the trial judge might have given the jury a cautionary and limiting instruction to forestall any prejudicial inference that the color of the bills remained unchanged through these tests. No such request was made, and the general objection that no proper foundation had been laid was correctly overruled.

Variance in Serial Numbers. Over defendant's objection, twenty-seven counterfeit $20 Federal Reserve notes were admitted into evidence. Except for serial numbers, the bills were identical. All purported to be notes drawn on the Federal Reserve Bank of Philadelphia, Series of 1969, Check Letter H., Face Plate No. 88, and Back Plate No. 120. Ten fictitious serial numbers were also identical except that two digits were transposed, so that some of the bills bore No. C20309642A while the remainder were numbered C 203 06942A. The indictment alleged that twenty-five of the bills bore the first number, and two the second. When they were offered into evidence, however, it appeared that the indictment's description was erroneous, reversing the quantities. Actually, twenty-five of the bills bore the serial number alleged to be the number appearing on the group of two, and only two contained the serial number described in the indictment as the number on the group of twenty-five. Upon defendant's objection to this variance, the district court granted the government's motion to strike the serial numbers from the indictment, and the numbers were physically obliterated by interlineation. Defendant's objections were overruled.

At the outset, it is clear and conceded that there was no necessity to set forth the fictitious serial numbers in the indictment, and that the indictment would have been legally sufficient without this descriptive surplusage. It is enough that the indictment sets forth "a plain, concise and definite written statement of the essential facts constituting the offense charged", Rule 7(c)(1), Fed.R.Crim.Pro., meeting "the requirement that the accused be informed of the charges against him, so that he can prepare his defense and so that he may be protected against a second prosecution for the same offense." United States v. Cassell, 452 F.2d 533, 536 (7th Cir. 1971). "Setting out the counterfeit bills or describing them by their fictitious serial numbers or otherwise would have afforded no real protection against a second prosecution for the same offense, because the number of identical facsimiles which might possibly be printed are limitless." Neville v. United States, 272 F.2d 414, 416 (5th Cir. 1959), certiorari denied 362 U.S. 924, 80 S.Ct. 678, 4 L.Ed.2d 743 (1960).

In several early cases decided a century ago, it was nonetheless held that if the indictment does set forth the serial numbers by way of description, they must be proved, although surplusage, according to the letter of the charge. See United States v. Hall, 26 Fed.Cas.No. 15,283, p. 82 (Cir.Ct.Dist.Col.1832); United States v. Mason, 26 Fed. Cas.No.15,736, p. 1192 (S.D.N.Y.1875). But see United States v. Howard, 26 Fed.Cas.No.15,403, p. 388 (C.C.Mass.1837) (Story, J.). This strict view was explained as merely an application of the prevailing rules against variance between pleading and proof, derived by analogy from the rules applicable in civil proceedings. United States v. Hardyman, 38 U.S. 176, 179, 10 L.Ed. 113 (1839). Today, such a requirement "may well be classed with what the late Justice Holmes designated as 'technicalities that were deemed vital a hundred or perhaps even fifty years ago.' " Simon v. United States, 78 F.2d 454, 455 (6th Cir. 1935). There the Sixth Circuit found no material or fatal variance when the indictment described the counterfeit bill as bearing Face Plate No. 1245 and the number on the bill offered into evidence was I–245. In Heisler v. United States, 394 F.2d 692 (9th Cir. 1968), the Ninth Circuit concluded the variance was not fatal in a bench trial when the indictment described the counterfeit note as a $20 bill and the evidence showed it to be a $10 bill. And in United States v. Taylor, 464 F.2d 240, 241–242 (2d Cir. 1972), the Second Circuit relegated to a footnote its rejection of the claim of variance when the indictment described the counterfeit bills as Treasury notes when the proof revealed them to be Federal Reserve notes. See also United States v. Cassell, 452 F.2d 533, 536 (7th Cir. 1971) (no variance when no proof was offered to show stolen Treasury checks were "genuine" as alleged in indictment). Cf. Graffi v. United States, 22 F.2d 593 (7th Cir. 1927).

Thus the deletion of the serial numbers did not impair the sufficiency of the indictment, and the clerical discrepancy between pleading and proof of the serial numbers did not amount to a fatal variance. Although the numbers were surplusage, unnecessary to plead or prove, defendant argues that it was error to implement these conclusions by the physical act of deleting the serial numbers from the indictment, marking them out. The argument builds upon the base of the constitutional guarantee of indictment by grand jury, as declared by the Fifth Amendment. To allow the prosecutor and court to amend the indictment, to change the nature or character of the crime charged by the grand jury, would be inconsistent with this guarantee. Ex parte Bain, 121 U.S. 1, 7 S.Ct. 781, 30 L.Ed. 849 (1887). Extending the rule, courts have held that an indictment cannot be amended even with the consent of the defendant. See, e. g. Carney v. United States, 163 F.2d 784 (9th Cir. 1947), certiorari denied 332 U.S. 824, 68 S.Ct. 165, 92 L.Ed. 400 (1948). In deference to this principle, the Federal Rules of Criminal Procedure, while generally authorizing amendment of an information (Rule 7(c)), provide only that "on motion of the defendant" the court may "strike surplusage from the indictment." Rule 7(d). The absence of specific authority for deletion of surplusage without defendant's consent has not been construed, however, to forbid the judge from instructing the jury to disregard descriptive surplusage in the indictment which varies from the proof when the written indictment itself remains untouched. United States v. Edwards, 465 F.2d 943, 950 (9th Cir. 1972). Nor does the rule prohibit correction of obvious clerical or typographical errors in the indictment, to change the initial letter of defendant's patronymic from K (Kenny) to D (Denny). United States v. Denny, 165 F.2d 668 (7th Cir. 1947), certiorari denied 333 U.S. 844, 68 S.Ct. 662, 92 L.Ed. 1127 (1948).

While the exceptions do not completely engulf the rule, we are not prepared to make a fetish of the prohibition against amendment of an indictment by holding that it is reversible error to interlineate fictitious serial numbers which are inaccurate solely because of the transposition of two digits in a ten digit string, which could have been omitted entirely from the indictment with no consequence, which need not be proved even if alleged, which the jury could have been instructed to ignore, which might have been corrected as typographical errors which correctly describe some of the bills in evidence, and which are incorrect only with respect to whether the quantity of bills bearing one number or the other is twenty-five or two. Neither the nature nor the gravity of the offense is affected by the discrepancy. Under the circumstances, any technical error that might have been committed by touching pen to paper to alter the indictment itself, is wholly without substance, and could not have prejudiced defendant's rights. In United States v. Buble, 440 F.2d 405 (9th Cir. 1971), the trial court had not merely stricken inaccurate numbers from the indictment, but had permitted the substitution of different numbers, to correct an obvious error in the dates on which allegedly false tax returns had been filed. The Ninth Circuit found no prejudicial error, observing that the "indictment did not require amendments, so amendments did not prejudice the defendant. The variance in the proof from the original indictment still could have permitted the case to go to the jury." 440 F.2d 406.

. . .

Affirmed.

BREEDING'S DANIA DRUG CO. v. RUNYON

Supreme Court of Florida, Division A, 1941.
2 So.2d 376.

Error to Circuit Court, Dade County; Arthur Gomez, Judge.

. . .

ADAMS Justice. Plaintiff recovered a $20,000 judgment against the defendants as joint tort feasors.

The plaintiff, a refrigeration man, was summoned by defendant, Breeding, to make certain repairs on some electrical refrigeration equipment in his drug store. Upon arriving plaintiff pulled the switch to disconnect the current from the compressor. Apparently the current was off, however, the pulling of the switch cut off only 110 of the 220 volts. In the course of the work the plaintiff's body came in contact with the compressor carrying 110 volts, resulting in his injury.

Negligence is charged to Lyon Electric Company for improper wiring. Jersey Ice Cream Company is charged with installing the refrigeration equipment and leaving it to be operated after having knowledge that the wiring was defective and dangerous. Liability is charged to Breeding and Breeding Dania Drug Company for using the aforesaid equipment without inspection as required by city ordinance.

The record convinces us that the equipment was defectively wired. We are also satisfied that the defective wiring was the proximate cause of plaintiff's injury. Did the plaintiff produce sufficient evidence to show the concurring negligence of all the defendants caused the injury? Louisville & N. R. R. Co. v. Allen, 67 Fla. 257, 65 So. 8, 12, L.R.A.1915C, 20 (1914):

> "If their acts of negligence, however separate and distinct in themselves, are concurrent in producing the injury, their liability is joint as well as several. . . . Each becomes liable because of his neglect of duty, and they are jointly liable for the single injury inflicted because the acts or omissions of both have contributed to it."

There was sufficient evidence before the jury that the electrical work was done by defendant, Lyon Electric Company. There was sufficient evidence before the jury that the refrigerating equipment was installed by defendant, Jersey Ice Cream Company, and that its agent knew of the dangerous condition.

The other defendants used the equipment approximately one year without an inspection as required by city ordinance. The occupant of premises is liable for latent defects which proximately cause injury to his invitees. The law fixes the duty of the occupant to exercise a reasonable degree of care commensurate with the surrounding circumstances. King v. Cooney-Eckstein Co., 66 Fla. 246, 63 So. 659, Ann.Cas.1916C, 163 (1914). The evidence is legally sufficient to submit the case to the jury. The probative weight of the testimony is for the jury. The verdict should not be set aside in the absence of a clear showing that it is contrary to the great weight of the evidence.

The defendant, Jersey Ice Cream Company, disclaims liability because the refrigerating equipment was installed by an independent contractor. With this we do not agree. The Ice Cream Company insists it did not make the electric connection and is for that reason not liable. The Ice Cream Company, having undertaken to install the equipment, is obligated to install same in a reasonably safe manner. Its servant gained knowledge, within the scope of his employment, that the equipment was dangerous. This notice was imputed to the Ice Cream Company. 2 Am.Jur., Agency, § 368. Neglecting to remove the danger contributing to plaintiff's injury makes a case against the Ice Cream Company.

We now consider whether the verdict is excessive. The burden is with him who assails the amount of the verdict to show that it is wholly unsupported by the evidence, or that the jury was influenced by passion, prejudice or other improper motive. Tampa Electric Company v. Bazemore, 85 Fla. 164, 96 So. 297 (1923).

The plaintiff's burn was described by the attending physician as a third degree burn, meaning a total destruction. Portions of the skull were burned so badly as to require removal. The plaintiff was 32 years of age and earning $27 per week at the time of injury. At the time of trial he had undergone four operations and required more. He will never be able to engage in normal work. His pain has obviously been great. Hospitalization and medical attention has been continuous and will continue for some time. The plaintiff will suffer ailments, lose of earnings, loss of personal appearance and inconvenience the remainder of his life. Our conclusion is that the verdict is not excessive. Courts are reluctant to substitute their judgment for that of the jury as to damages.

We now consider the propriety of exhibiting pictures of plaintiff's injury to the jury. In this we find no error. There was evidence that the pictures reflected the true condition of plaintiff.

The defendants had ample opportunity to cross examine the photographer; to explain or refute their genuineness. The fact that they might have been gruesome did not render them inadmissible. The purpose of all testimony is to reveal the truth to the end that courts and juries may be persuaded by it to a just decision.

Error is asserted for the refusal to give certain requested charges. We have examined them in the light of the charge given by the court and find no error.

Finding no reversible error in the record, the judgment is affirmed.

STATE OF NORTH CAROLINA v. STRICKLAND

Supreme Court of North Carolina, 1970.
276 N.C. 253, 173 S.E.2d 129.

. . .

BRANCH, Justice. The question presented for decision by this appeal is whether the North Carolina Court of Appeals erred in holding that sound motion pictures, taken of defendant approximately two hours after he was alleged to have operated an automobile upon the public highways of North Carolina while under the influence of intoxicating liquor, were properly admitted into evidence.

Defendant contends that the use of the sound moving pictures violated his Fifth Amendment privilege guaranteeing that a person cannot be "compelled in a criminal case to be a witness against himself" and the guarantee of Article I, Section 11 of the North Carolina Constitution that a person shall "not be compelled to give self-incriminating evidence."

The Federal courts have recognized that the Fifth Amendment privilege against self-incrimination relates only to testimonial or communicative acts of the person seeking to exercise the privilege and does not apply to acts not communicative in nature. Schmerber v.

California, 384 U.S. 757, 86 S.Ct. 1826, 16 L.Ed.2d 908 (1966); Holt v. United States, 218 U.S. 245, 31 S.Ct. 2, 54 L.Ed. 1021 (1910).

In the case of Schmerber v. California, supra, a physician withdrew blood from the defendant at the direction of a State officer, over objection of the accused, and in a State prosecution for driving an automobile while under the influence of intoxicating liquor offered in evidence an analysis of the blood so taken for the purpose of showing intoxication of accused. The defendant objected to the introduction of this evidence, contending that this violated his Fifth Amendment privilege against self-incrimination. Holding the blood test evidence competent because it was not his testimony or his communicative act, the United States Supreme Court stated:

> "(B)oth federal and state courts have usually held that it (Fifth Amendment) offers no protection against compulsion to submit to fingerprinting, photographing, or measurements, to write or speak for identification, to appear in court, to stand, to assume a stance, to walk, or to make a particular gesture. The distinction which has emerged, often expressed in different ways, is that the privilege is a bar against compelling 'communications' or 'testimony,' but that compulsion which makes a suspect or accused the source of 'real or physical evidence' does not violate it."

Another leading case in the federal court structure is Holt v. United States, supra, in which there was evidence that prior to the trial the accused, over his objection, was compelled to put on a blouse that "fitted" him. Mr. Justice Holmes, speaking for the Court, rejected the argument that this was a violation of Holt's right against self-incrimination as "based upon an extravagant extension of the 5th Amendment," and went on to say:

> "(T)he prohibition of compelling a man in a criminal court to be witness against himself is a prohibition of the use of physical or moral compulsion to extort communications from him, not an exclusion of his body as evidence when it may be material. The objection in principle would forbid a jury to look at a prisoner and compare his features with a photograph in proof." 218 U.S. at 252–253, 31 S.Ct. at 6, 54 L.Ed. at 1030.

Generally, the basic principles which govern the admissibility of photographs apply to motion pictures, and where they are relevant and have been properly authenticated, they are admissible in evidence. They have been used in both criminal and civil trials for many purposes, e. g., civil cases: Lehmuth v. Long Beach Unified School Dist., 53 Cal.2d 544, 2 Cal.Rptr. 279, 348 P.2d 887 (1960) (motion picture depicting condition of personal injury victim); McGoorty v. Benhart, 305 Ill.App. 458, 27 N.E.2d 289 (1940) (motion pictures admissible to discredit the testimony of a personal injury claimant by showing activity inconsistent with alleged injury);

Sparks v. Employers Mut. Liab. Ins. Co. of Wis., 83 So.2d 453 (La. Ct.App.1955) (motion picture admissible to show condition of a person, place, object, or activity). E. g., Criminal cases: People v. Hayes, 21 Cal.App.2d 320, 71 P.2d 321 (1937) (sound motion picture of confession held admissible); People v. Dabb, 32 Cal.2d 491, 197 P.2d 1 (1948) (sound pictures of re-enactment by defendants of a crime). 41 Notre Dame Lawyer, 1009, 1010, n. 6 (1965–66); Scott, Photographic Evidence, § 624; 62 A.L.R.2d 686. However, there is very little authority on the precise question of using moving pictures in cases in which a person is charged with driving on the public highways while under the influence of intoxicating liquor and asserts his constitutional right against self-incrimination. According to our research only one jurisdiction, Oklahoma, has adopted the view supporting defendant's position.

. . .

North Carolina has long recognized the distinction between compulsory testimonial evidence and compulsory physical disclosure. The North Carolina view is summarized in State v. Paschal, 253 N.C. 795, 117 S.E.2d 749 (1961), by Bobbitt, J. (now C. J.) as follows:

> "The established rule in this jurisdiction is that '(t)he scope of the privilege against self-incrimination, in history and in principle, includes only the process of testifying by word of mouth or in writing, i. e., the process of disclosure by utterance. It has no application to such physical, evidential circumstances as may exist on the accused's body or about his person.' State v. Rogers, 233 N.C. 390, 399, 64 S.E.2d 572, where Ervin, J., reviews prior decisions of this Court. See also State v. Grayson, 239 N.C. 453, 458, 80 S.E. 2d 387, opinion by Parker, J., and cases cited.
>
> "Where this rule applies, it is held that the admission of evidence of a defendant's *refusal to submit* to a chemical test designed to measure the alcoholic content of his blood does not violate his constitutional right against self-incrimination."

See also Branch v. State, 269 N.C. 642, 153 S.E.2d 343; State v. Gaskill, 256 N.C. 652, 124 S.E.2d 873.

Both better reasoning and the prevailing weight of authority lead us to follow the views adopted by Colorado, Texas and Ohio.

Brock, J., speaking for the Court of Appeals, correctly and concisely stated:

> "Talking motion pictures of an accused in a criminal action are not per se testimonial in nature, and, where they are properly used to illustrate competent and relevant testimony of a witness, their use does not violate accused's privilege against self-incrimination."

However, the State cannot introduce substantive evidence or add to the testimony of a witness under the guise of using a moving picture to illustrate the testimony of the witness. Nevertheless, if the testimony of a witness is generally consistent with the illustrative evidence, a slight variation only affects the credibility of the evidence. State v. Brooks, 260 N.C. 186, 132 S.E.2d 354 (1963).

The burden here was upon the State to prove that defendant operated his motor vehicle upon the public highways or streets while he was under the influence of intoxicating liquor. Defendant admitted that he had been drinking, but denied that he was operating his automobile when it was wrecked. He also defended upon the ground that even if the jury should find that he was the operator of the motor vehicle, his intoxication resulted from consuming alcoholic beverages in the two-hour period which elapsed between the wreck and the time when the sound moving pictures were made.

In the instant case the moving picture not only depicted defendant's physical condition and his ability (or inability) to coordinate his movements; its sound track recorded the following incriminating statement—"communicated by the accused from his knowledge of the offense": "Q. Have you had anything to drink since they stopped you? A. No, sir."

This question and answer presented testimony from defendant which tended to show not only that he was driving the motor vehicle but that he was under the influence of intoxicating liquor at that time. It placed him at the scene of the wreck and completely destroyed his contention that his intoxication resulted from drinking subsequent to the wreck. The statement was clearly substantive evidence, competent as an admission if competent at all. It certainly did not illustrate the testimony of any other witness.

It is the law in this state "that in-custody statements attributed to a defendant, when offered by the State and objected to by the defendant, 'are inadmissible *for any purpose* unless, after a voir dire hearing in the absence of the jury, the court, based upon sufficient evidence' makes factual findings that such statements were voluntarily and understandingly made by the defendant after he had been fully advised as to his constitutional rights." State v. Catrett, 276 N.C. 86, 171 S.E.2d 398, . . . This statement from *Catrett* was made with reference to the defendant's in-custody statements which were offered for *impeachment* purposes. *A fortiori*, it is applicable to the statement which defendant made in consequence of the interrogation quoted above.

The Oklahoma case of Stewart v. State, supra, cited as being contrary to the view adopted by this Court, is in partial accord with this decision, in that it holds that sound motion pictures taken of a defendant are inadmissible in evidence without a showing that prior to the taking he was advised of his right to counsel and given the admonitions required by Miranda v. State of Arizona, 384 U.S. 436, 86 S.Ct.

1602, 16 L.Ed.2d 694 (1966), and Escobedo v. State of Illinois, 378 U.S. 478, 84 S.Ct. 1758, 12 L.Ed.2d 977 (1964).

In the instant case, since no *voir dire* was held, there must be a new trial.

Aside from the constitutional and procedural questions here presented, we think it appropriate to observe that the use of properly authenticated moving pictures to illustrate a witness' testimony may be of invaluable aid in the jury's search for a verdict that speaks the truth. However, the powerful impact of this type of evidence requires the trial judge to examine carefully into its authenticity, relevancy, and competency, and—if he finds it to be competent—to give the jury proper limiting instructions at the time it is introduced. When a moving picture is offered into evidence, upon defendant's request the trial judge should allow defendant's counsel to preview it so that he can intelligently enter objections to those portions which he may deem uncorroborative or otherwise objectionable. Furthermore, when the sound motion picture contains incriminating statements by the defendant—made "from his knowledge of the offense" —upon defendant's objection, the judge must conduct a *voir dire* to determine the admissibility of the in-custody statements or admissions contained in the sound picture.

We find no fallacy in the reasoning of the North Carolina Court of Appeals to the effect that G.S. § 114–19 did not create a new rule of evidence. Even a cursory reading of this statute in connection with the chapter and article in which it is found leads to the conclusion that the statute is concerned with the compilation and preservation of statistics and records rather than the creation of a new rule of evidence.

For reasons stated, the decision of the Court of Appeals is reversed and the cause is remanded to that Court with direction to award a new trial, to be conducted in accordance with the principles herein set forth.

Reversed and remanded.

DECISIONS RELATING TO CHAPTER XVII, PRESUMPTIONS

NEELY v. PROVIDENT LIFE & ACCIDENT INS. CO. OF CHATTANOOGA, TENN.

Supreme Court of Pennsylvania, 1936.
322 Pa. 417, 185 A. 784.

. . .

MAXEY, Justice. Plaintiffs are beneficiaries in certain policies of accident insurance issued by the defendant to Dr. Edgar C. Neely, now deceased. One policy insured "against the effects of bodily injuries sustained directly, solely and exclusively through accidental means," in the principal sum of $15,000 and weekly benefits. The other policy insured in the principal sum of $1,500 and weekly sickness and accident benefits "against loss of life, limb, limbs, sight of time, resulting without other contributing cause from bodily injury . . . which is effected solely by the happening of a purely accidental event." Since the plaintiffs in the two cases claimed under the same policies, a stipulation was filed to try both cases together, and, in the event of a verdict for the plaintiffs, the latter by stipulation agreed as to how the proceeds should be divided.

The insured died on October 3, 1932. Plaintiffs' averment was that "on or about August 20, 1932, while Dr. Neely was treating a patient, a piece of glass from an ampoule accidently became imbedded in the forefinger of his right hand and that as a result the finger [later amputated] became infected with septic poisoning," which proved fatal.

Defendant denied these averments, and declared "that leukemia and diabetes fundamentally predisposed to the gangrene of the right forefinger, requiring amputation thereof." Defendant set forth that the insured did not die as a result of septic poisoning, but "from broncho-pneumonia, with leukemia as a secondary underlying cause." Webster's New International Dictionary (2d Ed.) defines "leukemia" as "a morbid state due to derangement of the blood-making organs and characterized by an excessive number of leucocytes [white corpuscles] in the blood."

After trial, the jury returned a verdict for plaintiffs in the sum of $18,975. Defendant made a motion for judgment n. o. v., having at the trial presented a point for binding instructions in its favor. The motion for judgment n. o. v. was later overruled. This appeal followed.

On August 21, 1932, Dr. Neely showed his right index finger to Miss Hancock, who was a registered, trained nurse attached to his office and who was in his employ for five years. Upon examining his finger, she found a small puncture about the size of a pinhead between the first joint and tip of his finger. Around this puncture there was an area of inflamed flesh about half the size of a dime. It was brought out on cross-examination of this witness that Dr. Neely had told her that he had loosened the flesh with a knife around the puncture. Miss Hancock sterilized a surgical knife, probed the wound, and therein felt a gritty substance of some kind which she was able to move backward and forward. She treated the wound with lysol and mercurochrome. She saw the wound the next day, at which time the inflammation had increased. She and Dr. Neely then probed it. She treated the wound until August 29th, when Dr. Neely consulted a physician. Dr. Neely was confined to his bed on September 3d, and on September 5th was taken to the hospital, where the wound in his finger was incised. Upon returning to his home, he was confined to his bed and left it only when he went to his physician's office, until September 9th, when the inflammation had progressed just beyond the third finger and a few red streaks appeared beyond this joint. On September 16th he was taken to the hospital; the inflammation had increased and red streaks appeared upon his arm. On this day his finger was amputated. He returned to his home on September 17th, and he was thereafter confined to his bed, and died on October 3d.

Dr. Lenker testified that, when Dr. Neely came to him as a patient, he found him suffering intensely with pain. The witness gave as his opinion that the puncture that he described was caused by "external violence of some kind." After describing his patient's condition, he testified that the center "of infection was the site of the injury, the opening in his finger." He said the patient "was suffering from an infected hand, which later on developed into an infection which extended up his arm, which resulted in blood poisoning or what we call septicemia." He was asked: "How did the infection get in his finger," and he answered: "Through the opening in his finger."

Dr. Smith testified that, after the incision was made on the 5th of September, Dr. Neely showed signs of improvement, "then the infection seemed to progress until the 16th." He described Dr. Neely as suffering from "an infected wound of the finger." When asked his opinion as to what caused Dr. Neely's death, he answered: "Infection of the finger, followed by a blood stream infection."

The jury was justified in coming to the conclusion from the evidence presented to it that the insured died of blood poisoning which was caused by an infection in his right forefinger. As to the further and fundamental question of whether or not this infection of the forefinger was caused by an accident, plaintiffs had to rely upon circumstantial evidence. As to that the learned trial judge said in his charge to the jury: "The several circumstances relied upon to support the fact [in issue] cannot be presumed, but must be established by proof of the same weight and force as if each were itself the main fact in issue, which here is: 'Was there an accident?' " The court then called attention to the fact that the evidence as to the accident was largely that of Miss Hancock, the nurse who probed the puncture she saw in the doctor's right forefinger and who felt therein a moveable gritty substance. In view of the fact that a moveable, gritty substance is not ordinarily found in a person's right forefinger, the jury were permitted to infer that this substance entered the finger by accidental means. In Watkins v. Prudential Ins. Co., 315 Pa. 497, 173 A. 644, 651, 95 A.L.R. 869 (1934), we said: "The operative facts of the insurance policy sued upon were 'external, violent and accidental means' causing the insured's death, and any evidence, whether direct or circumstantial, that tends to prove the operative facts, is admissible. . . . Causes of action are always set forth affirmatively and if they are to prevail they must be supported either (1) by facts tending to prove directly the cause of action pleaded or (2) by legitimate inferences from circumstances which have met the tests of admissibility." In Hill v. Central Accident Ins. Co., 209 Pa. 632, 59 A. 262 (1904), whether or not the gunshot wound which caused the death of the insured was caused by a pistol accidentally or intentionally discharged was left to the jury to decide from the attendant circumstances. Greenleaf on Evidence (15th ed.) § 13, was quoted as follows: "In civil cases it is sufficient, if the evidence on the whole agrees with and supports the hypothesis which it is adduced to prove. . . . In both cases [civil and criminal] the verdict may well be founded on circumstances alone, and these often lead to a conclusion more satisfactory than direct evidence." In Urian v. Equitable Life Assur. Soc., 310 Pa. 342, 165 A. 388 (1933), the jury were permitted to infer from circumstances whether the inhalation of the gas which caused the death of the insured was accidental or intentional. In Pomorskie v. Prudential Life Ins. Co., 318 Pa. 185, 177 A. 783 (1935), an accident policy case, this court held that the issue was for the jury on evidence that the body of deceased was found with signs of head injuries apparently caused by a fall, and an autopsy revealed no indications of death from disease. In Mars v. Philadelphia Rapid T. Co., 303 Pa. 80, 154 A. 290, 292 (1931), we stated that, where a fact is deducible as a reasonable inference from the facts and conditions directly proved, it cannot be classed as a mere conjecture or surmise or guess, and that "in both the civil and criminal law, circumstantial evidence is competent evidence."

In Com. v. Harman, 4 Pa. 269, 273 (1846), Chief Justice Gibson declared: "All evidence is more or less circumstantial, the difference being only in the degree." He used an illustration in which the cause of death was inferred, because, as he said, "we cannot account for the death on any other supposition." Chief Justice Bigelow, in Com. v. Jeffries, 7 Allen (Mass.) 548, 563, 83 Am.Dec. 712 (1863), said: "The process of ascertaining one fact from the existence of another is essential to the investigation of truth, and prevails in courts of law as well as in the ordinary affairs of life." In Gray v. Com., 101 Pa. 380, 47 Am.Rep. 733 (1882), in which a defendant was on trial for his life, Mr. Justice Paxson said:

> "We are not jurors, and are not called upon to weigh the evidence . . . further than to say . . . whether there

> is sufficient evidence to submit to the jury upon a particular question of fact." We also declared that absolute certainty is not required. Wigmore says in the second edition of his Evidence, vol. 1, § 27, p. 232: "The conclusions and tests of every day experience must constantly control the standards of legal logic."

Appellant in its paper book quotes from page 208 of Thayer's Preliminary Treatise on Evidence at the Common Law, that "the jury's verdict . . . must be defensible in point of sense; it must not be absurd or whimsical." The next sentence on the same page of Professor Thayer's book is not quoted by appellant. It reads as follows: "This, of course, is a different thing from imposing upon the jury the judge's own private standard of what is reasonable. . . . The judges are not an appellate jury." On pages 194 and 195, Thayer says in respect to inferences: "The right inference or conclusion, in point of fact, is itself matter of fact, and to be ascertained by the jury. As regards reasoning, the judges have no exclusive office; the jury also must perform it at every step. . . . Courts might always have done their own reasoning, after a fashion, if they had been in possession of a full supply of primary fact; but they were not; and when once juries were called in, at no period of their history could they discharge their special function of ascertaining and reporting facts, without going through a process of reasoning."

Defendant contends that, although the injury to the finger may have been accidental, the probing of the wound by Dr. Neely was an intentional and injurious act. The answer is that, if an accident to the finger started the sequence of events which terminated fatally, the company would be liable under these policies, even though the treatment invited by the trauma contributed to the fatal result. If the insured met with an accident to his finger, the probing of the wound, done admittedly by him, was a natural and probable result, and this probing, though a concurring cause of death, would not bar plaintiffs' recovery, for the accident was the proximate cause. In Jones v. Commonwealth Casualty Co., 255 Pa. 566, 571, 100 A. 450, 451 (1917), the insured's death through accidental means was the fact in issue, and this court held that, though peritonitis was the immediate cause of death and this was due to an operation, "the operation was made necessary by the injury, and defendant cannot escape liability so long as the operation was skillfully performed, as to which no question is raised." In 1 C.J. § 180, p. 470, the following is given as a definition of "proximate cause" as applied to accident policies, "that cause which directly produces the effect, as distinguished from the remote cause, the cause which sets in motion a train of events which brings about a result without the intervention of any force operating and working actively from a new and independent source." In Continental Casualty Co. v. Colvin, 77 Kan. 561, 95 Pac. 565 (1908), it was held that the requirement of an accident policy that death must have resulted "necessarily and solely" from accidental injury is satisfied where the injury was the predominating and efficient cause of the death, and that "other conditions were set in motion by the injury, which may have contributed to [the death], is immaterial." In Gardner v. United Surety Co., 110 Minn. 291, 125 N.W. 264, 266, 26 L.R.A. (N.S.) 1004 (1910), it was held that, when injury is caused by means insured against, and medical treatment administered is rendered necessary by the nature of the injury, the death of the insured, if caused by the injury and the medical treatment, was accidental, within a policy insuring against death caused by "external, violent, and accidental means." In Isitt et al., Exrs., v. The Railway Passengers Assurance Co. (1889) 22 Q.B.Div. 504, the question was whether or not the deceased had died from the effects of an injury caused by accident. The assured had fallen down and dislocated his shoulder. He was taken home and put to bed, where he died twenty-one days later from pneumonia. The court held: "The deceased would not have died as and when he did if it had not been for the accident. . . . He was reduced by the accident to a state of debility in which he was more susceptible of cold than he would have been but for the accident, and was also less able to resist the effects of any illness which might come to him. . . . These facts constitute a chain of circumstances leading naturally from the injury to the death. . . . The circumstances leading up to the death, including the cold which caused pneumonia, were the reasonable and natural consequences of the injury." In French v. Fidelity, etc., Co. of New York, 135 Wis. 259, 115 N.W. 869, 17 L.R.A.(N.S.) 1011 (1908), it was held that, where death results from disease which follows as a natural, although not as a necessary, consequence of an accidental physical injury, the death is within the terms of an accident policy insuring one against bodily injuries sustained through external means, independently of all other causes, the death being the proximate result of the injury, and not of the disease as an independent cause.

In the argument of appellant's counsel, the greatest stress is placed upon the proposition that "inferences cannot be based upon inferences." In another part of their paper book they express what they consider to be the identical proposition by saying that "presumptions cannot be based upon presumptions." While counsel treat these two quoted statements as meaning precisely the same thing, they are in fact two distinct propositions, respectively untenable and sound. As we pointed out in Watkins v. Prudential Ins. Co., supra, there is "a welter of loose language . . . concerning presumptions." We there attempted to make plain the distinction between a presumption and an inference. We said: "They [presumptions] are not evidence and should not be substituted for evidence. . . . Presumptions are not fact suppliers; they are guideposts indicating whence proof must come." We quoted from Professor Thayer in his Storrs Lectures in 1896 as follows: "A presumption itself contributes no evidence, and has no probative quality. . . . A presumption may be called 'an instrument of proof,' in the sense that it determines from whom evidence shall come. . . . The moment these conceptions give way to the perfectly distinct notion of evidence proper—i. e., probative matter, which may be a basis of inference something capable of being weighed in the scales of reason and compared and estimated with other matter of the probative sort—so that we get to treating the presumption of innocence or any other presumption, as being evidence in this its true sense, then we have wandered into the region of shadows and phantoms." Wigmore on Evidence (2d Ed.) vol. 5, § 2491 (also cited by us in the Watkins Case), says: "The distinction between presumptions 'of law' and presumptions 'of fact' is in truth the difference between things that are in reality presumptions and things that are not presumptions at all. . . . The presumption is not the fact itself, nor the inference itself, but the legal consequence attached to it. . . . A 'presumption of fact,' in the loose sense, is merely an improper term for the rational potency, or probative value, of the evidentiary fact, regarded as not having this necessary legal consequence. . . . There is but one kind of presumption, and the term 'presumption of fact' should be discarded as useless and confusing."

With the distinction clearly in mind between presumptions and inferences, it is obvious that no presumption can be founded on a presumption; and it is equally obvious that inferences may be founded on inferences, as they are in the investigations carried on by scientific men and in the everyday affairs of life. As to the proposition that inferences cannot be based on inferences, Wigmore on Evidence (2d Ed.) vol. 1, § 41, says: "There is no such rule; nor can be. If there were, hardly a single trial could be adequately prosecuted. For example, on a charge of murder, the defendant's gun is found discharged; from this we infer that he discharged it; and from this we infer that it was his bullet which struck and killed the deceased. Or, the defendant is shown to have been sharpening a knife; from this we argue that he had a design to use it upon the deceased; and from this we argue that the fatal stab was the result of this design. In these and innumerable daily instances we build up inference upon inference, and yet no court ever thought of forbidding it. All departments of reasoning, all scientific work, every day's life and every day's trials, proceed upon such data. The judicial utterances that sanction the fallacious and impracticable limitation, originally put forward without authority, must be taken as valid only for the particular evidentiary facts therein ruled upon." Dean William Tricket in an article published in The Forum of the Dickinson School of Law for March, 1906, vol. 10, p. 123, characterizes the postulate that, "when facts are to be inferred from other facts the latter must be established by direct evidence" as "error," and suggests that as a doctrine occasionally recognized as a principle of proof it ought to be "extirpated."

Both in the activities of laymen and in the administration of justice there are many examples of the permissible drawing of more than one inference from a primary established fact. When jurors in their deliberations arrive by a process of reasoning at an acceptable inference of fact, they have a right to add such fact to any previous facts found by them and proceed by ratiocination from such fact or facts to additional inferences of fact and then proceed still further by like process until they arrive at the ultimate conclusion on the issue trying.

In the instant case, the jury, starting with the primary fact testified to, namely, that a "foreign substance" was located in the insured's right forefinger on August 20, 1932, had a right to infer that this substance got in there accidentally; that it or the probe inserted therein as part of a treatment reasonably necessitated by its troublesome presence, caused an infection; that this infection reached the blood stream and caused septicemia; and that this led directly to the insured's death. This was all a legally permissible process of reasoning leading directly to the conclusion which found formal expression in the verdict.

The judgments are affirmed.

PEOPLE v. REDDY

Court of Appeals of New York, 1933.
261 N.Y. 479, 185 N.E. 705.

. . .

CROUCH, Judge. On the night of August 6, 1931, two robbers held up a cider stube, so called, on West Forty-fourth street in the city of New York. In the course of the robbery, one of the victims was shot and killed. The robber who fired the shots was pursued and captured. His name was Baumann. The other one escaped. Baumann and his companion, designated as John Doe, were indicted for murder in the first degree. Baumann was tried and convicted as charged. The judgment of conviction was affirmed by this court. People v. Baumann, 259 N.Y. 600, 182 N.E. 198 (1932). Subsequently the defendant here was arrested and brought to trial as being Baumann's companion and the person named as John Doe in the indictment. His appeal is from a judgment of conviction for murder in the first degree. That conviction was had upon the testimony of Baumann. Unless Baumann be corroborated by other evidence tending to connect the defendant with the commission of the crime, the conviction must be set aside. Code Cr.Proc. § 399.

Baumann testified that he was twenty-one years of age and had known the defendant Reddy, who was commonly called "Howie," for five or six years, although he had seen little of him during the year preceding the murder; that on the afternoon of the murder he had driven with Reddy from Keansburg, N. J., where they had both been staying for several days; that after they reached New York, Reddy suggested that they join in a holdup, to which Baumann agreed; that they separated with an understanding that they would meet at Tenth avenue and Forty-ninth street at 7 o'clock in the evening, Reddy in the meantime to get pistols and arrange for the use of a taxicab; that they met at the time and place stated, boarded a taxicab and drove off; that Reddy gave witness a pistol and some extra cartridges; that the taxicab stopped at Forty-fourth street about six doors from Ninth avenue; that Reddy alighted from the taxicab, followed by the witness, the motor being kept running; that the witness took out his pistol, opened the door, and went into the cider stube, followed by Reddy; that they ordered the people in the place to put up their hands and go to the rear of the store; that Reddy did most of the searching while the witness kept the victims covered with his pistol; that when the cash register had been rifled and the pockets of the victims searched, Reddy stepped past the witness saying, "Come on, let's go," and proceeded rapidly toward the front door; that as witness turned to follow, Munich, one of the victims, grappled with him; that at that time Reddy was close to the front door; that witness shouted out, "Wait a minute, Howie, this guy has got me," but Reddy proceeded out; that the struggle between witness and Munich ended after a short time with the firing of three shots, after which Munich fell away from the witness, whereupon the witness ran out and saw the taxicab turning into Ninth avenue; that the witness never saw Reddy again until the trial.

It further appears that when Baumann was searched, following his capture, there was found on him a small photograph of Reddy. He repeatedly denied that that was a photograph of the man who was with him; on the contrary, he asserted that his companion was an "Italian fellow." Baumann's conviction was affirmed by this court on June 1, 1932, and his execution was set for July 14, 1932. Within a few hours of the time set for execution, Baumann made a statement which for the first time implicated Reddy. A reprieve of twenty-four hours resulted, during which the district attorney took a statement from Baumann. A second reprieve put off execution until the night of August 18th. The statements which Baumann had made were not wholly true, and it was not until almost the moment of execution on the night of August 18th that Baumann sent for the district attorney and made still another statement which apparently satisfied that official. A further reprieve was thereupon granted to cover the time of Reddy's trial. After that trial, Baumann's sentence was commuted to life imprisonment. Baumann on this trial asserted that his testimony on his own trial and all statements made by him relating to the identity of his companion had been intentional and deliberate lies for the purpose of shielding Reddy. He frankly admitted that he finally implicated Reddy and became a witness for the people solely to save his own life, and to that end he would not hesitate to lie. The defendant did not take the stand.

. . .

The law of corroboration under section 399 of the Code of Criminal Procedure was concisely but comprehensively stated in People v. Dixon, 231 N.Y. 111, 116, 131 N.E. 752, 754 (1921). "The corroborative evidence," said the opinion, "need not show the commission of the crime; it need not show that defendant was connected with the commission of the crime. (People v. Mayhew, 150 N.Y. 346, 353 [44 N.E. 971]; People v. Cohen, 223 N.Y. 406, 426 [119 N.E. 886]). It is enough if it tends to connect the defendant with the commission of the crime in such a way as may reasonably satisfy the jury that the accomplice is telling the truth." Since the web of proof in every case is unique, corroboration "may vary in its nature according to the circumstances of the particular case." Id. When the trial judge finds that there is some corroborative evidence, it is his duty to submit it "to the jury for them to say first, whether it was worthy of belief, and secondly, whether if true it tended to connect defendant with the commission of the crime." Id., 231 N.Y. 117, 131 N.E. 752, 754 (1921).

The learned trial judge found the possibility of corroboration in evidence relating to two matters. One was the alleged flight of defendant following the crime; the other was Baumann's stronger motive for implicating as his companion in crime the man actually guilty, rather than one who was innocent. Accordingly, he submitted to the jury the evidence relating to each of these matters, to say whether it was true, and, if so, whether it tended to connect the defendant with the commission of the crime.

In respect to the matter of the stronger motive, the argument was that Baumann would naturally feel resentment against the man who, instead of responding to his appeal for help, had deserted him and fled in the taxicab with all the loot, leaving him to be hunted through the streets and captured; and hence that his testimony incriminating the defendant was credible in spite of the admitted character and interest of Baumann. So the trial judge charged the jury as follows: "If you find that that contention has merit, you may consider whether that is corroborated by the evidence of the other witnesses. . . . You have heard the testimony of several of the witnesses who were in the place, and of the officers. It is for you to say whether they establish, apart from Baumann, that the other man did escape, did get away in a taxicab, and that Baumann, in consequence of having no taxicab to get into, was captured. If you find that their testimony corroborates Baumann on the question that his accomplice abandoned him, thereby furnishing Baumann with a motive to testify truthfully against the accomplice, you may consider whether that is evidence that tends to connect this defendant with the crime; that is, to show that this defendant is that unknown man that escaped, and that the unknown man was not some other man, some guilty man whom Baumann is shielding."

. . .

In respect to the matter of flight, the general rule is well settled. Evidence of flight, concealment, or analogous conduct is always admissible. From of old, when unexplained, it has been deemed indicative of a consciousness of guilt, and hence of guilt itself. Proverbs, XXVIII, 1; People v. Ogle, 104 N.Y. 511, 514, 11 N.E. 53 (1887); People v. Fiorentino, 197 N.Y. 560, 567, 91 N.E. 195, 198 (1910);

Hickory v. United States, 160 U.S. 408, 16 S.Ct. 327, 40 L.Ed. 474 (1896). But "ordinarily it is of slight value, and of none whatever unless there are facts pointing to the motive which prompted it." People v. Fiorentino, supra; People v. Stilwell, 244 N.Y. 196, 199, 155 N.E. 98 (1927). Its consideration, as pointed out long ago, should not be pressed too far. Commonwealth v. Webster, 5 Cush. (Mass.) 295, 52 Am.Dec. 711 (1850). To the extent that it is evidence of guilt itself, it must be taken as corroborative of an accomplice's incriminating testimony. . . .

. . .

The judgment of conviction should be reversed and a new trial ordered.

SIMPSON v. SIMPSON

Court of Civil Appeals of Texas, 1964.
380 S.W.2d 855.

. . .

CLAUDE WILLIAMS, Justice. Letha Bethel Simpson brought this suit to establish and recover her undivided interest in the estate of Charles J. Simpson, deceased. She alleged that she was lawfully married to Charles J. Simpson (hereinafter referred to as decedent) on March 5, 1913 and remained his lawful wife until he died in December 1960. Plaintiff named Eloise Simpson as defendant, alleging that she was a putative wife of Charles J. Simpson at the time of his death, and was in physical possession of the property sought to be recovered by plaintiff. Defendant answered, asserting a general denial as well as affirmative defenses of laches, estoppel, *res judicata,* and limitations. Defendant then filed her motion for summary judgment which plaintiff opposed. The court, based upon supporting affidavits and depositions, sustained defendant's motion for summary judgment and plaintiff brings this appeal.

FACTS

Marriage, a status said to be of divine origin, is the pedestal around which the facts of this case revolve. The historical background of this case covers almost a half century (1913–1960). Affidavits and depositions reveal the following as a chronological history of relevant events relating to appellant.

Appellant married decedent on March 5, 1913 in the State of Arkansas. To this union there was born on August 26, 1914, a male child, Floyd Charles Simpson. In February 1917 decedent left her saying that he was going away to work and would send for her. She never saw him since that time. The first she heard from him was thirty years later, in 1947. Appellant attempted to locate decedent during World War I by communicating with the "War Board" who told her they would try to find decedent but such efforts were apparently fruitless. Appellant was never served with legal papers of any nature with regard to the decedent and appellant did not obtain a divorce or annulment from the decedent at any time prior to decedent's death in 1960. In 1920, having concluded that decedent was dead, appellant married one O'Donnell and lived with him until 1930 when they separated. O'Donnell died in 1941. On December 14, 1941, still under the impression she was a feme sole, appellant entered into a ceremonial marriage with Morrill Adams and continued to live with him, as husband and wife, in the State of Kansas, until this marriage was dissolved by court decree in 1954. In 1947, appellant was advised by her son that decedent was alive, living in Dallas, Texas, and married and had children by said marriage. Appellant, upon learning this information, continued to live with Morrill Adams for a period of seven years at which time she obtained a divorce from him in 1954. Charles J. Simpson died on December 21, 1960 in Dallas, Texas. This action was instituted on August 31, 1961.

Affidavits and depositions reveal the following chronological history of relevant events as to decedent and appellee Eloise Simpson. In 1924, approximately seven years after separating from appellant, decedent married Verda Mae Burton in Los Angeles, California. In applying for this marriage license, decedent certified that this marriage was his first marriage and that he was single, not divorced. Decedent and Verda Mae remained married until July 15, 1950 when she obtained a divorce from decedent. Three children were born to this union. In 1947 decedent located his son, Floyd Charles Simpson, in the State of Kansas, and visited with him in Dallas and elsewhere on several occasions. After the reunion of decedent and his son, Floyd Charles Simpson advised his mother concerning decedent's residence in Dallas, as well as his present marital status. On one occasion during a visit between decedent and his son, decedent stated to Floyd Charles Simpson that he, decedent, had never secured a divorce from appellant. In 1950 Verda Mae obtained a divorce from decedent in Dallas County. In 1950 decedent married appellee and such marriage continued until the date of decedent's death in December 1960. No children were born of this union. The official records of Los Angeles County, California, Denver County, Colorado, Tarrant County, Texas, and Dallas County Texas, the only places in which decedent lived from 1924 until the date of his death in 1960, reflect that decedent never procured an annulment or divorce from appellant.

OPINION

By her first point on appeal appellant contends that the trial court erred in granting appellee's motion for summary judgment for the reason that the record conclusively shows the existence of a genuine fact issue as to whether the appellant was lawfully married to decedent from 1913 until the date of decedent's death in 1960. By her counter points, appellee contends that the summary judgment was proper because the evidence presented does not overcome the presumption of the validity of the marriage between decedent and appellee. She also contends that the statement of Floyd Charles Simpson in his affidavit that his father told him in 1948 he had never secured a divorce from his mother, appellant, is not a statement of a fact that would be admissible as evidence as required by Rule 166–A (e), Texas Rules of Civil Procedure.

The institution of marriage is a status, more than a mere contract, and has been defined as the voluntary union for life of one man and one woman as husband and wife, to the exclusion of all others. 38 Tex.Jur.2d, pp. 28–29, Sec. 1; Grigsby v. Reib, 105 Tex. 597, 153 S.W. 1124 (1913). It has long been the established law of Texas that a ceremonial marriage entered into in accordance with legal forms will raise the presumption, or inference of its legality. One of the strongest presumptions of law is that a marriage, once being shown, is valid. However, as here, on proof of a second marriage by a party to a prior marriage, the question is presented as to whether a presumption of validity will attach to the second marriage. The generally accepted view is that a second marriage will be presumed to be valid and that such presumption is stronger than and overcomes the presumption of continuance of the prior marriage. 38 Tex.Jur. 2d, pp. 89–91, Sec. 44; 14 A.L.R.2d 10–11; . . .

However, such a presumption, strong though it may be, is a rebuttable one. Nixon, et al. v. Wichita Land & Cattle Co., 84 Tex. 408, 19 S.W. 560; . . . While it has been held that the presumption of validity of a subsequent marriage may be rebutted only by evidence that negatives every possible method by which the prior marriage could have been dissolved (Texas Employers Ins. Ass'n v. Gomez, 313 S.W.2d 956 (Tex.Civ.App.1958)) it has been ruled, with equal force, that in order to rebut the presumption of legality of the second marriage such need not be established absolutely or to a moral certainty, the plaintiff only being required to introduce sufficient evidence, standing alone, to negative such facts, in which case the weight of the evidence would be for the jury. Hudspeth v. Hudspeth, Tex.Civ.App., 206 S.W.2d 863 . . . .

. . .

Appellee argues forcefully that the language of the Supreme Court in Texas Employers Ins. Ass'n v. Elder, 155 Tex. 27, 282 S.W. 2d 371 (1955), to the effect that the presumption is one of the strongest known to law, and is, in itself, evidence, and may even outweigh positive evidence to the contrary, is controlling in this case. With full recognition of the forcefulness of the language utilized by our Supreme Court we must not blind ourselves to the pertinent fact that we are here dealing with a motion for summary judgment and not a trial on the merits, as was the Elder case, supra. The familiar rule has been announced repeatedly that in determining the question of whether or not material issues of fact were raised by the evidence, the court, on review, must review all the evidence in the light most favorable to the petitioners; disregard the conflicts in the testimony; and indulge, in favor of the petitioners, every intendment reasonably deducible from the evidence. Any doubt that exists in the mind of the reviewing court must be resolved in favor of the party against whom the motion was granted. Gulbenkian v. Penn, 151 Tex. 412, 252 S.W.2d 929 (1953).

Applying these rules to the factual situation here presented, we find that while appellant probably did not prove the continued existence of her marital relationship with decedent between 1917 and 1960 to a moral certainty, or beyond any doubt, yet she did introduce some evidence of probative force to negative the fact that her marriage to decedent had not been dissolved by divorce or annulment. While it is true that a jury weighing this evidence might be influenced greatly by the presumption of law relating to the validity of the second marriage, yet that is not the question for our decision. We must decide whether there are *any facts in evidence* in this record which would support appellant's contention and thereby which should have been submitted to a jury or a court, as triers of fact. In our opinion appellant has satisfied the law by producing sufficient evidence in the form of affidavits and depositions to create an issue of fact as to the dissolution of the prior marriage. As to appellee's counter point relating to the inadmissibility of the affidavit of appellant's son in which he relates that in 1948 his father told him that he, decedent, had never divorced appellant, we believe that such affidavit was admissible evidence. We think it was within the exception to the hearsay rule which permits testimony concerning declarations about pedigree and family history. Texas Law of Evidence, McCormick & Ray, Vol. 2, Sections 1341–1348, pp. 184–194, and cases there cited. Should we be mistaken in this regard, we feel that even without such affidavit appellant has met the burden imposed upon her to present sufficient evidence of probative force to create an issue of fact that should have been submitted to a jury. Appellant's first point is sustained.

. . .

The judgment of the trial court is reversed and remanded.

Reversed and remanded.

PEOPLE v. RUSSO

Supreme Court, Appellate Division, First Department, 1951.
278 App.Div. 98, 103 N.Y.S.2d 603.

John Russo and Milton Singer and another were prosecuted for an offense and from a judgment rendered in the Court of Special Sessions of the City of New York, New York County, Hoffman, Burlingam, Morrisey, JJ., convicting first named defendant of unlawfully possessing a firearm in violation of Penal Law, § 1897, the first named defendant appealed. . . .

. . .

COHN, Justice. At about 1:30 a. m. on April 7, 1949, in the City of New York, policemen in a patrol car observed appellant and the other two defendants seated in a parked car and saw a fourth man, Grubhofer, standing on the sidewalk with his head inside the window of the parked vehicle. Grubhofer was ordered to step aside and the three defendants were directed to come out of the car. After the four men had been searched for weapons, a loaded pistol was found in the automobile on the ledge behind the rear seat.

Shortly thereafter, when questioned in the police station, appellant Russo admitted to one of the arresting officers, Hladek by name, that he knew the gun was in the car; that he knew where it came from and how it had gotten in the auto. According to Hladek, appellant stated that his codefendant Singer brought the gun pursuant to a prearranged plan made earlier that night.

Defendants Singer and DePeralta and the fourth man, Grubhofer, were also questioned by Hladek in the police station. Their statements to the police were not binding upon appellant Russo. However, the statement of Grubhofer, who was not a defendant, was adduced at the trial through defense counsel's cross-examination of the officer in which counsel quoted some of Hladek's prior testimony given in the Magistrate's Court. This was to the effect that Grubhofer had told Hladek that while he (Grubhofer) was standing outside the car the gun was on his person, he having obtained it from Singer, and that upon seeing the officers drive up, he withdrew the weapon from inside his coat and threw it in back of the automobile.

Appellant did not take the stand and called no witnesses in his defense.

It is the contention of appellant that Section 1898–a of the Penal Law, upon which the People rely in part to sustain the conviction, is unconstitutional and, in any event, that the guilt of appellant was not established beyond a reasonable doubt.

Section 1897 of the Penal Law, so far as material here, prohibits the unlicensed possession of a pistol, Subd. 4. Section 1898–a as amended by Chapter 390 of the Laws of 1936 provides as follows: "The presence in an automobile, other than a public omnibus, of any of the following weapons, instruments or appliances, viz., a pistol . . . shall be presumptive evidence of its illegal possession by all the persons found in such automobile at the time such weapon, instrument or appliance is found."

Appellant's guilt, we think, was proven beyond a reasonable doubt. He and his co-defendants and the pistol were all in the automobile together immediately prior to the arrest. The testimony of the police officers sustains this view. Appellant admitted it, as did defendants Singer and DePeralta. Even the incompetent statement of Grubhofer, upon which appellant relies, places the appellant and the weapon in the automobile at the same time.

The statutory presumption of a gun's illegal possession by all persons found in an automobile is, of course, a rebuttable one. The evidence here, far from rebutting the presumption, served to confirm it. Possession as used in connection with the penal provisions relating to weapons is a knowing and voluntary possession "which places the weapon within the immediate control and reach of the accused, and where it is available for unlawful use if he so desires." People v. Persce, 204 N.Y. 397, 402, 97 N.E. 877, 878 (1912). In the case before us, the gun, as it lay on the back ledge of the automobile, was clearly "within the immediate control and reach of" the appellant and his companions and available for unlawful use if they so desired. Appellant knew the gun was in the car and he knew beforehand that it was going to be brought there. Indeed, the very purpose of the meeting at the place of the arrests was to have Singer bring it to the rendezvous after he had picked it up at his home. The evidence in this case disclosed constructive possession of the loaded revolver by appellant. The courts have so decided under similar circumstances. People v. Murphy, 276 N.Y. 612, 12 N.E.2d 602 (1938); People v. Amberg, 216 App.Div. 791, 214 N.Y.S. 896 (1926); People v. Birnbaum, 208 App.Div. 476, 203 N.Y.S. 697 (1924).

Appellant's assertion that Section 1898–a of the Penal Law is unconstitutional is apparently based upon the claim that it is in conflict with the Fourteenth Amendment of the Federal Constitution and Article 1, Section 6, of the Constitution of the State of New York, which provide in part that no person shall be compelled in any criminal case to be a witness against himself, nor deprived of life, liberty or property without due process of law.

It is well settled that statutes such as Section 1898–a of the Penal Law, providing that certain facts are presumptive evidence of one or more of the ultimate facts in issue, are not unconstitutional where, as here, there is a rational connection with the facts proved and the conclusion presumed, and where the presumptions themselves are neither conclusive nor arbitrary. Morrison v. People of State of California, 1934, 291 U.S. 82, 90, 54 S.Ct. 281, 78 L.Ed. 664 (1934); . . .

In People v. Cannon, 139 N.Y. 32, the court, at page 43, 34 N.E. 759, 762, stated the apposite law as to the power of the legislature to authorize a presumption, as follows: "The limitations are that the fact upon which the presumption is to rest must have some fair relation to, or natural connection with, the main fact. The inference of the existence of the main fact, because of the existence of the fact actually proved, must not be merely and purely arbitrary, or wholly unreasonable, unnatural, or extraordinary; and the accused must have in each case, a fair opportunity to make his defense, and to submit the whole case to the jury, to be decided by it after it has weighed all the evidence, and given such weight to the presumption as to it shall seem proper. A provision of this kind does not take away or impair the right of trial by jury. It does not in reality, [and finally] change the burden of proof. The people must at all times sustain the burden of proving the guilt of the accused beyond a reasonable doubt. It, in substance, enacts that, certain facts being proved, the jury may regard them, if believed, as sufficient to convict, in the absence of explanation or contradiction. Even in that case the court could not legally direct a conviction. It cannot do so in any criminal case. That is solely for the jury, and it could have the right, after a survey of the whole case, to refuse to convict unless satisfied beyond a reasonable doubt of the guilt of the accused, even though the statutory prima facie evidence were uncontradicted." See Commonwealth v. Williams, 72 Mass. 1, 6 Gray 1 (1856).

All presumptions arising from facts cast upon the defendant the burden of overcoming them. Here the statutory presumption merely assumes that in the absence of some explanation the occupants of an automobile in which a pistol is found are in illegal possession of it. If the persons in the automobile have no actual knowledge of its presence, there cannot be a conviction and the burden of establishing beyond a reasonable doubt their possession of the gun is nevertheless with the People.

In People v. Murphy, 276 N.Y. 612, 12 N.E.2d 602 (1938), the Court of Appeals had under consideration the constitutionality of a statute making the presence of a machine gun in any room or dwelling presumptive evidence of illegal possession by all occupying the place where the machine gun is found, Section 1897, subd. 1–a, Penal Law. In that case the Court affirmed a judgment of conviction for illegal possession by numerous defendants occupying the place where a quantity of the prohibited weapons was found.

. . .

Although the Court of Appeals in several somewhat recent cases has stated that in them it did not pass upon the constitutionality of Section 1898–a of the Penal Law, People ex rel. Dixon v. Lewis, 276 N.Y. 613, 12 N.E.2d 603 (1938); People v. Burt, 283 N.Y. 740, 28 N.E.2d 968 (1940), it would appear to have directly approved its constitutionality in People v. Rogalski, 281 N.Y. 581, 22 N.E.2d 160 (1939), where a conviction under Section 1897 of the Penal Law for carrying a dangerous weapon as a felony in circumstances very similar to those here was sustained. There the three convicted defendants, together with a fourth who was acquitted, were found in an automobile by police officers. Under the rear seat of that car was found a loaded gun and in the back of a front seat cushion was another loaded gun. In the pocket of defendant Rogalski were found two cartridges which might have been used in either gun. Each of the three convicted defendants stated to the police officers who apprehended them that he knew nothing about the presence of the guns in the car. An examination of the record on appeal in that case shows that the very first point argued by the three convicted defendants was that Section 1898–a was unconstitutional; "that the court erred and invaded the constitutional rights of the defendants by charging the jury the presumption of possession under Section 1898–a of the Penal Law"; and that the indictment should have been dismissed against all defendants. The charge of the Court to the jury instructing them, which followed the mandate of the statute, § 1898–a, was duly excepted to. Nevertheless the Court of Appeals affirmed the judgment of conviction, but without opinion. Cf. United States ex rel. Rogalski v. Jackson, 146 F.2d 251, 252 (2d Cir. 1945); People ex rel. Shinsky (Gerschinsky) v. Hunt, 178 Misc. 960, 36 N.Y.S.2d 801 (1942); People v. Burt, 258 App.Div. 896, 16 N.Y.S.2d 211 (1940), affirmed 283 N.Y. 740, 28 N.E.2d 968, supra.

It is common knowledge that the automobile is frequently employed as an agency in the furtherance of violent and serious crimes committed not by one but by several individuals. Before the enactment of Section 1898–a of the Penal Law in the year 1936, where a group of persons were about to embark on a mission of law-breaking in an automobile in which a revolver was placed, no law could reach any of the occupants unless it was established that the weapon was found on the person of an occupant. People v. Persce, 204 N.Y. 397, 97 N.E. 877 (1912), supra; People v. Andreacchi, 221 App.Div. 136, 222 N.Y.S. 610 (1927). Urgent need for legislation making the presence of a forbidden firearm in an automobile presumptive evidence of its possession by all occupants was judicially recognized. People ex rel. De Feo v. Warden of City Prison, 136 Misc. 836, 241 N.Y.S. 63 (1930), opinion by Lewis, J. It is not unreasonable to require, as the statute in effect commands, that those who occupy an automobile in which a revolver or other dangerous weapon is found should explain their knowledge of its presence in the automobile. An explanation by an innocent occupant of such a car of course, overcomes the presumption. There is thus no danger that an innocent person may become a victim of circumstances. In view of the facts of the case, and particularly the appellant's unsatisfactory explanation to the arresting officer, the triers of fact were warranted in according full effect to the statutory presumption.

The defendant, in our view, was properly convicted of the crime of Unlawfully Possessing A Firearm and the judgment of conviction should accordingly be affirmed.

Judgment affirmed. Order filed.

BORNHURST v. MASSACHUSETTS BONDING & INSURANCE CO.

Court of Appeals of New York, 1968.
21 N.Y.2d 581, 289 N.Y.S.2d 937.

Action against insurer to recover amount of judgment against driver of automobile upon ground that insured under garage liability policy was the owner of the vehicle involved. The Supreme Court, Trial and Special Term, Onondaga County, Richard Aronson, J., entered judgment for plaintiff and the Supreme Court, Appellate Division, 25 A.D.2d 479, 267 N.Y.S.2d 322, entered order reversing judgment and dismissing complaint and appeal was taken. . . .

KEATING, Judge. F. Richard Bornhurst was injured when the automobile he was operating collided with a vehicle operated by one

George Daniels. An action was commenced against Daniels and the alleged owner of the vehicle, Edmund Stearns, Catherine Stearns and Richard Stearns doing business as Edmund A. Stearns and Son Auto Sales. The plaintiff recovered a verdict against Daniels and "Stearns". The trial court set aside the verdict against "Stearns" and dismissed the complaint. The Appellate Division, however, reversed the order dismissing the complaint and ordered a new trial (Bornhurst v. Stearns, 4 A.D.2d 818, 164 N.Y.S.2d 303 (1917)).

Pursuant to Section 167 of the Insurance Law, Consol.Laws, c. 28 Bornhurst commenced the present action directly against the Massachusetts Bonding & Insurance Company to recover the amount of the judgment against Daniels upon the ground that the defendant having issued a garage liability policy to "Stearns", had refused to pay the judgment and that, at the time of the accident, "Stearns" was the owner of the vehicle involved in the accident.

After a trial by jury, a verdict was returned in the plaintiff's favor. The Appellate Division (4th Dept.) reversed on the law and facts and dismissed the complaint with one Justice concurring in reversal but voting for a new trial. The court held that the plaintiff had failed to establish that, at the time of the accident, title to the automobile driven by Daniels had passed to "Stearns".

The issue presented on this appeal is whether the plaintiff established a prima facie case and hence is entitled to a reversal and a new trial.

Former Section 99 of the Personal Property Law, Consol.Laws, c. 41, provided that:

> "1. Where there is a contract to sell specific or ascertained goods, the property in them is transferred to the buyer at such time as the parties to the contract intend it to be transferred.
>
> "2. For the purpose of ascertaining the intention of the parties, regard shall be had to the terms of the contract, the conduct of the parties, usages of trade and the circumstances of the case."

Viewing the evidence most favorably to the plaintiff, we conclude, as the Appellate Division did in its earlier decision, that "the question of [the] ownership of the . . . vehicle was one of fact for the determination of the jury" and that the complaint was improperly dismissed (Bornhurst v. Stearns, 4 A.D.2d 818, 164 N.Y.S.2d 303 (1957), supra).

There are essentially two conflicting stories regarding the circumstances surrounding Daniels' possession of the Ford vehicle. The defendant's version—corroborated by testimony of "Stearns" and its employee, one Machan—is that during the month of May Daniels had visited "Stearns" seeking to purchase a vehicle. An agreement was reached on the purchase of a 1946 Mercury on May 17, and partial financing through Onondaga Provident Loan Association had been arranged. The deal, however, fell through. Several days later, on May 21, 1954, Daniels appeared at "Stearns" and decided to purchase a 1941 Cadillac for $195. "Stearns' " employee, Machan, who handled the transaction, testified that he believed the deal would be for cash and a trade-in allowance on the Ford. Daniels then produced a registration certificate for the Ford. "Stearns' " stamp was placed on the back of the registration in that part providing for transfers.

According to Machan's testimony he believed that Daniels had at least $150 cash since, a few days earlier, Daniels had agreed to put up that amount in cash on the Mercury deal. Upon hearing that the deal was not to be for cash, but would require financing, he stated he would have to call the finance company and would write up an order for the Cadillac subject to approval. He then stated that he gave the registration back to Daniels who left, and the deal was never consummated.

Machan testified he called the finance company about five o'clock after Daniels had left and was advised that the loan was approved. A check for $144—dated May 21, 1954—was received on Monday, May 24, and eventually cashed.

The accident in question occurred shortly after Daniels left "Stearns" in the Ford.

Daniels' version of the events in question was that he had been at "Stearns" on May 20, and decided to purchase the Cadillac, that, sometime that day or next, he went to the finance company and obtained a check for $144 dated May 21, which was indorsed by him over to "Stearns". He testified that he then gave the registration certificate to Machan or Edmund Stearns who placed his company stamp thereon.

He testified further that he then went out and started the Cadillac and that it had a "knock" in it. He was told to leave it there and pick it up the next day, when it would be fixed, and to take the Ford in the meantime and bring it back the next day. The registration was then handed back to him.

There was testimony in the record that it was a general custom in the used car business that title to an automobile passed upon the stamping by the purchaser of registration and the signing by the transferor of his name at the appropriate part of the registration stub.

The foregoing evidence clearly establishes a prima facie case, and, while the testimony of Daniels, who is hardly a respectable character, is contradictory in places and certainly open to question, a dismissal of the complaint is not warranted.

The defendant recognizes that the issue is, in essence, one of credibility. It contends, however, that, even if Daniels' testimony be accepted as establishing the true facts, the proof herein falls far short of that required to prove a transfer of title to the Ford automobile from Daniels to "Stearns".

Initially the defendant argues that "the plaintiff is met by a number of presumptions which were not rebutted by the proof in this case". The first of these "presumptions" is that, since Daniels was shown to have been the owner of the vehicle prior to the date in question, his ownership is presumed to have continued until the contrary is shown (Richardson, Evidence [9th ed., Prince], § 73, p. 50). This presumption, it is urged, cannot be rebutted by Daniels' testimony since he is an interested witness.

This argument is without merit. The fact that Daniels may be an interested witness goes only to the issue of credibility. Where the evidence rebutting a presumption "presents an issue of credibility, it is for the jury to determine whether the rebuttal evidence is to be believed and, consequently, for the jury to determine whether the presumption has been destroyed" (Richardson, Evidence [9th ed., Prince], § 57).

The defendant next argues that "It has long been the law of this State that the license number of an automobile coupled with evidence as to the person who held such license, constitutes prima facie proof that such person was the owner of the vehicle. Ferris v. Sterling, 214 N.Y. 249, 108 N.E. 417 (1915). Lacking proof that title to a motor vehicle had previously actually been transferred, after it has been involved in an accident and has caused injury, the registered owner must be presumed to have been the owner thereof and will not be permitted to deny such ownership. Elfeld v. Burkham Auto Renting Co., 299 N.Y. 336, 87 N.E.2d 285, 13 A.L.R.2d 370 (1949); Shuba v. Greendonner, 271 N.Y. 189, 2 N.E.2d 536 (1936)."

Again the defendant's reliance is misplaced for the plaintiff introduced evidence which, if credited by the jury, would sustain a conclusion that title had in fact passed. Moreover, the rule that after an accident "the registered owner must be presumed to have been the owner thereof and will not be permitted to deny such ownership" would apply as a matter of policy only in an action by an injured party against the record owner—which is not the case here. As we have written: "To permit the [defendant] to relieve himself of liability by proving that he was not in fact the owner of the automobile and thereby establish his illegal and fraudulent act in procuring its registration in his own name would be against public policy and would encourage fraudulent and illegal deceptions on the state in procuring the registration of automobiles in the names of persons who were not the owners thereof, directly in violation of the statute." (Shuba v. Greendonner, 271 N.Y. 189, 194, 2 N.E.2d 536, 539 (1936).)

In the case at bar "Stearns" is not the record owner, and there are no policy considerations which prevent the plaintiff from establishing the true ownership of the vehicle. Indeed, there are strong policy considerations which favor a rule permitting an injured party to establish the true ownership of the vehicle. (Vehicle and Traffic Law, Consol.Laws, c. 71, § 388.)

The final argument of the defendant rests on an additional fact—not previously noted. It appears, for reasons not here relevant, that, when Daniels originally purchased the Ford, he registered it in the name of a third person (one Earl Pitts) without his consent. In transferring title on the registration, the name of Earl Pitts was signed —either by Daniels or another under his direction. The defendant argues that as a result "The attempted transfer of title to the Ford from Daniels to Stearns was permeated with fraud and trickery. [And] it has been held that there cannot be a sale of an automobile where such practices are involved. Davis [Damis] v. Barcia, 266 App.Div. 698, 40 N.Y.2d 107 (3rd Dept. 1943)"

It is sufficient to point out that the case on which the defendant relies is not only distinguishable but has since been expressly overruled (Stanton Motor Corp. v. Rosetti, 11 A.D.2d 296, 298, 203 N.Y.S.2d 273, 274 (3d Dept. 1960)). The transfer of title from Daniels to "Stearns"—assuming it occurred—did not result from any fraud perpetrated upon "Stearns". Daniels was the owner of the vehicle registered in the name of another and he could legally pass title to that vehicle. Indeed, Machan knew Daniels was not Pitts and nevertheless stamped the registration card which was in the name of one Pitts. Moreover, even if another person at Daniels' request signed the registration that could not affect the passage of title. In either case, "Stearns' " title could not have been challenged either by Pitts, Daniels or any other party.

To summarize, it seems clear to us that the Appellate Division erred in dismissing the complaint and that the order should be reversed and a new trial granted, with costs to abide the event, on the ground that the plaintiff established a prima facie case.

FULD, C. J., and BURKE, SCILEPPI, BERGAN, BREITEL and JASEN, JJ., concur.

Order reversed and a new trial granted, with costs to abide the event.

DECISIONS RELATING TO CHAPTER XVIII, JUDICIAL NOTICE

MANCUSO v. ROTHENBERG

Superior Court of New Jersey, Appellate Division, 1961.
67 N.J.Super. 248, 170 A.2d 482.

Action wherein defendant, who was driving plaintiffs' automobile at time of damage to it, impleaded his collision insurer as a third-party defendant. The trial court rendered judgment for this defendant against his insurer, and the insurer appealed. . . .

LEWIS, J. A. D. Plaintiffs Salvatore Mancuso and Ruby Mancuso, co-owners of a Fiat automobile, were insured against damages thereto, less $50 deductible, by Emmco Insurance Company (hereinafter referred to as Emmco).

On August 5, 1959 at 3:45 A.M., defendant Leonard Rothenberg, with the permission of the plaintiffs, was driving the Fiat, on a mission for his own benefit, when he became involved in a collision with another car owned by the defendant Alfred Bender and operated by his agent, defendant Louis Bender. The Fiat car was damaged. At the time of the accident, defendant Rothenberg owned a Plymouth automobile (not involved in the accident). He was at that time insured by Motors Insurance Corporation (hereinafter referred to as Motors) against damage from collision, less $50 deductible. This coverage extended to his Plymouth automobile and to any non-owned vehicle which he might have the occasion to operate.

The plaintiffs collected their loss (less $50) from Emmco, and instituted suit against Rothenberg for the full amount thereof, for the benefit of their carrier Emmco, as subrogee, and for themselves as to the $50 deducted. Defendant Rothenberg, pursuant to order for leave to file third-party complaint impleaded his insurance carrier, Motors, as a third-party defendant. Motors denied liability, maintaining that its policy did not afford coverage to the defendant Rothenberg relative to the matters set forth in the third-party complaint, that collision insurance covering the Fiat was issued and loss thereunder paid by Emmco (less $50), and that, under the circumstances, its coverage was excess insurance. The limits of the Emmco policy had not been exceeded.

The damages to the Fiat car were stipulated by the plaintiffs and the defendant Rothenberg to be $552.73. Motors agreed that such figure represented a fair and reasonable value of the repairs to the car. There was an additional towing charge of $25 covered by the policy of Motors. The case was tried without a jury, and the court found that there was no negligence on the part of the defendants Benders and, on their motion, without objection, judgment was entered in their favor. The court further found that the sole negligence and proximate cause of the accident rested with Rothenberg, and, accordingly, found for the plaintiffs and entered judgment against the defendant Rothenberg in the amount of $552.73. The court also found that the insurance policy of Motors "was issued for the protection of Rothenberg, not on a Fiat," and entered judgment for Rothenberg on the third-party complaint against Motors for $527.73, representing damages of $552.73 plus $25 towing charges less $50 which was deductible.

The contract of insurance contained a statement in bold red print: "This Policy DOES NOT PROVIDE bodily injury and property damage liability insurance or any other coverage for which a specific premium charge is not made, and does not comply with any Financial Responsibility Law." The declaration page of the policy indicates that premiums were paid for coverages including "E Collision or Upset (actual cash value less $50 deductible)" and "F Towing and Labor Costs." Under that portion of the policy relating to "Insuring Agreements," there is a provision as to "Coverage E-Collision" by which the insurance company agreed:

> "To pay for loss caused by collision to the owned automobile or to a non-owned automobile but only for the amount of each such loss in excess of the deductible amount stated in the declarations as applicable hereto."

Specific exclusions are enumerated, and item (c) is invoked. It reads: "to loss to a non-owned automobile arising out of its use by the insured in the automobile business." The recited conditions of the policy include, *inter alia,* a paragraph captioned "13. Other Insurance," which provides:

> "If the insured has other insurance against a loss covered by this policy, the company shall not be liable under this policy for a greater proportion of such loss than the applicable limit of liability of this policy bears to the total applicable limit of liability of all valid and collectible insurance against such loss; provided, however, the insurance with respect to a temporary substitute automobile or non-owned automobile shall be excess insurance over any other valid and collectible insurance."

It is uncontroverted that Rothenberg did not have any other collision insurance and that he was operating a non-owner's vehicle when the accident occurred. The court found as a matter of fact, supported by ample evidence, that he was engaged in a pleasure trip at the time of the accident, and that the loss sustained did not arise under circumstances that could be construed within the policy exclusion "use by the insured in the automobile business." Accordingly, the primary liability of Motors under the quoted provision of "Coverage E-Collision" is beyond question.

On the other hand, quoted condition 13 presents disputed language for construction. Motors maintains: (1) this provision is not limited to insurance by and for the insured; (2) the words "other insurance" as therein used should be liberally interpreted; and (3) the clause "provided, however, the insurance with respect to a temporary substitute automobile or non-owned automobile shall be excess insurance over any other valid and collectible insurance" is a lawful limitation which should be construed to mean "irrespective of whether other such insurance was procured by persons other than the named insured." In support of its contentions, reliance is placed upon Woodrich Construction Co. v. Indemnity Ins. Co., 252 Minn. 86, 89 N.W.2d 412 (Sup.Ct.1958). That case, however, is distinguishable in that it dealt with comprehensive liability and not collision insurance. Moreover, four employers' comprehensive general liability policies were before the court for analysis, comparison, and construction, and each of the four policies contained an "other insurance" clause.

The theory of Motors' defense at the trial level was that exclusion "C" of its policy relieved it of liability, and that, in any event, under condition 13 Motors could only be liable for excess insurance as the Fiat car was covered by an Emmco policy allegedly valid and collectible.

. . .

It is urged that the practice of insurance companies to include in their automobile insurance policies an "omnibus clause" insuring (in addition to the named insured) those who operate the insured vehicle, with the named insured's permission, is so common and widespread that this court may take judicial notice thereof. Insurance policies, and special clauses therein, are matters of contractual relationship between the parties, and their rights thereunder are ordinarily settled by the specific terms and conditions of their agreement. Judge (now Justice) Francis in the case of Mau v. Union Labor Life Ins. Co., 31 N.J.Super. 362, 106 A.2d 748 (App.Div.1954), refused to notice judicially that an inscription "WT–18 Ctf. No. 57," inserted under the designation "Number" on a policy of life insurance, indicated the existence of an employer's group insurance contract. *A fortiori*, this court should not take judicial notice of the existence of an "omnibus clause," or the terms and conditions of such a clause, or any part of an insurance contract which is not in evidence. Judicial notice is generally limited to facts of record and facts of general knowledge. "It is said that the term 'judicial notice' means no more than that the court will bring to its aid and consider, without proof of the facts, its knowledge of those matters of public concern which are known by all well-informed persons." C.J.S. Evidence § 6, p. 509. . . . The Emmco policy is not a matter of record or within common knowledge.

Motors advanced defenses at the trial level; interrogatories were propounded; and the Emmco policy was within reach of Motors by *subpoena duces tecum.* A review of the entire record does not reveal elements of surprise or injustice that would impel the exercise of our original jurisdiction under R.R. 1:5–4(a) and 2:5, as urged by Motors, or to invoke R.R. 1:27A and relax the rules that limit judicial review to matters presented to the trial court.

Judgment affirmed.

BERG v. ORIENTAL CONSOLIDATED MINING CO.

Supreme Court, Trial Term, New York County, 1947.
70 N.Y.S.2d 19.

. . .

BOTEIN, Justice. Plaintiff seeks in this action to recover from defendant, as paying agent of the Oriental Consolidated Mining Company, the sum of $23,016 allegedly due to him as liquidating dividends in dissolution upon certain shares of stock of that mining company.

These shares of stock were originally owned by plaintiff's aunt, to whom certificates were issued in October 1906. She was a resident of Switzerland; the certificates of stock were deposited in Switzerland. Plaintiff testified at the trial that in Switzerland in 1923 he acquired legal title to the shares from his aunt in consideration of his promise to support her for the rest of her life. He has bulwarked his testimony by proof that in December 1923 his aunt wrote the mining company a letter in which she stated that plaintiff "is now the owner of all my shares in your company." In addition he has had delivered to defendant the stock certificates, bearing an assignment in his favor dated May 8, 1933.

Defendant contends that plaintiff has failed to prove his title to the shares, arguing that the evidence fails to establish delivery of the certificates and of the assignment to plaintiff prior to his aunt's death in 1943. Defendant has established that on August 7, 1925 and again on September 14, 1932 plaintiff's aunt executed codicils to her will confirming a bequest of the shares to plaintiff, in the later of which codicils she stated that the certificates had been endorsed by her *in blank*. Defendant has submitted in evidence a document executed by plaintiff's aunt on August 1, 1939 in which she referred to plaintiff as her "heir presumptive" and in which she stated that he "has to dispose of *the income* of *my* Consolidated Mining Company Shares." It appears further that the certificates of stock were deposited by plaintiff's aunt in the Depositocasse of the City of Berne, Switzerland, some time prior to July 12, 1920 and remained there until 1945, when plaintiff arranged for their delivery to defendant. These facts, contends defendant, negative plaintiff's ownership as he has claimed it in this action and requires him to secure title to the shares by probate of his aunt's will. They at least raise an issue which can only be resolved by recourse to the laws of Switzerland.

It is well established that transfers of securities, checks and bills of exchange and shares of stock are governed by the laws of the country where the property is situated at the time of the transfer. 2 Beale, Treatise on the Conflict of Laws § 262.1; Weissman v. Banque de Bruxelles, 254 N.Y. 488, 494, 173 N.E. 835, 837 (1931); Hutchinson v. Ross, 262 N.Y. 381, 187 N.E. 65, 89 A.L.R. 1007 (1933); Direction der Disconto-Gesellschaft v. United States Steel Co., 267 U.S. 22, 28, 45 S.Ct. 207, 69 L.Ed. 495 (1925). Since the certificates of stock were physically present in Switzerland and the transfer to plaintiff is claimed to have been accomplished there, the law of that country must be applied to determine the validity of the transfer.

The plaintiff has claimed ownership and title to the stock under a contract made or transaction which took place in Switzerland, relating to certificates there situated. Considerations of justice and convenience require that plaintiff bear the burden of proving, in this case, that he acquired ownership and title in accordance with the laws of Switzerland and not that the defendant carry the burden of proving to the contrary. Arams v. Arams, 182 Misc. 328, 45 N.Y.S. 2d 251 (1944). The plaintiff's proof of the law of Switzerland is incomplete, is vigorously challenged by the defendant, and falls short of establishing his ownership and title under the facts which he has proved. While Section 344–a, Civil Practice Act, authorizes the court to take judicial notice of foreign law and to discover the same by independent research, nevertheless this right is to be exercised with caution in the discretion of the court. The section does not give "a judge the right to decide cases, not merely upon his own private discoveries of foreign law, but, also, upon his own translation of foreign languages . . . " and "must be applied with discriminating care and with due regard for all the 'legal niceties' of fair dealing and due process of law." Arams v. Arams, 182 Misc. 336, 45 N.Y.S.2d 251, 258 (1944).

Judgment is therefore directed for the defendant, and the complaint is dismissed, without prejudice.

PEOPLE OF THE STATE OF CALIFORNIA v. COWLES

Appellate Department, Superior Court, Alameda County, California, 1956.
142 Cal.App.2d Supp. 865, 298 P.2d 732.

Prosecution for parking violation. The Municipal Court of the Oakland-Piedmont Judicial District, Homer W. Buckley, J., rendered judgment of conviction and the defendant appealed on the ground that the Municipal Court being a court of record could not take judicial notice of a city ordinance. . . .

. . .

WAGLER, Presiding Judge. Defendant appeals from his conviction of a violation of Section 123 of the Oakland Municipal Code, which reads as follows:

> "It shall be unlawful for any person to park or leave standing any vehicle in any parking meter zone on any street, at any time during which the parking meter shows, indicates, registers or displays that the parking space is illegally in use,

> except during the time necessary to deposit United States coins in said parking meter so as to show, indicate, register, display or permit legal parking, and excepting also during the time from 6:00 P.M. to 8:00 A.M., and excepting also on holidays as designated in Section 128 of this Code when indicated by appropriate signs located on the parking meter."

Appellant does not question the sufficiency of the evidence. He contends, however, that the Municipal Court in which he was tried is a court of record; that as such, it does not take judicial notice of ordinances and his conviction must therefore be reversed, since no attempt was made on the part of the prosecution to prove either the contents or enactment of Section 123.

That the Municipal Court in question is a court of record, there can be no doubt. It was declared to be such by constitutional amendment enacted in 1924. See California Constitution, Article VI, § 12. That numerous cases categorically state that courts of record do not take judicial notice of ordinances, also cannot be doubted. See Grant v. California Bench Co., 76 Cal.App.2d 706, 173 P.2d 817 (1946); City of Tulare v. Hevren, 126 Cal. 226, 58 Pac. 530 (1899); Metteer v. Smith, 156 Cal. 572, 105 Pac. 735 (1910); Tilton v. Russek, 171 Cal. 731, 154 Pac. 860 (1916); Marysville Woolen Mills v. Smith, 178 Cal. 786, 175 Pac. 13 (1918).

This statement when originally made was no doubt factually correct. Its basis, however, is entirely historical, having been originally made when the only courts of record were courts of general jurisdiction. As such, they did not take judicial notice of ordinances which are private statutes.

Code of Civil Procedure, § 1875, subd. 2, provides that "courts take judicial notice of . . . whatever is established by law". Thus, in obedience to this section, the Superior Court as a court of general jurisdiction takes judicial notice of enactments of the State Legislature. By the same token, a Municipal Court which has exclusive jurisdiction of cases involving the violation of ordinances of cities or towns situated in the district in which it is established, P.C. § 1462, takes judicial notice of those ordinances.

. . .

> The rule is correctly stated in 18 Cal.Jur. (2) 452, as follows:
>
> "A municipal or justice court in which a proceeding is instituted for the express purpose of enforcing a city or county ordinance, which is the peculiar law of that forum, is bound to take notice of the ordinance. In such cases the rule that judicial notice will not be taken of ordinances does not apply. A municipal court holds the same relation to ordinances that the superior court holds to acts of the legislature, and the rule as to judicial notice of 'whatever is established by law' applies." See Ex parte Davis, 115 Cal. 445, 47 P. 258; Ex parte Hansen, 158 Cal. 494, 111 P. 528; People v. Mueller,

168 Cal. 521, 143 P. 748, L.R.A.1915B, 788; Ex parte Daniels, 183 Cal. 636, 192 P. 442, 21 A.L.R. 1172; People v. Crittenden, 93 Cal.App.2d Supp. 871, 209 P.2d 161.

Appellant makes the further point that even if the Municipal Court could take judicial notice of the ordinance in question, still the parking meter zone itself was not established by ordinance, but by mere *resolution* of the City Council. The court could not, says he, take judicial notice of a mere resolution. This presents an interesting question, which we do not here decide, because the record shows that "by stipulation a certified copy of an excerpt of the resolution" designating "14th Street, both sides from Jefferson to Harrison, as a parking meter zone" was in fact offered and received in evidence.

It is true, as appellant points out, that the record does not make it entirely clear that this resolution was adopted pursuant to the section of the Traffic Code which authorizes such resolutions. However, this is the only reasonable and logical inference. Furthermore, it must be presumed that official duty has been regularly performed. West's Ann.C.C.P. § 1963(15).

The judgment of conviction is affirmed.

PEOPLE OF THE STATE OF NEW YORK v. GERALD THOMAS PAYNE

District Court of New York, Suffolk County, Fifth District, 1969.
60 Misc.2d 830, 305 N.Y.S.2d 23.

. . .

DECISION

ANGELO MAUCERI, Judge. The defendant herein was charged with a violation of Section Six of the Vehicular Uses Great South Beach Ordinance of the Town of Islip, in particular "Vehicles for which a permit shall not have been issued are prohibited from being operated from May 15th to October 1st between the hours of 9 A.M. and 6 P.M. Between October 1st and May 15th, vehicles for which a permit shall have been issued are permitted to operate on the beach at any hour."

The definition of beach in the ordinance is "the beach shall encompass all real property at Fire Island and should include all of that area in the Town of Islip along the shore of the Atlantic Ocean lying between low water marks as a southerly boundary and the crest of the dunes as a northerly boundary".

The contention of the defendant in this matter is that the statute is unconstitutional, unreasonable, arbitrary and capricious and his argument in this regard is that the definition of the word beach is beyond any definitive scope, that the word has ever attained before in the English language and that this definition is arbitrary and unreasonable in that it has no foundation in fact or science that all the land on Fire Island is a beach.

The defendant further contends that the statute is arbitrary since there are no modes of transportation on Fire Island other than by vehicular travel and it is unreasonable to prohibit the residents of the island from said travel during the hours in the ordinance.

They further contend that since the ordinance doesn't prohibit all traffic during all hours, that the ordinance is not directed to its original purpose to prevent erosion of the dunes and of the sand areas on Fire Island. The Town of Islip is opposed to all of these contentions and feels that they have the right to declare as public policy the protection of a vital seashore area which can be eroded by extra heavy vehicular traffic. The Court has taken all of the arguments into consideration of both counsel and in considering the arguments of the defense counsel with regard to the validity of the instant statute, let it be said that it is the duty of the Court to sustain the police powers of the Legislature unless they are clearly, plainly and palpably in violation of the Constitution. (People v. Schweinler Press, 214 N.Y. 395, 108 N.E. 639, L.R.A.1918A, 1124 (1915)). Such enactment under the police power will not be invalidated merely because there is an earnest conflict of serious opinion as to its validity. Judicial review can only be limited to an inquiry as to whether there was a reasonable basis for the Legislature's determination. (People v. Ryan, 230 App.Div. 252, 243 N.Y.S.2d 644 (1963)). In order to invalidate the instant Legislation enacted under the police power of the Town of Islip, it must be shown as a matter of law, that the ordinance is not justifiable under any permissible or intelligent interpretation of all of the facts and is not a reasonable exercise of the police powers. (Wiggins v. Somers, 4 N.Y.2d 215, 173 N.Y.S.2d 579, 149 N.E.2d 869 (1958)). Reasonableness of necessity must be considered in the light of each problem as it is presented. (Town of Somers v. Camarco, 308 N.Y. 537, 127 N.E.2d 327 (1955)). And so, in this case the Court must consider the reasonableness of the exercise of the police powers of the Town of Islip in the Vehicular Ordinance in light of the problem presented. In L. I. Beach Buggy Association et al. v. Town of Islip et al., 58 Misc. 2d 295, 300, 295 N.Y.S.2d 268, 275–276 (1969), the Supreme Court of Suffolk County, Special Term, Justice Geiler presiding, the Court took judicial notice of the public policy of the United States with regard to the statement of the Secretary of the Interior who, on the 21st of July, 1967, stated the following:

> "The unrestricted use of motor vehicles in the Fire Island National Seashore, conflicts with the purposes of the Act of September 11th, 1964, authorizing the establishment of this Seashore, to conserve and preserve for the use of future generations certain relatively unspoiled and undeveloped beaches, dunes and other natural features within Suffolk County, N. Y., which possess high values to the Nation as examples of unspoiled areas of great natural beauty in close proximi-

> ty to large concentrations of urban population; conflicts with the administration of the Seashore to be established with the primary aim of conserving the natural resources located there; is inconsistent with statutory limitations on access to that section of the Seashore lying between the easterly boundary of the Brookhaven Town Park at Davis Park and the westerly boundary of the Smith Point County Park; and is incompatible with the preservation therein of the flora and fauna and the physiographic conditions now prevailing and conflicts with the preservation of such section and of the Sunken Forest Preserve in as nearly their present state and condition as possible".

This Court would be remiss if it did not extend that same judicial notice to the public policy of the United States and, it is clear to this Court that the Town of Islip has the police power to regulate vehicular traffic on Fire Island in order to protect the area from erosion, the municipality is justified in guarding against vehicles which, during the peak travel hours of the summer months, would contribute to erosion by continual travel over the sand area with distinct probability that the vehicles would traverse the dunes indiscriminately.

This ordinance is reasonably formulated to prevent as much as humanly possible in this regard. If the statute had prohibited vehicular traffic completely at all times, this certainly would be an arbitrary, unreasonable and capricious act.

The motions of the defendant to dismiss this information on the grounds of its unconstitutionality are denied. On the facts and on the law, after trial, the Court finds the defendant guilty as charged and sets the sentencing down before the Court on September 29th, 1969.

DECISIONS RELATING TO CHAPTER XIX, UNCONSTITUTIONALLY OBTAINED EVIDENCE

MAPP v. OHIO

Supreme Court of the United States, 1961.
367 U.S. 643, 81 S.Ct. 1684, 6 L.Ed.2d 1081.

. . .

Mr. Justice CLARK delivered the opinion of the Court.

Appellant stands convicted of knowingly having had in her possession and under her control certain lewd and lascivious books, pictures, and photographs in violation of § 2905.34 of Ohio's Revised Code.[1] As officially stated in the syllabus to its opinion, the Supreme Court of Ohio found that her conviction was valid though "based primarily upon the introduction in evidence of lewd and lascivious books and pictures unlawfully seized during an unlawful search of defendant's home . . . ." 170 Ohio St. 427–428, 166 N.E.2d 387, 388 (1960).

On May 23, 1957, three Cleveland police officers arrived at appellant's residence in that city pursuant to information that "a person [was] hiding out in the home, who was wanted for questioning in connection with a recent bombing, and that there was a large amount of policy paraphernalia being hidden in the home." Miss Mapp and her daughter by a former marriage lived on the top floor of the two-family dwelling. Upon their arrival at that house, the officers knocked on the door and demanded entrance but appellant, after telephoning her attorney, refused to admit them without a search warrant. They advised their headquarters of the situation and undertook a surveillance of the house.

The officers again sought entrance some three hours later when four or more additional officers arrived on the scene. When Miss Mapp did not come to the door immediately, at least one of the several doors to the house was forcibly opened[2] and the policemen gained admittance. Meanwhile Miss Mapp's attorney arrived, but the officers, having secured their own entry, and continuing in their defiance of the law, would permit him neither to see Miss Mapp nor to enter the house. It appears that Miss Mapp was halfway down

1. The statute provides in pertinent part that
"No person shall knowingly . . . have in his possession or under his control an obscene, lewd, or lascivious book [or] . . . picture . . . .
"Whoever violates this section shall be fined not less than two hundred nor more than two thousand dollars or imprisoned not less than one nor more than seven years or both."

2. A police officer testified that "we did pry the screen door to gain entrance"; the attorney on the scene testified that a policeman "tried . . . to kick in the door" and then "broke the glass in the door and somebody reached in and opened the door and let them in"; the appellant testified that "The back door was broken."

the stairs from the upper floor to the front door when the officers, in this highhanded manner, broke into the hall. She demanded to see the search warrant. A paper, claimed to be a warrant, was held up by one of the officers. She grabbed the "warrant" and placed it in her bosom. A struggle ensued in which the officers recovered the piece of paper and as a result of which they handcuffed appellant because she had been "belligerent" in resisting their official rescue of the "warrant" from her person. Running roughshod over appellant, a policeman "grabbed" her, "twisted [her] hand," and she "yelled [and] pleaded with him" because "it was hurting." Appellant, in handcuffs, was then forcibly taken upstairs to her bedroom where the officers searched a dresser, a chest of drawers, a closet and some suitcases. They also looked into a photo album and through personal papers belonging to the appellant. The search spread to the rest of the second floor including the child's bedroom, the living room, the kitchen and a dinette. The basement of the building and a trunk found therein were also searched. The obscene materials for possession of which she was ultimately convicted were discovered in the course of that widespread search.

At the trial no search warrant was produced by the prosecution, nor was the failure to produce one explained or accounted for. At best, "There is, in the record, considerable doubt as to whether there ever was any warrant for the search of defendant's home." 170 Ohio St. at page 430, 166 N.E.2d at page 389. The Ohio Supreme Court believed a "reasonable argument" could be made that the conviction should be reversed "because the 'methods' employed to obtain the [evidence] were such as to 'offend "a sense of justice,"'" but the court found determinative the fact that the evidence had not been taken "from defendant's person by the use of brutal or offensive physical force against defendant." 170 Ohio St. at page 431, 166 N.E.2d at pages 389–390.

The State says that even if the search were made without authority, or otherwise unreasonably, it is not prevented from using the unconstitutionally seized evidence at trial, citing Wolf v. People of State of Colorado, 338 U.S. 25, at page 33, 69 S.Ct. 1359, at page 1364, 93 L.Ed. 1782 (1949), in which this Court did indeed hold "that in a prosecution in a State court for a State crime the Fourteenth Amendment does not forbid the admission of evidence obtained by an unreasonable search and seizure." On this appeal, of which we have noted probable jurisdiction, 364 U.S. 868, 81 S.Ct. 111, 5 L.Ed.2d 90 (1960), it is urged once again that we review that holding.[3]

3. Other issues have been raised on this appeal but, in the view we have taken of the case, they need not be decided. Although appellant chose to urge what may have appeared to be the surer ground for favorable disposition and did not insist that Wolf be overruled, the *amicus curiae*, who was also permitted to participate in the oral argument, did urge the Court to overrule Wolf.

I.

Seventy-five years ago, in Boyd v. United States, 116 U.S. 616, 630, 6 S.Ct. 524, 532, 29 L.Ed. 746 (1886), considering the Fourth[4] and Fifth Amendments as running "almost into each other"[5] on the facts before it, this Court held that the doctrines of those Amendments

> "apply to all invasions on the part of the government and its employes of the sanctity of a man's home and the privacies of life. It is not the breaking of his doors, and the rummaging of his drawers, that constitutes the essence of the offence; but it is the invasion of his indefeasible right of personal security, personal liberty and private property . . . . Breaking into a house and opening boxes and drawers are circumstances of aggravation; but any forcible and compulsory extortion of a man's own testimony or of his private papers to be used as evidence to convict him of crime or to forfeit his goods, is within the condemnation . . . [of those Amendments]."

The Court noted that

> "constitutional provisions for the security of person and property should be liberally construed. . . . It is the duty of courts to be watchful for the constitutional rights of the citizen, and against any stealthy encroachments thereon." At page 635 of 116 U.S., at page 535 of 6 S.Ct.

In this jealous regard for maintaining the integrity of individual rights, the Court gave life to Madison's prediction that "independent tribunals of justice . . . will be naturally led to resist every enroachment upon rights expressly stipulated for in the Constitution by the declaration of rights." I Annals of Cong. 439 (1789). Concluding, the Court specifically referred to the use of the evidence there seized as "unconstitutional." At page 638 of 116 U.S., at page 536 of 6 S.Ct.

Less than 30 years after Boyd, this Court, in Weeks v. United States, 1914, 232 U.S. 383, at pages 391–392, 34 S.Ct. 341, at page 344, 58 L.Ed. 652, stated that

4. "The right of the people to be secure in their persons, houses, papers, and effects, against unreasonable searches and seizures, shall not be violated, and no warrants shall issue, but upon probable cause, supported by oath or affirmation, and particularly describing the place to be searched and the persons or things to be seized."

5. The close connection between the concepts later embodied in these two Amendments had been noted at least as early as 1765 by Lord Camden, on whose opinion in Entick v. Carrington, 19 Howell's State Trials 1029, the Boyd court drew heavily. Lord Camden had noted, at 1073:

"It is very certain, that the law obligeth no man to accuse himself; because the necessary means of compelling self-accusation, falling upon the innocent as well as the guilty, would be both cruel and unjust; and it should seem, that search for evidence is disallowed upon the same principle. There too the innocent would be confounded with the guilty."

> "the 4th Amendment . . . put the courts of the United States and Federal officials, in the exercise of their power and authority, under limitations and restraints [and] . . . forever secure[d] the people, their persons, houses, papers, and effects, against all unreasonable searches and seizures under the guise of law . . . and the duty of giving to it force and effect is obligatory upon all entrusted under our Federal system with the enforcement of the laws."

Specifically dealing with the use of the evidence unconstitutionally seized, the Court concluded:

> "If letters and private documents can thus be seized and held and used in evidence against a citizen accused of an offense, the protection of the Fourth Amendment declaring his right to be secure against such searches and seizures is of no value, and, so far as those thus placed are concerned, might as well be stricken from the Constitution. The efforts of the courts and their officials to bring the guilty to punishment, praiseworthy as they are, are not to be aided by the sacrifice of those great principles established by years of endeavor and suffering which have resulted in their embodiment in the fundamental law of the land." At page 393 of 232 U.S., at page 344 of 34 S.Ct.

Finally, the Court in that case clearly stated that use of the seized evidence involved "a denial of the constitutional rights of the accused." At page 398 of 232 U.S., at page 346 of 34 S.Ct. Thus, in the year 1914, in the Weeks case, this Court "for the first time" held that "in a federal prosecution the Fourth Amendment barred the use of evidence secured through an illegal search and seizure." Wolf v. People of State of Colorado, supra, 338 U.S. at page 28, 69 S.Ct. at page 1361. This Court has ever since required of federal law officers a strict adherence to that command which this Court has held to be a clear, specific, and constitutionally required—even if judicially implied—deterrent safeguard without insistence upon which the Fourth Amendment would have been reduced to "a form of words." Holmes J., Silverthorne Lumber Co. v. United States, 251 U.S. 385, 392, 40 S.Ct. 182, 183, 64 L.Ed. 319 (1920). It meant, quite simply, that "conviction by means of unlawful seizures and enforced confessions . . . should find no sanction in the judgments of the courts . . . ," Weeks v. United States, supra, 232 U.S. at page 392, 34 S.Ct. at page 344, and that such evidence "shall not be used at all." Silverthorne Lumber Co. v. United States, supra, 251 U.S. at page 392, 40 S.Ct. at page 183.

There are in the cases of this Court some passing references to the Weeks rule as being one of evidence. But the plain and unequivocal language of Weeks—and its later paraphrase in Wolf—to the effect that the Weeks rule is of constitutional origin, remains entirely undisturbed. In Byars v. United States, 273 U.S. 28, at pages 29–30, 47 S.Ct. 248, at pages 248–249, 71 L.Ed. 520 (1927), a unanimous Court declared that "the doctrine [cannot] . . . be tolerated *under our constitutional system,* that evidences of crime discovered by a federal officer in making a search without lawful warrant may be used against the victim of the unlawful search where a timely challenge has been interposed." (Emphasis added.) The Court, in Olmstead v. United States, 1928, 277 U.S. 438, at page 462, 48 S.Ct. 564, 567, 72 L.Ed. 944, in unmistakable language restated the Weeks rule:

> "The striking outcome of the Weeks case and those which followed it was the sweeping declaration that the Fourth Amendment, although not referring to or limiting the use of evidence in court, really forbade its introduction if obtained by government officers through a violation of the amendment."

In McNabb v. United States, 1943, 318 U.S. 332, at pages 339–340, 63 S.Ct. 608, at page 612, 87 L.Ed. 819, we note this statement:

> "[A] conviction in the federal courts, the foundation of which is evidence obtained in disregard of liberties deemed fundamental by the Constitution, cannot stand. Boyd v. United States . . . Weeks v. United States . . . . And this Court has, on Constitutional grounds, set aside convictions, both in the federal and state courts, which were based upon confessions 'secured by protracted and repeated questioning of ignorant and untutored persons, in whose minds the power of officers was greatly magnified' . . . or 'who have been unlawfully held incommunicado without advice of friends or counsel' . . . ."

. . .

II.

In 1949, 35 years after Weeks was announced, this Court, in Wolf v. People of State of Colorado, supra, again for the first time,[6] discussed the effect of the Fourth Amendment upon the States through the operation of the Due Process Clause of the Fourteenth Amendment. It said:

> "[W]e have no hesitation in saying that were a State affirmatively to sanction such police incursion into privacy it would run counter to the guaranty of the Fourteenth Amendment." At page 28 of 338 U.S., at page 1361 of 69 S.Ct.

Nevertheless, after declaring that the "security of one's privacy against arbitrary intrusion by the police" is "implicit in 'the concept of ordered liberty' and as such enforceable against the States through the Due Process Clause," cf. Palko v. State of Connecticut, 302 U.S. 319, 58 S.Ct. 149, 82 L.Ed. 288 (1937), and announcing that it "stout-

6. See, however, National Safe Deposit Co. v. Stead, 232 U.S. 58, 34 S.Ct. 209, 58 L.Ed. 504 (1914), and Adams v. People of State of New York, 192 U.S. 585, 24 S.Ct. 372, 48 L.Ed. 575 (1904).

ly adhere[d]" to the Weeks decision, the Court decided that the Weeks exclusionary rule would not then be imposed upon the States as "an essential ingredient of the right." 338 U.S. at pages 27–29, 69 S.Ct. at page 1362. The Court's reasons for not considering essential to the right to privacy, as a curb imposed upon the States by the Due Process Clause, that which decades before had been posited as part and parcel of the Fourth Amendment's limitation upon federal encroachment of individual privacy, were bottomed on factual considerations.

While they are not basically relevant to a decision that the exclusionary rule is an essential ingredient of the Fourth Amendment as the right it embodies is vouchsafed against the States by the Due Process Clause, we will consider the current validity of the factual grounds upon which Wolf was based.

The Court in Wolf first stated that "[t]he contrariety of views of the States" on the adoption of the exclusionary rule of Weeks was "particularly impressive" (338 U.S. at page 29, 69 S.Ct. at page 1362); and, in this connection, that it could not "brush aside the experience of States which deem the incidence of such conduct by the police too slight to call for a deterrent remedy . . . by overriding the [States'] relevant rules of evidence." At pages 31–32 of 338 U.S., at page 1363 of 69 S.Ct. While in 1949, prior to the Wolf case, almost two-thirds of the States were opposed to the use of the exclusionary rule, now, despite the Wolf case, more than half of those since passing upon it, by their own legislative or judicial decision, have wholly or partly adopted or adhered to the Weeks rule. See Elkins v. United States, 364 U.S. 206, Appendix, at pages 224–232, 80 S.Ct. 1437, at pages 1448–1453, 4 L.Ed.2d 1669 (1960). Significantly, among those now following the rule is California, which, according to its highest court, was "compelled to reach that conclusion because other remedies have completely failed to secure compliance with the constitutional provisions . . . ." People v. Cahan, 44 Cal.2d 434, 445, 282 P.2d 905, 911, 50 A.L.R.2d 513 (1955). In connection with this California case, we note that the second basis elaborated in Wolf in support of its failure to enforce the exclusionary doctrine against the States was that "other means of protection" have been afforded "the right to privacy."[7] 338 U.S. at page 30, 69 S.Ct. at page 1362.

7. Less than half of the States have any criminal provisions relating directly to unreasonable searches and seizures. The punitive sanctions of the 23 States attempting to control such invasions of the right of privacy may be classified as follows:

Criminal Liability of Affiant for Malicious Procurement of Search Warrant.—Ala.Code, 1958, Tit. 15, § 99; Alaska Comp.Laws Ann.1949, § 66-7-15; Ariz.Rev.Stat.Ann.1956, § 13-1454; Cal.Pen.Code § 170; Fla.Stat.1959, § 933.16, F.S.A.; Ga.Code Ann.1953, § 27-301; Idaho Code Ann.1948, § 18-709; Iowa Code Ann., 1950, § 751.38; Minn.Stat.Ann.1947, § 613.54; Mont. Rev.Codes Ann.1947, § 94-35-122; Nev. Rev.Stat. §§ 199.130, 199.140; N.J.Stat. Ann.1940, § 33:1-64; N.Y.Pen.Law, § 1786, N.Y.Code Crim.Proc. § 811; N.C. Gen.Stat.1953, § 15-27 (applies to "officers" only); N.D.Century Code Ann. 1960, §§ 12-17-08, 29-29-18; Okla.Stat. 1951, Tit. 21, § 585, Tit. 22, § 1239; Ore. Rev.Stat. § 141.990; S.D.Code, 1939 (Supp.1960) § 34.9904; Utah Code Ann. 1953, § 77-54-21.

The experience of California that such other remedies have been worthless and futile is buttressed by the experience of other States. The obvious futility of relegating the Fourth Amendment to the protection of other remedies has, moreover, been recognized by this Court since Wolf. See Irvine v. People of State of California, 347 U.S. 128, 137, 74 S.Ct. 381, 385, 98 L.Ed. 561 (1954).

Likewise, time has set its face against what Wolf called the "weighty testimony" of People v. Defore, 242 N.Y. 13, 150 N.E. 585 (1926). There Justice (then Judge) Cardozo, rejecting adoption of the Weeks exclusionary rule in New York, had said that "[t]he Federal rule as it stands is either too strict or too lax." 242 N.Y. at page 22, 150 N.E. at page 588. However, the force of that reasoning has been largely vitiated by later decisions of this Court. These include the recent discarding of the "silver platter" doctrine which allowed federal judicial use of evidence seized in violation of the Constitution by state agents, Elkins v. United States, supra; the relaxation of the formerly strict requirements as to standing to challenge the use of evidence thus seized, so that now the procedure of exclusion, "ultimately referable to constitutional safeguards," is available to anyone even "legitimately on [the] premises" unlawfully searched, Jones v. United States, 362 U.S. 257, 266–267, 80 S.Ct. 725, 734, 4 L.Ed.2d 697 (1960); and finally, the formulation of a method to prevent state use of evidence unconstitutionally seized by federal agents, Rea v. United States, 350 U.S. 214, 76 S.Ct. 292, 100 L.Ed. 233 (1956). Because there can be no fixed formula, we are admittedly met with "recurring questions of the reasonableness of searches," but less is not to be expected when dealing with a Constitution, and, at any rate, "[r]easonableness is in the first instance for the [trial court] to determine." United States v. Rabinowitz, 339 U.S. 56, 63, 70 S.Ct. 430, 434, 94 L.Ed. 653 (1950).

It, therefore, plainly appears that the factual considerations supporting the failure of the Wolf Court to include the Weeks exclusionary rule when it recognized the enforceability of the right to privacy against the States in 1949, while not basically relevant to the constitutional consideration, could not, in any analysis, now be deemed controlling.

Criminal Liability of Magistrate Issuing Warrant Without Supporting Affidavit.—N.C.Gen.Stat.1953, § 15–27; Va.Code Ann., 1960 Replacement Volume, § 19.1–89.

Criminal Liability of Officer Willfully Exceeding Authority of Search Warrant.—Fla.Stat.Ann.1944, § 933.17; Iowa Code Ann., 1950, § 751.39; Minn. Stat.Ann.1947, § 613.54; Nev.Rev.Stat. § 199.450; N.Y.Pen.Law, § 1847, N.Y. Code Crim.Proc. § 812; N.D.Century Code Ann.1960, §§ 12–17–07, 29–29–19; Okla.Stat.1951, Tit. 21, § 536, Tit. 22, § 1240; S.D.Code, 1939 (Supp.1960) § 34.9905; Tenn.Code Ann.1955, § 40–510; Utah Code Ann.1953, § 77–54–22.

Criminal Liability of Officer for Search with Invalid Warrant or no Warrant.—Idaho Code Ann.1948, § 18–703; Minn.Stat.Ann.1947, §§ 613.53, 621.17; Mo.Stat.Ann.1953, § 558.190; Mont.Rev. Codes Ann.1947, § 94–3506; N.J.Stat. Ann.1940, § 33:1–65; N.Y.Pen.Law, § 1846; N.D.Century Code Ann.1960, § 12–17–06; Okla.Stat.Ann.1958, Tit. 21, § 535; Utah Code Ann.1953, § 76–28–52; Va.Code Ann.1960 Replacement Volume, § 19.1–88; Wash.Rev.Code §§ 10.79.040, 10.79.045.

III.

Some five years after Wolf, in answer to a plea made here Term after Term that we overturn its doctrine on applicability of the Weeks exclusionary rule, this Court indicated that such should not be done until the States had "adequate opportunity to adopt or reject the [Weeks] rule." Irvine v. People of State of California, supra, 347 U.S. at page 134, 74 S.Ct. at page 384. There again it was said:

> "Never until June of 1949 did this Court hold the basic search-and-seizure prohibition in any way applicable to the states under the Fourteenth Amendment." Ibid.

And only last Term, after again carefully re-examining the Wolf doctrine in Elkins v. United States, supra, the Court pointed out that "the controlling principles" as to search and seizure and the problem of admissibility "seemed clear" (364 U.S. at page 212, 1441 of 80 S.Ct.) until the announcement in Wolf "that the Due Process Clause of the Fourteenth Amendment does not itself require state courts to adopt the exclusionary rule" of the Weeks case. At page 213 of 364 U.S., at page 1442 of 80 S.Ct. At the same time, the Court pointed out, "the underlying constitutional doctrine which Wolf established . . . that the Federal Constitution . . . prohibits unreasonable searches and seizures by state officers" had undermined the "foundation upon which the admissibility of state-seized evidence in a federal trial originally rested . . . ." Ibid. The Court concluded that it was therefore obliged to hold, although it chose the narrower ground on which to do so, that all evidence obtained by an unconstitutional search and seizure was inadmissible in a federal court regardless of its source. Today we once again examine Wolf's constitutional documentation of the right to privacy free from unreasonable state intrusion, and, after its dozen years on our books, are led by it to close the only courtroom door remaining open to evidence secured by official lawlessness in flagrant abuse of that basic right, reserved to all persons as a specific guarantee against that very same unlawful conduct. We hold that all evidence obtained by searches and seizures in violation of the Constitution is, by that same authority, inadmissible in a state court.

IV.

Since the Fourth Amendment's right of privacy has been declared enforceable against the States through the Due Process Clause of the Fourteenth, it is enforceable against them by the same sanction of exclusion as is used against the Federal Government. Were it otherwise, then just as without the Weeks rule the assurance against unreasonable federal searches and seizures would be "a form of words", valueless and undeserving of mention in a perpetual charter of inestimable human liberties, so too, without that rule the freedom from state invasions of privacy would be so ephemeral and so neatly severed from its conceptual nexus with the freedom from all brutish means of coercing evidence as not to merit this Court's high regard as a freedom "implicit in 'the concept of ordered liberty.'" At the time that the Court held in Wolf that the Amendment was applicable to the States through the Due Process Clause, the cases of this Court, as we have seen, had steadfastly held that as to federal officers the Fourth Amendment included the exclusion of the evidence seized in violation of its provisions. Even Wolf "stoutly adhered" to that proposition. The right to privacy, when conceded operatively enforceable against the States, was not susceptible of destruction by avulsion of the sanction upon which its protection and enjoyment had always been deemed dependent under the Boyd, Weeks and Silverthorne cases. Therefore, in extending the substantive protections of due process to all constitutionally unreasonable searches—state or federal—it was logically and constitutionally necessary that the exclusion doctrine—an essential part of the right to privacy—be also insisted upon as an essential ingredient of the right newly recognized by the Wolf case. In short, the admission of the new constitutional right by Wolf could not consistently tolerate denial of its most important constitutional privilege, namely, the exclusion of the evidence which an accused had been forced to give by reason of the unlawful seizure. To hold otherwise is to grant the right but in reality to withhold its privilege and enjoyment. Only last year the Court itself recognized that the purpose of the exclusionary rule "is to deter—to compel respect for the constitutional guaranty in the only effectively available way—by removing the incentive to disregard it." Elkins v. United States, supra, 364 U.S. at page 217, 80 S.Ct. at page 1444.

Indeed, we are aware of no restraint, similar to that rejected today, conditioning the enforcement of any other basic constitutional right. The right to privacy, no less important than any other right carefully and particularly reserved to the people, would stand in marked contrast to all other rights declared as "basic to a free society." Wolf v. People of State of Colorado, supra, 338 U.S. at page 27, 69 S.Ct. at page 1361. This Court has not hesitated to enforce as strictly against the States as it does against the Federal Government the rights of free speech and of a free press, the rights to notice and to a fair, public trial, including, as it does, the right not to be convicted by use of a coerced confession, however logically relevant it be, and without regard to its reliability. Rogers v. Richmond, 365 U.S. 534, 81 S.Ct. 735, 5 L.Ed.2d 760 (1961). And nothing could be more certain than that when a coerced confession is involved, "the relevant rules of evidence" are overridden without regard to "the incidence of such conduct by the police," slight or frequent. Why should not the same rule apply to what is tantamount to coerced testimony by way of unconstitutional seizure of goods, papers, effects, documents, etc.? . . . The philosophy of each Amendment and of each freedom is complementary to, although not dependent upon, that of the other in its sphere of influence—the very least that together they assure in either sphere is that no man is to be convicted on unconstitutional evidence. Cf. Rochin v. People of State of California, 342 U.S. 165, 173, 72 S.Ct. 205, 210, 96 L.Ed. 183 (1952).

V.

Moreover, our holding that the exclusionary rule is an essential part of both the Fourth and Fourteenth Amendments is not only the logical dictate of prior cases, but it also makes very good sense. There is no war between the Constitution and common sense. Presently, a federal prosecutor may make no use of evidence illegally seized, but a State's attorney across the street may, although he supposedly is operating under the enforceable prohibitions of the same Amendment. Thus the State, by admitting evidence unlawfully seized, serves to encourage disobedience to the Federal Constitution which it is bound to uphold. Moreover, as was said in Elkins, "[t]he very essence of a healthy federalism depends upon the avoidance of needless conflict between state and federal courts." 364 U.S. at page 221, 80 S.Ct. at page 1446. Such a conflict, hereafter needless, arose this very Term, in Wilson v. Schnettler, 365 U.S. 381, 81 S.Ct. 632, 5 L.Ed. 2d 620 (1961), in which, and in spite of the promise made by Rea, we gave full recognition to our practice in this regard by refusing to restrain a federal officer from testifying in a state court as to evidence unconstitutionally seized by him in the performance of his duties. Yet the double standard recognized until today hardly put such a thesis into practice. In non-exclusionary States, federal officers, being human, were by it invited to and did, as our cases indicate, step across the street to the State's attorney with their unconstitutionally seized evidence. Prosecution on the basis of that evidence was then had in a state court in utter disregard of the enforceable Fourth Amendment. If the fruits of an unconstitutional search had been inadmissible in both state and federal courts, this inducement to evasion would have been sooner eliminated. There would be no need to reconcile such cases as Rea and Schnettler, each pointing up the hazardous uncertainties of our heretofore ambivalent approach.

Federal-state cooperation in the solution of crime under constitutional standards will be promoted, if only by recognition of their now mutual obligation to respect the same fundamental criteria in their approaches. "However much in a particular case insistence upon such rules may appear as a technicality that inures to the benefit of a guilty person, the history of the criminal law proves that tolerance of shortcut methods in law enforcement impairs its enduring effectiveness." Miller v. United States, 357 U.S. 301, 313, 78 S.Ct. 1190, 1197, 2 L.Ed.2d 1332 (1958). Denying shortcuts to only one of two cooperating law enforcement agencies tends naturally to breed legitimate suspicion of "working arrangements" whose results are equally tainted. Byars v. United States, 273 U.S. 28, 47 S.Ct. 248, 71 L.Ed. 520 (1927); Lustig v. United States, 338 U.S. 74, 69 S.Ct. 1372, 93 L.Ed. 1819 (1949).

There are those who say, as did Justice (then Judge) Cardozo, that under our constitutional exclusionary doctrine "[t]he criminal is to go free because the constable has blundered." People v. Defore, 242 N.Y. at page 21, 150 N.E. at page 587. In some cases this will undoubtedly be the result.[9] But, as was said in Elkins, "there is another consideration—the imperative of judicial integrity." 364 U.S. at page 222, 80 S.Ct. at page 1447. The criminal goes free, if he must, but it is the law that sets him free. Nothing can destroy a government more quickly than its failure to observe its own laws, or worse, its disregard of the charter of its own existence. As Mr. Justice Brandeis, dissenting, said in Olmstead v. United States, 277 U.S. 438, 485, 48 S.Ct. 564, 575, 72 L.Ed. 944 (1928): "Our government is the potent, the omnipresent teacher. For good or for ill, it teaches the whole people by its example. . . . If the government becomes a lawbreaker, it breeds contempt for law; it invites every man to become a law unto himself; it invites anarchy." Nor can it lightly be assumed that, as a practical matter, adoption of the exclusionary rule fetters law enforcement. Only last year this Court expressly considered that contention and found that "pragmatic evidence of a sort" to the contrary was not wanting. Elkins v. United States, supra, 364 U.S. at page 218, 80 S.Ct. at page 1444. The Court noted that

> "The federal courts themselves have operated under the exclusionary rule of Weeks for almost half a century; yet it has not been suggested either that the Federal Bureau of Investigation [10] has thereby been rendered ineffective, or that the administration of criminal justice in the federal courts has thereby been disrupted. Moreover, the experience of the states is impressive . . . . . The movement towards the rule of exclusion has been halting but seemingly inexorable." Id., 364 U.S. at pages 218–219, 80 S.Ct. at pages 1444–1445.

The ignoble shortcut to conviction left open to the State tends to destroy the entire system of constitutional restraints on which the liberties of the people rest. Having once recognized that the right to privacy embodied in the Fourth Amendment is enforceable against the States, and that the right to be secure against rude invasions of

9. As is always the case, however, state procedural requirements governing assertion and pursuance of direct and collateral constitutional challenges to criminal prosecutions must be respected. We note, moreover, that the class of state convictions possibly affected by this decision is of relatively narrow compass when compared with Burns v. State of Ohio, 360 U.S. 252, 79 S.Ct. 1164, 3 L.Ed.2d 1209 (1959); Griffin v. People of State of Illinois, 351 U.S. 12, 76 S.Ct. 585, 100 L.Ed. 891 (1956) and Commonwealth of Pennsylvania ex rel. Herman v. Claudy, 350 U.S. 116, 76 S.Ct. 223, 100 L.Ed. 126 (1956). In those cases the same contention was urged and later proved unfounded. In any case, further delay in reaching the present result could have no effect other than to compound the difficulties.

10. See the remarks of Mr. Hoover, Director of the Federal Bureau of Investigation, FBI Law Enforcement Bulletin, September, 1952, pp. 1–2, quoted in Elkins v. United States, 364 U.S. 206, 218–219, 80 S.Ct. 1437, 1444–1445, note 8 (1960).

privacy by state officers is, therefore, constitutional in origin, we can no longer permit that right to remain an empty promise. Because it is enforceable in the same manner and to like effect as other basic rights secured by the Due Process Clause, we can no longer permit it to be revocable at the whim of any police officer who, in the name of law enforcement itself, chooses to suspend its enjoyment. Our decision, founded on reason and truth, gives to the individual no more than that which the Constitution guarantees him, to the police officer no less than that to which honest law enforcement is entitled, and, to the courts, that judicial integrity so necessary in the true administration of justice.

The judgment of the Supreme Court of Ohio is reversed and the cause remanded for further proceedings not inconsistent with this opinion.

Reversed and remanded.

. . .

Concurring opinions of Mr. Justice BLACK, Mr. Justice DOUGLAS, Memorandum of Mr. Justice STEWART and dissenting opinion of Mr. Justice HARLAN, joined by Mr. Justice FRANKFURTER and Mr. Justice WHITTAKER, deleted.

PEOPLE OF THE STATE OF NEW YORK v. MALINSKY

Court of Appeals of New York, 1967.
19 N.Y.2d 262, 279 N.Y.S.2d 20.

. . .

PER CURIAM. Upon the hearing which we directed when this case was previously before us (15 N.Y.2d 86, 262 N.Y.S.2d 65, 209 N.E.2d 694 (1965)), the People declined to disclose the name of the informer, offered no evidence of his reliability and failed to adduce any other evidence sufficient to establish the existence of probable cause for the arrests of the defendants (52 Misc.2d 717, 278 N.Y.S.2d 15 (1972)). Since then, the search incident to those arrests was illegal, the motion to suppress the evidence thereby obtained should have been granted. It follows that the proof upon which the convictions restεd fell short of establishing guilt beyond a reasonable doubt.

The defendants' motion to restore the appeal to the calendar is granted and, upon such restoration, the judgment of conviction should be reversed and the indictment dismissed.

FULD, C. J., and VAN VOORHIS, BURKE, SCILEPPI and BERGAN, JJ., concur.

KEATING and BREITEL, JJ., taking no part.

Motion to restore appeal to the calendar of the Court of Appeals granted.

Judgment reversed and indictment dismissed.

UNITED STATES v. VENTRESCA

Supreme Court of the United States, 1965.
380 U.S. 102, 85 S.Ct. 741, 13 L.Ed.2d 684.

Mr. Justice GOLDBERG delivered the opinion of the Court.

Respondent, Ventresca, was convicted in the United States District Court for the District of Massachusetts of possessing and operating an illegal distillery. The conviction was reversed by the Court of Appeals (one judge dissenting) on the ground that the affidavit for a search warrant pursuant to which the still was found was insufficient to establish probable cause. 324 F.2d 864.

The affidavit upon which the warrant was issued was made and submitted to a United States Commissioner on August 31, 1961, by Walter Mazaka, an Investigator for the Alcohol and Tobacco Tax Division of the Internal Revenue Service. He stated that he had reason to believe that an illegal distillery was in operation in respondent, Ventresca's, house at 148½ Coburn Avenue in Worcester, Massachusetts. The grounds for this belief were set forth in detail in the affidavit, prefaced with the following statement:

> "Based upon observations made by me, and based upon information received officially from other Investigators attached to the Alcohol and Tobacco Tax Division assigned to this investigation, and reports orally made to me describing the results of their observations and investigation, this request for the issuance of a search warrant is made."

The affidavit then described seven different occasions between July 28 and August 30, 1961, when a Pontiac car was driven into the yard to the rear of Ventresca's house. On four occasions the car carried loads of sugar in 60-pound bags; it made two trips loaded with empty tin cans; and once it was merely observed as being heavily laden. Garry, the car's owner, and Incardone, a passenger, were seen on several occasions loading the car at Ventresca's house and later unloading apparently full five-gallon cans at Garry's house late in the evening. On August 28, after a delivery of empty tin cans to Ventresca's house, Garry and Incardone were observed carrying from the house cans which appeared to be filled and placing them in the trunk of Garry's car. The affidavit went on to state that at about 4 a. m. on August 18, and at about 4 a. m. on August 30, "Investigators" smelled the odor of fermenting mash as they walked along the sidewalk in front of Ventresca's house. On August 18 they heard, "[a]t or about the same time, . . . certain metallic noises." On August 30, the day before the warrant was applied for, they heard (as they smelled the mash) "sounds similar to that of a motor or a pump coming from the direction of" Ventresca's house. The affidavit concluded: "The foregoing information is based upon personal knowledge and information which has been obtained from Investigators of the Alcohol and Tobacco Tax Division, Internal Revenue Service, who had been assigned to this investigation."

The District Court upheld the validity of the warrant on a motion to suppress. The divided Court of Appeals held the warrant insufficient because it read the affidavit as not specifically stating in so many words that the information it contained was based upon the personal knowledge of Mazaka or other reliable investigators. The Court of Appeals reasoned that all of the information recited in the affidavit might conceivably have been obtained by investigators other than Mazaka, and it could not be certain that the information of these other investigators was not in turn based upon hearsay received from unreliable informants rather than their own personal observations. For this reason the court found that probable cause had not been established. 324 F.2d, at 868–870. We granted certiorari to consider the standards by which a reviewing court should approach the interpretation of affidavits supporting warrants which have been duly issued by examining magistrates. 377 U.S. 989, 84 S.Ct. 1910, 12 L.Ed.2d 1043 (1963). For the reasons stated below, we reverse the judgment of the Court of Appeals.

I.

The Fourth Amendment states:

> "The right of the people to be secure in their persons, houses, papers, and effects, against unreasonable searches and seizures, shall not be violated, and no Warrants shall issue, but upon probable cause supported by Oath or affirmation, and particularly describing the place to be searched, and the persons or things to be seized."

We begin our analysis of this constitutional rule mindful of the fact that in this case a search was made pursuant to a search warrant. In discussing the Fourth Amendment policy against unnecessary invasions of privacy, we stated in Aguilar v. State of Texas, 378 U.S. 108, 84 S.Ct. 1509, 12 L.Ed.2d 723 (1949):

> "An evaluation of the constitutionality of a search warrant should begin with the rule that 'the informed and deliberate determinations of magistrates empowered to issue warrants . . . are to be preferred over the hurried action of officers . . . who may happen to make arrests.' United States v. Lefkowitz, 285 U.S. 452, 464, 52 S.Ct. 420, 423, 76 L.Ed. 877 (1944). The reasons for this rule go to the foundations of the Fourth Amendment." 378 U.S., at 110–111, 84 S.Ct., at 1512.

In Jones v. United States, 362 U.S. 257, 270, 80 S.Ct. 725, 735, 4 L.Ed.2d 697 (1948), this Court, strongly supporting the preference to be accorded searches under a warrant, indicated that in a doubtful or marginal case a search under a warrant may be sustainable where without one it would fall. In Johnson v. United States, 333 U.S. 10, 68 S.Ct. 367, 92 L.Ed. 436 (1946), and Chapman v. United States, 365 U.S. 610, 81 S.Ct. 776, 5 L.Ed.2d 828 (1948), the Court, in condemning searches by officers who invaded premises without a warrant, plainly intimated that had the proper course of obtaining a warrant from a magistrate been followed and had the magistrate on the same evidence available to the police made a finding of probable cause, the search under the warrant would have been sustained. Mr. Justice Jackson stated for the Court in Johnson:

> "The point of the Fourth Amendment, which often is not grasped by zealous officers, is not that it denies law enforcement the support of the usual inferences which reasonable men draw from evidence. Its protection consists in requiring that those inferences be drawn by a neutral and detached magistrate instead of being judged by the officer engaged in the often competitive enterprise of ferreting out crime. Any assumption that evidence sufficient to support a magistrate's disinterested determination to issue a search warrant will justify the officers in making a search without a warrant would reduce the Amendment to a nullity and leave the people's homes secure only in the discretion of police officers." Johnson v. United States, supra, 333 U.S. at 13–14, 68 S.Ct. at 369.

The fact that exceptions to the requirement that searches and seizures be undertaken only after obtaining a warrant are limited underscores the preference accorded police action taken under a warrant as against searches and seizures without one.

While a warrant may issue only upon a finding of "probable cause," this Court has long held that "the term 'probable cause' . . . means less than evidence which would justify condemnation," Locke v. United States, 7 Cranch 339, 348, 3 L.Ed. 364 (1813), and that a finding of "probable cause" may rest upon evidence which is not legally competent in a criminal trial. Draper v. United States, 358 U.S. 307, 311, 79 S.Ct. 329, 332, 3 L.Ed.2d 327 (1959). As the Court stated in Brinegar v. United States, 338 U.S. 160, 173, 69 S.Ct. 1302, 1309, 93 L.Ed. 1879 (1949), "There is a large difference between the two things to be proved [guilt and probable cause], as well as between the tribunals which determine them, and therefore a like difference in the *quanta* and modes of proof required to establish them." Thus hearsay may be the basis for issuance of the warrant "so long as there . . . [is] a substantial basis for crediting the hearsay." Jones v. United States, supra, 362 U.S. at 272, 80 S.Ct. at 736. And, in Aguilar we recognized that "an affidavit may be based on hearsay information and need not reflect the direct personal observations of the affiant," so long as the magistrate is "informed of some of the underlying circumstances" supporting the affiant's conclusions and his belief that any informant involved "whose identity need not be disclosed . . . was 'credible' or his information 'reliable.'" Aguilar v. State of Texas, supra, 378 U.S. at 114, 84 S.Ct. at 1514.

. . .

This is not to say that probable cause can be made out by affidavits which are purely conclusory, stating only the affiant's or an informer's belief that probable cause exists without detailing any of the "underlying circumstances" upon which that belief is based. See Aguilar v. State of Texas, supra. Recital of some of the underlying circumstances in the affidavit is essential if the magistrate is to perform his detached function and not serve merely as a rubber stamp for the police. However, where these circumstances are detailed, where reason for crediting the source of the information is given, and when a magistrate has found probable cause, the courts should not invalidate the warrant by interpreting the affidavit in a hypertechnical, rather than a commonsense, manner. Although in a particular case it may not be easy to determine when an affidavit demonstrates the existence of probable cause, the resolution of doubtful or marginal cases in this area should be largely determined by the preference to be accorded to warrants. Jones v. United States, supra, 362 U.S. at 270, 80 S.Ct. at 735.

II.

The application of the principles stated above leads us to reverse the Court of Appeals. The affidavit in this case, if read in a commonsense way rather than technically, shows ample facts to establish probable cause and allow the Commissioner to issue the search warrant. The affidavit at issue here, unlike the affidavit held insufficient in Aguilar, is detailed and specific. It sets forth not merely "some of the underlying circumstances" supporting the officer's belief, but a good many of them. This is apparent from the summary of the affidavit already recited and from its text which is reproduced in the Appendix.

The Court of Appeals did not question the specificity of the affidavit. It rested its holding that the affidavit was insufficient on the ground that "[t]he affidavit failed to clearly indicate which of the facts alleged therein were hearsay or which were within the affiant's own knowledge," and therefore "[t]he Commissioner could only conclude that the entire affidavit was based on hearsay." 324 F.2d at 868. While the Court of Appeals recognized that an affidavit based on hearsay will be sufficient, "so long as a substantial basis for crediting the hearsay is presented," Jones v. United States, supra, 362 U.S. at 269, 80 S.Ct. at 735, it felt that no such basis existed here because the hearsay consisted of reports by "Investigators," and the affidavit did not recite how the Investigators obtained their information. The Court of Appeals conceded that the affidavit stated that the Investigators themselves smelled the odor of fermenting mash, but argued that the rest of their information might itself have been based upon hearsay thus raising "the distinct possibility of hearsay-upon-hearsay." 324 F.2d at 869. For this reason, it held that the affidavit did not establish probable cause.

We disagree with the conclusion of the Court of Appeals. Its determination that the affidavit might have been based wholly upon hearsay cannot be supported in light of the fact that Mazaka, a Government Investigator, swore under oath that the relevant information was in part based "upon observations made by me" and "upon personal knowledge" as well as upon "information which has been obtained from Investigators of the Alcohol and Tobacco Tax Division, Internal Revenue Service, who have been assigned to this investigation." It also seems to us that the assumption of the Court of Appeals that all of the information in Mazaka's affidavit may in fact have come from unreliable anonymous informers passed on to Government Investigators, who in turn related this information to Mazaka is without foundation. Mazaka swore that, insofar as the affidavit was not based upon his own observations, it was "based upon information received officially from other Investigators attached to the Alcohol and Tobacco Tax Division assigned to this investigation, and reports orally made to me describing the results of their *observations* and investigation." (Emphasis added.) The Court of Appeals itself recognized that the affidavit stated that " 'Investigators' [employees of the Service] smelled the odor of fermenting mash in the vicinity of the suspected dwelling." 324 F.2d at 869. A qualified officer's detection of the smell of mash has often been held a very strong factor in determining that probable cause exists so as to allow issuance of a warrant. Moreover, upon reading the affidavit as a whole, it becomes clear that the detailed observations recounted in the affidavit cannot fairly be regarded as having been made in any significant part by persons other than full-time Investigators of the Alcohol and Tobacco Tax Division of the Internal Revenue Service. Observations of fellow officers of the Government engaged in a common investigation are plainly a reliable basis for a warrant applied for by one of their number. We conclude that the affidavit showed probable cause and that the Court of Appeals misapprehended its judicial function in reviewing this affidavit by giving it an unduly technical and restrictive reading.

This Court is alert to invalidate unconstitutional searches and seizures whether with or without a warrant. See Aguilar v. State of Texas, supra; Stanford v. State of Texas, 379 U.S. 476, 85 S.Ct. 506 (1949); Preston v. United States, 376 U.S. 364, 84 S.Ct. 881, 11 L.Ed.2d 777 (1949); Beck v. State of Ohio, 379 U.S. 89, 85 S.Ct. 223, 13 L.Ed.2d 142 (1949). By doing so, it vindicates individual liberties and strengthens the administration of justice by promoting respect for law and order. This Court is equally concerned to uphold the actions of law enforcement officers consistently following the proper constitutional course. This is no less important to the administration of justice than the invalidation of convictions because of disregard of individual rights or official overreaching. In our view the officers in this case did what the Constitution requires. They obtained a warrant from a judicial officer "upon probable cause, supported by Oath or affirmation, and particularly describing the place to be searched, and the . . . things to be seized." It is vital that having done so their actions should be sustained under a system of justice responsive both to the needs of individual liberty and to the rights of the community.

Reversed.

UNITED STATES v. ROBINSON

Supreme Court of the United States, 1973.
414 U.S. 218, 94 S.Ct. 467, 38 L.Ed.2d 427.

Mr. Justice REHNQUIST delivered the opinion of the Court.

Respondent Robinson was convicted in United States District Court for the District of Columbia of the possession and facilitation of concealment of heroin in violation of 26 U.S.C.A. § 4704(a) (1964 ed.), and 21 U.S.C.A. § 174 (1964 ed.). He was sentenced to concurrent terms of imprisonment for these offenses. On his appeal to the Court of Appeals for the District of Columbia Circuit, that court first remanded the case to the District Court for an evidentiary hearing concerning the scope of the search of respondent's person which had occurred at the time of his arrest. 145 U.S.App.D.C. 46, 447 F.2d 1215 (1971). The District Court made findings of fact and conclusions of law adverse to respondent, and he again appealed. This time the Court of Appeals en banc reversed the judgment of conviction, holding that the heroin introduced in evidence against respondent had been obtained as a result of a search which violated the Fourth Amendment to the United States Constitution. 153 U.S.App. D.C. 114, 471 F.2d 1082 (1972). We granted certiorari, 410 U.S. 982, 93 S.Ct. 1500, 36 L.Ed.2d 177 (1973), and set the case for argument together with Gustafson v. Florida, 414 U.S. 260, 94 S.Ct. 488, 38 L.Ed.2d 456, also decided today.

On April 23, 1968, at approximately 11 p. m., Officer Richard Jenks, a 15-year veteran of the District of Columbia Metropolitan Police Department, observed the respondent driving a 1965 Cadillac near the intersection of 8th and C Streets, N.E., in the District of Columbia. Jenks, as a result of previous investigation following a check of respondent's operator's permit four days earlier, determined there was reason to believe that respondent was operating a motor vehicle after the revocation of his operator's permit. This is an offense defined by statute in the District of Columbia which carries a mandatory minimum jail term, a mandatory minimum fine, or both. D.C.Code Ann. § 40–302(d) (1967).

Jenks signaled respondent to stop the automobile, which respondent did, and all three of the occupants emerged from the car. At that point Jenks informed respondent that he was under arrest for "operating after revocation and obtaining a permit by misrepresentation." It was assumed by the Court of Appeals, and is conceded by the respondent here, that Jenks had probable cause to arrest respondent, and that he effected a full-custody arrest.

In accordance with procedures prescribed in police department instructions, Jenks then began to search respondent. He explained at a subsequent hearing that he was "face-to-face" with the respondent, and "placed [his] hands on [the respondent], my right-hand to his left breast like this (demonstrating) and proceeded to pat him down thus [with the right hand]." During this patdown, Jenks felt an object in the left breast pocket of the heavy coat respondent was wearing, but testified that he "couldn't tell what it was" and also that he "couldn't actually tell the size of it." Jenks then reached into the pocket and pulled out the object, which turned out to be a "crumpled up cigarette package." Jenks testified that at this point he still did not know what was in the package:

> "As I felt the package I could feel objects in the package but I couldn't tell what they were. . . . I knew they weren't cigarettes."

The officer then opened the cigarette pack and found 14 gelatin capsules of white powder which he thought to be, and which later analysis proved to be, heroin. Jenks then continued his search of respondent to completion, feeling around his waist and trouser legs, and examining the remaining pockets. The heroin seized from the respondent was admitted into evidence at the trial which resulted in his conviction in the District Court.

The opinion for the plurality judges of the Court of Appeals, written by Judge Wright, the concurring opinion of Chief Judge Bazelon, and the dissenting opinion of Judge Wilkey, concurred in by three judges, gave careful and comprehensive treatment to the authority of a police officer to search the person of one who has been validly arrested and taken into custody. We conclude that the search conducted by Jenks in this case did not offend the limits imposed by the Fourth Amendment, and we therefore reverse the judgment of the Court of Appeals.

I.

It is well settled that a search incident to a lawful arrest is a traditional exception to the warrant requirement of the Fourth Amendment. This general exception has historically been formulated into two distinct propositions. The first is that a search may be made of the *person* of the arrestee by virtue of the lawful arrest. The second is that a search may be made of the area within the control of the arrestee.

Examination of this Court's decisions shows that these two propositions have been treated quite differently. The validity of the search of a person incident to a lawful arrest has been regarded as settled from its first enunciation, and has remained virtually unchallenged until the present case. The validity of the second proposition, while likewise conceded in principle, has been subject to differing interpretations as to the extent of the area which may be searched.

Because the rule requiring exclusion of evidence obtained in violation of the Fourth Amendment was first enunciated in Weeks v. United States, 232 U.S. 383, 34 S.Ct. 341, 58 L.Ed. 652 (1914), it is understandable that virtually all of this Court's search-and-seizure law has been developed since that time. In *Weeks,* the Court made clear its recognition of the validity of a search incident to a lawful arrest:

> "What then is the present case? Before answering that inquiry specifically, it may be well by a process of exclusion to state what it is not. It is not an assertion of the right on the part of the Government, always recognized under English and American law, to search the person of the accused when legally arrested to discover and seize the fruits or evidences of crime. This right has been uniformly maintained in many cases. 1 Bishop on Criminal Procedure, § 211; Wharton, Crim.Plead. and Practice, 8th ed., § 60; Dillon v. O'Brien and Davis, 16 Cox C.C. 245." Id., at 392, 34 S.Ct. at 344.

Agnello v. United States, 269 U.S. 20, 46 S.Ct. 4, 70 L.Ed. 145 (1925), decided 11 years after *Weeks,* repeats the categorical recognition of the validity of a search incident to lawful arrest:

> "The right without a search warrant contemporaneously to search persons lawfully arrested while committing crime and to search the place where the arrest is made in order to find and seize things connected with the crime as its fruits or as the means by which it was committed, as well as weapons and other things to effect an escape from custody, is not to be doubted." Id., at 30, 46 S.Ct. at 5.

Throughout the series of cases in which the Court has addressed the second proposition relating to a search incident to a lawful arrest—the permissible area beyond the person of the arrestee which such a search may cover—no doubt has been expressed as to the unqualified authority of the arresting authority to search the person of the arrestee. E. g., Carroll v. United States, 267 U.S. 132, 45 S.Ct. 280, 69 L.Ed. 543 (1925); Marron v. United States, 275 U.S. 192, 48 S.Ct. 74, 72 L.Ed. 231 (1927); Go-Bart Co. v. United States, 282 U.S. 344, 51 S.Ct. 153, 75 L.Ed. 374 (1931); United States v. Lefkowitz, 285 U.S. 452, 52 S.Ct. 420, 76 L.Ed. 877 (1932); Harris v. United States, 331 U.S. 145, 67 S.Ct. 1098, 91 L.Ed. 1399 (1947); Trupiano v. United States, 334 U.S. 699, 68 S.Ct. 1229, 92 L.Ed. 1663 (1948); United States v. Rabinowitz, 339 U.S. 56, 70 S.Ct. 430, 94 L.Ed. 653 (1950); Preston v. United States, 376 U.S. 364, 84 S.Ct. 881, 11 L.Ed.2d 777 (1964); Chimel v. California, 395 U.S. 752, 89 S.Ct. 2034, 23 L.Ed.2d 685 (1969). In *Chimel,* where the Court overruled *Rabinowitz* and *Harris* as to the area of permissible search incident to a lawful arrest, full recognition was again given to the authority to search the person of the arrestee:

> "When an arrest is made, it is reasonable for the arresting officer to search the person arrested in order to remove any weapons that the latter might seek to use in order to resist arrest or effect his escape. Otherwise, the officer's safety might well be endangered, and the arrest itself frustrated. In addition, it is entirely reasonable for the arresting officer to search for and seize any evidence on the arrestee's person in order to prevent its concealment or destruction." 395 U.S., at 762–763, 89 S.Ct. at 2040.

Three years after the decision in *Chimel,* supra, we upheld the validity of a search in which heroin had been taken from the person of the defendant after his arrest on a weapons charge, in Adams v. Williams, 407 U.S. 143, 92 S.Ct. 1921, 32 L.Ed.2d 612 (1972), saying:

> "Under the circumstances surrounding Williams' possession of the gun seized by Sgt. Connolly, the arrest on the weapons charge was supported by probable cause, and the search of his person and of the car incident to that arrest was lawful." Id., at 149, 92 S.Ct. at 1925.

Last Term in Cupp v. Murphy, 412 U.S. 291, 295, 93 S.Ct. 2000, 2003, 36 L.Ed.2d 900 (1973), we again reaffirmed the traditional statement of the authority to search incident to a valid arrest.

Thus the broadly stated rule, and the reasons for it, have been repeatedly affirmed in the decisions of this Court since Weeks v. United States, supra, nearly 60 years ago. Since the statements in the cases speak not simply in terms of an exception to the warrant requirement, but in terms of an affirmative authority to search, they clearly imply that such searches also meet the Fourth Amendment's requirement of reasonableness.

II.

In its decision of this case, the Court of Appeals decided that even after a police officer lawfully places a suspect under arrest for the purpose of taking him into custody, he may not ordinarily proceed to fully search the prisoner. He must, instead, conduct a limited frisk of the outer clothing and remove such weapons that he may, as a result of that limited frisk, reasonably believe and ascertain that the suspect has in his possession. While recognizing that Terry v. Ohio, 392 U.S. 1, 88 S.Ct. 1868, 20 L.Ed.2d 889 (1968), dealt with a permissible "frisk" incident to an investigative stop based on less than probable cause to arrest, the Court of Appeals felt that the principles of that case should be carried over to this probable-cause arrest for driving while one's license is revoked. Since there would be no further evidence of such a crime to be obtained in a search of the arrestee, the court held that only a search for weapons could be justified.

Terry v. Ohio, supra, did not involve an arrest for probable cause, and it made quite clear that the "protective frisk" for weapons which it approved might be conducted without probable cause. Id., at 21–22, 24–25, 88 S.Ct. at 1879–1880, 1881–1882. This Court's opinion explicitly recognized that there is a "distinction in purpose, character, and extent between a search incident to an arrest and a limited search for weapons."

> "The former, although justified in part by the acknowledged necessity to protect the arresting officer from assault with a concealed weapon, Preston v. United States, 376 U.S. 364, 367 [84 S.Ct. 881, 883, 11 L.Ed.2d 777] (1964), is also justified on other grounds, ibid., and can therefore involve a relatively extensive exploration of the person. A search for weapons in the absence of probable cause to arrest, however, must, like any other search, be strictly circumscribed by the exigencies which justify its initiation. Warden v. Hayden, 387 U.S. 294, 310 [87 S.Ct. 1642, 1652, 18 L.Ed.2d 782] (1967) (Mr. Justice Fortas, concurring). Thus it must be limited to that which is necessary for the discovery of weapons which might be used to harm the officer or others nearby, and may realistically be characterized as something less than a 'full' search, even though it remains a serious intrusion.
>
> " . . . An arrest is a wholly different kind of intrusion upon individual freedom from a limited search for weapons, and the interests each is designed to serve are likewise quite different. An arrest is the initial stage of a criminal prosecution. It is intended to vindicate society's interest in having its laws obeyed, and it is inevitably accompanied by future interference with the individual's freedom of movement, whether or not trial or conviction ultimately follows. The protective search for weapons, on the other hand, constitutes a brief, though far from inconsiderable, intrusion upon the sanctity of the person." Id., at 25–26, 88 S.Ct. at 1882 (footnote omitted).

Terry, therefore, affords no basis to carry over to a probable-cause arrest the limitations this Court placed on a stop-and-frisk search permissible without probable cause.

The Court of Appeals also relied on language in Peters v. New York, 392 U.S. 40, 66, 88 S.Ct. 1889, 1904, 20 L.Ed.2d 917 (1968), a companion case to *Terry.* There the Court held that the police officer had authority to search Peters because he had probable cause to arrest him, and went on to say:

> "[T]he incident search was obviously justified 'by the need to seize weapons and other things which might be used to assault an officer or effect an escape, as well as by the need

to prevent the destruction of evidence of the crime.' Preston v. United States, 376 U.S. 364, 367 [84 S.Ct. 881, 11 L.Ed.2d 777] (1964). Moreover, it was reasonably limited in scope by these purposes. Officer Lasky did not engage in an unrestrained and thorough-going examination of Peters and his personal effects." Id., at 67, 88 S.Ct. at 1905.

It is, of course, possible to read the second sentence from this quotation as imposing a novel limitation on the established doctrine set forth in the first sentence. It is also possible to read it as did Mr. Justice Harlan in his opinion concurring in the result:

> "The second possible source of confusion is the Court's statement that 'Officer Lasky did not engage in an unrestrained and thorough-going examination of Peters and his personal effects.' [392 U.S. at 67, 88 S.Ct.] at 1905. Since the Court found probable cause to arrest Peters, and since an officer arresting on probable cause is entitled to make a very full incident search, I assume that this is merely a factual observation. As a factual matter, I agree with it." Id., at 77, 88 S.Ct. at 1909 (footnote omitted).

We do not believe that the Court in *Peters* intended in one unexplained and unelaborated sentence to impose a novel and far-reaching limitation on the authority to search the person of an arrestee incident to his lawful arrest. While the language from *Peters* was quoted with approval in Chimel v. California, 395 U.S., at 764, 89 S.Ct. at 2040, it is preceded by a full exposition of the traditional and unqualified authority of the arresting officer to search the arrestee's person. Id., at 763, 89 S.Ct., at 2040. We do not believe that either *Terry* or *Peters,* when considered in the light of the previously discussed statements of this Court, justified the sort of limitation upon that authority which the Court of Appeals fashioned in this case.

III.

Virtually all of the statements of this Court affirming the existence of an unqualified authority to search incident to a lawful arrest are dicta. We would not, therefore, be foreclosed by principles of *stare decisis* from further examination into history and practice in order to see whether the sort of qualifications imposed by the Court of Appeals in this case were in fact intended by the Framers of the Fourth Amendment or recognized in cases decided prior to *Weeks.* Unfortunately such authorities as exist are sparse. Such common-law treatises as Blackstone's Commentaries and Holmes' Common Law are simply silent on the subject. Pollock and Maitland, in their History of English Law, describe the law of arrest as "rough and rude" before the time of Edward I, but do not address the authority to search incident to arrest. 2 F. Pollock & F. Maitland, The History of English Law 582 (2d ed. 1909).

. . .

Then Associate Judge Cardozo of the New York Court of Appeals summarized his understanding of the historical basis for the authority to search incident to arrest in these words:

> "The basic principle is this: Search of the person is unlawful when the seizure of the body is a trespass, and the purpose of the search is to discover grounds as yet unknown for arrest or accusation [citation omitted]. Search of the person becomes lawful when grounds for arrest and accusation have been discovered, and the law is in the act of subjecting the body of the accused to its physical dominion.
>
> "The distinction may seem subtle, but in truth it is founded in shrewd appreciation of the necessities of government. We are not to strain an immunity to the point at which human nature rebels against honoring it in conduct. The peace officer empowered to arrest must be empowered to disarm. If he may disarm, he may search, lest a weapon be concealed. The search being lawful, he retains what he finds if connected with the crime." People v. Chiagles, 237 N.Y. 193, 197, 142 N.E. 583, 584 (1923).

. . .

The justification or reason for the authority to search incident to a lawful arrest rests quite as much on the need to disarm the suspect in order to take him into custody as it does on the need to preserve evidence on his person for later use at trial. Agnello v. United States, 269 U.S. 20, 46 S.Ct. 4, 70 L.Ed. 145 (1925); Abel v. United States, 362 U.S. 217, 80 S.Ct. 683, 4 L.Ed.2d 668 (1960). The standards traditionally governing a search incident to lawful arrest are not, therefore, commuted to the stricter *Terry* standards by the absence of probable fruits or further evidence of the particular crime for which the arrest is made.

Nor are we inclined, on the basis of what seems to us to be a rather speculative judgment, to qualify the breadth of the general authority to search incident to a lawful custodial arrest on an assumption that persons arrested for the offense of driving while their licenses have been revoked are less likely to possess dangerous weapons than are those arrested for other crimes. It is scarcely open to doubt that the danger to an officer is far greater in the case of the extended exposure which follows the taking of a suspect into custody and transporting him to the police station than in the case of the relatively fleeting contact resulting from the typical *Terry*-type stop. This is an adequate basis for treating all custodial arrests alike for purposes of search justification.

But quite apart from these distinctions, our more fundamental disagreement with the Court of Appeals arises from its suggestion that there must be litigated in each case the issue of whether or not there was present one of the reasons supporting the authority for a search of the person incident to a lawful arrest. We do not think the long line of authorities of this Court dating back to *Weeks*, or what we can glean from the history of practice in this country and in England, requires such a case-by-case adjudication. A police officer's determination as to how and where to search the person of a suspect whom he has arrested is necessarily a quick *ad hoc* judgment which the Fourth Amendment does not require to be broken down in each instance into an analysis of each step in the search. The authority to search the person incident to a lawful custodial arrest, while based upon the need to disarm and to discover evidence, does not depend on what a court may later decide was the probability in a particular arrest situation that weapons or evidence would in fact be found upon the person of the suspect. A custodial arrest of a suspect based on probable cause is a reasonable intrusion under the Fourth Amendment; that intrusion being lawful, a search incident to the arrest requires no additional justification. It is the fact of the lawful arrest which establishes the authority to search, and we hold that in the case of a lawful custodial arrest a full search of the person is not only an exception to the warrant requirement of the Fourth Amendment, but is also a "reasonable" search under that Amendment.

IV.

The search of respondent's person conducted by Officer Jenks in this case and the seizure from him of the heroin, were permissible under established Fourth Amendment law. While thorough, the search partook of none of the extreme or patently abusive characteristics which were held to violate the Due Process Clause of the Fourteenth Amendment in Rochin v. California, 342 U.S. 165, 72 S.Ct. 205, 96 L.Ed. 183 (1952). Since it is the fact of custodial arrest which gives rise to the authority to search, it is of no moment that Jenks did not indicate any subjective fear of the respondent or that he did not himself suspect that respondent was armed. Having in the course of a lawful search come upon the crumpled package of cigarettes, he was entitled to inspect it; and when his inspection revealed the heroin capsules, he was entitled to seize them as "fruits, instrumentalities, or contraband" probative of criminal conduct. Harris v. United States, 331 U.S., at 154–155, 67 S.Ct., at 1103–1104; Warden v. Hayden, 387 U.S. 294, 299, 307, 87 S.Ct. 1642, 1646, 1650 (1967); Adams v. Williams, 407 U.S., at 149, 92 S.Ct., at 1924. The judgment of the Court of Appeals holding otherwise is reversed.

Reversed.

MIRANDA v. ARIZONA

Certiorari to the Supreme Court of Arizona, 1966.
384 U.S. 436, 86 S.Ct. 1602, 16 L.Ed.2d 694.

Mr. Chief Justice WARREN delivered the opinion of the Court.

The cases before us raise questions which go to the roots of our concepts of American criminal jurisprudence: the restraints society must observe consistent with the Federal Constitution in prosecuting individuals for crime. More specifically, we deal with the admissibility of statements obtained from an individual who is subjected to custodial police interrogation and the necessity for procedures which assure that the individual is accorded his privilege under the Fifth Amendment to the Constitution not to be compelled to incriminate himself.

We dealt with certain phases of this problem recently in Escobedo v. Illinois, 378 U.S. 478, 84 S.Ct. 1758, 12 L.Ed.2d 977 (1964). There, as in the four cases before us, law enforcement officials took the defendant into custody and interrogated him in a police station for the purpose of obtaining a confession. The police did not effectively advise him of his right to remain silent or of his right to consult with his attorney. Rather, they confronted him with an alleged accomplice who accused him of having perpetrated a murder. When the defendant denied the accusation and said "I didn't shoot Manuel, you did it," they handcuffed him and took him to an interrogation room. There, while handcuffed and standing, he was questioned for four hours until he confessed. During this interrogation, the police denied his request to speak to his attorney, and they prevented his retained attorney, who had come to the police station, from consulting with him. At his trial, the State, over his objection, introduced the confession against him. We held that the statements thus made were constitutionally inadmissible.

This case has been the subject of judicial interpretation and spirited legal debate since it was decided two years ago. Both state and federal courts, in assessing its implications, have arrived at varying conclusions. A wealth of scholarly material has been written tracing its ramifications and underpinnings. Police and prosecutor have speculated on its range and desirability. We granted certiorari in these cases, 382 U.S. 924, 925, 937, in order further to explore some facets of the problems, thus exposed, of applying the privilege against self-incrimination to in-custody interrogation, and to give concrete constitutional guidelines for law enforcement agencies and courts to follow.

We start here, as we did in *Escobedo,* with the premise that our holding is not an innovation in our jurisprudence, but is an application of principles long recognized and applied in other settings. We have undertaken a thorough re-examination of the *Escobedo* decision and the principles it announced, and we reaffirm it. That case was but an explication of basic rights that are enshrined in our Constitution—that "No person . . . shall be compelled in any criminal case to be a witness against himself," and that "the accused shall . . .

have the Assistance of Counsel"—rights which were put in jeopardy in that case through official overbearing. These precious rights were fixed in our Constitution only after centuries of persecution and struggle. And in the words of Chief Justice Marshall, they were secured "for ages to come, and . . . designed to approach immortality as nearly as human institutions can approach it," Cohens v. Virginia, 6 Wheat. 264, 387 (1821).

Over 70 years ago, our predecessors on this Court eloquently stated:

> "The maxim *nemo tenetur seipsum accusare* had its origin in a protest against the inquisitorial and manifestly unjust methods of interrogating accused persons, which [have] long obtained in the continental system, and, until the expulsion of the Stuarts from the British throne in 1688, and the erection of additional barriers for the protection of the people against the exercise of arbitrary power, [were] not uncommon even in England. While the admissions or confessions of the prisoner, when voluntarily and freely made, have always ranked high in the scale of incriminating evidence, if an accused person be asked to explain his apparent connection with a crime under investigation, the ease with which the questions put to him may assume an inquisitorial character, the temptation to press the witness unduly, to browbeat him if he be timid or reluctant, to push him into a corner, and to entrap him into fatal contradictions, which is so painfully evident in many of the earlier state trials, notably in those of Sir Nicholas Throckmorton, and Udal, the Puritan minister, made the system so odious as to give rise to a demand for its total abolition. The change in the English criminal procedure in that particular seems to be founded upon no statute and no judicial opinion, but upon a general and silent acquiescence of the courts in a popular demand. But, however adopted, it has become firmly embedded in English, as well as in American jurisprudence. So deeply did the iniquities of the ancient system impress themselves upon the minds of the American colonists that the States, with one accord, made a denial of the right to question an accused person a part of their fundamental law, so that a maxim, which in England was a mere rule of evidence, became clothed in this country with the impregnability of a constitutional enactment." Brown v. Walker, 161 U.S. 591, 596–597, 16 S.Ct. 644, 40 L.Ed. 819 (1896).

In stating the obligation of the judiciary to apply these constitutional rights, this Court declared in Weems v. United States, 217 U.S. 349, 373, 30 S.Ct. 544, 54 L.Ed. 793 (1910):

> ". . . our contemplation cannot be only of what has been but of what may be. Under any other rule a constitution would indeed be as easy of application as it would be

deficient in efficacy and power. Its general principles would have little value and be converted by precedent into impotent and lifeless formulas. Rights declared in words might be lost in reality. And this has been recognized. The meaning and vitality of the Constitution have developed against narrow and restrictive construction."

This was the spirit in which we delineated, in meaningful language, the manner in which the constitutional rights of the individual could be enforced against overzealous police practices. It was necessary in *Escobedo*, as here, to insure that what was proclaimed in the Constitution had not become but a "form of words," Silverthorne Lumber Co. v. United States, 251 U.S. 385, 392, 40 S.Ct. 182, 64 L.Ed. 319 (1920), in the hands of government officials. And it is in this spirit, consistent with our role as judges, that we adhere to the principles of *Escobedo* today.

Our holding will be spelled out with some specificity in the pages which follow but briefly stated it is this: the prosecution may not use statements, whether exculpatory or inculpatory, stemming from custodial interrogation of the defendant unless it demonstrates the use of procedural safeguards effective to secure the privilege against self-incrimination. By custodial interrogation, we mean questioning initiated by law enforcement officers after a person has been taken into custody or otherwise deprived of his freedom of action in any significant way. As for the procedural safeguards to be employed, unless other fully effective means are devised to inform accused persons of their right of silence and to assure a continuous opportunity to exercise it, the following measures are required. Prior to any questioning, the person must be warned that he has a right to remain silent, that any statement he does make may be used as evidence against him, and that he has a right to the presence of an attorney, either retained or appointed. The defendant may waive effectuation of these rights, provided the waiver is made voluntarily, knowingly and intelligently. If, however, he indicates in any manner and at any stage of the process that he wishes to consult with an attorney before speaking there can be no questioning. Likewise, if the individual is alone and indicates in any manner that he does not wish to be interrogated, the police may not question him. The mere fact that he may have answered some questions or volunteered some statements on his own does not deprive him of the right to refrain from answering any further inquiries until he has consulted with an attorney and thereafter consents to be questioned.

I.

The constitutional issue we decide in each of these cases is the admissibility of statements obtained from a defendant questioned while in custody or otherwise deprived of his freedom of action in any significant way. In each, the defendant was questioned by police officers, detectives, or a prosecuting attorney in a room in which he was cut off from the outside world. In none of these cases was the defendant given a full and effective warning of his rights at the outset of the interrogation process. In all the cases, the questioning elicited oral admissions, and in three of them, signed statements as well which were admitted at their trials. They all thus share salient features—incommunicado interrogation of individuals in a police-dominated atmosphere, resulting in self-incriminating statements without full warnings of constitutional rights.

An understanding of the nature and setting of this in-custody interrogation is essential to our decisions today. The difficulty in depicting what transpires at such interrogations stems from the fact that in this country they have largely taken place incommunicado. From extensive factual studies undertaken in the early 1930's, including the famous Wickersham Report to Congress by a Presidential Commission, it is clear that police violence and the "third degree" flourished at that time. In a series of cases decided by this Court long after these studies, the police resorted to physical brutality—beating, hanging, whipping—and to sustained and protracted questioning incommunicado in order to extort confessions. The Commission on Civil Rights in 1961 found much evidence to indicate that "some policemen still resort to physical force to obtain confessions," 1961 Comm'n on Civil Rights Rep., Justice, pt. 5, 17. The use of physical brutality and violence is not, unfortunately, relegated to the past or to any part of the country. Only recently in Kings County, New York, the police brutally beat, kicked and placed lighted cigarette butts on the back of a potential witness under interrogation for the purpose of securing a statement incriminating a third party. People v. Portelli, 15 N.Y.2d 235, 205 N.E.2d 857, 257 N.Y.S.2d 931 (1965).

The examples given above are undoubtedly the exception now, but they are sufficiently widespread to be the object of concern. Unless a proper limitation upon custodial interrogation is achieved—such as these decisions will advance—there can be no assurance that practices of this nature will be eradicated in the foreseeable future. The conclusion of the Wickersham Commission Report, made over 30 years ago, is still pertinent:

> "To the contention that the third degree is necessary to get the facts, the reporters aptly reply in the language of the present Lord Chancellor of England (Lord Sankey): 'It is not admissible to do a great right by doing a little wrong. . . . It is not sufficient to do justice by obtaining a proper result by irregular or improper means.' Not only does the use of the third degree involve a flagrant violation of law by the officers of the law, but it involves also the dangers of false confessions, and it tends to make police and prosecutors less zealous in the search for objective evidence. As the New York prosecutor quoted in the report said, 'It is a short cut and makes the police lazy and unenterprising.' Or, as another official quoted remarked: 'If you use your fists, you are not so likely to use your wits.' We agree with the conclusion ex-

> pressed in the report, that 'The third degree brutalizes the police, hardens the prisoner against society, and lowers the esteem in which the administration of justice is held by the public.' " IV National Commission on Law Observance and Enforcement, Report on Lawlessness in Law Enforcement 5 (1931).

Again we stress that the modern practice of in-custody interrogation is psychologically rather than physically oriented. As we have stated before, "Since Chambers v. Florida, 309 U.S. 227, this Court has recognized that coercion can be mental as well as physical, and that the blood of the accused is not the only hallmark of an unconstitutional inquisition." Blackburn v. Alabama, 361 U.S. 199, 206, 80 S.Ct. 274, 4 L.Ed.2d 242 (1960). Interrogation still takes place in privacy. Privacy results in secrecy and this in turn results in a gap in our knowledge as to what in fact goes on in the interrogation rooms. A valuable source of information about present police practices, however, may be found in various police manuals and texts which document procedures employed with success in the past, and which recommend various other effective tactics. These texts are used by law enforcement agencies themselves as guides. It should be noted that these texts professedly present the most enlightened and effective means presently used to obtain statements through custodial interrogation. By considering these texts and other data, it is possible to describe procedures observed and noted around the country.

The officers are told by the manuals that the "principal psychological factor contributing to a successful interrogation is *privacy*—being alone with the person under interrogation." The efficacy of this tactic has been explained as follows:

> "If at all practicable, the interrogation should take place in the investigator's office or at least in a room of his own choice. The subject should be deprived of every psychological advantage. In his own home he may be confident, indignant, or recalcitrant. He is more keenly aware of his rights and more reluctant to tell of his indiscretions or criminal behavior within the walls of his home. Moreover his family and other friends are nearby, their presence lending moral support. In his own office, the investigator possesses all the advantages. The atmosphere suggests the invincibility of the forces of the law."

To highlight the isolation and unfamiliar surroundings, the manuals instruct the police to display an air of confidence in the suspect's guilt and from outward appearance to maintain only an interest in confirming certain details. The guilt of the subject is to be posited as a fact. The interrogator should direct his comments toward the reasons why the subject committed the act, rather than court failure by asking the subject whether he did it. Like other men, perhaps the subject has had a bad family life, had an unhappy childhood, had too much to drink, had an unrequited desire for women. The officers are instructed to minimize the moral seriousness of the offense, to cast blame on the victim or on society. These tactics are designed to put the subject in a psychological state where his story is but an elaboration of what the police purport to know already—that he is guilty. Explanations to the contrary are dismissed and discouraged.

The texts thus stress that the major qualities an interrogator should possess are patience and perseverance. One writer describes the efficacy of these characteristics in this manner:

> "In the preceding paragraphs emphasis has been placed on kindness and strategems. The investigator will, however, encounter many situations where the sheer weight of his personality will be the deciding factor. Where emotional appeals and tricks are employed to no avail, he must rely on an oppressive atmosphere of dogged persistence. He must interrogate steadily and without relent, leaving the subject no prospect of surcease. He must dominate his subject and overwhelm him with his inexorable will to obtain the truth. He should interrogate for a spell of several hours pausing only for the subject's necessities in acknowledgment of the need to avoid a charge of duress that can be technically substantiated. In a serious case, the interrogation may continue for days, with the required intervals for food and sleep, but with no respite from the atmosphere of domination. It is possible in this way to induce the subject to talk without resorting to duress or coercion. The method should be used only when the guilt of the subject appears highly probable."

The manuals suggest that the suspect be offered legal excuses for his actions in order to obtain an initial admission of guilt. Where there is a suspected revenge-killing, for example, the interrogator may say:

> "Joe, you probably didn't go out looking for this fellow with the purpose of shooting him. My guess is, however, that you expected something from him and that's why you carried a gun—for your own protection. You knew him for what he was, no good. Then when you met him he probably started using foul, abusive language and he gave some indication that he was about to pull a gun on you, and that's when you had to act to save your own life. That's about it, isn't it, Joe? "

Having then obtained the admission of shooting, the interrogator is advised to refer to circumstantial evidence which negates the self-defense explanation. This should enable him to secure the entire story. One text notes that "Even if he fails to do so, the inconsistency between the subject's original denial of the shooting and his present admission of at least doing the shooting will serve to deprive him of a self-defense 'out' at the time of trial."

When the techniques described above prove unavailing, the texts recommend they be alternated with a show of some hostility. One ploy often used has been termed the "friendly-unfriendly" or the "Mutt and Jeff" act:

> ". . . In this technique, two agents are employed. Mutt, the relentless investigator, who knows the subject is guilty and is not going to waste any time. He's sent a dozen men away for this crime and he's going to send the subject away for the full term. Jeff, on the other hand, is obviously a kindhearted man. He has a family himself. He has a brother who was involved in a little scrape like this. He disapproves of Mutt and his tactics and will arrange to get him off the case if the subject will cooperate. He can't hold Mutt off for very long. The subject would be wise to make a quick decision. The technique is applied by having both investigators present while Mutt acts out his role. Jeff may stand by quietly and demur at some of Mutt's tactics. When Jeff makes his plea for cooperation, Mutt is not present in the room."

The interrogators sometimes are instructed to induce a confession out of trickery. The technique here is quite effective in crimes which require identification or which run in series. In the identification situation, the interrogator may take a break in his questioning to place the subject among a group of men in a line-up. "The witness or complainant (previously coached, if necessary) studies the line-up and confidently points out the subject as the guilty party." Then the questioning resumes "as though there were now no doubt about the guilt of the subject." A variation on this technique is called the "reverse line-up":

> "The accused is placed in a line-up, but this time he is identified by several fictitious witnesses or victims who associated him with different offenses. It is expected that the subject will become desperate and confess to the offense under investigation in order to escape from the false accusations."

The manuals also contain instructions for police on how to handle the individual who refuses to discuss the matter entirely, or who asks for an attorney or relatives. The examiner is to concede him the right to remain silent. "This usually has a very undermining effect. First of all, he is disappointed in his expectation of an unfavorable reaction on the part of the interrogator. Secondly, a concession of this right to remain silent impresses the subject with the apparent fairness of his interrogator." After this psychological conditioning, however, the officer is told to point out the incriminating significance of the suspect's refusal to talk:

> "Joe, you have a right to remain silent. That's your privilege and I'm the last person in the world who'll try to take it away from you. If that's the way you want to leave this, O. K. But let me ask you this. Suppose you were in my shoes and I were in yours and you called me in to ask me about this and I told you, 'I don't want to answer any of your questions.'

> You'd think I had something to hide, and you'd probably be right in thinking that. That's exactly what I'll have to think about you, and so will everybody else. So let's sit here and talk this whole thing over."

Few will persist in their initial refusal to talk, it is said, if this monologue is employed correctly.

In the event that the subject wishes to speak to a relative or an attorney, the following advice is tendered:

> "[T]he interrogator should respond by suggesting that the subject first tell the truth to the interrogator himself rather than get anyone else involved in the matter. If the request is for an attorney the interrogator may suggest that the subject save himself or his family the expense of any such professional service, particularly if he is innocent of the offense under investigation. The interrogator may also add, 'Joe, I'm only looking for the truth, and if you're telling the truth, that's it. You can handle this by yourself.' "

From these representative samples of interrogation techniques, the setting prescribed by the manuals and observed in practice becomes clear. In essence, it is this: To be alone with the subject is essential to prevent distraction and to deprive him of any outside support. The aura of confidence in his guilt undermines his will to resist. He merely confirms the preconceived story the police seek to have him describe. Patience and persistence, at times relentless questioning, are employed. To obtain a confession, the interrogator must "patiently maneuver himself or his quarry into a position from which the desired objective may be attained." When normal procedures fail to produce the needed result, the police may resort to deceptive stratagems such as giving false legal advice. It is important to keep the subject off balance, for example, by trading on his insecurity about himself or his surroundings. The police then persuade, trick, or cajole him out of exercising his constitutional rights.

Even without employing brutality, the "third degree" or the specific stratagems described above, the very fact of custodial interrogation exacts a heavy toll on individual liberty and trades on the weakness of individuals. This fact may be illustrated simply by referring to three confession cases decided by this Court in the Term immediately preceding our *Escobedo* decision. In Townsend v. Sain, 372 U.S. 293, 83 S.Ct. 745, 9 L.Ed.2d 770 (1963), the defendant was a 19-year-old heroin addict, described as a "near mental defective," id., at 307–310. The defendant in Lynumn v. Illinois, 372 U.S. 528, 83 S.Ct. 917, 9 L.Ed.2d 922 (1963), was a woman who confessed to the arresting officer after being importuned to "cooperate" in order to prevent her children from being taken by relief authorities. This Court as in those cases reversed the conviction of a defendant in Haynes v. Washington, 373 U.S. 503, 83 S.Ct. 1336, 10 L.Ed.2d 513 (1963), whose persistent request during his interrogation was to phone his wife or attorney. In other settings, these individuals might have exercised their constitutional rights. In the incommunicado police-dominated atmosphere, they succumbed.

In the cases before us today, given this background, we concern ourselves primarily with this interrogation atmosphere and the evils it can bring. In No. 759, Miranda v. Arizona, the police arrested the defendant and took him to a special interrogation room where they secured a confession. In No. 760, Vignera v. New York, the defendant made oral admissions to the police after interrogation in the afternoon, and then signed an inculpatory statement upon being questioned by an assistant district attorney later the same evening. In No. 761, Westover v. United States, the defendant was handed over to the Federal Bureau of Investigation by local authorities after they had detained and interrogated him for a lengthy period, both at night and the following morning. After some two hours of questioning, the federal officers had obtained signed statements from the defendant. Lastly, in No. 584, California v. Stewart, the local police held the defendant five days in the station and interrogated him on nine separate occasions before they secured his inculpatory statement.

In these cases, we might not find the defendants' statements to have been involuntary in traditional terms. Our concern for adequate safeguards to protect precious Fifth Amendment rights is, of course, not lessened in the slightest. In each of the cases, the defendant was thrust into an unfamiliar atmosphere and run through menacing police interrogation procedures. The potentiality for compulsion is forcefully apparent, for example, in *Miranda,* where the indigent Mexican defendant was a seriously disturbed individual with pronounced sexual fantasies, and in *Stewart,* in which the defendant was an indigent Los Angeles Negro who had dropped out of school in the sixth grade. To be sure, the records do not evince overt physical coercion or patent psychological ploys. The fact remains that in none of these cases did the officers undertake to afford appropriate safeguards at the outset of the interrogation to insure that the statements were truly the product of free choice.

It is obvious that such an interrogation environment is created for no purpose other than to subjugate the individual to the will of his examiner. This atmosphere carries its own badge of intimidation. To be sure, this is not physical intimidation, but it is equally destructive of human dignity. The current practice of incommunicado interrogation is at odds with one of our Nation's most cherished principles—that the individual may not be compelled to incriminate himself. Unless adequate protective devices are employed to dispel the compulsion inherent in custodial surroundings, no statement obtained from the defendant can truly be the product of his free choice.

From the foregoing, we can readily perceive an intimate connection between the privilege against self-incrimination and police custodial questioning. It is fitting to turn to history and precedent underlying the Self-Incrimination Clause to determine its applicability in this situation.

II.

We sometimes forget how long it has taken to establish the privilege against self-incrimination, the sources from which it came and the fervor with which it was defended. Its roots go back into ancient times. Perhaps the critical historical event shedding light on its origins and evolution was the trial of one John Lilburn, a vocal anti-Stuart Leveller, who was made to take the Star Chamber Oath in 1637. The oath would have bound him to answer to all questions posed to him on any subject. The Trial of John Lilburn and John Wharton, 3 How. St.Tr. 1315 (1637). He resisted the oath and declaimed the proceedings, stating:

> "Another fundamental right I then contended for, was, that no man's conscience ought to be racked by oaths imposed, to answer to questions concerning himself in matters criminal, or pretended to be so." Haller & Davies, The Leveller Tracts 1647–1653, p. 454 (1944).

On account of the Lilburn Trial, Parliament abolished the inquisitorial Court of Star Chamber and went further in giving him generous reparation. The lofty principles to which Lilburn had appealed during his trial gained popular acceptance in England. These sentiments worked their way over to the Colonies and were implanted after great struggle into the Bill of Rights. Those who framed our Constitution and the Bill of Rights were ever aware of subtle encroachments on individual liberty. They knew that "illegitimate and unconstitutional practices get their first footing . . . by silent approaches and slight deviations from legal modes of procedure." Boyd v. United States, 116 U.S. 616, 635, 6 S.Ct. 524, 29 L.Ed. 746 (1886). The privilege was elevated to constitutional status and has always been "as broad as the mischief against which it seeks to guard." Counselman v. Hitchcock, 142 U.S. 547, 562, 12 S.Ct. 195, 35 L.Ed. 1110 (1892). We cannot depart from this noble heritage.

Thus we may view the historical development of the privilege as one which groped for the proper scope of governmental power over the citizen. As a "noble principle often transcends its origins," the privilege has come rightfully to be recognized in part as an individual's substantive right, a "right to a private enclave where he may lead a private life. That right is the hallmark of our democracy." United States v. Grunewald, 233 F.2d 556, 579, 581–582 (2d Cir. 1956) (Frank, J., dissenting), reversed 353 U.S. 391, 77 S.Ct. 963, 1 L.Ed.2d 931 (1957). We have recently noted that the privilege against self-incrimination—the essential mainstay of our adversary system—is founded on a complex of values. Murphy v. Waterfront Comm'n, 378 U.S. 52, 55–57, n. 5, 84 S.Ct. 1594, 12 L.Ed.2d 678 (1964); Tehan v. Shott, 382 U.S. 406, 414–415, n. 12, 86 S.Ct. 459, 15 L.Ed.2d 453 (1966). All these policies point to one overriding thought: the constitutional foundation underlying the privilege is the respect a government—state or federal—must accord to the dignity and integrity of its citizens. To maintain a "fair state-individual balance," to require the government "to shoulder the entire load," 8 Wigmore, Evidence 317 (McNaughton rev. 1961), to respect the inviolability of the human personality, our accusatory system of criminal justice demands that the government seeking to punish an individual produce the evidence against him by its own independent labors, rather than by the cruel, simple expedient of compelling it from his own mouth. Chambers v. Florida, 309 U.S. 227, 235–238, 60 S.Ct. 472, 84 L.Ed. 716 (1940). In sum, the privilege is fulfilled only when the person is guaranteed the right "to remain silent unless he chooses to speak in the unfettered exercise of his own will." Malloy v. Hogan, 378 U.S. 1, 8, 84 S.Ct. 1489, 12 L.Ed.2d 653 (1964).

The question in these cases is whether the privilege is fully applicable during a period of custodial interrogation. In this Court, the privilege has consistently been accorded a liberal construction. Albertson v. SACB, 382 U.S. 70, 81, 86 S.Ct. 194, 15 L.Ed.2d 165 (1965); Hoffman v. United States, 341 U.S. 479, 486, 71 S.Ct. 814, 97 L.Ed. 1118 (1951); Arndstein v. McCarthy, 254 U.S. 71, 72–73, 41 S.Ct. 26, 65 L. Ed.2d 138 (1920); Counselman v. Hitchcock, 142 U.S. 547, 562, 12 S. Ct. 195, 35 L.Ed. 1110 (1892). We are satisfied that all the principles embodied in the privilege apply to informal compulsion exerted by law-enforcement officers during in-custody questioning. An individual swept from familiar surroundings into police custody, surrounded by antagonistic forces, and subjected to the techniques of persuasion described above cannot be otherwise than under compulsion to speak. As a practical matter, the compulsion to speak in the isolated setting of the police station may well be greater than in courts or other official investigations, where there are often impartial observers to guard against intimidation or trickery.

This question, in fact, could have been taken as settled in federal courts almost 70 years ago, when, in Bram v. United States, 168 U.S. 532, 542, 18 S.Ct. 183, 42 L.Ed. 568 (1897), this Court held:

> "In criminal trials, in the courts of the United States, wherever a question arises whether a confession is incompetent because not voluntary, the issue is controlled by that portion of the Fifth Amendment . . . commanding that no person 'shall be compelled in any criminal case to be a witness against himself.' "

In *Bram*, the Court reviewed the British and American history and case law and set down the Fifth Amendment standard for compulsion which we implement today:

> "Much of the confusion which has resulted from the effort to deduce from the adjudged cases what would be a sufficient quantum of proof to show that a confession was or was not voluntary, has arisen from a misconception of the subject to which the proof must address itself. The rule is not that in order to render a statement admissible the proof must be adequate to establish that the particular communications contained in a statement were voluntarily made, but it must be sufficient to establish that the making of the statement was

voluntary; that is to say, that from the causes, which the law treats as legally sufficient to engender in the mind of the accused hope or fear in respect to the crime charged, the accused was not involuntarily impelled to make a statement, when but for the improper influences he would have remained silent. . . ." 168 U.S. at 549. And see, id. at 542.

The Court has adhered to this reasoning. In 1924, Mr. Justice Brandeis wrote for a unanimous Court in reversing a conviction resting on a compelled confession, Wan v. United States, 266 U.S. 1, 45 S.Ct. 1, 69 L.Ed. 131. He stated:

> "In the federal courts, the requisite of voluntariness is not satisfied by establishing merely that the confession was not induced by a promise or a threat. A confession is voluntary in law if, and only if, it was, in fact, voluntarily made. A confession may have been given voluntarily, although it was made to police officers, while in custody, and in answer to an examination conducted by them. But a confession obtained by compulsion must be excluded whatever may have been the character of the compulsion, and whether the compulsion was applied in a judicial proceeding or otherwise. Bram v. United States, 168 U.S. 532." 266 U.S. at 14–15.

In addition to the expansive historical development of the privilege and the sound policies which have nurtured its evolution, judicial precedent thus clearly establishes its application to incommunicado interrogation. In fact, the Government concedes this point as well established in No. 761, Westover v. United States, stating: "We have no doubt . . . that it is possible for a suspect's Fifth Amendment right to be violated during in-custody questioning by a law-enforcement officer."

Because of the adoption by Congress of Rule 5(a) of the Federal Rules of Criminal Procedure, and this Court's effectuation of that Rule in McNabb v. United States, 318 U.S. 332, 63 S.Ct. 608, 87 L.Ed. 819 (1943), and Mallory v. United States, 354 U.S. 449, 77 S.Ct. 1356, 1 L.Ed.2d 1479 (1957), we have had little occasion in the past quarter century to reach the constitutional issues in dealing with federal interrogations. These supervisory rules, requiring production of an arrested person before a commissioner "without unnecessary delay" and excluding evidence obtained in default of that statutory obligation, were nonetheless responsive to the same considerations of Fifth Amendment policy that unavoidably face us now as to the States. In McNabb, 318 U.S. at 343–344, and in Mallory, 354 U.S. at 455–456, we recognized both the dangers of interrogation and the appropriateness of prophylaxis stemming from the very fact of interrogation itself.

Our decision in Malloy v. Hogan, 378 U.S. 1, 84 S.Ct. 1489, 12 L.Ed.2d 653 (1964), necessitates an examination of the scope of the privilege in state cases as well. In *Malloy*, we squarely held the privilege applicable to the States, and held that the substantive standards underlying the privilege applied with full force to state court proceedings. There, as in Murphy v. Waterfront Comm'n, 378 U.S. 52, 84 S.Ct. 1594, 12 L.Ed.2d 678 (1964), and Griffin v. California, 380 U.S. 609, 85 S.Ct. 1229, 14 L.Ed.2d 106 (1965), we applied the existing Fifth Amendment standards to the case before us. Aside from the holding itself, the reasoning in *Malloy* made clear what had already become apparent—that the substantive and procedural safeguards surrounding admissibility of confessions in state cases had become exceedingly exacting, reflecting all the policies embedded in the privilege, 378 U.S. at 7–8. The voluntariness doctrine in the state cases, as *Malloy* indicates, encompasses all interrogation practices which are likely to exert such pressure upon an individual as to disable him from making a free and rational choice. The implications of this proposition were elaborated in our decision in Escobedo v. Illinois, 378 U.S. 478, 84 S.Ct. 1758, 12 L.Ed.2d 977, decided one week after *Malloy* applied the privilege to the States.

Our holding there stressed the fact that the police had not advised the defendant of his constitutional privilege to remain silent at the outset of the interrogation, and we drew attention to that fact at several points in the decision, 378 U.S. at 483, 485, 491. This was no isolated factor, but an essential ingredient in our decision. The entire thrust of police interrogation there, as in all the cases today, was to put the defendant in such an emotional state as to impair his capacity for rational judgment. The abdication of the constitutional privilege—the choice on his part to speak to the police—was not made knowingly or competently because of the failure to apprise him of his rights; the compelling atmosphere of the in-custody interrogation, and not an independent decision on his part, caused the defendant to speak.

A different phase of the *Escobedo* decision was significant in its attention to the absence of counsel during the questioning. There, as in the cases today, we sought a protective device to dispel the compelling atmosphere of the interrogation. In *Escobedo*, however, the police did not relieve the defendant of the anxieties which they had created in the interrogation rooms. Rather, they denied his request for the assistance of counsel, 378 U.S. at 481, 488, 491. This heightened his dilemma, and made his later statements the product of this compulsion. Cf. Haynes v. Washington, 373 U.S. 503, 514, 83 S.Ct. 1336, 10 L.Ed.2d 513 (1963). The denial of the defendant's request for his attorney thus undermined his ability to exercise the privilege—to remain silent if he chose or to speak without any intimidation, blatant or subtle. The presence of counsel, in all the cases before us today, would be the adequate protective device necessary to make the process of police interrogation conform to the dictates of the privilege. His presence would insure that statements made in the government-established atmosphere are not the product of compulsion.

It was in this manner that *Escobedo* explicated another facet of the pre-trial privilege, noted in many of the Court's prior decisions: the protection of rights at trial. That counsel is present when statements are taken from an individual during interrogation obviously enhances the integrity of the fact-finding processes in court. The presence of an attorney, and the warnings delivered to the individual, enable the defendant under otherwise compelling circumstances to tell his story without fear, effectively, and in a way that eliminates the evils in the interrogation process. Without the protections flowing from adequate warnings and the rights of counsel, "all the careful safeguards erected around the giving of testimony, whether by an accused or any other witness, would become empty formalities in a procedure where the most compelling possible evidence of guilt, a confession, would have already been obtained at the unsupervised pleasure of the police." Mapp v. Ohio, 367 U.S. 643, 685, 81 S.Ct. 1684, 6 L.Ed.2d 1081 (1961) (HARLAN, J., dissenting). Cf. Pointer v. Texas, 380 U.S. 400, 85 S.Ct. 1065, 14 L.Ed.2d 923 (1965).

III.

Today, then, there can be no doubt that the Fifth Amendment privilege is available outside of criminal court proceedings and serves to protect persons in all settings in which their freedom of action is curtailed in any significant way from being compelled to incriminate themselves. We have concluded that without proper safeguards the process of in-custody interrogation of persons suspected or accused of crime contains inherently compelling pressures which work to undermine the individual's will to resist and to compel him to speak where he would not otherwise do so freely. In order to combat these pressures and to permit a full opportunity to exercise the privilege against self-incrimination, the accused must be adequately and effectively apprised of his rights and the exercise of those rights must be fully honored.

It is impossible for us to foresee the potential alternatives for protecting the privilege which might be devised by Congress or the States in the exercise of their creative rule-making capacities. Therefore we cannot say that the Constitution necessarily requires adherence to any particular solution for the inherent compulsions of the interrogation process as it is presently conducted. Our decision in no way creates a constitutional straitjacket which will handicap sound efforts at reform, nor is it intended to have this effect. We encourage Congress and the States to continue their laudable search for increasingly effective ways of protecting the rights of the individual while promoting efficient enforcement of our criminal laws. However, unless we are shown other procedures which are at least as effective in apprising accused persons of their right of silence and in assuring a continuous opportunity to exercise it, the following safeguards must be observed.

At the outset, if a person in custody is to be subjected to interrogation, he must first be informed in clear and unequivocal terms that he has the right to remain silent. For those unaware of the privilege, the warning is needed simply to make them aware of it—the threshold requirement for an intelligent decision as to its exercise. More important, such a warning is an absolute prerequisite in overcoming the inherent pressures of the interrogation atmosphere. It is not just the subnormal or woefully ignorant who succumb to an interrogator's imprecations, whether implied or expressly stated, that the interrogation will continue until a confession is obtained or that silence in the face of accusation is itself damning and will bode ill when presented to a jury. Further, the warning will show the individual that his interrogators are prepared to recognize his privilege should he choose to exercise it.

The Fifth Amendment privilege is so fundamental to our system of constitutional rule and the expedient of giving an adequate warning as to the availability of the privilege so simple, we will not pause to inquire in individual cases whether the defendant was aware of his rights without a warning being given. Assessments of the knowledge the defendant possessed, based on information as to his age, education, intelligence, or prior contact with authorities, can never be more than speculation; a warning is a clearcut fact. More important, whatever the background of the person interrogated, a warning at the time of the interrogation is indispensable to overcome its pressures and to insure that the individual knows he is free to exercise the privilege at that point in time.

The warning of the right to remain silent must be accompanied by the explanation that anything said can and will be used against the individual in court. This warning is needed in order to make him aware not only of the privilege, but also of the consequences of forgoing it. It is only through an awareness of these consequences that there can be any assurance of real understanding and intelligent exercise of the privilege. Moreover, this warning may serve to make the individual more acutely aware that he is faced with a phase of the adversary system—that he is not in the presence of persons acting solely in his interest.

The circumstances surrounding in-custody interrogation can operate very quickly to overbear the will of one merely made aware of his privilege by his interrogators. Therefore, the right to have counsel present at the interrogation is indispensable to the protection of the Fifth Amendment privilege under the system we delineate today. Our aim is to assure that the individual's right to choose between silence and speech remains unfettered throughout the interrogation process. A once-stated warning, delivered by those who will conduct the interrogation, cannot itself suffice to that end among those who most require knowledge of their rights. A mere warning given by the interrogators is not alone sufficient to accomplish that end. Prosecutors themselves claim that the admonishment of the right to remain silent without more "will benefit only the recidivist and the professional." Brief for the National District Attorneys Association as *amicus curiae,* p. 14. Even preliminary advice given to the accused by his own attorney can be swiftly overcome by the secret interrogation process. Cf. Escobedo v. Illinois, 378 U.S. 478, 485, n. 5, 84 S.Ct. 1758, 12 L.Ed.2d 977. Thus, the need for counsel to protect the Fifth Amendment privilege comprehends not merely a right to consult with counsel prior to questioning, but also to have counsel present during any questioning if the defendant so desires.

The presence of counsel at the interrogation may serve several significant subsidiary functions as well. If the accused decides to talk to his interrogators, the assistance of counsel can mitigate the dangers of untrustworthiness. With a lawyer present the likelihood that the police will practice coercion is reduced, and if coercion is nevertheless exercised the lawyer can testify to it in court. The presence of a lawyer can also help to guarantee that the accused gives a fully accurate statement to the police and that the statement is rightly reported by the prosecution at trial. See Crooker v. California, 357 U.S. 433, 443–448, 78 S.Ct. 1287, 2 L.Ed.2d 1448 (1958) (DOUGLAS, J., dissenting).

An individual need not make a pre-interrogation request for a lawyer. While such request affirmatively secures his right to have one, his failure to ask for a lawyer does not constitute a waiver. No effective waiver of the right to counsel during interrogation can be recognized unless specifically made after the warnings we here delineate have been given. The accused who does not know his rights and therefore does not make a request may be the person who most needs counsel. As the California Supreme Court has aptly put it:

> "Finally, we must recognize that the imposition of the requirement for the request would discriminate against the defendant who does not know his rights. The defendant who does not ask for counsel is the very defendant who most needs counsel. We cannot penalize a defendant who, not understanding his constitutional rights, does not make the formal request and by such failure demonstrates his helplessness. To require the request would be to favor the defendant whose sophistication or status had fortuitously prompted him to make it." People v. Dorado, 62 Cal.2d 338, 351, 398 P.2d 361, 369–370, 42 Cal.Rptr. 169, 177–178 (1965) (Tobriner, J.).

In Carnley v. Cochran, 369 U.S. 506, 513, 82 S.Ct. 884, 8 L.Ed.2d 70 (1962), we stated: "[I]t is settled that where the assistance of counsel is a constitutional requisite, the right to be furnished counsel does not depend on a request." This proposition applies with equal force in the context of providing counsel to protect an accused's Fifth Amendment privilege in the face of interrogation. Although the role of counsel at trial differs from the role during interrogation, the differences are not relevant to the question whether a request is a prerequisite.

Accordingly we hold that an individual held for interrogation must be clearly informed that he has the right to consult with a lawyer and to have the lawyer with him during interrogation under the system for protecting the privilege we delineate today. As with the warnings of the right to remain silent and that anything stated can be used in evidence against him, this warning is an absolute prerequisite to interrogation. No amount of circumstantial evidence that the person may have been aware of this right will suffice to stand in its stead. Only through such a warning is there ascertainable assurance that the accused was aware of this right.

If an individual indicates that he wishes the assistance of counsel before any interrogation occurs, the authorities cannot rationally ignore or deny his request on the basis that the individual does not have or cannot afford a retained attorney. The financial ability of the individual has no relationship to the scope of the rights involved here. The privilege against self-incrimination secured by the Constitution applies to all individuals. The need for counsel in order to protect the privilege exists for the indigent as well as the affluent. In fact, were we to limit these constitutional rights to those who can retain an attorney, our decisions today would be of little significance. The cases before us as well as the vast majority of confession cases with which we have dealt in the past involve those unable to retain counsel. While authorities are not required to relieve the accused of his poverty, they have the obligation not to take advantage of indigence in the administration of justice. Denial of counsel to the indigent at the time of interrogation while allowing an attorney to those who can afford one would be no more supportable by reason or logic than the similar situation at trial and on appeal struck down in Gideon v. Wainwright, 372 U.S. 335, 83 S.Ct. 792, 9 L.Ed.2d 799 (1963), and Douglas v. California, 372 U.S. 353, 83 S.Ct. 814, 9 L.Ed.2d 811 (1963).

In order fully to apprise a person interrogated of the extent of his rights under this system then, it is necessary to warn him not only that he has the right to consult with an attorney, but also that if he is indigent a lawyer will be appointed to represent him. Without this additional warning, the admonition of the right to consult with counsel would often be understood as meaning only that he can consult with a lawyer if he has one or has the funds to obtain one. The warning of a right to counsel would be hollow if not couched in terms that would convey to the indigent—the person most often subjected to interrogation—the knowledge that he too has a right to have counsel present. As with the warnings of the right to remain silent and of the general right to counsel, only by effective and express explanation to the indigent of this right can there be assurance that he was truly in a position to exercise it.

Once warnings have been given, the subsequent procedure is clear. If the individual indicates in any manner, at any time prior to or during questioning, that he wishes to remain silent, the interrogation must cease. At this point he has shown that he intends to exercise his Fifth Amendment privilege; any statement taken after the person invokes his privilege cannot be other than the product of compulsion, subtle or otherwise. Without the right to cut off questioning, the setting of in-custody interrogation operates on the individual to overcome free choice in producing a statement after the privilege has been once invoked. If the individual states that he wants an attorney, the interrogation must cease until an attorney is present. At that time, the individual must have an opportunity to confer with the attorney and to have him present during any subsequent questioning. If the individual cannot obtain an attorney and he indicates that he wants one before speaking to police, they must respect his decision to remain silent.

This does not mean, as some have suggested, that each police station must have a "station house lawyer" present at all times to advise prisoners. It does mean, however, that if police proposed to interrogate a person they must make known to him that he is entitled to a lawyer and that if he cannot afford one, a lawyer will be provided for him prior to any interrogation. If authorities conclude that they will not provide counsel during a reasonable period of time in which investigation in the field is carried out, they may refrain from doing so without violating the person's Fifth Amendment privilege so long as they do not question him during that time.

If the interrogation continues without the presence of an attorney and a statement is taken, a heavy burden rests on the government to demonstrate that the defendant knowingly and intelligently waived his privilege against self-incrimination and his right to retained or appointed counsel. Escobedo v. Illinois, 378 U.S. 478, 490, n. 14, 84 S.Ct. 1758, 12 L.Ed.2d 977. This Court has always set high standards of proof for the waiver of constitutional rights, Johnson v. Zerbst, 304 U.S. 458, 58 S.Ct. 1019, 82 L.Ed. 1461 (1938), and we re-assert these standards as applied to in-custody interrogation. Since the State is responsible for establishing the isolated circumstances under which the interrogation takes place and has the only means of making available corroborated evidence of warnings given during incommunicado interrogation, the burden is rightly on its shoulders.

An express statement that the individual is willing to make a statement and does not want an attorney followed closely by a statement could constitute a waiver. But a valid waiver will not be presumed simply from the silence of the accused after warnings are given or simply from the fact that a confession was in fact eventually obtained. A statement we made in Carnley v. Cochran, 369 U.S. 506, 516, 82 S.Ct. 884, 8 L.Ed.2d 70 (1962), is applicable here:

> "Presuming waiver from a silent record is impermissible. The record must show, or there must be an allegation and evidence which show, that an accused was offered counsel but intelligently and understandingly rejected the offer. Anything less is not waiver."

See also Glasser v. United States, 315 U.S. 60, 62 S.Ct. 457, 86 L.Ed. 680 (1942). Moreover, where in-custody interrogation is involved, there is no room for the contention that the privilege is waived if the individual answers some questions or gives some information on his own prior to invoking his right to remain silent when interrogated.

Whatever the testimony of the authorities as to waiver of rights by an accused, the fact of lengthy interrogation or incommunicado incarceration before a statement is made is strong evidence that the accused did not validly waive his rights. In these circumstances the fact that the individual eventually made a statement is consistent with the conclusion that the compelling influence of the interrogation finally forced him to do so. It is inconsistent with any notion of a voluntary relinquishment of the privilege. Moreover, any evidence that the accused was threatened, tricked, or cajoled into a waiver will, of course, show that the defendant did not voluntarily waive his privilege. The requirement of warnings and waiver of rights is a fundamental with respect to the Fifth Amendment privilege and not simply a preliminary ritual to existing methods of interrogation.

The warnings required and the waiver necessary in accordance with our opinion today are, in the absence of a fully effective equivalent, prerequisites to the admissibility of any statement made by a defendant. No distinction can be drawn between statements which are direct confessions and statements which amount to "admissions" of part or all of an offense. The privilege against self-incrimination protects the individual from being compelled to incriminate himself in any manner; it does not distinguish degrees of incrimination. Similarly, for precisely the same reason, no distinction may be drawn between inculpatory statements and statements alleged to be merely "exculpatory." If a statement made were in fact truly exculpatory it would, of course, never be used by the prosecution. In fact, statements merely intended to be exculpatory by the defendant are often used to impeach his testimony at trial or to demonstrate untruths in the statement given under interrogation and thus to prove guilt by implication. These statements are incriminating in any meaningful sense of the word and may not be used without the full warnings and effective waiver required for any other statement. In *Escobedo* itself, the defendant fully intended his accusation of another as the slayer to be exculpatory as to himself.

The principles announced today deal with the protection which must be given to the privilege against self-incrimination when the individual is first subjected to police interrogation while in custody at the station or otherwise deprived of his freedom of action in any significant way. It is at this point that our adversary system of criminal proceedings commences, distinguishing itself at the outset from the inquisitorial system recognized in some countries. Under the system of warnings we delineate today or under any other system which may be devised and found effective, the safeguards to be erected about the privilege must come into play at this point.

Our decision is not intended to hamper the traditional function of police officers in investigating crime. See Escobedo v. Illinois, 378 U.S. 478, 492, 84 S.Ct. 1758, 12 L.Ed.2d 277. When an individual is in custody on probable cause, the police may, of course, seek out evidence in the field to be used at trial against him. Such investigation may include inquiry of persons not under restraint. General on-the-scene questioning as to facts surrounding a crime or other general questioning of citizens in the fact-finding process is not affected by our holding. It is an act of responsible citizenship for individuals to give whatever information they may have to aid in law enforcement. In such situations the compelling atmosphere inherent in the process of in-custody interrogation is not necessarily present.

In dealing with statements obtained through interrogation, we do not purport to find all confessions inadmissible. Confessions remain a proper element in law enforcement. Any statement given freely and voluntarily without any compelling influences is, of course, admissible in evidence. The fundamental import of the privilege while an individual is in custody is not whether he is allowed to talk to the police without the benefit of warnings and counsel, but whether he can be interrogated. There is no requirement that police stop a person who enters a police station and states that he wishes to confess to a crime, or a person who calls the police to offer a confession or any other statement he desires to make. Volunteered statements of any kind are not barred by the Fifth Amendment and their admissibility is not affected by our holding today.

To summarize, we hold that when an individual is taken into custody or otherwise deprived of his freedom by the authorities in any significant way and is subjected to questioning, the privilege against self-incrimination is jeopardized. Procedural safeguards must be employed to protect the privilege, and unless other fully effective means are adopted to notify the person of his right of silence and to assure that the exercise of the right will be scrupulously honored, the following measures are required. He must be warned prior to any questioning that he has the right to remain silent, that anything he says can be used against him in a court of law, that he has the right to the presence of an attorney, and that if he cannot afford an attorney one will be appointed for him prior to any questioning if he so desires. Opportunity to exercise these rights must be afforded to him throughout the interrogation. After such warnings have been given, and such opportunity afforded him, the individual may knowingly and intelligently waive these rights and agree to answer questions or make a statement. But unless and until such warnings and waiver are demonstrated by the prosecution at trial, no evidence obtained as a result of interrogation can be used against him.

IV.

A recurrent argument made in these cases is that society's need for interrogation outweighs the privilege. This argument is not unfamiliar to this Court. See, e. g., Chambers v. Florida, 309 U.S. 227, 240–241, 60 S.Ct. 472, 84 L.Ed. 716 (1940). The whole thrust of our foregoing discussion demonstrates that the Constitution has prescribed the rights of the individual when confronted with the power of government when it provided in the Fifth Amendment that an individual cannot be compelled to be a witness against himself. That right cannot be abridged. As Mr. Justice Brandeis once observed:

> "Decency, security and liberty alike demand that government officials shall be subjected to the same rules of conduct that are commands to the citizen. In a government of laws, existence of the government will be imperilled if it fails to observe the law scrupulously. Our Government is the potent, the omnipresent teacher. For good or for ill, it teaches the whole people by its example. Crime is contagious. If the Government becomes a lawbreaker, it breeds contempt for law; it invites every man to become a law unto himself; it invites anarchy. To declare that in the administration of the criminal law the end justifies the means . . . would bring terrible retribution. Against that pernicious doctrine this Court should resolutely set its face." Olmstead v. United States, 277 U.S. 438, 485 (1928) (dissenting opinion).

In this connection, one of our country's distinguished jurists has pointed out: "The quality of a nation's civilization can be largely measured by the methods it uses in the enforcement of its criminal law."

If the individual desires to exercise his privilege, he has the right to do so. This is not for the authorities to decide. An attorney may advise his client not to talk to police until he has had an opportunity to investigate the case, or he may wish to be present with his client during any police questioning. In doing so an attorney is merely exercising the good professional judgment he has been taught. This is not cause for considering the attorney a menace to law enforcement. He is merely carrying out what he is sworn to do under his oath—to protect to the extent of his ability the rights of his client. In fulfilling this responsibility the attorney plays a vital role in the administration of criminal justice under our Constitution.

In announcing these principles, we are not unmindful of the burdens which law enforcement officials must bear, often under trying circumstances. We also fully recognize the obligation of all citizens to aid in enforcing the criminal laws. This Court, while protecting individual rights, has always given ample latitude to law enforcement agencies in the legitimate exercise of their duties. The limits we have placed on the interrogation process should not constitute an undue interference with a proper system of law enforcement. As we have noted, our decision does not in any way preclude police from carrying out their traditional investigatory functions. Although confessions may play an important role in some convictions, the cases before us present graphic examples of the overstatement of the "need" for confessions. In each case authorities conducted interrogations ranging up to five days in duration despite the presence, through standard investigating practices, of considerable evidence against each defendant. Further examples are chronicled in our prior cases. See, e. g., Haynes v. Washington, 373 U.S. 503, 518–519, 83 S.Ct. 1336, 10 L.Ed.2d 513 (1963); Rogers v. Richmond, 365 U.S. 534, 541, 81 S.Ct. 735, 5 L.Ed.2d 760 (1961); Malinski v. New York, 324 U.S. 401, 402, 65 S.Ct. 781, 89 L.Ed. 1029 (1945).

It is also urged that an unfettered right to detention for interrogation should be allowed because it will often redound to the benefit of the person questioned. When police inquiry determines that there is no reason to believe that the person has committed any crime, it is said, he will be released without need for further formal procedures. The person who has committed no offense, however, will be better able to clear himself after warnings with counsel present than without. It can be assumed that in such circumstances a lawyer would advise his client to talk freely to police in order to clear himself.

Custodial interrogation, by contrast, does not necessarily afford the innocent an opportunity to clear themselves. A serious consequence of the present practice of the interrogation alleged to be beneficial for the innocent is that many arrests "for investigation" subject large numbers of innocent persons to detention and interrogation. In one of the cases before us, No. 584, California v. Stewart, police held four persons, who were in the defendant's house at the time of the arrest, in jail for five days until defendant confessed. At that time they were finally released. Police stated that there was "no evidence to connect them with any crime." Available statistics on the extent of this practice where it is condoned indicate that these four are far from alone in being subjected to arrest, prolonged detention, and interrogation without the requisite probable cause.

Over the years the Federal Bureau of Investigation has compiled an exemplary record of effective law enforcement while advising any suspect or arrested person, at the outset of an interview, that he is not required to make a statement, that any statement may be used against him in court, that the individual may obtain the services of an attorney of his own choice and, more recently, that he has a right to free counsel if he is unable to pay. A letter received from the Solicitor General in response to a question from the Bench makes it clear that the present pattern of warnings and respect for the rights of the individual followed as a practice by the FBI is consistent with the procedure which we delineate today. It states:

> "At the oral argument of the above cause, Mr. Justice Fortas asked whether I could provide certain information as to the practices followed by the Federal Bureau of Investigation. I have directed these questions to the attention of the Director of the Federal Bureau of Investigation and am submitting herewith a statement of the questions and of the answers which we have received.
>
> "'(1) When an individual is interviewed by agents of the Bureau, what warning is given to him?

" 'The standard warning long given by Special Agents of the FBI to both suspects and persons under arrest is that the person has a right to say nothing and a right to counsel, and that any statement he does make may be used against him in court. Examples of this warning are to be found in the *Westover* case at 342 F.2d 684 (1965), and Jackson v. U. S., 337 F.2d 136 (1964), cert. den. 380 U.S. 935.

" 'After passage of the Criminal Justice Act of 1964, which provides free counsel for Federal defendants unable to pay, we added to our instructions to Special Agents the requirement that any person who is under arrest for an offense under FBI jurisdiction, or whose arrest is contemplated following the interview, must also be advised of his right to free counsel if he is unable to pay, and the fact that such counsel will be assigned by the Judge. At the same time, we broadened the right to counsel warning to read counsel of his own choice, or anyone else with whom he might wish to speak.

" '(2) When is the warning given?

" 'The FBI warning is given to a suspect at the very outset of the interview, as shown in the *Westover* case, cited above. The warning may be given to a person arrested as soon as practicable after the arrest, as shown in the *Jackson* case, also cited above, and in U. S. v. Konigsberg, 336 F.2d 844 (1964), cert. den. 379 U.S. 933, but in any event it must precede the interview with the person for a confession or admission of his own guilt.

" '(3) What is the Bureau's practice in the event that (a) the individual requests counsel and (b) counsel appears?

" 'When the person who has been warned of his right to counsel decides that he wishes to consult with counsel before making a statement, the interview is terminated at that point, Shultz v. U. S., 351 F.2d 287 (1965). It may be continued, however, as to all matters *other* than the person's own guilt or innocence. If he is indecisive in his request for counsel, there may be some question on whether he did or did not waive counsel. Situations of this kind must necessarily be left to the judgment of the interviewing Agent. For example, in Hiram v. U. S., 354 F.2d 4 (1965), the Agent's conclusion that the person arrested had waived his right to counsel was upheld by the courts.

" 'A person being interviewed and desiring to consult counsel by telephone must be permitted to do so, as shown in Caldwell v. U. S., 351 F.2d 459 (1965). When counsel appears in person, he is permitted to confer with his client in private.

" '(4) What is the Bureau's practice if the individual requests counsel, but cannot afford to retain an attorney?

" 'If any person being interviewed after warning of counsel decides that he wishes to consult with counsel before proceeding further the interview is terminated, as shown above. FBI Agents do not pass judgment on the ability of the person to pay for counsel. They do, however, advise those who have been arrested for an offense under FBI jurisdiction, or whose arrest is contemplated following the interview, of a right to free counsel *if* they are unable to pay, and the availability of such counsel from the Judge.' "

The practice of the FBI can readily be emulated by state and local enforcement agencies. The argument that the FBI deals with different crimes than are dealt with by state authorities does not mitigate the significance of the FBI experience.

The experience in some other countries also suggests that the danger to law enforcement in curbs on interrogation is overplayed. The English procedure since 1912 under the Judges' Rules is significant. As recently strengthened, the Rules require that a cautionary warning be given an accused by a police officer as soon as he has evidence that affords reasonable grounds for suspicion; they also require that any statement made be given by the accused without questioning by police. The right of the individual to consult with an attorney during this period is expressly recognized.

The safeguards present under Scottish law may be even greater than in England. Scottish judicial decisions bar use in evidence of most confessions obtained through police interrogation. In India, confessions made to police not in the presence of a magistrate have been excluded by rule of evidence since 1872, at a time when it operated under British law. Identical provisions appear in the Evidence Ordinance of Ceylon, enacted in 1895. Similarly, in our country the Uniform Code of Military Justice has long provided that no suspect may be interrogated without first being warned of his right not to make a statement and that any statement he makes may be used against him. Denial of the right to consult counsel during interrogation has also been proscribed by military tribunals. There appears to have been no marked detrimental effect on criminal law enforcement in these jurisdictions as a result of these rules. Conditions of law enforcement in our country are sufficiently similar to permit reference to this experience as assurance that lawlessness will not result from warning an individual of his rights or allowing him to exercise them. Moreover, it is consistent with our legal system that we give at least as much protection to these rights as is given in the jurisdictions described. We deal in our country with rights grounded in a specific requirement of the Fifth Amendment of the Constitution, whereas other jurisdictions arrived at their conclusions on the basis of principles of justice not so specifically defined.

It is also urged upon us that we withhold decision on this issue until state legislative bodies and advisory groups have had an opportunity to deal with these problems by rule making. We have already pointed out that the Constitution does not require any specific code of procedures for protecting the privilege against self-incrimination during custodial interrogation. Congress and the States are free to develop their own safeguards for the privilege, so long as they are fully as effective as those described above in informing accused persons of their right of silence and in affording a continuous opportunity to exercise it. In any event, however, the issues presented are of constitutional dimensions and must be determined by the courts. The admissibility of a statement in the face of a claim that it was obtained in violation of the defendant's constitutional rights is an issue the resolution of which has long since been undertaken by this Court. See Hopt v. Utah, 110 U.S. 574, 4 S.Ct. 202, 28 L. Ed. 262 (1884). Judicial solutions to problems of constitutional dimension have evolved decade by decade. As courts have been presented with the need to enforce constitutional rights, they have found means of doing so. That was our responsibility when *Escobedo* was before us and it is our responsibility today. Where rights secured by the Constitution are involved, there can be no rule making or legislation which would abrogate them.

V.

Because of the nature of the problem and because of its recurrent significance in numerous cases, we have to this point discussed the relationship of the Fifth Amendment privilege to police interrogation without specific concentration on the facts of the cases before us. We turn now to these facts to consider the application to these cases of the constitutional principles discussed above. In each instance, we have concluded that statements were obtained from the defendant under circumstances that did not meet constitutional standards for protection of the privilege.

No. 759. *Miranda v. Arizona.*

On March 13, 1963, petitioner, Ernesto Miranda, was arrested at his home and taken in custody to a Phoenix police station. He was there identified by the complaining witness. The police then took him to "Interrogation Room No. 2" of the detective bureau. There he was questioned by two police officers. The officers admitted at trial that Miranda was not advised that he had a right to have an attorney present. Two hours later, the officers emerged from the interrogation room with a written confession signed by Miranda. At the top of the statement was a typed paragraph stating that the confession was made voluntarily, without threats or promises of immunity and "with full knowledge of my legal rights, understanding any statement I make may be used against me."

At his trial before a jury, the written confession was admitted into evidence over the objection of defense counsel, and the officers testified to the prior oral confession made by Miranda during the interrogation. Miranda was found guilty of kidnapping and rape. He was sentenced to 20 to 30 years' imprisonment on each count, the sentences to run concurrently. On appeal, the Supreme Court of Arizona held that Miranda's constitutional rights were not violated in obtaining the confession and affirmed the conviction. 98 Ariz. 18, 401 P.2d 721 (1965). In reaching its decision, the court emphasized heavily the fact that Miranda did not specifically request counsel.

We reverse. From the testimony of the officers and by the admission of respondent, it is clear that Miranda was not in any way apprised of his right to consult with an attorney and to have one present during the interrogation, nor was his right not to be compelled to incriminate himself effectively protected in any other manner. Without these warnings the statements were inadmissible. The mere fact that he signed a statement which contained a typed-in clause stating that he had "full knowledge" of his "legal rights" does not approach the knowing and intelligent waiver required to relinquish constitutional rights. Cf. Haynes v. Washington, 373 U.S. 503, 512–513, 83 S.Ct. 1336, 10 L.Ed.2d 513 (1963); Haley v. Ohio, 332 U.S. 596, 601, 68 S.Ct. 302, 92 L.Ed. 224 (1948) (opinion of Mr. Justice DOUGLAS).

No. 760. *Vignera v. New York.*

Petitioner, Michael Vignera, was picked up by New York police on October 14, 1960, in connection with the robbery three days earlier of a Brooklyn dress shop. They took him to the 17th Detective Squad headquarters in Manhattan. Sometime thereafter he was taken to the 66th Detective Squad. There a detective questioned Vignera with respect to the robbery. Vignera orally admitted the robbery to the detective. The detective was asked on cross-examination at trial by defense counsel whether Vignera was warned of his right to counsel before being interrogated. The prosecution objected to the question and the trial judge sustained the objection. Thus, the defense was precluded from making any showing that warnings had not been given. While at the 66th Detective Squad, Vignera was identified by the store owner and a saleslady as the man who robbed the dress shop. At about 3 p. m. he was formally arrested. The police then transported him to still another station, the 70th Precinct in Brooklyn, "for detention." At 11 p. m. Vignera was questioned by an assistant district attorney in the presence of a hearing reporter who transcribed the questions and Vignera's answers. This verbatim account of these proceedings contains no statement of any warnings given by the assistant district attorney. At Vignera's trial on a charge of first degree robbery, the detective testified as to the oral confession. The transcription of the statement taken was also introduced in evidence. At the conclusion of the testimony, the trial judge charged the jury in part as follows:

> "The law doesn't say that the confession is void or invalidated because the police officer didn't advise the defendant as to his rights. Did you hear what I said? I am telling you what the law of the State of New York is."

Vignera was found guilty of first degree robbery. He was subsequently adjudged a third-felony offender and sentenced to 30 to 60 years' imprisonment. The conviction was affirmed without opinion by the Appellate Division, Second Department, 21 App.Div.2d 752, 252 N.Y.S.2d 19 (1964), and by the Court of Appeals, also without opinion, 15 N.Y.2d 970, 207 N.E.2d 527, 259 N.Y.S.2d 857 (1965), remittitur amended, 16 N.Y.2d 614, 209 N.E.2d 110, 261 N.Y.S.2d 65 (1965). In argument to the Court of Appeals, the State contended that Vignera had no constitutional right to be advised of his right to counsel or his privilege against self-incrimination.

We reverse. The foregoing indicates that Vignera was not warned of any of his rights before the questioning by the detective and by the assistant district attorney. No other steps were taken to protect these rights. Thus he was not effectively apprised of his Fifth Amendment privilege or of his right to have counsel present and his statements are inadmissible.

No. 761. *Westover v. United States.*

At approximately 9:45 p. m. on March 20, 1963, petitioner, Carl Calvin Westover, was arrested by local police in Kansas City as a suspect in two Kansas City robberies. A report was also received from the FBI that he was wanted on a felony charge in California. The local authorities took him to a police station and placed him in a line-up on the local charges, and at about 11:45 p. m. he was booked. Kansas City police interrogated Westover on the night of his arrest. He denied any knowledge of criminal activities. The next day local officers interrogated him again throughout the morning. Shortly before noon they informed the FBI that they were through interrogating Westover and that the FBI could proceed to interrogate him. There is nothing in the record to indicate that Westover was ever given any warning as to his rights by local police. At noon, three special agents of the FBI continued the interrogation in a private interview room of the Kansas City Police Department, this time with respect to the robbery of a savings and loan association and a bank in Sacramento, California. After two or two and one-half hours, Westover signed separate confessions to each of these two robberies which had been prepared by one of the agents during the interrogation. At trial one of the agents testified, and a paragraph on each of the statements states, that the agents advised Westover that he did not have to make a statement, that any statement he made could be used against him, and that he had the right to see an attorney.

Westover was tried by a jury in federal court and convicted of the California robberies. His statements were introduced at trial.

He was sentenced to 15 years' imprisonment on each count, the sentences to run consecutively. On appeal, the conviction was affirmed by the Court of Appeals for the Ninth Circuit. 342 F.2d 684.

We reverse. On the facts of this case we cannot find that Westover knowingly and intelligently waived his right to remain silent and his right to consult with counsel prior to the time he made the statement. At the time the FBI agents began questioning Westover, he had been in custody for over 14 hours and had been interrogated at length during that period. The FBI interrogation began immediately upon the conclusion of the interrogation by Kansas City police and was conducted in local police headquarters. Although the two law enforcement authorities are legally distinct and the crimes for which they interrogated Westover were different, the impact on him was that of a continuous period of questioning. There is no evidence of any warning given prior to the FBI interrogation nor is there any evidence of an articulated waiver of rights after the FBI commenced its interrogation. The record simply shows that the defendant did in fact confess a short time after being turned over to the FBI following interrogation by local police. Despite the fact that the FBI agents gave warnings at the outset of their interview, from Westover's point of view the warnings came at the end of the interrogation process. In these circumstances an intelligent waiver of constitutional rights cannot be assumed.

We do not suggest that law enforcement authorities are precluded from questioning any individual who has been held for a period of time by other authorities and interrogated by them without appropriate warnings. A different case would be presented if an accused were taken into custody by the second authority, removed both in time and place from his original surroundings, and then adequately advised of his rights and given an opportunity to exercise them. But here the FBI interrogation was conducted immediately following the state interrogation in the same police station—in the same compelling surroundings. Thus, in obtaining a confession from Westover the federal authorities were the beneficiaries of the pressure applied by the local in-custody interrogation. In these circumstances the giving of warnings alone was not sufficient to protect the privilege.

No. 584. *California v. Stewart.*

In the course of investigating a series of purse-snatch robberies in which one of the victims had died of injuries inflicted by her assailant, respondent, Roy Allen Stewart, was pointed out to Los Angeles police as the endorser of dividend checks taken in one of the robberies. At about 7:15 p. m., January 31, 1963, police officers went to Stewart's house and arrested him. One of the officers asked Stewart if they could search the house, to which he replied, "Go ahead." The search turned up various items taken from the five robbery victims. At the time of Stewart's arrest, police also arrested Stewart's wife and three other persons who were visiting him. These four were jailed along with Stewart and were interrogated. Stewart was taken to the University Station of the Los Angeles Police Department where he was placed in a cell. During the next five days, police interrogated Stewart on nine different occasions. Except during the first interrogation session, when he was confronted with an accusing witness, Stewart was isolated with his interrogators.

During the ninth interrogation session, Stewart admitted that he had robbed the deceased and stated that he had not meant to hurt her. Police then brought Stewart before a magistrate for the first time. Since there was no evidence to connect them with any crime, the police then released the other four persons arrested with him.

Nothing in the record specifically indicates whether Stewart was or was not advised of his right to remain silent or his right to counsel. In a number of instances, however, the interrogating officers were asked to recount everything that was said during the interrogations. None indicated that Stewart was ever advised of his rights.

Stewart was charged with kidnapping to commit robbery, rape, and murder. At his trial, transcripts of the first interrogation and the confession at the last interrogation were introduced in evidence. The jury found Stewart guilty of robbery and first degree murder and fixed the penalty as death. On appeal, the Supreme Court of California reversed. 62 Cal.2d 571, 400 P.2d 97, 43 Cal.Rptr. 201 (1965). It held that under this Court's decision in *Escobedo,* Stewart should have been advised of his right to remain silent and of his right to counsel and that it would not presume in the face of a silent record that the police advised Stewart of his rights.

We affirm. In dealing with custodial interrogation, we will not presume that a defendant has been effectively apprised of his rights and that his privilege against self-incrimination has been adequately safeguarded on a record that does not show that any warnings have been given or that any effective alternative has been employed. Nor can a knowing and intelligent waiver of these rights be assumed on a silent record. Furthermore, Stewart's steadfast denial of the alleged offenses through eight of the nine interrogations over a period of five days is subject to no other construction than that he was compelled by persistent interrogation to forgo his Fifth Amendment privilege.

Therefore, in accordance with the foregoing, the judgments of the Supreme Court of Arizona in No. 759, of the New York Court of Appeals in No. 760, and of the Court of Appeals for the Ninth Circuit in No. 761 are reversed. The judgment of the Supreme Court of California in No. 584 is affirmed.

It is so ordered.

Concurring decision of Mr. Justice CLARK No. 584, and dissenting Nos. 759, 760, 761 omitted, dissenting decision of Mr. Justice HARLAN, joined by Mr. Justice STEWART and Mr. Justice WHITE, deleted. Dissenting decision of Mr. Justice WHITE, joined by Mr. Justice HARLAN and Mr. Justice STEWART are not included.

UNITED STATES v. WATSON

Supreme Court of the United States, 1976.
423 U.S. 411, 96 S.Ct. 820, 46 L.Ed.2d 598.

Mr. Justice WHITE delivered the opinion of the Court.

This case presents questions under the Fourth Amendment as to the legality of a warrantless arrest and of an ensuing search of the arrestee's automobile carried out with his purported consent.

I.

The relevant events began on August 17, 1972, when an informant, one Khoury, telephoned a postal inspector informing him that respondent Watson, was in possession of a stolen credit card and had asked Khoury to cooperate in using the card to their mutual advantage. On five to 10 previous occasions Khoury had provided the inspector with reliable information on postal inspection matters, some involving Watson. Later that day Khoury delivered the card to the inspector. On learning that Watson had agreed to furnish additional cards, the inspector asked Khoury to arrange to meet with Watson. Khoury did so, a meeting being scheduled for August 22. Watson cancelled that engagement, but at noon on August 23, Khoury met with Watson at a restaurant designated by the latter. Khoury had been instructed that if Watson had additional stolen credit cards, Khoury was to give a designated signal. The signal was given, the officers closed in and Watson was forthwith arrested. He was removed from the restaurant to the street where he was given the warnings required by Miranda v. Arizona, 384 U.S. 436, 86 S.Ct. 1602, 16 L.Ed.2d 694 (1966). A search having revealed that Watson had no credit cards on his person, the inspector asked if he could look inside Watson's car, which was standing within view. Watson said, "Go ahead," and repeated these words when the inspector cautioned that "[i]f I find anything, it is going to go against you." Using keys furnished by Watson, the inspector entered the car and found under the floor mat an envelope containing two credit cards in the names of other persons. These cards were the basis for two counts of a four-count indictment charging Watson with possessing stolen mail in violation of 18 U.S.C.A. § 1708.

Prior to trial, Watson moved to suppress the cards, claiming that his arrest was illegal for want of probable cause and an arrest warrant and that his consent to search the car was involuntary and ineffective because he had not been told that he could withhold consent. The motion was denied, and Watson was convicted of illegally possessing the two cards seized from his car.

A divided panel of the Court of Appeals for the Ninth Circuit reversed, 504 F.2d 849 (1974), ruling that the admission in evidence of the two credit cards found in the car was prohibited by the Fourth Amendment. In reaching this judgment, the court decided two issues in Watson's favor. First, notwithstanding its agreement with the District Court that Khoury was reliable and that there was probable cause for arresting Watson, the court held the arrest unconstitutional because the postal inspector had failed to secure an arrest warrant although he concededly had time to do so. Second, based on the totality of the circumstances, one of which was the illegality of the arrest, the court held Watson's consent to search had been coerced and hence was not a valid ground for the warrantless search of the automobile. We granted certiorari. 420 U.S. 924, 95 S.Ct. 1117, 43 L.Ed.2d 392 (1975).

II.

A major part of the Court of Appeals' opinion was its holding that Watson's warrantless arrest violated the Fourth Amendment. Although it did not expressly do so, it may have intended to overturn the conviction on the independent ground that the two credit cards were the inadmissible fruits of an unconstitutional arrest. Cf. Brown v. Illinois, 422 U.S. 590, 95 S.Ct. 2254, 45 L.Ed.2d 416 (1975). However that may be, the Court of Appeals treated the illegality of Watson's arrest as an important factor in determining the voluntariness of his consent to search his car. We therefore deal first with the arrest issue.

Contrary to the Court of Appeals' view, Watson's arrest was not invalid because executed without a warrant. Section 3061(a) of Title 18 U.S.C. expressly empowers the Board of Governors of the Postal Service to authorize Postal Service officers and employees "performing duties related to the inspection of postal matters" to

> "(3) make arrests without warrant for felonies cognizable under the laws of the United States if they have reasonable grounds to believe that the person to be arrested has committed or is committing such a felony."

By regulation, 39 CFR § 232.5(a) (1975), and in identical language the Board of Governors has exercised that power and authorized warrantless arrests. There being probable cause in this case to believe that Watson had violated § 1708, the inspector and his subordinates, in arresting Watson, were acting strictly in accordance with the governing statute and regulations. The effect of the judgment of the Court of Appeals was to invalidate the statute as applied in this case and as applied to all the situations where a court fails to find exigent circumstances justifying a warrantless arrest. We reverse that judgment.

Under the Fourth Amendment, the people are to be "secure in their persons, houses, papers, and effects, against unreasonable searches and seizures, . . . and no Warrants shall issue, but upon probable cause . . .." Section 3061 represents a judgment by Congress that it is not unreasonable under the Fourth Amendment for postal inspectors to arrest without a warrant provided they have probable cause to do so. This was not an isolated or quixotic judgment of the legislative branch. Other federal law enforcement officers have been expressly authorized by statute for many years to make felony arrests on probable cause but without a warrant. This is true of United States Marshals, 18 U.S.C.A. § 3053, and of agents of the Federal Bureau of Investigation, 18 U.S.C.A. § 3052; the Drug Enforcement Administration, 84 Stat. 1273, 21 U.S.C.A. § 878; the Secret Service, 18 U.S.C.A. § 3056(a); and the Customs Service, 26 U.S.C.A. § 7607.

Because there is a "strong presumption of constitutionality due to an Act of Congress, especially when it turns on what is 'reasonable,' . . . [o]bviously the Court should be reluctant to decide that a search thus authorized by Congress was unreasonable and that the Act was therefore unconstitutional." United States v. Di Re, 332 U.S. 581, 585, 68 S.Ct. 222, 224, 92 L.Ed. 210 (1948). Moreover, there is nothing in the Court's prior cases indicating that under the Fourth Amendment a warrant is required to make a valid arrest for a felony. Indeed, the relevant prior decisions are uniformly to the contrary.

"The usual rule is that a police officer may arrest without warrant one believed by the officer upon reasonable cause to have been guilty of a felony . . . ." Carroll v. United States, 267 U.S. 132, 156, 45 S.Ct. 280, 286, 69 L.Ed. 543 (1925). In Henry v. United States, 361 U.S. 98, 80 S.Ct. 168, 4 L.Ed.2d 134 (1959), the Court dealt with an FBI agent's warrantless arrest under 18 U.S.C.A. § 3052 which authorizes a warrantless arrest where there are reasonable grounds to believe that the person to be arrested has committed a felony. The Court declared that "[t]he statute states the constitutional standard . . . ." Id., at 100, 80 S.Ct. at 170. The necessary inquiry, therefore, was not whether there was a warrant or whether there was time to get one but whether there was probable cause for the arrest. In Abel v. United States, 362 U.S. 217, 232, 80 S.Ct. 683, 693, 4 L.Ed. 2d 668 (1960), the Court sustained an administrative arrest made without "a judicial warrant within the scope of the Fourth Amendment". The crucial question in Draper v. United States, 358 U.S. 307, 79 S.Ct. 329, 3 L.Ed.2d 327 (1959), was whether there was probable cause for the warrantless arrest. If there was, the Court said, "the arrest, though without a warrant, was lawful . . . ." Id. at 310, 79 S.Ct. at 331. Ker v. California, 374 U.S. 23, 34–35, 83 S.Ct. 1623, 1630, 10 L.Ed.2d 726 (1963), reiterated the rule that "[t]he lawfulness of the arrest without warrant, in turn, must be based upon probable cause . . ." and went on to sustain the warrantless arrest over other claims going to the mode of entry. Just last Term, while recognizing that maximum protection of individual rights could be assured by requiring a magistrate's review of the factual justification prior to any arrest, we stated that "such a requirement would constitute an intolerable handicap for legitimate law enforcement" and noted that the Court "has never invalidated an arrest supported by probable cause solely because the officers failed to secure a warrant." Gerstein v. Pugh, 420 U.S. 103, 113, 95 S.Ct. 854, 862, 43 L.Ed.2d 54 (1975).

The cases construing the Fourth Amendment thus reflect the ancient common-law rule that a peace officer was permitted to arrest without a warrant for a misdemeanor or felony committed in his presence as well as for a felony not committed in his presence if there was reasonable grounds for making the arrest. 10 Halsbury's Laws of England 344–345 (3d ed. 1955); 4 Blackstone's Commentaries 292–293 (Lewis ed. 1902); 1 J. Stephen, A History of the Criminal Law of England 193 (1883); 2 M. Hale, Historia Placitorum Coronae 72–74 (new ed. 1800); Wilgus, Arrest Without a Warrant, 22 Mich. L.Rev. 541, 547–550, 686–688 (1924); Samuel v. Payne, 1 Dougl. 359, 99 Eng.Rep. 230 (K.B.1780); Beckwith v. Philby, 6 Barn. & Cress. 635, 108 Eng.Rep. 585 (K.B.1827). This has also been the prevailing rule under state constitutions and statutes "The rule of the common law, that a peace officer or a private citizen may arrest a felon without a warrant, has been generally held by the courts of the several States to be in force in cases of felony punishable by the civil tribunals." Kurtz v. Moffitt, 115 U.S. 487, 504, 6 S.Ct. 148, 154, 29 L.Ed. 458 (1885).

. . .

Because the common-law rule authorizing arrests without warrant generally prevailed in the States, it is important for present purposes to note that in 1792 Congress invested United States Marshals and their deputies with "the same powers in executing the laws of the United States, as sheriffs and their deputies in their several states have by law, in executing the laws of their respective states." Act of May 2, 1792, c. 28, § 9, 1 Stat. 265. The Second Congress thus saw no inconsistency between the Fourth Amendment and giving United States Marshals the same power as local peace officers to arrest for a felony without a warrant. This provision equating the power of federal marshals to those of local sheriffs was several times re-enacted and is today § 570 of Title 28. That provision, however, was supplemented in 1935 by § 504a of the Judicial Code which in its essential elements is now 18 U.S.C.A. § 3053 and which expressly empowered marshals to make felony arrests without warrant and on probable cause. It was enacted to furnish a federal standard independent of the vagaries of state laws, the Committee Report remarking that under existing law a "marshal or deputy marshal may make an arrest without a warrant within his district in all cases where the sheriff might do so under the State statutes." H.R.Rep.No.283, 74th Cong., 1st Sess., 1 (1935). See United States v. Riggs, 474 F.2d 699, 702–703 n. 2 (2d Cir. 1973), certiorari denied, 414 U.S. 820, 94 S.Ct. 115, 38 L.Ed.2d 53 (1973).

The balance struck by the common law in generally authorizing felony arrests on probable cause, but without warrant, has survived substantially intact. It appears in almost all of the States in the form of express statutory authorization. In 1963, the American Law Institute undertook the task of formulating a model statute governing police powers and practice in criminal law enforcement and related aspects of pretrial procedure. In 1975, after years of discussion, A Model Code of Pre-arraignment Procedure was proposed. Among its provisions was § 120.1 which authorized an officer to take a person into custody if the officer has reasonable cause to believe that the person to be arrested has committed a felony, or has committed a misdemeanor or petty misdemeanor in his presence. The commentary to this section said: "The Code thus adopts the traditional and almost universal standard for arrest without a warrant."

This is the rule Congress has long directed its principal law enforcement officers to follow. Congress has plainly decided against conditioning warrantless arrest power on proof of exigent circumstances. Law enforcement officers may find it wise to seek arrest warrants where practicable to do so, and their judgments about probable cause may be more readily accepted where backed by a warrant issued by a magistrate. See United States v. Ventresca, 380 U.S. 102, 106, 85 S.Ct. 741, 744–745, 13 L.Ed.2d 684 (1965); Aguilar v. Texas, 378 U.S. 108, 111, 84 S.Ct. 1509, 1512, 12 L.Ed.2d 723 (1964); Wong Sun v. United States, 371 U.S. 471, 479–480, 83 S.Ct. 407, 412–413, 9 L.Ed.2d 441 (1963). But we decline to transform this judicial preference into a constitutional rule when the judgment of the Nation and Congress has for so long been to authorize warrantless public arrests on probable cause rather than to encumber criminal prosecutions with endless litigation with respect to the existence of exigent circumstances, whether it was practicable to get a warrant, whether the suspect was about to flee, and the like.

Watson's arrest did not violate the Fourth Amendment, and the Court of Appeals erred in holding to the contrary.

III.

Because our judgment is that Watson's arrest comported with the Fourth Amendment, Watson's consent to the search of his car was not the product of an illegal arrest. To the extent that the issue of the voluntariness of Watson's consent was resolved on the premise that his arrest was illegal, the Court of Appeals was also in error.

We are satisfied in addition that the remaining factors relied upon by the Court of Appeals to invalidate Watson's consent are inadequate to demonstrate that, in the totality of the circumstances, Watson's consent was not his own "essentially free and unconstrained choice" because his "will ha[d] been overborne and his capacity for self-determination critically impaired." Schneckloth v. Bustamonte, 412 U.S. 218, 225, 93 S.Ct. 2041, 2047, 36 L.Ed.2d 854 (1973). There was no overt act or threat of force against Watson proved or claimed. There were no promises made to him and no indication of more subtle forms of coercion that might flaw his judgment. He had been arrested and was in custody, but his consent was given while on a public street, not in the confines of the police station. Moreover, the fact of custody alone has never been enough in itself to demonstrate a coerced confession or consent to search. Similarly, under *Schneck-*

loth, the absence of proof that Watson knew he could withhold his consent, though it may be a factor in the overall judgment, is not to be given controlling significance. There is no indication in this record that Watson was a newcomer to the law, mentally deficient or unable in the face of a custodial arrest to exercise a free choice. He was given *Miranda* warnings and was further cautioned that the results of the search of his car could be used against him. He persisted in his consent.

In these circumstances, to hold that illegal coercion is made out from the fact of arrest and the failure to inform the arrestee that he could withhold consent would not be consistent with *Schneckloth* and would distort the voluntariness standard that we reaffirmed in that case.

In consequence, we reverse the judgment of the Court of Appeals.

So ordered.

Reversed.

. . .

APPENDIX

Rules of Evidence for United States Courts and Magistrates

Rule 101.

SCOPE

These rules govern proceedings in the courts of the United States and before United States magistrates, to the extent and with the exceptions stated in rule 1101.

Rule 102.

PURPOSE AND CONSTRUCTION

These rules shall be construed to secure fairness in administration, elimination of unjustifiable expense and delay, and promotion of growth and development of the law of evidence to the end that the truth may be ascertained and proceedings justly determined.

Rule 103.

RULINGS ON EVIDENCE

(a) Effect of erroneous ruling. Error may not be predicated upon a ruling which admits or excludes evidence unless a substantial right of the party is affected, and

> **(1) Objection.** In case the ruling is one admitting evidence, a timely objection or motion to strike appears of record, stating the specific ground of objection, if the specific ground was not apparent from the context; or
>
> **(2) Offer of proof.** In case the ruling is one excluding evidence, the substance of the evidence was made known to the court by offer or was apparent from the context within which questions were asked.

(b) Record of offer and ruling. The court may add any other or further statement which shows the character of the evidence, the form in which it was offered, the objection made, and the ruling thereon. It may direct the making of an offer in question and answer form.

(c) Hearing of jury. In jury cases, proceedings shall be conducted, to the extent practicable, so as to prevent inadmissible evidence from being suggested to the jury by any means, such as making statements or offers of proof or asking questions in the hearing of the jury.

(d) Plain error. Nothing in this rule precludes taking notice of plain errors affecting substantial rights although they were not brought to the attention of the court.

Rule 104.

PRELIMINARY QUESTIONS

(a) Questions of admissibility generally. Preliminary questions concerning the qualification of a person to be a witness, the existence of a privilege, or the admissibility of evidence shall be determined by the court, subject to the provisions of subdivision (b). In making its determination it is not bound by the rules of evidence except those with respect to privileges.

(b) Relevancy conditioned on fact. When the relevancy of evidence depends upon the fulfillment of a condition of fact, the court shall admit it upon, or subject to, the introduction of evidence sufficient to support a finding of the fulfillment of the condition.

(c) Hearing of jury. Hearings on the admissibility of confessions shall in all cases be conducted out of the hearing of the jury. Hearings on other preliminary matters shall be so conducted when the interests of justice require or, when an accused is a witness, if he so requests.

(d) Testimony by accused. The accused does not, by testifying upon a preliminary matter, subject himself to cross-examination as to other issues in the case.

(e) Weight and credibility. This rule does not limit the right of a party to introduce before the jury evidence relevant to weight or credibility.

Rule 105.

LIMITED ADMISSIBILITY

When evidence which is admissible as to one party or for one purpose but not admissible as to another party or for another purpose is admitted, the court, upon request, shall restrict the evidence to its proper scope and instruct the jury accordingly.

Rule 106.

REMAINDER OF OR RELATED WRITINGS OR RECORDED STATEMENTS

When a writing or recorded statement or part thereof is introduced by a party, an adverse party may require him at that time to introduce any other part or any other writing or recorded statement which ought in fairness to be considered contemporaneously with it.

Rule 201.

JUDICIAL NOTICE OF ADJUDICATIVE FACTS

(a) Scope of rule. This rule governs only judicial notice of adjudicative facts.

(b) Kinds of facts. A judicially noticed fact must be one not subject to reasonable dispute in that it is either (1) generally known within the territorial jurisdiction of the trial court or (2) capable of accurate and ready determination by resort to sources whose accuracy cannot reasonably be questioned.

(c) When discretionary. A court may take judicial notice, whether requested or not.

(d) When mandatory. A court shall take judicial notice if requested by a party and supplied with the necessary information.

(e) Opportunity to be heard. A party is entitled upon timely request to an opportunity to be heard as to the propriety of taking judicial notice and the tenor of the matter noticed. In the absence of prior notification, the request may be made after judicial notice has been taken.

(f) Time of taking notice. Judicial notice may be taken at any stage of the proceeding.

(g) Instructing jury. In a civil action or proceeding, the court shall instruct the jury to accept as conclusive any fact judicially noticed. In a criminal case, the court shall instruct the jury that it may, but is not required to, accept as conclusive any fact judicially noticed.

Rule 301.

PRESUMPTIONS IN GENERAL IN CIVIL ACTIONS AND PROCEEDINGS

In all civil actions and proceedings not otherwise provided for by Act of Congress or by these rules, a presumption imposes on the party against whom it is directed the burden of going forward with evidence to rebut or meet the presumption, but does not shift to such party the burden of proof in the sense of the risk of nonpersuasion, which remains throughout the trial upon the party on whom it was originally cast.

Rule 302.

APPLICABILITY OF STATE LAW IN CIVIL ACTIONS AND PROCEEDINGS

In civil actions and proceedings, the effect of a presumption respecting a fact which is an element of a claim or defense as to which

State law supplies the rule of decision is determined in accordance with State law.

Rule 401.

DEFINITION OF "RELEVANT EVIDENCE"

"Relevant evidence" means evidence having any tendency to make the existence of any fact that is of consequence to the determination of the action more probable or less probable than it would be without the evidence.

Rule 402.

RELEVANT EVIDENCE GENERALLY ADMISSIBLE; IRRELEVANT EVIDENCE INADMISSIBLE

All relevant evidence is admissible, except as otherwise provided by the Constitution of the United States, by Act of Congress, by these rules, or by other rules prescribed by the Supreme Court pursuant to statutory authority. Evidence which is not relevant is not admissible.

Rule 403.

EXCLUSION OF RELEVANT EVIDENCE ON GROUNDS OF PREJUDICE, CONFUSION, OR WASTE OF TIME

Although relevant, evidence may be excluded if its probative value is substantially outweighed by the danger of unfair prejudice, confusion of the issues, or misleading the jury, or by considerations of undue delay, waste of time, or needless presentation of cumulative evidence.

Rule 404.

CHARACTER EVIDENCE NOT ADMISSIBLE TO PROVE CONDUCT; EXCEPTIONS; OTHER CRIMES

(a) Character evidence generally. Evidence of a person's character or a trait of his character is not admissible for the purpose of proving that he acted in conformity therewith on a particular occasion, except:

(1) Character of accused. Evidence of a pertinent trait of his character offered by an accused, or by the prosecution to rebut the same;

(2) Character of victim. Evidence of a pertinent trait of character of the victim of the crime offered by an accused, or by the prosecution to rebut the same, or evidence of a character trait of peacefulness of the victim, offered by the prosecution in a homicide case to rebut evidence that the victim was the first aggressor;

(3) Character of witness. Evidence of the character of a witness, as provided in rules 607, 608, and 609.

(b) Other crimes, wrongs, or acts. Evidence of other crimes, wrongs, or acts is not admissible to prove the character of a person in order to show that he acted in conformity therewith. It may, however, be admissible for other purposes, such as proof of motive, opportunity, intent, preparation, plan, knowledge, identity, or absence of mistake or accident.

Rule 405.

METHODS OF PROVING CHARACTER

(a) Reputation or opinion. In all cases in which evidence of character or a trait of character of a person is admissible, proof may be made by testimony as to reputation or by testimony in the form of an opinion. On cross-examination, inquiry is allowable into relevant specific instances of conduct.

(b) Specific instances of conduct. In cases in which character or a trait of character of a person is an essential element of a charge, claim, or defense, proof may also be made of specific instances of his conduct.

Rule 406.

HABIT; ROUTINE PRACTICE

Evidence of the habit of a person or of the routine practice of an organization, whether corroborated or not and regardless of the presence of eyewitnesses, is relevant to prove that the conduct of the person or organization on a particular occasion was in conformity with the habit or routine practice.

Rule 407.

SUBSEQUENT REMEDIAL MEASURES

When, after an event, measures are taken which, if taken previously would have made the event less likely to occur, evidence of the subsequent measures is not admissible to prove negligence or culpable conduct in connection with the event. This rule does not require the exclusion of evidence of subsequent measures when offered for another purpose, such as proving ownership, control, or feasibility of precautionary measures, if controverted, or impeachment.

Rule 408.

COMPROMISE AND OFFERS TO COMPROMISE

Evidence of (1) furnishing or offering or promising to furnish, or (2) accepting or offering or promising to accept, a valuable consideration in compromising or attempting to compromise a claim which was disputed as to either validity or amount, is not admissible to prove liability for or invalidity of the claim or its amount. Evidence of conduct or statements made in compromise negotiations is likewise not admissible. This rule does not require the exclusion of any evidence otherwise discoverable merely because it is presented in the course of compromise negotiations. This rule also does not require exclusion when the evidence is offered for another purpose, such as proving bias or prejudice of a witness, negativing a contention of undue delay, or proving an effort to obstruct a criminal investigation or prosecution.

Rule 409.

PAYMENT OF MEDICAL AND SIMILAR EXPENSES

Evidence of furnishing or offering or promising to pay medical, hospital, or similar expenses occasioned by an injury is not admissible to prove liability for the injury.

Rule 410.

INADMISSIBILITY OF PLEAS, OFFERS OF PLEAS, AND RELATED STATEMENTS

Except as otherwise provided in this rule, evidence of a plea of guilty, later withdrawn, or a plea of nolo contendere, or of an offer to plead guilty or nolo contendere to the crime charged or any other crime, or of statements made in connection with, and relevant to, any of the foregoing pleas or offers, is not admissible in any civil or criminal proceeding against the person who made the plea or offer. However, evidence of a statement made in connection with, and relevant to, a plea of guilty, later withdrawn, a plea of nolo contendere, or an offer to plead guilty or nolo contendere to the crime charged or any other crime, is admissible in a criminal proceeding for perjury or false statement if the statement was made by the defendant under oath, on the record, and in the presence of counsel.

Rule 411.

LIABILITY INSURANCE

Evidence that a person was or was not insured against liability is not admissible upon the issue whether he acted negligently or otherwise wrongfully. This rule does not require the exclusion of evidence of insurance against liability when offered for another purpose, such as proof of agency, ownership, or control, or bias or prejudice of a witness.

Rule 501.

GENERAL RULE

Except as otherwise required by the Constitution of the United States or provided by Act of Congress or in rules prescribed by the Supreme Court pursuant to statutory authority, the privilege of a witness, person, government, State, or political subdivision thereof shall be governed by the principles of the common law as they may be interpreted by the courts of the United States in the light of reason and experience. However, in civil actions and proceedings, with respect to an element of a claim or defense as to which State law supplies the rule of decision, the privilege of a witness, person, government, State, or political subdivision thereof shall be determined in accordance with State law.

Rule 601.

GENERAL RULE OF COMPETENCY

Every person is competent to be a witness except as otherwise provided in these rules. However, in civil actions and proceedings, with respect to an element of a claim or defense as to which State law supplies the rule of decision, the competency of a witness shall be determined in accordance with State law.

Rule 602.

LACK OF PERSONAL KNOWLEDGE

A witness may not testify to a matter unless evidence is introduced sufficient to support a finding that he has personal knowledge of the matter. Evidence to prove personal knowledge may, but need not, consist of the testimony of the witness himself. This rule is subject to the provisions of rule 703, relating to opinion testimony by expert witnesses.

Rule 603.

OATH OR AFFIRMATION

Before testifying, every witness shall be required to declare that he will testify truthfully, by oath or affirmation administered in a form calculated to awaken his conscience and impress his mind with his duty to do so.

Rule 604.

INTERPRETERS

An interpreter is subject to the provisions of these rules relating to qualification as an expert and the administration of an oath or affirmation that he will make a true translation.

Rule 605.

COMPETENCY OF JUDGE AS WITNESS

The judge presiding at the trial may not testify in that trial as a witness. No objection need be made in order to preserve the point.

Rule 606.

COMPETENCY OF JUROR AS WITNESS

(a) At the trial. A member of the jury may not testify as a witness before that jury in the trial of the case in which he is sitting as a juror. If he is called so to testify, the opposing party shall be afforded an opportunity to object out of the presence of the jury.

(b) Inquiry into validity of verdict or indictment. Upon an inquiry into the validity of a verdict or indictment, a juror may not testify as to any matter or statement occurring during the course of the jury's deliberations or to the effect of anything upon his or any other juror's mind or emotions as influencing him to assent to or dissent from the verdict or indictment or concerning his mental processes in connection therewith, except that a juror may testify on the question whether extraneous prejudicial information was improperly brought to the jury's attention or whether any outside influence was improperly brought to bear upon any juror. Nor may his affidavit or evidence of any statement by him concerning a matter about which he would be precluded from testifying be received for these purposes.

Rule 607.

WHO MAY IMPEACH

The credibility of a witness may be attacked by any party, including the party calling him.

Rule 608.

EVIDENCE OF CHARACTER AND CONDUCT OF WITNESS

(a) Opinion and reputation evidence of character. The credibility of a witness may be attacked or supported by evidence in the form of opinion or reputation, but subject to these limitations: (1) the evidence may refer only to character for truthfulness or untruthfulness, and (2) evidence of truthful character is admissible only after the character of the witness for truthfulness has been attacked by opinion or reputation evidence or otherwise.

(b) Specific instances of conduct. Specific instances of the conduct of a witness, for the purpose of attacking or supporting his credibility, other than conviction of crime as provided in rule 609, may not be proved by extrinsic evidence. They may, however, in the discretion of the court, if probative of truthfulness or untruthfulness, be inquired into on cross-examination of the witness (1) concerning his character for truthfulness or untruthfulness, or (2) concerning the character for truthfulness or untruthfulness of another witness as to which character the witness being cross-examined has testified.

The giving of testimony, whether by an accused or by any other witness, does not operate as a waiver of his privilege against self-incrimination when examined with respect to matters which relate only to credibility.

Rule 609.

IMPEACHMENT BY EVIDENCE OF CONVICTION OF CRIME

(a) General rule. For the purpose of attacking the credibility of a witness, evidence that he has been convicted of a crime shall be admitted if elicited from him or established by public record during cross-examination but only if the crime (1) was punishable by death or imprisonment in excess of one year under the law under which he was convicted, and the court determines that the probative value of admitting this evidence outweighs its prejudicial effect to the defendant, or (2) involved dishonesty or false statement, regardless of the punishment.

(b) Time limit. Evidence of a conviction under this rule is not admissible if a period of more than ten years has elapsed since the date of the conviction or of the release of the witness from the confinement imposed for that conviction, whichever is the later date, unless the court determines, in the interests of justice, that the probative value of the conviction supported by specific facts and circumstances substantially outweighs its prejudicial effect. However, evidence of a conviction more than 10 years old as calculated herein, is not admissible unless the proponent gives to the adverse party sufficient advance written notice of intent to use such evidence to provide the adverse party with a fair opportunity to contest the use of such evidence.

(c) Effect of pardon, annulment, or certificate of rehabilitation. Evidence of a conviction is not admissible under this rule if (1) the conviction has been the subject of a pardon, annulment, certificate of rehabilitation, or other equivalent procedure based on a finding of the rehabilitation of the person convicted, and that person has not been convicted of a subsequent crime which was punishable by death or imprisonment in excess of one year, or (2) the conviction has been the subject of a pardon, annulment, or other equivalent procedure based on a finding of innocence.

(d) Juvenile adjudications. Evidence of juvenile adjudications is generally not admissible under this rule. The court may, however, in a criminal case allow evidence of a juvenile adjudication of a witness other than the accused if conviction of the offense would be admissible to attack the credibility of an adult and the court is satisfied that admission in evidence is necessary for a fair determination of the issue of guilt or innocence.

(e) Pendency of appeal. The pendency of an appeal therefrom does not render evidence of a conviction inadmissible. Evidence of the pendency of an appeal is admissible.

Rule 610.

RELIGIOUS BELIEFS OR OPINIONS

Evidence of the beliefs or opinions of a witness on matters of religion is not admissible for the purpose of showing that by reason of their nature his credibility is impaired or enhanced.

Rule 611.

MODE AND ORDER OF INTERROGATION AND PRESENTATION

(a) Control by court. The court shall exercise reasonable control over the mode and order of interrogating witnesses and presenting evidence so as to (1) make the interrogation and presentation effective for the ascertainment of the truth, (2) avoid needless consumption of time, and (3) protect witnesses from harassment or undue embarrassment.

(b) Scope of cross-examination. Cross-examination should be limited to the subject matter of the direct examination and matters affecting the credibility of the witness. The court may, in the exercise of discretion, permit inquiry into additional matters as if on direct examination.

(c) Leading questions. Leading questions should not be used on the direct examination of a witness except as may be necessary to develop his testimony. Ordinarily leading questions should be permitted on cross-examination. When a party calls a hostile witness, an adverse party, or a witness identified with an adverse party, interrogation may be by leading questions.

Rule 612.

WRITING USED TO REFRESH MEMORY

Except as otherwise provided in criminal proceedings by section 3500 of title 18, United States Code, if a witness uses a writing to refresh his memory for the purpose of testifying, either—

(1) while testifying, or

(2) before testifying, if the court in its discretion determines it is necessary in the interests of justice,

an adverse party is entitled to have the writing produced at the hearing, to inspect it, to cross-examine the witness thereon, and to introduce in evidence those portions which relate to the testimony of the witness. If it is claimed that the writing contains matters not related to the subject matter of the testimony the court shall examine the writing in camera, excise any portions not so related, and order delivery of the remainder to the party entitled thereto. Any portion withheld over objections shall be preserved and made available to the appellate court in the event of an appeal. If a writing is not produced or delivered pursuant to order under this rule, the court shall make any order justice requires, except that in criminal cases when the prosecution elects not to comply, the order shall be one striking the testimony or, if the court in its discretion determines that the interests of justice so require, declaring a mistrial.

Rule 613.

PRIOR STATEMENTS OF WITNESSES

(a) Examining witness concerning prior statement. In examining a witness concerning a prior statement made by him, whether written or not, the statement need not be shown nor its contents disclosed to him at that time, but on request the same shall be shown or disclosed to opposing counsel.

(b) Extrinsic evidence of prior inconsistent statement of witness. Extrinsic evidence of a prior inconsistent statement by a witness is not admissible unless the witness is afforded an opportunity to explain or deny the same and the opposite party is afforded an opportunity to interrogate him thereon, or the interests of justice otherwise require. This provision does not apply to admissions of a party-opponent as defined in rule 801(d)(2).

Rule 614.

CALLING AND INTERROGATION OF WITNESSES BY COURT

(a) Calling by court. The court may, on its own motion or at the suggestion of a party, call witnesses, and all parties are entitled to cross-examine witnesses thus called.

(b) Interrogation by court. The court may interrogate witnesses, whether called by itself or by a party.

(c) Objections. Objections to the calling of witnesses by the court or to interrogation by it may be made at the time or at the next available opportunity when the jury is not present.

Rule 615.

EXCLUSION OF WITNESSES

At the request of a party the court shall order witnesses excluded so that they cannot hear the testimony of other witnesses, and it may make the order of its own motion. This rule does not authorize exclusion of (1) a party who is a natural person, or (2) an officer or employee of a party which is not a natural person designated as its representative by its attorney, or (3) a person whose presence is shown by a party to be essential to the presentation of his cause.

Rule 701.

OPINION TESTIMONY BY LAY WITNESSES

If the witness is not testifying as an expert, his testimony in the form of opinions or inferences is limited to those opinions or inferences which are (a) rationally based on the perception of the witness and (b) helpful to a clear understanding of his testimony or the determination of a fact in issue.

Rule 702.

TESTIMONY BY EXPERTS

If scientific, technical, or other specialized knowledge will assist the trier of fact to understand the evidence or to determine a fact in issue, a witness qualified as an expert by knowledge, skill, experience, training, or education, may testify thereto in the form of an opinion or otherwise.

Rule 703.

BASES OF OPINION TESTIMONY BY EXPERTS

The facts or data in the particular case upon which an expert bases an opinion or inference may be those perceived by or made known to him at or before the hearing. If of a type reasonably relied upon by experts in the particular field in forming opinions or inferences upon the subject, the facts or data need not be admissible in evidence.

Rule 704.

OPINION ON ULTIMATE ISSUE

Testimony in the form of an opinion or inference otherwise admissible is not objectionable because it embraces an ultimate issue to be decided by the trier of fact.

Rule 705.

DISCLOSURE OF FACTS OR DATA UNDERLYING EXPERT OPINION

The expert may testify in terms of opinion or inference and give his reasons therefor without prior disclosure of the underlying facts or data, unless the court requires otherwise. The expert may in any event be required to disclose the underlying facts or data on cross-examination.

Rule 706.

COURT APPOINTED EXPERTS

(a) Appointment. The court may on its own motion or on the motion of any party enter an order to show cause why expert witnesses should not be appointed, and may request the parties to submit nominations. The court may appoint any expert witnesses agreed upon by the parties, and may appoint expert witnesses of its own selection. An expert witness shall not be appointed by the court unless he consents to act. A witness so appointed shall be informed of his duties by the court in writing, a copy of which shall be filed with the clerk, or at a conference in which the parties shall have opportunity to participate. A witness so appointed shall advise the parties of his findings, if any; his deposition may be taken by any party; and he may be called to testify by the court or any party. He shall be subject to cross-examination by each party, including a party calling him as a witness.

(b) Compensation. Expert witnesses so appointed are entitled to reasonable compensation in whatever sum the court may allow. The compensation thus fixed is payable from funds which may be provided by law in criminal cases and civil actions and proceedings involving just compensation under the fifth amendment. In other civil actions and proceedings the compensation shall be paid by the parties in such proportion and at such time as the court directs, and thereafter charged in like manner as other costs.

(c) Disclosure of appointment. In the exercise of its discretion, the court may authorize disclosure to the jury of the fact that the court appointed the expert witness.

(d) Parties' experts of own selection. Nothing in this rule limits the parties in calling expert witnesses of their own selection.

Rule 801.

DEFINITIONS

The following definitions apply under this article:

(a) Statement. A "statement" is (1) an oral or written assertion or (2) nonverbal conduct of a person, if it is intended by him as an assertion.

(b) Declarant. A "declarant" is a person who makes a statement.

(c) Hearsay. "Hearsay" is a statement, other than one made by the declarant while testifying at the trial or hearing, offered in evidence to prove the truth of the matter asserted.

(d) Statements which are not hearsay. A statement is not hearsay if—

(1) Prior statement by witness. The declarant testifies at the trial or hearing and is subject to cross-examination concerning the statement, and the statement is (A) inconsistent with his testimony, and was given under oath subject to the penalty of perjury at a trial, hearing, or other proceeding, or in a deposition, or (B) consistent with his testimony and is offered to rebut an express or implied charge against him of recent fabrication or improper influence or motive, or (C) one of identification of a person made after perceiving him; or

(2) Admission by party-opponent. The statement is offered against a party and is (A) his own statement, in either his individual or a representative capacity or (B) a statement of which he has manifested his adoption or belief in its truth, or (C) a statement by a person authorized by him to make a statement concerning the subject, or (D) a statement by his agent or servant concerning a matter within the scope of his agency or employment, made during the existence of the relationship, or (E) a statement by a coconspirator of a party during the course and in furtherance of the conspiracy.

Rule 802.

HEARSAY RULE

Hearsay is not admissible except as provided by these rules or by other rules prescribed by the Supreme Court pursuant to statutory authority or by Act of Congress.

Rule 803.

HEARSAY EXCEPTIONS; AVAILABILITY OF DECLARANT IMMATERIAL

The following are not excluded by the hearsay rule, even though the declarant is available as a witness:

(1) Present sense impression. A statement describing or explaining an event or condition made while the declarant was perceiving the event or condition, or immediately thereafter.

(2) Excited utterance. A statement relating to a startling event or condition made while the declarant was under the stress of excitement caused by the event or condition.

(3) Then existing mental, emotional, or physical condition. A statement of the declarant's then existing state of mind, emotion, sensation, or physical condition (such as intent, plan, motive, design, mental feeling, pain, and bodily health), but not including a statement of memory or belief to prove the fact remembered or believed unless it relates to the execution, revocation, identification, or terms of declarant's will.

(4) Statements for purposes of medical diagnosis or treatment. Statements made for purposes of medical diagnosis or treatment and describing medical history, or past or present symptoms, pain, or sensations, or the inception or general character of the cause or external source thereof insofar as reasonably pertinent to diagnosis or treatment.

(5) Recorded recollection. A memorandum or record concerning a matter about which a witness once had knowledge but now has insufficient recollection to enable him to testify fully and accurately, shown to have been made or adopted by the witness when the matter was fresh in his memory and to reflect that knowledge correctly. If admitted, the memorandum or record may be read into evidence but may not itself be received as an exhibit unless offered by an adverse party.

(6) Records of regularly conducted activity. A memorandum, report, record, or data compilation, in any form, of acts, events, conditions opinions, or diagnoses, made at or near the time by, or from information transmitted by, a person with knowledge, if kept in the course of a regularly conducted business activity, and if it was the regular practice of that business activity to make the memorandum, report, record, or data compilation, all as shown by the testimony of the custodian or other qualified witness, unless the source of information or the method or circumstances of preparation indicate lack of trustworthiness. The term "business" as used in this paragraph includes business, institution, association, profession, occupation, and calling of every kind, whether or not conducted for profit.

(7) Absence of entry in records kept in accordance with the provisions of paragraph (6). Evidence that a matter is not included in the memoranda reports, records, or data compilations, in any form, kept in accordance with the provisions of paragraph (6), to prove the nonoccurrence or nonexistence of the matter, if the matter was of a kind of which a memorandum, report, record, or data compilation was regularly made and preserved, unless the sources of information or other circumstances indicate lack of trustworthiness.

(8) Public records and reports. Records, reports, statements, or data compilations, in any form, of public offices or agencies, setting forth (A) the activities of the office or agency, or (B) matters observed pursuant to duty imposed by law as to which matters there was a duty to report, excluding, however, in criminal cases matters observed by police officers and other law enforcement personnel, or (C) in civil actions and proceedings and against the Government in criminal cases, factual findings resulting from an investigation made pursuant to authority granted by law, unless the sources of information or other circumstances indicate lack of trustworthiness.

(9) Records of vital statistics. Records or data compilations, in any form, of births, fetal deaths, deaths, or marriages, if the report thereof was made to a public office pursuant to requirements of law.

(10) Absence of public record or entry. To prove the absence of a record, report, statement, or data compilation, in any form, or the nonoccurrence or nonexistence of a matter of which a record, report, statement, or data compilation, in any form, was regularly made and preserved by a public office or agency, evidence in the form of a certification in accordance with rule 902, or testimony, that diligent search failed to disclose the record, report, statement, or data compilation, or entry.

(11) Records of religious organizations. Statements of births, marriages, divorces, deaths, legitimacy, ancestry, relationship by blood or marriage, or other similar facts of personal or family history, contained in a regularly kept record of a religious organization.

(12) Marriage, baptismal, and similar certificates. Statements of fact contained in a certificate that the maker performed a marriage or other ceremony or administered a sacrament, made by a clergyman, public official, or other person authorized by the rules or practices of a religious organization or by law to perform the act certified, and purporting to have been issued at the time of the act or within a reasonable time thereafter.

(13) **Family records.** Statements of fact concerning personal or family history contained in family Bibles, genealogies, charts, engravings on rings, inscriptions on family portraits, engravings on urns, crypts, or tombstones, or the like.

(14) **Records of documents affecting an interest in property.** The record of a document purporting to establish or affect an interest in property, as proof of the content of the original recorded document and its execution and delivery by each person by whom it purports to have been executed, if the record is a record of a public office and an applicable statute authorizes the recording of documents of that kind in that office.

(15) **Statements in documents affecting an interest in property.** A statement contained in a document purporting to establish or affect an interest in property if the matter stated was relevant to the purpose of the document, unless dealings with the property since the document was made have been inconsistent with the truth of the statement or the purport of the document.

(16) **Statements in ancient documents.** Statements in a document in existence twenty years or more the authenticity of which is established.

(17) **Market reports, commercial publications.** Market quotations, tabulations, lists, directories, or other published compilations, generally used and relied upon by the public or by persons in particular occupations.

(18) **Learned treatises.** To the extent called to the attention of an expert witness upon cross-examination or relied upon by him in direct examination, statements contained in published treatises, periodicals, or pamphlets on a subject of history, medicine, or other science or art, established as a reliable authority by the testimony or admission of the witness or by other expert testimony or by judicial notice. If admitted, the statements may be read into evidence but may not be received as exhibits.

(19) **Reputation concerning personal or family history.** Reputation among members of his family by blood, adoption, or marriage, or among his associates, or in the community, concerning a person's birth, adoption, marriage, divorce, death, legitimacy, relationship by blood, adoption, or marriage, ancestry, or other similar fact of his personal or family history.

(20) **Reputation concerning boundaries or general history.** Reputation in a community, arising before the controversy, as to boundaries of or customs affecting lands in the community, and reputation as to events of general history important to the community or State or nation in which located.

(21) **Reputation as to character.** Reputation of a person's character among his associates or in the community.

(22) Judgment of previous conviction. Evidence of a final judgment, entered after a trial or upon a plea of guilty (but not upon a plea of nolo contendere), adjudging a person guilty of a crime punishable by death or imprisonment in excess of one year, to prove any fact essential to sustain the judgment, but not including, when offered by the Government in a criminal prosecution for purposes other than impeachment, judgments against persons other than the accused. The pendency of an appeal may be shown but does not affect admissibility.

(23) Judgment as to personal, family, or general history, or boundaries. Judgments as proof of matters of personal, family or general history, or boundaries, essential to the judgment, if the same would be provable by evidence of reputation.

(24) Other exceptions. A statement not specifically covered by any of the foregoing exceptions but having equivalent circumstantial guarantees of trustworthiness, if the court determines that (A) the statement is offered as evidence of a material fact; (B) the statement is more probative on the point for which it is offered than any other evidence which the proponent can procure through reasonable efforts; and (C) the general purposes of these rules and the interests of justice will best be served by admission of the statement into evidence. However, a statement may not be admitted under this exception unless the proponent of it makes known to the adverse party sufficiently in advance of the trial or hearing to provide the adverse party with a fair opportunity to prepare to meet it, his intention to offer the statement and the particulars of it, including the name and address of the declarant.

Rule 804.

HEARSAY EXCEPTIONS; DECLARANT UNAVAILABLE

(a) Definition of unavailability. "Unavailability as a witness" includes situations in which the declarant—

(1) is exempted by ruling of the court on the ground of privilege from testifying concerning the subject matter of his statement; or

(2) persists in refusing to testify concerning the subject matter of his statement despite an order of the court to do so; or

(3) testifies to a lack of memory of the subject matter of his statement; or

(4) is unable to be present or to testify at the hearing because of death or then existing physical or mental illness or infirmity; or

(5) is absent from the hearing and the proponent of his statement has been unable to procure his attendance (or in the

case of a hearsay exception under subdivision (b) (2), (3), or (4), his attendance or testimony) by process or other reasonable means.

A declarant is not unavailable as a witness if his exemption, refusal, claim of lack of memory, inability, or absence is due to the procurement or wrongdoing of the proponent of his statement for the purpose of preventing the witness from attending or testifying.

(b) Hearsay exceptions. The following are not excluded by the hearsay rule if the declarant is unavailable as a witness:

(1) Former testimony. Testimony given as a witness at another hearing of the same or a different proceeding, or in a deposition taken in compliance with law in the course of the same or another proceeding, if the party against whom the testimony is now offered, or, in a civil action or proceeding, a predecessor in interest, had an opportunity and similar motive to develop the testimony by direct, cross, or redirect examination.

(2) Statement under belief of impending death. In a prosecution for homicide or in a civil action or proceeding, a statement made by a declarant while believing that his death was imminent, concerning the cause or circumstances of what he believed to be his impending death.

(3) Statement against interest. A statement which was at the time of its making so far contrary to the declarant's pecuniary or proprietary interest, or so far tended to subject him to civil or criminal liability, or to render invalid a claim by him against another, that a reasonable man in his position would not have made the statement unless he believed it to be true. A statement tending to expose the declarant to criminal liability and offered to exculpate the accused is not admissible unless corroborating circumstances clearly indicate the trustworthiness of the statement.

(4) Statement of personal or family history. (A) A statement concerning the declarant's own birth, adoption, marriage, divorce, legitimacy, relationship by blood, adoption, or marriage, ancestry, or other similar fact of personal or family history, even though declarant had no means of acquiring personal knowledge of the matter stated; or (B) a statement concerning the foregoing matters, and death also, of another person, if the declarant was related to the other by blood, adoption, or marriage or was so intimately associated with the other's family as to be likely to have accurate information concerning the matter declared.

(5) Other exceptions. A statement not specifically covered by any of the foregoing exceptions but having equivalent circumstantial guarantees of trustworthiness, if the court determines that (A) the statement is offered as evidence of a material fact; (B) the statement is more probative on the point for which it is offered than any other evidence which the proponent can procure through reasonable efforts; and (C) the general purposes of these rules and the interests of justice will best be served by admission of the statement into evidence. However, a statement may not be admitted under this exception unless the proponent of it makes known to the adverse party sufficiently in advance of the trial or hearing to provide the adverse party with a fair opportunity to prepare to meet it, his intention to offer the statement and the particulars of it, including the name and address of the declarant.

Rule 805.

HEARSAY WITHIN HEARSAY

Hearsay included within hearsay is not excluded under the hearsay rule if each part of the combined statements conforms with an exception to the hearsay rule provided in these rules.

Rule 806.

ATTACKING AND SUPPORTING CREDIBILITY OF DECLARANT

When a hearsay statement, or a statement defined in Rule 801 (d)(2), (C), (D), or (E), has been admitted in evidence, the credibility of the declarant may be attacked, and if attacked may be supported, by any evidence which would be admissible for those purposes if declarant had testified as a witness. Evidence of a statement or conduct by the declarant at any time, inconsistent with his hearsay statement, is not subject to any requirement that he may have been afforded an opportunity to deny or explain. If the party against whom a hearsay statement has been admitted calls the declarant as a witness, the party is entitled to examine him on the statement as if under cross-examination.

Rule 901.

REQUIREMENT OF AUTHENTICATION OR IDENTIFICATION

(a) General provision. The requirement of authentication or identification as a condition precedent to admissibility is satisfied by evidence sufficient to support a finding that the matter in question is what its proponent claims.

(b) Illustrations. By way of illustration only, and not by way of limitation, the following are examples of authentication or identification conforming with the requirements of this rule:

(1) Testimony of witness with knowledge. Testimony that a matter is what it is claimed to be.

(2) Nonexpert opinion on handwriting. Nonexpert opinion as to the genuineness of handwriting, based upon familiarity not acquired for purposes of the litigation.

(3) Comparison by trier or expert witness. Comparison by the trier of fact or by expert witnesses with specimens which have been authenticated.

(4) Distinctive characteristics and the like. Appearance, contents, substance, internal patterns, or other distinctive characteristics, taken in conjunction with circumstances.

(5) Voice identification. Identification of a voice, whether heard firsthand or through mechanical or electronic transmission or recording, by opinion based upon hearing the voice at any time under circumstances connecting it with the alleged speaker.

(6) Telephone conversations. Telephone conversations, by evidence that a call was made to the number assigned at the time by the telephone company to a particular person or business, if (A) in the case of a person, circumstances, including self-identification, show the person answering to be the one called, or (B) in the case of a business, the call was made to a place of business and the conversation related to business reasonably transacted over the telephone.

(7) Public records or reports. Evidence that a writing authorized by law to be recorded or filed and in fact recorded or filed in a public office, or a purported public record, report, statement, or data compilation, in any form, is from the public office where items of this nature are kept.

(8) Ancient documents or data compilation. Evidence that a document or data compilation, in any form, (A) is in such condition as to create no suspicion concerning its authenticity, (B) was in a place where it, if authentic, would likely be, and (C) has been in existence 20 years or more at the time it is offered.

(9) Process or system. Evidence describing a process or system used to produce a result and showing that the process or system produces an accurate result.

(10) Methods provided by statute or rule. Any method of authentication or identification provided by Act of Congress or by other rules prescribed by the Supreme Court pursuant to statutory authority.

Rule 902.

SELF-AUTHENTICATION

Extrinsic evidence of authenticity as a condition precedent to admissibility is not required with respect to the following:

(1) Domestic public documents under seal. A document bearing a seal purporting to be that of the United States, or of any State, district, Commonwealth, territory, or insular possession thereof, or the Panama Canal Zone, or the Trust Territory of the Pacific Islands, or of a political subdivision, department, officer, or agency thereof, and a signature purporting to be an attestation or execution.

(2) **Domestic public documents not under seal.** A document purporting to bear the signature in his official capacity of an officer or employee of any entity included in paragraph (1) hereof, having no seal, if a public officer having a seal and having official duties in the district or political subdivision of the officer or employee certifies under seal that the signer has the official capacity and that the signature is genuine.

(3) **Foreign public documents.** A document purporting to be executed or attested in his official capacity by a person authorized by the laws of a foreign country to make the execution or attestation, and accompanied by a final certification as to the genuineness of the signature and official position (A) of the executing or attesting person, or (B) of any foreign official whose certificate of genuineness of signature and official position relates to the execution or attestation or is in a chain of certificates of genuineness of signature and official position relating to the execution or attestation. A final certification may be made by a secretary of embassy or legation, consul general, consul, vice consul, or consular agent of the United States, or a diplomatic or consular official of the foreign country assigned or accredited to the United States. If reasonable opportunity has been given to all parties to investigate the authenticity and accuracy of official documents, the court may, for good cause shown, order that they be treated as presumptively authentic without final certification or permit them to be evidenced by an attested summary with or without final certification.

(4) **Certified copies of public records.** A copy of an official record or report or entry therein, or of a document authorized by law to be recorded or filed and actually recorded or filed in a public office, including data compilations in any form, certified as correct by the custodian or other person authorized to make the certification, by certificate complying with paragraph (1), (2), or (3) of this rule or complying with any Act of Congress or rule prescribed by the Supreme Court pursuant to statutory authority.

(5) **Official publications.** Books, pamphlets, or other publications purporting to be issued by public authority.

(6) **Newspapers and periodicals.** Printed materials purporting to be newspapers or periodicals.

(7) **Trade inscriptions and the like.** Inscriptions, signs, tags, or labels purporting to have been affixed in the course of business and indicating ownership, control, or origin.

(8) Acknowledged documents. Documents accompanied by a certificate of acknowledgment executed in the manner provided by law by a notary public or other officer authorized by law to take acknowledgments.

(9) Commercial paper and related documents. Commercial paper, signatures thereon, and documents relating thereto to the extent provided by general commercial law.

(10) Presumptions under Acts of Congress. Any signature, document, or other matter declared by Act of Congress to be presumptively or prima facie genuine or authentic.

Rule 903.

SUBSCRIBING WITNESS' TESTIMONY UNNECESSARY

The testimony of a subscribing witness is not necessary to authenticate a writing unless required by the laws of the jurisdiction whose laws govern the validity of the writing.

Rule 1001.

DEFINITIONS

For purposes of this article the following definitions are applicable:

(1) Writings and recordings. "Writings" and "recordings" consist of letters, words, or numbers, or their equivalent, set down by handwriting, typewriting, printing, photostating, photographing, magnetic impulse, mechanical or electronic recording, or other form of data compilation.

(2) Photographs. "Photographs" include still photographs, X-ray films, video tapes, and motion pictures.

(3) Original. An "original" of a writing or recording is the writing or recording itself or any counterpart intended to have the same effect by a person executing or issuing it. An "original" of a photograph includes the negative or any print therefrom. If data are stored in a computer or similar device, any printout or other output readable by sight, shown to reflect the data accurately, is an "original".

(4) Duplicate. A "duplicate" is a counterpart produced by the same impression as the original, or from the same matrix, or by means of photography, including enlargements and miniatures, or by mechanical or electronic re-recording, or by chemical reproduction, or by other equivalent techniques which accurately reproduces the original.

Rule 1002.

REQUIREMENT OF ORIGINAL

To prove the content of a writing, recording, or photograph, the original writing, recording, or photograph is required, except as otherwise provided in these rules or by Act of Congress.

Rule 1003.

ADMISSIBILITY OF DUPLICATES

A duplicate is admissible to the same extent as an original unless (1) a genuine question is raised as to the authenticity of the original or (2) in the circumstances it would be unfair to admit the duplicate in lieu of the original.

Rule 1004.

ADMISSIBILITY OF OTHER EVIDENCE OF CONTENTS

The original is not required, and other evidence of the contents of a writing, recording, or photograph is admissible if—

(1) **Originals lost or destroyed.** All originals are lost or have been destroyed, unless the proponent lost or destroyed them in bad faith; or

(2) **Original not obtainable.** No original can be obtained by any available judicial process or procedure; or

(3) **Original in possession of opponent.** At a time when an original was under the control of the party against whom offered, he was put on notice, by the pleadings or otherwise, that the contents would be a subject of proof at the hearing, and he does not produce the original at the hearing; or

(4) **Collateral matters.** The writing, recording, or photograph is not closely related to a controlling issue.

Rule 1005.

PUBLIC RECORDS

The contents of an official record, or of a document authorized to be recorded or filed and actually recorded or filed, including data compilations in any form, if otherwise admissible, may be proved by copy, certified as correct in accordance with rule 902 or testified to be correct by a witness who has compared it with the original. If a copy which complies with the foregoing cannot be obtained by the exercise of reasonable diligence, then other evidence of the contents may be given.

Rule 1006.

SUMMARIES

The contents of voluminous writings, recordings, or photographs which cannot conveniently be examined in court may be presented in the form of a chart, summary, or calculation. The originals, or duplicates, shall be made available for examination or copying, or both, by other parties at reasonable time and place. The court may order that they be produced in court.

Rule 1007.

TESTIMONY OR WRITTEN ADMISSION OF PARTY

Contents of writings, recordings, or photographs may be proved by the testimony or deposition of the party against whom offered or by his written admission, without accounting for the nonproduction of the original.

Rule 1008.

FUNCTIONS OF COURT AND JURY

When the admissibility of other evidence of contents of writings, recordings, or photographs under these rules depends upon the fulfillment of a condition of fact, the question whether the condition has been fulfilled is ordinarily for the court to determine in accordance with the provisions of rule 104. However, when an issue is raised (a) whether the asserted writing ever existed, or (b) whether another writing, recording, or photograph produced at the trial is the original, or (c) whether other evidence of contents correctly reflects the contents, the issue is for the trier of fact to determine as in the case of other issues of fact.

Rule 1101.

APPLICABILITY OF RULES

(a) Courts and magistrates. These rules apply to the United States district courts, the District Court of Guam, the District Court of the Virgin Islands, the District Court for the District of the Canal Zone, the United States courts of appeals, the Court of Claims, and to United States magistrates, in the actions, cases, and proceedings and to the extent hereinafter set forth. The terms "judge" and "court" in these rules include United States magistrates, referees in bankruptcy, and commissioners of the Court of Claims.

(b) Proceedings generally. These rules apply generally to civil actions and proceedings, including admiralty and maritime cases, to criminal cases and proceedings, to contempt proceedings except those in which the court may act summarily, and to proceedings and cases under the Bankruptcy Act.

(c) Rule of privilege. The rule with respect to privileges applies at all stages of all actions, cases, and proceedings.

(d) Rules inapplicable. The rules (other than with respect to privileges) do not apply in the following situations:

(1) Preliminary questions of fact. The determination of questions of fact preliminary to admissibility of evidence when the issue is to be determined by the court under rule 104.

(2) Grand jury. Proceedings before grand juries.

(3) Miscellaneous proceedings. Proceedings for extradition or rendition; preliminary examinations in criminal cases; sentencing, or granting or revoking probation; issuance of warrants for arrest, criminal summonses, and search warrants; and proceedings with respect to release on bail or otherwise.

(e) Rules applicable in part. In the following proceedings these rules apply to the extent that matters of evidence are not provided for in the statutes which govern procedure therein or in other rules prescribed by the Supreme Court pursuant to statutory authority: the trial of minor and petty offenses by United States magistrates; review of agency actions when the facts are subject to trial de novo under section 706(2)(F) of title 5, United States Code; review of orders of the Secretary of Agriculture under section 2 of the Act entitled "An Act to authorize association of producers of agricultural products" approved February 18, 1922 (7 U.S.C. 292), and under sections 6 and 7(c) of the Perishable Agricultural Commodities Act, 1930 (7 U.S.C. 499f, 499g(c)); naturalization and revocation of naturalization under sections 310–318 of the Immigration and Nationality Act (8 U.S.C. 1421–1429); prize proceedings in admiralty under sections 7651–7681 of title 10, United States Code; review of orders of the Secretary of the Interior under section 2 of the Act entitled "An Act authorizing associations of producers of aquatic products" approved June 25, 1934 (15 U.S.C. 522); review of orders of petroleum control boards under section 5 of the Act entitled "An Act to regulate interstate and foreign commerce in petroleum and its products by prohibiting the shipment in such commerce of petroleum and its products produced in violation of State law, and for other purposes", approved February 22, 1935 (15 U.S.C. 715d); actions for fines, penalties, or forfeitures under part V of title IV of the Tariff Act of 1930 (19 U.S.C. 1581–1624), or under the Anti-Smuggling Act (19 U.S.C. 1701–1711); criminal libel for condemnation, exclusion of imports, or other proceedings under the Federal Food, Drug, and Cosmetic Act (21 U.S.C. 301–392); disputes between seamen under sections 4079, 4080, and 4081 of the Revised Statutes (22 U.S.C. 256–258); habeas corpus under sections 2241–2254 of title 28, United States Code; motions to vacate, set aside or correct sentence under section 2255 of title 28, United States Code;

actions for penalties for refusal to transport destitute seamen under section 4578 of the Revised Statutes (46 U.S.C. 679); actions against the United States under the Act entitled "An Act authorizing suits against the United States in admiralty for damage caused by and salvage service rendered to public vessels belonging to the United States, and for other purposes", approved March 3, 1925 (46 U.S.C. 781–790), as implemented by section 7730 of title 10, United States Code.

Rule 1102.

AMENDMENTS

Amendments to the Federal Rules of Evidence may be made as provided in section 2076 of title 28 of the United States Code.

Rule 1103.

TITLE

These rules may be known and cited as the Federal Rules of Evidence.

Sec. 2. (a) Title 28 of the United States Code is amended—

(1) by inserting immediately after section 2075 the following new section:

"§ 2076. Rules of evidence

"The Supreme Court of the United States shall have the power to prescribe amendments to the Federal Rules of Evidence. Such amendments shall not take effect until they have been reported to Congress by the Chief Justice at or after the beginning of a regular session of Congress but not later than the first day of May, and until the expiration of one hundred and eighty days after they have been so reported; but if either House of Congress within that time shall by resolution disapprove any amendment so reported it shall not take effect. The effective date of any amendment so reported may be deferred by either House of Congress to a later date or until approved by Act of Congress. Any rule whether proposed or in force may be amended by Act of Congress. Any provision of law in force at the expiration of such time and in conflict with any such amendment not disapproved shall be of no further force or effect after such amendment has taken effect. Any such amendment creating, abolishing, or modifying a privilege shall have no force or effect unless it shall be approved by act of Congress"; and

(2) by adding at the end of the table of sections of chapter 131 the following new item:

"2076. Rules of evidence."

(b) Section 1732 of title 28 of the United States Code is amended by striking out subsection (a), and by striking out "(b)".

(c) Section 1733 of title 28 of the United States Code [3] is amended by adding at the end thereof the following new subsection:

"(c) This section does not apply to cases, actions, and proceedings to which the Federal Rules of Evidence apply."

Sec. 3. The Congress expressly approves the amendments to the Federal Rules of Civil Procedure, and the amendments to the Federal Rules of Criminal Procedure, which are embraced by the orders entered by the Supreme Court of the United States on November 20, 1972, and December 18, 1972, and such amendments shall take effect on the one hundred and eightieth day beginning after the date of the enactment of this Act.

TABLE OF CASES

The principal cases are in italic type. Cases cited or discussed are in roman type. References are to Pages.

INDEX

References are to Pages

References are to Pages

WEST PUBLISHING CO